netw⊙rks™
A Social Studies Learning System

GO online

MEETS YOU ANYWHERE —
TAKES YOU EVERYWHERE

start netw⊙rking

networks™
A Social Studies Learning System

MEETS YOU ANYWHERE —
TAKES YOU EVERYWHERE

It's **ALL** online

1. Go to *connected.mcgraw-hill.com.*

2. Get your User Name and Password from your teacher and enter them.

3. Click on your **Networks** book.

4. Select your chapter and lesson.

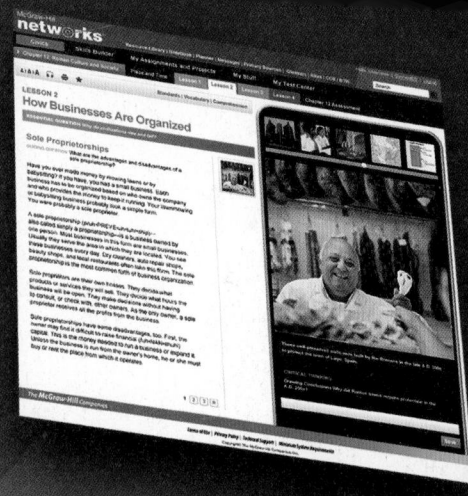

HOW do you learn?

Read • Reflect • Watch • Listen • Connect • Discover • Interact

The Presidential Pardon

On September 8, 1974, President Gerald Ford issued a presidential pardon of Richard Nixon for crimes he may have committed while president. Though Nixon had not yet been formally charged with any crime, Ford though it would be best for the country to put the matter behind us and move ahead.

Over the years, the use of the presidential pardon has changed from the use that may have been intended by the founders. Presidents today have the power to grant full pardons (officially removing the crime and the conviction from any record, as if they had never occurred) or to commute sentences (shorten or lessen the sentence imposed).

Pardons are also more common today than they were in the past. The first six presidents pardoned a total of eleven people; the most recent six presidents (before Barack Obama), together pardoned or commuted the

© White House Historical Association

networks

BUILDING CITIZENSHIP

CIVICS & ECONOMICS

McGraw Hill Education

start **networ**king

networks™
A Social Studies Learning System

**MEETS YOU ANYWHERE —
TAKES YOU EVERYWHERE**

WHO is in your network?

People Past and Present • Places • Events

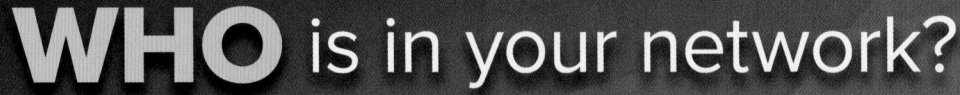

WHAT do you learn?

History · Geography · Economics · Government · Culture

start **network**ing

networks™
A Social Studies Learning System

MEETS YOU ANYWHERE —
TAKES YOU EVERYWHERE

HOW do you make Networks yours?

Organize • Take Notes • Study • Submit • Message

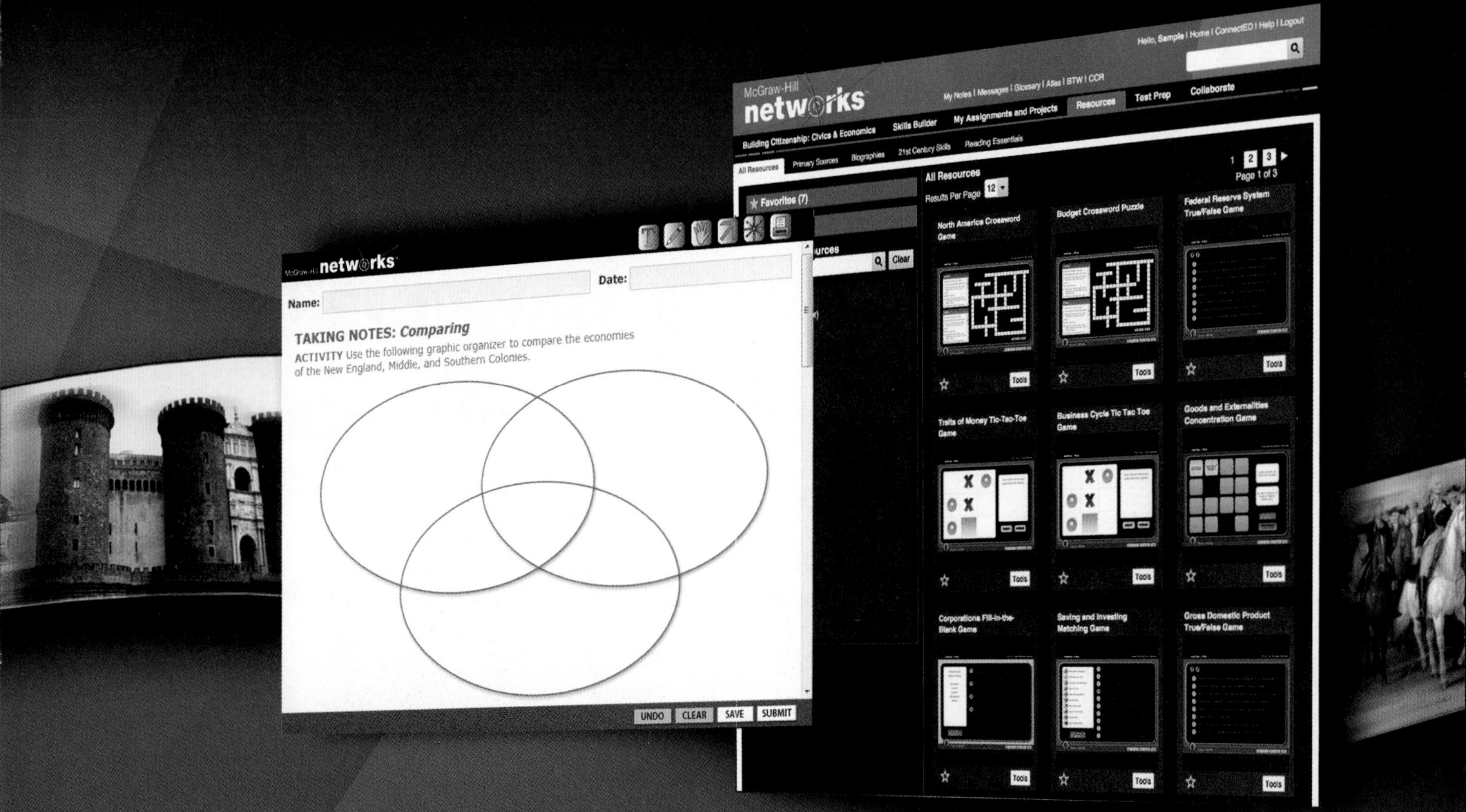

WHAT do you use?

Graphic Organizers • Primary Sources • Videos • Games • Photos

start**netw🔍rk**ing

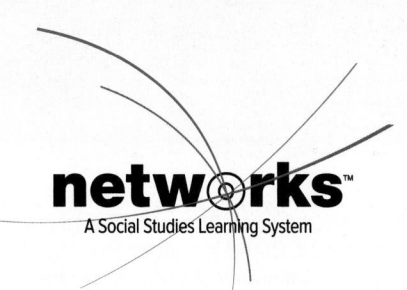

networks™
A Social Studies Learning System

BUILDING CITIZENSHIP

CIVICS & ECONOMICS

Richard C. Remy, Ph.D.

John J. Patrick, Ed.D.

David C. Saffell, Ph.D.

Gary E. Clayton, Ph.D.

Mc
Graw
Hill
Education

www.mheonline.com/networks

Send all inquiries to:
McGraw-Hill Education
8787 Orion Place
Columbus, OH 43240

ISBN: 978-0-07-660120-2
MHID: 0-07-660120-x

Printed in the United States of America.

2 3 4 5 6 7 8 9 QVS 20 19 18 17 16 15

AUTHORS

Richard C. Remy, Ph.D., is Professor Emeritus in the College of Education at The Ohio State University. He served for two decades as Director of the Civic Education Program at the Mershon Center for International Security and Public Policy at Ohio State. Remy received his Ph.D. in political science from Northwestern University. His books include *United States Government: Democracy in Action, Building Civic Education for Democracy in Poland, American Government and National Security*, and *Lessons on the Constitution*. In the 1990s Remy created and codirected a long-term project with the Polish Ministry of National Education and the Center for Citizenship Education, Warsaw, to develop new civic education programs for Polish students, teachers, and teacher educators.

John J. Patrick, Ed.D., is a Professor Emeritus of Education at Indiana University, Bloomington. He is the author of many publications about civics and government, such as *The Oxford Guide to the United States Government, The Supreme Court of the United States: A Student Companion, The Bill of Rights: A History in Documents, Founding the Republic, Constitutional Debates on Freedom of Religion, Understanding Democracy,* and *The Pursuit of Justice: Supreme Court Decisions That Shaped America*. From 1996–2009, Patrick was a member of the Standing Committee on Civics of the National Assessment of Educational Progress (NAEP). From 1992–2004, he participated in several international civic education projects involving post-Communist countries. In 2002 Patrick received Indiana University's John W. Ryan Award for distinguished achievements in International Programs. In 2003 he received the Sagamore of the Wabash Award from the Governor of Indiana in recognition of his long-term contributions to civic

education in Indiana. In 2005 he was the original recipient of the Indiana State Bar Association's Civic Education Award. In 2007 he presented the inaugural Claude Moore Endowed Lecture at the Center for the Constitution at James Madison's Montpelier.

David C. Saffell, Ph.D., received his Ph.D. in political science from the University of Minnesota. He is Professor of Political Science Emeritus at Ohio Northern University, where he served as chair of the Social Science Division for 15 years. Saffell is coauthor of *State of Local Government: Politics and Public Policies*, 9th edition, published by McGraw-Hill. He has authored and edited several other books about American government, and has written opinion pieces for various newspapers, including the *Chicago Tribune* and *Baltimore Sun*.

Gary E. Clayton, Ph.D., currently teaches economics at Northern Kentucky University. He received his Ph.D. in economics from the University of Utah. He has taught economics and finance at several universities in the United States and abroad and has authored a number of books. Clayton has appeared on numerous radio and television programs and was a frequent guest commentator for NPR's *Marketplace*. Clayton has a long-standing interest in economic education. He has participated in numerous economic education workshops, and is a National Council on Economic Education Kazanjian Award winner. Clayton also received the year 2000 Leavey Award for Excellence in Private Enterprise Education from the Freedoms Foundation at Valley Forge. Most recently, Clayton was the recipient of Northern Kentucky University's 2005 Frank Sinton Milburn Outstanding Professor Award.

CONTRIBUTING AUTHORS

Jay McTighe has published articles in a number of leading educational journals and coauthored 10 books, including the best-selling *Understanding by Design* series with Grant Wiggins. McTighe also has an extensive background in professional development and is a featured speaker at national, state, and district conferences and workshops. He received his undergraduate degree from The College of William and Mary, earned a Masters degree from the University of Maryland, and completed postgraduate studies at the Johns Hopkins University.

Dinah Zike, M.Ed., is an award-winning author, educator, and inventor recognized for designing three-dimensional, hands-on manipulatives and graphic organizers known as Foldables™. Foldables are used nationally and internationally by parents, teachers, and other professionals in the education field. Zike has developed more than 150 supplemental educational books and materials. Her two latest books, *Notebook Foldables®* and *Foldables®, Notebook Foldables®, & VKV®s for Spelling and Vocabulary 4th-12th* were each awarded *Learning Magazine's*

Teacher's Choice Award for 2011. In 2004 Zike was honored with the CESI Science Advocacy Award. She received her M.Ed. from Texas A&M, College Station, Texas.

Doug Fisher, Ph.D., and Nancy Frey, Ph.D., are professors in the School of Teacher Education at San Diego State University. Fisher's focus is on literacy and language, with an emphasis on students who are English Learners. Frey's focus is on literacy and learning, with a concentration in how students acquire content knowledge. Both teach elementary and secondary teacher preparation courses, in addition to their work with graduate and doctoral programs. Their shared interests include supporting students with diverse learning needs, instructional design, and curriculum development. They are coauthors of numerous articles and books, including *Better Learning Through Structured Teaching, Checking for Understanding, Background Knowledge,* and *Improving Adolescent Literacy*. They are coeditors (with Diane Lapp) of the NCTE journal *Voices from the Middle*.

CONSULTANTS AND REVIEWERS

ACADEMIC CONSULTANTS

Jody Baumgartner, Ph.D.
Associate Professor of Political
 Science
East Carolina University
Greenville, NC

David Berger, Ph.D.
Ruth and I. Lewis Gordon Professor
 of Jewish History
Dean, Bernard Revel Graduate School
Yeshiva University
New York, NY

Stephen Cunha, Ph.D.
Professor and Director, California
 Geographic Alliance
Humboldt State University
Arcata, CA

Tom Daccord
Educational Technology Specialist
Co-Director, EdTech Teacher
Boston, MA

Nancy Lind, Ph.D.
Associate Department Chair, Professor
 of Political Science
Illinois State University
Carbondale, IL

Irfan Nooruddin, Ph.D.
Associate Professor of Political
 Science
The Ohio State University
Columbus, OH

Tom Reich
Educational Technology Specialist
Co-Director, EdTech Teacher
Boston, MA

Donald A. Ritchie, Ph.D.
Associate Historian of the United
 States Senate Historical Office
Washington, DC

William Shapiro
Professor of Political Science
Oxford College of Emory University
Oxford, GA

TEACHER REVIEWERS

Christine Disinger
DeLand Middle School
DeLand, FL

Jon-Maria Ramseur
West Charlotte High School
Charlotte, NC

Cathy Schroepfer
Deerlake Middle School
Tallahassee, FL

Michael Singh
Victoria Fertitta Middle School
Las Vegas, NV

Donald Thornton
Ovey Comeaux School
Rayne, LA

Aaron Webb
Miguel Juarez Middle School
Waukegan, IL

CONTENTS

v

CONTENTS

AP Photo/George Widman

CHAPTER 4

Getty Images

CHAPTER 5

Brooks Kraft/Corbis

CHAPTER 6

Kenneth Garrett/Getty Images

CHAPTER 7

The Judicial Branch **215**

Chip Somodevilla/Getty Images

CHAPTER 8

Political Parties **245**

ROBYN BECK/AFP/Getty Images

CHAPTER 9

Voting and Elections **265**

CONTENTS

Jim West/PhotoEdit

Ilene MacDonald/Alamy

Barry Winiker/Getty Images

Joe Raedle/Getty Images

CHAPTER 13

Blend Images/SuperStock

CHAPTER 14

Dan Bannister/Getty Images

CHAPTER 15

CONTENTS

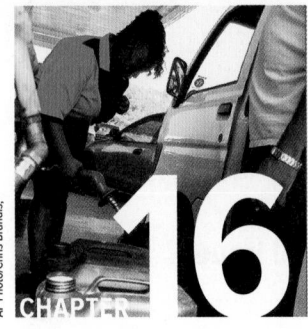

AP Photo/Chris Brandis;

CHAPTER 16

AP Photo/LM Otero

CHAPTER 17

Jemal Countess/Getty Images

CHAPTER 18

Michael Ventura/Alamy

CHAPTER 19

Business in America **513**

Essential Questions

Why and how do people make economic choices? • How do economic systems influence societies?

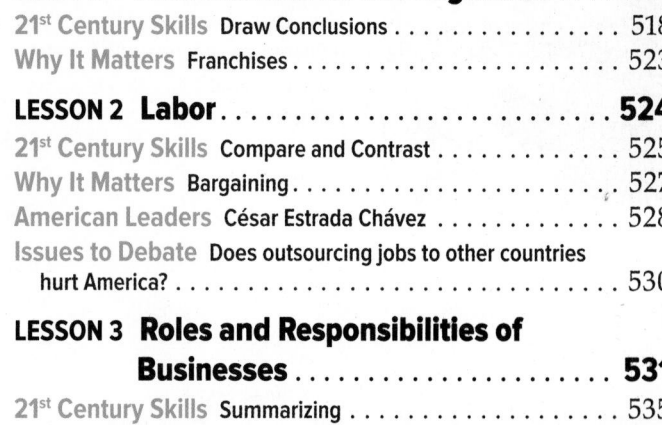

Jin Lee/Bloomberg via Getty Images

CHAPTER 20

Government's Role in the Economy **539**

Essential Question

How does government influence the economy and economic institutions?

CONTENTS

Stephen Hilger/Getty Images

CHAPTER 21

The Government and Banking 565

Essential Question

How does government influence the economy and economic institutions?

Jim Richardson/Getty Images

CHAPTER 22

Financing the Government 587

Essential Question

How does government influence the economy and economic institutions?

Iain Masterton/Alamy

CHAPTER 23

International Trade and Economic Systems 607

Essential Questions

Why do people trade? • Why and how do people make economic choices?

PEDRO UGARTE/AFP/Getty Images

CHAPTER **24**

FEATURES

Landmark Supreme Court Cases

teen citizens in action

Political Cartoons

Issues to Debate

American Leaders/ American Entrepreneurs

21st Century SKILLS

FEATURES

Why It MATTERS

MAPS, CHARTS, and GRAPHS

MAPS

CHARTS AND GRAPHS

MAPS, CHARTS, and GRAPHS

Charts and Graphs *(continued)*

networks ONLINE RESOURCES

Videos

Every lesson has a video to help you learn more about civics or economics.

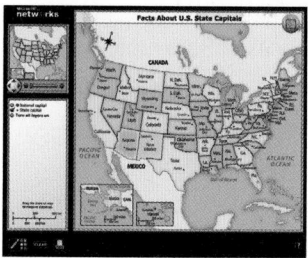

⌄ Maps

All maps that appear in your printed textbook are also available in an interactive format in your Online Student Edition.

⌄ Slide Shows

networks ONLINE RESOURCES

Interactive Graphs and Charts

Interactive Graphic Organizers

HOW TO USE THE ONLINE STUDENT EDITION

TO THE STUDENT

Welcome to McGraw-Hill Education's **Networks** online student learning center. Here you will access your Online Student Edition as well as many other learning resources.

1 **LOGGING ON TO THE STUDENT LEARNING CENTER**

Using your internet browser, go to connected.mcgraw-hill.com.

Enter your username and password

or

Create a new account using the redemption code your teacher gave you.

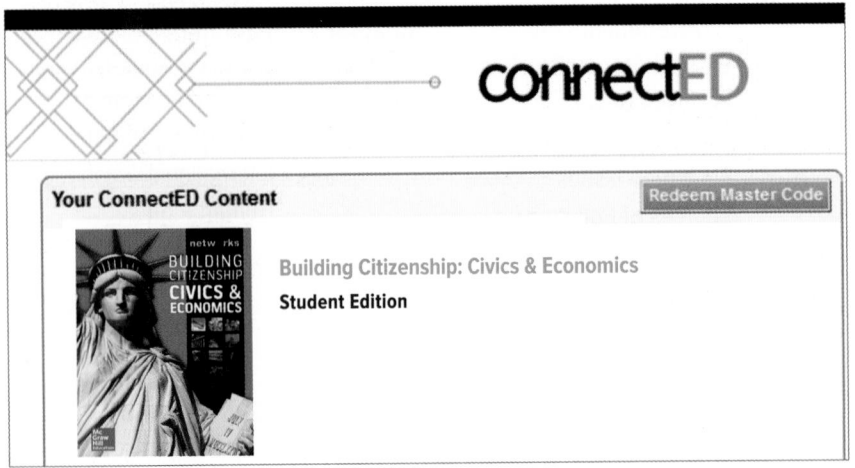

2 **SELECT YOUR PROGRAM**

Click your program to launch the home page of your Online Student Learning Center.

(t) McGraw-Hill Education

HOW TO USE THE ONLINE STUDENT EDITION

Using Your Home Page

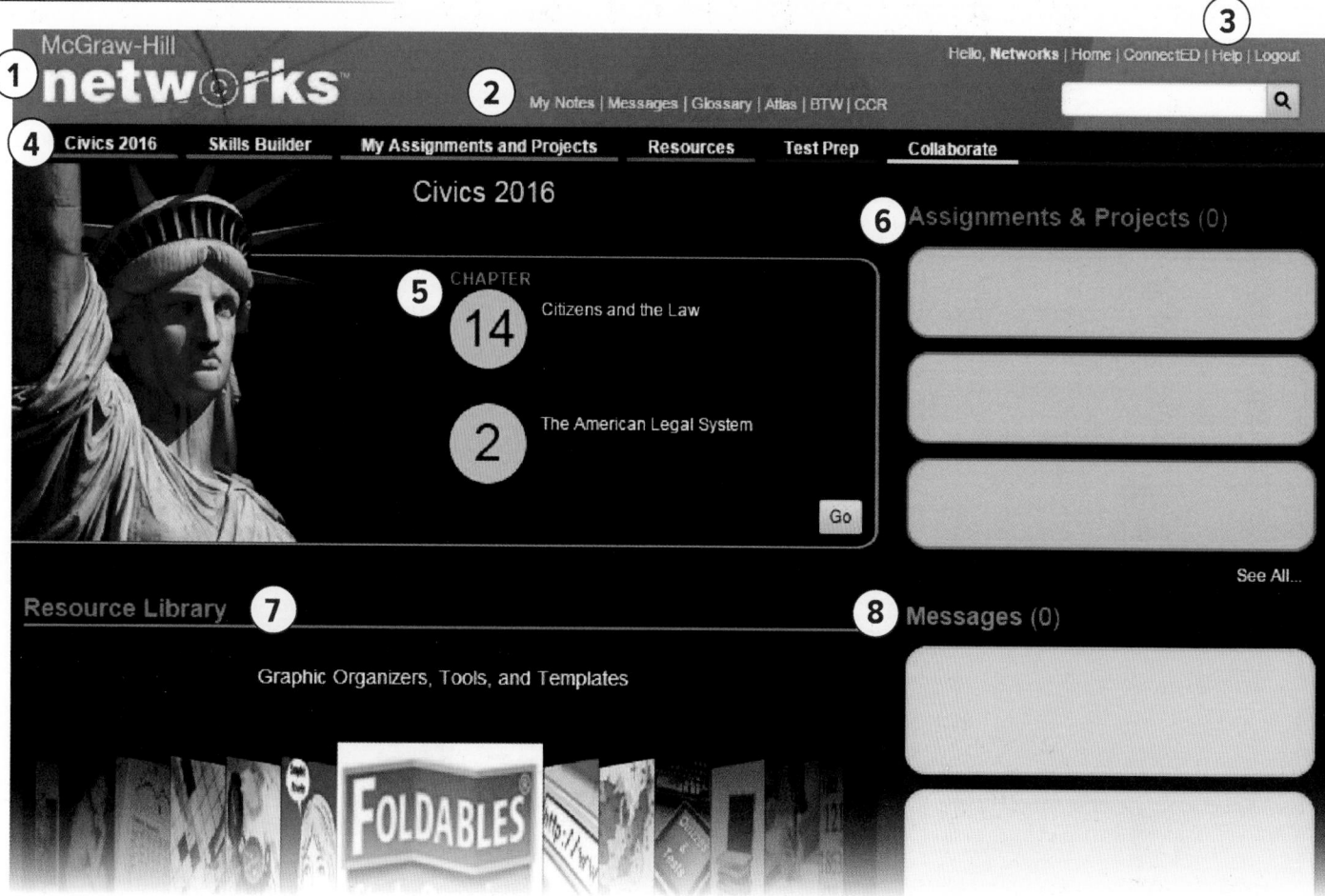

1 HOME PAGE

To return to your home page at any time, click the Networks logo in the top-left corner of the page.

2 QUICK LINKS MENU

Use this menu to access:
- My Notes (your personal notepad)
- Messages
- The online Glossary
- The online Atlas
- BTW (current events Web-site for social studies)
- College and Career Readiness (CCR) materials

3 HELP

For videos and assistance with the various features of the Networks system, click Help.

4 MAIN MENU

Use the menu bar to access:
- The Online Student Edition
- Skills Builder (for activities to improve your skills)
- Assignments and Projects
- Resource Library
- Test Prep
- Collaborate with Classmates

5 ONLINE STUDENT EDITION

Go to your Online Student Edition by selecting the chapter and lesson and then click Go.

6 ASSIGNMENTS

Recent assignments from your teacher will appear here. Click the assignment or click See All to see the details.

7 RESOURCE LIBRARY

Use the carousel to browse the Resource Library.

8 MESSAGES

Recent messages from your teacher will appear here. To view the full message, click the message or click See All.

HOW TO USE THE ONLINE STUDENT EDITION

Using Your Online Student Edition

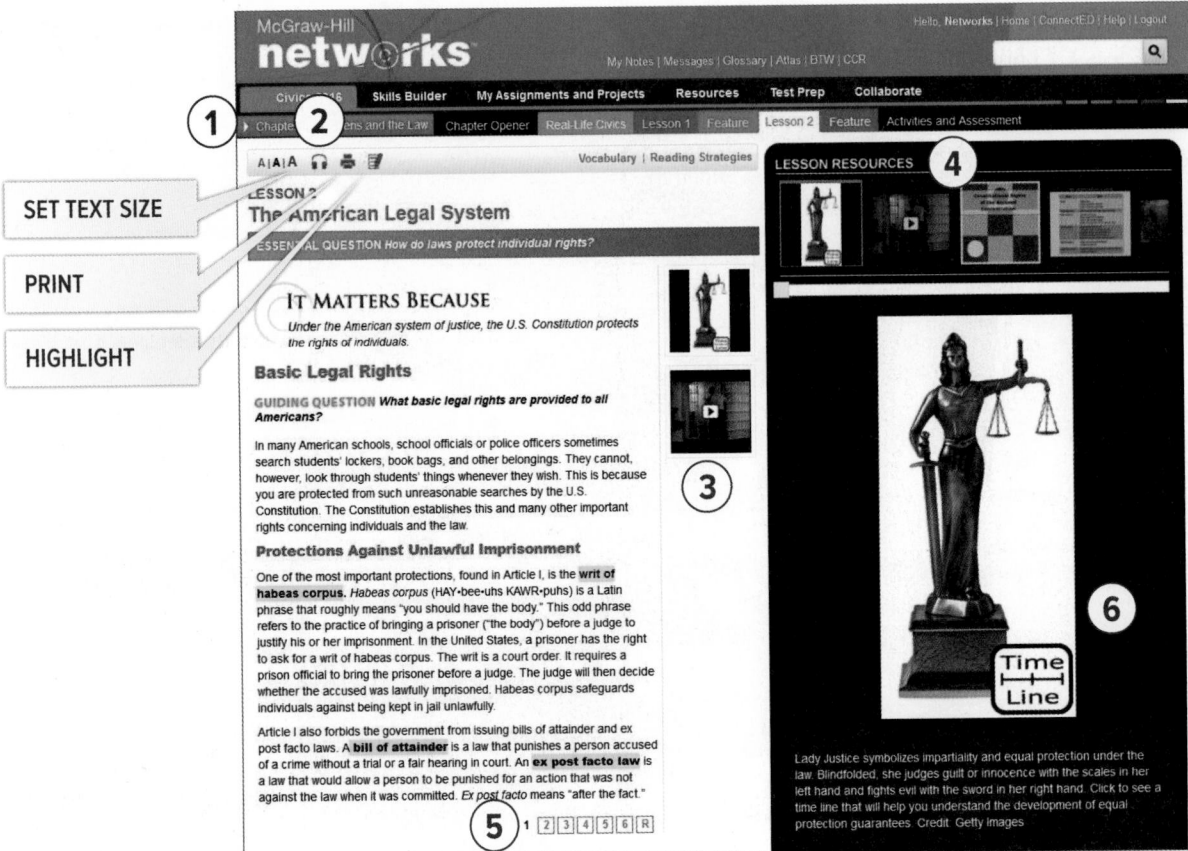

1 LESSON MENU

- Use the tabs to open the different lessons and special features in a chapter.
- Clicking on the chapter title will open the table of contents.

2 AUDIO EDITION

Click on the headphones symbol to have the page read to you. MP3 files for downloading each lesson are also available in the Resource Library.

3 RESOURCES FOR THIS PAGE

Resources appear in the middle column to show that they go with the text on this page. Click the images to open them in the viewer.

4 LESSON RESOURCES

Use the carousel to browse the interactive resources available in this lesson. Click on a resource to open it in the viewer below.

5 CHANGE PAGES

Click here to move to the next page in the lesson.

6 RESOURCE VIEWER

Click on the image that appears in the viewer to launch an interactive resource, including:

- Lesson Videos
- Interactive Photos and Slide Shows
- Interactive Maps
- Interactive Charts and Graphs
- Games
- Self-Check Quizzes for each lesson

HOW TO USE THE ONLINE STUDENT EDITION

Reading Support in the Online Student Edition

Your Online Student Edition contains several features to help improve your reading skills and understanding of the content.

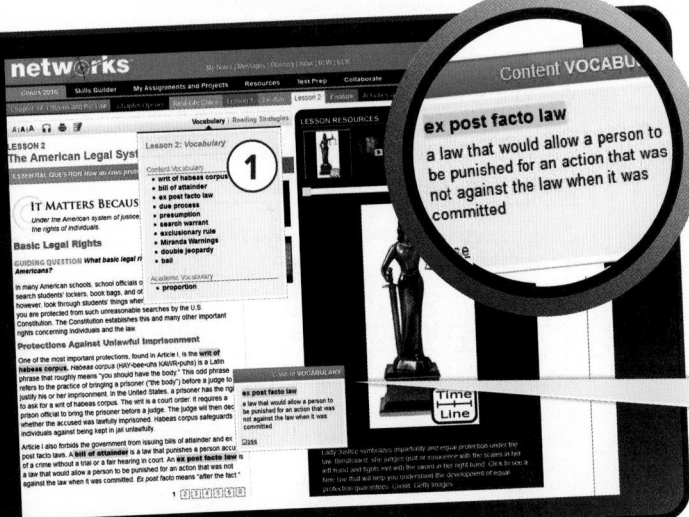

(1) LESSON VOCABULARY

Click Vocabulary to bring up a list of terms introduced in this lesson.

VOCABULARY POP-UP

Click on any term highlighted in yellow to open a window that gives the definition of the term.

(2) MY NOTES

Click My Notes to open the note-taking tool. You can write and save any notes you want in the Lesson Notes tab.

Click on the Guided Notes to view the Guided Reading Questions. Answering these questions will help you build a set of notes about the lesson.

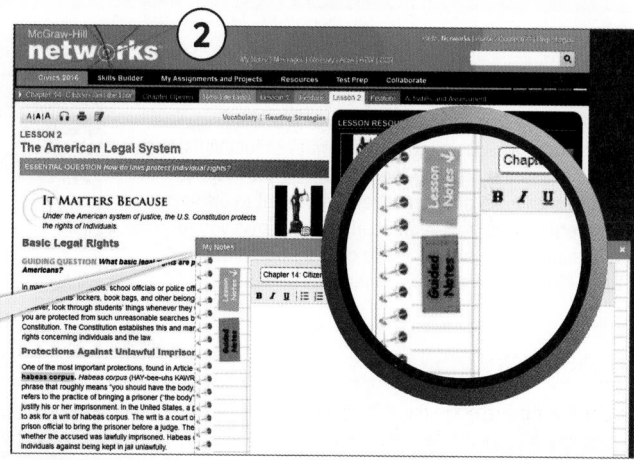

(3) GRAPHIC ORGANIZER

Click Reading Strategies to open a note-taking activity using a graphic organizer.

Click the image of the graphic organizer to make it interactive. You can type directly into the graphic organizer and save or print your notes.

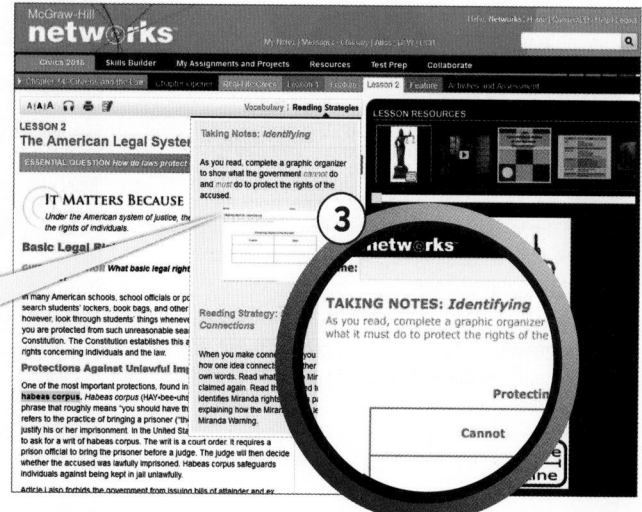

(t) McGraw-Hill Education

Go Online! connected.mcgraw-hill.com **XXV**

HOW TO USE THE ONLINE STUDENT EDITION

Using Interactive Resources in the Online Student Edition

Each lesson of your Online Student Edition contains many resources to help you learn the content and skills you need to know for this subject.

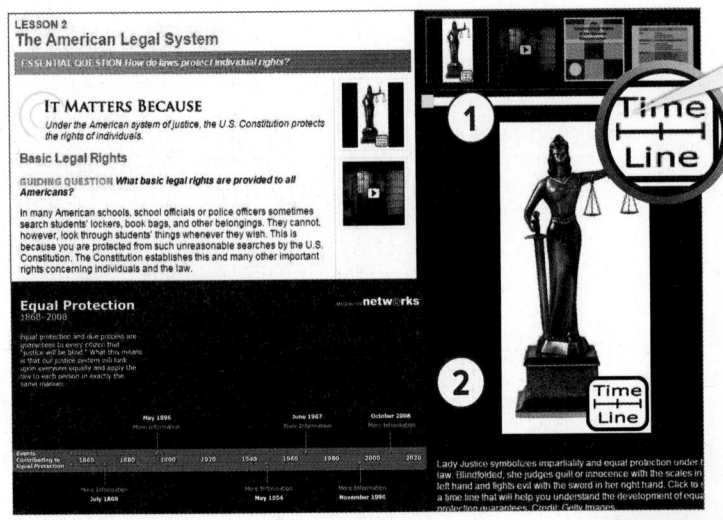

Networks features many kinds of resources. This symbol shows that the resource is a time line.

1 LAUNCHING RESOURCES

Clicking a resource in the viewer launches an interactive resource.

2 QUESTIONS AND ACTIVITIES

When a resource appears in the viewer, one or two questions or activities typically appear beneath it. You can type and save your answers in the answer boxes and submit them to your teacher.

3 INTERACTIVE MAPS

Most maps in the program are interactive. Clicking on the map allows you to use a number of functions. You can use the drawing tool to mark up the map. You can also zoom in and turn layers on and off to display different information. A measuring tool allows you to find the distance between two or more points on the map. Maps may also have animations or audio.

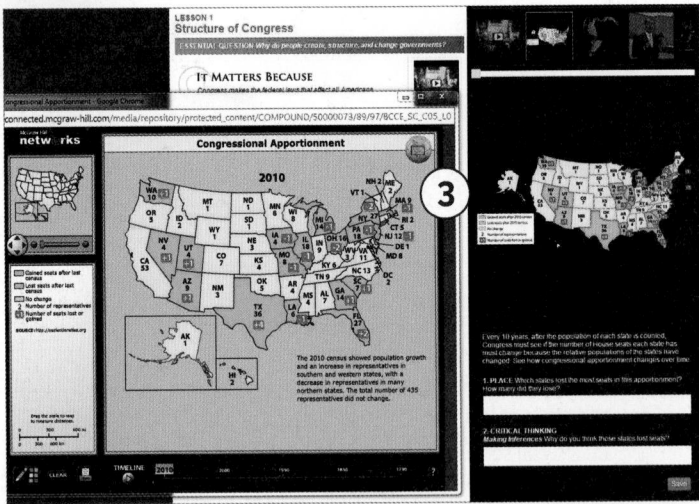

4 CHAPTER FEATURE

Each chapter begins with a feature called *Real-Life Civics*. This feature examines a real issue in government or economics, making important connections and setting the stage for the chapter. The questions in Civic Literacy ask you to analyze and provide your opinion about the featured issue.

The images are interactive. You can click on the photos, charts, graphs, or maps to access an interactive version.

HOW TO USE THE ONLINE STUDENT EDITION

Activities and Assessment

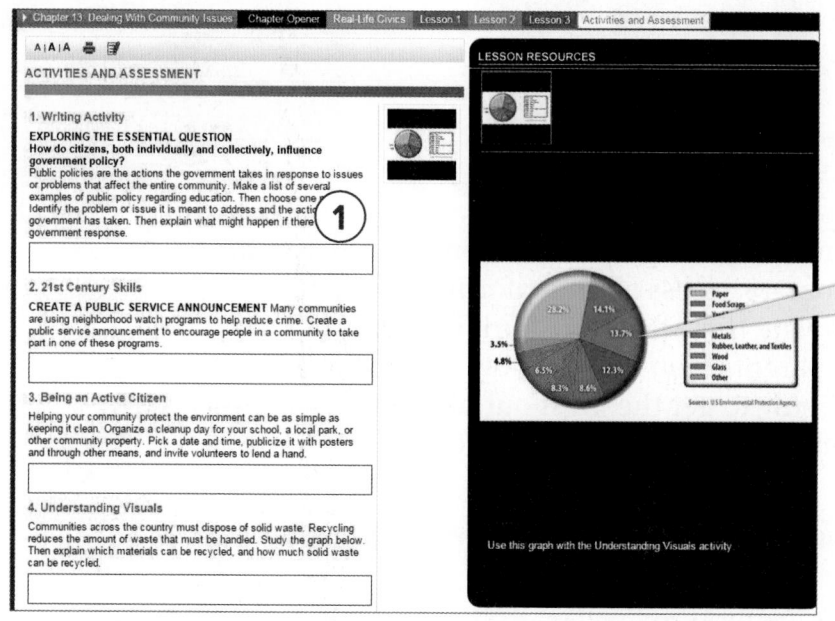

1 CHAPTER ACTIVITIES AND ASSESSMENT

At the end of each chapter is the Activities and Assessment tab. Here you can test your understanding of what you have learned. You can type and save answers in the answer boxes and submit them to your teacher.

When a question or an activity requires an image or graph or map, it will appear in the viewer.

Finding Other Resources

There are hundreds of additional resources available in the Resource Library. Click the Resources tab to enter the library.

2 RESOURCE LIBRARY

Click the Resource tabs to find collections of Primary Sources, Biographies, Skills Activities, and the Reading Essentials and Study Guide.

You can search the Resource Library by lesson or keyword.

Click the star to mark a resource as a favorite.

SCAVENGER HUNT

NETWORKS contains a wealth of information. The trick is to know where to look to access all the information in the book. If you complete this scavenger hunt exercise with your teachers or parents, you will see how the textbook is organized and how to get the most out of your reading and studying time. Let's get started!

1 How many chapters and how many lessons are in this book?

2 How are the content vocabulary words *liberty, duty*, and *boycott* in Chapter 2 called out?

3 You want to read the Declaration of Independence. How will you find it?

4 In what chapter would you learn about federal courts?

5 What is the topic of the Real-Life Civics on pages 126–127?

6 Who is the topic of the Teen Citizens in Action on page 498?

7 Where can you find the Essential Questions for each chapter?

8 Where would you look to quickly find reference maps?

9 Where in the back of the book can you quickly find the meaning of important vocabulary words such as *docket*?

10 What is the topic of the Landmark Supreme Court Case in Chapter 20?

Americans, Citizenship, and Governments

ESSENTIAL QUESTIONS • *What are the characteristics that make up a culture?*
• *What is a citizen?* • *Why do people create, structure, and change governments?*

The Story Matters...

American citizens are a diverse group of people. On a stroll through New York City, for example, you might see a woman in traditional Indian clothing or a man wearing a kippah, or Jewish skullcap. You might hear people speaking Chinese or Greek. You might taste a Syrian falafel or a Mexican tortilla.

The 2010 U.S. Census says 12 percent of Americans are immigrants and 11 percent have at least one immigrant parent. About 98 percent of us have a foreign-born ancestor. Many of them entered the United States through Ellis Island in New York City. This immigration station processed some 12 million immigrants into the nation. Most became U.S. citizens.

◀ *This hologram represents the diversity of the American people. It is located at the Ellis Island Immigration Museum in New York Harbor.*

PHOTO: John Moore/Getty Images

1

Real-Life Civics

> **THEN** Americans of varied heritages do their duty as citizens by serving in the U.S. armed forces. But this has not always been easy for some Americans. The 1941 Japanese attack on Pearl Harbor in Hawaii led President Franklin D. Roosevelt to force 120,000 innocent American citizens of Japanese descent, including 60,000 children, into internment camps. Soldiers of Japanese descent were called "enemy aliens," and had to leave their units.

In 1942, the U.S. military allowed Nisei (second-generation Japanese Americans) to serve in a separate battalion. More than 2,300 Nisei from internment camps volunteered. Their 442nd Regimental Combat Team became the most decorated unit in U.S. history. They fought in seven European campaigns. Despite the difficult circumstances, the Nisei proved themselves to be loyal American citizens.

Japanese Americans served in the 442nd Regimental Combat Team during World War II.

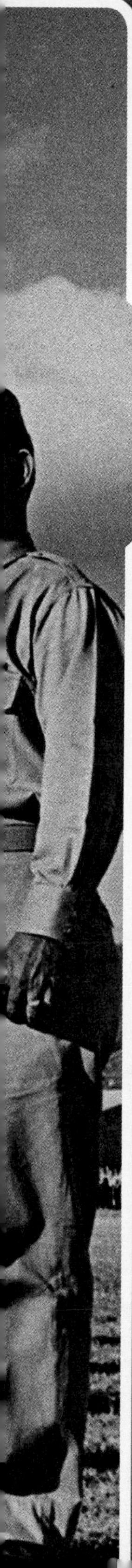

These men and women of the U.S. armed forces stationed in Afghanistan prepare to go out on patrol.

> **NOW** For much of our nation's history, most citizens who did their duty by serving in the U.S. military were white males. But over time the armed forces have come to reflect the diversity of Americans. One group whose role in the military has grown is women. At first women were limited to nursing. Then they began to work in administration and communications. In World War II some women became civil service pilots. But not until the 1960s and 1970s did women enjoy a full range of opportunities. Today women play a vital role in the military in locations around the world, although they still are not permitted to perform many combat jobs.

PHOTOS: (l) Time & Life Pictures/Getty Images; (tr) Paula Bronstein/Getty Images

CIVIC LITERACY

★ ★ ★ ★

Analyzing What difficulties have some citizens, such as Nisei or women, experienced in past decades while attempting to serve their country in the U.S. military?

Your Opinion Why do you think citizens choose to serve our country in the armed forces? Why is their choice important for the United States?

netw⊙rks
There's More Online!

☑ **GRAPHIC ORGANIZER**
American Population

☑ **GRAPHS**
U.S. Foreign-Born Population,
1850–2020
Ethnic Diversity of the
United States, 2010
Foreign-Born Population by
Nation of Origin

☑ **MAP**
United States Immigration, 2009

☑ **VIDEO**

Lesson 1
Being an American

ESSENTIAL QUESTION *What are the characteristics that make up a culture?*

IT MATTERS BECAUSE
The United States is enriched by its diversity and unified by its shared values.

A Diverse Population

GUIDING QUESTION *From what areas did early Americans come?*

Do you celebrate your birthday with a cake, a piñata, or a bowl of noodles? People in the United States share many traditions, such as watching parades or fireworks displays on the Fourth of July. They also enjoy different traditions that their families brought with them from other countries. Some of those special traditions were brought by people who came to this country in recent years. About 13 percent of all Americans were born in another country. These foreign-born people are **immigrants** (IH•muh•gruhnts), or people who move permanently to a new country.

The movement of people to the United States has been taking place for a few hundred years. About 98 percent of all the people now living in the United States are descended from families who once lived in another country. Immigrants have come to this country from nations located all over the world. Once in the United States, they have worked together to build a nation.

PHOTOS: (tl) Stewart Cohen/Blend Images/Corbis; (tc) Philip Scalia/Alamy; (tr) Richard Lewisohn/Getty Images

Reading **HELP**DESK

Taking Notes: *Identifying*
As you read, complete a graphic organizer like the one shown here by identifying characteristics of the American population.

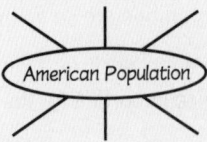
American Population

Content Vocabulary
- immigrant
- ethnic group
- values
- institution
- popular sovereignty

immigrant an individual who moves permanently to a new country

A History of Immigration

Most scholars believe that the very first people to live in what is now the United States came from Asia. They first arrived about 20,000 years ago. Over time they spread across North America. They developed a variety of cultures and spoke hundreds of different languages. Although these groups formed **distinct,** or separate, identities, together they are called Native Americans.

In the 1500s, the Spanish first made permanent homes in what is today the United States. The earliest of these settlers lived in what is now Florida. Later, Spanish-speaking people settled in the Southwest, including the present-day states of Texas and California.

Beginning in the 1600s, people from France, the Netherlands, and England also came to North America. The French settled mainly in what is now Canada. Some also made homes around the Great Lakes and along the Mississippi River. The Dutch established New Amsterdam, which we now know as New York City, and started farms along the Hudson River. English immigrants settled all along the east coast of North America. By the late 1600s and the 1700s, people started arriving from Germany, Sweden, Ireland, and Scotland. These early immigrants created the thirteen colonies that became the United States.

Some people who came to the Americas did not come willingly. Many people from western and central Africa were taken by force from their homes. Then they were brought by ship across the Atlantic Ocean to the Americas and sold into slavery. In 1807 Congress passed a law that stopped the practice of bringing enslaved people to the United States. By then, some 500,000 Africans had arrived and become part of the United States.

The *piñata*, a colorful figure filled with treats, is a tradition most associated with Mexico and other Latin American countries. At special celebrations, children have fun trying to break open the *piñata* with sticks.

▶ CRITICAL THINKING

Identifying What is another example of a tradition from another culture that has been adopted in the United States?

PHOTO: Stewart Cohen/Blend Images/Corbis

Academic Vocabulary

distinct separate or noticeably different

U.S. FOREIGN-BORN POPULATION, 1850–2020

The number of Americans born in another country and the percentage they represent of the whole population has changed greatly over the years.

1 *Identifying* What do the bars show? What does the line show?

▶ CRITICAL THINKING

2 *Making Generalizations* After 2009, what trend would you expect in terms of the percentage of the population that is foreign-born?

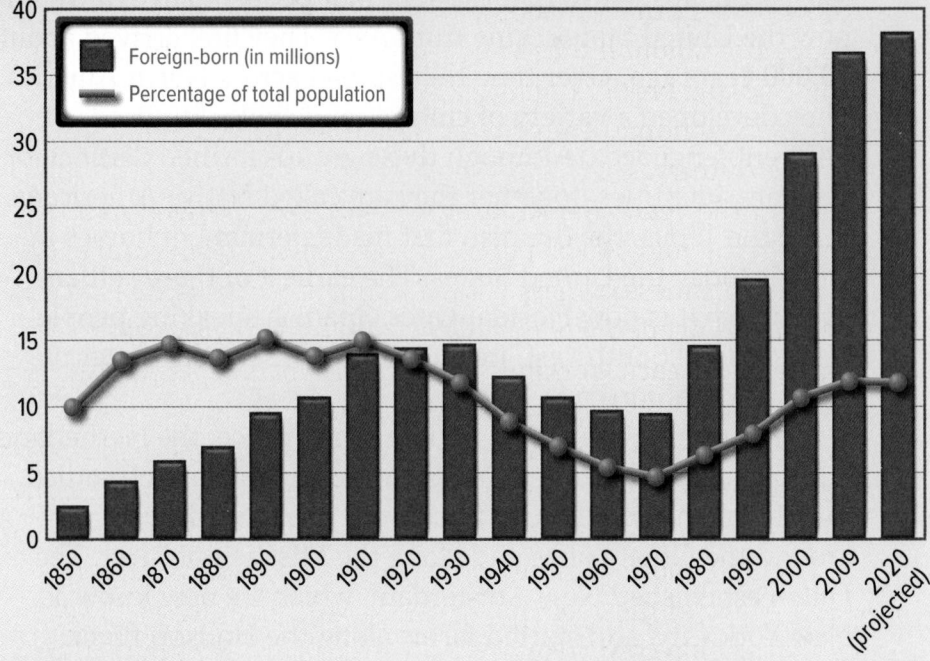

Source: U.S. Census Bureau; Urban Institute.

From the 1830s to the 1860s, more than 5 million people came to the United States. Most of these new settlers came from Ireland and Germany. They were fleeing poverty and disease at home. The discovery of gold in California in 1848 led many people from around the world to move to that area in hopes of becoming rich. Thousands of these new immigrants came from China.

Between 1860 and 1890, another 10 million Europeans streamed into the country. Many of the new settlers in this period came from Denmark, Norway, and Sweden. Then a shift in immigration followed. Up until the 1890s, most European immigrants had come from northern or western Europe. From 1890 to 1924, though, a majority of immigrants came from southern and eastern Europe. In those years, about 22 million immigrants arrived from countries such as Italy, Greece, Poland, and Russia.

The later 1900s saw another change in the source of immigration. A larger share of immigrants than before came from Asia and Latin America. Today, more than half of all the people in the United States who were born in another country come from Latin America.

Reading HELPDESK

Reading Strategy: *Organizing*

Create a three-column table to take notes on the history of immigration to the United States. Label the columns "Years," "Sources of Immigration," and "Number of Immigrants." Then fill in details from the text.

Ongoing Transformation

Between 1830 and 1930, the nation's population grew from about 12 million people to nearly 120 million people. About 40 million of those new Americans were immigrants. These people brought many different foods and ways of life to their new home. They helped make the United States a diverse country.

Over the years, the American population changed in other ways. In the mid-1800s, people began moving from rural areas to cities. Business owners were building new industries in this period and needed workers. They paid higher wages than people could earn working on a farm. Many people left the farms for cities in hopes of making a better living.

Following the Civil War, African Americans who had been enslaved were freed. Many of them left the South for Northern cities. They hoped to find jobs and a new way of life.

By 1920, more than half of all Americans lived in towns or cities. Many of these people worked in factories. They became known as blue-collar workers. The term *blue-collar* refers to the blue shirts workers wore. Others found jobs in schools, offices, and stores. These workers were called white-collar workers.

PHOTOS: (tl) Freeman Patterson/Masterfile; (bl) Moreleaze Tropicana/Alamy; (tr) CORBIS; (br) blickwinkel/Alamy

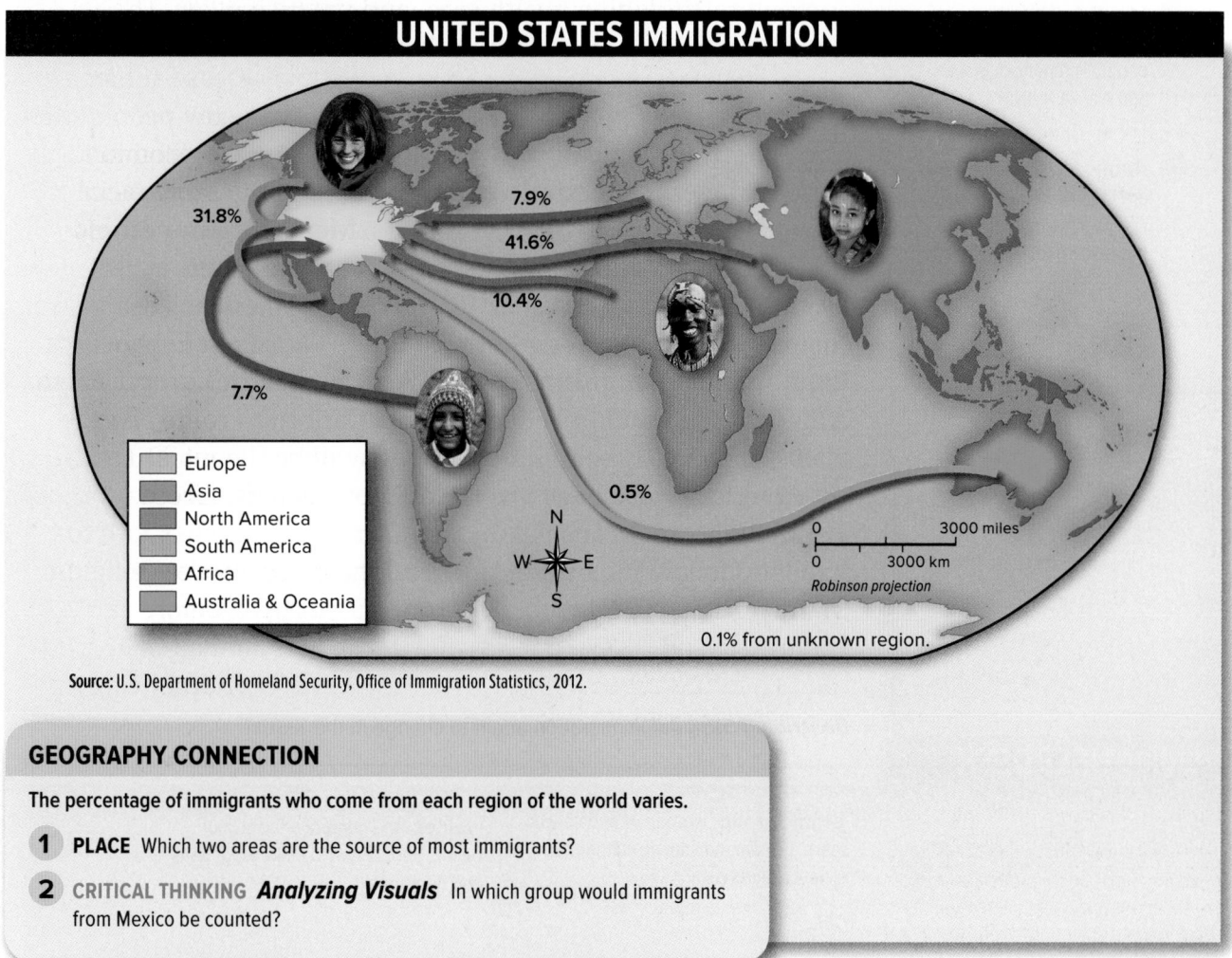

UNITED STATES IMMIGRATION

31.8%

7.9%

41.6%

10.4%

7.7%

0.5%

Europe
Asia
North America
South America
Africa
Australia & Oceania

N
W E
S

0   3000 miles
0   3000 km
Robinson projection

0.1% from unknown region.

Source: U.S. Department of Homeland Security, Office of Immigration Statistics, 2012.

GEOGRAPHY CONNECTION

The percentage of immigrants who come from each region of the world varies.

1 **PLACE** Which two areas are the source of most immigrants?

2 **CRITICAL THINKING** *Analyzing Visuals* In which group would immigrants from Mexico be counted?

21ˢᵗ Century SKILLS

Determine Cause and Effect

The population of the United States underwent great transformations from 1830 to 1930. Make a two column chart listing causes and effects of these population changes.

Two or more Races Non-Hispanic 1.7%

Native Hawaiian and other Pacific Islander 0.2%

American Indian and Alaskan Native 0.8%

Asian 4.4%

African American 12.3%

65.1% White, non-Hispanic

15.5% Hispanic

Source: U.S. Census Bureau, *Statistical Abstract of the United States: 2011.*

PHOTO: Philip Scalia/Alamy

GRAPH SKILLS

Native Americans, who make up a small percentage of the population, and members of other groups sometimes hold public ceremonies that include traditional music, dancing, and clothing.

1 Identifying What percentage of the American people is American Indian and Alaska Native?

▶ CRITICAL THINKING

2 Analyzing Visuals What are the two largest groups represented in the graph, besides White, non-Hispanic?

Over the past few decades, the working world has continued to change. More women are in the labor force than before. The number of factory jobs has decreased. Those jobs have been replaced by "the service economy." Service jobs are work that is done for someone else. They include teaching, programming computers, providing health care, and practicing law. The number of people who work in their homes has risen as well.

American Diversity

The American population is very diverse. People belong to a variety of racial and ethnic groups. People of the same racial group share distinctive physical traits. Members of an **ethnic** (EHTH•nihk) **group** share a common national, cultural, or racial background. About 16 percent of Americans call themselves Latinos. Their heritage traces back to Latin America. Latinos and other groups such as African Americans and Asian Americans are said to be members of minority groups. By the 2040s, though, these minority groups will be the majority.

Americans also have diverse religious beliefs. About 173 million Americans belong to a Christian church. Close to 9 million follow Judaism, Islam, Buddhism, or another religion. Many practice no religion.

✓ PROGRESS CHECK

Describing How did immigration begin to change in the 1890s?

Reading**HELP**DESK

ethnic group a group of people who share a common national, cultural, or racial background

values the general principles or beliefs people use to make judgments and decisions

Values and Institutions

GUIDING QUESTION *What do Americans value?*

Do you agree with most of your friends about what is good and what is bad? The general principles, or beliefs, you use to make these judgments are your **values.** Values are broad ideas about what is good or desirable and what is bad or not desirable. People's values are important because they influence how people act.

People with different beliefs and backgrounds have made lives for themselves in the United States. They have helped make this nation a land of great diversity. Certain shared values, however, help unite all these Americans. These values include freedom, equality, opportunity, justice, and democracy. Other shared American values include unity, respect for one another, and tolerance. It is these values that allow American diversity to prosper. At the same time, they give Americans a shared identity.

Many of these values are stated in the country's founding document. The Declaration of Independence states, for instance, that all people are equal. This statement means that everyone should be treated equally by the law. The Declaration also states how important freedom is to Americans. It says that all people have the right to "life, liberty, and the pursuit of happiness." *Liberty* is another word for freedom. With these words, the Declaration makes clear how important freedom is to all Americans.

Some female Muslims, or believers in the religion of Islam, follow religious rules about covering their heads.

▶ CRITICAL THINKING

Making Connections What are some religious or cultural practices that you or someone you know follows? Why is it important to be able to practice these freely?

PHOTO: Richard Lewisohn/Getty Images

Lesson 1 **9**

You can learn how to work with others by participating in groups at school. You can also take part in a sports team, a social group, or some other organization outside school. These experiences can teach cooperation, group decision making, and recognizing the abilities of others. Think of a group that you belong to. Make a list of three skills you have learned by taking part in that group.

institution a key practice, relationship, or organization in a society

Academic Vocabulary

arbitrary not agreed upon; seemingly random

popular sovereignty the idea that government receives its power from the people

Social Institutions

Our shared values are reflected in the important institutions of American life. **Institutions** are the key practices, relationships, and organizations in a society. The most important institution in American life is the family. The family is the center of social life. In families, parents and older family members teach children their values, both personal and national.

Religious institutions, such as churches, temples, and mosques, give a sense of meaning and belonging to the people who worship there. Schools reflect society's culture, history, and knowledge. They do more than teach students. They also help those students develop a shared sense of being American. Social institutions such as clubs and volunteer groups bring together people who have similar values or who believe in the same cause.

Government Institutions

American government institutions reflect how strongly Americans value freedom. Freedom is the right to make one's own choices in life without **arbitrary,** or unrestrained, interference from the government. American government is based on the principle of popular sovereignty. **Popular sovereignty** (PAH•pyuh•luhr SAH•vuhr•uhn•tee) is the idea that the government receives its power from the people. The people choose the nation's leaders, and those leaders must face the people again to stay in office.

The Constitution reflects another key principle. It makes sure that government is limited in its power. It sets up a three-part government in which no one part can have more power than the other two. In addition, the Bill of Rights makes sure that the government cannot abuse its power over the individual.

✔ **PROGRESS CHECK**

Explaining Why is the family an important institution?

LESSON 1 REVIEW

Review Vocabulary

1. What is an *immigrant*? What areas have been the main sources of immigrants in recent years?

2. What are *values*? What are three examples of shared American values?

Answer the Guiding Questions

3. *Explaining* Why is the population of the United States so diverse?

4. *Making Generalizations* What are three ways the American workforce has changed recently?

5. *Describing* How does American government reflect shared values?

6. **INFORMATIVE/EXPLANATORY** Describe some traditions practiced in your family or community. In what ways do they reflect American diversity? In what ways do they reflect American unity?

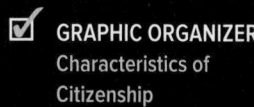
netw⊙rks

There's More Online!

☑ **GRAPHIC ORGANIZER**
   Characteristics of
   Citizenship

☑ **VIDEO**

☑ **GAMES**

Lesson 2
Becoming a Citizen

ESSENTIAL QUESTION *What is a citizen?*

IT MATTERS BECAUSE
In the United States there are two ways to become a citizen.

What Is Civics?

GUIDING QUESTION *How does a person become a citizen of the United States?*

At home you might have certain responsibilities that you are supposed to carry out. For example, you might have to do chores like walking the dog or washing the dishes. You may also have certain privileges. For instance, you might be allowed to use the computer after finishing your homework or to go with friends to see a movie.

In a similar way, citizens have both duties and rights. **Citizens** (SIH•tuh•zuhnz) are members of a community who owe loyalty to a government and, in turn, are entitled to the protection of that government. **Civics** (SIH•vihks) is the study of the duties and rights of citizens.

The Founders of the United States believed strongly in the value of civics. Thomas Jefferson wrote, "Whenever the people are well-informed, they can be trusted with their own government." In other words, to have an effective government, citizens must understand their rights and responsibilities. Informed citizens are able to make wise decisions about public questions. They are also better prepared to make choices about who should serve in public office.

Reading **HELP**DESK

Taking Notes: *Summarizing*

As you read, complete a web diagram like the one shown here to summarize the characteristics of citizenship.

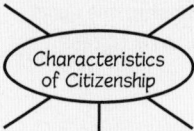
Characteristics of Citizenship

Content Vocabulary

- citizen
- civics
- citizenship
- government
- naturalization
- alien
- refugee

Roots of Citizenship

The idea of **citizenship** (SIH•tuh•zuhn•SHIHP), or the rights and duties of citizens, dates back more than 2,500 years to ancient Greece and Rome. Citizenship gave people legal rights and allowed them to take part in government. In those days, citizenship was only for men who owned property. Citizens' duties to the **government** included paying taxes and serving in the armed forces.

Over the centuries, other ideas about citizenship replaced the Greek and Roman views. In the 1700s, though, revolutionary thinkers in America and France brought back the ancient ideas, with some changes to the old definition. First, they defined citizens in terms of belonging to a nation. Second, they said that the power of government comes from the people governed. This idea is known as the "consent of the governed." Citizens give their consent, or agreement, by participating in government.

This new idea had the chance to give much power to the people. Still, that power had limits. For many years, U.S. citizenship was limited largely to white men. Gradually, and with much struggle, other groups gained full citizenship. African Americans were made citizens through the Fourteenth Amendment in 1868. Women gained the right to vote in 1920. That right came as a result of the Nineteenth Amendment. Members of a few Native American groups became citizens through treaties with the federal government. Not until 1924 did Congress pass the Indian Citizenship Act making all Native Americans citizens.

In the United States today, citizenship is not based on wealth, gender, race, or religion. A person can become an American citizen in either of two ways. They are by birth or by going through a particular process.

After signing the bill that gave citizenship to all Native Americans, President Calvin Coolidge (center) posed with four members of the Osage nation. The law gave all Native Americans the right to vote.

▶ CRITICAL THINKING
Speculating Is it surprising that Native Americans, who were the continent's first inhabitants, were the last to gain the right to vote? Explain.

PHOTO: Library of Congress, National Photo Company Collection

Natural-Born Citizens

Any person born in any of the 50 states or in the District of Columbia automatically becomes an American citizen at birth. The same is true of someone born in an American territory, such as Puerto Rico, or on a U.S. military base overseas. This rule also applies to children born on American soil to people who are not U.S. citizens. Those children become citizens at birth.

A person born in another country can claim American citizenship in two cases. He or she can be a citizen if both parents are U.S. citizens or if one parent is a citizen who has lived in the United States.

Someone who is born in another country may choose to hold dual citizenship. He or she can be a citizen of both the United States and the country where he or she was born.

Naturalized Citizens

Naturalization (NA•chuh•ruh•luh•ZAY•shuhn) is a legal process to obtain citizenship. More than 40 percent of the foreign-born people who live in the United States are naturalized citizens. Immigrants who want to become United States citizens must meet certain requirements:

- They must be age 18 or older.
- They must have been a lawful permanent resident for five years.
- They must be able to read, write, and speak English.
- They must be of good moral character.
- They must show an understanding of U.S. civics.

The first step in this process is to complete an application and send it to the U.S. Citizenship and Immigration Services (USCIS). Next, a USCIS official talks to the applicant to make sure that the person meets all five requirements.

The next step is to take a citizenship exam. The exam tests the applicant's ability to read, write, and speak English. It also asks the applicant about the history and government of the United States. Many people take classes to prepare for this test.

The banner hanging at this voter registration drive says "Your Vote Is Your Voice" in Spanish.

▶ CRITICAL THINKING
Explaining In what way is the statement on the banner true?

PHOTO: Marc Pokempner/Getty Images

Reading Strategy: *Sequencing*

With a process, like the steps of naturalization, you can take notes by drawing a series of boxes connected by arrows and writing a description of each step in a box in the correct order. Doing so will help you visualize and remember the steps.

naturalization a legal process to obtain citizenship

From 1995 to 2009, at least 461,000 people became naturalized citizens each year. The last step in the naturalization process is taking an oath of loyalty to the United States.

▶ **CRITICAL THINKING**
Drawing Conclusions Why do you think the government requires naturalized citizens to take such an oath?

PHOTO: Richard Ellis/Getty Images

The last step is a special ceremony. At this event, applicants take an oath in which they swear to be loyal to the United States above all other countries. They make other promises, too. For instance, they swear to obey the Constitution and the country's laws. After taking this oath and signing a document, they are citizens. If they have children under 18, the children automatically become citizens too.

Losing Citizenship

Americans can lose their citizenship in three ways:

- *Expatriation.* Someone who gives his or her allegiance to a foreign country is expatriated. An example is a person who becomes a naturalized citizen of another country.
- *Denaturalization.* Naturalized citizens who are found to have lied on their citizenship application are denaturalized. That is, they lose their naturalization. They may then be deported, or sent out of the country.
- *Being convicted of certain crimes.* Those guilty of any of three very serious crimes can lose citizenship. The crimes are treason, taking part in a rebellion, and trying to overthrow the government by violent means.

Only the federal government can grant citizenship or take it away. States can **deny**, or take away, some privileges of citizenship. For instance, states can take away the right to vote from some criminals. States cannot take away citizenship itself, however.

✓ **PROGRESS CHECK**

Identifying the Main Idea Why do we study civics?

Academic Vocabulary
deny to take away a right or privilege

 alien a foreign-born resident of the United States who has not been naturalized

Foreign-Born Residents

GUIDING QUESTION *In what ways can a foreign person enter the United States?*

Not everyone who lives and works in the United States is a citizen of the country. Many people are **aliens** (AY•lee•uhnz), or foreign-born residents who have not been naturalized. The government identifies two other groups of foreign-born persons living in the country. People in one group are, like aliens, in the country legally. People in the other group are not here legally.

Legal Aliens

There are two categories of legal aliens. A *resident alien* is a legal immigrant who permanently lives in the United States. Resident aliens may stay in the country as long as they wish. A *nonresident alien* is someone who expects to stay in the United States for a short, specified period. For instance, a foreign newspaper reporter who has come to report on an election would be a nonresident alien.

Like citizens, legal aliens may hold jobs, own property, attend public schools, and receive other government services. They pay taxes to the government, and they have the right to be protected by the law. They cannot vote in elections or run for office, however. They may not serve on juries or work in most government jobs. In addition, aliens must carry identification cards at all times. Those cards show that they are legal aliens.

Refugees

The United States accepts some people as refugees. A **refugee** (REH•fyoo•JEE) is a person fleeing his or her country to escape danger. For example, he or she might be subject to persecution by the government. Or the person might be fleeing a disaster, such as an earthquake or a war. When someone is a political refugee, the government promises to protect him or her. The government grants this status to people only if they can prove that they really are in danger if they return to their homeland.

Resident aliens have many rights of citizens, such as holding jobs.

▶ CRITICAL THINKING

Analyzing Why is this an important right for resident aliens to have?

refugee a person who has left his or her home to escape danger such as persecution by the government, war, or natural disaster

Illegal Aliens

Currently, the United States limits the number of immigrants who can enter the country each year to about 1 million people. The relatives of U.S. citizens receive the highest **priority,** or highest ranking. So do people who have job skills that are needed by employers in the United States. The law also makes room for immigrants from countries that have provided fewer numbers of immigrants in the past.

Many more people want to come to the United States to live than the law allows, however. As a result, some people decide to come to the country without the government allowing it. Each year, about 1 million aliens enter or remain in the nation illegally. Some of these people were refused permission to immigrate, but they come anyway. Others have never applied for permission but simply cross our borders with Mexico and Canada illegally. Some are nonresident aliens who stay longer than their legal time limit for living in the country. No matter how they arrived in the United States, these illegal aliens can be arrested and deported back to their home countries if they are discovered.

Today, close to 12 million people are living in the United States illegally. Most came to look for work and a better life. Yet illegal aliens often have a difficult time living in the United States. Many have no friends or family here, no place to live, and no sure way to earn money. Getting a job can be difficult for them because it is against the law to hire illegal aliens. Those who do find work usually receive low pay and no benefits. Every day illegal aliens live with the fear that government officials will discover them and send them back to their own countries.

☑ **PROGRESS CHECK**

Comparing and Contrasting How do the rights of legal aliens differ from those of U.S. citizens?

LESSON 2 REVIEW

Review Vocabulary

1. What is a *citizen*? What is the meaning of *citizenship*?

2. What is a *refugee*?

Answer the Guiding Questions

3. ***Identifying*** Name two ways a person can become a U.S. citizen.

4. ***Contrasting*** What is the difference between a legal alien and an illegal alien?

5. **INFORMATIVE/EXPLANATORY** Write a brief essay describing how the definition of citizenship has changed over time. Describe also the ways in which citizenship has remained the same.

Dred Scott v. Sandford

Before the Civil War, Americans were asking: Are African Americans citizens of the United States? May Congress prohibit enslavement of African Americans in U.S. territories?

Dred Scott

Background of the Case

Dred Scott was an African American who was enslaved to a physician named John Emerson. An army doctor, Emerson moved often and took Scott with him. As a result, Scott lived for a time in the state of Illinois and in the territory of Wisconsin. Neither of these regions had slavery. Both regions were also north of a boundary line set by Congress in the Missouri Compromise of 1820. That compromise allowed slavery south of the line and banned it north of the line.

Emerson died in 1843. Scott tried to buy his freedom from Emerson's widow, but she refused. In 1846 Scott sued for his freedom in Missouri. He claimed that since he had lived in a free state and a free territory, he was free. Scott's case moved slowly through Missouri's court system. He won his case in a lower court, but the ruling was overturned by Missouri's state supreme court in 1852. Mrs. Emerson eventually left the state. When she did, she gave control of her late husband's property to her brother, John Sanford.

Scott's lawyers filed a lawsuit against Sanford. The case eventually reached the U.S. Supreme Court.

The Decision

The Supreme Court decided the case on March 6, 1857. Chief Justice Roger B. Taney spoke for the seven-justice majority. Taney first stated his own view of the Framers' "original intent" when they wrote the Constitution. He said it was "absolutely certain that the African race were not included under the name of citizens of a State." He wrote further:

▐▐ [I]t is the opinion of the Court that the act of Congress which prohibited . . . [slaveholding] north of the line therein mentioned is . . . void; and that neither Dred Scott himself, nor any member of his family were made free by being carried into this territory. ▐▐

—Chief Justice Roger B. Taney

The Court ruled on two issues. First, it said that Scott was not a citizen and thus did not have the right to bring a lawsuit. Second, it ruled that the Missouri Compromise was unconstitutional. Therefore, Scott was not free.

Why It Matters

The ruling added to the tensions that led to the Civil War. In 1868, three years after the end of that war, the Fourteenth Amendment to the Constitution overruled the Dred Scott decision. It said that African Americans were citizens.

Analyzing the Case

1. **Explaining** Why was Dred Scott not freed as a result of the Supreme Court's decision?
2. **Inferring** What is your opinion of Justice Taney's view of the Framers' "original intent"?

PHOTO: Bettmann/Corbis

netw🔘rks
There's More Online!

☑ **GRAPHIC ORGANIZER**
Taking Part in Civic Life

☑ **CHART**
Citizens' Duties and
Responsibilities

☑ **INFOGRAPHIC**
Volunteering in America

☑ **VIDEO**

☑ **GAME**

Lesson 3
Duties and Responsibilities of American Citizens

ESSENTIAL QUESTION *What is a citizen?*

⊙ IT MATTERS BECAUSE
Democracy depends on citizens fulfilling their duties and acting responsibly.

Duties of Citizens

GUIDING QUESTION *What are the duties of American citizens?*

What comes to mind when you hear the word *community?* Do you think of your neighborhood or your town? Actually, each of us belongs to many communities—our school or workplace, our place of worship, our state, and our country as a whole. We are also members of the global, or worldwide, community of all humans.

We all play a part in making our communities safe and successful. All of us have certain responsibilities to fulfill. **Responsibilities** (rih•SPAHN•suh•BIH•luh•teez) are things we should do. They are obligations that we meet of our own free will. As American citizens, we also have legal duties that we have to carry out. **Duties** are actions that we are required to perform.

National, state, and local governments require American citizens to perform certain duties. Those duties are set by laws. Anyone who fails to perform those duties is subject to penalties under the law. Those penalties can include fines and time in prison. Five of our most important duties are discussed next.

PHOTOS: (tl) Alan Schein/Corbis; (tc) moodboard/Getty Images; (tr) Viviane Moos/Corbis

Reading**HELP**DESK

Taking Notes: *Organizing*

As you read, complete a graphic organizer, like the one shown here, by listing the duties and responsibilities of citizens.

Duties	Responsibilities

Content Vocabulary

- responsibility
- duty
- tolerance
- welfare
- volunteerism

Obey Laws

A citizen's most important duty is to obey the law. Laws are sets of rules that allow people to live together peacefully. Laws keep order in society by letting people know which actions are acceptable and which are not. If we do not obey laws, communities cannot maintain order or protect our health, safety, and property. Think of the conflict that would arise if people did not respect each other's right to their own property.

Pay Taxes

Taxes provide most of the money government needs to keep running. Without taxes, the federal government could not pay its employees, defend the country, or help those in need. Taxes allow your local community to hire police officers and firefighters, run schools, and pave roads. Local, state, and federal governments collect a variety of taxes. Taxes on income, property, and the sale of goods are just a few ways governments raise money. People who try to avoid paying taxes face stiff fines and other penalties.

Defend the Nation

In the United States, the law requires most male citizens aged 18 to 25 to **register** with the Selective Service System (SSS). The SSS is a government agency that keeps a record of all males in this age span. In the event of war or extreme national emergency, the government may need to **draft,** or call for military service, men from this list.

Registering with the SSS does not mean that a person will necessarily be drafted. In fact, the United States has not had a draft since 1973. Since then, volunteers have met the needs of the armed forces. In a recent year, nearly 75,000 people volunteered to join the U.S. Army. Thousands also volunteer each year for the U.S. Navy, the Marine Corps, the U.S. Air Force, or the Coast Guard.

Laws, such as traffic laws, keep order in society.

▶ CRITICAL THINKING
Analyzing Give an example of how traffic laws make travel safer.

PHOTO: Alan Schein/Corbis

---

responsibility an obligation that we meet of our own free will

duty an action we are required to perform

Academic Vocabulary

register to record or enroll formally

draft to call for military service

PHOTO: moodboard/Getty Images

A person called for jury duty might not necessarily hear a case. Lawyers can question jurors to determine which ones to select.

▶ CRITICAL THINKING

Evaluating Do you think serving on a jury is an important duty? Why or why not?

Serve in Court

The U.S. Constitution guarantees anyone accused of a crime the right to a trial by jury. A jury is a group of citizens who hear evidence in a case and decide whether the accused is guilty. Every adult citizen must be prepared to serve on a jury. The accused also has the right to hear and present witnesses. Citizens have the duty to serve as witnesses at a trial if they are called to do so.

Attend School

The government provides free public elementary and secondary education. Most states have laws that require children to attend school between the ages of 7 and 16. In school, students are taught the knowledge and skills they need to become good citizens. Students learn to resolve problems in thoughtful ways, to form opinions, and to express their views clearly.

Public school and higher education also have another benefit. They prepare students for their work life. In school, students gain skills that will help them become productive workers who can help keep the economy strong. For instance, students learn how to work together on group projects.

✓ PROGRESS CHECK

Explaining Why must we obey laws?

ReadingHELPDESK

Reading Strategy: *Organizing*

Organizing information in a passage helps you identify and remember main ideas. Make a two-column chart with the headings "Duty" and "Benefit." List the duties and benefits of citizens in the appropriate column.

Responsibilities of Citizens

GUIDING QUESTION *What are American citizens' responsibilities?*

Your teacher may assign you to work in a small group with other students. Each person is responsible for his or her participation and for the success of the entire group. Group members must help one another and allow one another to voice their ideas and concerns. Citizenship works much the same way. Everyone needs to participate to meet a shared goal: having a society that works well.

Be an Informed and Active Citizen

Government decisions affect your life. The state legislature, for example, might pass a law changing the rate of sales tax you pay. Your school board might vote to start the school day earlier. Your town council might set aside funds for a new recreation center. You have a responsibility to know what the government is doing so that you can voice your opinion on those matters.

Citizens are also responsible for making sure that the government is working properly. If you expect public officials to act in your interests, you must make your concerns known. You can make your voice heard by supporting a cause that you care about, contacting elected officials, and, above all, by voting.

Voting is one of American citizens' most important responsibilities. By electing leaders and voting on proposed measures, Americans give their consent to the government. As President Franklin D. Roosevelt said,

PRIMARY SOURCE

"The ultimate rulers of our democracy are not a President and Senators and Congressmen and Government officials but the voters of this country."
—Franklin D. Roosevelt (1938)

21st Century SKILLS

Paraphrasing

Reread the primary source quotation from Franklin D. Roosevelt. What did Roosevelt mean? Write a paraphrase putting Roosevelt's idea in your own words.

CITIZENS' DUTIES AND RESPONSIBILITIES

DUTIES	RESPONSIBILITIES
Obey the law	Be informed and vote
Pay taxes	Participate in your community and government
Defend the nation	
Serve in court	Respect the rights and property of others
Attend school	Respect different opinions and ways of life

CHART SKILLS

Citizenship involves duties and responsibilities.

▶ CRITICAL THINKING

1. *Speculating* Why do you think voting is a responsibility and not a duty?

2. *Evaluating* Add another responsibility to the chart. Explain why you added it.

Some people choose not to vote because they say that their vote does not count. However, as illustrated in many cases, every vote really does count. In 2008, for example, voters in Minnesota went to the polls to elect someone to represent them in the U.S. Senate. More than 2.4 million voters cast their ballots in that election. The winner won by just 225 of those votes.

Many Americans contribute to their community by giving their time to groups like food banks that help those who are in need.

► **CRITICAL THINKING**
Analyzing How does this kind of activity benefit the person taking the action?

In the United States, all citizens 18 years of age and older have the right to vote. Each Election Day, citizens have the opportunity to shape the future of their communities, states, and nation by voting. Thoughtful voters study the candidates and the issues carefully before casting their votes.

Responsible voters also remain aware of what their elected leaders are doing while holding office. If an official performs poorly, it is up to the voters to replace him or her in the next election. Voting ensures that leadership is changed in a peaceful and orderly manner.

Respect the Rights of Others

Treating others politely and respectfully is also part of being a good citizen. Society runs smoothly when individuals respect one another's rights. The United States has a very diverse population. It is important to remember that everyone has the right to his or her opinions, beliefs, and practices. Respecting and accepting others, regardless of differences, is called **tolerance.** Tolerance includes respecting private and public property as well.

Contribute to the Common Good

What would your community be like if no one supported charities or volunteered for community projects? What if no one ever spoke out about community problems? In order for communities and governments to grow, people need to participate.

Responsible citizens show concern for others as well as for themselves. They are willing to give time, effort, and money to improve community life. The members of a community must contribute to the common good, or the things that benefit all members of the community. For example, everyone benefits from having safe streets, good schools, and a clean environment.

 PROGRESS CHECK

Explaining Why is voting important?

PHOTO: Viviane Moos/Corbis

tolerance respecting and accepting others, regardless of their beliefs, practices, or differences

welfare the health, prosperity, and happiness of the members of a community

volunteerism the practice of offering your time and services to others without receiving payment

teen citizens in action

Amy Chyao knows how to spell success. She should. When she was 13, she placed eighth in the National Spelling Bee championship and twice won regional spelling contests. Amy then began to help the children of immigrant parents in her hometown improve their reading, spelling, and writing skills.

One year later, Amy started a study group called Spell Success. The group, consisting of students

from kindergarten through eighth grade, meets monthly at the local public library. Sometimes their parents sit in as well. Each August, a Spell

Success weekend summer camp helps students learn study methods, vocabulary, and public speaking skills. Amy also prepares students for her annual Spell Success Spelling Bee. The top three winners receive trophies and scholarship awards of $100, $50, or $25. Other awards go to the top spellers at each age level.

"The most important thing," says Amy, "is not that the students become better spellers, but that they laugh and make friends while learning. I hope that by showing them the fun in learning at a young age, students will grow to become lifelong learners who can make a difference in our society."

Citizenship and Teens

How would seeing the fun in learning help make students better learners?

Being Involved

GUIDING QUESTION *How can citizens make their community a better place to live?*

Have you volunteered to help out at school or in your community? By volunteering, we make our communities better places to live. We can also learn valuable skills.

We rely on government to provide many services, from police protection to collecting trash. Citizens also share responsibility for meeting community needs. Good citizens care about the **welfare**—the health, prosperity, and happiness—of all members of their community.

Donating Time and Money

Giving your time to work in the community is the heart of **volunteerism** (VAH•luhn•TIHR•IH•zuhm). This is the practice of offering your time and services to others without receiving payment. More than 63 million people, aged 16 and up, do volunteer work. Without the efforts of so many citizens, many important needs would not be met.

People do many kinds of volunteer work. Neighbors gather on a Saturday to clean up a park. Church groups make holiday baskets for needy families. Retirees teach schoolchildren or record books for the blind. You and your fellow students might visit nursing homes or collect food for a local pantry.

Percentage of Adults Active in Volunteer Work

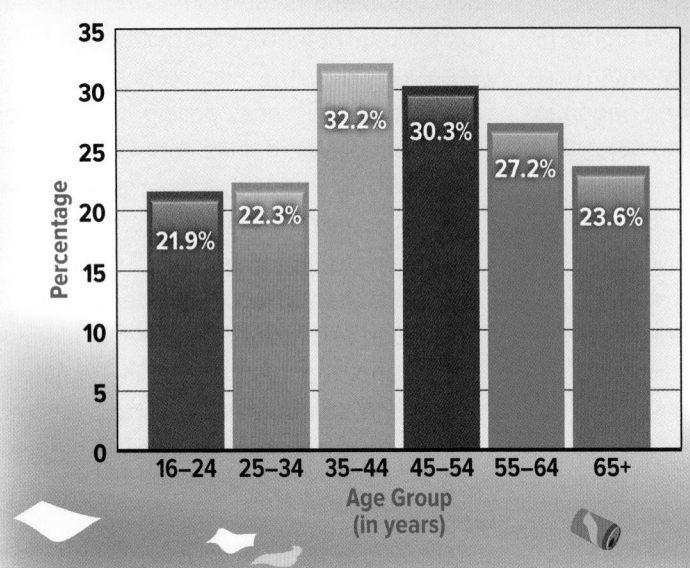

Volunteers by Type of Organization

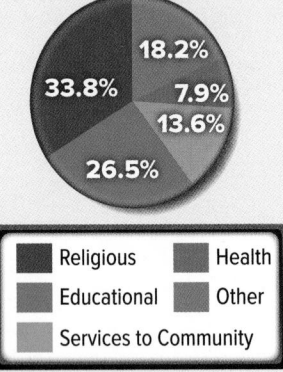

18.2%

33.8%   7.9%
        13.6%

26.5%

- Religious
- Educational
- Services to Community
- Health
- Other

National Service Programs	
Peace Corps	Advises farmers, teaches children, starts small businesses, and fights serious diseases worldwide
AmeriCorps	Meets community needs, helps victims of natural disasters, cleans polluted rivers, and assists disabled people
Senior Corps	Volunteer opportunities for Americans 55 and older: • Foster Grandparents–help special needs kids • Senior Companions– help other seniors at home • Retired and Senior Volunteer Program (RSVP)– connects seniors to volunteer opportunities in their own communities

Source for graphs: Bureau of Labor Statistics, 2010

INFOGRAPHIC SKILLS

Millions of Americans of all ages do many different kinds of volunteer work. Opportunities to help your community are easy to find.

▶ CRITICAL THINKING

1 **Analyzing Visuals** Which age group has the highest percentage of volunteering?

2 **Making Inferences** Why do you think the field of education is so popular among volunteers?

Reading**HELP**DESK

Reading Strategy: *Finding the Main Idea*

One way of making sure you understand a chart or graph is to state the main idea in words. For each part of the infographic, write the main idea. Then list at least two details from the chart or graph that support that main idea.

People also support causes by giving money. Americans give more than $300 billion to charity each year. Much of this money comes from small gifts made by ordinary people.

The Spirit of Volunteerism

Americans have a long history of volunteering. In the 1830s, French political writer Alexis de Tocqueville visited America. He was amazed to see citizens solving community problems rather than relying on the government. He said it was "self-interest rightly understood." In other words, by banding together to serve the community, we really serve ourselves.

The United States has more than 1 million charities. Many are small and local, such as animal shelters and food pantries. Some are local branches of national organizations, such as Boys and Girls Clubs. Other groups serve large numbers of people. Habitat for Humanity, for example, has built more than 350,000 homes for low-income families.

National Service Programs

The government has a long history of supporting volunteerism. Today, the Corporation for National and Community Service provides money, training, and other help for volunteer groups. This government agency also manages three national volunteer organizations. They are AmeriCorps, Senior Corps, and Learn and Serve America.

AmeriCorps members work in education, public safety, health, and the environment. For a year of service, they receive money to help them live and to pay for college. Older Americans can serve in Senior Corps to help their communities. Learn and Serve America promotes service learning in schools. Service learning programs, such as analyzing the local water supply, link community service with classroom work.

✓ PROGRESS CHECK

Defining What is volunteerism?

LESSON 3 REVIEW

Review Vocabulary

1. What is the difference between a *duty* and a *responsibility*?

2. What is *tolerance*?

Answer the Guiding Questions

3. *Drawing Conclusions* Why do you think serving on a jury is a civic duty?

4. *Explaining* Why is it every citizen's responsibility to be informed?

5. *Finding the Main Idea* Why do Americans volunteer?

6. **ARGUMENT** What do you think is the most important duty or responsibility of a citizen? Explain the reasons for your choice.

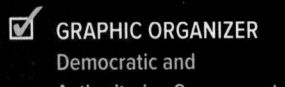

netw⊙rks

There's More Online!

☑ **GRAPHIC ORGANIZER**
Democratic and
Authoritarian Governments

☑ **CHARTS**
Functions of Government
Principles of American
Democracy
Comparing Democratic and
Authoritarian Systems

☑ **VIDEO**

☑ **GAMES**

Lesson 4

Forms of Government

ESSENTIAL QUESTION *Why do people create, structure, and change governments?*

IT MATTERS BECAUSE

People form governments to establish order, provide security, and accomplish common goals.

The Importance of Government

GUIDING QUESTION *What is the purpose of government?*

Think about playing basketball with no rules or referees. The game would probably be a free-for-all. Similarly, if there were no government to make and enforce laws, people would face a time of confusion, violence, and fear. Government makes it possible for people to live together peacefully and productively.

A government is the ruling authority for a community. Any organization that has the power to make and carry out laws and decisions for all those living in a community is a government.

Keep Order and Provide Security

Conflicts will always arise when people live together. The most important purpose of a government is to provide laws, or rules of conduct, for people to follow. These laws serve to prevent conflicts between individuals, groups, or nations. Some laws protect the safety of members of the society by making it a crime to attack or harm another person. Some laws protect people's property by making it a crime to steal. Other laws protect people's right to speak their minds. When conflicts do occur, laws help **resolve**, or find a solution, for them.

Reading**HELP**DESK

Taking Notes: *Categorizing*

As you read, complete a graphic organizer like this one to identify the differences between democratic and authoritarian governments.

Democratic	
Authoritarian	

Content Vocabulary

- public policy
- representative democracy
- constitutional monarchy
- majority rule
- authoritarian regime

Governments have the power to enforce the laws they make. For example, police officers can ticket or arrest drivers who break traffic laws. Courts decide whether people accused of crimes are guilty. For those who are found guilty, courts decide how they should be punished.

Along with the need for law and order, societies also have a need for security. That is, they need to be protected from attacks from other societies. Governments also meet this need. They set up armed forces to defend citizens from foreign enemies.

Provide Services

Governments provide many services that people would not get otherwise. Governments run libraries, schools, hospitals, and parks. They build and repair streets and bridges, collect garbage, and deliver the mail.

Many government services keep the public safe and healthy. Local governments set up police and fire departments. State governments license drivers and doctors. Government agencies make sure that food, medicines, and products from cars to cribs are safe. When a disease threatens large numbers of people, governments take steps to try to limit its spread.

Governments also give help to people who are very needy. For example, state governments give food, monetary support, or other kinds of help to poor families and people who are out of work. They also supply housing, health care, and special programs for people with disabilities.

FUNCTIONS OF GOVERNMENT

KEEP ORDER	PROVIDE SECURITY
Pass and enforce laws to deter crime	Establish armed forces
Establish courts	Protect citizens from foreign attacks
PROVIDE SERVICES	**GUIDE THE COMMUNITY**
Protect public health	Develop public policy
Protect public safety	Manage the economy
Provide public welfare	Conduct foreign relations

CHART SKILLS

Governments serve many different purposes.

► CRITICAL THINKING

1 *Identifying* What are the four broad functions of government?

2 *Evaluating* Which one of the functions of government do you think is the most important? Why?

Academic Vocabulary

- totalitarian
- ideology
- socialism

resolve to find a solution to a disagreement

Guide the Community

Governments develop public policy. **Public policy** refers to the decisions and actions a government takes to solve problems in the community. Protecting consumers from unsafe products is a public policy goal. So is making the nation more secure from attacks. When governments pass laws or develop plans to reach these goals, they make public policy.

Most public policy decisions involve financial planning. Governments have limited amounts of money. They must use their resources wisely. Creating a plan for collecting and spending money is a key to the government's success.

Governments also guide the community by handling relations with neighboring countries and other outsiders. Governments talk to and work with other governments on such matters as trade and travel for the benefit of their citizens. They sometimes make agreements to share resources that two or more governments have a claim to, such as fisheries or oil located under bodies of water. Governments also sometimes make agreements to help each other if attacked.

In 2010 in Seoul, South Korea, U.S. president Barack Obama (left) met with other world leaders, including South Korea's president Lee Myung-bak (center) and Canada's prime minister Stephen Harper (right).

▶ CRITICAL THINKING
Determining Cause and Effect Why do you think world leaders meet to conduct foreign policy?

Reading**HELP**DESK

public policy the decisions and actions a government takes to solve problems in the community

Levels of Government

The United States has a federal system of government. This means that government power is divided between the federal, or national, government and the states. In addition, local governments serve towns, cities, and counties.

The national government has the highest level of authority over its citizens. It makes and enforces laws for the entire country. A state or local government cannot make any laws that would go against the laws of the national government. The national government also sets the basic rules for citizenship.

Each of the 50 states has its own government. These governments decide matters for the people of their state. States set marriage laws, make rules for schooling, and hold elections. They manage public health and safety and build roads and bridges. They also have the power to set up local governments.

Local governments can be found in counties, cities, and towns. They are the level of government closest to citizens. They provide schools, police and fire departments, emergency medical services, and local courts. They perform public services such as providing outdoor lighting and removing snow from streets. Like the states, local governments cannot take actions that go against the laws or authority of the national government.

PHOTO: Peter Steiner/Alamy

Local governments help ensure that roads are maintained properly.

► CRITICAL THINKING
Drawing Conclusions How do services such as maintaining roads help our society function more smoothly?

✓ PROGRESS CHECK

Identifying How do governments keep order in society?

The Types of Government

GUIDING QUESTION *What are the types of government?*

Do you belong to a club or take part in student government? How do these groups make decisions? How do you and your friends or family make decisions? These groups may have different ways of governing themselves. Nations, too, have different forms of government.

Many Americans express their views on public issues and other matters by writing blog entries. These posts are like mini-essays. They use thoughtful, lively writing to state an idea and support it with strong reasons and examples. Choose one of the seven principles of American democracy from the chart. Write a blog entry identifying and explaining why you think the principle is important. Remember to make your entry lively and well reasoned.

Democratic Government

Democracy began in the ancient Greek city of Athens some 2,500 years ago. Athens had a direct, or pure, democracy. All citizens met to discuss government matters and voted to decide what to do.

Today nations have large areas and many people. As a result, direct democracy is not practical. Instead, many countries that want a democratic government choose to have a **representative democracy** (reh•pree•ZEHN•tuh•tihv dih•MAH•kruh•see). In this kind of democracy, citizens choose a group of people to represent them, make laws, and govern on their behalf. The United States has this form of government. It is the world's oldest representative democracy.

There are two kinds of representative democracies. Some, like the United States, are republics. In republics, citizens have a role in choosing the person who will be the head of the government or the head of state. In the United States and in many other republics, that leader is called the president. The second kind of representative democracy is a **constitutional monarchy** (kahn•stuh•TOO•shnuhl MAH•nuhr•kee), also known as a limited monarchy. The word *monarchy* describes a government with a hereditary ruler, such as a king or queen. In most European countries with monarchs today, the power of this hereditary ruler is limited by the country's constitution. For that reason, they are called constitutional monarchies.

CHART SKILLS

The seven principles that underlie American democracy reflect American values.

▶ CRITICAL THINKING

1. *Explaining* Use your own words to explain what is meant by "free, fair, and competitive elections."

2. *Making Inferences* How is the principle of limited government related to the principle of individual rights?

PRINCIPLES OF AMERICAN DEMOCRACY

RULE OF LAW	All people, including those who govern, are bound by the law.
LIMITED GOVERNMENT	Government is not all-powerful. It may do only those things that the people have given it the power to do.
CONSENT OF THE GOVERNED	American citizens are the source of all government power.
INDIVIDUAL RIGHTS	In American democracy, individual rights are protected by government.
REPRESENTATIVE GOVERNMENT	People elect government leaders to make the laws and govern on their behalf.
FREE, FAIR, AND COMPETITIVE ELECTIONS	Every citizen's vote has equal value. They choose between candidates and parties. They vote by secret ballot free from government interference.
MAJORITY RULE	A majority of the members of a community has the power to make laws binding upon all the people.

Reading**HELP**DESK

representative democracy
a government in which citizens choose a smaller group to govern on their behalf

constitutional monarchy
monarchy in which the power of the hereditary ruler is limited by the country's constitution and laws

majority rule political principle providing that a majority of the members of a community has the power to make laws binding upon all the people

Academic Vocabulary

regime a government that is in power

COMPARING DEMOCRATIC AND AUTHORITARIAN SYSTEMS

	SELECTION OF LEADERS	EXTENT OF GOVERNMENT POWER	MEANS OF ENSURING OBEDIENCE	POLITICAL PARTIES
Democracy (including republic, constitutional monarchy)	Leaders are chosen in free and fair elections.	The government is limited in power by the constitution and laws; citizens' rights and freedoms are protected.	The government relies on the rule of law.	Multiple parties compete for power.
Authoritarianism (including absolute monarchy, dictatorship, and totalitarianism)	Rulers inherit their positions or take power by force.	Rulers have unlimited power; the government may impose an official ideology and control all aspects of political, economic, and civic life.	The government relies on state control of the media, propaganda, military or police power, and terror.	Power lies with a single party.

CHART SKILLS

Differences in four key areas reveal the fundamental differences between democracies and authoritarian governments.

▶ **CRITICAL THINKING**

① *Analyzing Visuals* What kind of a government can a monarchy be?

② *Making Inferences* Sometimes authoritarian governments stage elections. Do you think they would be free and fair? Why or why not?

In a modern constitutional monarchy, the monarch has a limited role that is often just ceremonial. Voters elect representatives to sit in a lawmaking body. The representatives choose a prime minister to head the government.

Democracy works on the principle of **majority rule.** This principle means that a majority, or more than half, of the members of a community has the power to make laws that everyone in the community must follow. Under this principle, citizens agree to abide by what more than half the people want. At the same time, members of the minority keep all their basic rights as citizens. In a democracy, ruling majorities are determined through free and fair elections in which candidates from two or more political parties vie for the voters' approval.

Authoritarian Government

In democratic **regimes,** the people rule. In **authoritarian regimes** (aw•THAHR•uh•TEHR•ee•uhn ray•ZHEEMZ), power is held by a person or a group not accountable to the people.

Until about the 1600s, most monarchs could rule as they wished. With unlimited power, they were absolute monarchs in a form of government called an autocracy. Today, there are few absolute monarchs. In the Middle East, the king of Saudi Arabia and the emir of Qatar might still be seen as absolute monarchs. Their power is officially without limits. Their decisions are supposed to follow Islamic law, however.

Another form of authoritarian government is a dictatorship. Dictators, like absolute monarchs, exercise complete control over the state. Dictators often come to power by the use of force. They overthrow an existing government and seize power. Sometimes, when a serious situation demands a strong leader, government officials may welcome rule by a dictator.

Once they have power, though, dictators rarely give it up. To stay in power, most dictators rely on the police and the military. They often refuse to hold elections. When they do allow elections, they usually take steps to make the result suit them. If it does not, they may ignore the voters' choice.

In a dictatorship, people do not have freedom. They can be jailed for criticizing the government and are forbidden from forming opposition groups. Scores of dictators have ruled throughout history. Modern dictatorships include North Korea and Turkmenistan.

Many dictators force their people to accept **totalitarian** (toh•TA•luh•TEHR•ee•uhn) rule. In a totalitarian state, the government controls almost all aspects of people's lives. Totalitarian leaders ban any efforts to oppose them. They take away individual freedom, telling people what they can believe and what groups they may join. These rulers often have an **ideology** (EYE•dee•AH•luh•jee), or a strict idea about life and society. To force the people to obey this ideology, totalitarian leaders control the media, and they often rely on scare tactics and violence.

Some totalitarian states practice the system of **socialism.** In a socialist state, society controls all aspects of the economy, either directly or indirectly through the government. The government, rather than private owners, decides what items industries will produce and what jobs workers will have. Under socialism it was hoped that a nation's wealth would be more evenly divided among its citizens. This, however, was not the case in totalitarian states.

Three infamous totalitarian regimes arose in the 1920s and 1930s. They were Nazi Germany under Adolf Hitler, Fascist Italy under Benito Mussolini, and the Soviet Union under Joseph Stalin. Today the nations of Cuba, North Korea, and Myanmar are thought to be totalitarian states.

Cuba's Fidel Castro seized power in 1959, when he and his supporters overthrew Cuba's existing government. Castro ruled Cuba until he stepped down from power in 2008 due to ill health. That year, he was replaced by his brother.

▶ **CRITICAL THINKING**

Making Inferences Based on this information about how Castro obtained and held power, what kind of government do you think Cuba had under him? Why?

PHOTO: Sven Creutzmann/Mambo Photo/Getty Images

Reading**HELP**DESK

authoritarian regime a government in which one leader or group of people holds absolute power

totalitarian describes a system in which government control extends to almost all aspects of people's lives

ideology a body of ideas about life and society

socialism system in which society, either directly or indirectly through the government, controls all aspects of the economy

Authoritarian governments have also included oligarchies and theocracies. An oligarchy is a form of government in which a small group of people holds power. Often, such power was based on wealth. Most, but not all, oligarchies have been viewed as authoritarian. A government that is ruled by religious leaders is a theocracy. In such a government, religious law is the basis of all of society's laws. Often, religious law is absolute and forced upon all of a nation's citizens.

Systems of Government

Nations also differ in their systems of government and how power is shared or not shared among various levels of government. The United States has a federal system of government. In a federal system, power is divided among a central, national government and smaller self-governing political units such as states. The central government cannot dissolve or take power from the smaller units. Germany, Brazil, and India are other countries that have federal systems of government.

Most nations do not divide governmental power in this way. They have unitary systems of government. In a unitary system, the central government is supreme. It may create smaller administrative units to carry out some of its functions. But those smaller units are not protected by a constitution. The central government can dissolve them or reallocate their powers as it sees fit. France, Japan, and Great Britain have unitary systems of government.

The United States did not always have a federal system of government. When it achieved its independence, it was governed under a confederal system of government. A confederal system consists of member states that have agreed to join together voluntarily. The states or nations create a common body to carry out certain functions, but they retain their powers.

☑ PROGRESS CHECK

Comparing and Contrasting How does an absolute monarchy differ from a constitutional monarchy?

LESSON 4 REVIEW

Review Vocabulary

1. How does *representative democracy* differ from direct democracy?

2. What is the role of *majority rule*?

Answer the Guiding Questions

3. *Identifying* What types of services does our government provide at the national, state, and local levels?

4. *Contrasting* Which principles of democracy are not followed in an authoritarian state? Explain why.

5. *Comparing* How are federal and unitary systems of government different? Explain.

6. **INFORMATIVE/EXPLANATORY** In a short essay, explain how the ideology of a totalitarian regime differs from that of a democratic regime.

Activities

Write your answers on a separate sheet of paper.

1 **Writing Activity**

EXPLORING THE ESSENTIAL QUESTION
What is a citizen?

Write a paragraph describing what it means to be a citizen of the United States.

2 **21st Century Skills**

IDENTIFY PROBLEMS AND SOLUTIONS Think about some ways to improve your community. Your community can include your school, your neighborhood, or the whole town or city. Use local news sources, such as newspapers, newsletters, and the Internet, to identify problems in your community. Then with a group of friends, brainstorm possible solutions. On your own, choose the problem you think is the most important one to solve. Write a paragraph explaining what the problem is and which solution you think will work best. Explain why you think that is the best solution.

3 **Being an Active Citizen**

There are many ways to be an active citizen. People do not always think their contribution matters, though. Write a 30-second public service announcement (PSA) aimed at convincing people to be active and responsible citizens. Try to be as persuasive as you can be. Deliver your PSA to the rest of the class.

4 **Understanding Visuals**

Study the circle graph. Then, in one or two sentences, describe the religious diversity of the United States.

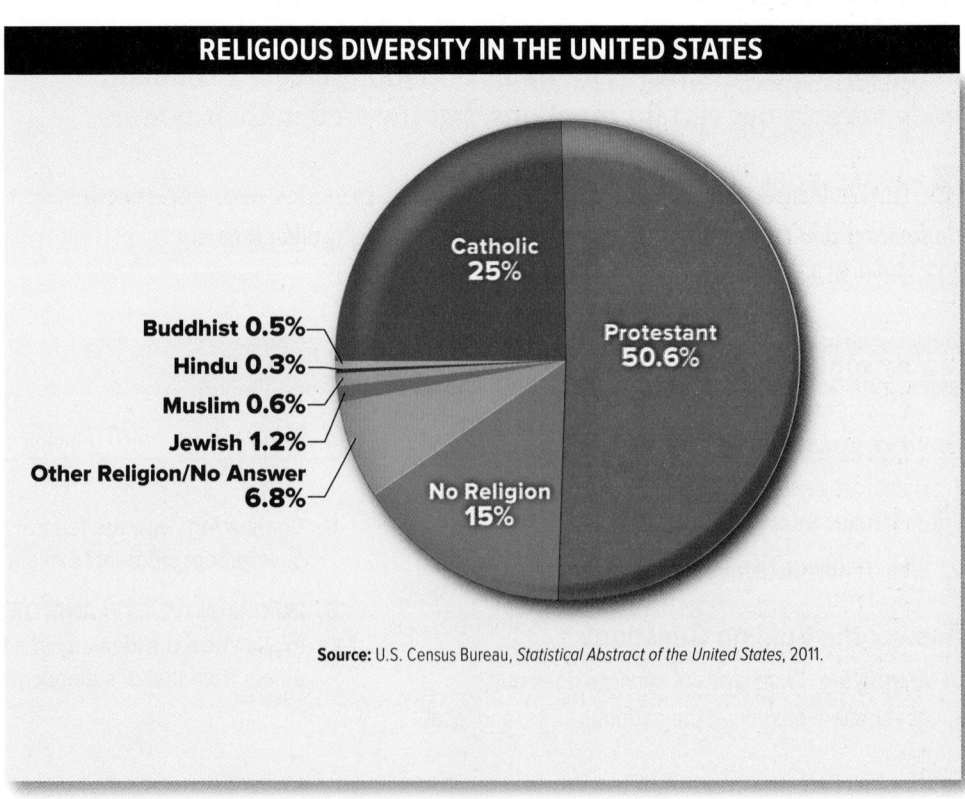

RELIGIOUS DIVERSITY IN THE UNITED STATES

Catholic 25%

Protestant 50.6%

Buddhist 0.5%
Hindu 0.3%
Muslim 0.6%
Jewish 1.2%
Other Religion/No Answer 6.8%

No Religion 15%

Source: U.S. Census Bureau, *Statistical Abstract of the United States*, 2011.

REVIEW THE GUIDING QUESTIONS

Directions: Choose the best answer for each question.

1 Which areas are the main sources of immigration to the United States today?

   A. Africa and the Pacific Islands

   B. western and northern Europe

   C. Asia and North America

   D. southern and eastern Europe

2 Naturalization is a legal process to obtain

   F. a birth certificate.

   G. citizenship.

   H. residency.

   I. a work permit.

3 Which describes a resident alien?

   A. a legal alien who has made residence in the United States permanent

   B. a foreigner who expects to stay in the United States for a short period

   C. someone with full political rights

   D. someone who is a refugee

4 Which of the following is a duty of citizenship?

   F. being informed and voting

   G. respecting differences of opinion and ways of life

   H. participating in the community

   I. obeying the law

5 In the United Kingdom, the king or queen presides over ceremonies, but elected officials run the government. What type of government does the United Kingdom have?

   A. absolute monarchy

   B. constitutional monarchy

   C. dictatorship

   D. republic

6 Authoritarian governments

   F. protect the rights of individuals.

   G. derive power from the people.

   H. have all been replaced by democratic governments.

   I. often rely on propaganda, military power, and terror.

DBQ ANALYZING DOCUMENTS

Directions: Analyze the excerpt and answer the questions that follow.

A home owner talks about volunteers after a fire destroyed her community.

> *"We needed their youthful hope, energy, and optimism as much as we needed their strong, physical help. As I looked up from down in the rubble and saw these AmeriCorps kids' faces . . . they reminded me . . . of all that can be accomplished . . . when we are willing to use our hands and hearts and minds in creative caring and generosity—together."*
>
> —Margaret Nes, New Mexico, 2010

7 **Identifying the Main Idea** Which states the main idea of this passage?
- **A.** The AmeriCorps volunteers showed a belief in civic responsibility.
- **B.** The AmeriCorps volunteers were fulfilling a civic duty.
- **C.** The AmeriCorps volunteers were too young to help.
- **D.** The AmeriCorps volunteers worked by majority rule.

8 **Analyzing** Which statement does the passage support?
- **F.** Only the young can perform hard physical labor.
- **G.** The government is not doing its job.
- **H.** A lot can be accomplished when people work together.
- **I.** Most young people only talk about helping.

SHORT RESPONSE

> *"I . . . declare . . . that I will support and defend the Constitution and laws of the United States . . . against all enemies, foreign and domestic; [and] that I will bear arms on behalf of the United States when required by law."*
>
> —Oath of Citizenship

9 Explain why you think people who are about to become citizens must take this oath.

10 Do you think people who are citizens by birth should have to take an oath like this also? Why or why not?

EXTENDED RESPONSE

11 **Argument** By 1920 millions of Americans, representing a wide variety of cultures, had migrated from rural areas to cities. How do you think this affected their individual cultures and that of the United States in general?

TEXT: A Letter of Thanks, by Margaret "Peggy" Nes. Stories of Service. AmeriCorps. http://www.americorps.gov/for_individuals/current/stories_detail.asp?tbl_stories_id=30

Need Extra Help?

If You've Missed Question	**1**	**2**	**3**	**4**	**5**	**6**	**7**	**8**	**9**	**10**	**11**
Review Lesson	1	2	2	3	4	4	3	3	1, 2, 3	1, 2, 3	1

The American Colonies and Their Government

ESSENTIAL QUESTIONS · *How does geography influence the development of communities?* · *Why do people create, structure, and change governments?*

The Story Matters...

In 1776 a group of determined American colonists met. Risking their freedom and perhaps their lives, they defied Great Britain, the world's most powerful nation. Most of these men had come from Great Britain, or had British ancestors. They had grown up valuing the English traditions of law and limited government. As a result, when they felt that their freedoms were being denied, they took decisive action.

America's political leaders came together to write a document explaining their desire for and right to freedom. Their words became a unique political statement in history—the Declaration of Independence.

◄ *Colonial leaders including Benjamin Franklin, Thomas Jefferson, and John Adams met to create the Declaration of Independence.*

PHOTO: Getty Images

Real-Life Civics

▶ **TODAY** Each year, Americans across the land celebrate the birth of their nation on the 4th of July. The day commemorates the official signing of the Declaration of Independence, announcing the American colonies' intent to form a nation separate from Great Britain. In towns large and small, from the East Coast to the West Coast, crowds gather for a day marked by fireworks, flag-raisings, family picnics, parades, and community band concerts. One of the grandest celebrations takes place on the National Mall in Washington, D.C., the capital of the United States. Here famous monuments to many major events in the nation's history provide dramatic reminders of those who have sacrificed greatly to preserve our country.

A spectacular fireworks display lights up the night sky above the United States Marine Corps War Memorial in Washington, D.C.

George Washington, the Marquis de Lafayette, and the Continental Army endured a bitter winter at Valley Forge.

LONG AGO American independence was not easily won. In order to become a nation independent from Great Britain, the colonists waged a war lasting eight years. Perhaps the lowest point of the American Revolution came at Valley Forge, Pennsylvania, during the winter of 1777 and 1778. Low on food, clothing, and other supplies, several thousand American troops died of exposure to frigid temperatures and of disease. Yet the soldiers who survived this terrible ordeal emerged confident that their army could fight and win against the highly trained and well-armed British forces.

CIVIC LITERACY

★ ★ ★ ★

Analyzing Do you think the words of the Declaration of Independence helped the American soldiers to endure the brutal conditions at Valley Forge and to continue their fight for freedom? Why or why not?

Your Opinion Is there a cause for which you might be willing to make a great sacrifice? Explain.

networks

There's More Online!

☑ **GRAPHIC ORGANIZER**
Limiting the Power of Government

☑ **CHARTS**
English Bill of Rights
Enlightenment Thinkers

☑ **TIME LINE**
The Glorious Revolution Era

Lesson 1

Influences on American Colonial Government

ESSENTIAL QUESTIONS • *How does geography influence the development of communities?* • *Why do people create, structure, and change governments?*

IT MATTERS BECAUSE

Ancient peoples and the great thinkers of the Enlightenment influenced how the Founders shaped our government in ways that still affect us today.

The Foundations of Democracy

GUIDING QUESTION *What ancient principles, traditions, and events have shaped the system of government we have today?*

The rights, freedoms, and form of government that we enjoy as Americans did not begin with the adoption of the United States Constitution in 1788. Nor did they begin with our Declaration of Independence from Great Britain in 1776. In fact, the origins of the American political system can be traced to ancient times.

The growth of **democracy**, or rule by the people, has not occurred at a steady pace over those thousands of years. There have been long periods of time when little democracy existed. During some of these periods, people were governed by monarchs, or single rulers who held great power. At other times, however, the ideas and practices of democracy have developed, spread, and grown strong.

Ancient Democracies

One of the earliest foundations for democracy can be found in the Jewish religion. Since ancient times, Judaism has taught

PHOTO: (tl) Ancient Art and Architecture Collection Ltd./The Bridgeman Art Library International; (tcl) The Stapleton Collection/The Bridgeman Art Library International; (tcr) Bettmann/CORBIS; (tr) AP Photo/Lee Marriner

Reading**HELP**DESK

Taking Notes: *Relating*

As you read, create a graphic organizer showing how events limited government power.

Event	Effect
Magna Carta →	
Petition of Right →	
English Bill of Rights →	
social contract theory →	

Content Vocabulary

- **democracy**
- **direct democracy**
- **representative democracy**
- **republic**
- **limited government**
- **legislature**

(and teaches today) that every person has worth and is equal before the law. This belief is a basic principle of democracy.

Centuries later, in the 400s B.C., the Greek city-state of Athens created the world's first democracy. All free men over 18 were considered citizens. They could take part in the Athens assembly. This was a gathering at which any citizen had the right to speak. Its decisions were carried out by a council of 500 members. This council governed Athens. Citizens took turns serving on the council. Since this required taking time off from work, council members were paid for their service.

This system, in which the people govern themselves, is called **direct democracy.** It was possible in Athens because the city-state was small. In places with large populations, direct democracy is not practical. In such places, people choose leaders to govern for them. This form of democracy is called **representative democracy.** A government based on representative democracy is called a **republic.** The United States is a republic.

As the ancient Greeks were creating democracy, the ancient Romans were creating the world's first republic. In 509 B.C. the Romans overthrew their king. Government was put in the hands of a senate. Members of this body were chosen from among Rome's wealthy upper class, called *patricians*. The senators elected two members, called *consuls*, to lead the government. Both consuls had to agree. Each consul had the power to block the actions of the other by saying *veto*, meaning "I forbid!"

Persuasive speech-making was one of the key skills of a Roman senator. This painting shows a famous incident in which the consul Cicero (left) accuses a politician named Catiline (extreme right) of being a traitor.

▶ CRITICAL THINKING
Speculating Why do you think the artist showed all the other senators on one side of the room and Catiline on the other?

PHOTO: Ancient Art and Architecture Collection Ltd./The Bridgeman Art Library International

- **social contract**
- **natural right**

democracy a government in which citizens hold the power to rule

direct democracy a form of democracy in which the people vote firsthand

representative democracy a government in which citizens choose a smaller group to govern on their behalf

Rome's common citizens, called *plebeians*, soon tired of the rule of the patricians. A long struggle followed. The plebeians finally gained political equality in 287 B.C.

Rome continued as a republic until General Julius Caesar took control around 50 B.C. After his death, monarchs called emperors ruled Rome and its empire for more than 500 years.

Early English Influences

The Roman Empire collapsed around A.D. 476. For the next 700 years, kings and lords ruled most of Europe. Lords were noblemen who usually inherited land, wealth, and power. Over time the growth of towns as business and trade centers weakened the power of the lords. The kings gained greater control of their kingdoms. Many nobles resisted this change. In England they rose up against King John in 1215. They forced him to sign a **document** called the Magna Carta (Latin for "Great Charter").

The Magna Carta limited the king's power. It forbade him from placing certain taxes on the nobles without their consent. It gave rights to free men. These included the rights to equal treatment under the law and to trial by one's peers. The Magna Carta also gave nobles the right to rebel if the king broke his part of the agreement.

The Magna Carta is important because it established the principle of **limited government.** This is the idea that a ruler or a government is not all-powerful. At first, many of the rights protected by the Magna Carta applied only to nobles. Over time, however, those rights came to apply to all English people.

Kings who came after John were advised by nobles and church officials. Gradually this group grew to include representatives of the common people, as well. By the late 1300s the advisers had become a **legislature,** or lawmaking body. It was called Parliament.

Parliament had some influence, but England's monarchs remained strong for the next 300 years. In the mid-1600s, a power struggle developed between the monarch and Parliament. In 1625 King Charles I dismissed Parliament and ruled alone.

English nobles forced King John to sign the Magna Carta limiting the monarch's power.

► CRITICAL THINKING
Cause and Effect How did this event affect future English kings?

PHOTO: The Stapleton Collection/The Bridgeman Art Library International

Reading**HELP**DESK

republic a representative democracy where citizens choose their lawmakers

Academic Vocabulary
document an official paper or form that is a record of something

limited government the principle that a ruler or a government is not all-powerful

legislature a group of people that makes laws

When he recalled the members in 1628, they forced him to sign the Petition of Right. Like the Magna Carta, this document limited the king's power. When Charles failed to uphold the terms of the agreement, a civil war broke out. Eventually, Parliament removed the king and ruled without a monarch for about 20 years.

The English Bill of Rights

In 1688 Parliament forced King James II, the son of Charles I, from the throne. It asked James's daughter Mary and her husband, William, to rule instead. This transfer of power is known as the Glorious Revolution.

But first William and Mary had to accept rules set by Parliament. They agreed that English citizens had rights that no king could violate. Citizens had the right to a fair trial. They also could not be taxed unless Parliament agreed. The rights set out by Parliament became known as the English Bill of Rights.

The signing of the English Bill of Rights signaled the end of the struggle between Parliament and the monarch. Parliament had won. It was now the leading force in English government. Such events changed English government. They also received much notice in the English colonies in North America.

✓ PROGRESS CHECK

Explaining How did the Magna Carta establish the principle of limited government?

English Bill of Rights (1689)

- No imprisonment without due process of law.
- No loss of property without due process of law.
- No cruel punishment.
- No standing army in time of peace without Parliament's consent.
- No taxation without Parliament's consent.
- Subjects [people] have the right to bear arms.
- Subjects [people] have the right to petition the king.
- Freedom of speech in Parliament.

The English Bill of Rights built on the gains won in the Petition of Right.

▶ CRITICAL THINKING
Classifying What rights listed here do you recognize as rights modern Americans enjoy?

Influence of the Enlightenment

GUIDING QUESTION *How did Europe's Enlightenment influence ideas about government in what became the United States?*

The conflict between the monarch and Parliament produced new ideas about government. These new ideas were part of a larger cultural movement in Europe known as the Enlightenment.

During the 1600s, scientific discoveries led to the belief that God had created an orderly universe. Some people thought that its laws could be discovered through human reason.

This change in how some people saw their world is called the Enlightenment. These thinkers wanted to apply the laws that ruled nature to people and society. These new ideas had a great effect on political thinking in Europe and the Americas.

PHOTO: Bettmann/CORBIS

Members of Parliament look on as William and Mary accept the English crown.

▶ CRITICAL THINKING

Making Connections How did the Glorious Revolution inspire Enlightenment thinkers?

Enlightenment Thinkers

In their writings on government, many Enlightenment thinkers looked back to Niccolò Machiavelli (1469–1527). Machiavelli was an Italian Renaissance writer and thinker best known today for his book *The Prince*. In it, he argued that it is safer for a ruler to be feared than loved. Elsewhere, however, he praised republics as the best form of government.

An early Enlightenment thinker, Thomas Hobbes (1588–1679), experienced the English Civil War firsthand. Hobbes believed that an agreement, called a **social contract,** existed between government and the people. In this contract, the people agreed to give up some freedom and be ruled by government. In return, government had to protect the people's rights. But Hobbes thought that people needed a strong leader because they were too selfish to be able to rule themselves.

Another English thinker, John Locke (1632–1704), was influenced by the events of the Glorious Revolution. In 1690 he published *Two Treatises of Government*. (A treatise is a long essay.) Locke wrote that all people were born equal with certain

Reading**HELP**DESK

social contract an agreement among people in a society with their government

natural right a freedom people possess relating to life, liberty, and property

God-given rights, called **natural rights.** These included the rights to life, to freedom, and to own property. Like Hobbes, Locke believed in a form of social contract. Locke believed that people agreed to give up some rights and to be ruled by a government. But he believed that if the ruler failed to protect the rights of the people, the social contract was broken. Then the people could choose new leaders.

Some years later, a French thinker named Jean-Jacques Rousseau (1712–1778) wrote *The Social Contract.* It was published in 1762. In it, he said that "man is born free, yet everywhere he is found in chains." He referred to the many Europeans living with little freedom. Rousseau thought people had the right to decide how they should be governed.

At about this time, another French writer named Baron de Montesquieu (1689–1755) developed the idea that the power of government should be divided into branches. Then, Montesquieu believed, no one branch would become too strong and threaten people's rights. Montesquieu called this idea the separation of powers.

French writer Francois-Marie Arouet (1694–1778), who wrote under the name Voltaire, also believed people should have liberty. He supported freedom of religion and freedom of trade.

Colonists' views about government were shaped by the Enlightenment thinkers. Ideas about a social contract, natural rights, and separation of powers influenced the writers of the Declaration of Independence and the U.S. Constitution.

☑ PROGRESS CHECK

Listing What natural rights did John Locke believe all people had?

21ˢᵗ Century
SKILLS
Compare and Contrast

Develop and complete a Venn diagram comparing and contrasting the ideas of Thomas Hobbes and John Locke.

ENLIGHTENMENT THINKERS

NAME	YEARS LIVED	BELIEFS
Thomas Hobbes	1588–1679	People agree to be ruled because their ruler pledges to protect their rights.
John Locke	1632–1704	People have rights to life, liberty, and property that the government must protect for the common good.
Baron de Montesquieu	1689–1755	Separate the parts of government so no one part can become too powerful.
Voltaire	1694–1778	People have the right to speak freely, and this right should be defended by everyone.
Jean-Jacques Rousseau	1712–1778	The legislative power belongs to the people.

CHART SKILLS

Although Enlightenment thinkers had different ideas about how people should be governed, they also shared some basic beliefs.

1 *Summarizing* What rights do people have, according to these thinkers?

2 CRITICAL THINKING *Identifying Central Issues* What did these Enlightenment thinkers believe the relationship between the people and government should be?

Student Government

The forms of government that were created in the early colonies have been adapted to many other areas of American life. Find out about student government at your school. Does it include any of the features of the governments that developed in the colonies?

The First Colonial Governments

GUIDING QUESTION *How were the first English colonies in America shaped by earlier ideas about democracy and government?*

England founded colonies in America throughout the 1600s. A colony is an area of settlement in one place that is controlled by a country in another place. The early colonists were loyal to England. They brought to America the traditions, beliefs, and changes that had shaped England's government. These included a strong belief in their rights and representative government.

Jamestown

The first permanent English settlement in North America was Jamestown. It was located in what is now Virginia. Jamestown was founded in 1607 by the Virginia Company. The Virginia Company was a business owned by a group of London merchants. They asked King James I to allow them to send some colonists to North America. The company provided the supplies and settlers for the colony. The owners hoped the colony would make money for the company.

At first, Jamestown was ruled by a governor and a council. The company appointed these officials. To attract more settlers, in 1619 the company allowed the colony to make its own laws. The colonists elected leaders to represent them in an assembly. These leaders were called burgesses. The assembly was named the House of Burgesses. This legislature marked the beginning of self-government and representative democracy in colonial America.

The Mayflower Compact

Soon after the House of Burgesses was formed, another group of English colonists arrived in America. In 1620 these Pilgrims set sail for Virginia, seeking religious freedom. A storm in the Atlantic blew their small ship, the *Mayflower,* off course. They anchored off the coast of what is now Massachusetts instead.

The Pilgrims knew they had reached a land that had no English government. They knew that to survive they needed to form their own government. So they drew up a **compact,** or written agreement. All the Pilgrim men aboard the ship signed. They agreed to choose leaders and work together to make their own laws for the colony. They also agreed to obey the laws that were made. Then the colonists went ashore and founded the town of Plymouth.

Reading**HELP**DESK

Academic Vocabulary

compact an agreement, or contract, among a group of people

The signers of the Mayflower Compact established a direct democracy in colonial America. The people of Plymouth held town meetings to discuss problems and make decisions. Anyone in the town could attend and express his or her views. However, only some male members of the colony could vote. The tradition of the town meeting continues in much of New England today.

Residents listen to a speaker at a town hall meeting in Grafton, New Hampshire. Many New England towns preserve the tradition of direct democracy.

☑ PROGRESS CHECK

Summarizing What beliefs about government did early English colonists bring to America?

▶ CRITICAL THINKING
Evaluating What are some advantages and disadvantages of direct democracy?

LESSON 1 REVIEW

Review Vocabulary

1. How could a *legislature* restrain a monarch and establish *limited government*?

2. How do *direct democracy* and *representative democracy* differ?

Answer the Guiding Questions

3. *Identifying* What two ancient democracies helped shape the system of government we have today?

4. *Explaining* How did the writings of John Locke and Baron de Montesquieu influence ideas about government in what became the United States?

5. *Contrasting* How did lawmaking at Jamestown differ from lawmaking at Plymouth?

6. **ARGUMENT** Write a short speech convincing William and Mary to accept the English Bill of Rights.

netw⊙rks

There's More Online!

☑ **GRAPHIC ORGANIZER**
The Colonial Economy

☑ **MAP**
Colonial Economy, c. 1750

☑ **GRAPH**
Indentured Servants

☑ **VIDEO**

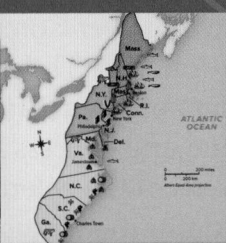

Lesson 2

Settlement, Culture, and Government of the Colonies

ESSENTIAL QUESTIONS • *How does geography influence the development of communities?* • *Why do people create, structure, and change governments?*

IT MATTERS BECAUSE

The reasons early settlers came to America and the economies and governments that grew helped to shape the new United States and continue to influence American culture today.

Settling the English Colonies

GUIDING QUESTION *Why did people settle in England's colonies in America?*

Where did the colonists who settled in England's American colonies come from? Most were from England. Others came from Scotland, Ireland, and Wales. Settlers also arrived from other parts of Europe, such as Germany. Over time, thousands of enslaved Africans were brought to the colonies against their will. They worked in the fields, shops, and homes of the European settlers.

Some colonies along the Atlantic Coast were not founded by English people. The Dutch started a colony that England later took over and renamed New York. Sweden founded a colony that became part of the English colonies of Delaware and New Jersey.

Economic Opportunity

People came to America for several reasons. For many settlers, the chance to earn a living was the main one. America offered land for farming and other jobs too.

Reading **HELP** DESK

Taking Notes: *Comparing*

As you read, create a graphic organizer. Compare the economies of the New England, Middle, and Southern Colonies.

The Colonial Economy	
Region	Economic Activities

Content Vocabulary

- **indentured servant**
- **dissenter**
- **economy**
- **cash crop**
- **plantation**

Those too poor to pay for their trip to America came as **indentured servants.** Colonists in America agreed to pay the costs of bringing the servants to the colonies and promised to provide food and shelter in return for work. The servants worked from four to seven years, until their debt was paid. Then the workers were free to make better lives for themselves.

Religious Freedom

Other people wanted religious freedom. At this time, there was religious unrest in Europe, especially in England. Some groups were persecuted, or treated harshly, because of their religious beliefs. To find a place where they could worship in their own way, some groups decided to come to the English colonies.

The Puritans founded Massachusetts for this reason. The Puritans got their name because they wanted to reform, or purify, the church in England. They also called themselves Pilgrims. It was a group of Pilgrims who founded Plymouth colony in 1620. Soon after this, another group of Puritans started the Massachusetts Bay Colony nearby. The Puritans were religious **dissenters.** A dissenter is one who opposes official or commonly held views. The Puritans left England because they wanted to worship God in their own way. Yet, they did not allow others that freedom. Instead, the Puritans forced people to leave their colony if they did not wish to worship as the Puritans did.

Some colonists who were forced to leave Massachusetts started the colonies of Rhode Island and Connecticut. Rhode Island became known for the freedoms its colonists enjoyed. Connecticut developed America's first written constitution in 1639. It was called the Fundamental Orders of Connecticut. This document said that the colonists would elect an assembly of representatives from each town to pass laws. The colonists also elected their governor and judges.

☑ **PROGRESS CHECK**

Explaining Why did some people come to the colonies as indentured servants?

Why It
MATTERS

Forms of Government in Your Life

When people come together for a common purpose, they often draw up a list of rules to govern their actions. What organized clubs or organizations do you belong to? Find out if they have any rules or by-laws.

The English colonies provided economic opportunity for many people. Small farms, like this one in Virginia, offered a way for many to improve their lives.

▶ **CRITICAL THINKING**
Speculating What obstacles did new settlers overcome to begin a new life in America?

indentured servant a worker who contracted with American colonists for food and shelter in return for his or her labor

dissenter one who opposes official or commonly held views

PHOTO: The Granger Collection, NYC. All rights reserved.

The economy of the New England Colonies was tied to the sea. Shipbuilding, shown above, and fishing were important industries.

▶ CRITICAL THINKING
Making Connections How did the geographic features of New England affect the economy that developed there?

Colonial Life

GUIDING QUESTION *How was life in the colonies shaped by where people lived?*

As you have read, the colonists came to America from many places and for a variety of reasons. They lived in different ways depending on where they settled. By 1733 England had 13 colonies along the Atlantic Coast of North America. The features of its geography influenced each colony's **economy.** These factors shaped how people lived. Over time, three economic regions developed. Each had its own way of life.

The New England Colonies

The New England Colonies were located farthest north. They were Massachusetts Bay, New Hampshire, Connecticut, and Rhode Island. Most people in this region lived in towns. The cold climate and rocky soil made large-scale farming difficult. So farms were small and located near towns. Most farmers lived in town and went out to the countryside to work in their fields.

Many colonists in New England were Puritans. The Puritan religion stressed the values of thrift and hard work. A number of New Englanders worked as shopkeepers or in other small businesses. Others were employed in shipbuilding and fishing. The region's forests provided wood for boats. Fur-bearing animals were another important natural resource. Colonists hunted and trapped these animals. They also traded with Native Americans for furs. Then they shipped the furs to Europe. There the furs were made into coats and hats.

The Middle Colonies

New York, Pennsylvania, New Jersey, and Delaware were English colonies located south of New England. These colonies were known as the Middle Colonies. The climate and soil in this region were better for agriculture. Farmers raised wheat and other **cash crops.** Cash crops are grown in large quantities to be sold rather than to feed the farmer's family.

Cash crops were often sold overseas. This trade helped turn New York City and Philadelphia into busy port cities. Many of

ReadingHELPDESK

economy a system for making choices about ways to use scarce resources to make and distribute goods and services to fulfill people's needs and wants

cash crop a crop produced mainly for sale

plantation a large estate

the port businesses, as well as the region's farms, were owned by hardworking colonists from Germany, Holland, and other European countries.

The Middle Colonies were also rich in natural resources. Sawmills, mines, ironworks, and other businesses grew in the region. The colonists here depended upon such resources as lumber, metals, and natural harbors.

The Southern Colonies

The English colonies farthest south along the Atlantic Coast were Maryland, Virginia, North Carolina, South Carolina, and Georgia. A warm climate, a long growing season, and rich soil made large-scale agriculture successful in the Southern Colonies. Tobacco became the main cash crop in some of these colonies. In others it was rice. Both crops grew best on the low, flat coastal plains of the region.

Large farms called **plantations** developed on the coastal plains. Many workers were needed to plant, tend, and harvest the large fields of crops. At first, indentured servants did much of this work. Over time, however, plantation owners came to depend on the labor of enslaved Africans.

21st Century
SKILLS

Analyzing Historical Maps

Study the map and summarize the kinds of economic activity popular in each region. Then create a three-column chart in which you list products for each region. Highlight those products that are distinct to each region.

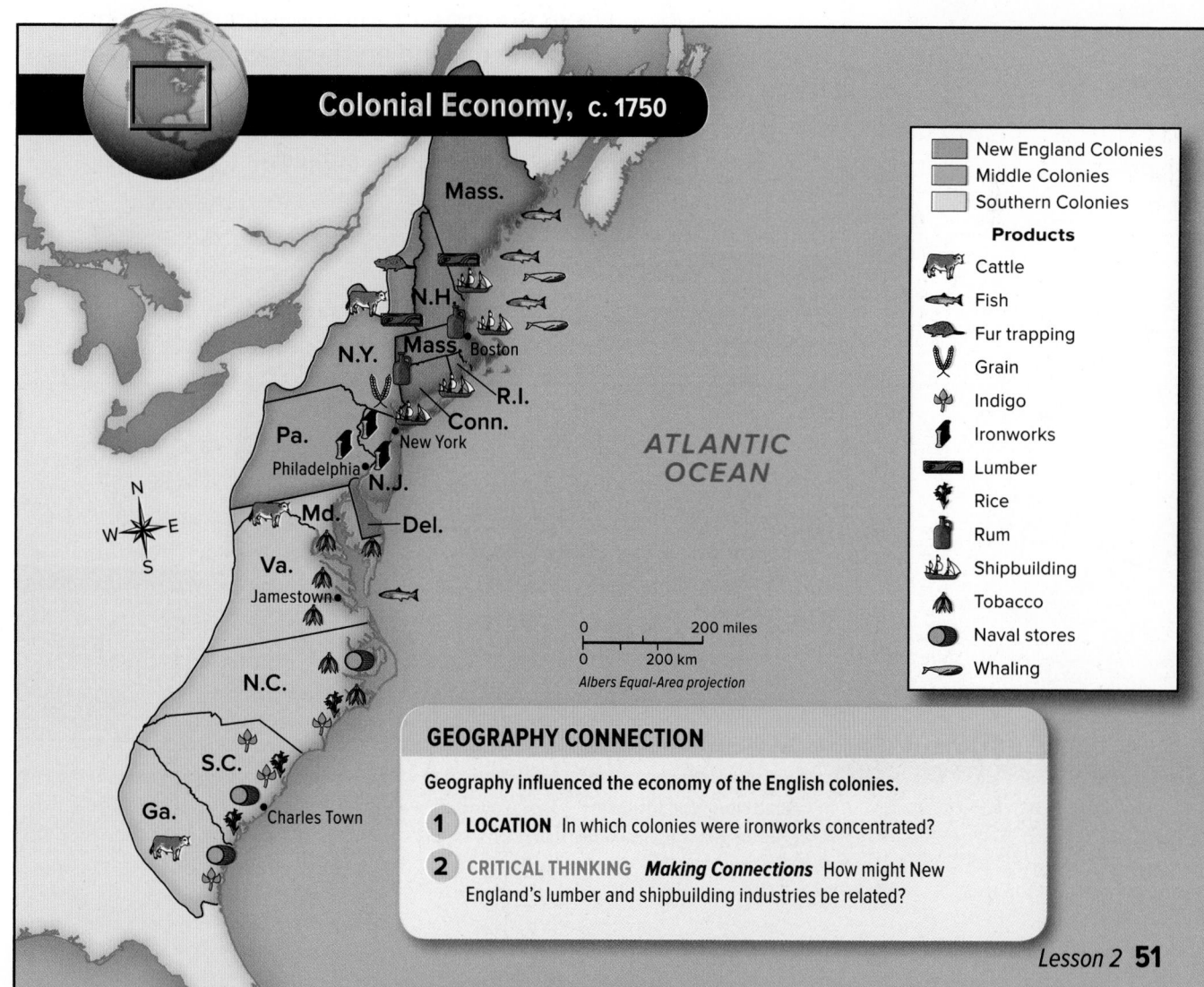

Colonial Economy, c. 1750

New England Colonies
Middle Colonies
Southern Colonies

Products
Cattle
Fish
Fur trapping
Grain
Indigo
Ironworks
Lumber
Rice
Rum
Shipbuilding
Tobacco
Naval stores
Whaling

ATLANTIC OCEAN

0   200 miles
0   200 km
Albers Equal-Area projection

GEOGRAPHY CONNECTION

Geography influenced the economy of the English colonies.

1 **LOCATION** In which colonies were ironworks concentrated?

2 **CRITICAL THINKING** *Making Connections* How might New England's lumber and shipbuilding industries be related?

Farther inland, away from the coast, the soil was poorer and farms were smaller. Farmers here mainly grew only what they needed to feed their families. They also depended less on enslaved labor.

Small farmers outnumbered plantation owners, but the plantation owners had greater wealth and power. As a result, they were able to sway the decisions of the representative assemblies. They also controlled the region's economy. Due in part to the influence of plantation owners, few large towns and little industry developed in the Southern Colonies.

☑ **PROGRESS CHECK**

Explaining Who controlled the elected assemblies in the Southern Colonies and why?

Colonial Government

GUIDING QUESTION *What factors weakened the ties between England and its colonies?*

The colonies developed different economies and ways of life. But one thing they shared was their English heritage. Most colonists were loyal to England. They valued their rights as English subjects.

But England was far away. Messages took weeks to arrive. Over the years, the colonists began to depend on their own governments— and their elected legislatures—for leadership. They began to see themselves as Americans rather than English subjects.

Completed in 1722, the Capitol in Williamsburg was the seat of royal power in the Virginia colony.

▶ **CRITICAL THINKING**
Analyzing How did the actions of colonial legislatures toward colonial governors show weakening ties to England in the colonies?

PHOTO: © Matt Purciel/Alamy

Reading**HELP**DESK

Academic Vocabulary

benefit to be useful or profitable to

Governing the Colonies

When the colonies were first founded, England's government paid little attention to them. One reason was political unrest in England. Members of Parliament were in a power struggle with the king. Nevertheless, English leaders always believed that the main purpose of the colonies was to **benefit** England. Therefore, in the 1650s Parliament began passing laws to regulate the colonies' trade.

But these laws were hard to enforce. In the colonies south of New England, few people lived along the coast. So colonists' ships could secretly load or unload goods without being seen. In this way, colonial traders ignored English trade laws intended to control their actions.

Most colonies eventually had a governor who had been appointed by the king. The royal governor took orders from the English king and Parliament. He enforced England's laws in his colony. But local laws were usually passed by the colony's elected assembly.

A Time of Change

As time passed, the colonists' elected assemblies grew strong. Assemblies and governors sometimes fought for control of the colonies. The assemblies had the power to tax and to decide how the money would be spent. They used these powers to weaken the royal governors.

By the mid 1700s, the colonies had become used to governing themselves through their elected legislatures. Colonists knew of the writings of John Locke. He said that governments existed to serve the people. Many colonists felt that their governor put British interests ahead of their own. They began to resent the fact that they had fewer rights than people living in Great Britain.

☑ PROGRESS CHECK

Evaluating How did the distance between England and America influence colonists' ideas about leadership?

LESSON 2 REVIEW

Review Vocabulary

1. What reasons did *dissenters* and *indentured servants* have for coming to the American colonies?

2. Use the terms *plantation* and *cash crop* in a sentence about the colonies' economy.

Answer the Guiding Questions

3. *Explaining* How did the writings of people like John Locke lead colonists to resent the British government?

4. *Analyzing* How did geographic features influence life in the colonies?

5. *Identifying* How do John Locke's ideas help explain why the colonists looked to their legislatures for leadership instead of to the colony's governor?

6. **NARRATIVE** You have decided to move from Great Britain to America in the 1700s. Write a letter to a friend explaining which colony you have chosen to settle in and why.

netw⊙rks
There's More Online!

☑ **GRAPHIC ORGANIZER**
British Action and
Colonial Response

☑ **MAP**
The Proclamation Line of 1763

☑ **POLITICAL CARTOON**
The Stamp Act

☑ **CHART**
Taxing the Colonies

☑ **VIDEO**

Lesson 3
Disagreements with Great Britain

ESSENTIAL QUESTION *Why do people create, structure, and change governments?*

⊙ IT MATTERS BECAUSE

The events that led American colonists to declare independence affected the choices they made about a new government.

Social and Political Changes in the Colonies

GUIDING QUESTION *What events and movements affected colonial attitudes?*

From the 1740s through the 1760s there was a religious movement called the Great Awakening. It swept across the colonies. Fiery preachers stressed the value of personal religious experience. They rejected the teachings of church leaders. Instead, they urged people to build a direct relationship with God.

The Great Awakening pressed colonists to question traditional religious **authority.** Enlightenment leaders urged people to question accepted political authority. Together, these social and political movements created a strong spirit of **liberty,** or personal freedom. This spirit strengthened the colonists' belief that they should have the same rights as people in Great Britain.

Colonists believed that Parliament should protect the rights of British people from abuses by the king. Yet the king and Parliament made laws for the colonists. Also, America was far away, so the colonists had little voice in what happened in England. In addition, the king's governors ruled many of the

Reading **HELP**DESK

Taking Notes: *Describing*

As you read, complete a graphic organizer to explain how the colonists responded to British actions.

British Action	Colonists' Response

Content Vocabulary

- **liberty**
- **proclamation**
- **boycott**
- **repeal**
- **duty**
- **smuggling**
- **delegate**

colonies. That meant colonists had little voice in choosing these leaders. Moreover, their policies favored British interests over the colonists' needs. These concerns combined with a series of events in the 1760s to cause growing resentment against British rule.

The French and Indian War

As the colonies grew, they expanded westward. By the 1750s, British colonists were moving into areas also claimed by France. The increasing tensions soon led to war. In 1754, French forces joined with some Native American groups. Together they drove British colonists from land west of the Appalachian Mountains. The conflict was called the French and Indian War. It led to war between Great Britain and France in Europe.

Britain sent troops to the colonies. Finally, the British army won the war in 1763. Britain took control of French lands all the way to the Mississippi River. The colonists wanted to move into those lands. The French were now gone, so the colonists felt that they did not need British troops to protect them. However, British king George III had other plans for the colonies.

New Laws and Taxes

The French and Indian War had been long and costly. Fighting it had left Britain deep in debt. The colonists had caused the war by moving west. Therefore, King George decided they should pay for it. He also wanted to end the fighting in America. The French were gone, but Native Americans remained in the region. So he issued a **proclamation,** or an official statement. It forbade the colonists from settling in the lands won from France. He placed over 10,000 British troops in the colonies to keep order.

The king's actions enraged the colonists. Many felt that their only hope of owning land was now gone. Others suspected that the king was punishing the colonies. They thought he was trying to limit the economic growth they might achieve through expansion into the new lands.

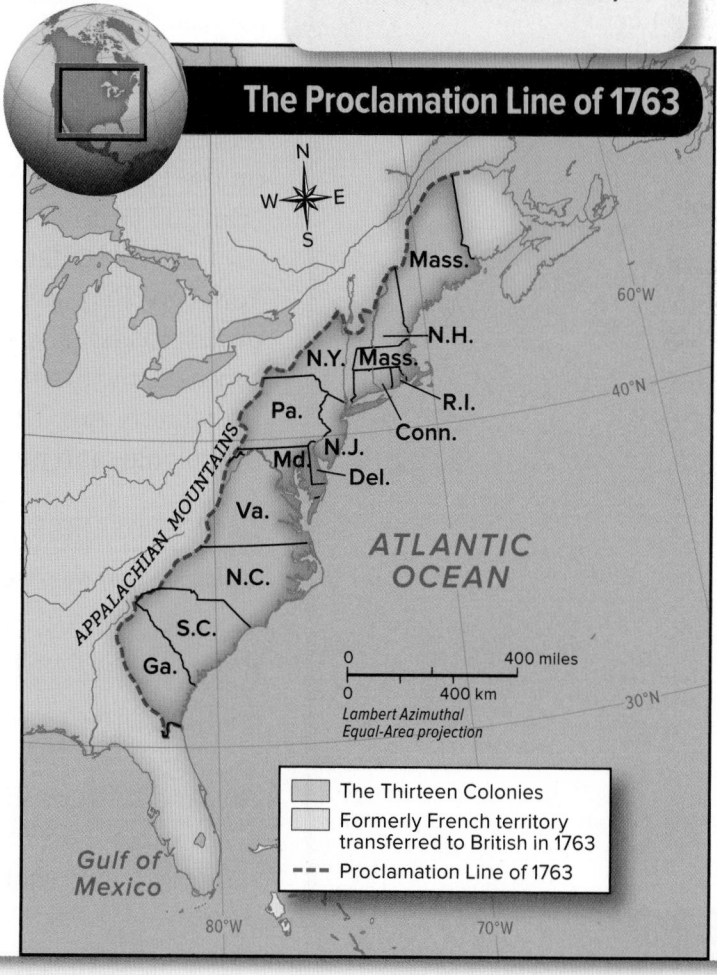

GEOGRAPHY CONNECTION

The Proclamation line of 1763 set a limit to where colonists could legally settle.

1 **LOCATION** What physical feature did the Proclamation line follow?

2 **CRITICAL THINKING**
Speculating Why do you think the British would use a physical characteristic to set a boundary?

The Proclamation Line of 1763

N W E S

Mass.

60°W

N.H.

N.Y. Mass.

R.I.

40°N

Pa.

Conn.

N.J.

Md. Del.

Va.

APPALACHIAN MOUNTAINS

N.C.

ATLANTIC OCEAN

S.C.

Ga.

0   400 miles
0   400 km
Lambert Azimuthal Equal-Area projection

30°N

The Thirteen Colonies
Formerly French territory transferred to British in 1763
- - - Proclamation Line of 1763

Gulf of Mexico

80°W   70°W

Academic Vocabulary

authority the power to make others obey

liberty the quality or state of being free

proclamation an official, formal public announcement

PHOTO: The Repeal, or the Funeral Procession of Miss Americ-Stamp, pub. 1766 (etching) (b&w photo), Wilson, Benjamin (1721-88) / Private Collection / The Bridgeman Art Library

Next, King George asked Parliament to tax the colonies. The money would help pay off Great Britain's war debts. In 1765 Parliament passed the Stamp Act. The law required that the colonists buy and place tax stamps on many kinds of documents. These included legal papers and even newspapers. The colonies protested this tax.

Colonial leaders called on the colonists to **boycott,** or refuse to buy, British goods. They claimed that only their elected representatives had the right to tax them. Leaders based the claim on the English Bill of Rights and on political traditions. For more than 100 years only their own legislatures had taxed the colonists.

Colonial leaders also organized a Stamp Act Congress in New York City. Representatives from nine colonies met to write a united protest to Parliament and the king. In 1766 Parliament **repealed,** or canceled, the Stamp Act. The same day, however, it passed the Declaratory Act. This law stated that Parliament had the right to tax the colonies and make decisions for them "in all cases whatsoever."

☑ PROGRESS CHECK

Explaining Why were the colonists angered by the Proclamation of 1763?

Colonial Dissatisfaction Grows

GUIDING QUESTION *What events increased colonists' anger toward British rule?*

A year after repealing the Stamp Act, Parliament levied a new set of taxes. The Townshend Acts placed **duties** on a wide range of goods that the colonies imported from overseas. Once again the colonists resisted with boycotts and protests. In 1770 Parliament repealed all the duties except for a tax on tea.

One of the Townshend Acts allowed general search warrants. British officials used these to combat **smuggling**— illegally moving goods in or out of a country. These warrants were called writs of assistance. They made it lawful for officers to enter any business or home to look for goods on which the import duty had not been paid. These searches greatly angered the colonists. Nearly 20 years later, Americans remembered writs of assistance. They even demanded that a protection against "unreasonable searches and seizures" be added to the United States Constitution.

In 1773 Parliament passed the Tea Act. This measure was not a tax. In fact, it allowed a British company that grew tea in India to import its tea into the colonies without paying the existing tea tax. This made the British company's tea cheaper than other tea sold in the colonies. Still, Parliament's control of taxes angered the colonists.

In December 1773, some angry colonists boarded several ships in Boston Harbor. These ships carried the British company's tea waiting to be unloaded. The group of protesters had disguised themselves as Native Americans. Urged on by a large crowd onshore, the protesters dumped 342 chests of the company's tea into the water. This protest became known as the Boston Tea Party.

How did Parliament respond to the Boston Tea Party? It passed laws called the Coercive Acts. These laws were meant to punish Massachusetts—and especially Boston—for resisting Great Britain's rule. The Coercive Acts were so harsh that the colonists called them the Intolerable Acts. Some of the laws violated the English Bill of Rights that the colonists held so dear.

✓ PROGRESS CHECK

Specifying Why did the colonists refer to the Coercive Acts as the Intolerable Acts?

Identifying Points of View

If you had been a British colonist in the 1700s, what side do you think you would have been on in the argument over independence? Prepare a list of arguments for that point of view—either supporting loyalty to the king and Parliament in their decisions to tax the colonists or agreeing with the colonists who were rebelling against the king and his actions.

While only about 100 protesters destroyed the tea, hundreds more looked on.

► CRITICAL THINKING
Drawing Conclusions What do you think the protesters hoped to achieve by dumping the tea?

smuggling the act of importing or exporting secretly, in violation of law and especially without paying duty on goods

1764

Sugar Act (1764)
The Sugar Act put a three-cent tax on foreign refined sugar and increased taxes on coffee, indigo, and certain kinds of wine.

1765

Stamp Act (1765)
The Stamp Act imposed the first direct British tax on the American colonists. It required them to pay a tax on every piece of printed paper they used. Ships' papers, legal documents, licenses, newspapers, and other publications were all included.

1766

1767

Declaratory Act (1766)
Stated that Great Britain had full rights to tax and govern the colonies as it saw fit.

Townshend Acts (1767)
Named for Charles Townshend, British Treasurer, the Townshend Acts placed new taxes on glass, lead, paints, paper, and tea.

Coercive Acts (Intolerable Acts) (1774)
- **The Boston Port Act** closed Boston's harbor until the tea that was used in the Boston Tea Party was fully paid for.
- **The Massachusetts Government Act** made town meetings illegal except by the written consent of the colony's British governor.
- **The Quartering Act** required the colonists to provide housing for British soldiers.
- **The Impartial Administration of Justice Act** allowed trials of British officials from Massachusetts to be held in other colonies or in Great Britain.
- **The Quebec Act** extended the Canadian border southward to the Ohio River, eliminating the colonies' claim to the land.

1773

Tea Act (1773)
The Tea Act required American colonists to buy tea only from the British East India Company. While taxes on some goods had been lifted, the tax on tea was still in place.

1774

1776

Declaration of Independence

CHART SKILLS

Taxes were a main source of tension between Great Britain and the colonies.

1 *Identifying* Which acts listed on the chart were not designed to raise taxes?

2 CRITICAL THINKING
Contrasting How were the Coercive Acts different from the other acts that Parliament had passed?

delegate a representative to a meeting

Academic Vocabulary
debate to discuss or argue

Steps Toward Independence

GUIDING QUESTION *What ideas about government influenced the Declaration of Independence?*

Parliament thought the Coercive Acts would frighten the colonists into respecting British rule. Instead, the reverse occurred. The other colonies banded together to help Massachusetts and challenge British authority.

The First Continental Congress

In September 1774, **delegates,** or representatives, from 12 colonies met in Philadelphia to plan a united response to the Coercive Acts. Although the group was called the Continental Congress, it did not pass laws like Congress does today. Instead, the delegates discussed what to do about the colonies' issues with Great Britain. They decided to send a letter to the king. In it they would ask that Britain respect the colonists' rights as British citizens. They also organized a total boycott of British goods and a ban on all trade with Britain. They agreed to meet again in the spring if British policies had not improved.

King George responded by calling for even stronger measures. "The New England governments are in a state of rebellion," he declared. "Blows [a fight] must decide whether they are subject to this country or independent."

The Second Continental Congress

The first "blows" had been struck when the delegates met again in May 1775. In April, British troops and colonial militiamen had fought at Lexington and Concord, in Massachusetts. Congress had to decide whether to continue working towards peace or to split with Great Britain.

This time the Congress acted as a governing body for the colonies. Not every member favored a split with Great Britain. Some delegates remained loyal to Britain and the king. Others feared that the colonies could not defeat Great Britain in a war. For months, Congress **debated** what to do.

Meanwhile, support for independence grew in the colonies. In January 1776, Thomas Paine published a pamphlet titled *Common Sense.* Paine had recently moved to the colonies from Great Britain. He used the ideas of John Locke to make the case for independence. He argued that "common sense" called for the colonists to rebel against the king's "violent abuse of power." Paine continued,

PRIMARY SOURCE

"The cause of America is in a great measure the cause of all mankind. . . . We have it in our power to begin the world over again.**"**

The text of the Declaration of Independence was quickly printed and distributed throughout the colonies. The first official public reading took place on July 8, 1776, in front of Independence Hall in Philadelphia, as shown.

▶ CRITICAL THINKING

Hypothesizing What do you think the colonists felt as they heard the words of the Declaration for the first time? Why?

PHOTO: Library of Congress, Prints & Photographs Division, LC-DIG-pga-03091

More than 500,000 copies of *Common Sense* were sold in 1776. By spring more than half the delegates of the Second Continental Congress favored independence.

The Declaration of Independence

The Congress chose a committee to draft a document to explain to the world why the colonies should be free. The committee consisted of John Adams, Benjamin Franklin, Thomas Jefferson, Robert Livingston, and Roger Sherman. The committee chose Jefferson to write the document.

The words Jefferson wrote show that his thinking was greatly influenced by John Locke. In fact, a passage in the second paragraph of the Declaration clearly was inspired by Locke's ideas about natural rights in *Two Treatises of Government*.

PRIMARY SOURCE

*"*We hold these truths to be self-evident, that all men are created equal, that they are endowed by their Creator with certain unalienable Rights, that among these are Life, Liberty, and the pursuit of Happiness.*"*

Reading HELP DESK

Reading Strategy: *Summarizing*

When you summarize a reading, you find the main idea of the passage and restate it in your own words. Read about the steps leading toward American independence. On a separate sheet of paper, summarize the reading in one or two sentences.

Then, drawing on Locke's views about the social contract, Jefferson wrote:

"[T]o secure these rights, Governments are instituted among Men, deriving [getting] their just powers from the consent of the governed, That whenever any form of government becomes destructive of these ends, it is the Right of the People to alter or abolish it, and to institute [create] new Government."

Later in the Declaration, Jefferson offered proof that the social contract had been broken. He put together a long list of ways in which King George had abused his power.

Jefferson was clearly influenced by the political thoughts of Locke. But he also drew ideas from other times in history. You read earlier that ideas about democracy began with the ancient Greeks. In addition, Jefferson was inspired by the writings of other Enlightenment thinkers. For instance, Jean-Jacques Rousseau wrote that if a government did not protect its people's freedom, it should not exist. Voltaire also believed that people had a right to liberty. The Declaration of Independence reflects many of these old and new beliefs.

The Second Continental Congress approved the Declaration of Independence on July 4, 1776. John Hancock, the president of the Congress, was first to sign it.

The Declaration of Independence was a revolutionary document. No other nation's government at that time was based on the principles of government by consent of the governed. Over the years, many other nations have used the Declaration of Independence as a model in their own efforts to gain freedom.

☑ PROGRESS CHECK

Identifying How did Thomas Paine use John Locke's ideas in his pamphlet *Common Sense*?

LESSON 3 REVIEW

Review Vocabulary

1. Describe the relationship between a *boycott* and a *repeal*.

2. Write a sentence that shows how these words are related: *duty, smuggling*.

Answer the Guiding Questions

3. *Summarizing* How were the ideas of colonists affected by events in the American colonies?

4. *Labeling* What were the key events that led to growing colonial support for independence?

5. *Identifying* What ideas about government did Jefferson draw on in writing the Declaration of Independence?

6. **ARGUMENT** Suppose you are a member of the Second Continental Congress. Write a speech using ideas of natural rights that supports the Declaration of Independence.

Write your answers on a separate sheet of paper.

1 Writing Activity

EXPLORING THE ESSENTIAL QUESTION
Why do people create, structure, and change governments?

In making the case for American independence from Great Britain, the Declaration of Independence states that "governments long established should not be changed for light [unimportant] and transient [temporary] causes." By the time these words were written, the colonies had been under British rule for more than 150 years. In your opinion, did the colonists who called for independence have good reasons for doing so? Had you been a colonist, would you have supported independence or remained loyal to Great Britain? Think about these questions and answer them in an essay. Support your position with facts you have learned about what was happening in the colonies in the mid-1700s.

2 21st Century Skills

CONDUCT RESEARCH Ideas expressed in the Declaration of Independence have inspired many other peoples to seek the rights and freedoms that Americans enjoy. Go online to find a nation whose people have set up a democratic government in the 1900s or 2000s. Some possible nations to research include Ireland, India, Algeria, Singapore, and Nepal. Find out where the country is located, what kind of rule it has had over its history, and what efforts its people have made to gain rights and freedom in recent times. Then create a media presentation for the class about that nation's history and comparing its old form of government to its current form of government.

3 Being an Active Citizen

In 1690, in his *Two Treatises of Government*, John Locke wrote that the purpose of government is to serve the people and protect their natural rights. Identify a problem in your community or in the news where government could be doing a better job of fulfilling that responsibility. Develop a plan to address the problem by researching different policy options and determining a course of action. Your plan should also identify the appropriate government agency to put the plan into effect.

4 Understanding Visuals

Political cartoons are a type of art. They express political opinions in a visual form. As this cartoon shows, the art form is hundreds of years old. Some cartoons are easily understood. Others are more complicated. Examine this political cartoon. What is its subject? What opinion does it express? How would this cartoon have influenced the colonists' attitudes about British rule?

THE HORSE AMERICA, *throwing his Master.*

REVIEW THE GUIDING QUESTIONS

Directions: Choose the best answer for each question.

1 Why was the government of ancient Athens called a direct democracy?

    A. The people chose representatives to make laws for them.

    B. The people governed themselves.

    C. The people directly chose their king.

    D. The government directed all aspects of life.

2 How did the English Bill of Rights change the nature of English government?

    F. It made England a direct democracy.

    G. It increased the power of the monarch.

    H. It made Parliament more powerful than the monarch.

    I. It set the principle of taxing people in return for having rights.

3 Which condition in the Middle Colonies encouraged the growth of Philadelphia and New York as busy ports?

    A. an ideal location for fishing

    B. a large population of enslaved Africans

    C. soil and climate suited to cash crops

    D. a large supply of wood to use for shipbuilding

4 Why did colonists dislike how governors were chosen in many colonies?

    F. They did not understand the process.

    G. Since governors were named by the king, they favored the king.

    H. The colonists did not trust the colonial legislatures.

    I. They preferred a system of direct democracy.

5 How did the Second Continental Congress respond to British policies?

    A. They started the French and Indian War.

    B. They chose a committee to write the Declaration of Independence explaining why the colonies should be free.

    C. They passed the Tea Act, allowing a British company to import tea to the colonies without paying taxes.

    D. They hired Thomas Paine to write *Common Sense*.

6 Which legislation by Parliament stated its right to pass laws and make decisions for the colonies?

    F. the Declaratory Act

    G. the Proclamation of 1763

    H. the Stamp Act

    I. the Coercive Acts

DBQ **ANALYZING DOCUMENTS**

Directions: Analyze the document and answer the questions that follow.

"[I]n the Presence of God and one another, [we] . . . combine ourselves together into a civil Body Politick, for our better Ordering and Preservation, and . . . to enact, constitute, and frame such just and equal Laws, Ordinances, Acts, Constitutions, and Offices, from time to time, as shall be thought most meet [proper] and convenient for the general Good of the Colony; unto which we promise all due Submission and Obedience."

—The Mayflower Compact (1620)

7 Identifying What action were the writers and signers of this document taking?

A. starting an unlimited government   C. stating their natural rights

B. creating a social contract   D. declaring independence

8 Summarizing What is the main purpose of this agreement?

F. to choose a leader

G. to set down economic rules

H. to create a court system

I. to maintain unity and order

SHORT RESPONSE

"We hold these truths to be self-evident, that all men are created equal, that they are endowed by their Creator with certain unalienable Rights, that among these are Life, Liberty, and the pursuit of Happiness. That to secure these rights, Governments are instituted among Men, deriving [obtaining] their just powers from the consent of the governed, That whenever any form of government becomes destructive of those ends, it is the Right of the People to alter or to abolish it, and to institute new Government."

—The Declaration of Independence (1776)

9 What truths does this passage say are obvious?

10 Following this passage, the Declaration of Independence has a long list of ways that King George abused his power. What was the purpose of this list?

EXTENDED RESPONSE

11 Informative/Explanatory Explain John Locke's ideas about natural rights and social contracts. Then explain how and where these ideas are found in the Declaration of Independence.

Need Extra Help?

If You've Missed Question	1	2	3	4	5	6	7	8	9	10	11
Review Lesson	1	1	2	2	3	3	1	1	3	3	1, 3

THE DECLARATION of INDEPENDENCE

Words are spelled as originally written.

In Congress, July 4, 1776. The unanimous Declaration of the thirteen United States of America,

[Preamble]

When in the Course of human events, it becomes necessary for one people to dissolve the political bands which have connected them with another, and to assume among the Powers of the earth, the separate and equal station to which the Laws of Nature and of Nature's God entitle them, a decent respect to the opinions of mankind requires that they should declare the causes which **impel** them to the separation.

> **The Preamble** The Declaration of Independence has four parts. The Preamble explains why the Continental Congress drew up the Declaration.

> **impel:** force

[Declaration of Natural Rights]

We hold these truths to be self-evident, that all men are created equal, that they are **endowed** by their Creator with certain unalienable Rights, that among these are Life, Liberty, and the pursuit of Happiness.

> **Natural Rights** The second part, the Declaration of Natural Rights, lists the rights of the citizens. It goes on to explain that, in a republic, people form a government to protect their rights.

That to secure these rights, Governments are instituted among Men, deriving their just powers from the consent of the governed,

That whenever any Form of Government becomes destructive of these ends, it is the Right of the People to alter or to abolish it, and to institute new Government, laying its foundation on such principles and organizing its powers in such form, as to them shall seem most likely to effect their Safety and Happiness. Prudence, indeed, will dictate that Governments long established should not be changed for light and transient causes; and accordingly all experience hath shown, that mankind are more disposed to suffer, while evils are sufferable, than to right themselves by abolishing the forms to which they are accustomed. But when a long train of abuses and **usurpations,** pursuing invariably the same Object evinces a design to reduce them under absolute **Despotism,** it is their right, it is their duty, to throw off such Government, and to provide new Guards for their future security.

> **endowed:** provided

> **usurpations:** unjust uses of power

> **despotism:** unlimited power

[List of Grievances]

Such has been the patient sufferance of these Colonies; and such is now the necessity which constrains them to alter their former Systems of Government. The history of the present King of Great Britain is a history of repeated injuries and usurpations, all having in direct object the establishment of an absolute Tyranny over these States. To prove this, let Facts be submitted to a candid world.

> **List of Grievances** The third part of the Declaration lists the colonists' complaints against the British government. Notice that King George III is singled out for blame.

He has refused his Assent to Laws, the most wholesome and necessary for the public good.

He has forbidden his Governors to pass Laws of immediate and pressing importance, unless suspended in their operation till his Assent should be obtained; and when so suspended, he has utterly neglected to attend to them.

He has refused to pass other Laws for the accommodation of large districts of people, unless those people would **relinquish** the right of Representation in the Legislature, a right **inestimable** to them and formidable to tyrants only.

relinquish: give up
inestimable: priceless

He has called together legislative bodies at places unusual, uncomfortable, and distant from the depository of their Public Records, for the sole purpose of fatiguing them into compliance with his measures.

He has dissolved Representative Houses repeatedly, for opposing with manly firmness his invasions on the rights of the people.

He has refused for a long time, after such dissolutions, to cause others to be elected; whereby the Legislative Powers, incapable of **Annihilation,** have returned to the People at large for their exercise; the State remaining in the mean time exposed to all the dangers of invasion from without, and **convulsions** within.

annihilation: destruction

convulsions: violent disturbances

He has endeavoured to prevent the population of these States; for that purpose obstructing the **Laws for Naturalization of Foreigners;** refusing to pass others to encourage their migrations hither, and raising the conditions of new Appropriations of Lands.

Laws for Naturalization of Foreigners: process by which foreign-born persons become citizens

He has obstructed the Administration of Justice, by refusing his Assent to Laws for establishing Judiciary Powers.

He has made Judges dependent on his Will alone, for the **tenure** of their offices, and the amount and payment of their salaries.

tenure: term

quartering: lodging

He has erected a multitude of New Offices, and sent hither swarms of Officers to harass our people, and eat out their substance.

He has kept among us, in times of peace, Standing Armies without the Consent of our legislature.

He has affected to render the Military independent of and superior to the Civil Power.

He has combined with others to subject us to a jurisdiction foreign to our constitution, and unacknowledged by our laws; giving his Assent to their acts of pretended legislation:

For **quartering** large bodies of troops among us:

For protecting them, by a mock Trial, from Punishment for any Murders which they should commit on the Inhabitants of these States:

For cutting off our Trade with all parts of the world:

For imposing taxes on us without our Consent:

For depriving us in many cases, of the benefits of Trial by Jury:

For transporting us beyond Seas to be tried for pretended offences:

For abolishing the free System of English Laws in a neighbouring Province, establishing therein an Arbitrary government, and enlarging its Boundaries so as to **render** it at once an example and fit instrument for introducing the same absolute rule into these Colonies:

For taking away our Charters, abolishing our most valuable Laws, and altering fundamentally the Forms of our Governments:

For suspending our own Legislature, and declaring themselves invested with Power to legislate for us in all cases whatsoever.

He has **abdicated** Government here, by declaring us out of his Protection and waging War against us.

He has plundered our seas, ravaged our Coasts, burnt our towns, and destroyed the lives of our people.

He is at this time transporting large armies of foreign mercenaries to compleat the works of death, desolation and tyranny, already begun with circumstances of Cruelty & **perfidy** scarcely paralleled in the most barbarous ages, and totally unworthy the Head of a civilized nation.

He has constrained our fellow Citizens taken Captive on the high Seas to bear Arms against their Country, to become the executioners of their friends and Brethren, or to fall themselves by their Hands.

He has excited domestic **insurrections** amongst us, and has endeavoured to bring on the inhabitants of our frontiers, the merciless Indian Savages, whose known rule of warfare, is an undistinguished destruction of all ages, sexes and conditions.

In every stage of these Oppressions We have **Petitioned for Redress** in the most humble terms: Our repeated Petitions have been answered only by repeated injury. A Prince, whose character is thus marked by every act which may define a Tyrant, is unfit to be the ruler of a free People.

Nor have We been wanting in attention to our British brethren. We have warned them from time to time of attempts by their legislature to extend an **unwarrantable jurisdiction** over us. We have reminded them of the circumstances of our emigration and settlement here. We have appealed to their native justice and magnanimity, and we have conjured them by the ties of our common kindred to disavow these usurpations, which, would inevitably interrupt our connections and correspondence. They too have been deaf to the voice of justice and of **consanguinity**.

render: make

abdicated: given up

perfidy: violation of trust

insurrections: rebellions

petitioned for redress: asked formally for a correction of wrongs

unwarrantable jurisdiction: unjustified authority

consanguinity: originating from the same ancestor

We must, therefore, acquiesce in the necessity, which denounces our Separation, and hold them, as we hold the rest of mankind, Enemies in War, in Peace Friends.

[Resolution of Independence by the United States]

We, therefore, the Representatives of the united States of America, in General Congress, Assembled, appealing to the Supreme Judge of the world for the **rectitude** of our intentions, do, in the Name, and by Authority of the good People of these Colonies, solemnly publish and declare, That these United Colonies are, and of Right ought to be Free and Independent States; that they are Absolved from all Allegiance to the British Crown, and that all political connection between them and the State of Great Britain, is and ought to be totally dissolved; and that as Free and Independent States, they have full Power to levy War, conclude Peace, contract Alliances, establish Commerce, and to do all other Acts and Things which Independent States may of right do.

And for the support of this Declaration, with a firm reliance on the Protection of Divine Providence, we mutually pledge to each other our Lives, our Fortunes and our sacred Honor.

Resolution of Independence The final section declares that the colonies are "Free and Independent States" with the full power to make war, to form alliances, and to trade with other countries.

rectitude: rightness

Signers of the Declaration The signers, as representatives of the American people, declared the colonies independent from Great Britain. Most members signed the document on August 2, 1776.

John Hancock
  President from
  Massachusetts

Georgia
Button Gwinnett
Lyman Hall
George Walton

North Carolina
William Hooper
Joseph Hewes
John Penn

South Carolina
Edward Rutledge
Thomas Heyward, Jr.
Thomas Lynch, Jr.
Arthur Middleton

Maryland
Samuel Chase
William Paca
Thomas Stone
Charles Carroll
  of Carrollton

Virginia
George Wythe
Richard Henry Lee
Thomas Jefferson
Benjamin Harrison
Thomas Nelson, Jr.
Francis Lightfoot Lee
Carter Braxton

Pennsylvania
Robert Morris
Benjamin Rush
Benjamin Franklin
John Morton
George Clymer
James Smith
George Taylor
James Wilson
George Ross

Delaware
Caesar Rodney
George Read
Thomas McKean

New York
William Floyd
Philip Livingston
Francis Lewis
Lewis Morris

New Jersey
Richard Stockton
John Witherspoon
Francis Hopkinson
John Hart
Abraham Clark

New Hampshire
Josiah Bartlett
William Whipple
Matthew Thornton

Massachusetts
Samuel Adams
John Adams
Robert Treat Paine
Elbridge Gerry

Rhode Island
Stephen Hopkins
William Ellery

Connecticut
Samuel Huntington
William Williams
Oliver Wolcott
Roger Sherman

The Constitution

ESSENTIAL QUESTIONS • *Why do people create, structure, and change governments?*
• *How do societies balance individual and community rights?*
• *How does social change influence government?*

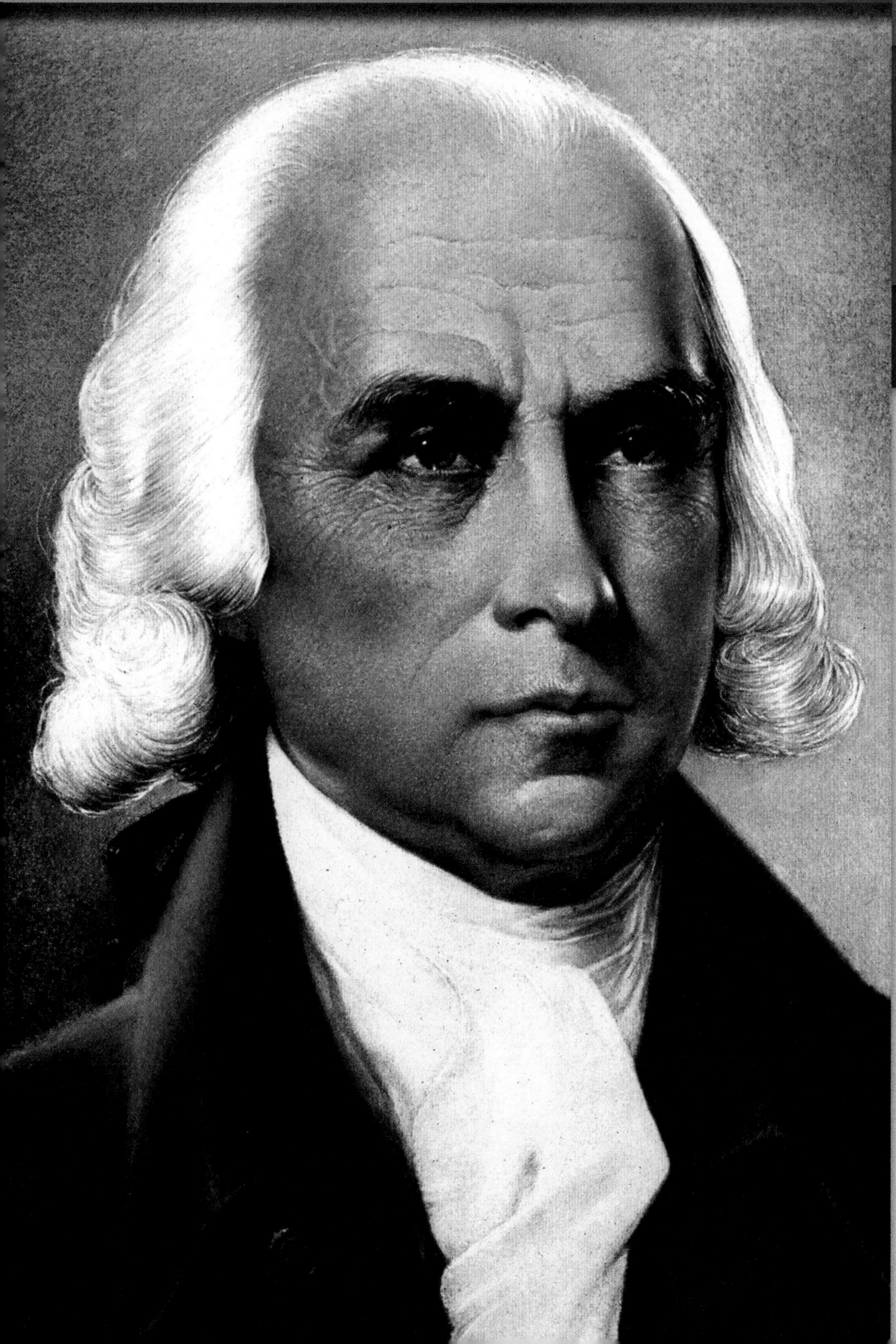

networks

There's More Online about the Constitution.

CHAPTER 3

The Story Matters...

Before arriving at Independence Hall in Philadelphia in 1787 to help create a new U.S. government, James Madison had already had an impressive political career. He helped write Virginia's state constitution. He also served in the Virginia House of Delegates and the Continental Congress.

Madison realized that the country needed a stronger central government. He had studied forms of government. This helped him develop a plan that carefully balanced national, state, and individual interests. In 1787, many of Madison's ideas became part of the new blueprint for the federal government—the U.S. Constitution.

◄ *James Madison earned the title "Father of the Constitution" for the many significant contributions he made to this important document.*

PHOTO: The Granger Collection

Real-Life Civics

▷ **NOW** Though written more than 200 years ago, the Constitution is a document of enduring importance. It still structures our government. Criminal court judges and Supreme Court justices rely on it as they make legal decisions about everything from cell phone communications and laser technology to the rights of students in schools, privacy on the Internet, and the sale of DVDs with violent content. At Philadelphia's National Constitution Center, visitors can learn much about the Constitution and how it was created through a variety of interactive exhibits. In Signers' Hall at the Center, visitors enjoy posing among these statues of the nation's delegates to the Constitutional Convention that took place in nearby Independence Hall.

Life-size bronze statues of delegates to the Constitutional Convention include Benjamin Franklin, George Washington, and James Madison.

In 1975, people in Ohio lined up for hours for a chance to board the second Freedom Train and view original copies of the Constitution, the Declaration of Independence, and other historical documents.

PHOTO: (l) Robert Harding Picture Library Ltd/Alamy; (tr) AP Photo

▶ **THEN** The men who drafted the Constitution in the 1780s could not have foreseen how much would change in the centuries after it was written. What has not changed is Americans' respect for their Constitution. In the late 1940s, a traveling exhibition on American history crossed the country. The Freedom Train carried original copies of such documents as the Constitution, the Mayflower Compact, and the Magna Carta. During the U.S. bicentennial celebrations in 1975 and 1976, another Freedom Train made stops in 48 states. As in the late 1940s, millions of people lined up to view these precious pieces of history.

CIVIC LITERACY
★★★★

Analyzing What might Americans gain from visiting displays such as Signers' Hall and the Freedom Train that deal with the history of our nation and its government?

Your Opinion What sorts of displays would you be interested in seeing that relate to the formation of our country? Why?

netw☺rks
There's More Online!

☑ **GRAPHIC ORGANIZER**
Shays's Rebellion

☑ **MAP**
Northwest Territory, 1785

☑ **CHART**
Weaknesses of the Articles of Confederation

☑ **GAME**

☑ **VIDEO**

 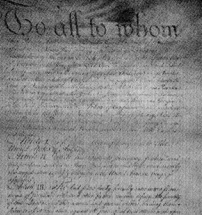  

Lesson 1

The Country's First Governments

ESSENTIAL QUESTION *Why do people create, structure, and change governments?*

⊚ IT MATTERS BECAUSE

The weaknesses of the first U.S. government shaped the way our government works today.

State Constitutions

GUIDING QUESTION *How did citizens set up governments as they transitioned from colonies to states?*

Even before the Declaration of Independence was signed, American colonists thought about independence. Independence would mean an end to colonial charters. New plans of government would have to replace them. The Second Continental Congress urged colonists to form governments, "as shall . . . best conduce [contribute] to the happiness and safety of their constituents [voters]."

In January 1776, New Hampshire became the first colony to organize as a state. Leaders wrote a **constitution:** a detailed, written plan for government. Within a few years, all the other former colonies had their own state constitutions.

State Governments

All of the state constitutions set up a similar form of government. Each state had a legislature to make laws. Most of these legislatures

PHOTO: (tl) David R. Frazier Photolibrary, Inc./Alamy; (tcl) National Archives and Records Administration (Public); (tr) Bettmann/Corbis

Reading **HELP**DESK

Taking Notes: *Asking Questions*

As you read, fill in a table about Shays's Rebellion.

Shays's Rebellion

Question Word	Question	Answer
Who?		
What?		
When?		
Why?		
How?		

Content Vocabulary

- **constitution**
- **bicameral**
- **confederation**
- **Articles of Confederation**
- **ratify**

were **bicameral.** This means they were divided into two parts, or houses. The members of each house or state legislature were chosen by different methods.

Each state also had a governor. This official was elected either by the legislature or by the citizens. The governor's job was to carry out the laws. Finally, each state had courts. Judges in the courts decided what the laws meant and how to apply them to each new situation.

Bills of Rights

The new state governments were based upon ideals stated in the Declaration of Independence. These included the American ideals of individual rights to "life, liberty, and the pursuit of happiness." Most state constitutions contained a bill, or list, of rights. This list guaranteed the basic freedoms and legal protections that the state's citizens would enjoy. Among these rights were trial by jury and protection of personal property. They can be traced all the way back to the Magna Carta and the English Bill of Rights.

✓ **PROGRESS CHECK**

Identifying What is a constitution?

The Articles of Confederation

GUIDING QUESTION *How did the Articles of Confederation create problems for the United States?*

Each state was ready to govern itself when independence was declared. However, some tasks were too big for individual states to handle on their own. A state could not raise and support a large army, for example. Americans realized that 13 small, separate forces could not fight the mighty British army. To win the war, American leaders knew they needed a single, strong army under central control.

For this and other reasons, the Second Continental Congress planned for a confederation of states. A **confederation** is a group of individual state governments that unite for a common purpose. In 1777 the Congress wrote out these plans in the **Articles of Confederation.** This document became the first constitution of the United States of America.

New Hampshire was the first of the 13 colonies to declare independence and adopt a state constitution.

In 1781 the Articles of Confederation, shown here, established a weak central authority.

► CRITICAL THINKING

Analyzing Why were the Articles of Confederation necessary for the new nation?

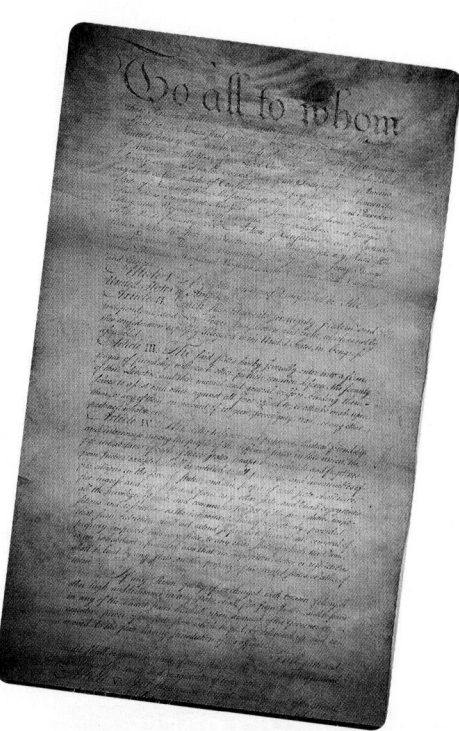

PHOTO: (tr) David R. Frazier Photolibrary, Inc./Alamy; (br) National Archives and Records Administration (Public)

- ordinance
- Ordinance of 1785
- Northwest Ordinance
- Shays's Rebellion

constitution a detailed, written plan for government

bicameral a legislature consisting of two parts, or houses

confederation a group of individuals or state governments

Articles of Confederation the first constitution of the United States

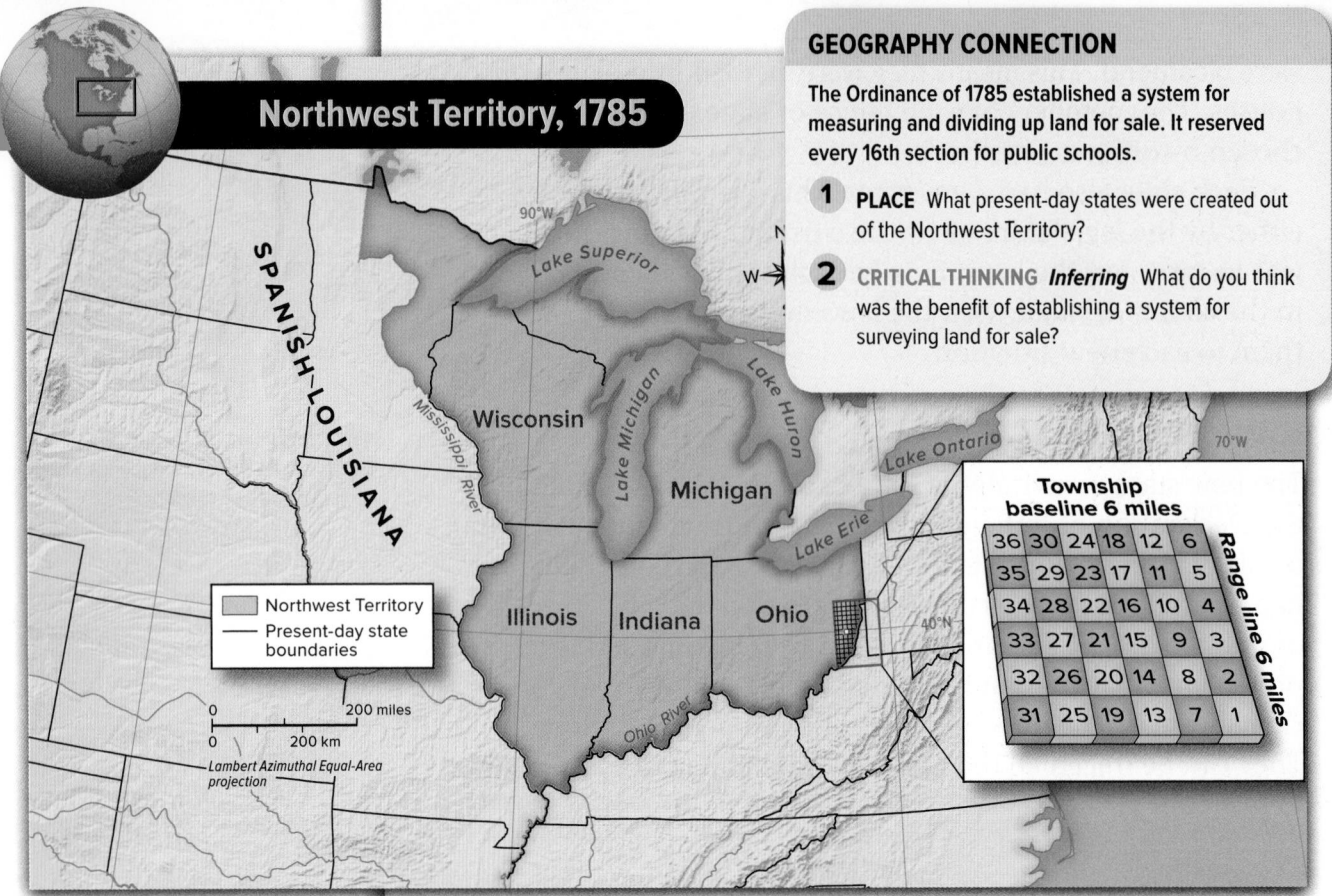

Northwest Territory, 1785

GEOGRAPHY CONNECTION

The Ordinance of 1785 established a system for measuring and dividing up land for sale. It reserved every 16th section for public schools.

1 PLACE What present-day states were created out of the Northwest Territory?

2 CRITICAL THINKING *Inferring* What do you think was the benefit of establishing a system for surveying land for sale?

Township baseline 6 miles

Range line 6 miles

36	30	24	18	12	6
35	29	23	17	11	5
34	28	22	16	10	4
33	27	21	15	9	3
32	26	20	14	8	2
31	25	19	13	7	1

Northwest Territory
Present-day state boundaries

0   200 miles
0   200 km
Lambert Azimuthal Equal-Area projection

The Articles of Confederation set up a "league of friendship" among independent states. By 1781 all 13 states had **ratified**, or approved, the Articles.

The Articles of Confederation created a one-house legislature in which each state had one vote. The legislature was known as the Confederation Congress. It controlled the army and had the power to deal with foreign countries on behalf of the states.

The Northwest Ordinances

The Confederation Congress passed two laws, or **ordinances,** that would have a major effect on the history of the United States. Both of these ordinances were about the Old Northwest. This **area** included present-day Ohio, Indiana, Illinois, Michigan, Wisconsin, and part of Minnesota.

The first ordinance, the **Ordinance of 1785,** set up a plan for surveying western lands. Surveying means measuring a piece of land. The ordinance also described how western lands were to be sold. It divided the land into townships six miles square. Each township was further divided into 36 sections, each one mile square. This way of surveying is still used today.

Reading**HELP**DESK

ratify to vote approval of

ordinance a law, usually of a city or county

Academic Vocabulary

area a region

Ordinance of 1785 a law that set up a plan for surveying western lands

The second ordinance was passed in 1787. It was known as the **Northwest Ordinance.** This law set up a government for this area, which was called the Northwest Territory. Officials later used the ordinance as a model to organize governments for other new territories. The ordinance also provided a plan for admitting new states to the Union. Because of these plans, the Northwest Ordinance was perhaps the most important action of Congress under the Articles.

Another clause in the ordinance that would have a significant **impact** on U.S. history in the 1800s said:

PRIMARY SOURCE

"There shall be neither slavery nor involuntary servitude in said territory."

—the Northwest Ordinance

The Ordinance of 1785 and the Northwest Ordinance helped people settle the Northwest Territory in an orderly way. During the American Revolution, only a few thousand settlers lived there. By the 1790s, their numbers had grown to about 120,000.

Weaknesses of the Articles

These two Northwest Territory ordinances were important laws. The Confederation Congress, however, had few other successes. Why was this so? First, the Congress could not pass a law unless nine states voted for it. Also, any attempt to amend, or change, the Articles required all 13 states to agree. Such strict voting rules made it hard for the Congress to do anything.

WEAKNESSES OF THE ARTICLES OF CONFEDERATION
LACK OF POWER AND MONEY
• Congress had no power to collect taxes.
• Congress had no power to regulate trade.
• Congress had no power to enforce its laws.
LACK OF CENTRAL POWER
• No single leader or group directed government policy.
• No national court system existed.
RULES TOO RIGID
• Congress could not pass laws without the approval of 9 states.
• The Articles could not be changed without the agreement of all 13 states.

CHART SKILLS

The Articles of Confederation were aimed at setting up a new government but had some serious weaknesses.

1. *Explaining* Under the Articles of Confederation, on whom did the Confederation Congress have to depend to enforce its laws?
2. CRITICAL THINKING
   Analyzing Why was it a serious problem that the Articles were almost impossible to change?

Northwest Ordinance 1787 law that set up a government for the Northwest Territory and a plan for admitting new states to the Union

Academic Vocabulary
impact an effect

The power of the Confederation Congress was strictly limited. The colonists had disliked strong British rule. As a result, the 13 states gave the Confederation Congress little power. Even when the Congress passed laws, it could not enforce them. Unlike state constitutions, the Articles did not allow for a governor. If a state ignored a law, Congress could do nothing. There was no one to ensure the law was obeyed.

The Confederation Congress also did not have the power to tax. The Articles allowed the Congress to ask the states for money but not to demand it. The Congress could not, in fact, require the states to do anything.

Shays's Rebellion

The Articles were too weak to deal with many of the problems facing the new country. However, the United States was able to achieve some success. The states forced the British to accept their independence. The Treaty of Paris was signed in 1783. It ended the fighting between Great Britain and the new nation.

Independence, however, did not put an end to the country's struggles. For one thing, the United States faced serious financial troubles. It was unable to collect taxes. Yet, the Confederation Congress had borrowed money to pay for the American Revolution. It had run up a large debt.

PHOTO: Bettmann/Corbis

Because they could not pay high state taxes after the war, some farmers risked losing their land. In Shays's Rebellion, Massachusetts farmers revolted.

► **CRITICAL THINKING**
Determining Cause and Effect How did uprisings like Shays's Rebellion help lead to a change in the nation's government?

Shays's Rebellion an uprising of Massachusetts farmers who did not want to lose their farms because of debt caused by heavy state taxes after the American Revolution

The state governments had also fallen into deep debt. They taxed their citizens heavily. Meanwhile, trade slowed and people lost jobs. Farmers could not sell their crops and went into debt. Some even lost their lands. The states also taxed goods imported from other states and countries. These taxes hurt trade. Merchants and businesspeople suffered. The Confederation Congress had no power to fix these problems.

Even worse, the Congress could do nothing to calm the public's worries. Above all, Americans feared that the government could not protect them. During 1786 and 1787, riots broke out in several states.

One alarming uprising took place in Massachusetts. There, a farmer named Daniel Shays owed money because of heavy state taxes. Massachusetts courts threatened to take his farm to pay for his debts. Shays felt the state had no right to punish him for a problem it had created. Many others agreed. Shays led about 1,200 protestors, including a number of free African Americans, in an attack on a federal arsenal. The uprising, known as **Shays's Rebellion,** was quickly stopped. But it was a warning to the country. Could the government maintain law and order?

Many political leaders, merchants, and writers began calling for a stronger national government.

PRIMARY SOURCE

"I do not conceive we can exist long as a nation, without having lodged somewhere a power which will pervade the whole Union."

—George Washington's papers

In 1787 representatives, called delegates, from 12 of the states attended a meeting in Philadelphia. Their plan was to revise, or change, the Articles of Confederation.

✓ PROGRESS CHECK

Explaining Why was it difficult to pass laws under the Articles of Confederation?

21ˢᵗ Century
SKILLS

Articulate Thoughts and Ideas

Daniel Shays took arms against the government. However, people have many peaceful ways to make themselves heard. A petition, for example, is a formal written request made to an official or organization. Suppose you are Daniel Shays. Draft a petition to present to the governor of Massachusetts.

LESSON 1 REVIEW

Review Vocabulary

1. What is a *confederation*?

2. What were two successful *ordinances* created under the *Articles of Confederation*? What did they achieve?

Answer the Guiding Questions

3. *Identifying* State constitutions based their bills of rights on what English document?

4. *Determining Cause and Effect* What problems after the war caused Shays's Rebellion?

5. **ARGUMENT** Suppose that you are on a committee to write a new state constitution. Identify three freedoms you want the constitution to guarantee. Explain why it is important to guarantee these rights.

networks

There's More Online!

☑ **GRAPHIC ORGANIZER**
The Great Compromise

☑ **MAP**
Ratification of the Constitution

☑ **AMERICAN LEADERS**
James Madison

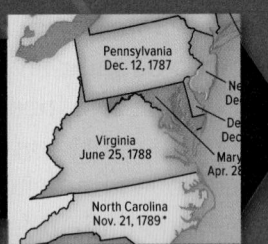

Lesson 2
Creating a New Constitution

ESSENTIAL QUESTION *Why do people create, structure, and change governments?*

IT MATTERS BECAUSE

In creating the Constitution, the basis for our government today, the Framers reached important compromises that had lasting legacies.

The Constitutional Convention

GUIDING QUESTION *Why did American leaders decide to create a new plan of government?*

In 1777, the Articles of Confederation had loosely joined 13 independent states. After almost 10 years, American leaders decided that the national government needed to be stronger. In the spring of 1787, delegates from the states met in Philadelphia to fix the Articles. Only Rhode Island did not take part. Its leaders opposed a stronger central government.

The Delegates

The convention, or meeting, took place in Independence Hall. It began on May 25, 1787. Many delegates traveled long distances and arrived late. But the group that finally gathered was special.

Most of the 55 men present were well educated. They were lawyers, merchants, college presidents, physicians, generals, governors, and planters. They all had political experience. Eight had signed the Declaration of Independence. Seven had been state governors, and 41 were or had been members of the Continental Congress. Native Americans, African Americans, and women were not allowed to take part in the meeting.

Reading**HELP**DESK

Taking Notes: *Comparing and Contrasting*

As you read, compare and contrast the Virginia Plan and the New Jersey Plan by completing a Venn diagram like the one shown.

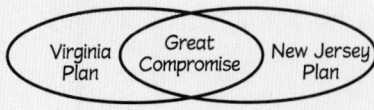

Content Vocabulary

- **Constitutional Convention**
- **Great Compromise**
- **Three-Fifths Compromise**

Benjamin Franklin of Pennsylvania, at 81, was the oldest delegate. He was a diplomat, writer, inventor, and scientist. Most delegates, however, were younger men in their thirties or forties. Their careers were ahead of them. George Washington and James Madison would become presidents of the United States. Nineteen delegates would become U.S. senators and 13 would serve in the House of Representatives. Four men would be federal judges. Four others would be Supreme Court justices.

A few key leaders were not there. Thomas Jefferson and John Adams were in Europe, representing the U.S. government. Patrick Henry, a Virginian and a leader during the Revolution, was also absent. Henry was elected as a delegate. However, he was against a stronger central government and did not attend.

The First Decisions

The delegates chose George Washington to guide the convention. He was respected for his leadership during the American Revolution. Washington ran the meetings in an orderly way. He reminded the delegates that their task was vital. He warned that if they could not come up with an acceptable plan of government, "perhaps another dreadful conflict is to be sustained [suffered]."

As the convention **process** began, the delegates made some key decisions. Each state would have one vote, no matter how many delegates represented that state. Also, a simple majority—in this case, seven votes— would decide any issue.

The delegates wished to keep the work of the convention secret. This would enable delegates to talk freely. The public was not allowed into meetings. Doors were guarded. Windows were shut **despite** the summer heat. Delegates agreed not to discuss the meeting with outsiders.

Because of this secrecy, we have few written records of the convention. The most detailed account comes from a notebook kept by James Madison, a delegate from Virginia.

PHOTO: Mira/Alamy

Independence Hall in Philadelphia, Pennsylvania, stands today as a proud monument to the nation's founding.

▶ CRITICAL THINKING

Drawing Conclusions What belief united the delegates to the Constitutional Convention that met in Independence Hall?

- Electoral College
- Federalist
- federalism
- The Federalist Papers
- Anti-Federalist

Academic Vocabulary

process a series of steps taken to achieve something
despite regardless of; in spite of

PHOTO: PoodlesRock/Corbis Art/Corbis

The Constitutional Convention, shown here in a 1940 painting, consisted of experienced political leaders, including George Washington (standing at right) and Benjamin Franklin (center).

▶ CRITICAL THINKING
Hypothesizing Why do you think it was important for the delegates at the Constitutional Convention to have political experience?

The delegates' original job was to revise the Articles of Confederation. However, they decided that greater changes were needed. They felt that the current government was too weak to deal with the nation's many problems. As a result, the delegates soon agreed to begin anew. They would work to strengthen the national government. To do this, they would need an entirely new plan of government—a new constitution. Thus, the meeting in Philadelphia came to be known as the **Constitutional Convention.**

✅ PROGRESS CHECK

Explaining Why did the delegates want to write a new plan instead of making changes to the Articles of Confederation?

Compromising for a Constitution

GUIDING QUESTION *Why were compromises made at the Constitutional Convention?*

The delegates wanted a government plan that all states could accept. Failure could mean disaster. According to James Madison's notes, George Mason of Virginia said the following:

PRIMARY SOURCE

❝[I] would bury [my] bones in this city rather than [leave] . . . the Convention without any thing being done.❞

—George Mason, remarks at the Constitutional Convention

As the Convention began its work, the Virginia delegates presented a surprise. James Madison had written a plan for a strong national government. This is known as the Virginia Plan.

Constitutional Convention meetings of state delegates in 1787 leading to adoption of a new Constitution

Great Compromise agreement providing a dual system of congressional representation

The Virginia Plan

The Virginia Plan had a federal government much like ours. It had a president, courts, and a congress with two houses. State population would decide how many representatives were in each house. Larger states would have more votes than smaller states.

Delegates from states with more people liked the plan. These states were Massachusetts, Pennsylvania, Virginia, and New York. Delegates from smaller states were opposed. They felt the larger states would ignore the interests of the smaller states.

The New Jersey Plan

Two weeks of heated debate passed. Then, William Paterson of New Jersey offered the New Jersey Plan. It was based on the Articles of Confederation, with some changes. The plan kept the Confederation's one-house congress. Each state would have one vote. But Congress could set taxes and regulate, or control, trade. These were powers it did not have under the Articles. Also, instead of a strong president, a less powerful committee named by Congress would carry out laws.

Delegates from the smaller states backed this plan. These states were Delaware, Maryland, and New Jersey. In the New Jersey Plan, smaller states had the same power as larger states. Of course, delegates from the larger states opposed the plan. They wanted states with more people to have more power.

The Great Compromise

Finally, a committee headed by Roger Sherman of Connecticut found an answer. The committee decided that Congress would have two houses—a Senate and a House of Representatives. In the Senate, each state would have two members. This pleased the smaller states. In the House, the number of seats for each state would reflect the state's population. This pleased the larger states.

No group was fully satisfied. Yet, all could accept the committee's plan. Historians call Sherman's plan the Connecticut Compromise, or the **Great Compromise.** A compromise is an agreement between two or more sides. Each side gives up something but gains something else.

The Three-Fifths Compromise

Still, other issues remained. One concerned slavery and representation in Congress. In 1787, more than 550,000 African Americans were enslaved. Most of them lived in southern states. These states hoped to count the enslaved people in their populations. Then they would have more votes in the House of Representatives.

Connecticut's Roger Sherman had a long career in public service but is best remembered for saving the Constitutional Convention from failure with his Great Compromise.

▶ CRITICAL THINKING
Analyzing How did the Great Compromise please both large and small states?

Roger Sherman

The North had few enslaved persons. Therefore, Northern delegates argued that enslaved persons were legally property and did not vote or share in government. Therefore, they said, enslaved people should not be counted for representation.

The delegates worked out an agreement. It became known as the **Three-Fifths Compromise.** The delegates decided that every five enslaved persons would equal three free persons. Thus, three-fifths of the enslaved population in each state would count for representation in Congress. The same rule was also used for assessing taxes on the states.

Other Compromises

Delegates compromised on trade matters, too. Northern states felt that Congress should be able to regulate foreign trade and trade between the states. Southern states feared that Congress would then tax exports—goods sold to other countries. This would hurt the Southern economy. The South exported large amounts of tobacco, rice, and other products.

Southerners also worried that Congress might stop traders from bringing enslaved people into the nation. The South's economy depended on this labor. Another compromise would settle the issue.

The Southern delegates agreed that Congress could regulate trade between the states, as well as with other countries. In return, the North agreed that Congress could not tax exports. Congress also could not ban the slave trade before 1808—about 20 years in the future.

Southern states wanted the slave population counted for purposes of representation. In some Southern states, enslaved African Americans made up as much as 45 percent of the population. Alabama had more than 125,000 people in 1820, a year after it became a state. Nearly a third of them were enslaved African Americans.

▶ CRITICAL THINKING
Analyzing Why did Southern states want to count enslaved people?

PHOTO: File Photo

Three-Fifths Compromise agreement providing that enslaved persons would count as three-fifths of other persons in determining representation in Congress

The delegates also made compromises about the national government. Some thought Congress should elect the president. Others wanted the people to have this right. The solution was the **Electoral College.** This group would select a president and a vice president. It would be made up of electors, or delegates, named by each state legislature. The Electoral College still exists today. However, voters in each state now choose electors.

✓ PROGRESS CHECK

Inferring What does the Three-Fifths Compromise show about how most free Americans viewed enslaved people?

Federalists and Anti-Federalists

GUIDING QUESTION *How did Federalist and Anti-Federalist viewpoints differ?*

Throughout the long, hot summer, the delegates to the Constitutional Convention worked out the details of the new government. As their task came to an end, some delegates headed home. However, 42 of the original 55 remained. On September 17, 1787, they met for the last time. A committee headed by Gouverneur Morris had written down the Convention's ideas. The Constitution was ready to be signed. All but three delegates wrote their names at the bottom. The delegates at Philadelphia had produced the Constitution. The document's acceptance, however, rested on the will of the American people.

The next step was to win the Constitution's ratification, or approval. The delegates had decided that each state would set up a ratifying convention to vote "yes" or "no." At least nine of the 13 states were required to ratify the Constitution. Only then would it become the supreme law of the land.

Who Were the Federalists?

Americans held different views about the proposed Constitution. Those who supported it called themselves **Federalists.** They chose this name because they believed the Constitution would create a system of **federalism,** that is, a form of government in which power is divided between the federal, or national, government and the states. They believed, however, that federal law should be supreme over state law.

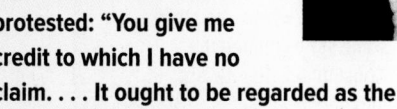

American Leaders
James Madison (1751–1836)

Even in his day, James Madison was known as the "Father of the Constitution." Madison protested: "You give me credit to which I have no claim. . . . It ought to be regarded as the work of many heads and many hands."

When it came to creating the Constitution, however, Madison had few equals. He contributed greatly to the debates at the Constitutional Convention in Philadelphia. Nonetheless, Madison at first opposed the addition of a bill of rights. He feared that future governments might honor only those rights listed in the bill. When some leaders continued to insist on a bill of rights, Madison finally agreed.

To make sure the amendments did not weaken the new government, Madison helped write them himself. Then, as the U.S. representative from Virginia, Madison pushed the amendments through Congress, fulfilling the Constitution's promise to create a "more perfect union."

In later years, Madison continued to play a large role in the nation's political life. With Thomas Jefferson, he founded the Democratic-Republican Party. It opposed what they saw as a dangerous growth of federal power at the expense of the states. In 1801 he became President Thomas Jefferson's secretary of state. In 1808 Madison was elected the fourth president of the United States.

Looking at Leadership

James Madison wrote: "Liberty may be endangered by the abuse of liberty, but also by the abuse of power."
EXPLAINING *Put this statement in your own words.*

Electoral College a group of people named by each state legislature to select the president and vice president

Federalist a supporter of the Constitution

federalism a form of government in which power is divided between the federal, or national, government and the states

Nine of the 13 states were needed to ratify the Constitution in order for it to take effect.

1 LOCATION Which states were most supportive of the Constitution?

2 CRITICAL THINKING
Anaylzing Why do you think some states ratified the Constitution after it went into effect?

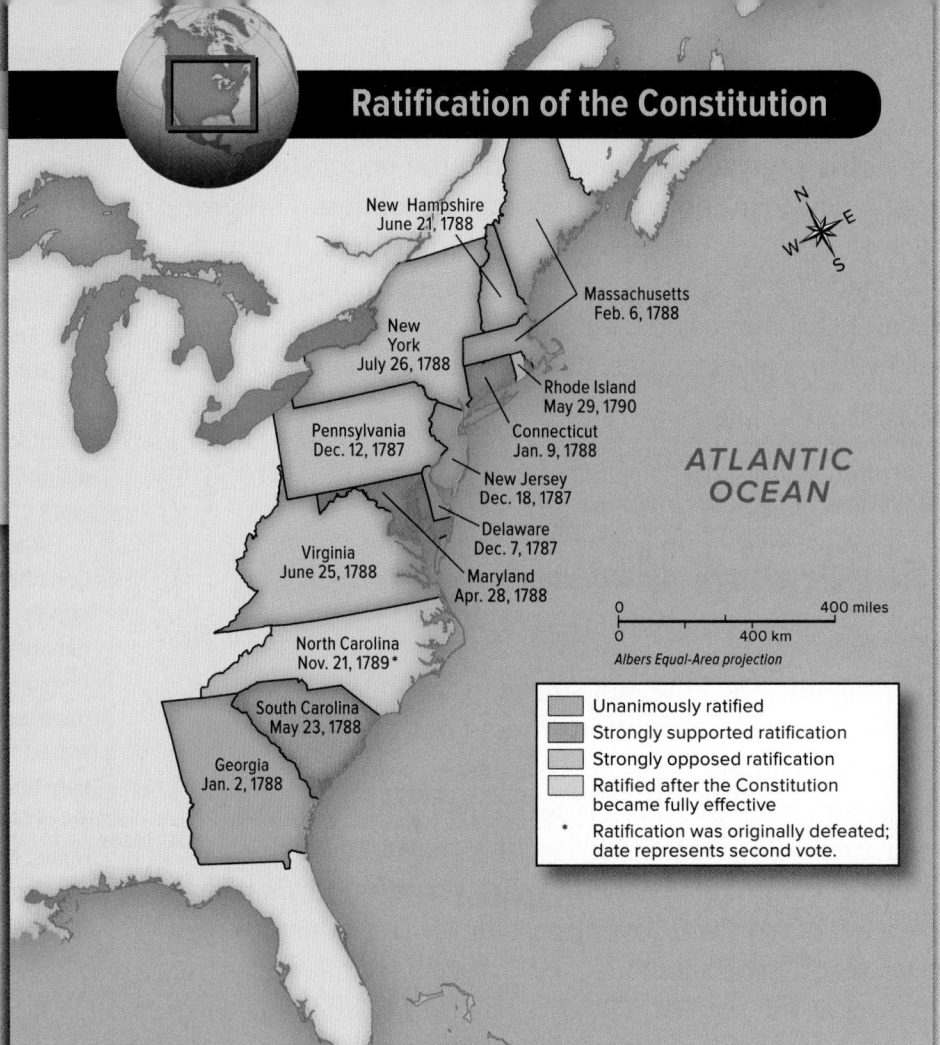

Ratification of the Constitution

New Hampshire
June 21, 1788

Massachusetts
Feb. 6, 1788

New York
July 26, 1788

Rhode Island
May 29, 1790

Pennsylvania
Dec. 12, 1787

Connecticut
Jan. 9, 1788

New Jersey
Dec. 18, 1787

Delaware
Dec. 7, 1787

Virginia
June 25, 1788

Maryland
Apr. 28, 1788

North Carolina
Nov. 21, 1789 *

South Carolina
May 23, 1788

Georgia
Jan. 2, 1788

ATLANTIC OCEAN

0 ___ 400 miles
0 ___ 400 km
Albers Equal-Area projection

- Unanimously ratified
- Strongly supported ratification
- Strongly opposed ratification
- Ratified after the Constitution became fully effective
- * Ratification was originally defeated; date represents second vote.

To win support, the Federalists reminded Americans of the weaknesses in the Articles of Confederation. They argued that the United States could not survive without a strong national government. They believed a strong national government was needed to protect property rights. The Federalists also claimed that only a strong national government could solve the country's problems at home and defend its interests abroad.

The main leaders of the Federalists were Alexander Hamilton, James Madison, and John Jay. To defend the Constitution, they wrote essays called **the Federalist Papers,** or *The Federalist*. In one essay, James Madison argued that:

PRIMARY SOURCE

❝[a] Republic, by which I mean a Government in which the scheme of representation takes place . . . promises the cure for which we are seeking.❞

—James Madison, *The Federalist*, No. 10

ReadingHELPDESK

The Federalist Papers a series of essays written to defend the Constitution

Anti-Federalist a person who opposed ratification of the Constitution

Who Were the Anti-Federalists?

Some Americans opposed the Constitution. They were called **Anti-Federalists.** The Anti-Federalists argued that the new Constitution would destroy the liberties won in the American Revolution. They believed the new Constitution would create a national government so powerful that it would ignore the rights of the states. Some feared that such a government would also favor the wealthy few over the common people. They felt that the power of the national government should not extend beyond what was necessary to preserve the union.

The Anti-Federalists saw a key weakness of the new Constitution. It had no bill of rights to protect individual freedoms. Several state conventions declared they would not ratify the Constitution without a bill of rights.

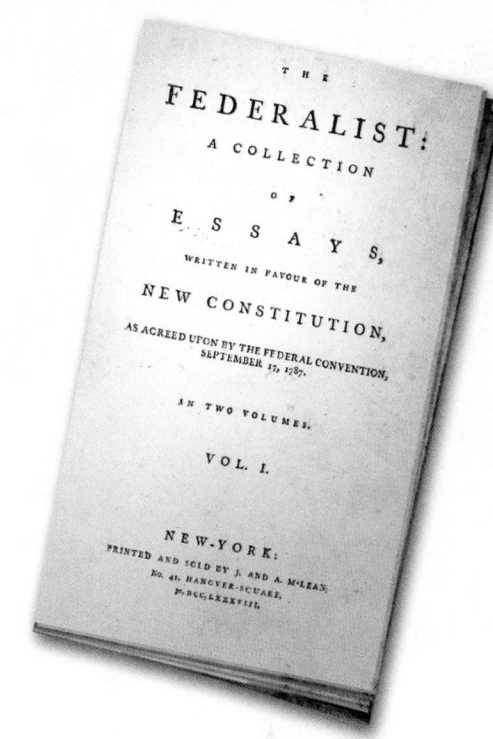

Launching a New Nation

The Federalists at last agreed with the Anti-Federalists. A bill of rights was needed. The Federalists vowed that the new government would quickly add such a bill if the Constitution was adopted.

That promise helped win public support for the Constitution. Several states had already voted for ratification. New Hampshire became the ninth state to do so. The Constitution took effect in June 1788. In time, the remaining four states also ratified it. The last state was Rhode Island in May 1790. The 13 independent states were now one nation, the United States of America.

The Federalist Papers helped explain the proposed Constitution to people. Its arguments proved persuasive at the time and continue to be relevant today.

▶ **CRITICAL THINKING**
Speculating In what way do you think the Federalist Papers continue to be useful today?

PROGRESS CHECK

Explaining Describe the views of the Federalists. How did they feel about ratifying the Constitution?

PHOTO: Fotosearch/Archive Photos/Getty Images

LESSON 2 REVIEW

Review Vocabulary

1. How were both the *Great Compromise* and the *Three-Fifths Compromise* related to population?

2. What was the purpose of *the Federalist Papers*?

Answer the Guiding Questions

3. *Explaining* Why did delegates think the Articles of Confederation needed to be replaced?

4. *Describing* What issue did the Three-Fifths Compromise solve?

5. *Analyzing* Who opposed ratifying the Constitution? What was their major argument against ratification?

6. **ARGUMENT** Put yourself in the position of an Anti-Federalist. You think that a strong national government is a mistake. You believe it would be as abusive as the British government was. Write a short letter or speech expressing your view.

netw⊚rks

There's More Online!

☑ **GRAPHIC ORGANIZER**
Organization of the
U.S. Constitution

☑ **CHARTS**
Comparing Governments
Amending the Constitution

☑ **VIDEO**

A constitutional conventio

Lesson 3
The Structure of the Constitution

ESSENTIAL QUESTION *Why do people create, structure, and change governments?*

IT MATTERS BECAUSE
The U.S. Constitution sets up the structure of our government and the basic laws of our nation.

The Parts of the Constitution

GUIDING QUESTION *How does the U.S. Constitution organize the government?*

The main purpose of the United States Constitution is to provide a plan of government. However, the document is much more. It is the highest authority in the nation. It is the basic law of the United States. The powers of the three branches of the federal government come from it. Like the American flag, the U.S. Constitution is a symbol of our nation. It represents our system of government. It also stands for our basic ideals, such as personal liberty and democracy.

The Constitution has three main parts. First is an introduction called the **Preamble** (PREE•AM•buhl). It states the goals and purposes of the government. Next are seven **articles,** or main parts. They describe the way the government is set up. Third are 27 **amendments.** These are additions and changes to the Constitution.

As plans of government go, the Constitution is fairly brief. It contains a little less than 7,000 words. Unlike most other constitutions, it does not go into a lot of detail. This flexibility has proved a strength over the years.

PHOTO: (tl) Michael Ventura/Alamy; (tr) MPI/Getty Images

Reading**HELP**DESK

Taking Notes: *Summarizing*

As you read, complete a table about the three parts of the U.S. Constitution.

Organization of the U.S. Constitution

Major Part	Purpose
1. Preamble	
2. Articles	
3. Amendments	

Content Vocabulary

- Preamble
- article
- amendment

- legislative branch
- executive branch
- judicial branch

The Preamble

The Preamble consists of a single, powerful sentence. It begins and ends as follows:

PRIMARY SOURCE

❝ We the People of the United States . . . do ordain and establish this Constitution for the United States of America. ❞

—Preamble of the U.S. Constitution

These carefully chosen words make clear that the power of government comes from the people. The middle part of the Preamble states six purposes of the government:

1. To "form a more perfect Union"—to unite the states so they can act as a single nation, for the good of all
2. To "establish Justice"—to make sure that all citizens are treated equally
3. To "insure domestic Tranquility"—to provide peace and order, keeping citizens and their property from harm
4. To "provide for the common [defense]"—to be ready militarily to protect the country and its citizens from attack
5. To "promote the general Welfare"—to help people live healthy, happy, and prosperous lives
6. To "secure the Blessings of Liberty to ourselves and our Posterity"—to guarantee the basic rights of all Americans, including future generations (posterity)

The Seven Articles

The seven articles after the Preamble begin with the Roman numerals I through VII. The first three articles state the powers and responsibilities of each branch of government.

Article I outlines the lawmaking powers of the **legislative branch,** or Congress. It states that Congress, made up of the Senate and the House of Representatives, will have all lawmaking authority. It describes how members of each house will be chosen and what rules they must follow in making laws.

Article II sets out an **executive branch,** or law-enforcing part of government headed by a president and vice president. It explains how these leaders are to be elected and how they can be removed from office.

Visitors to the National Archives Building in Washington, D.C., can view a carefully preserved Constitution. President Hoover called the Constitution and the Declaration of Independence "the most sacred Documents of our history."

▶ CRITICAL THINKING

Assessing Which part of the Constitution do you think has most helped the document adapt to changing times?

PHOTO: Michael Ventura/Alamy

Preamble the opening section of the Constitution

article one of several main parts of the Constitution

amendment any change in the Constitution

legislative branch the lawmaking branch of government

executive branch the branch of government that carries out laws

COMPARING GOVERNMENTS

► CRITICAL THINKING

1 *Analyzing* How did the
Constitution strengthen the
power of the national
government?

2 *Comparing* What were
some powers that the
national government had
under both the Articles and
the Constitution?

ARTICLES OF CONFEDERATION

Organization

- Strong independent states with
  weak central government
- One-house legislature with equal
  representation for each state

Congress

- Declare war
- Make treaties
- Coin and borrow money
- Make laws, although not
  empowered to enforce them
- No power to tax
- No power to regulate trade

No executive branch
No judicial branch

CONSTITUTION

- Strong central government with certain
  powers reserved to states
- Two-house legislature: House of
  Representatives, with representation
  based on state population; Senate, with
  equal representation for all states

Powers

Congress

- Declare war
- Make treaties
- Coin and borrow money
- Make nation's laws
- Tax
- Regulate trade

President

- Commander in chief of armed forces
- Carries out the nation's laws

Supreme Court and lower federal courts

- Interpret the law

Article II lists the president's powers. They include leading
the armed forces and making treaties with other nations.

Article III sets up the **judicial branch** of government. This
branch interprets the laws and sees that they are fairly applied.
The article calls for "one supreme Court" and lower courts as
Congress determines. It lists the powers of the federal courts.
Article III also describes the kinds of cases the courts may hear.

Article IV explains the relationship between the states
and the national government. Article V describes when and
how the Constitution can be changed. Article VI declares
the Constitution the "supreme Law of the Land." Article VII
describes how the Constitution was to be ratified.

The Amendments

Amendments form the last part of the Constitution. There are 27
of them. The first 10 amendments make up the Bill of Rights.

✓ PROGRESS CHECK

Identifying What branches of government does the Constitution establish?

judicial branch the branch of
government that interprets laws

Amending and Interpreting the Constitution

GUIDING QUESTION *In what ways can the Constitution be changed?*

Any change made to the Constitution is called an amendment. Would it surprise you to know that thousands of amendments to the Constitution have been considered over the years? Yet only 27 have been ratified. Few proposed amendments achieve ratification because the Framers—the delegates who framed, or wrote, the Constitution—deliberately made the amendment process difficult. After much debate and compromise, they understood that the Constitution was delicately balanced. Changing even one small detail could have dramatic effects throughout the government. Therefore, the Framers made sure the Constitution could not be amended without the overwhelming support of the people.

At the same time, the ability to change the Constitution is necessary. The Framers had seen how, under the Articles of Confederation, the opposition of only one state made it almost impossible to make important changes to the structure of government. Moreover, amending the Constitution allows for changing social conditions. For example, it took amendments to the Constitution to free enslaved people and give women the right to vote. If the Constitution could not have been changed to protect the rights of African Americans, women, and other groups, it—and our government—might not have lasted.

Why It MATTERS

Changing the Rules

The Constitution provides a method for changing, or amending, the document. Find out if your school, club, or other organization has a formal method for changing its rules. How difficult is it to make rule changes?

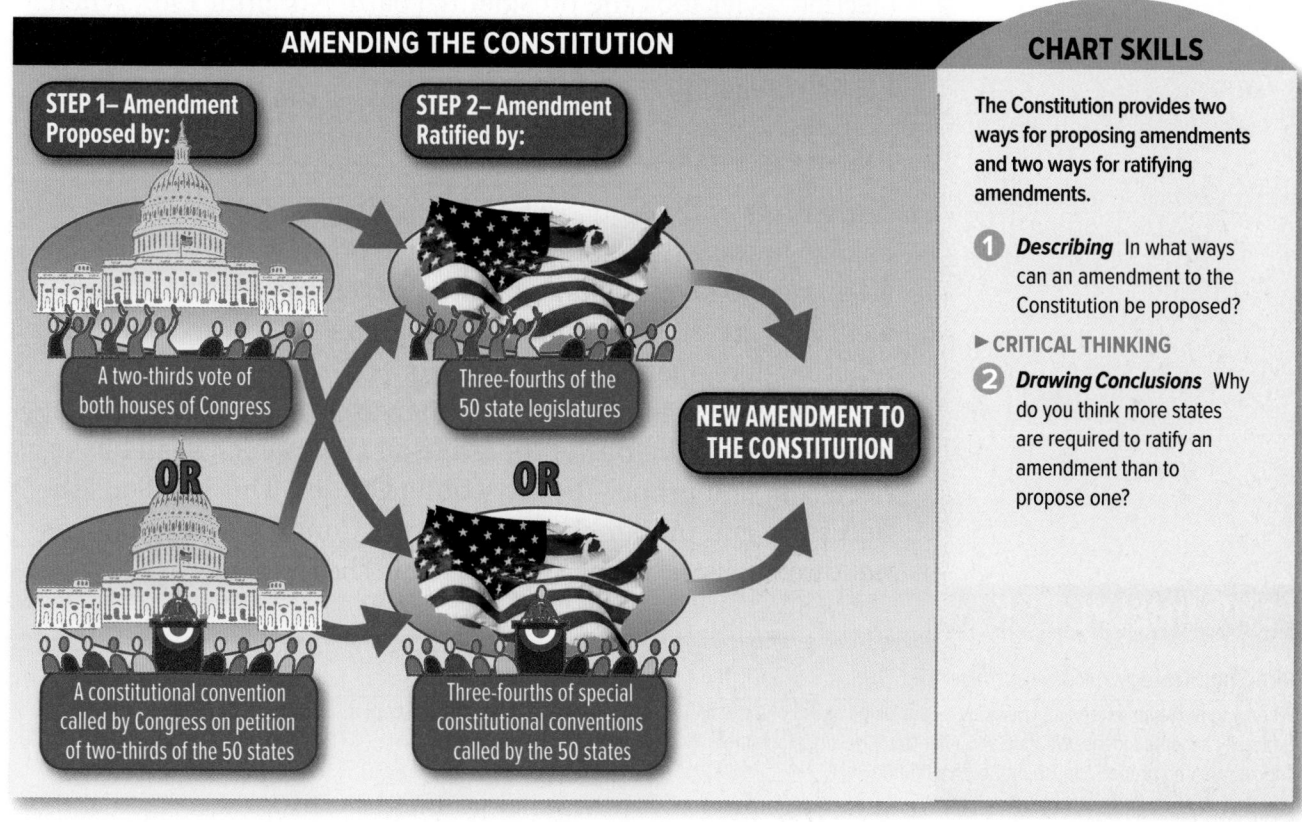

AMENDING THE CONSTITUTION

STEP 1– Amendment Proposed by:

A two-thirds vote of both houses of Congress

OR

A constitutional convention called by Congress on petition of two-thirds of the 50 states

STEP 2– Amendment Ratified by:

Three-fourths of the 50 state legislatures

OR

Three-fourths of special constitutional conventions called by the 50 states

NEW AMENDMENT TO THE CONSTITUTION

CHART SKILLS

The Constitution provides two ways for proposing amendments and two ways for ratifying amendments.

1 *Describing* In what ways can an amendment to the Constitution be proposed?

▶ CRITICAL THINKING

2 *Drawing Conclusions* Why do you think more states are required to ratify an amendment than to propose one?

PHOTO: MPI/Getty Images

Only Congress has the power to declare war. Yet President Thomas Jefferson used his power as commander in chief to send a squadron of naval ships to defend U.S. ships from pirates in the North African port city of Tripoli.

▶ CRITICAL THINKING

Evaluating How have presidential actions like Jefferson's changed the meaning of the Constitution?

Formal and Informal Amendments

Amending the Constitution, as stated in Article V, is a process made up of two steps. These are proposal and ratification. An amendment may be proposed in either of two ways. The first method— used for all amendments so far—is by an act of Congress. A vote of two-thirds of the members of both houses of Congress is required. The second method is by a national convention called by two-thirds of the state legislatures.

Once an amendment has been proposed, three-fourths of the states must ratify it. Ratification can be voted on by the state legislature or by a special state convention. Only one amendment, the Twenty-first Amendment, has been ratified by means of state conventions.

Official, or formal, amendments are part of the Constitution. However, certain actions by the president have led to informal, or unofficial, changes as well. For example, in 1841 William Henry Harrison became the first president to die in office. Vice President John Tyler **assumed,** or accepted, the powers of the president as authorized by the Constitution. The Constitution, however, was not clear on whether Tyler automatically became president or he was merely acting as president until the next election. Tyler took the presidential oath. Not until 1967, when the Twenty-fifth Amendment was ratified, was Tyler's action formally made part of the Constitution.

Interpreting the Constitution

The writers of the Constitution knew that the world would change in ways they could not predict. For this reason, they attempted to keep the document as general as possible. They went into great detail about some matters. However, they left other matters open for interpretation, or explanation.

Article I lists the powers of Congress. The Constitution gives Congress the power to "make all Laws which shall be necessary and proper" to carry out its duties. This is called "the necessary and proper clause." It allows Congress to use powers not directly listed in the Constitution. These powers are known as "implied powers." Much of what the federal government does today—from licensing television stations to regulating air pollution—is based on the implied powers of Congress.

Of course, not everyone agrees on which laws are "necessary and proper." Some people think Congress should be allowed to make any laws the Constitution does not forbid and that fit its purposes. These people believe in a "loose" interpretation of the Constitution. Others think Congress should make only the kinds of laws mentioned in the Constitution. They believe in a "strict" interpretation of the Constitution.

The final authority for interpreting the Constitution is the Supreme Court. Over the years, the Supreme Court has interpreted the Constitution in different ways—sometimes strictly, sometimes loosely. With each new interpretation by the Court, our government changes.

Congress and the president also interpret the Constitution by taking actions not directed by it. For example, nowhere in the Constitution does it state that the president should propose bills or budgets to Congress. Yet since the presidency of George Washington, each year the president has proposed hundreds of bills to Congress.

The interpretation of the Constitution has also changed as customs have changed. For example, the Constitution does not mention political parties. However, political parties quickly became an important part of our political system. These days, they help organize the government and conduct elections.

The Constitution in the present day includes many changes from the document written in 1787. In the next 200 years, it will probably go through many more changes. However, the basic organization and principles of our government will likely remain.

21st Century
SKILLS

Summarizing

How has the "necessary and proper clause" affected the role of government today? Prepare an oral summary and present it to a partner.

✔ **PROGRESS CHECK**

Summarizing How can Congress change the Constitution? Are these types of changes formal or informal?

LESSON 3 REVIEW

Review Vocabulary

1. Describe the organization of the Constitution using the words *Preamble*, *article*, and *amendment*.

2. What is the purpose of the *legislative branch*? The *executive branch*? The *judicial branch*?

Answer the Guiding Questions

3. *Identifying* What are the purposes of Articles I, II, and III of the Constitution?

4. *Describing* How are the states involved in the process of ratifying an amendment to the Constitution?

5. **INFORMATIVE/EXPLANATORY** Do you think that informal changes to the Constitution are as important as formal amendments? Explain why, using supporting information from your reading.

networks

There's More Online!

☑ **GRAPHIC ORGANIZER**
Principles in the Constitution

☑ **CHARTS**
A System of Checks and Balances
Federal and State Powers

Lesson 4

Principles of the Constitution

ESSENTIAL QUESTIONS • *How do societies balance individual and community rights?*
• *How does social change influence government?*

IT MATTERS BECAUSE

Every aspect of our lives is affected by the principles set down in the Constitution by the Framers.

Major Principles of Government

GUIDING QUESTION *What are the principles of United States government?*

Principles are basic beliefs by which people live their lives. Countries can have principles, too. Many of our nation's principles are stated in the U.S. Constitution. Often people take these principles for granted. However, they are some of the most important ideas in human history. Countless people have fought and died for them. People all over the world still dream of living in a country with such noble principles.

The U.S. Constitution seems filled with details about how our government should be structured. However, these details fall under five basic principles of government. The five principles are

- popular sovereignty
- limited government and the rule of law
- separation of powers
- checks and balances
- federalism

They are the foundation on which our government is built.

PHOTO: (tl) ROBERTO SCHMIDT/AFP/Getty Images; (tc) Lebrecht Music and Arts Photo Library/Alamy

Taking Notes: *Organizing*

As you read, complete a graphic organizer to identify principles of the Constitution.

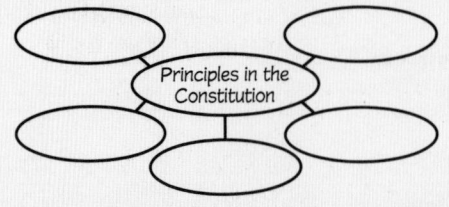

Principles in the Constitution

Content Vocabulary

- **popular sovereignty**
- **limited government**
- **rule of law**

Popular Sovereignty

Article IV of the Constitution guarantees the American people "a Republican Form of Government." Today the word *republic* can mean any representative government headed by a president or other elected leader. This differs from a government in which the leader, such as a king or queen, inherits his or her position. The Framers of the Constitution, however, used the term *republic* to describe a representative democracy. In this kind of government, power belongs to the people. The people state their will through elected representatives. This idea was valued by the early English colonists who came to America.

The idea that the power of government lies with the people is called **popular sovereignty** (SAH•vuhrn•tee). Sovereignty means "the right to rule." The word *popular,* in this case, means "the people or public." Thus, *popular* sovereignty means "the people's right to rule."

The Declaration of Independence is a statement about popular sovereignty. It says that governments should draw their powers "from the consent of the governed." The same idea is echoed in the "We the People" phrase with which the Constitution begins.

Further, the Constitution includes several parts that protect and **ensure**, or guarantee, the sovereignty of the people. Under the Constitution, the will of the people is stated most strongly through elections. By a majority vote, citizens decide who will represent them in Congress. Through the Electoral College, voters also choose the president and vice president. Elected officials must always answer to the people. Elections are held at set times. Voters can reject and replace representatives who serve them poorly.

PHOTO: ROBERTO SCHMIDT/AFP/Getty Images

These voters in Coral Gables, Florida, cast their votes using electronic voting machines. The Constitution ensures that all citizens 18 and older have the right to select their representatives.

▶ CRITICAL THINKING
Analyzing How does voting ensure "the consent of the governed"?

- separation of powers
- checks and balances
- enumerated powers
- reserved powers
- concurrent powers
- supremacy clause

popular sovereignty the idea that power lies with the people

Academic Vocabulary

ensure to make sure of; to guarantee

Limited Government and the Rule of Law

The Framers firmly believed that the government should be strong, but not too strong. They therefore included in the Constitution the principle of **limited government.** This means that government can do only what the people allow it to do.

PRIMARY SOURCE

❝ In framing a government which is to be administered [run] by men over men, the great difficulty lies in this: you must first enable the government to control the governed; and in the next place oblige [require] it to control itself. ❞

—James Madison, *The Federalist*, No. 51

The Constitution limits the power of both the federal and state governments. It says what each may and may not do. English monarchs, before the Magna Carta, headed unlimited governments. The powers of these rulers had few limits.

Under the Constitution, the U.S. government is also limited by the **rule of law.** This means that the law applies to everyone, even those who govern. No one may break the law. No one, even at the highest level of government, can escape its reach. Thus, limited government and the rule of law may prevent tyranny by the government and protect the liberty of the people.

Separation of Powers

The Framers acted to protect Americans against the abuse, or misuse, of power. They also took steps to keep any one person or group from gaining too much power. To set limits on power, the Framers divided the federal government into three branches. Each branch would have different tasks. The Framers' ideas were influenced by French thinker Baron de Montesquieu.

Montesquieu believed that the people's liberty could be protected by separating the legislative, executive, and judicial tasks of government. He thought each task should be **assigned** to a separate branch of government. This division of authority is called **separation of powers.**

This separation of powers, the Framers believed, would limit the ability of any one branch from gaining too much power in another way. The Framers relied on human nature. The ambition of people serving in each branch will lead them to guard their own power from attempts by another branch to expand its power.

Montesquieu, shown here, studied the governments of Europe. After traveling to England, he concluded that the separation of powers was key to liberty.

▶ **CRITICAL THINKING**
Analyzing How does the separation of powers try to prevent abuse of power?

Reading HELP DESK

limited government a government that can do only what the people allow it to do

rule of law the principle that the law applies to everyone, even those who govern

separation of powers the split of authority among the legislative, executive, and judicial branches

Academic Vocabulary

assign to give

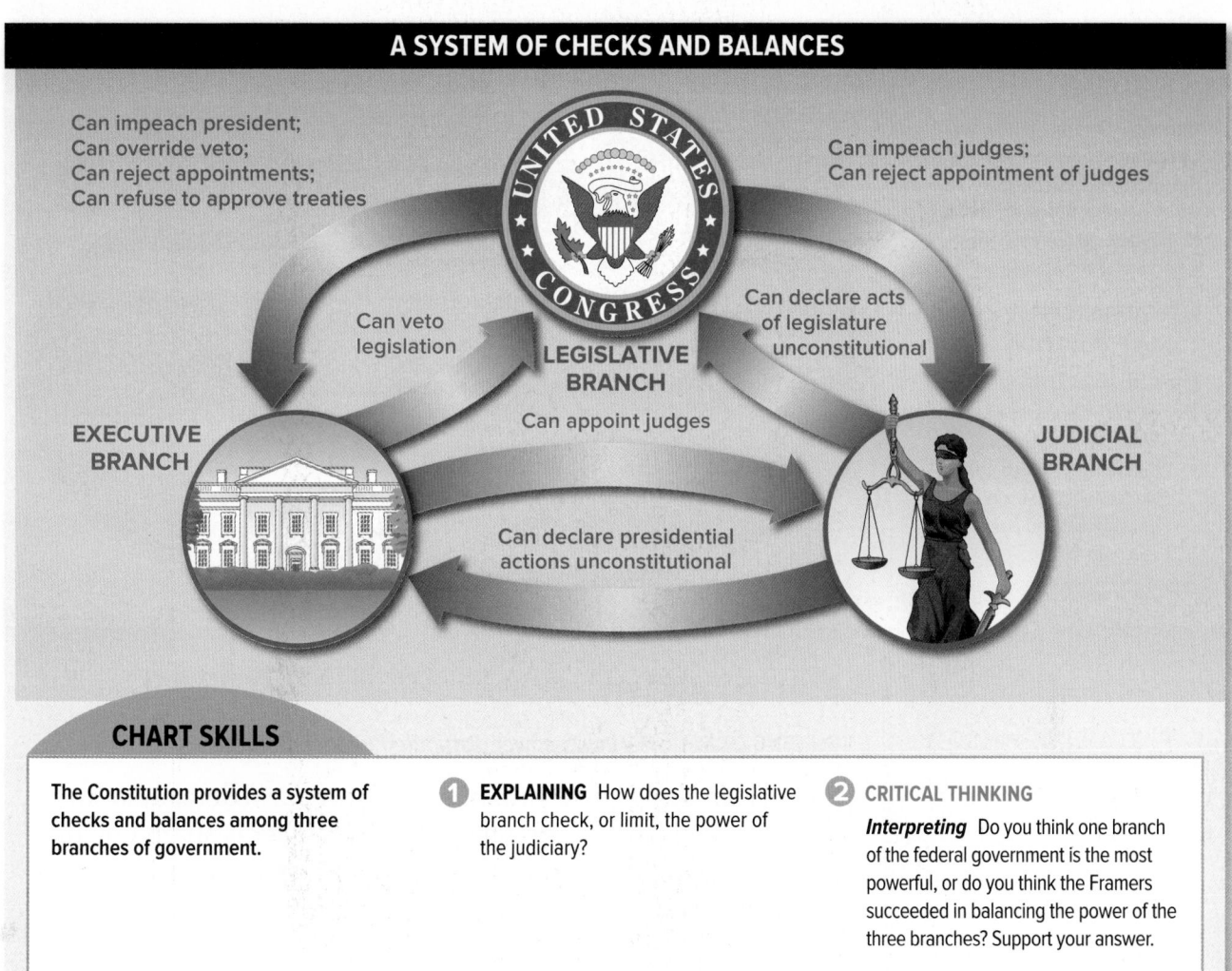

A SYSTEM OF CHECKS AND BALANCES

Can impeach president;
Can override veto;
Can reject appointments;
Can refuse to approve treaties

Can impeach judges;
Can reject appointment of judges

Can veto legislation

Can declare acts of legislature unconstitutional

LEGISLATIVE BRANCH

Can appoint judges

EXECUTIVE BRANCH

JUDICIAL BRANCH

Can declare presidential actions unconstitutional

CHART SKILLS

The Constitution provides a system of checks and balances among three branches of government.

1 EXPLAINING How does the legislative branch check, or limit, the power of the judiciary?

2 CRITICAL THINKING

Interpreting Do you think one branch of the federal government is the most powerful, or do you think the Framers succeeded in balancing the power of the three branches? Support your answer.

Checks and Balances

Separation of powers was set up to check unlimited authority. However, the Framers feared that one branch of government could still gain control of the other two. Therefore, they developed another plan. Its goal was to keep any one of the three branches from becoming too powerful.

This plan was called **checks and balances.** Under a system of checks and balances, each branch of government is able to check, or limit, the power of the other two branches in a number of ways. The chart of checks and balances shows you how each branch interacts with the other two.

✓ PROGRESS CHECK

Synthesizing How is the will of the people, or popular sovereignty, most strongly expressed according to the Constitution?

checks and balances a system in which each branch of government is able to check, or restrain, the power of the others

Under our federal system, some government powers are shared by the state and national governments. Other powers, however, are limited to the national government or reserved for the states.

1 CATEGORIZING What powers are reserved for the states?

2 CRITICAL THINKING

Making Generalizations What characterizes the difference between powers limited to the national government and powers reserved for the states?

NATIONAL GOVERNMENT

- Coin money
- Maintain army and navy
- Declare war
- Regulate trade between states and with foreign nations
- Carry out all expressed powers

NATIONAL AND STATE GOVERNMENTS

- Establish courts
- Enforce laws
- Collect taxes
- Borrow money
- Provide for general welfare

STATE GOVERNMENTS

- Regulate trade within a state
- Protect public welfare and safety
- Conduct elections
- Establish local governments

Federalism

GUIDING QUESTION *How is power distributed under federalism?*

Further limits on government arise from our federal system. Under federalism, as you have learned, power is shared by the national government and the states. Each level of government—national and state—has independent authority over people at the same time.

Three Types of Power

In creating a federal system, the writers of the Constitution divided the powers of government into three types. The powers directly granted to the national government are called the **enumerated powers.** The word *enumerated* means "listed" or "spelled out." Enumerated powers are also called the expressed powers. You will read more about them in another chapter.

There are certain powers that the Constitution does not give to the national government. Instead, they are set aside, or reserved, for the states. These **reserved powers** include regulating trade within state borders, setting up schools, and making rules for marriage and divorce.

The authority of the national and state governments overlap in some cases. Powers that both levels of government carry out are **concurrent powers.** Examples include collecting taxes, borrowing money, and setting up courts and prisons.

Reading**HELP**DESK

enumerated powers powers directly granted to the national government by the Constitution

reserved powers powers the Constitution does not give to the federal government; powers set aside for the states

concurrent powers powers shared by the state and federal governments

supremacy clause a clause stating that the Constitution and other laws and treaties made by the national government are "the supreme Law of the Land"

The Supremacy Clause

In a federal system, the laws of a state and the laws of the nation may conflict. The Framers dealt with this possibility. They included a statement called the **supremacy clause** in the Constitution. It is found in Article VI. The supremacy clause states that the Constitution and other laws and treaties made by the national government "shall be the supreme Law of the Land."

Because the Constitution is the highest law, the national government is not supposed to act against it. Likewise, states may do nothing that goes against either the Constitution or federal law.

The Constitution Today

The entire system of government in the United States rests on a single document: the Constitution. Thomas Jefferson admired the Constitution. He wrote,

PRIMARY SOURCE

" I am persuaded no constitution was ever before so well calculated [thought out] as ours for . . . self-government. "

Jefferson has been proven right. The Constitution is both lasting and adaptable. It has served as the "supreme law of the land" for more than 200 years.

The five principles that support it—popular sovereignty, limited government and the rule of law, separation of powers, checks and balances, and federalism—ensure government limits as well as strength. The Constitution gives our elected representatives enough power to defend our country's freedom and to keep order. At the same time, it sets limits to protect Americans from tyranny, or unlimited and unjust power. The U.S. Constitution stands as a powerful symbol of American values. It is a source of pride and unity to the nation's citizens.

✓ PROGRESS CHECK

Categorizing What are two examples of concurrent powers?

Why It MATTERS

Which Principle Matters Most to You?

Five principles underlie the United States government under the Constitution. They are popular sovereignty, limited government and the rule of law, separation of powers, checks and balances, and federalism. Which matters most to you? Write a paragraph identifying the principle that matters most to you and explaining why.

LESSON 4 REVIEW

Review Vocabulary

1. Use the terms *separation of powers* and *checks and balances* to describe how the U.S. Constitution set up the three branches of the federal government.

2. What is the *supremacy clause* and why is it important to maintaining order in the United States?

Answer the Guiding Questions

3. *Identifying Key Ideas* What are the five principles of government expressed in the Constitution?

4. *Comparing and Contrasting* How are enumerated powers, reserved powers, and concurrent powers similar to and different from one another?

5. **INFORMATIVE/EXPLANATORY** James Madison wrote: "If men were angels, no government would be necessary." How do you think these words relate to the principles of limited government and popular sovereignty?

Write your answers on a separate sheet of paper.

1 Writing Activity

EXPLORING THE ESSENTIAL QUESTION
Why do people create, structure, and change governments?

The government created under the Articles of Confederation was ineffective, so the Framers wrote an entirely new Constitution and fundamentally changed the government. They did this "to form a more perfect Union, establish Justice, insure domestic Tranquility," and for other reasons. Yet they purposely made the new Constitution extremely difficult to change. (That is why there are so few amendments.) In a short essay, explain why a group of people who saw the value of changing a government would create such a difficult process for making future changes to the new government.

2 21st Century Skills

COMPARE AND CONTRAST Americans argued about how much power the national government should have even before the Constitution was adopted. That debate continues today. Conduct online research to learn more. Identify three major arguments for greater national government power and three major arguments for greater state power. Organize each side's arguments in a media presentation. Provide examples and illustrations, and present both sides of the argument to the class.

3 Being an Active Citizen

The Preamble to the Constitution is a single sentence of 52 words. Yet this sentence ranks among the most important pieces of writing in political science, in philosophy, in American history, and even in world history. Rarely has so much thinking about people and government been so beautifully expressed in so few words. Cooperate with classmates, family members, and other community members to commit to memorizing the Preamble within one school week. Work on learning one line each day. Practice it by yourself and for others. Then invite your teacher or some classmates to hear you recite the entire Preamble.

4 Understanding Visuals

The Constitution is an important historical document. Although it is a written work, it has a visual aspect as well. Look at the picture of the first page of the Constitution. Describe in writing what you see that relates to the principle of popular sovereignty.

REVIEW THE GUIDING QUESTIONS

Directions: Choose the best answer for each question.

1 Which of the following did Congress have the power to do under the Articles of Confederation?

   A. pass laws

   B. collect taxes

   C. ignore debts

   D. enforce laws

2 What agreement at the Constitutional Convention concerned the way to represent enslaved persons in the House of Representatives?

   F. the separation of powers

   G. the Electoral College

   H. the Great Compromise

   I. the Three-Fifths Compromise

3 Which statement best reflects the views of an Anti-Federalist?

   A. "I demand a new constitution."

   B. "I support ratification."

   C. "I fear a strong government."

   D. "I oppose a bill of rights."

4 Where in the Constitution are the three branches of government described?

   F. in the Preamble

   G. in the articles

   H. in the amendments

   I. in the Bill of Rights

5 To be ratified, how many states must approve a proposed amendment to the Constitution?

   A. half

   B. two-thirds

   C. three-fourths

   D. all

6 What powers are held only by the federal government?

   F. legislative powers

   G. reserved powers

   H. concurrent powers

   I. enumerated powers

DBQ **ANALYZING DOCUMENTS**

Directions: Analyze the excerpt and answer the questions that follow.

"We the People of the United States, in Order to form a more perfect Union, establish Justice, insure domestic Tranquility, provide for the common defence, promote the general Welfare, and secure the Blessings of Liberty to ourselves and our Posterity, do ordain and establish this Constitution for the United States of America."

—Preamble to the U.S. Constitution

7 **Interpreting** What information does the Preamble provide?

A. the reasons for establishing the Constitution

B. the weaknesses of the Articles of Confederation

C. the arguments for American independence

D. the rights of the American people

8 **Identifying** According to the Preamble, who created the Constitution?

F. posterity

G. the union

H. the people

I. the government

SHORT RESPONSE

"The powers delegated by the proposed Constitution to the federal government are few and defined. Those which are to remain in the State governments are numerous and indefinite."

—James Madison, *The Federalist*, No. 45

9 What form of government is Madison discussing?

10 Madison wrote these words while attempting to convince people to support the proposed Constitution. Why might Madison have thought this statement would help?

EXTENDED RESPONSE

11 **Argument** How well do you think the Framers succeeded in setting up a government that is strong enough to rule but does not interfere with the rights of states and individual citizens? Write a paragraph stating your opinion and supporting it. Include information about the principles in the Constitution that you think do or do not work well.

Need Extra Help?

If You've Missed Question	**1**	**2**	**3**	**4**	**5**	**6**	**7**	**8**	**9**	**10**	**11**
Review Lesson	1	2	2	3	3	4	3	3	4	4	4

THE CONSTITUTION
of the UNITED STATES

The Constitution of the United States is truly a remarkable document. It was one of the first written constitutions in modern history. The Framers wanted to devise a plan for a strong central government that would unify the country, as well as preserve the ideals of the Declaration of Independence.

The entire text of the Constitution and its amendments follows. For easier study, those passages that have been set aside or changed by the adoption of amendments are printed in blue. Also included are explanatory notes that will help clarify the meaning of each article and section.

The Preamble introduces the Constitution and sets forth the general purposes for which the government was established. The Preamble also declares that the power of the government comes from the people.

The printed text of the document shows the spelling and punctuation of the parchment original.

Article I. The Legislative Branch
The Constitution contains seven divisions called articles. Each article covers a general topic. For example, Articles I, II, and III create the three branches of the national government—the legislative, executive, and judicial branches. Most of the articles are divided into sections.

Representation The number of representatives from each state is based on the size of the state's population. Each state is entitled to at least one representative. *What are the qualifications for members of the House of Representatives?*

Vocabulary

preamble: introduction
constitution: principles and laws of a nation
enumeration: census or population count

Preamble

We the People of the United States, in Order to form a more perfect Union, establish Justice, insure domestic Tranquility, provide for the common defence, promote the general Welfare, and secure the Blessings of Liberty to ourselves and our Posterity, do ordain and establish this Constitution for the United States of America.

Article I

Section 1

All legislative Powers herein granted shall be vested in a Congress of the United States, which shall consist of a Senate and House of Representatives.

Section 2

[1.] The House of Representatives shall be composed of Members chosen every second Year by the People of the several States, and the Electors in each State shall have the Qualifications requisite for Electors of the most numerous Branch of the State Legislature.

[2.] No person shall be a Representative who shall not have attained the Age of twenty five Years, and been seven Years a Citizen of the United States, and who shall not, when elected, be an Inhabitant of that State in which he shall be chosen.

[3.] Representatives and direct Taxes shall be apportioned among the several States which may be included within this Union, according to their respective Numbers, which shall be determined by adding to the whole Number of free Persons, including those bound to Service for a Term of Years, and excluding Indians not taxed, three fifths of all other Persons. The actual **Enumeration** shall be made within three Years after the first Meeting of the Congress of the United States, and within every subsequent Term of ten Years, in such Manner as they shall by Law direct. The Number of Representatives shall not exceed one for every thirty Thousand, but each State shall have at Least one Representative; and until such enumeration shall be made, the State of New Hampshire shall be entitled to chuse three, Massachusetts eight, Rhode-Island and Providence Plantations one, Connecticut five, New-York six, New Jersey four, Pennsylvania eight, Delaware one, Maryland six, Virginia ten, North Carolina five, South Carolina five, and Georgia three.

[4.] When vacancies happen in the Representation from any State, the Executive Authority thereof shall issue Writs of Election to fill such Vacancies.

[5.] The House of Representatives shall chuse their Speaker and other Officers; and shall have the sole Power of **Impeachment**.

Section 3

[1.] The Senate of the United States shall be composed of two Senators from each State, chosen by the Legislature thereof, for six Years; and each Senator shall have one Vote.

[2.] Immediately after they shall be assembled in Consequence of the first Election, they shall be divided as equally as may be into three Classes. The Seats of the Senators of the first Class shall be vacated at the Expiration of the second Year, of the second Class at the Expiration of the fourth Year, and of the third Class at the Expiration of the sixth Year, so that one third may be chosen every second Year; and if Vacancies happen by Resignation, or otherwise, during the Recess of the Legislature of any State, the Executive thereof may make temporary Appointments until the next Meeting of the Legislature, which shall then fill such Vacancies.

[3.] No Person shall be a Senator who shall not have attained to the Age of thirty Years, and been nine Years a Citizen of the United States, and who shall not, when elected, be an Inhabitant of that State for which he shall be chosen.

[4.] The Vice President of the United States shall be President of the Senate, but shall have no Vote, unless they be equally divided.

[5.] The Senate shall chuse their other Officers, and also a **President pro tempore**, in the Absence of the Vice President, or when he shall exercise the Office of the President of the United States.

[6.] The Senate shall have the sole Power to try all Impeachments. When sitting for that Purpose, they shall be on Oath or Affirmation. When the President of the United States is tried, the Chief Justice shall preside: And no Person shall be convicted without the Concurrence of two thirds of the Members present.

[7.] Judgment in Cases of Impeachment shall not extend further than to removal from Office, and disqualification to hold and enjoy any Office of honor, Trust or Profit under the United States: but the Party convicted shall nevertheless be liable and subject to **Indictment**, Trial, Judgment and Punishment, according to Law.

PHOTO: White House Historical Association (White House Collection) (detail)

Electing Senators Originally, senators were chosen by the state legislators of their own states. The Seventeenth Amendment changed this, so that senators are now elected by the people. There are 100 senators, 2 from each state. The vice president serves as president of the Senate.

▲ John Adams, the first vice president

Impeachment One of Congress's powers is the power to impeach— to accuse government officials of wrongdoing, put them on trial, and if necessary remove them from office. *Which body has the power to decide the official's guilt or innocence?*

Vocabulary

impeachment: bringing charges against an official

president pro tempore: presiding officer of Senate who serves when the vice president is absent

indictment: charging a person with an offense

Section 4

[1.] The Times, Places and Manner of holding Elections for Senators and Representatives, shall be prescribed in each State by the Legislature thereof; but the Congress may at any time by Law make or alter such Regulations, except as to the Places of chusing Senators.

[2.] The Congress shall assemble at least once in every Year, and such Meeting shall be on the first Monday in December, unless they shall by Law appoint a different Day.

Section 5

[1.] Each House shall be the Judge of the Elections, Returns and Qualifications of its own Members, and a Majority of each shall constitute a **Quorum** to do Business; but a smaller Number may **adjourn** from day to day, and may be authorized to compel the Attendance of absent Members, in such Manner, and under such Penalties as each House may provide.

[2.] Each House may determine the Rules of its Proceedings, punish its Members for disorderly Behaviour, and, with the Concurrence of two thirds, expel a Member.

[3.] Each House shall keep a Journal of its Proceedings, and from time to time publish the same, excepting such Parts as may in their Judgment require Secrecy; and the Yeas and Nays of the Members of either House on any question shall, at the Desire of one fifth of those Present, be entered on the Journal.

[4.] Neither House, during the Session of Congress, shall, without the Consent of the other, adjourn for more than three days, nor to any other Place than that in which the two Houses shall be sitting.

Section 6

[1.] The Senators and Representatives shall receive a Compensation for their Services, to be ascertained by Law, and paid out of the Treasury of the United States. They shall in all Cases, except Treason, Felony and Breach of the Peace, be privileged from Arrest during their Attendance at the Session of their respective Houses, and in going to and returning from the same; and for any Speech or Debate in either House, they shall not be questioned in any other Place.

[2.] No Senator or Representative shall, during the Time for which he was elected, be appointed to any civil Office under the Authority of the United States, which shall have been created, or the **Emoluments** whereof shall have been encreased during such time; and no Person holding any Office under the United States, shall be a Member of either House during his Continuance in Office.

Congressional Salaries To strengthen the federal government, the Founders set congressional salaries to be paid by the United States Treasury rather than by members' respective states. Originally, members were paid $6 per day. In 2011, all members of Congress received a base salary of $174,000.

Vocabulary

quorum: minimum number of members that must be present to conduct sessions

adjourn: to suspend a session

emoluments: salaries

Section 7

[1.] All **Bills** for raising **Revenue** shall originate in the House of Representatives; but the Senate may propose or concur with Amendments as on other Bills.

[2.] Every Bill which shall have passed the House of Representatives and the Senate, shall, before it become a Law, be presented to the President of the United States; If he approve he shall sign it, but if not he shall return it, with his Objections to that House in which it shall have originated, who shall enter the Objections at large on their Journal, and proceed to reconsider it. If after such Reconsideration two thirds of that House shall agree to pass the Bill, it shall be sent, together with the Objections, to the other House, by which it shall likewise be reconsidered, and if approved by two thirds of that House, it shall become a Law. But in all such Cases the Votes of both Houses shall be determined by yeas and Nays, and the Names of the Persons voting for and against the Bill shall be entered on the Journal of each House respectively. If any Bill shall not be returned by the President within ten Days (Sundays excepted) after it shall have been presented to him, the Same shall be a Law, in like Manner as if he had signed it, unless the Congress by their Adjournment prevent its Return, in which Case it shall not be a Law.

[3.] Every Order, **Resolution**, or Vote to which the Concurrence of the Senate and House of Representatives may be necessary (except on a question of Adjournment) shall be presented to the President of the United States; and before the Same shall take Effect, shall be approved by him, or being disapproved by him, shall be repassed by two thirds of the Senate and House of Representatives, according to the Rules and Limitations prescribed in the Case of a Bill.

Section 8

[1.] The Congress shall have the Power To lay and collect Taxes, Duties, Imposts and Excises, to pay the Debts and provide for the common Defence and general Welfare of the United States; but all Duties, Imposts and Excises shall be uniform throughout the United States;

[2.] To borrow Money on the credit of the United States;

[3.] To regulate Commerce with foreign Nations, and among the several States, and with the Indian Tribes;

[4.] To establish an uniform Rule of **Naturalization**, and uniform Laws on the subject of Bankruptcies throughout the United States;

[5.] To coin Money, regulate the Value thereof, and of foreign Coin, and fix the Standard of Weights and Measures;

[6.] To provide for the Punishment of counterfeiting the Securities and current Coin of the United States;

[7.] To establish Post Offices and post Roads;

Where Tax Laws Begin All tax laws must originate in the House of Representatives. This ensures that the branch of Congress that is elected by the people every two years has the major role in determining taxes.

How Bills Become Laws A bill may become a law only by passing both houses of Congress and by being signed by the president. The president can check Congress by rejecting—vetoing—its legislation. *How can Congress override the president's veto?*

Powers of Congress Expressed powers are those powers directly stated in the Constitution. Most of the expressed powers of Congress are listed in Article I, Section 8. These powers are also called enumerated powers because they are numbered 1 through 18. *Which clause gives Congress the power to declare war?*

Vocabulary

bill: draft of a proposed law

revenue: income raised by government

resolution: legislature's formal expression of opinion

naturalization: procedure by which a citizen of a foreign nation becomes a citizen of the United States.

Elastic Clause The final enumerated power is often called the "elastic clause." This clause gives Congress the right to make all laws "necessary and proper" to carry out the powers expressed in the other clauses of Article I. It is called the elastic clause because it lets Congress "stretch" its powers to meet situations the Founders could never have anticipated.

Necessary and Proper What does the phrase "necessary and proper" in the elastic clause mean? Almost from the beginning, this phrase was a subject of dispute. The issue was whether a strict or a broad interpretation of the Constitution should be applied. The dispute was first addressed in 1819, in the case of *McCulloch* v. *Maryland*, when the Supreme Court ruled in favor of a broad interpretation.

Habeas Corpus A writ of habeas corpus issued by a judge requires a law official to bring a prisoner to court and show cause for holding the prisoner. A bill of attainder is a bill that punished a person without a jury trial. An "ex post facto" law is one that makes an act a crime after the act has been committed. *What does the Constitution say about bills of attainder?*

Vocabulary

tribunal: a court
insurrection: rebellion

[8.] To promote the Progress of Science and useful Arts, by securing for limited Times to Authors and Inventors the exclusive Right to their respective Writings and Discoveries;

[9.] To constitute **Tribunals** inferior to the supreme Court;

[10.] To define and punish Piracies and Felonies committed on the high Seas, and Offences against the Law of Nations;

[11.] To declare War, grant Letters of Marque and Reprisal, and make Rules concerning Captures on Land and Water;

[12.] To raise and support Armies, but no Appropriation of Money to that Use shall be for a longer Term than two Years;

[13.] To provide and maintain a Navy;

[14.] To make Rules for the Government and Regulation of the land and naval Forces;

[15.] To provide for calling forth the Militia to execute the Laws of the Union, suppress **Insurrections** and repel Invasions;

[16.] To provide for organizing, arming, and disciplining, the Militia, and for governing such Part of them as may be employed in the Service of the United States, reserving to the States respectively, the Appointment of the Officers, and the Authority of training the Militia according to the discipline prescribed by Congress;

[17.] To exercise exclusive Legislation in all Cases whatsoever, over such District (not exceeding ten Miles square) as may, by Cession of particular States, and the Acceptance of Congress, become the Seat of the Government of the United States, and to exercise like Authority over all Places purchased by the Consent of the Legislature of the State in which the Same shall be, for the Erection of Forts, Magazines, Arsenals, dock-Yards, and other needful Buildings; —And

[18.] To make all Laws which shall be necessary and proper for carrying into Execution the foregoing Powers, and all other Powers vested by this Constitution in the Government of the United States, or in any Department or Officer thereof.

Section 9

[1.] The Migration or Importation of such Persons as any of the States now existing shall think proper to admit, shall not be prohibited by the Congress prior to the Year one thousand eight hundred and eight, but a Tax or duty may be imposed on such Importation, not exceeding ten dollars for each Person.

[2.] The Privilege of the Writ of Habeas Corpus shall not be suspended, unless when in Cases of Rebellion or Invasion the public Safety may require it.

[3.] No Bill of Attainder or ex post facto Law shall be passed.

[4.] No Capitation, or other direct, Tax shall be laid, unless in Proportion to the Census or Enumeration herein before directed to be taken.

[5.] No Tax or Duty shall be laid on Articles exported from any State.

[6.] No Preference shall be given by any Regulation of Commerce or Revenue to the Ports of one State over those of another: nor shall Vessels bound to, or from, one State, be obliged to enter, clear, or pay Duties in another.

[7.] No Money shall be drawn from the Treasury, but in Consequence of **Appropriations** made by Law; and a regular Statement and Account of the Receipts and Expenditures of all public Money shall be published from time to time.

[8.] No Title of Nobility shall be granted by the United States: And no Person holding any Office of Profit or Trust under them, shall, without the Consent of the Congress, accept of any present, Emolument, Office, or Title, of any kind whatever, from any King, Prince, or foreign State.

Section 10

[1.] No State shall enter into any Treaty, Alliance, or Confederation; grant Letters of Marque and Reprisal; coin Money; emit Bills of Credit; make any Thing but gold and silver Coin a Tender in Payment of Debts; pass any Bill of Attainder, ex post facto Law, or Law impairing the Obligation of Contracts, or grant any Title of Nobility.

[2.] No State shall, without the Consent of the Congress, lay any **Imposts** or **Duties** on Imports or Exports, except what may be absolutely necessary for executing it's inspection Laws: and the net Produce of all Duties and Imposts, laid by any State on Imports and Exports, shall be for the Use of the Treasury of the United States; and all such Laws shall be subject to the Revision and Controul of the Congress.

[3.] No State shall, without the Consent of Congress, lay any Duty of Tonnage, keep Troops, or Ships of War in time of Peace, enter into any Agreement or Compact with another State, or with a foreign Power, or engage in War, unless actually invaded, or in such imminent Danger as will not admit of delay.

Article II

Section 1

[1.] The executive Power shall be vested in a President of the United States of America. He shall hold his Office during the Term of four Years, and, together with the Vice President, chosen for the same Term, be elected, as follows.

[2.] Each State shall appoint, in such Manner as the Legislature thereof may direct, a Number of Electors, equal to the whole Number of Senators and Representatives to which the State may be entitled in the Congress: but no Senator or Representative, or Person holding an Office of Trust or Profit under the United States, shall be appointed an Elector.

Limitations on the States Section 10 lists limits on the states. These restrictions were designed, in part, to prevent an overlapping in functions and authority with the federal government.

Article II. The Executive Branch Article II creates an executive branch to carry out laws passed by Congress. Article II lists the powers and duties of the presidency, describes qualifications for office and procedures for electing the president, and provides for a vice president.

Vocabulary

appropriations: funds set aside for a specific use

impost: tax

duty: tax

[3.] The Electors shall meet in their respective States, and vote by Ballot for two Persons, of whom one at least shall not be an Inhabitant of the same State with themselves. And they shall make a List of all the Persons voted for, and of the Number of Votes for each; which List they shall sign and certify, and transmit sealed to the Seat of the Government of the United States, directed to the President of the Senate. The President of the Senate shall, in the Presence of the Senate and House of Representatives, open all the Certificates, and the Votes shall then be counted. The Person having the greatest Number of Votes shall be the President, if such Number be a Majority of the whole Number of Electors appointed; and if there be more than one who have such Majority, and have an equal Number of Votes, then the House of Representatives shall immediately chuse by Ballot one of them for President; and if no person have a Majority, then from the five highest on the List the said House shall in like Manner chuse the President. But in chusing the President, the Votes shall be taken by States, the Representation from each State having one Vote; A quorum for this Purpose shall consist of a Member or Members from two thirds of the States, and a Majority of all the States shall be necessary to a Choice. In every Case, after the Choice of the President, the Person having the greatest Number of Votes of the Electors shall be the Vice President. But if there should remain two or more who have equal Votes, the Senate shall chuse from them by Ballot the Vice President.

[4.] The Congress may determine the Time of chusing the Electors, and the Day on which they shall give their Votes; which Day shall be the same throughout the United States.

[5.] No Person except a natural born Citizen, or a Citizen of the United States, at the time of the Adoption of this Constitution, shall be eligible to the Office of President; neither shall any Person be eligible to that Office who shall not have attained to the Age of thirty five Years, and been fourteen Years a Resident within the United States.

[6.] In Case of the Removal of the President from Office, or of his Death, Resignation, or Inability to discharge the Powers and Duties of the said Office, the Same shall devolve on the Vice President, and the Congress may by Law provide for the Case of Removal, Death, Resignation or Inability, both of the President and Vice President, declaring what Officer shall then act as President, and such Officer shall act accordingly, until the Disability be removed, or a President shall be elected.

[7.] The President shall, at stated Times, receive for his Services, a Compensation, which shall neither be increased nor diminished during the Period for which he shall have been elected, and he shall not receive within that Period any other Emolument from the United States, or any of them.

Previous Elections The Twelfth Amendment, added in 1804, changed the method of electing the president stated in Article II, Section 3. The Twelfth Amendment requires that the electors cast separate ballots for president and vice president.

Qualifications The president must be a citizen of the United States by birth, at least 35 years of age, and a resident of the United States for 14 years.

Vacancies If the president dies, resigns, is removed from office by impeachment, or is unable to carry out the duties of the office, the vice president becomes president. The Twenty-fifth Amendment sets procedures for presidential succession.

Salary Originally, the president's salary was $25,000 per year. The president's current salary is $400,000 plus a $50,000 nontaxable expense account per year. The president also receives living accommodations in two residences—the White House and Camp David.

[8.] Before he enter on the Execution of his Office, he shall take the following Oath or Affirmation:—"I do solemnly swear (or affirm) that I will faithfully execute the Office of President of the United States, and will to the best of my Ability, preserve, protect and defend the Constitution of the United States."

Section 2

[1.] The President shall be Commander in Chief of the Army and Navy of the United States, and of the Militia of the several States, when called into the actual Service of the United States; he may require the Opinion, in writing, of the principal Officer in each of the executive Departments, upon any Subject relating to the Duties of their respective Offices, and he shall have Power to grant Reprieves and Pardons for Offences against the United States, except in Cases of Impeachment.

[2.] He shall have Power, by and with the Advice and Consent of the Senate, to make Treaties, provided two thirds of the Senators present concur; and he shall nominate, and by and with the Advice and Consent of the Senate, shall appoint Ambassadors, other public Ministers and Consuls, Judges of the supreme Court, and all other Officers of the United States, whose Appointments are not herein otherwise provided for, and which shall be established by Law: but the Congress may by Law vest the Appointment of such inferior Officers, as they think proper, in the President alone, in the Courts of Law, or in the Heads of Departments.

[3.] The President shall have Power to fill up all Vacancies that may happen during the Recess of the Senate, by granting Commissions which shall expire at the End of their next Session.

Section 3

He shall from time to time give to the Congress Information of the State of the Union, and recommend to their Consideration such Measures as he shall judge necessary and expedient; he may, on extraordinary Occasions, convene both Houses, or either of them, and in Case of Disagreement between them, with Respect to the Time of Adjournment, he may adjourn them to such Time as he shall think proper; he shall receive Ambassadors and other public Ministers; he shall take Care that the Laws be faithfully executed, and shall Commission all the Officers of the United States.

The Cabinet Mention of "the principal officer in each of the executive departments" is the only suggestion of the president's cabinet to be found in the Constitution. The cabinet is an advisory body, and its power depends on the president. Section 2, Clause 1 also makes the president—a civilian—the head of the armed services. This established the principle of civilian control of the military.

Presidential Powers An executive order is a command issued by a president to exercise a power which he or she has been given by the U.S. Constitution or by a federal statute. In times of emergency, presidents sometimes have used the executive order to override the Constitution and Congress. During the Civil War, President Lincoln suspended many fundamental rights, closing down newspapers that opposed his policies and imprisoning people who disagreed with him. Lincoln said that these actions were justified to preserve the Union.

▲ **President Bill Clinton during impeachment proceedings**

Article III. The Judicial Branch The term *judicial* refers to courts. The Constitution set up only the Supreme Court, but provided for the establishment of other federal courts. The judiciary of the United States has two different systems of courts. One system consists of the federal courts, whose powers derive from the Constitution and federal laws. The other includes the courts of each of the 50 states, whose powers derive from state constitutions and laws.

Statute Law Federal courts deal mostly with "statute law," or laws passed by Congress, treaties, and cases involving the Constitution itself.

The Supreme Court A Court with "original jurisdiction" has the authority to be the first court to hear a case. The Supreme Court has "appellate jurisdiction" and mostly hears cases appealed in lower courts.

Vocabulary

original jurisdiction: authority to be the first court to hear a case

appellate jurisdiction: authority to hear cases that have been appealed in lower courts

Section 4

The President, Vice President and all civil Officers of the United States, shall be removed from Office on Impeachment for, and Conviction of, Treason, Bribery, or other high Crimes and Misdemeanors.

Article III

Section 1

The judicial Power of the United States, shall be vested in one supreme Court, and in such inferior Courts as the Congress may from time to time ordain and establish. The Judges, both of the supreme and inferior Courts, shall hold their Offices during good Behaviour, and shall, at stated Times, receive for their Services, a Compensation, which shall not be diminished during their Continuance in Office.

Section 2

[1.] The judicial Power shall extend to all Cases, in Law and Equity, arising under this Constitution, the Laws of the United States, and Treaties made, or which shall be made, under their Authority;—to all Cases affecting Ambassadors, other public Ministers and Consuls;—to all Cases of admiralty and maritime Jurisdiction;—to Controversies to which the United States shall be a Party;—to Controversies between two or more States;—between a State and Citizens of another State;—between Citizens of different States,—between Citizens of the same State claiming Lands under Grants of different States, and between a State, or the Citizens thereof, and foreign States, Citizens or Subjects.

[2.] In all Cases affecting Ambassadors, other public Ministers and Consuls, and those in which a State shall be Party, the supreme Court shall have **original Jurisdiction**. In all the other Cases before mentioned, the supreme Court shall have **appellate Jurisdiction**, both as to Law and Fact, with such Exceptions, and under such Regulations as the Congress shall make.

[3.] The Trial of all Crimes, except in Cases of Impeachment, shall be by Jury; and such Trial shall be held in the State where the said Crimes shall have been committed; but when not committed within any State, the Trial shall be at such Place or Places as the Congress may by Law have directed.

Section 3

[1.] **Treason** against the United States, shall consist only in levying War against them, or in adhering to their Enemies, giving them Aid and Comfort. No Person shall be convicted of Treason unless on the Testimony of two Witnesses to the same overt Act, or on Confession in open Court.

[2.] The Congress shall have Power to declare the Punishment of Treason, but no Attainder of Treason shall work Corruption of Blood, or Forfeiture except during the Life of the Person attainted.

Article IV

Section 1

Full Faith and Credit shall be given in each State to the public Acts, Records, and judicial Proceedings of every other State. And the Congress may by general Laws prescribe the Manner in which such Acts, Records and Proceedings shall be proved, and the Effect thereof.

Section 2

[1.] The Citizens of each State shall be entitled to all Privileges and Immunities of Citizens in the several States.

[2.] A Person charged in any State with Treason, Felony, or other Crime, who shall flee from Justice, and be found in another State, shall on Demand of the executive Authority of the State from which he fled, be delivered up, to be removed to the State having Jurisdiction of the Crime.

[3.] No Person held to Service of Labour in one State, under the Laws thereof, escaping into another, shall, in Consequence of any Law or Regulation therein, be discharged from such Service or Labour, but shall be delivered up on Claim of the Party to whom such Service or Labour may be due.

Section 3

[1.] New States may be admitted by the Congress into this Union; but no new State shall be formed or erected within the Jurisdiction of any other State; nor any State be formed by the Junction of two or more States, or Parts of States, without the Consent of the Legislatures of the States concerned as well as of the Congress.

[2.] The Congress shall have Power to dispose of and make all needful Rules and Regulations respecting the Territory or other Property belonging to the United States; and nothing in this Constitution shall be so construed as to Prejudice any Claims of the United States, or of any particular State.

Article IV. Relations Among the States Article IV explains the relationship of the states to one another and to the national government. This article requires each state to give citizens of other states the same rights as its own citizens, addresses admitting new states, and guarantees that the national government will protect the states.

New States Congress has the power to admit new states. It also determines the basic guidelines for applying for statehood. Two states, Maine and West Virginia, were created within the boundaries of another state. In the case of West Virginia, President Lincoln recognized the West Virginia government as the legal government of Virginia during the Civil War. This allowed West Virginia to secede from Virginia without obtaining approval from the Virginia legislature.

Vocabulary

treason: violation of the allegiance owed by a person to his or her own country; for example, by aiding an enemy

Section 4

The United States shall guarantee to every State in this Union a Republican Form of Government, and shall protect each of them against Invasion; and on Application of the Legislature, or of the Executive (when the Legislature cannot be convened) against domestic Violence.

Article V

The Congress, whenever two thirds of both Houses shall deem it necessary, shall propose **Amendments** to this Constitution, or, on the Application of the Legislatures of two thirds of the several States, shall call a Convention for proposing Amendments, which, in either Case, shall be valid to all Intents and Purposes, as Part of this Constitution, when ratified by the Legislatures of three fourths of the several States, or by Conventions in three fourths thereof, as the one or the other Mode of **Ratification** may be proposed by the Congress; Provided that no Amendment which may be made prior to the Year One thousand eight hundred and eight shall in any Manner affect the first and fourth Clauses in the Ninth Section of the first Article; and that no State, without its Consent, shall be deprived of its equal Suffrage in the Senate.

Article VI

[1.] All Debts contracted and Engagements entered into, before the Adoption of this Constitution, shall be as valid against the United States under this Constitution, as under the Confederation.

[2.] This Constitution, and the Laws of the United States which shall be made in Pursuance thereof; and all Treaties made, or which shall be made, under the Authority of the United States, shall be the supreme Law of the Land; and the Judges in every State shall be bound thereby, any Thing in the Constitution or Laws of any State to the Contrary notwithstanding.

[3.] The Senators and Representatives before mentioned, and the Members of the several State Legislatures, and all executive and judicial Officers, both of the United States and of the several States, shall be bound by Oath or Affirmation, to support this Constitution; but no religious Test shall ever be required as a Qualification to any Office or public Trust under the United States.

Vocabulary

amendment: a change to the Constitution

ratification: process by which an amendment is approved

Article VII

The Ratification of the Conventions of nine States, shall be sufficient for the Establishment of this Constitution between the States so ratifying the Same.

Done in Convention by the Unanimous Consent of the States present the Seventeenth Day of September in the Year of our Lord one thousand seven hundred and Eighty seven and of the Independence of the United States of America the Twelfth. In witness whereof We have hereunto subscribed our Names,

Article VII. Ratification Article VII addresses ratification and declares that the Constitution would take effect after it was ratified by nine states.

Signers

George Washington, President and Deputy from Virginia

New Hampshire
John Langdon
Nicholas Gilman

Massachusetts
Nathaniel Gorham
Rufus King

Connecticut
William Samuel Johnson
Roger Sherman

New York
Alexander Hamilton

New Jersey
William Livingston
David Brearley
William Paterson
Jonathan Dayton

Pennsylvania
Benjamin Franklin
Thomas Mifflin
Robert Morris
George Clymer
Thomas FitzSimons
Jared Ingersoll
James Wilson
Gouverneur Morris

Delaware
George Read
Gunning Bedford, Jr.
John Dickinson
Richard Bassett
Jacob Broom

Maryland
James McHenry
Daniel of St. Thomas Jenifer
Daniel Carroll

Virginia
John Blair
James Madison, Jr.

North Carolina
William Blount
Richard Dobbs Spaight
Hugh Williamson

South Carolina
John Rutledge
Charles Cotesworth
  Pinckney
Charles Pinckney
Pierce Butler

Georgia
William Few
Abraham Baldwin

Attest: William Jackson, Secretary

◀ Re-creating colonial response to the signing at Independence Hall

PHOTO: George Widman/AP Images

The Amendments This part of the Constitution consists of amendments, or changes. The Constitution has been amended 27 times throughout the nation's history.

Amendment I

Congress shall make no law respecting an establishment of religion, or prohibiting the free exercise thereof; or abridging the freedom of speech, or of the press; or the right of the people peaceably to assemble, and to petition the Government for a redress of grievances.

Bill of Rights The first 10 amendments are known as the Bill of Rights (1791). These amendments limit the powers of government. The First Amendment protects the civil liberties of individuals in the United States. The amendment freedoms are not absolute, however. They are limited by the rights of other individuals. *What freedoms does the First Amendment protect?*

Amendment II

A well regulated Militia, being necessary to the security of a free State, the right of the people to keep and bear Arms, shall not be infringed.

Amendment III

No Soldier shall, in time of peace be **quartered** in any house, without the consent of the Owner, nor in time of war, but in a manner to be prescribed by law.

Amendment IV

The right of the people to be secure in their persons, houses, papers, and effects, against unreasonable searches and seizures, shall not be violated, and no **Warrants** shall issue, but upon **probable cause**, supported by Oath or affirmation, and particularly describing the place, to be searched, and the persons or things to be seized.

Rights of the Accused This amendment contains important protections for people accused of crimes. One of the protections is that government may not deprive any person of life, liberty, or property without due process of law. This means that the government must follow proper constitutional procedures in trials and in other actions it takes against individuals. *According to Amendment V, what is the function of a grand jury?*

Amendment V

No person shall be held to answer for a capital, or otherwise infamous crime, unless on a presentment or indictment of a Grand Jury, except in cases arising in the land or naval forces, or in the Militia, when in actual service in time of War or public danger; nor shall any person be subject for the same offence to be twice put in jeopardy of life or limb; nor shall be compelled in any criminal case to be a witness against himself, nor be deprived of life, liberty, or property, without due process of law; nor shall private property be taken for public use without just compensation.

Vocabulary

quarter: to provide living accommodations

warrant: document that gives police particular rights or powers

probable cause: police must have a reasonable basis to believe a person is linked to a crime

common law: law established by previous court decisions

bail: money that an accused person provides to the court as a guarantee that he or she will be present for a trial

Amendment VI

In all criminal prosecutions, the accused shall enjoy the right to a speedy and public trial, by an impartial jury of the State and district wherein the crime shall have been committed, which district shall have been previously ascertained by law, and to be informed of the nature and cause of the accusation; to be confronted with the witnesses against him; to have compulsory process for obtaining witnesses in his favor, and to have the assistance of counsel for his defence.

Amendment VII

In Suits at **common law**, where the value in controversy shall exceed twenty dollars, the right of trial by jury shall be preserved, and no fact tried by a jury, shall be otherwise re-examined in any Court of the United States, than according to the rules of common law.

Amendment VIII

Excessive **bail** shall not be required, nor excessive fines imposed, nor cruel and unusual punishments inflicted.

Amendment IX

The enumeration in the Constitution, of certain rights, shall not be construed to deny or disparage others retained by the people.

Amendment X

The powers not delegated to the United States by the Constitution, nor prohibited by it to the States, are reserved to the States respectively, or to the people.

Amendment XI

The Judicial power of the United States shall not be construed to extend to any suit in law or equity, commenced or prosecuted against one of the United States by Citizens of another State, or by Citizens or Subjects of any Foreign State.

Rights to a Speedy, Fair Trial A basic protection is the right to a speedy, public trial. The jury must hear witnesses and evidence on both sides before deciding the guilt or innocence of a person charged with a crime. This amendment also provides that legal counsel must be provided to a defendant. In 1963, the Supreme Court ruled, in *Gideon* v. *Wainwright*, that if a defendant cannot afford a lawyer, the government must provide one to defend him or her. *Why is the right to a "speedy" trial important?*

Powers Reserved to the People
This amendment prevents government from claiming that the only rights people have are those listed in the Bill of Rights.

Powers Reserved to the States
The final amendment of the Bill of Rights protects the states and the people from an all-powerful federal government. It establishes that powers not given to the national government—or denied to the states—by the Constitution belong to the states or to the people.

Suits Against States The Eleventh Amendment (1795) limits the jurisdiction of the federal courts. The Supreme Court had ruled that a federal court could try a lawsuit brought by citizens of South Carolina against a citizen of Georgia. This case, *Chisholm* v. *Georgia*, decided in 1793, raised a storm of protest, leading to passage of the Eleventh Amendment.

Election of President and Vice President The Twelfth Amendment (1804) corrects a problem that had arisen in the method of electing the president and vice president. This amendment provides for the Electoral College to use separate ballots in voting for president and vice president. *If no candidate receives a majority of the electoral votes, who elects the president?*

Amendment XII

The electors shall meet in their respective states and vote by ballot for President and Vice-President, one of whom, at least, shall not be an inhabitant of the same state with themselves; they shall name in their ballots the person voted for as President, and in distinct ballots the person voted for as Vice-President, and they shall make distinct lists of all persons voted for as President, and of all persons voted for as Vice-President, and of the number of votes for each, which lists they shall sign and certify, and transmit sealed to the seat of the government of the United States, directed to the President of the Senate;—The President of the Senate shall, in the presence of the Senate and House of Representatives, open all the certificates and the votes shall then be counted;—The person having the greatest number of votes for President, shall be the President, if such number be a majority of the whole number of Electors appointed; and if no person have such majority, then from the persons having the highest numbers not exceeding three on the list of those voted for as President, the House of Representatives shall choose immediately, by ballot, the President. But in choosing the President, the votes shall be taken by states, the representation from each state having one vote; a quorum for this purpose shall consist of a member or members from two-thirds of the states, and a **majority** of all the states shall be necessary to a choice. And if the House of Representatives shall not choose a President whenever the right of choice shall **devolve** upon them, before the fourth day of March next following, then the Vice-President shall act as President, as in the case of the death or other constitutional disability of the President— The person having the greatest number of votes as Vice-President, shall be the Vice-President, if such number be a majority of the whole number of Electors appointed, and if no person have a majority, then from the two highest numbers on the list, the Senate shall choose the Vice-President; a quorum for the purpose shall consist of two-thirds of the whole number of Senators, and a majority of the whole number shall be necessary to a choice. But no person constitutionally ineligible to the office of President shall be eligible to that of Vice-President of the United States.

Vocabulary

majority: more than half

devolve: to pass on

Amendment XIII

Section 1

Neither slavery nor involuntary servitude, except as a punishment for crime whereof the party shall have been duly convicted, shall exist within the United States, or any place subject to their jurisdiction.

Section 2

Congress shall have power to enforce this article by appropriate legislation.

Amendment XIV

Section 1

All persons born or naturalized in the United States, and subject to the jurisdiction thereof, are citizens of the United States and of the State wherein they reside. No State shall make or enforce any law which shall **abridge** the privileges or immunities of citizens of the United States; nor shall any State deprive any person of life, liberty, or property, without due process of law; nor deny to any person within its jurisdiction the equal protection of the laws.

Section 2

Representatives shall be apportioned among the several States according to their respective numbers, counting the whole number of persons in each State, excluding Indians not taxed. But when the right to vote at any election for the choice of electors for President and Vice President of the United States, Representatives in Congress, the Executive and Judicial officers of a State, or the members of the Legislature thereof, is denied to any of the male inhabitants of such State, being twenty-one years of age, and citizens of the United States, or in any way abridged, except for participation in rebellion, or other crime, the basis of representation therein shall be reduced in the proportion which the number of such male citizens shall bear to the whole number of male citizens twenty-one years of age in such State.

Section 3

No person shall be a Senator or Representative in Congress, or elector of President and Vice President, or hold any office, civil or military, under the United States, or under any State, who, having previously taken an oath, as a member of Congress, or as an officer of the United States, or as a member of any State legislature, or as an executive or judicial officer of any State, to support the Constitution

Abolition of Slavery Amendments Thirteen (1865), Fourteen (1868), and Fifteen (1870) often are called the Civil War amendments because they grew out of that great conflict. The Thirteenth Amendment outlaws slavery.

Rights of Citizens The Fourteenth Amendment (1868) originally was intended to protect the legal rights of the freed slaves. Today it protects the rights of citizenship in general by prohibiting a state from depriving any person of life, liberty, or property without "due process of law." In addition, it states that all citizens have the right to equal protection of the law in all states.

Representation in Congress This section reduced the number of members a state had in the House of Representatives if it denied its citizens the right to vote. Later civil rights laws and the Twenty-fourth Amendment guaranteed the vote to African Americans.

Vocabulary
abridge: to reduce

Public Debt The public debt acquired by the federal government during the Civil War was valid and could not be questioned by the South. However, the debts of the Confederacy were declared to be illegal. *Could former slaveholders collect payment for the loss of their slaves?*

of the United States, shall have engaged in insurrection or rebellion against the same, or given aid or comfort to the enemies thereof. But Congress may by a vote of two-thirds of each House, remove such disability.

Section 4

The validity of the public debt of the United States, authorized by law, including debts incurred for payment of pensions and bounties for service in suppressing insurrection or rebellion, shall not be questioned. But neither the United States nor any State shall assume or pay any debt or obligation incurred in aid of insurrection or rebellion against the United States, or any claim for the loss or **emancipation** of any slave; but all such debts, obligations and claims shall be held illegal and void.

Section 5

The Congress shall have power to enforce, by appropriate legislation, the provisions of this article.

Amendment XV

Right to Vote The Fifteenth Amendment (1870) prohibits the government from denying a person's right to vote on the basis of race. Despite the law, many states denied African Americans the right to vote by such means as poll taxes, literacy tests, and white primaries. During the 1950s and 1960s, Congress passed successively stronger laws to end racial discrimination in voting rights.

Section 1

The right of citizens of the United States to vote shall not be denied or abridged by the United States or by any State on account of race, color, or previous condition of servitude.

Section 2

The Congress shall have power to enforce this article by appropriate legislation.

Amendment XVI

The Congress shall have power to lay and collect taxes on incomes, from whatever source derived, without apportionment among the several States and without regard to any census or enumeration.

Amendment XVII

Election of Senators The Seventeenth Amendment (1913) states that the people, instead of state legislatures, elect United States senators. *How many years are in a Senate term?*

Section 1

The Senate of the United States shall be composed of two Senators from each State, elected by the people thereof, for six years; and each Senator shall have one vote. The electors in each State shall have the qualifications requisite for electors of the most numerous branch of the State legislatures.

Vocabulary

emancipation: freedom from slavery

Section 2

When vacancies happen in the representation of any State in the Senate, the executive authority of such State shall issue writs of election to fill such vacancies: *Provided,* That the legislature of any State may empower the executive thereof to make temporary appointments until the people fill the vacancies by election as the legislature may direct.

Section 3

This amendment shall not be so construed as to affect the election or term of any Senator chosen before it becomes valid as part of the Constitution.

▲ **Dumping illegal liquor**

Amendment XVIII
Section 1

After one year from ratification of this article the manufacture, sale, or transportation of intoxicating liquors within, the importation thereof into, or the exportation thereof from the United States and all territory subject to the jurisdiction thereof for beverage purposes is hereby prohibited.

Section 2

The Congress and the several States shall have concurrent power to enforce this article by appropriate legislation.

Section 3

This article shall be inoperative unless it shall have been ratified as an amendment to the Constitution by the legislatures of the several States, as provided in the Constitution, within seven years from the date of the submission hereof to the States by the Congress.

Prohibition The Eighteenth Amendment (1919) prohibited the production, sale, or transportation of alcoholic beverages in the United States. Prohibition proved to be difficult to enforce. This amendment was later repealed by the Twenty-first Amendment.

Amendment XIX
Section 1

The right of citizens of the United States to vote shall not be denied or abridged by the United States or by any State on account of sex.

Section 2

Congress shall have power to enforce this article by appropriate legislation.

Women's Suffrage The Nineteenth Amendment (1920) guaranteed women the right to vote. By then women had already won the right to vote in many state elections, but the amendment put their right to vote in all state and national elections on a constitutional basis.

Amendment XX

Section 1

The terms of the President and Vice President shall end at noon on the 20th day of January, and the terms of the Senators and Representatives at noon on the 3d day of January, of the years in which such terms would have ended if this article had not been ratified; and the terms of their successors shall then begin.

Section 2

The Congress shall assemble at least once in every year, and such meeting shall begin at noon on the 3d day of January, unless they shall by law appoint a different day.

Section 3

If, at the time fixed for the beginning of the term of the President, the **President elect** shall have died, the Vice President elect shall become President. If a President shall not have been chosen before the time fixed for the beginning of his term, or if the President elect shall have failed to qualify, then the Vice President elect shall act as President until a President shall have qualified; and the Congress may by law provide for the case wherein neither a President elect nor a Vice President elect shall have qualified, declaring who shall then act as President, or the manner in which one who is to act shall be selected, and such person shall act accordingly until a President or Vice President shall have qualified.

Section 4

The Congress may by law provide for the case of the death of any of the persons from whom the House of Representatives may choose a President whenever the right of choice shall have devolved upon them, and for the case of the death of any of the persons from whom the Senate may choose a Vice President whenever the right of choice shall have devolved upon them.

Section 5

Section 1 and 2 shall take effect on the 15th day of October following the ratification of this article.

Vocabulary

president-elect: individual who is elected president but has not yet begun serving his or her term

Section 6

This article shall be inoperative unless it shall have been ratified as an amendment to the Constitution by the legislatures of three-fourths of the several States within seven years from the date of its submission.

Amendment XXI

Section 1

The eighteenth article of amendment to the Constitution of the United States is hereby repealed.

Section 2

The transportation or importation into any State, Territory, or possession of the United States for delivery or use therein of intoxicating liquors, in violation of the laws thereof, is hereby prohibited.

Section 3

This article shall be inoperative unless it shall have been ratified as an amendment to the Constitution by conventions in the several States, as provided in the Constitution, within seven years from the date of the submission hereof to the States by the Congress.

Amendment XXII

Section 1

No person shall be elected to the office of the President more than twice, and no person who had held the office of President, or acted as President, for more than two years of a term to which some other person was elected President shall be elected to the office of the President more than once. But this Article shall not apply to any person holding the office of President when this Article was proposed by the Congress, and shall not prevent any person who may be holding the office of President, or acting as President, during the term within which this Article becomes operative from holding the office of President or acting as President during the remainder of such term.

Section 2

This article shall be inoperative unless it shall have been ratified as an amendment to the Constitution by the legislatures of three-fourths of the several States within seven years from the date of its submission to the States by the Congress.

Repeal of Prohibition The Twenty-first Amendment (1933) repeals the Eighteenth Amendment. It is the only amendment ever passed to overturn an earlier amendment. It is also the only amendment ratified by special state conventions instead of state legislatures.

Term Limit The Twenty-second Amendment (1951) limits presidents to a maximum of two elected terms. It was passed largely as a reaction to Franklin D. Roosevelt's election to four terms between 1933 and 1945.

Amendment XXIII

Section 1

The District constituting the seat of Government of the United States shall appoint in such manner as the Congress may direct:

A number of electors of President and Vice President equal to the whole number of Senators and Representatives in Congress to which the District would be entitled if it were a State, but in no event more than the least populous State; they shall be in addition to those appointed by the States, but they shall be considered, for the purposes of the election of President and Vice President, to be electors appointed by a State; and they shall meet in the District and perform such duties as provided by the twelfth article of amendment.

Section 2

The Congress shall have power to enforce this article by appropriate legislation.

Amendment XXIV

Section 1

The right of citizens of the United States to vote in any primary or other election for President or Vice President, for electors for President or Vice President, or for Senator or Representative in Congress, shall not be denied or abridged by the United States or any State by reason of failure to pay any poll tax or other tax.

Section 2

The Congress shall have power to enforce this article by appropriate legislation.

Amendment XXV

Section 1

In case of the removal of the President from office or of his death or resignation, the Vice President shall become President.

Section 2

Whenever there is a vacancy in the office of the Vice President, the President shall nominate a Vice President who shall take the office upon confirmation by a majority vote of both Houses of Congress.

Section 3

Whenever the President transmits to the President pro tempore of the Senate and the Speaker of the House of Representatives his written declaration that he is unable to discharge the powers and duties of his office, and until he transmits to them a written declaration to the contrary, such powers and duties shall be discharged by the Vice President as Acting President.

Section 4

Whenever the Vice President and a majority of either the principal officers of the executive departments or of such other body as Congress may by law provide, transmit to the President pro tempore of the Senate and the Speaker of the House of Representatives their written declaration that the President is unable to discharge the powers and duties of his office, the Vice President shall immediately assume the power and duties of the office of Acting President.

Thereafter, when the President transmits to the President pro tempore of the Senate and the Speaker of the House of Representatives his written declaration that no inability exists, he shall resume the powers and duties of his office unless the Vice President and a majority of either the principal officers of the executive department or of such other body as Congress may by law provide, transmit within four days to the President pro tempore of the Senate and the Speaker of the House of Representatives their written declaration that the President is unable to discharge the powers and duties of his office. Thereupon Congress shall decide the issue, assembling within forty-eight hours for that purpose if not in session. If the Congress, within twenty-one days after receipt of the latter written declaration, or, if Congress is not in session, within twenty-one days after Congress is required to assemble, determines by two-thirds vote of both Houses that the President is unable to discharge the powers and duties of his office, the Vice President shall continue to discharge the same as Acting President; otherwise, the President shall resume the power and duties of his office.

Amendment XXVI

Section 1

The right of citizens of the United States, who are eighteen years of age or older, to vote shall not be denied or abridged by the United States or by any State on account of age.

▲ Lyndon B. Johnson is sworn in to office after the assassination of President John F. Kennedy.

Voting Age The Twenty-sixth Amendment (1971) lowered the voting age in both federal and state elections to 18.

The Congress shall have power to enforce this article by appropriate legislation.

Amendment XXVII

No law, varying the compensation for the services of Senators and Representatives, shall take effect, until an election of representatives shall have intervened.

Congressional Pay Raises The Twenty-seventh Amendment (1992) makes congressional pay raises effective during the term following their passage. James Madison offered the amendment in 1789, but it was never adopted. In 1982 Gregory Watson, then a student at the University of Texas, discovered the forgotten amendment while doing research for a school paper. Watson made the amendment's passage his crusade.

▼ Joint meeting of Congress

PHOTO: Sandy Schaeffer/Mai/Mai/Time Life Pictures/Getty Images

The Bill of Rights

ESSENTIAL QUESTIONS • *How do societies balance individual and community rights?*
• *How does social change influence governments?*

The Story Matters...

In 2007 immigrant rights supporters in Kennett Square, Pennsylvania, and across the United States joined marches and rallies. Carrying signs in English and other languages, the demonstrators urged Congress to reform laws affecting the nation's 12 million illegal immigrants.

Throughout our history, Americans have rallied and marched to raise awareness for issues. People have supported women's right to vote, civil rights, and ending unpopular wars. Americans make use of two vital freedoms guaranteed in the Bill of Rights. The First Amendment grants the right to speak out and to join together in rallies or marches.

◀ *Immigrant rights supporters march through Kennett Square, Pennsylvania, after a rally calling for a path to citizenship for illegal immigrants.*

PHOTO: AP Photo/George Widman

125

Real-Life Civics

> **THE PRESS**   The earliest colonial newspapers began in the late 1600s. In the 1700s, people were reading newspaper accounts about events that led to the American Revolution. The Framers firmly believed that a free press was vital to a democracy. It would inform citizens about key issues and serve as a watchdog over government. The Framers guaranteed this freedom in the Bill of Rights.

In our nation's first 150 years, most Americans learned the news, such as election results and the progress of various wars, from newspapers. During the late 1800s and early 1900s, people in most small towns read two or three daily and weekly papers. Many read a morning and an evening paper. Cities like New York and Chicago offered 20 or more papers with diverse points of view.

A vendor sells daily newspapers at a San Francisco newsstand.

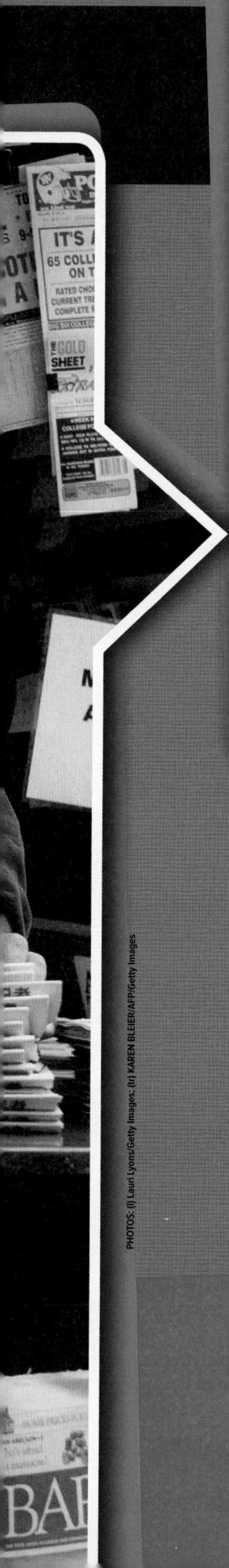

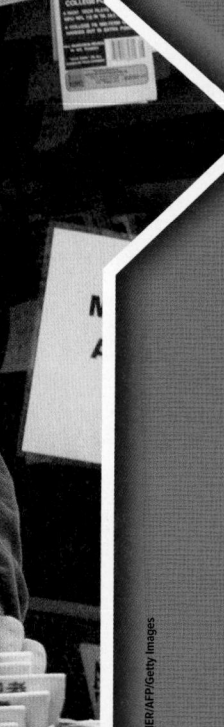

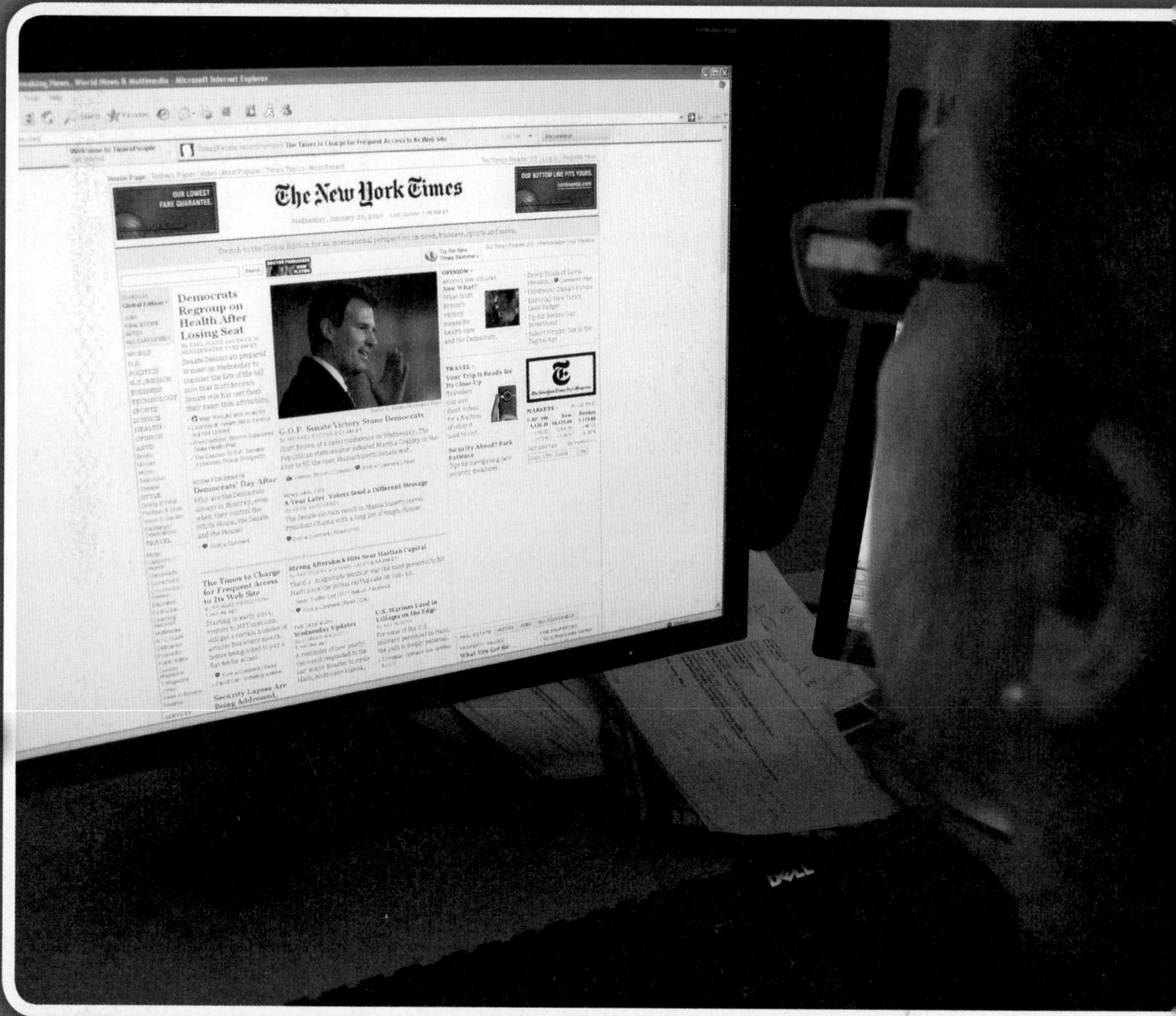

This woman uses her computer to read her newspaper online.

CHANGING MEDIA For much of U.S. history, the "free press" meant newspapers. Then, during the 1900s, inventions such as radio and television found their way into American homes. Suddenly, people could get breaking news more quickly. Still, newspapers continued to provide in-depth reporting. In the late 1900s, technology such as personal computers and the World Wide Web again changed the way Americans accessed the news. Many people today check their computers and cell phones to stay informed. They rely on 24-hour television news channels, blogs, and Internet news outlets to instantly learn what is happening around the world. The concept of "free press" applies to all of these media formats. With so much media to choose from, the challenge in the 2000s is not access to information, but determining which news sources are accurate and unbiased, or fair.

PHOTOS: (l) Lauri Lyons/Getty Images; (tr) KAREN BLEIER/AFP/Getty Images

CIVIC LITERACY

★★★★

Analyzing What role should the media have in a democracy?

Your Opinion Which media do you turn to for information about politics, government, or current events? Explain your choices.

netwⓞrks

There's More Online!

☑ **GRAPHIC ORGANIZER**
First Amendment Rights

☑ **GRAPHS**
U.S. Adult Religious
Affiliation 2008
Selected Peaceful Protests
in U.S. History

☑ **POLITICAL CARTOON**
Free Speech

Lesson 1
The First Amendment

ESSENTIAL QUESTION *How do societies balance individual and community rights?*

IT MATTERS BECAUSE
The rights granted under the First Amendment are among our most basic freedoms.

Guaranteeing Civil Liberties

GUIDING QUESTION *Which individual rights are protected by the First Amendment?*

Have you ever seen people protesting a law? Have you ever wondered why police officers in a movie have to tell a suspect of his or her rights? Have you ever thought about who can vote?

All these questions have to do with certain basic civil liberties we have. **Civil liberties** are the freedoms we have to think and to act without interference from the government or without fearing that we will be treated unfairly. They are the cornerstone of our way of life. They are called **civil** liberties because they are connected with being a citizen.

Many of these civil liberties are protected under the Bill of Rights, the first 10 amendments to the Constitution. Lesson 2 will talk about the rights covered in the Second through the Tenth Amendments. In this lesson, you will learn the importance of the First Amendment. It allows us to follow our own beliefs and express ourselves freely.

The First Amendment protects five basic freedoms. These are freedom of religion, freedom of speech, freedom of the press, freedom of assembly, and freedom to petition the government.

Reading**HELP**DESK

Taking Notes: *Identifying*

As you read, complete a graphic organizer like the one shown to identify the meaning of each of the five rights protected by the First Amendment.

First Amendment Right	Meaning
1.	
2.	

Content Vocabulary

- civil liberty
- free speech
- censorship
- petition
- slander
- libel

Freedom of Religion

The First Amendment protects freedom of religion in two ways. First, it says that Congress cannot establish, or support, any religion as the official faith of the United States. Because it stops the government from establishing a state religion, this rule is called the establishment clause. In 1802 President Thomas Jefferson called this clause a "wall of separation between church and state." Because of this clause, the United States does not have an official religion as Iran and Egypt do.

The second way the First Amendment protects freedom of religion is in how people express their faith. Under the First Amendment, Americans have the right to practice their faith in the way that they want. The government cannot make laws that would stop them from worshipping as they choose. People in some nations do not have these rights. For instance, the People's Republic of China puts limits on some religions.

Freedom of religion has long been part of United States history. Many of the people who first settled here left their homes because they did not have religious freedom. In 1649 Maryland made a law that allowed people in the colony to follow any Christian faith. In 1682 William Penn made freedom of religion a basic right for everyone in Pennsylvania.

The First Amendment's guarantee of freedom of worship is one reason why the United States has attracted people from around the world. Here a Greek Orthodox priest conducts a church service.

▶ CRITICAL THINKING
Making Connections In what way is freedom of religion rooted in U.S. history?

Freedom of Speech

In some countries, people can be jailed for criticizing the government. They worry even when speaking in private that their words can be used against them. In the United States, the First Amendment guarantees our right of **free speech.** We can state our opinions, in public or in private, without fear of being punished by the government.

Free speech covers what we say in meetings, conversations, speeches, and lectures. It includes words spoken in radio and television broadcasts as well. The Supreme Court has judged many cases that are connected to this freedom. Its decisions have shown that "speech" can mean more than just using words. Internet messages, art, music, and even clothing are protected.

PHOTO: World Religions Photo Library/Alamy

civil liberty the freedom to think and act without government interference or fear of unfair legal treatment

Academic Vocabulary

civil of or relating to citizens

free speech the right to say our opinions, in public or in private, without fear of being stopped or punished by the government for those ideas

This cartoon is a comment on the importance of the right to free speech. This freedom includes the right to express our views with actions as well as with words. For example, flag burning in protest is protected under the First Amendment.

► CRITICAL THINKING
Analyzing Visuals Why does the sign say to read the Bill of Rights "in case of fire"?

PHOTO: Gary McCoy/Political Cartoons.com

Freedom of the Press

In 1733, publisher John Peter Zenger criticized the governor of New York in his newspaper. As a result, Zenger was arrested. Lawyer Andrew Hamilton agreed to defend Zenger at his trial. He argued that only a press that was free to criticize the government can keep that government from misusing its power. Hamilton's argument worked. Zenger was found not guilty. The case is seen as a big step in the rise of a free press in America.

Because we have freedom of the press, the government cannot censor news reports. **Censorship** means banning printed materials or films because they have alarming or offensive ideas. The government is also blocked from another kind of censorship. It cannot prevent information from being published or broadcast. Reporters in many other countries are not protected in these ways. Their stories are reviewed by government officials, who take out parts they do not approve of. Reporters also run the risk of being arrested if they publish stories their leaders do not like.

When the Bill of Rights was written, "the press" referred to printed materials such as books, newspapers, and magazines. Today the press includes many other media sources, such as

censorship the banning of printed materials or films due to alarming or offensive ideas they contain

petition a formal request for government action

radio, television, and the Internet. Because of freedom of the press, Americans have a chance to hear a range of views on public issues.

Freedom of Assembly

The First Amendment protects our right to gather in groups for any reason, as long as the groups are peaceful. We can attend meetings, rallies, celebrations, and parades. The government has the power to make rules about when and where these activities are held. It cannot ban them, though.

This right includes the freedom of association. That is, the First Amendment protects our right to form and join clubs, political parties, labor unions, and other groups.

Freedom to Petition

The First Amendment gives us the right to send petitions to the government. A **petition** is a formal request for the government to act. Often the word is used to mean a written statement that hundreds or thousands of people sign. Even a simple letter or e-mail from one person is a petition, though.

Petition gives us the right to express ourselves to the government. Suppose you are not happy about overcrowded schools. You have the right to send a complaint to members of the school board. If enough people express similar views, the board may act.

☑ **PROGRESS CHECK**

Analyzing How are Americans' rights to express themselves protected by the First Amendment?

When the Framers wrote the First Amendment, the Internet did not exist. Freedom of the press first emerged for printed news. Today's instant sources of news mean citizens must quickly figure out if information is accurate. Americans can compare what we read in many sources. But in some countries, such as China, the government limits Internet access to control the news that people get. What do you think are the benefits of having open access to Internet information? What might be some risks?

Tens of thousands of African American men and supporters gathered at the Million Man March on October 16, 1995. Its purpose was to unify African American men and encourage them to work to improve their communities and build their political power and businesses.

▶ **CRITICAL THINKING**
Drawing Conclusions What First Amendment right are the people in this photo exercising, and why is it important?

PHOTO: AP Photo/Charles Tasnadi

Limits on Civil Liberty

GUIDING QUESTION *Why are limits placed on individual rights?*

The First Amendment gives very broad rights to all Americans. By the same token, it was never intended to allow citizens to do whatever they please. The rights of one individual must be balanced against the rights of others. Individual rights must also be balanced against the rights of the community. When there is a conflict, the rights of the community often come first. If that were not the case, society would break apart.

Citizens are expected to use their civil liberties responsibly. This means that in exercising their individual rights, they should not interfere with the rights of others. For example, you are free to campaign for causes, but you may not disturb your neighbors with blaring loudspeaker broadcasts.

Similar limits apply to larger groups as well. As you read earlier, the government has the power to set some limits on the right of assembly. If an organization wants to stage a parade, the government can determine when and where the parade can be held.

Some **restrictions,** or limits, can even be placed on free speech rights. Those limits have to be reasonable, though. You have the right to criticize public officials, but you do not have the right to spread lies that will harm a person's reputation. Spreading such lies in speech is a crime called **slander.** It is the crime of **libel** if the lies are printed.

Free speech is limited in other ways as well. No person, for example, has the right to speak or write in a way that directly leads to criminal acts. Also, people do not have the right to make a speech that will lead to efforts to overthrow the government by force. These kinds of speech are illegal.

✓ PROGRESS CHECK

Explaining Do Americans enjoy unlimited civil liberties? Explain.

Academic Vocabulary

restriction a limit placed on something

slander spoken untruths that are harmful to someone's reputation

libel written untruths that are harmful to someone's reputation

---

LESSON 1 REVIEW

Review Vocabulary

1. Why are *civil liberties* important to democracy?

2. What is the difference between *slander* and *libel*?

Answer the Guiding Questions

3. ***Identifying*** Name the individual rights protected by the First Amendment.

4. ***Evaluating*** Why is it necessary to limit individual rights?

5. **ARGUMENT** Write a paragraph to explain why you think the First Amendment is necessary for a democracy.

Tinker v. Des Moines School District

Public school officials set standards of behavior that students are expected to follow. Does this arrangement leave students with any rights? Sometimes the Supreme Court must decide.

Mary Beth and John Tinker

PHOTO: Bettmann/CORBIS

Background of the Case

One night in December 1965, a group of public school students, led by high school sophomores Christopher Eckhardt and John Tinker and eighth-grader Mary Beth Tinker, wore black armbands to protest the Vietnam War. As other students joined the armband protest, principals and members of the school board met the growing protest with a ban on armbands—to prevent "disturbing influences" at school.

On December 16, 1965, Christopher, John, and Mary Beth were suspended for wearing their armbands to school. Their parents protested the suspensions in federal court. They contended that the students' First Amendment right of free speech had been violated.

The Decision

On February 24, 1969, the United States Supreme Court in a 7–2 decision declared the school suspensions unconstitutional. Justice Abe Fortas, who wrote the majority opinion, first established that the students' action was "akin [similar] to pure speech." Even though their protest involved no speaking, he argued, it deserved "protection under the First Amendment." In the key passage of the opinion, Justice Fortas wrote:

▎▎It can hardly be argued that either students or teachers shed their constitutional rights to freedom of speech or expression at the schoolhouse gate.▎▎

Why It Matters

Supporters of the young protesters saluted the Court decision that "students are entitled to freedom of expression of their views." Critics who opposed the wearing of the armbands predicted harmful consequences.

Justice Hugo Black dissented from the majority opinion. He suggested that the Court's decision was "the beginning of a new revolutionary era of permissiveness in this country fostered by the judiciary." He argued that no one has a complete right to freedom of speech and expression.

Later decisions, such as *Bethel School District* v. *Fraser* (1986) and *Hazelwood School District* v. *Kuhlmeier* (1988), narrowed students' First Amendment rights. These rulings by their nature also expanded the authority of school officials.

Analyzing the Case

1. **Explaining** Why did the students' lawyers argue that wearing the armbands was protected by the First Amendment?

2. **Inferring** How did Justice Fortas's concept of "pure speech" extend First Amendment free-speech rights?

networks
There's More Online!

☑ **GRAPHIC ORGANIZER**
Constitutional Protections
for the Accused

☑ **CHART**
Rights of the Accused

Lesson 2

Other Bill of Rights Protections

ESSENTIAL QUESTION *How do societies balance individual and community rights?*

IT MATTERS BECAUSE
Other parts of the Bill of Rights provide important protections.

Rights of the Accused

GUIDING QUESTION *How does the Bill of Rights protect the rights of the accused?*

The First Amendment protects five basic freedoms for all Americans. Equally precious, however, is the right to fair treatment in the legal system. This is the subject of other parts of the Bill of Rights. The Fourth, Fifth, Sixth, and Eighth Amendments protect the rights of the **accused,** people officially charged with crimes.

The Fourth Amendment

The Fourth Amendment protects us against "unreasonable searches and seizures." No officer of the government can search a person's property or take his or her possessions at will. The officer must have **probable cause,** or strong reasons to think that the person or property was involved in a crime.

When law enforcement officers want to do a search for evidence, they must first get approval. They must ask a judge to issue a **search warrant.** This court order allows officers to search a suspect's home, business, or other property and take certain items as evidence. Only items listed in the warrant can be taken. Judges do not give out search warrants easily. They must be convinced that a search is likely to yield evidence.

Reading **HELP**DESK

Taking Notes: *Categorizing*

As you read, note constitutional protections for the accused and amendments.

Protection	Amendment
1.	
2.	

Content Vocabulary

- accused
- probable cause
- search warrant
- indictment
- double jeopardy
- self-incrimination
- due process
- eminent domain
- bail

The Fifth Amendment

The Fifth Amendment protects several rights of an accused person. First, it states that no one can be tried for a serious crime without an indictment. An **indictment** (ihn•DITE•muhnt) is a document issued by a body called a grand jury that formally charges someone with a crime. Members of the grand jury first review all the evidence against an accused person before deciding to indict him or her. Someone who is indicted is not necessarily guilty. This document simply states the grand jury's belief that he or she may have carried out a crime. A trial will decide whether he or she did.

The Fifth Amendment prevents putting people on trial more than once for the same crime. Putting someone on trial for a crime of which he or she was previously found innocent is called **double jeopardy.** The Fifth Amendment blocks the government from that action.

The Fifth Amendment also protects an accused person's right to remain silent. Throughout history, governments have sometimes forced people to confess to crimes they did not really commit. To prevent this, the Fifth Amendment states that people cannot be made to testify against themselves. This protects them against **self-incrimination.**

Law enforcement officers must have probable cause in order to conduct a search. Here a police officer and his bomb-sniffing dog conduct a search at the Detroit Metropolitan Airport.

▶ CRITICAL THINKING
Assessing In the Fourth Amendment, how did the Framers balance keeping people safe with keeping people free?

PHOTO: Bill Pugliano/Getty Images

accused a person officially charged with a crime

probable cause a strong reason to think that a person or property was involved in a crime

search warrant a court order allowing police to search property and seize evidence

indictment a document issued by a grand jury to charge someone with a crime

double jeopardy putting someone on trial for a crime of which he or she was previously found innocent

PHOTO: David R. Frazier Photolibrary, Inc.

A citizen's public service on a jury is necessary to the American system of justice. A juror must generally be at least 18 years old, a U.S. citizen, and a resident of the county where the trial takes place.

▶ CRITICAL THINKING
Evaluating How does a jury trial help protect the rights of the accused?

The Fifth Amendment states that no one may be denied life, liberty, or property "without due process of law." **Due process** means following set legal procedures. It includes the idea that the laws to be followed must be reasonable.

Finally, the Fifth Amendment protects property rights. It limits the government's power of eminent domain. **Eminent domain** (EH•mih•nehnt doh•MAYN) is the government's right to take private property—usually land—for public use. For example, if your home lies in the path of a proposed highway, it may be legally taken and destroyed. The Fifth Amendment limits this power. It requires the government to pay a fair price for the property.

The Sixth Amendment

The Sixth Amendment guarantees other rights to the accused. First, it requires that persons be clearly told what the charges against them are.

The Sixth Amendment also covers trials. It requires that the accused be allowed a trial by jury, although he or she may choose to be tried by only a judge. If the person asks for a jury trial, that trial must be speedy and held in public. In addition, the jurors must be fair. If possible, the trial should be held in the community where the crime took place.

An accused person has the right to hear and question all witnesses against him or her. He or she must be allowed to call witnesses in defense. Finally, he or she has the right to a lawyer. The Supreme Court has said that when an accused cannot afford a lawyer, the government must pay for one.

The Eighth Amendment

Sometimes months can pass before a trial can be held. During that time, the accused may have the choice to remain free by paying bail. **Bail** is a sum of money used as a security deposit. In exchange for being let out of jail, the person pays the sum and promises to appear at the trial. When the accused comes to court for the trial, the bail is returned. If the person fails to appear, he or she loses the money.

Reading **HELP**DESK

self-incrimination giving evidence about yourself that could lead to you being found guilty of a crime

due process following established legal procedures

eminent domain the right of the government to take private property— usually land—for public use

bail a sum of money used as a security deposit to ensure that an accused person who is released from jail returns for his or her trial

A judge decides how much bail a person must pay. The Eighth Amendment, however, forbids "excessive" bail—that is, an amount that is much too high. Excessive does not just refer to what a person is able to pay. In setting bail, a judge weighs several matters. These include the type of crime committed, the record of the accused person, and the likelihood that he or she will appear in court. Sometimes judges deny bail. They do so when they think the accused will try to flee, or escape, rather than show up for the trial.

When a person is found guilty of a crime, the Eighth Amendment protects him or her from punishment that is too harsh. It also bars fines from being too high.

This amendment also forbids "cruel and unusual punishments." Americans have long debated what punishments are cruel and unusual. Many agree that punishment should be in proportion to, or fit, the crime committed. For example, a sentence of life imprisonment for stealing a loaf of bread would be too harsh. People disagree strongly, though, about whether the death penalty is cruel and unusual punishment.

✓ PROGRESS CHECK

Categorizing Which of the Fourth, Fifth, Sixth, and Eighth Amendments apply to the police? Which apply to the courts?

Additional Protections

GUIDING QUESTION *Which other protections does the Bill of Rights offer?*

When the Founders wrote the Bill of Rights, they remembered the events that had led to the American Revolution. They felt that certain actions taken by the British government were abuses of power. The Founders wanted to prevent the American government from taking such actions.

The Second Amendment

The Second Amendment says this: "A well regulated Militia being necessary to the security of a free State, the right of the people to keep and bear Arms shall not be infringed." To infringe a right is to put limits on it.

When the Second Amendment was written, a state's militia was made up of a small army of people who served as soldiers when needed.

Why It MATTERS

The Rights of the Accused

Have you ever thought a friend or sibling had done something wrong, only to find out that you were mistaken? Sometimes people accused of crimes are innocent. The rights of the accused help protect innocent people from being convicted. These rights act as a check on the power of the government that helps ensure justice for all.

Over the years, there has been intense debate over whether the death penalty is constitutional. Here, protesters against the death penalty march and carry signs in front of the U.S. Supreme Court in Washington, D.C.

▶ CRITICAL THINKING
Interpreting To whom do you think the protesters are directing their signs?

Opinion is divided over the meaning of the Second Amendment. Gun advocates argue for responsible use of guns (above). Opponents link guns to violence (right).

PHOTO: (tl) AP Photo/Jay LaPrete; (tr) AP Photo/Mark Stehle

▶ CRITICAL THINKING
Drawing Conclusions Why do you think gun ownership is regulated by the government?

People have long debated what rights, exactly, this amendment protects. Then in 2008 the Supreme Court commented on the Second Amendment. The Court stated that the Second Amendment means that individuals have a constitutional right to keep firearms in their homes for personal safety.

Courts have generally ruled that the government can pass laws to control gun ownership. For example, federal and state governments can spell out who can have a **license** to own firearms.

The Third Amendment

In the years before the American Revolution, the British required colonists to shelter British soldiers in their own homes and feed them. The Third Amendment bans that practice in peacetime. It says that, when there is no war, soldiers may not stay in people's homes without permission of the home owner.

The Seventh Amendment

The Seventh Amendment concerns civil cases. Civil cases are lawsuits that arise when people's rights are in conflict.

The amendment guarantees the right to a jury trial in most of these disputes heard in the federal courts. This guarantee specifically applies to disputes about property worth more than $20. Today, however, nearly all such disputes involve sums larger than $20. As a result, this requirement of the amendment is almost always met.

Reading**HELP**DESK

Academic Vocabulary

license a document granting the holder permission to do something

retain to keep

The Seventh Amendment also sets separate roles for judges and juries in these cases. The judge has the duty to solve issues of law. For example, a judge determines whether or not certain evidence is allowed. The jury is to listen to evidence and consider the facts presented. From this information, the jury must then draw reasonable conclusions to reach a verdict, or decision. If both parties in a conflict agree, the trial can be held without a jury. When this happens, a judge hears the evidence and decides the case.

The Ninth Amendment

The Ninth Amendment states that all other rights not spelled out in the Constitution are **retained,** or kept, by the people. This amendment prevents the government from claiming that the only rights people have are those listed in the Bill of Rights. The Ninth Amendment makes it clear that citizens have other rights beyond those listed in the Constitution, and they may not be taken away.

The Tenth Amendment

The last amendment in the Bill of Rights did not add anything to the ratified Constitution. Instead, the Tenth Amendment recognizes that the power of the federal government is limited.

The Tenth Amendment states that any powers the Constitution does not specifically give to the federal government belong to the states or the people. The amendment expresses the idea that the federal government is limited in power. In this way, the amendment is intended to prevent Congress and the president from becoming too strong. The government of the United States can have only the powers the people give it.

✔ PROGRESS CHECK

Comparing In what ways do the Ninth and Tenth Amendments protect citizens?

LESSON 2 REVIEW

Review Vocabulary

1. How is a *search warrant* related to *probable cause*?

2. How does *due process* limit *eminent domain*?

Answer the Guiding Questions

3. *Reviewing* What are the rights of the accused found in the Bill of Rights?

4. *Identifying* What protections do the Second, Third, Seventh, Ninth, and Tenth Amendments offer?

5. **ARGUMENT** Is the death penalty "cruel and unusual punishment"? Take a position on the issue and write an essay to convince readers of your opinion.

PHOTO: Nivek Neslo/Getty Images

Is the Patriot Act an infringement of privacy?

A terrorist attack shocked the United States on September 11, 2001. Congress quickly responded to the attorney general's call for changes in the law to combat terrorism. President George W. Bush signed the Patriot Act as a new tool to fight "a threat like no other our Nation has ever seen." Later, some members of Congress and concerned citizens said some parts of the act violated the Fourth Amendment's protection against unreasonable searches and seizures. Before most searches, officers must obtain a warrant from a judge, showing "probable cause" and describing the place to be searched and the persons or things to be seized. The Patriot Act made exceptions to these requirements. Section 215 permitted the FBI to go before the Foreign Intelligence Surveillance Court for an order to search for "any tangible things" connected to a terrorism suspect.

> The Patriot Act made it legal for the government to access Internet communications, medical records, and even your home, all without notice or a search warrant.

Yes

In November 2003, the American Civil Liberties Union contended that the Patriot Act contains "flaws that threaten your fundamental freedoms by giving the government the power to access your medical records, tax records, information about the books you buy or borrow without probable cause, and the power to break into your home and conduct secret searches without telling you for weeks, months, or indefinitely." In 2004 the ACLU filed a lawsuit to overturn a Patriot Act provision that gave the government authority to obtain customer records from Internet service providers and other businesses without a warrant.

—American Civil Liberties Union

No

Senator Orrin Hatch of Utah voted for the Patriot Act and defended it when Congress voted to renew most of its provisions. In 2003 he said, "The Patriot Act has not eroded any of the rights we hold dear as Americans. I would be the first to call for corrective action, were that the case. Yet not one of the civil liberties groups has cited one instance of abuse of our constitutional rights. . . . We should not undermine or limit our law enforcement and intelligence agencies' efforts by imposing requirements that go above and beyond those required by the Constitution. That would only have the effect of protecting terrorists and criminals while endangering the lives of innocent Americans."

—Senator Orrin Hatch

Debating the Issue

1. **Describing** How does the Fourth Amendment attempt to protect Americans' privacy?

2. **Describing** What must an officer of the law normally do to obtain a warrant for a search?

3. **Explaining** Why are some people concerned about the provisions in Section 215?

4. **Drawing Conclusions** Are the concerns of people who opposed some provisions of the Patriot Act justified? Explain.

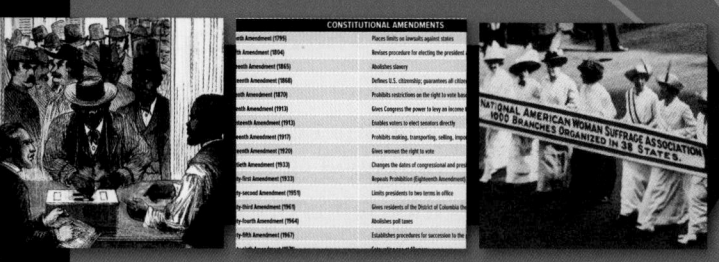

Lesson 3
Furthering Civil Liberties

ESSENTIAL QUESTION *How do societies balance individual and community rights?*

IT MATTERS BECAUSE
Voting is the way the people in a democracy make their wishes known.

Civil War Amendments

GUIDING QUESTION *How were civil rights extended following the Civil War?*

The 10 amendments that make up the Bill of Rights are not the only changes that have been made to the Constitution. Seventeen other amendments have been added over the years. Three from the mid-1800s aimed mainly to give more rights to African Americans.

Before 1865, many African Americans were enslaved. Enslaved people had almost no rights. Slavery divided the Northern states, which did not have it, and the Southern states, which did. It grew to be a serious national problem.

Then, in 1860 and 1861, 11 Southern states tried to leave the Union and form a new country. From 1861 to 1865, the North and South fought a war—called the Civil War—over whether the states could do this. When it ended, the South had lost and slavery had been **eliminated,** or taken away.

Three amendments were passed after the Civil War. All of them tried in some way to help African Americans. However, unfair treatment of this group did not end. States kept African Americans separated from whites. New laws denied them basic rights. Not until the 1900s were African Americans able to enjoy the rights guaranteed by the Civil War amendments.

PHOTOS: (tl) North Wind Picture Archives—All rights reserved.; (tr) Paul Thompson/Topical Press Agency/Getty Images

Reading HELP DESK

Taking Notes: *Summarizing*

As you read, complete a diagram to summarize each of the Civil War amendments.

Civil War Amendments
↓
↓

Content Vocabulary
- **black codes**
- **suffrage**
- **poll tax**

Academic Vocabulary
eliminate to take away or to end

For years after the Civil War, Union soldiers protected the rights of African Americans in the South. When the troops left, new laws took away many of these rights. Above, an African American election official supervises the first black voters in Washington, D.C., in 1867.

► CRITICAL THINKING
Determining Cause and Effect Why was the Fourteenth Amendment needed to make sure African Americans had full voting rights?

The Thirteenth Amendment

The Thirteenth Amendment was the first of the Civil War amendments. Approved after the war in 1865, it outlawed slavery. In effect, it freed hundreds of thousands of enslaved African Americans.

The Thirteenth Amendment also banned forced labor, which means forcing someone to work. The only legal forced labor was as a punishment for committing a crime. Because of this exception, prisoners can be made to work in prison workshops. This wording also makes it possible for judges to order some people who break the law to do community service.

The Fourteenth Amendment

The Thirteenth Amendment ended slavery. However, it did not guarantee full rights for African Americans. Many Southern states soon passed laws known as **black codes.** These laws kept African Americans from holding certain jobs, gave them few property rights, and limited their rights in other ways.

The Fourteenth Amendment was approved in 1868 to try to protect African Americans from these laws. First, it defined an American citizen as anyone "born or naturalized in the United States." This definition included most African Americans.

Second, the amendment said that every state must give all citizens "equal protection of the laws." The purpose was to force states to end unfair laws that hurt African Americans. That goal was not achieved until the late 1900s. In those years, this clause was also used to help other unequally treated groups. Those groups included women and people with disabilities.

Third, the amendment forbade state governments from unreasonable action or interference with U.S. citizens. Finally, the amendment said that states cannot take a person's "life, liberty, or property" unless they follow due process. As you learned earlier, due process means fair procedures set by law. The "due process" clause proved very important.

Over time, the courts have used the "due process" wording to redefine the reach of the Bill of Rights. When it was first approved, the Bill of Rights was thought to apply only to the federal government. That changed in 1925, when the Supreme Court decided the case *Gitlow* v. *New York*. The Court ruled that

Reading**HELP**DESK

black codes laws from after the Civil War that kept African Americans from holding certain jobs, gave them few property rights, and limited their rights in other ways

suffrage the right to vote

CONSTITUTIONAL AMENDMENTS

Eleventh Amendment (1795)	Places limits on lawsuits against states
Twelfth Amendment (1804)	Revises procedure for electing the president and vice president
Thirteenth Amendment (1865)	Abolishes slavery
Fourteenth Amendment (1868)	Defines U.S. citizenship; guarantees all citizens "equal protection of the laws"
Fifteenth Amendment (1870)	Prohibits restrictions on the right to vote based on race and color
Sixteenth Amendment (1913)	Gives Congress the power to levy an income tax
Seventeenth Amendment (1913)	Enables voters to elect senators directly
Eighteenth Amendment (1917)	Prohibits making, transporting, selling, importing, and exporting alcoholic beverages
Nineteenth Amendment (1920)	Gives women the right to vote
Twentieth Amendment (1933)	Changes the dates of congressional and presidential terms
Twenty-first Amendment (1933)	Repeals Prohibition (Eighteenth Amendment)
Twenty-second Amendment (1951)	Limits presidents to two terms in office
Twenty-third Amendment (1961)	Gives residents of the District of Columbia the right to vote
Twenty-fourth Amendment (1964)	Abolishes poll taxes
Twenty-fifth Amendment (1967)	Establishes procedures for succession to the presidency
Twenty-sixth Amendment (1971)	Sets voting age at 18 years
Twenty-seventh Amendment (1992)	Delays congressional pay raises until the term following their passage

CHART SKILLS

Since the addition of the Bill of Rights, only 17 more amendments have been added to the Constitution.

1. *Identifying* What amendments affected the office of the president? In what ways?

2. CRITICAL THINKING *Speculating* Why do you think women were given the right to vote before 18-year-olds?

the due process clause protected free speech and a free press from *state* law. The Court said that the due process clause requires states to respect these First Amendment rights.

Since the *Gitlow* case, the Supreme Court has used the Fourteenth Amendment to apply other rights in the Bill of Rights to the states. This legal interpretation means that citizens in every part of the country have the same basic rights.

The Fifteenth Amendment

The Fifteenth Amendment, ratified in 1870, was the last of the Civil War amendments. It says that no state may deny a person the right to vote because of race. The amendment was meant to guarantee **suffrage**—the right to vote—for African Americans. Still, many states found other ways to keep African Americans from voting.

The Fifteenth Amendment was aimed only at African American men. The various states had the power to decide whether women could vote. Most did not give women that right for many decades.

✔ PROGRESS CHECK

Explaining What was the purpose of the Civil War amendments?

Members of the National American Woman Suffrage Association march in support of giving women the right to vote at the New York Suffrage Parade in 1913. Women worked to get the vote for about 80 years.

▶ CRITICAL THINKING
Theorizing Why do you think a parade would help the cause of giving women voting rights?

Electoral Process and Voting Rights

GUIDING QUESTION *In what ways have twentieth-century amendments affected voting rights and changed elections?*

During the 1900s, new amendments made important changes in voting and elections. Some made clear who had the right to vote in every state. Others changed the way elections were **conducted,** or carried out. Together, these new amendments put more power in the hands of the people.

The Seventeenth Amendment

Article I of the Constitution says that members of the House of Representatives shall be elected by the people. However, it calls for members of the Senate to be chosen by the state legislatures. The Seventeenth Amendment, ratified in 1913, changed that. It allowed voters to elect their senators directly. This change gave Americans a greater voice in their government.

The Nineteenth Amendment

The Constitution did not guarantee women the right to vote. However, it did not clearly deny the vote to them. Using the powers set aside for them under the Tenth Amendment, states could make their own laws on woman suffrage. As early as the 1840s, leaders Elizabeth Cady Stanton and Susan B. Anthony campaigned for woman suffrage. Many Americans did not think women should have the same rights as men, however.

That began to change in the late 1800s. The territory of Wyoming gave women the vote in 1869. Several other territories and states also did so in the years that followed. In 1920, the Nineteenth Amendment was approved. That finally protected the right of women to vote in all national and state elections.

The Twenty-third Amendment

Another group that was denied full voting rights was citizens living in our nation's capital, Washington, D.C. For many years, they could not vote for president or vice president. "D.C." stands for the District of Columbia, an area between Maryland and

PHOTO: Paul Thompson /Topical Press Agency/Getty Images

Virginia. Since the District is not a state, people there could not vote in national elections. The Twenty-third Amendment changed that situation in 1961. It said that people in the District may vote for president and vice president. It gave the District the same number of electoral votes as the smallest state. District residents still do not have a voting representative in Congress, however.

The Twenty-fourth Amendment

The Fifteenth Amendment gave African American men the right to vote. However, Southern states found ways to block African Americans from voting. Many Southern states required a **poll tax.** This was a fee people had to pay to vote. Because the fee had to be paid not only for the current year but for previous unpaid years as well, it was a great financial burden. Many African Americans could not afford to pay the tax. Therefore, they could not vote. Poor whites, too, could not afford the tax and could not vote.

The Twenty-fourth Amendment, passed in 1964, made poll taxes illegal in national elections. Two years later, the Supreme Court banned poll taxes in state elections too. As a result, many African Americans were able to vote for the first time.

The Twenty-sixth Amendment

Throughout our nation's history, many teens have bravely fought for our country. By law, however, they were not old enough to vote for the leaders who sent them into battle. Most states set the minimum age for voting at 21.

That changed in 1971, at a time when many young Americans were fighting in the Vietnam War. The Twenty-sixth Amendment guaranteed the right to vote to citizens 18 years of age and older. As a result, you can register, or sign up, to vote once you turn 18.

✓ PROGRESS CHECK

Analyzing How did eliminating the poll tax affect voting rights?

21ˢᵗ *Century*
SKILLS

Make an Argument

Due to the Twenty-third Amendment, residents of the District of Columbia can vote for president and vice president. They also elect a delegate to the House of Representatives who has limited voting rights. The District residents choose a second, nonvoting member of the House and two nonvoting senators. Many residents of the District argue that they are denied rights of citizens because they do not have full representation in Congress. Many want the District to gain statehood. Write an argument for or against statehood for the District.

LESSON 3 REVIEW

Review Vocabulary

1. What were *black codes*?

2. What amendment extended *suffrage* to nearly half of all American citizens? Why did it affect so many?

Answer the Guiding Questions

3. *Explaining* How did the Thirteenth, Fourteenth, and Fifteenth Amendments extend African Americans' rights?

4. *Identifying* What election laws were affected by the Seventeenth, Nineteenth, Twenty-third, Twenty-fourth, and Twenty-sixth Amendments?

5. **INFORMATIVE/EXPLANATORY** What led the Supreme Court to rule that the Bill of Rights applied to the states?

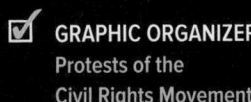

netw❂rks
There's More Online!

☑ **GRAPHIC ORGANIZER**
Protests of the
Civil Rights Movement

☑ **VIDEO**

☑ **SLIDESHOW**

Lesson 4
The Civil Rights Movement

ESSENTIAL QUESTIONS • *How do societies balance individual and community rights?*
• *How does social change influence government?*

IT MATTERS BECAUSE

The civil rights movement helped convince Americans in other groups to push for their rights.

Origins of the Civil Rights Movement

GUIDING QUESTION *Why did the civil rights movement occur?*

The Fourteenth Amendment says that all Americans should have the equal protection of the laws. How would you feel, then, if you were told you could not eat in a certain restaurant? What if you were told you had to sit in one certain part of a movie theater? Would you feel that you were being treated equally?

For many years African Americans faced **discrimination,** or unfair treatment based on prejudice, every day. The Civil War amendments were meant to protect African Americans' rights. They did not do the job, though. Southern states passed laws to separate African Americans and whites in most public places. This practice is called **segregation.** These segregation laws were known as **"Jim Crow" laws.** The name came from a well-known stage character who presented a negative image of African Americans.

These unfair laws **persisted,** or lasted, for decades. African Americans were forced to ride in the back of buses. They were sent to separate schools. They had to drink from separate

PHOTO: (tl) Ted Russell/Time Life Pictures/Getty Images; (tcl) AP Photo/Gene Herrick; (tcr) Bettmann/Corbis; (tr) Tom Williams/Roll Call via Getty Images

---

Why It MATTERS

Fulfilling the Promise of the Declaration

The Declaration of Independence states the belief that "all men are created equal" and says they all have certain civil rights. For more than a century, though, African Americans were denied many rights. The civil rights movement was an effort to secure those rights, fulfilling the promise of the Declaration.

Reading**HELP**DESK

Taking Notes: *Identifying*

As you read, complete a diagram to show examples of segregation and resulting protests during the civil rights movement. Add boxes as needed.

Issue		Resulting Event/Protest
Segregation on buses	→	

Content Vocabulary

- discrimination
- segregation
- "Jim Crow" law
- civil rights
- nonviolent resistance
- sit-in
- hate crime

drinking fountains. Even in the North, prejudice put limits on the opportunities African Americans had in life. It took a long time for African Americans to win their **civil rights**—the rights of full citizenship and equality under the law. They finally gained those rights in part because they started a movement to win them.

The *Brown* Decision

The courts let the segregation laws stand. An important Supreme Court case set a standard it said states should meet: "separate, but equal." In real life that was hardly the case, however. The services given to African Americans were far from equal to those given to whites. For example, states in the South spent far more on schools for whites than they did on schools for African Americans.

As early as the 1930s, African Americans began to challenge the idea of "separate, but equal." A key case came from Topeka, Kansas, in the 1950s. There, a seven-year-old African American girl named Linda Brown could not attend the school near her home because it was for white students. Instead, she had to go to a school across the city meant for African Americans. Her family sued the school system to try to change this, but they lost the case. The family turned for help to the National Association for the Advancement of Colored People (NAACP). Lawyers for this civil rights group took the case all the way to the Supreme Court. They argued that the education being given Brown and other African American students was not equal to the one given to white students. They said segregation had to end.

The Court made its decision in 1954. *Brown* v. *Board of Education of Topeka, Kansas* was a great victory for civil rights. The Court said that separating children in school by race went against the Constitution. Segregated schools were not equal and could not be made equal. Segregation, the Court said, went against the call for equal protection found in the Fourteenth Amendment.

In 1946, the U.S. Supreme Court made segregation illegal on buses that crossed state lines. In 1960, the Court ruled that segregation in bus stations was also illegal. Nonetheless, bus companies operating in the South ignored these rulings, inspiring "Freedom Rides" in 1961. In the "Freedom Rides," civil rights workers challenged segregation by these companies to push the federal government to enforce the Court's rulings.

▶ CRITICAL THINKING

Inferring In what part of the country do you think the "Freedom Riders" traveled? Why?

PHOTO: Ted Russell/Time Life Pictures/Getty Images

discrimination unfair treatment based on prejudice against a certain group

segregation the social separation of the races

"Jim Crow" law Southern segregation law

civil rights the rights of full citizenship and equality under the law

Academic Vocabulary

persist to last or to continue

Rosa Parks is fingerprinted in Montgomery, Alabama, after her arrest. Even before her arrest, Parks, a member of her local chapter of the NAACP, was active in working for civil rights.

▶ CRITICAL THINKING
Draw Conclusions How did Rosa Parks's action lead to the Montgomery bus boycott?

Students stage a peaceful protest at a lunch counter in Greensboro, North Carolina, that refused to serve African Americans. The Greensboro protest began on February 1, 1960, with four students. It quickly attracted many more and eventually inspired similar actions throughout the South. Students braved arrest and, sometimes, violent attacks for their beliefs.

▶ CRITICAL THINKING
Inferring How did peaceful protests such as sit-ins help the civil rights cause?

Montgomery Bus Boycott

Soon after *Brown* came another important event in the civil rights movement. In 1955 an African American woman named Rosa Parks got on a city bus in Montgomery, Alabama. She sat in the area set aside for whites. When white passengers got on the bus, the driver told Parks to move. She refused. At the next bus stop, police took Parks off the bus and arrested her. She was charged with breaking the law that segregated city buses.

Parks's arrest led African Americans in Montgomery to boycott the city's buses. For a year, they refused to ride them. Finally, the Supreme Court ruled that segregation in public buses was against the Constitution. Both Parks and Dr. Martin Luther King, Jr., gained fame across the nation. King had been a leader of the boycott.

Peaceful Protests

King was a young minister and a stirring speaker. He believed in confronting injustice through **nonviolent resistance**—peaceful protest against laws believed to be unfair. For the next several years, King led marches, boycotts, and demonstrations. These protests drew growing support.

PHOTO: (tr) AP Photo/Gene Herrick; (bl) Bettmann/Corbis

Reading**HELP**DESK

nonviolent resistance peaceful protest against laws believed to be unfair

Many others also pushed for civil rights. African American students held **sit-ins,** sitting at lunch counters that served only whites. They refused to leave until they were served. Their actions forced businesses to change. In 1961, whites and African Americans traveled together through the South by bus on "Freedom Rides." They wanted to end the segregation found in bus stations across the South.

There were marches too. In 1963 more than 200,000 people took part in a march on Washington, D.C. Their goal was to show support for a new civil rights bill. At this gathering, King gave his famous "I Have a Dream" speech, full of hope for racial equality.

Civil Rights Act of 1964

The movement led to a growing public demand for government action. As a result, Congress passed the Civil Rights Act of 1964. This law banned segregation in stores, restaurants, hotels, and theaters. It ended discrimination in decisions about hiring workers. The law did not apply just to African Americans. It also outlawed discrimination based on gender, religion, and national origin.

Voting Rights Act of 1965

This law was a major gain for African Americans. Still, most of those who lived in the South were not able to vote. State laws required them to pay a poll tax. The Twenty-fourth Amendment ended poll taxes in national elections, but other laws kept African Americans from the polls. Many states said voters had to pass a literacy, or reading, test. White officials made it very difficult for African Americans to pass these tests.

Seeing that more had to be done, Congress passed the Voting Rights Act of 1965. It banned the unfair use of literacy tests. Many people see the Voting Rights Act of 1965 as one of the most effective civil rights laws. After it passed, the number of African American voters in the South finally rose.

☑ PROGRESS CHECK

Describing What are some of the methods African Americans used to secure their civil rights?

PHOTO: MPI/Getty Images

American Leaders
Martin Luther King, Jr. (1929–1968)

Martin Luther King, Jr., pulled at the nation's conscience. He urged people to work to make the American ideal of justice and equality for all citizens come true. His words and efforts moved many Americans. What drove him to take on this demanding role?

King was born in Atlanta, Georgia, in 1929. The son of a Baptist minister, he decided when he was 18 years old to become a minister also. King's ideals came from his Christian belief that all people were children of God. He based his methods on the work of Mohandas Gandhi of India. Gandhi had used nonviolent resistance to win his country's freedom from British rule.

King applied the idea of nonviolent resistance to the struggle for civil rights. He first gained national prominence in 1955, when he led the Montgomery Bus Boycott. In 1957 King founded the Southern Christian Leadership Conference. This group helped organize civil rights protests throughout the South. King's efforts to eliminate "Jim Crow" laws and to gain voting rights for African Americans won him the Nobel Peace Prize in 1964.

Though King always preached nonviolence, he was often the target of violent attacks. The last of those came in April 1968, when he was shot and killed. Though millions were saddened by his death, King's message of inspiration and hope lived on.

Looking at Leadership

Why do you think Martin Luther King inspired people?

---

sit-in the act of occupying seats or sitting down on the floor of an establishment as a form of organized protest

The Struggle Continues

GUIDING QUESTION *What other groups of citizens have struggled to win civil rights?*

The civil rights gains of the 1960s helped other groups, too. The way the Civil Rights Act of 1964 was written assured that it would apply to many groups. The civil rights movement also convinced other groups to work for their own rights. Women, Latinos, Native Americans, and the disabled all called for more equal treatment.

Even today the struggle for equal rights goes on. About 82,000 people per year complain that they have been harmed by discrimination where they work. Each year some people are subjected to unfair treatment by police. One practice is called *racial profiling*. This means that police single out certain people as suspects because of the way they look. Each year, some people are the victims of **hate crimes.** These are violent acts against people because of a group that they belong to.

Affirmative Action

In 1961 President John F. Kennedy wanted to see African Americans enter new kinds of jobs in growing numbers. He urged companies to take what he called affirmative action to make that happen. The term refers to a policy meant to increase the number of minorities and women at work and in colleges.

This effort hopes to make up for past actions that blocked people in these groups. Colleges use these programs to help minority students and women enter college in larger numbers than before. Companies use them to hire and promote members of minority groups and women.

From the start, affirmative action had its critics. They called the idea "reverse discrimination." They said that giving special treatment to people from minority groups or to women meant that whites and men were now being treated unfairly.

Representative Jim Langevin of Rhode Island speaks at an event in 2010 celebrating the 20th anniversary of the enactment of the Americans with Disabilities Act. The ADA extends protections to people with disabilities across broad areas of life, including education, recreation, transportation, dining in restaurants, and visiting a museum.

▶ **CRITICAL THINKING**
Analyzing How does protecting the rights of people with disabilities help protect the rights of all?

Americans with Disabilities Act

ADA:
Advancing Equal Rights
for All Americans

PHOTO: Tom Williams/Roll Call via Getty Images

Reading**HELP**DESK

hate crime a violent act against a person because of his or her race, color, national origin, gender, or disability

Academic Vocabulary

exploit to use unfairly for someone else's gain

Other Civil Rights Gains

Other groups saw that the civil rights movement had met some success. They, too, had suffered injustice. They, too, raised their voices in hopes of gaining rights long denied to them.

In 1968 several Native Americans came together to form a group. They called it the American Indian Movement. Its goal was to improve the lives of Native Americans, many of whom were poor. It worked to protect the rights granted to Native American peoples by treaties. It has also tried to keep native culture alive.

The Chicano Movement was formed by Mexican Americans. It tried to fight segregation against this group in the Southwest. Other Mexican American leaders worked for fair treatment of farm workers, most of whom were from this group. These workers were **exploited,** or used unfairly, by the companies they worked for. César Chávez and Dolores Huerta used strikes and boycotts to gain better working conditions and pay for these workers.

The movement for women's rights gained new energy in 1966. That year, the National Organization for Women was formed. The group dealt with many issues important to women. It worked to end discrimination on the job and to pass laws against domestic violence. Many people worked hard to get an Equal Rights Amendment, or ERA, added to the Constitution. An ERA had first been suggested back in 1923. It said that no state could deny any person equal rights because of gender. In 1972 Congress approved the ERA, but it was never ratified by enough states to be come an amendment.

People who have disabilities have also won rights. More than 20 years ago, Congress passed a law called the Americans with Disabilities Act. This important law protects the rights of people with disabilities in the workplace and elsewhere.

✔ PROGRESS CHECK

Summarizing What other groups were inspired by the civil rights movement to work for equality for themselves?

LESSON 4 REVIEW

Review Vocabulary

1. How did "*Jim Crow*" laws formalize *segregation*?

2. Explain how *sit-ins* are examples of *nonviolent resistance*.

Answer the Guiding Questions

3. *Describing* What were the conditions that led to the civil rights movement?

4. *Explaining* Why does the struggle for civil rights continue?

5. **INFORMATIVE/EXPLANATORY** Write a brief essay that describes the different tactics of the civil rights movement.

1 Writing Activity

EXPLORING THE ESSENTIAL QUESTION

How do societies balance individual and community rights?

In an essay, explain how the Bill of Rights protects citizens. Describe how these rights are limited. Using concrete examples, show how these limits help keep order in society.

2 21st Century Skills

MEDIA PRESENTATION Create a media presentation summarizing the milestones of the civil rights movement of the 1950s and 1960s, including the Montgomery bus boycott and the "Freedom Rides" through Alabama. Search the Internet to find at least ten events to include.

3 Being an Active Citizen

For the 2008 presidential election, only 71 percent of eligible citizens were registered to vote, and only 64 percent of voting-age citizens turned up at the polls. Working in small groups, brainstorm ways to encourage people in your community to register to vote. For example, you can research the times and places people can register to vote or the steps they must go through. Publicize your findings in a creative way. You could also identify any barriers that exist to voter registration in your community and find ways to overcome them.

4 Understanding Visuals

Study the photograph. Write a paragraph describing what you think is going on in the photograph. What objects in it signal to you what the situation is and the relationship between the individuals? Your paragraph should address how the Fifth Amendment protects people accused of a crime.

Kim Kulish/CORBIS

REVIEW THE GUIDING QUESTIONS

Directions: Choose the best answer for each question.

1 Freedom of assembly implies freedom of
   A. choice.
   B. speech.
   C. association.
   D. the press.

2 The Fourth Amendment prevents soldiers, government agents, and police officers from searching your home or taking your property without a(n)
   F. bail.
   G. double jeopardy.
   H. indictment.
   I. search warrant.

3 Which of the following is a Fifth Amendment protection?
   A. guarantee of due process
   B. no cruel and unusual punishment
   C. probable cause
   D. trial by jury

4 The Fifteenth Amendment extended suffrage to
   F. all women.
   G. all white women.
   H. poor whites.
   I. African American men.

5 Segregation is
   A. a civil right.
   B. the social separation of the races.
   C. a form of protest.
   D. nonviolent resistance.

6 The Civil Rights Act of 1964
   F. banned discrimination by race, color, sex, religion, and national origin.
   G. created the Equal Rights Amendment.
   H. eliminated burdensome voting requirements.
   I. segregated public schools.

DBQ ANALYZING DOCUMENTS

Directions: Analyze the excerpt and answer the questions that follow.

"In all criminal prosecutions, the accused shall enjoy the right to a speedy and public trial, by an impartial jury . . . ; to be confronted with the witnesses against him; to have compulsory process for obtaining witnesses in his favor, and to have the Assistance of Counsel for his defence."

—U. S. Constitution, Sixth Amendment

7 Analyzing Which of the following is prevented by the amendment's requirement that an accused person "shall enjoy a speedy and public trial, by an impartial jury"?

A. juries smaller than 12 people

B. trials in local courts

C. secret trials

D. trials without juries

8 Synthesizing According to the Supreme Court, what is the meaning of the right to "the Assistance of Counsel for his defence"?

F. Anyone who cannot afford to pay a lawyer will not be tried.

G. If an accused person cannot afford a lawyer, the government must pay for one.

H. Men are entitled to be helped by a lawyer, but not women.

I. An accused person can call on the judge for advice.

SHORT RESPONSE

"All persons born or naturalized in the United States, and subject to the jurisdiction thereof, are citizens of the United States and of the State wherein they reside. No State shall . . . deprive any person of life, liberty, or property, without due process of law; nor deny to any person within its jurisdiction the equal protection of the laws."

—U.S. Constitution, Fourteenth Amendment, Section 1

9 Why was the Fourteenth Amendment passed?

10 Why is the "due process" clause of this amendment so important in terms of the Bill of Rights?

EXTENDED RESPONSE

11 Argument Which of the amendments studied in this chapter do you think is the most important? Why? Support your position with historical evidence.

Need Extra Help?

If You've Missed Question	**1**	**2**	**3**	**4**	**5**	**6**	**7**	**8**	**9**	**10**	**11**
Review Lesson	1	2	2	3	4	4	2	2	3	3	1,2,3, 4

The Legislative Branch

ESSENTIAL QUESTION
Why do people create, structure, and change governments?

The Story Matters...

Who makes our laws? Congress is the lawmaking branch of the federal government. It consists of the Senate and the House of Representatives. John Lewis has served in the House of Representatives since 1986. He represents the people of the Georgia congressional district that includes Atlanta and parts of three surrounding counties.

Lewis was born into a family of poor Alabama sharecroppers. As a young man, he was a key civil rights leader. Lewis first held political office in the Atlanta city government. As a member of Congress, he champions causes he passionately believes in: human rights and civil liberties.

◄ *Representative John Lewis has gained great respect throughout the nation's political community because of his high standards and moral principles. He has been called "the conscience of the U.S. Congress."*
PHOTO: Getty Images

155

Real-Life Civics

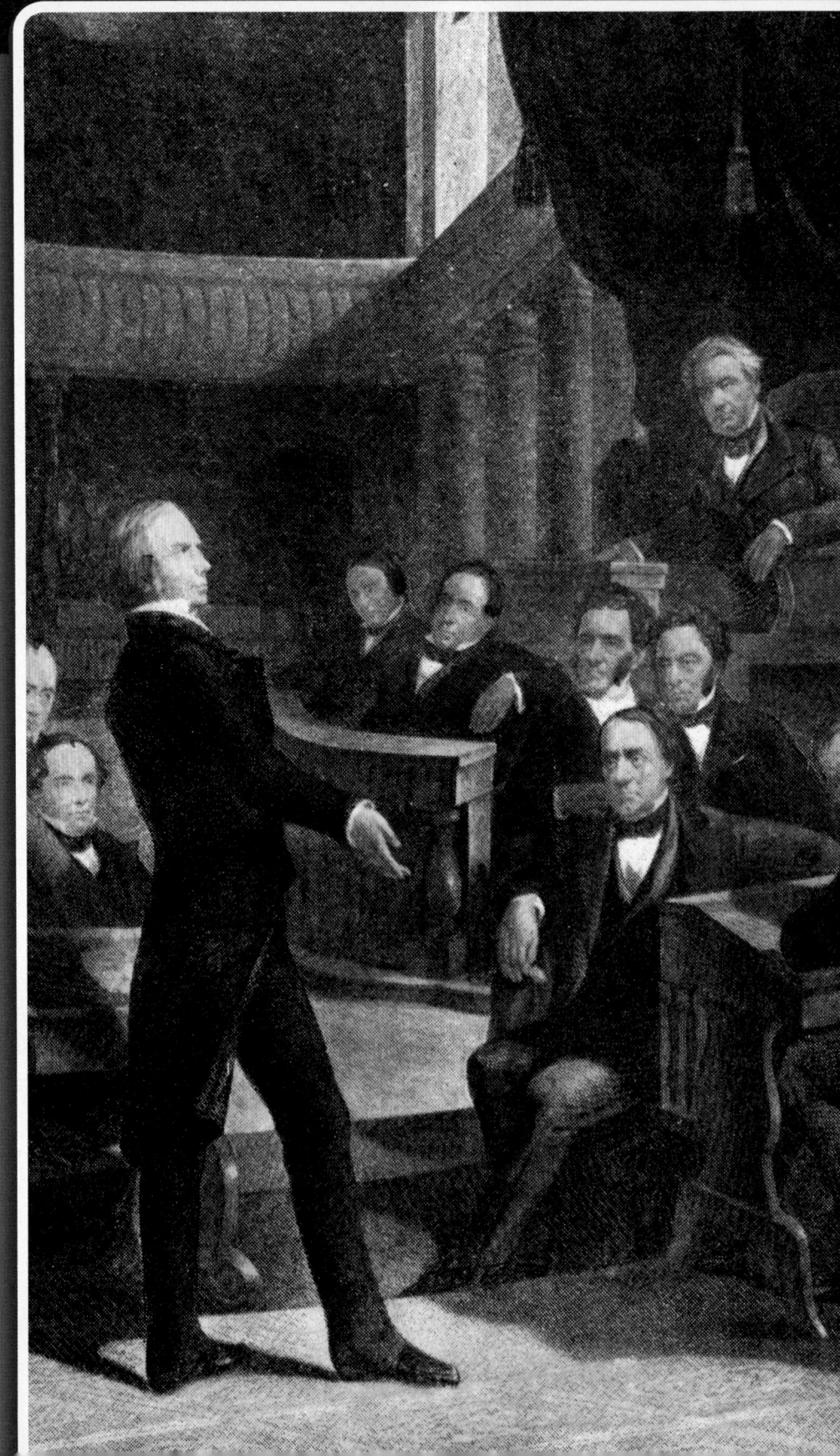

> **THEN** In 1850, the issue of slavery threatened to tear the nation apart. Many in Congress from Northern states wanted to stop the spread of slavery, while those from Southern states resisted. To ease the tension, Kentucky senator Henry Clay proposed several measures that became known as the Compromise of 1850. Clay's skillful speech making before the Senate led to the compromise bill's passage and helped to maintain peace during a turbulent time.

In our history, many of the country's most pressing issues have been discussed and decided in Congress. Senators and representatives come before their fellow members to present impassioned pleas for causes they believe are vital to the nation. They hope to convince other members to vote for or against a particular bill or law.

In his long career, Henry Clay served in both the U.S. Senate and House of Representatives.

MR. BYRD
CHAIRMAN

△ In 2008 Senator Robert Byrd expressed his strong opposition to spending more money on the war in Iraq.

> **NOW** The country's critical issues continue to be discussed and argued in Congress in modern times. One dramatic example occurred in October 2002. Senator Robert Byrd of West Virginia rose to give an eloquent speech against allowing President George W. Bush to use military force against Iraq. Byrd was 83 years old, the longest-serving member of Congress at the time. His knowledge of constitutional law and Senate rules helped make him a respected figure in Congress. Although he failed to convince his fellow senators that day, he continued to strongly oppose the war in Iraq until his death in 2010. Heated debates among lawmakers, as well as compromise, negotiation, and behind-the-scenes deal making, are as important today as they were more than 160 years ago when Henry Clay spoke on the Senate floor.

CIVIC LITERACY

★ ★ ★ ★

Analyzing How were the goals of Henry Clay and Robert Byrd similar and different?

Your Opinion What do you think are the most important skills a member of Congress needs in order to effectively represent the people of his or her state or district?

netw⊙rks
There's More Online!

☑ **GRAPHIC ORGANIZER**
The United States Congress

☑ **MAP**
Congressional Apportionment

☑ **POLITICAL CARTOON**
Gerrymandering

☑ **CHART**
Congressional Committees

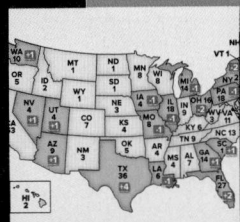

Lesson 1
Structure of Congress

ESSENTIAL QUESTION *Why do people create, structure, and change governments?*

IT MATTERS BECAUSE
Congress makes the federal laws that affect all Americans.

The Two Houses of Congress

GUIDING QUESTION *Why is Congress composed of a House of Representatives and a Senate?*

Congress creates our nation's laws. Both the Senate and the House of Representatives have their own special rules and procedures. Why is Congress divided into two houses, each with its own special character?

When writing the Constitution in 1787, the Framers wanted to create a Congress with the power to pass laws. They had a problem, however. They could not agree about how the states should be represented in this Congress. Delegates from the smaller states wanted each state to have equal representation. Those from the larger states wanted votes in Congress to be based on population. This would give them more power. In the end, the Framers reached a compromise. They made Congress a two-part, or bicameral, body. In the **Senate,** each state would have an equal number of representatives—two. In the **House of Representatives,** the number of members for each state would be based on its population.

The Framers wanted the legislative branch of government to have more power than the other two branches. They described

PHOTO: (tcl) North Wind/North Wind Picture Archives—All rights reserved.; (tcr) McGraw-Hill Companies, Inc./Jill Braaten, photographer; (tr) Congressional Quarterly/Getty Images

Congress in the first part of the Constitution, Article I. As James Madison said, Congress is "the First Branch of this Government."

Every year, 535 of our fellow citizens gather inside the U.S. Capitol in Washington, D.C. There, they make new laws and address the many issues facing our country. These are our elected representatives, the members of Congress.

Terms and Sessions

The government calendar is set by law. Each Congress lasts for a term, or a period of time, of two years. Each Congress usually starts on January 3 of odd-numbered years and lasts for two years. Each "new" Congress is numbered to identify its two-year term. For example, the first Congress met in 1789, and the 114th Congress is in session from January 2015 to January 2017.

Each Congress is divided into two sessions, or meetings. A typical session of Congress today lasts from January until November or December. Congress may also meet during special sessions or in times of crisis. A joint session **occurs**, or happens, when the House and Senate meet together. The two chambers have joint sessions to do business as a unit or to hear a presidential speech.

GEOGRAPHY CONNECTION

Every 10 years, after the population of each state is counted, Congress must see if the number of House seats each state has must change because the relative populations of the states have changed.

1 **PLACE** Which states lost the most seats in this apportionment? How many did they lose?

2 **CRITICAL THINKING** *Making Inferences* Why do you think these states lost seats?

CONGRESSIONAL APPORTIONMENT

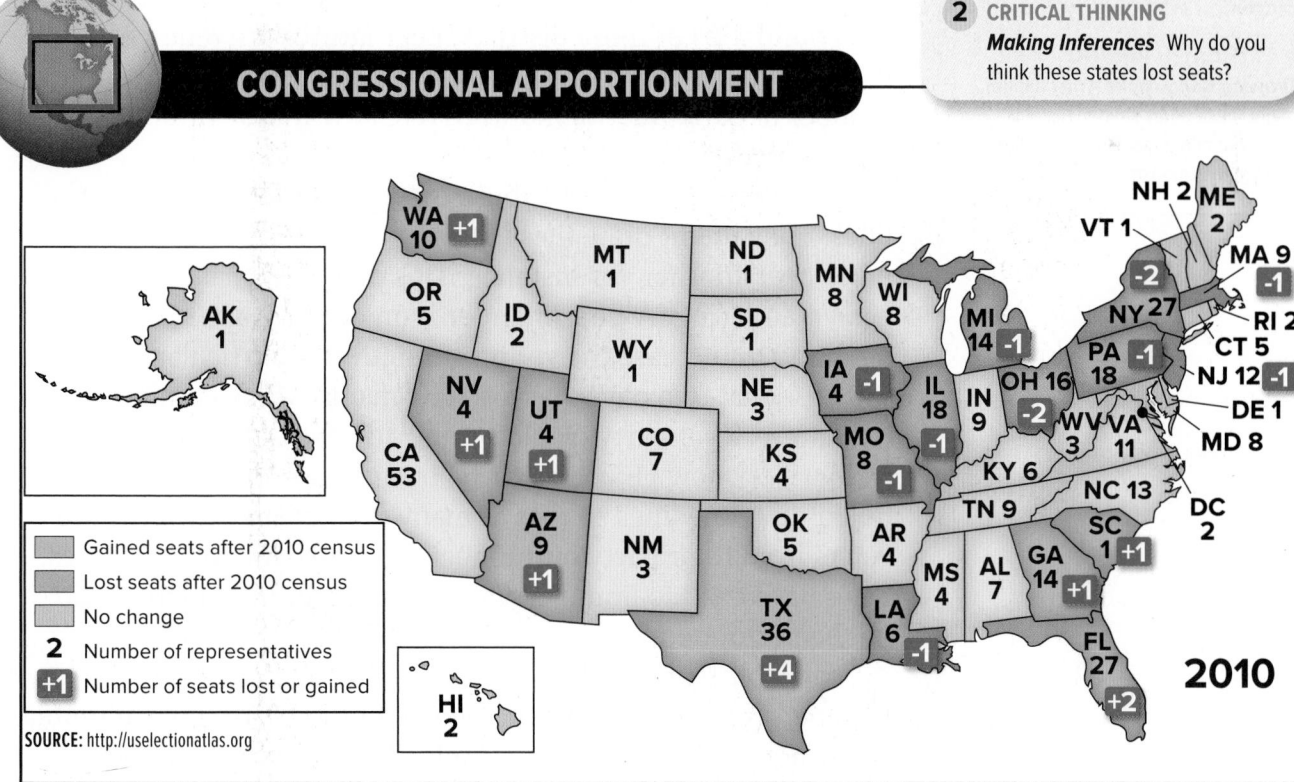

Gained seats after 2010 census
Lost seats after 2010 census
No change
2 Number of representatives
+1 Number of seats lost or gained

SOURCE: http://uselectionatlas.org

2010

Senate the upper house of Congress, consisting of two representatives from each state

House of Representatives the lower house of Congress, consisting of a different number of representatives from each state, depending on population

Academic Vocabulary

occur to happen or take place

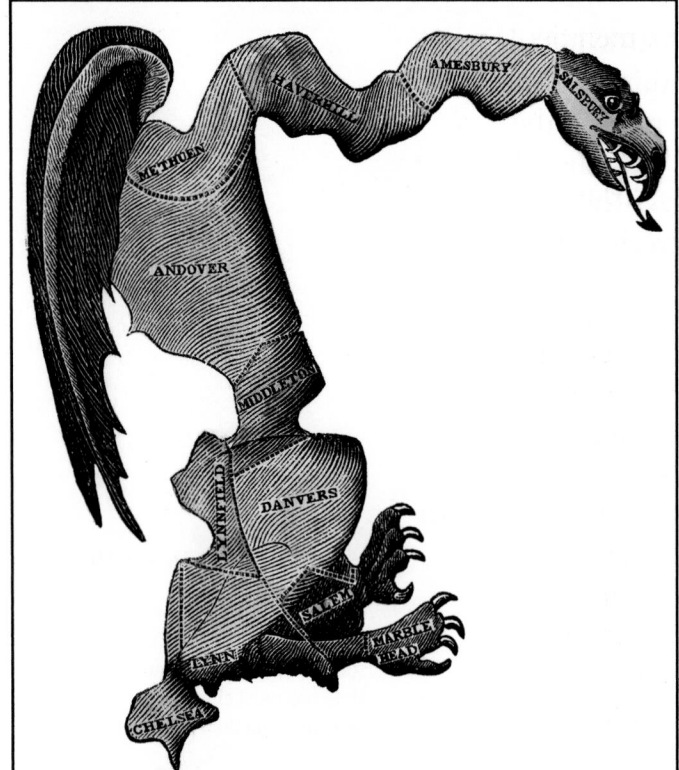

Gerrymandering after a census often leads to oddly shaped districts such as this one, shown in an 1812 cartoon.

▶ CRITICAL THINKING

Drawing Conclusions What danger might these oddly shaped districts pose that might make the cartoonist see them as monsters?

The House of Representatives

The House of Representatives is the larger of the two houses of Congress. It has 435 voting members who are divided among the states on the basis of their population. These representatives serve two-year terms.

The United States Constitution allows each state at least one representative, no matter how small its population. Every 10 years, a **census,** or population count, is taken by the Census Bureau. Congress then **adjusts**, or changes, the number of representatives given to each state based on the census results. States that have gained enough people since the last census might get one or even two more House members. Those that lose people might lose one or more seats.

Each state is divided into one or more congressional districts. One representative, or House member, is elected by the voters of each district. State legislatures must draw the boundaries of these districts. Legislatures are required to draw the districts so that they each include roughly the same number of **constituents** (kuhn•STIHCH•wuhnts), or people represented.

Sometimes lawmakers abuse their power to draw district lines. They might draw these lines to favor one political party over another, for instance. This practice is called gerrymandering. A **gerrymander** is an oddly shaped district designed to increase the voting strength of a particular group. Suppose that one party has a strong majority in the state legislature. That party would be able to control how the map is drawn for new House districts. In that case, party members might draw the lines so that as many districts as possible have voters from their party outnumbering those from other parties. Laws have tried to limit gerrymandering, but the practice has not been stopped.

The House of Representatives also has six nonvoting members. One represents the people of the District of Columbia. The other five represent the people of Puerto Rico and four

Reading**HELP**DESK

census a population count taken by the Census Bureau

Academic Vocabulary

adjust to change or alter in order to fit or conform

constituent a person from a legislator's district

gerrymander an oddly shaped election district designed to increase the voting strength of a particular group

island territories in the Pacific Ocean. These six members do not vote on bills being considered in the House.

The Senate

The Senate has 100 members, with two coming from each of the 50 states. Each senator represents his or her entire state rather than a particular district. Senators serve six-year terms. However, elections are staggered. This means that no more than one-third of the senators are running for reelection at any one time. The remaining two-thirds of the senators ensure that the Senate is stable through each election. This helps shield the Senate from sudden shifts in public opinion.

A senator may die or resign before the end of his or her term. How the vacant seat is filled depends on state law. In most states, the governor can name someone to fill the empty position. That person will hold the office until there is an election. Most states wait until the next regular election to choose a permanent new senator. Other states will call for a special election to be held sooner.

Congressional Leadership

In both the House of Representatives and the Senate, the political party to which more than half of the members belong is known as the **majority party.** The other party, with less than half of the members, is called the **minority party.** At the beginning of each new Congress, each party's members in each house choose the party's leaders to direct its activities.

Each political party chooses its leader, called either the majority or the minority leader, depending on that party's position in the new Congress. Each leader speaks for his or her party on issues that come up in that house. Each leader tries to push along and sway votes in favor of bills supported by his or her party. An assistant leader, called a "whip," helps each party leader. For example, the whip makes sure legislators are present for key votes.

Top Leadership in the House

In addition to these party leaders, each house of Congress has one presiding officer. In the House of Representatives, this leader is called the Speaker of the House. Members of the majority party choose the Speaker at a caucus, or closed meeting. The rest of the House then approves the choice of Speaker.

In January 2011, John Boehner, a Republican from Ohio, became the Speaker of the House.

▶ CRITICAL THINKING
Making Inferences Which political party do you think had a majority in the House in 2011, the Republicans or the Democrats? Why?

PHOTO: McGraw-Hill Companies, Inc./Jill Braaten, photographer

majority party in both the House of Representatives and the Senate, the political party to which more than half the members belong

minority party in both the House of Representatives and the Senate, the political party to which fewer than half the members belong

PHOTO: Congressional Quarterly/Getty Images

During the two terms of President George W. Bush (2001–2009), Vice President Richard Cheney (top center) was the presiding officer of the Senate.

► **CRITICAL THINKING**
Speculating Why do you think the vice president is allowed to vote to break a tie in the Senate?

The Speaker of the House has great power. He or she presides over the House and leads its majority party. The Speaker guides legislation through the House and leads floor debates. If anything happens to the president and vice president, the Speaker is next in line to become president, provided he or she is legally qualified.

Speakers rely on persuasion and the power of their position to influence other House members. On a typical day, the Speaker may talk with dozens of members of Congress. Often the Speaker listens to requests for a favor. In return for meeting such requests, the Speaker expects the representatives' support on important issues.

The office of the Speaker is mentioned in the Constitution. That document gives no other details about the office or its powers, however. The duties of the office have developed over time, shaped by the actions of the people who have served as Speaker.

Top Leadership in the Senate

Like the House, the Senate needs a presiding officer. That person runs the sessions of the Senate and keeps order. The presiding officer in the Senate is the vice president. The vice president differs from the Speaker of the House in an important way. The Speaker can vote on any matter before the House. The vice president, however, can vote in the Senate only when there is a tie.

The vice president cannot always be present when the Senate is in session, though. When he or she is absent, a temporary officer fills in. That officer is named the president pro tempore (proh TEHM•puh•ree)—meaning "for the time being." He or she is from the majority party and is usually its most senior member. The president pro tempore is also in the line of succession to fill the presidency, coming after the Speaker of the House.

☑ **PROGRESS CHECK**

Recalling How many members are there in the House? The Senate?

The Committee System

GUIDING QUESTION *Why are members of Congress assigned to work on committees?*

In a single session, each house of Congress handles thousands of bills, or proposed laws. In order to carefully consider so many bills at one time, each house has set up many different committees. The committee system makes Congress's large workload easier. President Woodrow Wilson noted the importance of committees.

PRIMARY SOURCE

" It is not far from the truth to say that Congress in session is Congress on public exhibition, whilst Congress in its committee rooms is Congress at work. "

—Woodrow Wilson, *Congressional Government*, 1885

Types of Committees

Congress has three types of committees. They are standing committees, select committees, and joint committees. Standing committees are permanent, meaning they are used each term. They focus on specific areas of government work. For example, both the Senate and the House have standing committees to deal with agriculture, commerce, and veterans' affairs.

The House and Senate sometimes form temporary committees to deal with special issues. These select committees meet for a limited time until they complete their assigned task.

Occasionally, the Senate and the House form joint committees, which include members of both houses. Joint committees meet to consider specific issues.

21st Century SKILLS

Paraphrasing

Reread the primary source quotation from Woodrow Wilson's *Congressional Government*. What did Wilson mean? Write a paraphrase putting Wilson's idea in your own words.

CONGRESSIONAL COMMITTEES

House of Representatives
STANDING COMMITTEES

- Agriculture
- Appropriations
- Armed Services
- Budget
- Education and Labor
- Energy and Commerce
- Financial Services
- Foreign Affairs
- Homeland Security
- House Administration
- Judiciary
- Natural Resources
- Oversight and Government Reform
- Rules
- Science and Technology
- Small Business
- Standards of Official Conduct
- Transportation and Infrastructure
- Veterans Affairs
- Ways and Means

Senate
STANDING COMMITTEES

- Agriculture, Nutrition, and Forestry
- Appropriations
- Armed Services
- Banking, Housing, and Urban Affairs
- Budget
- Commerce, Science, and Transportation
- Energy and Natural Resources
- Environmental and Public Works
- Finance
- Foreign Relations
- Health, Education, Labor, and Pensions
- Homeland Security and Governmental Affairs
- Judiciary
- Rules and Administration
- Small Business and Entrepreneurship
- Veterans Affairs

CHART SKILLS

The House and Senate have their own standing committees.

▶ CRITICAL THINKING
1. *Identifying* Which type of committee has members from both houses?
2. *Drawing Conclusions* Why do you think both the House and Senate have committees that cover the same issues?

JOINT COMMITTEES

- Economic
- Printing
- Taxation
- Library

seniority years of service, which is used as a consideration for assigning committee members

Serving on Committees

Newly elected senators and representatives try to get placed on committees that affect the people who elected them. For example, members of Congress from farm areas might want to serve on agriculture committees. Those with many factories in their districts might be interested in serving on labor committees.

It is the task of party leaders to make committee assignments. In doing so, they consider members' interests, experience, and loyalty to their party. Another key factor is **seniority,** or years of service. The senators and representatives who have been in Congress longest usually get to serve on the most favored or most powerful committees.

The longest-serving committee member from the majority party usually becomes the chairperson. The person in this position has a great deal of power. Chairpersons decide when and if a committee will meet. They also decide which bills will be studied and who will serve on each of the subcommittees. The longest-serving committee member from the minority party leads the members of that party in the committee. He or she is called the ranking minority member.

Some people think the seniority system is a good idea. They say that it prevents fights over committee jobs. They also say it ensures that chairpersons will have experience. Opponents complain that talented committee members may be overlooked in favor of those who have simply been around for a while. There has been so much criticism of the seniority system over the years that both political parties have moved slightly away from it. The senior majority party member still usually becomes the committee chair. It is no longer guaranteed, however.

✓ **PROGRESS CHECK**

Identifying What are the three types of committees?

LESSON 1 REVIEW

Review Vocabulary

1. How does the *census* affect representation in the *House of Representatives*?

2. How do states divide the number of *constituents* in their congressional districts? How are constituents divided in a *gerrymander*?

3. What determines which is the *majority party* and which is the *minority party* in each house?

Answer the Guiding Questions

4. ***Expressing*** Why are the two houses of Congress good places to discuss issues that might require new laws?

5. ***Explaining*** Why does Congress rely on the committee system?

6. **ARGUMENT** Do you think that government by committee makes the role of individual members of Congress less important? Express your opinion in a paragraph. Give reasons to support your opinion.

er Legislative Pow

Lesson 2
Powers of Congress

ESSENTIAL QUESTION *Why do people create, structure, and change governments?*

IT MATTERS BECAUSE

The Framers gave Congress many powers and also placed some limits on those powers.

Legislative Powers

GUIDING QUESTION *What kinds of lawmaking powers were given to Congress by the Constitution?*

Have you noticed the rating given to a video game? That rating is required by law. You can thank Congress for that law.

Congress has enormous influence over life in the United States. Its decisions affect our nation's society and economy. Its actions also affect your family and your life. In fact, the actions taken by Congress even affect many people living in other nations. Understanding what powers Congress has—and how those powers are limited—is vital knowledge for every American citizen.

Expressed Powers

Most of the powers that the Constitution gives to Congress are listed in Article I, Section 8. These powers that are clearly stated in that document are called the **expressed powers** or the **enumerated powers** of Congress. There are 18 clauses listing powers specifically given to Congress. Clause 5, for example, says, "The Congress shall have the Power . . . To coin Money."

Reading**HELP**DESK

Taking Notes: *Identifying*

Create a graphic organizer similar to the one shown. As you read, write each important power of Congress.

Powers of Congress

Content Vocabulary

- **expressed power**
- **enumerated power**
- **implied power**
- **elastic clause**
- **nonlegislative power**
- **impeach**

SELECTED EXPRESSED POWERS

SELECTED IMPLIED POWERS

Money Powers

- Lay and collect taxes to provide for the defense and general welfare of the United States (Clause 1)
- Borrow money (Clause 2)
- Establish bankruptcy laws (Clause 4)
- Coin, print, and regulate money (Clause 5)
- Punish counterfeiters of American currency (Clause 6)

- Lay and collect taxes implies the power to support public schools, welfare programs, public housing, etc.
- Borrow money implies the power to maintain the Federal Reserve Board

Commerce Powers

- Regulate foreign and interstate commerce (Clause 3)

- Regulate commerce implies the power to prohibit discrimination in restaurants, hotels, and other public accommodations

Military and Foreign Policy Powers

- Declare war (Clause 11)
- Raise, support, and regulate an army and navy (Clauses 12, 13, & 14)
- Provide, regulate, and call into service a militia, known as the National Guard (Clauses 15 &16)
- Punish acts committed on international waters and against the laws of nations (Clause 10)

- Raise and support an army implies the right to draft people into the armed services

Other Legislative Powers

- Establish laws of naturalization (Clause 4)
- Establish post offices and post roads (Clause 7)
- Grant copyrights and patents (Clause 8)
- Create lower federal courts (Clause 9)
- Govern Washington, D.C. (Clause 17)
- Provide for laws necessary and proper for carrying out of all other listed powers (Clause 18)

- Establish laws of naturalization implies the power to limit the number of immigrants to the United States

Source: *Congress A to Z,* 4th ed. (Washington, D.C.: CQ Press 2003.).

CHART SKILLS

The 18 clauses of Article I, Section 8 of the Constitution spell out the expressed powers of Congress.

▶ CRITICAL THINKING

1 *Explaining* Why is the power to lay and collect taxes the one that the Constitution places in the very first clause?

2 *Synthesizing* Why are there no clauses listed for each of the implied powers on the right-hand side of the chart?

ReadingHELPDESK

Content Vocabulary (cont.)

- **writ of habeas corpus**
- **bill of attainder**
- **ex post facto law**

expressed power power that the U.S. Congress has that is specifically listed in the Constitution

enumerated power another name for expressed power

Implied Powers

Certain powers are given to Congress even though they are not specifically stated in the Constitution. The source of these powers is Article I, Section 8, Clause 18. This clause says that Congress has the power to do whatever is "necessary and proper" to carry out its expressed powers. The powers that Congress has because of Clause 18 are called **implied powers.** This means they are not stated directly in the Constitution but can be understood to be granted.

Clause 18 is often called the **elastic clause** because it has allowed Congress to stretch its powers to meet new needs. For instance, the Constitution does not state that Congress has the power to hire millions of people to work in the Defense Department. Under the elastic clause, though, Congress has done just that. It did so as part of its expressed power to support the armed forces.

Lawmaking Powers

Most of Congress's powers relate to making laws. As the chart on the powers of Congress shows, many lawmaking powers fall into one of three major categories—money, commerce, and military and foreign policy.

Congress has the power to raise and spend money. That includes the power to require people to pay taxes and the power to print money. Congress can also **regulate**, or manage, commerce that takes place across state lines. Commerce is the business of buying and selling goods and services. Finally, Congress makes laws about defense matters, war, and foreign policy issues. Congress has the power to create and maintain armed forces. Congress alone has the power to declare war.

Other lawmaking powers do not fit into these categories. The Constitution also gives Congress the power to create a postal service and a federal court system. In addition, Congress has the power to set up the government of Washington, D.C.

The Constitution gives Congress expressed and implied powers. Setting up a national postal service is one of the expressed powers in Article 1, Section 8, Clause 7. At the time the Constitution was written, there were no electronic forms of communication.

▶ **CRITICAL THINKING**
Making Inferences Why do you think this power was considered important enough to be listed as an expressed power in the Constitution?

✔ **PROGRESS CHECK**

Expressing Why is the "necessary and proper" clause also called the elastic clause?

---

implied power power that Congress has that is not stated explicitly in the Constitution

elastic clause clause in Article I, Section 8 of the Constitution that gives Congress the right to make all laws "necessary and proper" to carry out its expressed powers

Academic Vocabulary

regulate to manage or to control

GUILTY
30
0
30

NOT GUILTY
3
31
34

CLINTON ACQUITTED

SENATE VOTE
67 VOTES TO CONVICT
IMPEACHMENT ARTICLE 2
LIEBERMAN D OBSTRUCTION OF JUSTICE

CNN LIVE

PHOTO: CNN/AFP/Getty Images

While the House starts the impeachment process, the actual trial and determination of guilt take place in the Senate.

▶ CRITICAL THINKING
Making Inferences After President Bill Clinton was impeached and tried, he was not removed from office. Based on that context information, what do you think acquitted means?

Other Powers and Limits

GUIDING QUESTION *What powers does Congress have to check the powers of the other branches of government?*

The most important duty of Congress is to legislate, or make laws. Congress also has a number of duties and responsibilities besides making laws. These powers are called **nonlegislative powers.**

Nonlegislative Powers

One nonlegislative power is the ability of Congress to suggest amendments to the Constitution. Among the most important nonlegislative powers of Congress, though, are those that allow it to check the other branches of government. Some of these are set forth in the Constitution. Others have developed over time.

The Senate has the power to approve or reject the president's nominees for various offices. The offices include Supreme Court justices, federal judges, and ambassadors.

The Constitution also allows Congress to remove from office any federal official involved in serious wrongdoing. This action must follow a two-step process. The House has the power to **impeach,** or accuse officials of misconduct in office. A majority vote of the House is needed to impeach an official. The Senate then holds a trial of the official. The Senate also acts as a jury to decide the official's guilt or innocence. A two-thirds vote in the Senate is necessary to convict an official and remove him or her from office.

The House of Representatives has rarely used its right to impeach. Most often, the power is used for federal judges. Only two presidents have been impeached: Andrew Johnson in 1868 and Bill Clinton in 1998. Both presidents stood trial in the Senate. In both cases, the Senate did not find them guilty. As a result, they were not removed from office.

Limits on Congressional Powers

The Constitution explains not only what Congress may do but also what it may *not* do. Some limits are imposed by the Bill of Rights. The purpose of the Bill of Rights was to limit or deny certain powers to the federal government. For example, Congress may not pass laws that restrict freedom of speech or freedom of religion.

Reading HELPDESK

nonlegislative power duty Congress holds besides lawmaking

impeach to accuse government officials of misconduct in office

The Constitution places other limits on the powers of Congress. Many of these limits are found in Article I, Section 9. For instance, Congress may not favor one state over another, tax interstate commerce, or tax exports.

The Framers wanted to be sure to prevent Congress from abusing power. As a result, Section 9 also forbids Congress from passing laws that would hurt the legal rights of individuals. For example, Congress cannot block the **writ of habeas corpus** (HAY•bee•uhs KAWR•puhs), except in times of rebellion or invasion to protect public safety. This writ is a court order that requires police to bring a prisoner to court to explain why they are holding the person. In addition, Congress cannot pass **bills of attainder.** These are laws that punish a person without a trial. Congress is also prevented from passing **ex post facto laws.** These are laws declaring that an act is a crime after the act has been committed.

Other limits on the powers of Congress result from the fact that the Constitution sets aside many powers for the state governments. Those powers are denied to the federal government. Congress cannot interfere with these powers, such as the right to regulate public schools.

Further limits come from the powers that are given to the other branches to check the powers of Congress. The Supreme Court can declare laws passed by Congress to be unconstitutional. The president can veto, or say no to, bills passed by Congress. This prevents those bills from becoming laws. In this case, Congress has its own check on the power of the president. If both the Senate and the House of Representatives can get a two-thirds vote, they can override the president's veto.

✅ PROGRESS CHECK

Considering Why do you think the Constitution forbids Congress from passing ex post facto laws?

writ of habeas corpus a court order that requires police to bring a prisoner to court to explain why they are holding the person

bill of attainder a law that punishes a person accused of a crime without a trial or a fair hearing in court

ex post facto law a law that allows a person to be punished for an action that was not against the law when it was committed

LESSON 2 REVIEW

Review Vocabulary

1. How is the *elastic clause* related to Congress's *implied powers*?

2. Why do you think that the House rarely *impeaches* a top government official?

3. How does preventing Congress from passing a *bill of attainder* help safeguard rights?

Answer the Guiding Questions

4. *Specifying* What are three examples of expressed powers of Congress?

5. *Describing* What are two nonlegislative powers given to Congress?

6. **ARGUMENT** Should representatives always vote as their constituents want, or according to their own best judgment? Write a paragraph in which you express and defend your position.

networks

There's More Online!

☑ **GRAPHIC ORGANIZER**
Congressional
Requirements and
Privileges

☑ **INFOGRAPHIC**
Profile of Congress

☑ **POLITICAL CARTOON**
Bringing Home the Bacon

☑ **TIME LINE**
Women in Congress

Lesson 3

How Congress Works

ESSENTIAL QUESTION *Why do people create, structure, and change governments?*

IT MATTERS BECAUSE

In making laws, Congress makes decisions that affect all Americans.

Qualifications and Staffing

GUIDING QUESTION *What are the qualifications for becoming a member of Congress?*

Would you like to be a member of Congress someday? You would belong to one of the most powerful lawmaking bodies in the world. You would have a nice salary and good health care. You would have the opportunity to meet with and talk to the president. You would also work with other powerful members of our government—and the governments of other nations. You would have a chance to do good things to help the people of your state or district. Does that sound exciting and rewarding?

Of course, there is another side to the job. You would carry the responsibility of serving your constituents and the nation as a whole. You would be busy almost all the time. You would have to make difficult decisions. Your choices would be constantly watched by the media and your constituents. You would know that any decision, no matter how much you believed in it, would not satisfy everyone. You might be voted out of office in two or six years.

Who would choose this life? What kinds of people are the members of Congress? What challenges do they face? How do they go about doing their jobs? Who helps them do their work?

PHOTO: (tl) Congressional Quarterly Inc.; (tc) Getty Images; (tr) Ed Fischer, and CartoonStock.com

Taking Notes: *Comparing*

Use a Venn diagram to note the basic requirements for running for each house of Congress and the privileges shared by all members.

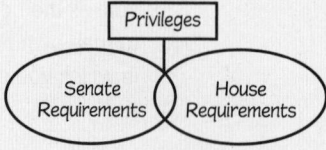

Content Vocabulary

- **franking privilege**
- **lobbyist**
- **casework**
- **pork-barrel project**

Requirements and Benefits

The Constitution describes the qualifications for members of Congress. To run for senator, you must be at least 30 years old and live in the state you plan to represent. You also must have been a U.S. citizen for at least nine years before being elected. Members of the House of Representatives have to be at least 25 years old and live in the state they represent. In addition, they must have been a U.S. citizen for at least seven years before being elected.

The members of Congress have more in common than meeting these legal qualifications. In the previous 113th Congress, about 200 senators and House members—almost two out of every five—were lawyers. There was a great mix of occupations, though, including farmers, doctors, homemakers, and former members of the armed forces. There were even a few former entertainers and professional athletes.

Members of Congress tend to be "joiners." They are more likely than the average citizen to be active in community organizations.

In the 114th Congress, senators had an average age of 61 and House members an average age of 56. Only about 30 House members and senators in total were younger than 40.

Members of Congress receive many benefits. In 2014, both senators and representatives were paid $174,000 a year. Further, they receive free office space, parking, and trips to their home states. Senators and representatives can send job-related mail without paying postage. This is called the **franking privilege.** Members of Congress have life and health insurance. They also have the use of a gymnasium, special restaurants, and a clinic.

Another benefit is that senators and representatives have immunity, or legal protection, in certain situations. This allows them to say and do what they believe is right without fear of interference from outsiders. Of course, this protection does not mean that they are free to break the law.

Before taking office, members of Congress must take an oath to uphold the Constitution. Carte Goodwin of West Virginia took the oath in June 2010 to fill the Senate seat made vacant by the death of Senator Robert Byrd.

▶ **CRITICAL THINKING**
Making Inferences Why do you think members of Congress must take such an oath?

PHOTO: Congressional Quarterly Inc.

franking privilege the right of senators and representatives to send job-related mail without paying postage

Congressional Staffs

Serving in Congress is a full-time job. To get help with their workload, members of Congress hire a staff of clerks, secretaries, and special assistants.

Members of Congress have offices in or near the Capitol in Washington, D.C. They also have one or more offices in their home district or state. The members rely on the people on their personal staffs to run these offices.

What do these personal staffs do? These workers gather information on new bills and issues. They handle requests for help from constituents. They deal with news reporters and **lobbyists.** Lobbyists are people who represent interest groups. They contact lawmakers or other government officials in an effort to influence their policy making. Staff members also work to help the member of Congress win reelection. The law, however, requires staff to do this work on their own time.

Why It
MATTERS

Location, Location, Location

All members of Congress have at least one office in their home district. If you or your family needs information or help from your representative, you can contact the staff at the district office for assistance. Go online to the senate.gov or house.gov Web site to find the office nearest you.

CHART SKILLS

These graphs show some facts about the makeup of the 114th Congress.

▶ CRITICAL THINKING

1 *Comparing* What is the percentage of women in the House? In the Senate?

2 *Making Inferences* Why do you think such a high percentage of members of Congress are lawyers?

PROFILE OF CONGRESS

GENDER

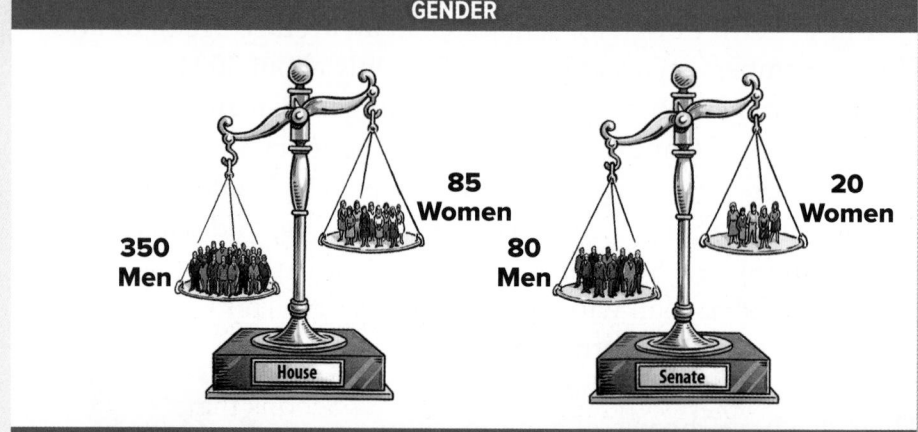

350 Men

85 Women

House

80 Men

20 Women

Senate

PARTY AFFILIATION

House of Representatives

Senate

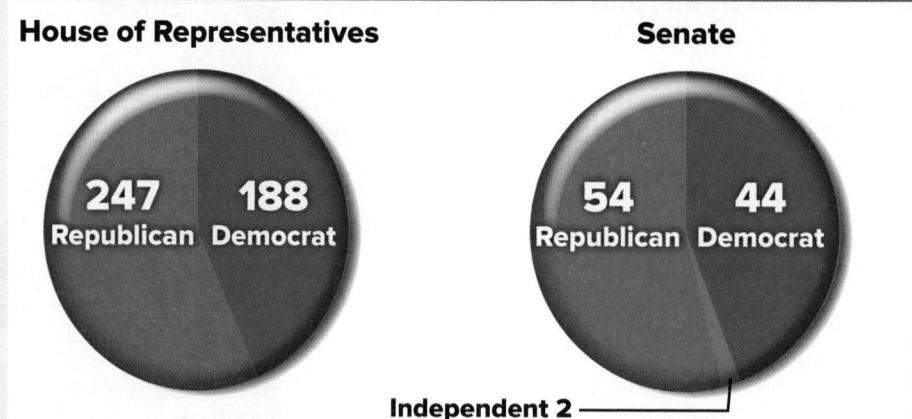

247 Republican   188 Democrat

54 Republican   44 Democrat

Independent 2

lobbyist representative of an interest group who contacts lawmakers or other government officials directly to influence their policy making

Academic Vocabulary

draft to make an outline or a rough version
estimate to judge the approximate nature, value, quality, or amount of a thing

In addition, many members of Congress hire students from their districts to work as volunteers. The students serve as interns and pages. Interns help with research and office duties. Pages deliver messages and run other errands. This experience gives young people a firsthand look at the political process. One former intern commented, "I felt like I had a backstage pass to the greatest show in the world."

Congressional committees also need staffs. Committee staff members do many day-to-day lawmaking chores. They gather information on issues the committee will handle. They organize committee hearings and negotiate with lobbyists. They also **draft**, or outline, bills. In short, they keep the long and complex process of making laws moving.

Agencies of Congress

Congress has also created agencies to support its work. The Library of Congress is the largest library in the world. At least one copy of every book published in the United States is kept there. The Library of Congress is an important source of information for members of Congress and their staffs.

The Government Accountability Office (GAO) looks into financial matters for Congress. It reviews spending by federal agencies to make sure that funds are being used well. It studies federal programs to see if they are working properly. The GAO also suggests ways to improve how the government spends money. The GAO helps Congress when it is considering new laws. It studies problems and analyzes different actions that can be taken to address them. The GAO does not work only with Congress. It can also give advice to executive departments.

The Congressional Budget Office (CBO) is another agency that helps members of Congress. The CBO provides information needed by Congress to develop the government's budget. Budgeting is an important activity of Congress that takes place every year. It helps Congress come up with—and stick to—a budget plan. The CBO also looks at the possible costs and benefits of different actions Congress is considering. It does not suggest policies. Instead it **estimates**, or tries to identify the amount of, the costs of programs and their possible effects.

✔ **PROGRESS CHECK**

Concluding Why might the franking privilege help a member of Congress get reelected?

---

teen citizens in action

Serving as a House Page

Leland Chapman, 17
Salisbury, North Carolina

Leland Chapman thought it was a dream come true. After trying for three years, he was finally selected to serve in the House Page Program in Washington, D.C.

Every summer, teenagers ages 16 and 17 from across the United States apply to come to the nation's capital to serve as pages. Pages serve on the support staff of the members of Congress. To serve in the House Page Program, applicants must be sponsored by the representative from their local district.

Teens accepted into the program live in the House Page Residence Hall a few blocks from the Capitol. They study such subjects as government and foreign affairs at the House Page School. Most of the time, they work for House members on the House floor. Leland loved it. "I saw the lawmaking process in action," he said.

Leland and other pages carried out a wide variety of jobs, from answering phones in the members' cloakroom and delivering mail to collecting documents to be placed in the Congressional Record, the official record of the work of Congress. Leland learned a lot. "It's important to understand how government works," he says, "because you want your voice to be heard. The only way your voice will be heard is if you get involved in politics. I want to be a changemaker."

Citizenship and Teens

What did Leland learn as a page that he thinks will help him in the future?

Lesson 3 **173**

Congress at Work

GUIDING QUESTION *How do members of Congress exercise their responsibilities?*

Today, the United States has more than 310 *million* people. Only 535 members of Congress represent them. The many demands of our nation on Congress are mind-boggling. How does Congress handle its huge workload?

The basic job of senators and representatives is to represent the people of their states and districts. They are responsible for reflecting and putting into action their constituents' interests and concerns. Congress does its work in regular time periods, or sessions, that begin each January 3 and last most of the year.

Making Laws

As representatives, members of Congress carry out many different tasks. Making laws is perhaps the best-known one. In fact, members of Congress are often called "lawmakers."

Congress considers different kinds of legislation each year. Most legislation is in the form of bills, which are drafts of proposed laws presented to the House and Senate. You will learn more about this process in Lesson 4.

As lawmakers, members of Congress fill various roles. They act as investigators and thinkers, studying issues to understand them—and to try to come up with ways to address them. When they propose a law, they take the role of writer. Once the bill is written, they must work to promote it to other members to gain support for it. Finally, they are evaluators. They examine proposed bills, thinking about how those bills will affect the people they represent and the nation.

Doing Casework

Members of Congress often help people from their home districts and states in dealing with the federal government. This help is called **casework.** Some members receive as many as 10,000 requests a year for this help. These requests cover a range of issues.

> **PRIMARY SOURCE**
>
> " The casework requests are as diverse as the federal government: a lost Social Security check; a veteran's widow requesting burial assistance for her deceased spouse; . . . immigration; farmers' loans; Medicare claims; railroad retirement; and federal rental housing. "
>
> —Anonymous congressional staff member, quoted in **Congressional Research Service,** *Congressional Member Office Operations,* **2003**

Members of Congress often hear testimony from the public, including celebrities, about issues they are studying. Here, performer Harry Connick, Jr., testifies about rebuilding the Gulf Coast following Hurricane Katrina.

▶ **CRITICAL THINKING**
Making Inferences Why is it important for congressional committees to listen to testimony from members of the public?

PHOTO: Getty Images

casework the work that a lawmaker does to help constituents with a problem

pork-barrel project government project grant that primarily benefits a congressperson's home district or state

Why do lawmakers spend so much time on casework? First, casework helps lawmakers to get reelected because it increases popular support. Second, casework helps lawmakers see how well the executive branch is handling programs such as Social Security or veterans' benefits. Third, casework provides a way to help citizens deal with federal agencies. One member of Congress was asked about the importance of casework. He called casework "about second to breathing."

Helping the District or State

Besides serving their constituents, members of Congress also try to bring federal government projects to their districts and states. Projects funded by government spending that mainly benefit the home district or state are often called **pork-barrel projects.** To understand this term, think of a member of Congress dipping into the "pork barrel" (the federal treasury) and pulling out a piece of "fat" (a federal project for his or her district). Critics say that this spending is a waste of taxpayers' money.

Many lawmakers see the situation differently. To them, bringing federal dollars to their own state or district is not doing anything wrong. Rather, they see it as trying to help people or groups in their state or district who have a need. They believe it is a way of helping their constituents win a fair share of government spending. A goal of many members of Congress is to work to give their constituents a share in the money the national government spends every year.

This cartoon shows a congressman returning home riding on top of his pork-barrel projects.

▶ CRITICAL THINKING
Predicting How do you think pork-barrel projects affect the view of constituents toward their representative?

Think of a public works project that you believe would benefit your community. Suppose that a lawmaker encouraged you to contact an agency official to help make the need for the project known. Make an argument in favor of the project, focusing on why it would be a good use of public money.

Every year, Congress passes public works bills. These bills set aside billions of dollars for local projects. Such projects might include building dams, military bases, veterans' hospitals, or highways. The construction work brings jobs and money into a state or district, sometimes for a period of several years. In addition, these projects can create jobs in the future, to run or maintain whatever has been built.

Lawmakers use several different methods to try to win projects for their district or state. They cannot simply decide to grant the money, of course. They do not have direct control over grants and contracts. Executive branch agencies, such as the Department of Labor, make these decisions.

Lawmakers can, however, try to influence agency decisions. Members of Congress may try to convince agency officials to give a favorable hearing to their state's requests. Lawmakers may also encourage their constituents to contact agency officials in order to make their needs known. Sometimes, public pressure can affect the choices that executive agencies make.

Senators and House members can also add wording to bills to provide funds for specific projects they favor. These additions are called "earmarks." Of course, the funding only goes through if both chambers pass the bill.

Members of Congress want their districts or states to get a fair share of the available grants and contracts funded through the federal budget. These grants and contracts are important to lawmakers and the people in their districts or states. These federal funds are a major source of money and jobs and can greatly improve the economy of a district or state.

✓ **PROGRESS CHECK**

Evaluating Do you think pork-barrel projects are a good idea? Or should such projects be distributed evenly among states and districts?

LESSON 3 REVIEW

Review Vocabulary

1. What is the *franking privilege*?

2. Why do members of Congress believe that *casework* is important?

3. Why might a *lobbyist* work to get a member of Congress to support a particular *pork-barrel project*?

Answer the Guiding Questions

4. ***Identifying*** What qualifications must a person have to be a candidate for the House of Representatives? The Senate?

5. ***Summarizing*** What are three major responsibilities of members of Congress?

6. **INFORMATIVE/EXPLANATORY** Describe the job of a member of the House or Senate by creating a want ad for a member of Congress. In the ad, include qualifications, benefits and salary, and skills needed. Also include facts that demonstrate the typical responsibilities of members.

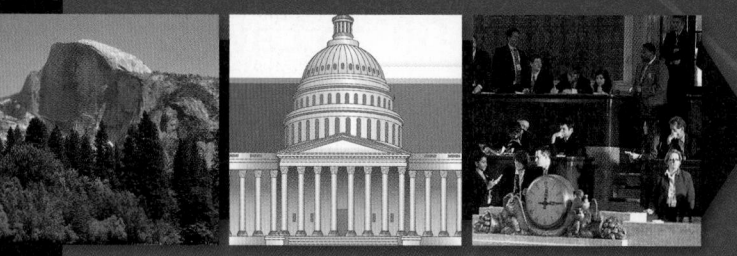

Lesson 4

How a Bill Becomes a Law

ESSENTIAL QUESTION *Why do people create, structure, and change governments?*

IT MATTERS BECAUSE
The process Congress follows to make laws is complex.

Types of Bills

GUIDING QUESTION *What kinds of bills come before Congress?*

As Congress is a legislature, its major job is passing laws. Each session, more than 10,000 bills—proposals for new laws—are introduced. Only a small percentage—just a few hundred—actually become law. The process is designed to be long and complicated to make sure that bills are considered carefully.

Bills generally fall into two categories, or types. Private bills concern individual people or places. They usually deal with people's claims against the government. Public bills apply to the entire nation and involve general matters such as taxation or farm policy or highway building.

Along with bills, Congress also considers resolutions. These are formal statements expressing lawmakers' opinions or decisions. Many resolutions do not have the power of law. **Joint resolutions**—those passed by both houses of Congress—do become law if they are signed by the president. Congress uses joint resolutions to propose constitutional amendments and to designate money for a special purpose.

☑ **PROGRESS CHECK**

Identifying What are the two types of bills?

Reading**HELP**DESK

Taking Notes: *Sequencing*

As you read, create a sequencing diagram to track the major steps an idea takes to become a law.

Content Vocabulary

- joint resolution
- special-interest group
- rider
- filibuster
- cloture
- voice vote
- standing vote
- roll-call vote
- pocket veto

Each year, Congress votes on bills that set aside, or appropriate, money for different purposes. One such purpose is to maintain national parks, such as Yosemite in California.

▶ **CRITICAL THINKING**
Explaining Why are bills that appropriate funding an important responsibility of Congress?

From Bill to Law

GUIDING QUESTION *How does a bill become a law?*

Every bill starts with an idea. Ideas for new bills come from three main sources. Private citizens may suggest bills. Other proposals may come from the president. The third source of ideas is special-interest groups. **Special-interest groups** are organizations made up of people who share common interests.

Whatever its source, a bill can only be **submitted**, or offered for consideration, by a member of Congress. The member who introduces a bill is known as its sponsor. A bill can have more than one sponsor. Every bill is given a title and a number when it is submitted. During the first session of Congress, the first bill introduced is called S.1 in the Senate and H.R.1 in the House.

Committee Action

After a bill is introduced in Congress, it is sent to the standing committee that handles the subject of the bill. Standing committees have life-and-death power over bills. Only if the committee approves a bill will it go to the floor for a vote by the full House or Senate.

If the committee members think that the bill is worth considering, they may hold hearings about it. After gathering information in hearings, committee members discuss the bill.

The committee can take one of five actions on a bill:

- pass the bill, which sends it to the full chamber
- make changes to the bill and then pass it and send it to the full House or Senate
- replace the original bill with a new bill on the same subject
- "pigeonhole" the bill, which means to ignore the bill and let it die in committee
- kill the bill outright by having a majority vote against it

Debating a Bill

Bills approved in committee are then considered by the full House or Senate. This stage of the process is called the floor debate. During the debate, members argue the bill's pros and cons. They also discuss amendments. The House accepts only amendments relevant to the bill. The Senate, however, allows **riders**—completely unrelated amendments—to be added.

PHOTO: BananaStock/Alamy

ReadingHELPDESK

joint resolution a resolution that is passed by both houses of Congress

special-interest group an organization of people with some common interest who try to influence government decisions

Academic Vocabulary

submit to offer a bill for consideration

rider a completely unrelated amendment added to a bill

HOW A BILL BECOMES A LAW

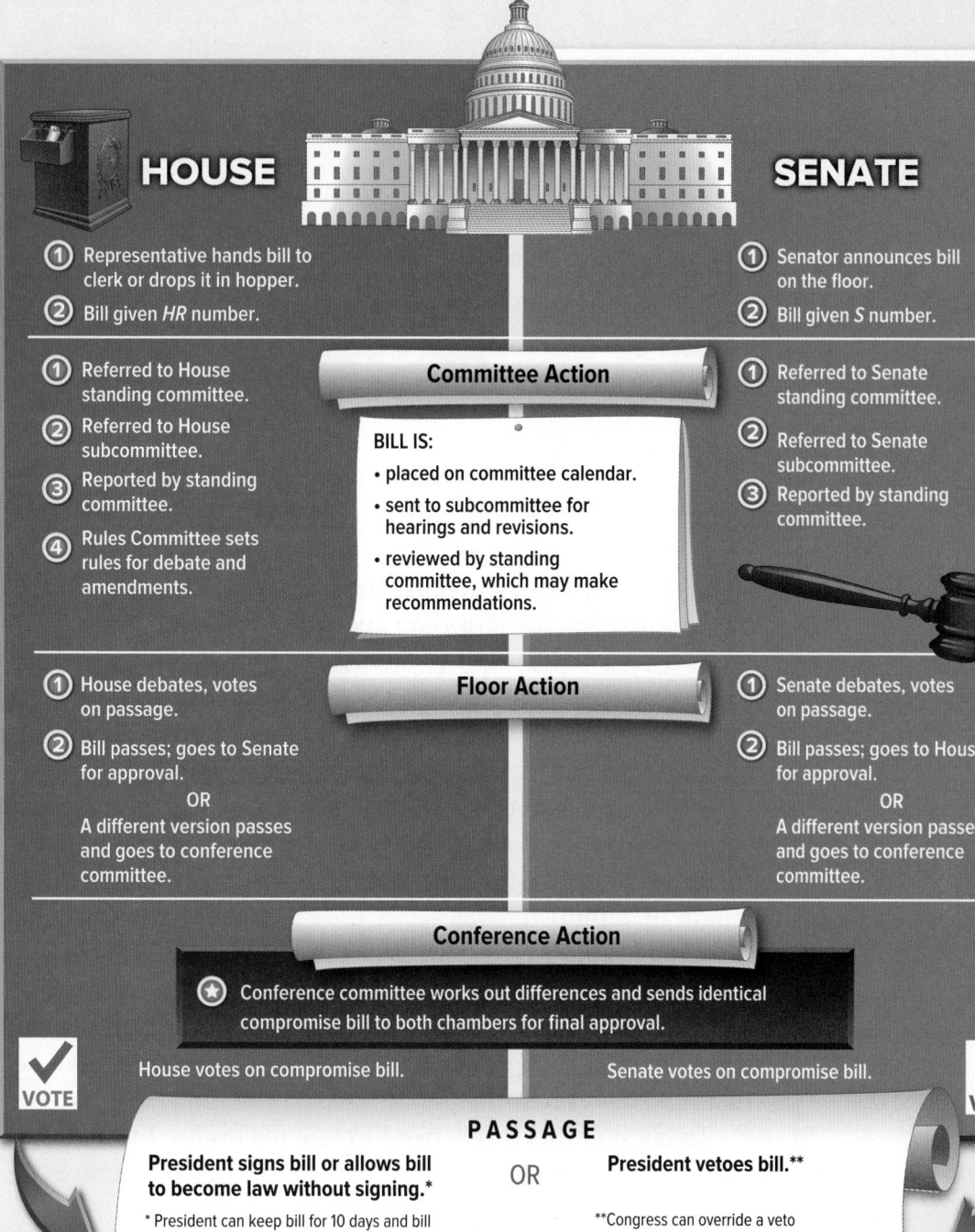

HOUSE

SENATE

1. Representative hands bill to clerk or drops it in hopper.
2. Bill given *HR* number.

1. Senator announces bill on the floor.
2. Bill given *S* number.

Committee Action

1. Referred to House standing committee.
2. Referred to House subcommittee.
3. Reported by standing committee.
4. Rules Committee sets rules for debate and amendments.

BILL IS:
- placed on committee calendar.
- sent to subcommittee for hearings and revisions.
- reviewed by standing committee, which may make recommendations.

1. Referred to Senate standing committee.
2. Referred to Senate subcommittee.
3. Reported by standing committee.

Floor Action

1. House debates, votes on passage.
2. Bill passes; goes to Senate for approval.
   OR
   A different version passes and goes to conference committee.

1. Senate debates, votes on passage.
2. Bill passes; goes to House for approval.
   OR
   A different version passes and goes to conference committee.

Conference Action

★ Conference committee works out differences and sends identical compromise bill to both chambers for final approval.

House votes on compromise bill.   Senate votes on compromise bill.

✓ VOTE   ✓ VOTE

PASSAGE

President signs bill or allows bill to become law without signing.*   OR   **President vetoes bill.****

* President can keep bill for 10 days and bill becomes law. If Congress adjourns before the 10 days (Sundays excluded), the bill does not become law.

**Congress can override a veto by a 2/3 majority in both chambers. If either fails to override, the bill dies.

LAW

Source:
Congress A to Z,
4th ed., 2003.

CHART SKILLS

The general procedures followed in both the House and the Senate are very similar.

▶ CRITICAL THINKING

1 *Contrasting* How do the steps of committee action in the House differ from those in the Senate?

2 *Making Inferences* Why does the language approved in both the House and Senate have to be the same?

The electronic tally board at the top of the photograph displays the vote cast by each member of the House on the bill that is being considered. The board also tracks the number of votes for and against the bill.

The way the debate is carried out differs in the two chambers. In the House, the Rules Committee sets the terms for debate. It usually puts time limits on the discussion, for example, to speed up action. The Senate, because it is smaller, has fewer rules. Senators can speak for as long as they wish. At times they use this right to **filibuster** against a bill, or to talk a bill to death. In a filibuster, a senator holds the floor by talking for hour after hour. The goal of a filibuster is to delay a vote on a bill until the bill's sponsor is persuaded to withdraw it.

The Senate can end a filibuster if three-fifths of the members vote for **cloture** (KLOH•chuhr). Under this procedure, no senator may speak for more than one hour. A record for the length of a filibuster was set in 1964 as the Senate was debating the Civil Rights Act. Senators opposed to the bill staged a filibuster that lasted for 57 days of the Senate's session. The senators who were in favor of the bill finally were able to gather enough supporters to win a cloture vote and end the debate. Just nine days later, the Senate passed the bill and it became law.

Today senators rarely need to talk for hours. Instead, they vote against cloture resolutions and use other procedures to prevent a majority vote.

Voting and Vetoes

After a bill is debated, it is brought to a vote. Voting in the House is done in one of three ways. The simplest is a **voice vote**. Those in favor of the bill say "Aye" and those against the bill say "No." The Speaker then decides which side has the most

filibuster a tactic for defeating a bill in the Senate by talking until the bill's sponsor withdraws it

cloture a procedure used in the Senate to limit debate on a bill

voice vote a voting method in which those in favor say "Aye" and those against say "No"

votes. A second method is by **standing vote.** Those in favor of a bill stand to be counted. Then, those members of the House who are against it stand to be counted. The third method is a recorded vote, in which votes are recorded electronically.

The Senate also has three methods of voting: a voice vote, a standing vote, and a roll call. In a **roll-call vote,** senators respond "Aye" or "No" as their names are called.

A simple majority of all members present is needed to pass a bill. If a bill passes in one house, it is sent to the other. If either the Senate or the House rejects a bill, it dies.

The Senate and House must pass a bill in exactly the same form. Sometimes each house passes a different version of the same bill. When this happens, a conference committee usually meets. The committee, which has members from each house, works out compromises on the differences and makes changes to the bill. Both the House and the Senate must then either accept the revised bill just as it is or reject it.

After a bill is approved by both houses, it goes to the president. The president may sign the bill and declare it a new law. The president may veto, or refuse to sign, the bill. The president may also do nothing for 10 days. At that point, if Congress is in session, the bill becomes law without the president's signature. If Congress has adjourned, the bill dies. Killing legislation in this indirect way is called a **pocket veto.**

If the president vetoes a bill, Congress has one final chance to save it. Members of Congress can override the veto with a two-thirds vote of each house. This is not an easy task, though. From 1789 through July 2010, Congress overturned only 109 out of 2,560 vetoes.

☑ PROGRESS CHECK

Speculating Why do you think senators attach riders to bills?

standing vote in Congress, when members stand to be counted for a vote on a bill

roll-call vote a voting method in the Senate in which members voice their votes in turn

pocket veto president's power to kill a bill, if Congress is not in session, by not signing it for 10 days

LESSON 4 REVIEW

Review Vocabulary

1. Why might a *special-interest group* work hard to get a *rider* attached to a bill?

2. How does *cloture* affect a *filibuster*?

3. What is the difference between a veto and a *pocket veto*?

Answer the Guiding Questions

4. *Contrasting* What is the difference between public and private bills?

5. *Hypothesizing* Why do you think a bill has to pass both houses of Congress to reach the president's desk?

6. **INFORMATIVE/EXPLANATORY** Suppose you needed to explain how a bill becomes a law to a younger student. Write a short, easy-to-understand paragraph that explains the major steps in the process.

Write your answers on a separate sheet of paper.

❶ Writing Activity

EXPLORING THE ESSENTIAL QUESTION
Why do people create, structure, and change governments?

Sir Winston Churchill, who served as prime minister of the United Kingdom during World War II, stated, "It has been said that democracy is the worst form of government except all the others that have been tried." Think about the complex process by which a bill becomes a law. Then write a paragraph that explains how Churchill's quote could apply to this process.

❷ 21st Century Skills

INVESTIGATING Congress represents the people, yet most Americans rarely see or communicate with their senators and representatives. Modern technology has helped close this gap. The House and the Senate, as well as individual representatives and senators, all have their own Web sites. Visit the sites of the U.S. House of Representatives and the U.S. Senate. Tell the class what each site is like. Describe the type of information you found.

❸ Being an Active Citizen

Do you know who your representatives in Congress are? A member of the House and two senators are there to look out for *your* interests. Find out who they are and some information about them. On a note card, write their names, the political party they belong to, their ideas about government, information about how to contact them, and some important facts about them. Then, the next time a public issue about which you have a strong opinion comes up, contact these representatives and tell them what you think about it!

❹ Understanding Visuals
Congress is an institution of people and of rules. Which house of Congress is this political cartoon about? Which rule does it refer to? What is the cartoonist saying about that rule?

PHOTO: JOHN COLE, and PoliticalCartoons.com

REVIEW THE GUIDING QUESTIONS

Directions: Choose the best answer for each question.

1 Which pairing is correct?

  A. Senate—based on population

  B. Senate—lower house

  C. House—six-year terms

  D. House—435 members

2 Which type of congressional committee is permanent?

  F. standing committee

  G. constitutional committee

  H. select committee

  I. conference committee

3 What does Congress rely on to stretch its powers?

  A. the enumerated powers

  B. the elastic clause

  C. bills of attainder

  D. ex post facto laws

4 Which of these is a major responsibility of members of Congress?

  F. deciding who will receive federal grants

  G. finding jobs for constituents

  H. giving help to constituents

  I. providing analysis for the CBO

5 The House of Representatives passes a bill changing income tax rates. Which statement about the bill *must* be true?

  A. The president will veto the bill.

  B. The bill is a public bill.

  C. The same bill passed the Senate.

  D. The bill will be amended.

6 What happens to a bill in the House after it leaves the committee?

  F. Representatives add riders to the bill.

  G. The House clerk assigns a number to the bill.

  H. The Rules Committee sets the rules for debating the bill.

  I. Representatives vote for cloture to limit debate on the bill.

DBQ **ANALYZING DOCUMENTS**

Directions: Analyze the document and answer the questions that follow.

"Every bill which shall have passed the House of Representatives and the Senate, . . . [and] Every order, resolution, or vote to which the concurrence [agreement] of the Senate and House of Representatives may be necessary (except on a question of adjournment) shall be presented to the President."

—Article 1, Section 7, U.S. Constitution

7 Summarizing Which statement best summarizes this excerpt from the Constitution?

A. The House and Senate have joint committees.

B. The president must review all passed bills.

C. Congress is a bicameral body.

D. Laws must be constitutional.

8 Identifying Which of these actions by Congress would go to the president for signing?

F. a bill passed by the House and defeated in the Senate

G. a bill passed by both houses

H. a vote in the House to change its rules

I. a vote in the Senate to adjourn for a week

SHORT RESPONSE

"[Congress is] functioning the way the founding fathers intended—not very well. . . . They understood that if you move too quickly, our democracy will be less responsible to the majority. I don't think it's the function of Congress to function well. It should drag its heels on the way to decision."

—Barber Benjamin Conable, Jr., U.S. Congressman, 1956–1985

9 What is Conable saying about the way bills become laws?

10 Do you agree with Conable's statement? In a few sentences, explain why or why not.

EXTENDED RESPONSE

11 Argument Which official is more powerful in Congress, the Speaker of the House or the vice president? Why do you think so? Support your opinion with examples.

Need Extra Help?

If You've Missed Question	1	2	3	4	5	6	7	8	9	10	11
Review Lesson	1	1	2	3	4	4	3	3	3	3	2

The Executive Branch

ESSENTIAL QUESTIONS • *What is required of leaders?*
• *Why do nations interact with each other?*

The Story Matters...

In 2008 Americans made history by electing Barack Obama as the 44th president and the first African American to hold the office. In 2012 he was reelected. Before becoming president, Obama served as an Illinois state senator and as a U.S. senator from Illinois.

Obama's father was from Kenya and his mother was American. He grew up in Hawaii and Indonesia. After attending college in California and New York, he worked to improve life in poor Chicago communities. He later became a civil rights lawyer and a law professor before running for the Illinois Senate. When he became president, Obama brought a unique and varied set of skills and experiences to this difficult job.

◀ *As president, President Obama is leader of not only the Democratic Party, but the nation as a whole.*
PHOTO: Brooks Kraft/Corbis

185

Real-Life Civics

▶ **NOW** One of any president's most challenging jobs is the role of commander in chief of our nation's military forces. President Obama entered office with wars raging in Iraq and Afghanistan. He had little prior experience with military affairs. But even presidents with military backgrounds must rely on military analysts and advisers, as well as American uniformed officers, to help shape policy and carry out their orders.

As commander in chief, President Obama travels to war zones to speak with generals and soldiers. At home he visits military hospitals to talk with wounded soldiers and meets with families whose relatives have died while serving in the armed forces.

▷ President Obama receives a fist bump greeting from a U.S. soldier as he visits with troops at Camp Victory in Baghdad, Iraq.

PHOTOS: (l) Pete Souza/White House via Getty Images; (tr) Washington Reviewing the Western Army at Fort Cumberland, Maryland; after 1795 (oil on canvas), Frederick Kemmelmeyer (d.1821) (attr. to)/Metropolitan Museum of Art, New York, USA/Giraudon/The Bridgeman Art Library

President Washington reviews the troops at Fort Cumberland in Maryland.

THEN The nation's first commander in chief was George Washington. For most of his presidency, Washington overcame threats to peace and security through diplomacy and persuasion. In 1789, however, Washington called on several governors to send troops from their state militias. He assembled an army of 13,000 soldiers to stop the Whiskey Rebellion, a protest by Pennsylvania farmers against a tax on whiskey. He took direct command of the troops. The arrival of this force in western Pennsylvania, led by the hero of the American Revolution, quickly ended the uprising. The last president to lead troops in battle was James Madison. His efforts to defend Washington, D.C., were not as successful. British troops burned the capital in 1814. Since then, presidents have focused on setting broad policy goals while leaving the actual fighting to those in the military.

CIVIC LITERACY

★ ★ ★ ★

Analyzing Do you think President Obama has the same goals and duties as commander in chief as did President Washington? Explain.

Your Opinion What do you think is the hardest part of the president's role as commander in chief? Why?

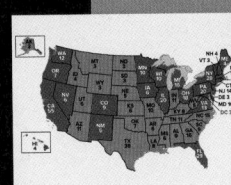  

netw🔵rks

There's More Online!

☑ **GRAPHIC ORGANIZER**
The President:
Requirements
and Characteristics

☑ **MAP**
Presidential Election of 2012

☑ **CHART**
Presidential Succession

Lesson 1

The President and Vice President

ESSENTIAL QUESTION *What is required of leaders?*

IT MATTERS BECAUSE

The president and vice president are the only leaders elected by the entire nation.

Office of the President

GUIDING QUESTION *How does a citizen become president?*

Would you want to be a U.S. president some day? You would have great power—and heavy responsibility. The president heads the executive branch of the national government. He or she bears the chief burden for protecting the nation and its more than 310 million people. Many Americans look to the president as the person to take the lead in solving the nation's problems. Because of the power and global influence of the United States, the president may hold the most important job in the world.

The U.S. Constitution lists only three rules for being president. A president must be at least 35 years old. He or she must be a native-born American citizen. He or she must have lived in the United States for at least 14 years.

Characteristics of Presidents

Almost all our presidents have shared similar characteristics, or features. So far, each has been male. All but one have been Protestant Christians. Most have had a college education. Many were lawyers. Most came from states with large populations.

PHOTO: (tcl) Getty Images; (tcr) Saul Loeb/AFP/Getty Images; (tr) Eric Draper/The White House via Getty Image

Reading **HELP**DESK

Taking Notes: *Describing*

As you read, create a graphic organizer listing the requirements for becoming president and the characteristics of persons who have held the office.

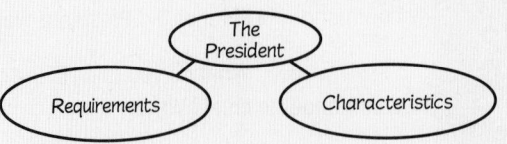

Content Vocabulary
• elector

In recent years, a more diverse group of Americans has run for high office. In 1960 John F. Kennedy became the first Roman Catholic elected as president. In 2008 Barack Obama became the first African American elected as president. In 2012 Republican Mitt Romney became the first Mormon to run as a major-party presidential nominee. Two women have run for vice president on a major-party ticket: Democrat Geraldine Ferraro in 1984 and Republican Sarah Palin in 2008. In 2000 Joseph Lieberman was the first Jewish candidate for vice president.

Electing a President

Every four years, the nation elects a president. The elections take place in years that can be divided by the number four. For example, 2004, 2008, and 2012 are all election years.

It may surprise you to learn that the president is not chosen directly by voters. Instead, he or she is elected by a group called the Electoral College. Each state and the District of Columbia have a certain number of **electors.** The number of electoral votes is equal to the total number of senators and representatives a state has. The District of Columbia also has three of them. As a result, there are 538 members of the Electoral College.

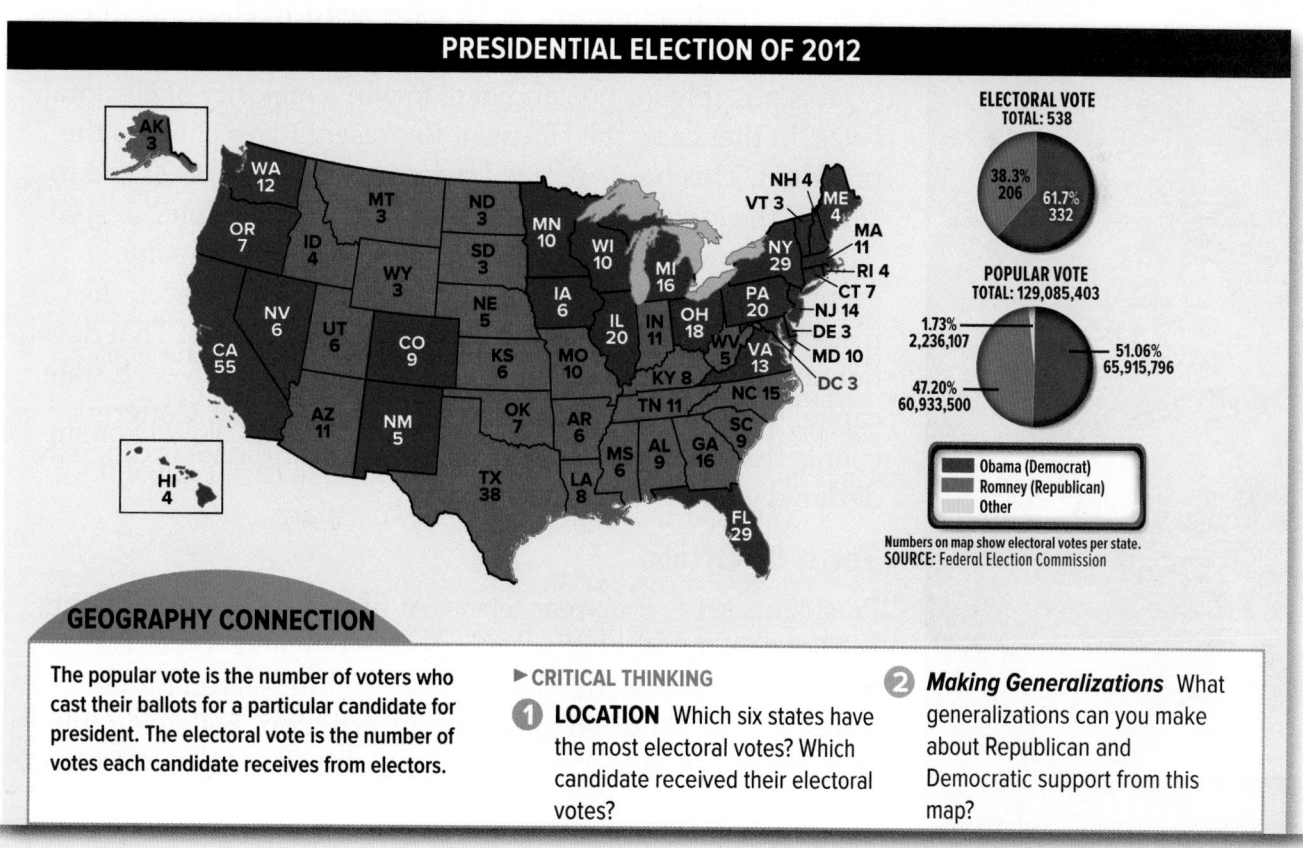

PRESIDENTIAL ELECTION OF 2012

ELECTORAL VOTE
TOTAL: 538
38.3% 206
61.7% 332

POPULAR VOTE
TOTAL: 129,085,403
1.73% 2,236,107
51.06% 65,915,796
47.20% 60,933,500

Obama (Democrat)
Romney (Republican)
Other

Numbers on map show electoral votes per state.
SOURCE: Federal Election Commission

GEOGRAPHY CONNECTION

The popular vote is the number of voters who cast their ballots for a particular candidate for president. The electoral vote is the number of votes each candidate receives from electors.

▶ CRITICAL THINKING

① **LOCATION** Which six states have the most electoral votes? Which candidate received their electoral votes?

② *Making Generalizations* What generalizations can you make about Republican and Democratic support from this map?

elector person appointed to vote in presidential elections for president or vice president

The method for selecting electors varies. In most states, the political parties nominate electors at their state party conventions or by committee. Electors almost always vote for their party's candidate. On the day of the general election in November, the voters in each state choose the electors. In some states, the ballot **displays,** or shows, electors' names below the name of the candidates running for president. In other states, only the names of the candidates appear. A vote for the candidate is really a vote for the electors. The electors actually elect the president.

Most states give their electoral votes using a rule of "winner-take-all." In this method, the candidate who wins the most popular votes in the state gets all of its electoral votes. This is true even if the candidate wins by only a small margin. As a result, a change in a small number of votes can make a big difference. In the election of 2000, for instance, one candidate or the other won six states by fewer than 10,000 votes each. Two of those states, worth 30 electoral votes, were won by fewer than 600 votes.

To win the election, a candidate must win more than half of the 538 electoral votes. This means the winner must have at least 270 votes. In a very close election, a few small states can decide the **outcome,** or result. The 2000 election was won by Republican George W. Bush by only five electoral votes. A different result in any one of 13 states with 10 electoral votes or fewer would have changed the outcome of the election.

It is possible for no candidate to win a majority of electoral votes. In that case, the House of Representatives chooses the president. This has happened twice in history—in 1800 and in 1824. If the House votes, each state has only one vote.

The winning candidate is usually known on the same evening that the popular election takes place. However, the result is not official until the Electoral College votes. That does not take place until December. The electors meet in each state capital to cast their ballots. The following January, Congress counts the electoral votes. At that time, a candidate is officially declared winner of the election.

Term of Office

Presidents serve four-year terms. At first, the Constitution did not limit the number of terms a president could serve. The nation's first president, George Washington, served for two terms. He then refused to run for a third term. Following this example, no president served more than two terms until 1940.

President Franklin Roosevelt waves to onlookers after being sworn in for a third term in office.

▶ CRITICAL THINKING
Assessing Do you think term limits are necessary? Explain your reasoning.

PHOTO: Getty Images

Reading **HELP**DESK

Reading Strategy: *Sequencing*

Understanding the sequence, or order, of events in a presidential election will help you understand the role of the Electoral College. As you read, note the sequence of events, from the nomination of electors to the counting of electoral votes.

Academic Vocabulary

display to show or list
outcome a result or consequence

190 *The Executive Branch*

In 1940, Franklin D. Roosevelt broke with tradition to run for a third term. He won that year and again in 1944. Some people worried that a person could hold too much power if there were no term limits. That concern led to the Twenty-second Amendment in 1951. It limits a president to two elected terms in office. However, a person may serve almost 10 years if he or she becomes president with less than two years remaining in the term of the previous president.

Salary and Benefits

The president is paid $400,000 per year. He or she also receives some money for personal costs and for travel. The president lives and works in the White House. A staff of more than 80 people takes care of the president's family.

The president has use of Camp David. This is an estate in the Catoctin Mountains of Maryland. The complex is about 60 miles northwest of Washington, D.C. Presidents travel with afleet of special cars, helicopters, and airplanes. For long trips, the president uses *Air Force One*, a specially equipped jet.

The Vice President

The vice president is elected with the president. He or she is also chosen by the Electoral College. The rules for becoming vice president are the same as those for the presidency.

The Constitution gives little power to the vice president. Article I states that the vice president shall preside over, or oversee, the Senate. It also says that the vice president can vote in that body in case of a tie. Finally, the vice president becomes president if the president dies, is removed from office, falls seriously ill, or resigns.

President Obama (top) boards the presidential helicopter, *Marine One*. The use of presidential helicopters dates back to 1957. President George W. Bush (inset) spent many days at Camp David, which is managed by the White House Military Office. Presidents often host foreign leaders and hold special meetings at the presidential retreat.

▶ **CRITICAL THINKING**
Making Connections Why do you think presidential transportation and the presidential retreat are the responsibility of the military?

✓ **PROGRESS CHECK**

Identifying How many votes are needed to win in the Electoral College?

Presidential Succession

GUIDING QUESTION *What happens if the president must step down from office?*

In 1841 William Henry Harrison became the first president to die in office. His death raised many questions. The Constitution says that the vice president should take on the "powers and duties" of the presidency. But no one was sure what that meant. Should the vice president remain as vice president but do the president's job? Should the vice president become president? Should a special election be called to elect a new president?

Vice President John Tyler settled these questions. He declared himself president and took the oath of office. Then he served out the rest of Harrison's term. Since Tyler's time, eight other vice presidents have taken over the presidency after a president has either died or **resigned.**

The Presidential Succession Act

In 1947, Congress passed the Presidential Succession Act. It lists the line of succession after the vice president. A line of succession is the order in which officials are expected to succeed, or come next, to an office. The chart shows the current line of succession.

CHART SKILLS

The Presidential Succession Act sets the order of succession for the office of president. The vice president is first in the line of succession.

1 **Identifying** Which two officials come after the vice president in the line of succession?

2 **CRITICAL THINKING**
Making Inferences Why is it important to have the order of succession clearly set?

PRESIDENTIAL SUCCESSION

1 Vice President

2 Speaker of the House

3 President *pro tempore* of the Senate

4 Secretary of State

5 Secretary of the Treasury

6 Secretary of Defense

7 Attorney General

8 Secretary of the Interior

9 Secretary of Agriculture

10 Secretary of Commerce

11 Secretary of Labor

12 Secretary of Health and Human Services

13 Secretary of Housing and Urban Development

14 Secretary of Transportation

15 Secretary of Energy

16 Secretary of Education

17 Secretary of Veterans Affairs

18 Secretary of Homeland Security

Source: Nelson, Ed. *The Presidency A to Z*, 3rd ed. (Washington, D.C.: CQ Press, 2003)

Reading HELPDESK

Academic Vocabulary

resign to give up one's office or position

The Twenty-fifth Amendment

Other questions about presidential succession were answered by the Twenty-fifth Amendment. It was ratified in 1967. The Twenty-fifth Amendment makes it clear that if the president dies or leaves office, the vice president becomes president. It goes further, though. In the past, when a vice president became president, the office of vice president was left empty. This amendment changed that. It said that the new president should choose a new vice president with the help of Congress. The process has two steps. First, the new president names someone to the office. Second, both the Senate and the House of Representatives must then vote to approve this choice.

This part of the Twenty-fifth Amendment has been used twice. In 1973 Vice President Spiro Agnew resigned. President Richard Nixon named Gerald Ford of Michigan to replace him. Congress approved the choice, and Ford became vice president. The next year, Nixon resigned from office, making Ford president. That left the vice presidency vacant again. Ford named Nelson A. Rockefeller of New York to be his vice president. He, too, was approved by the House and the Senate.

The Twenty-fifth Amendment made another important change. It gives the vice president a role in deciding whether a president is disabled and cannot do the job. If that occurs, the vice president serves as acting president until the president is able to go back to work. This feature has been used once in history. In 1985 President Ronald Reagan needed to have some surgery. Before he did, he told Congress that he would be unable to carry out his duties during the surgery. As a result, Vice President George H. W. Bush served as acting president for about eight hours.

☑ PROGRESS CHECK

Summarizing What problem with the vice presidency was the Twenty-fifth Amendment meant to solve?

The "Why It Matters" sidebar:

Why It MATTERS

Successsion Rules

Sometimes leaders in government or other organizations leave office unexpectedly. Succession rules help to keep order. If you belong to any clubs or organizations, find out if they have an established order of succession.

LESSON 1 REVIEW

Review Vocabulary

1. Write a sentence that explains the role of *electors* in choosing the president.

Answer the Guiding Questions

2. *Explaining* What three requirements must a person meet to become president or vice president of the United States?

3. *Summarizing* What role is given to the vice president in the constitution?

4. *Speculating* For what reasons might the Twenty-fifth Amendment be used to replace a president?

5. **ARGUMENT** Which characteristic do you think is most important in a president? Is it the president's profession, education, religion, or some other characteristic? Explain your reasoning in a paragraph.

netw⦿rks
There's More Online!

☑ **GRAPHIC ORGANIZER**
Roles of the President

☑ **CHART**
Fun Facts About the
State of the Union

☑ **SLIDESHOW**
Executive Privilege

Lesson 2
The President's Powers and Roles

ESSENTIAL QUESTION *What is required of leaders?*

IT MATTERS BECAUSE
The president has many important duties that affect all Americans.

Presidential Powers

GUIDING QUESTION *What are the duties of the president?*

Fewer than 50 men have known what it feels like to be president of the United States. Some former presidents' thoughts are revealing.

PRIMARY SOURCE

❝The presidency has made every man who occupied it, no matter how small, bigger than he was; and no matter how big, not big enough for its demands.❞
—Lyndon B. Johnson

The president is the head of just one of the three branches of government. However, he or she is one of only two officials in the federal government elected by the entire nation. The other official is the vice president. As a result, the president is a symbol of both the federal government and the entire nation.

The president is the most powerful public official in the United States. The U.S. Constitution is the basis of the president's power. Article II says that "Executive Power shall be invested in a President." Thus, the president's main job is to execute, or carry out, the laws passed by Congress.

Reading HELPDESK

Taking Notes: *Categorizing*

Create a graphic organizer like the one shown. As you read this lesson, fill it out with roles of the president.

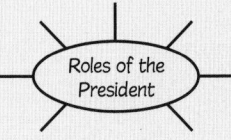
Roles of the President

Content Vocabulary
- **executive order**
- **pardon**
- **reprieve**
- **amnesty**
- **ambassador**

Academic Vocabulary
require to have a need for, or to order

Beyond the responsibility to carry out the laws, the Constitution gives the president several specific powers:

- He or she can veto, or reject, bills passed in Congress.
- He or she can call Congress into special session.
- He or she serves as commander in chief of the armed forces.
- He or she receives leaders and other officials of foreign countries.
- He or she can make treaties with other countries, although they need approval by the Senate.
- He or she names the heads of executive agencies, judges of the federal court, ambassadors, and other top government officials. These appointments need Senate approval.
- He or she can pardon or reduce the penalties against people convicted of federal crimes.

The Constitution **requires,** or calls for, the president to tell Congress about the "state of the union." Each year, then, the president gives the State of the Union address. In this speech, the president discusses the nation's most important issues and his or her plans to address them.

✔ PROGRESS CHECK

Identifying What are the president's powers as stated in the Constitution?

President Obama (center), like presidents before him, delivered his first State of the Union address shortly after taking office. George Washington delivered the very first State of the Union address, then called the Annual Message.

► CRITICAL THINKING
Finding the Main Idea What do you think is the purpose of the State of the Union address?

Presidential Roles

GUIDING QUESTION *What roles does the president have?*

Under the Constitution, the president is responsible for carrying out the duties of the executive branch. As the nation has grown, the president has taken on other roles.

Chief Executive

The president's most important job is to carry out the nation's laws. To do this, the president is in charge of 15 cabinet departments and many agencies. The president names people to head the departments and the agencies. The Senate has to approve all of these choices. About 3 million workers—not counting people in the armed forces—help carry out this work.

One tool presidents use to carry out the law is the executive order. An **executive order** is a rule or command the president gives out that has the same power and force as a law. Presidents use executive orders to spell out details of the policies set by Congress. They are part of the president's duty to "take care that the laws are faithfully executed." These orders also make it possible for presidents to act quickly when they must do so.

Many executive orders concern the everyday work of the executive branch. Some have had a much greater effect, though. In 1948, for example, President Harry S. Truman used an executive order to end the separation of races in the military. This order gave Americans of all races the same opportunity to serve in the armed forces.

Another power of the chief executive is to name people to serve as justices of the Supreme Court and judges of other federal courts. Supreme Court justices decide whether a law follows the Constitution or not. This power is very important. In addition, once appointed, Supreme Court justices serve for life. Thus, most presidents try to name justices who share views close to their own. That way, they can ensure that their views continue to influence government long after they leave office.

The Constitution also gives the president the power to grant pardons. A **pardon** declares forgiveness and freedom from punishment. The president may also issue a **reprieve.** This order delays punishing a person until a higher court can hear the case. The president can also grant **amnesty,** a pardon for a large group of people.

In 1974 President Ford granted a pardon to former president Nixon, who resigned from office following a political scandal. Ford felt the pardon was necessary to spare the nation further turmoil.

▶ **CRITICAL THINKING**
Making Connections Why is the power to pardon given to the president and not to Congress?

PHOTO: Bettmann/Corbis

Reading HELPDESK

executive order a rule or command the president gives out that has the force of law

pardon a declaration of forgiveness and freedom from punishment

reprieve an order to delay a person's punishment until a higher court can hear the case

amnesty a pardon to a group of people

ambassador an official representative of a country's government

PHOTO: DMITRY ASTAKHOV/AFP/Getty Images

Chief Diplomat

The president leads the foreign policy of the United States. In this role, the president decides how the United States acts toward other countries. This role includes naming people to serve as **ambassadors.** These officials represent the United States government in other nations.

Head of State

The president is the living symbol of the nation. In this role, he or she tries to build goodwill with other countries by greeting their leaders when they visit the United States. The president also represents all Americans at important ceremonies. For example, the president awards medals to the country's heroes and places a wreath at Memorial Day ceremonies at Arlington National Cemetery.

Commander in Chief

Under the Constitution, the president is commander in chief of the nation's armed forces. This allows presidents to back up foreign policy decisions with force when they need to. The president and Congress share the power to make war. Congress has the power to declare war. Yet, only the president can order troops into battle. The commanders of the army, navy, air force, marines, and coast guard all follow the orders of the president.

Congress has declared war just five times. Presidents, however, have sent troops into action more than 150 times. For example, Congress never declared war on Iraq. Nonetheless, American troops invaded that nation in 2003 on orders of President George W. Bush.

In 1973, after the Vietnam War, Congress passed the War Powers Resolution. This law says that the president must let Congress know within 48 hours when troops are sent into battle.

The troops must be brought home after 60 days unless Congress approves their use or declares war. Since the law's passage, however, troops have never been recalled due to congressional disapproval, nor has war been declared.

Legislative Leader

Only members of Congress can introduce bills. But Congress expects the president to propose new laws. Every president has goals that include new laws he or she wants Congress to pass. The president makes speeches to build support for these goals. He or she also meets with key senators and representatives. The president tries to convince them to support the proposed laws.

The president and Congress often disagree over what laws Congress should pass. One reason is that the president represents the whole nation, while members of Congress represent only their states or districts.

Economic Leader

Every president tries to help the country's economy prosper. Voters expect the president to deal with such problems as lack of jobs, rising prices, and high taxes. One key task for the president each year is to plan the federal government's budget. The president meets with budget officials. Together, they decide what programs to support and what programs to cut back. Budget decisions have a great effect on the nation's economy.

Party Leader

The president is generally regarded as the leader of his or her political party. The president gives speeches to help fellow party members who are running for office as members of Congress, governors, and mayors. The president also helps the party to raise money.

✔ **PROGRESS CHECK**

Explaining Why is the War Powers Resolution important?

LESSON 2 REVIEW

Review Vocabulary

1. Write a sentence comparing an *executive order* to a law.

2. Use the terms *pardon*, *reprieve*, and *amnesty* in a paragraph.

Answer the Guiding Questions

3. *Summarizing* What influence does the president have over Congress?

4. *Analyzing* How is the president's role as chief diplomat connected with the roles of head of state and commander in chief?

5. **ARGUMENT** Many people consider carrying out the nation's laws to be the president's most important job. If you agree, explain why in a paragraph. If you do not agree, explain which role you think is the president's most important job.

United States v. Nixon, 1974

Presidents have claimed a right to keep discussions with their aides private. Under what circumstances, if any, must the courts honor that claim?

President Richard M. Nixon

Background of the Case

In 1972, President Richard Nixon was trying to win reelection. One of his campaign workers hired some men to break into the offices of the Democratic Party in Washington, D.C. The offices were in a group of buildings called the Watergate. The break-in and what followed became known as the Watergate scandal.

The Senate began to investigate the crime. So did a special prosecutor working in the Justice Department. They learned that some officials in the White House might have been involved. They also learned that the president had a taping system in his White House office. With this system, he had taped his conversations with aides. They thought that the tapes would show what the president and his aides had known about the crime. When they asked for the tapes, though, the president refused to release them. He based his claim on what he called *executive privilege*. This is the right of a president to keep his conversations private.

The special prosecutor went to court, and a federal judge ordered President Nixon to turn over the tapes. Nixon refused. The case was appealed to the Supreme Court.

The Decision

Nixon's lawyers argued that executive privilege applied. They said presidents had to be able to protect the privacy of their conversations with top aides. The Court rejected this argument. Chief Justice Warren Burger wrote the decision. He said that the situation might be different if holding back the tapes was to protect "military, diplomatic or sensitive national security secrets." Claiming

executive privilege for general discussions, though, "would upset the constitutional balance of a 'workable government.'"

Eight justices took part in the decision. They all agreed that the president had to turn over the tapes. Meanwhile, the House of Representatives had begun the process for impeaching Nixon. The president finally released the tapes, which revealed his role in the cover-up. He lost most of his remaining support in Congress. Four days later, he resigned from the office of president.

Why It Matters

United States v. *Nixon* made it clear that in the American system of government, even the most powerful person, the president, is not above the law and beyond the power of the courts.

Analyzing the Case

1. **Explaining** What reason did Nixon give to support his claim of executive privilege?

2. **Analyzing** What is your opinion of the Court's decision? Do you agree or disagree that presidents should have a right of executive privilege?

networks

There's More Online!

☑ **GRAPHIC ORGANIZER**
Foreign Policy Goals
and Tools

☑ **POLITICAL CARTOON**
Tightening the Belt

Lesson 3
Making Foreign Policy

ESSENTIAL QUESTIONS • *What is required of leaders?*
• *Why do nations interact with each other?*

IT MATTERS BECAUSE
The president makes the key decisions about our relations with other countries.

The President and Foreign Policy

GUIDING QUESTION *What are the goals of foreign policy?*

A nation's plan for dealing with other nations is called its **foreign policy.** In making this policy, presidents hope to achieve several goals.

The main goal of American foreign policy is **national security.** This means the ability to keep the country safe from attack or harm. No government can meet other goals, such as educating children, if the nation is under attack.

Another major goal is to build trade with other nations. Trade is important to a strong economy. It creates markets for American products. It also provides jobs for American workers.

A third goal is to promote world peace. Any war, even one far away, can disrupt trade and put the nation's safety at risk. When other nations are at peace, there is less risk that the United States will be drawn into war.

A fourth goal of foreign policy is to advance democracy around the world. Promoting democracy and human rights in other countries encourages peace. This also helps protect our own national security.

PHOTO: (tl) Eric Draper/White House/Getty Images; (tc) Fischer - Ed/Cartoonstock; (tr) Bullit Marquez/AP Photo

---

Reading **HELP**DESK

Taking Notes: *Categorizing*

As you read, create a graphic organizer like this one to show the president's foreign policy goals and tools.

Foreign Policy Goals	Foreign Policy Tools

Content Vocabulary

- **foreign policy**
- **national security**
- **treaty**
- **executive agreement**
- **trade sanctions**
- **embargo**

The Foreign Policy Team

The president leads the way in trying to achieve these goals. He or she does not work alone, though. The president is helped by close aides in the White House like the National Security Advisor. This official studies foreign policy questions. Then he or she gives advice to the president.

A large team also works on foreign policy. The State Department, the Defense Department, and the National Security Council are all part of this team. Officials in these organizations give their ideas to the president. The Office of the Director of National Intelligence (ODNI) and Central Intelligence Agency (CIA) also serve on this team. They provide important background information.

In the end, though, the president must make the final decisions. President Harry S. Truman noted,

PRIMARY SOURCE

❝No one who has not had the responsibility can really understand what it is like to be President, not even his closest aides. . . . [H]e is never allowed to forget that he is President.❞

—Harry S. Truman

Once the president decides on a policy, this foreign policy team works to carry it out.

President George Bush (center) meets with the National Security Council in September 2001. The National Security Council includes senior national security advisers and cabinet officials who help the president manage national security and foreign policy matters.

▶ **CRITICAL THINKING**
Drawing Conclusions Why do you think the president has both military and nonmilitary foreign policy advisers?

foreign policy a nation's overall plan for dealing with other nations

national security the ability to keep the country safe from attack or harm

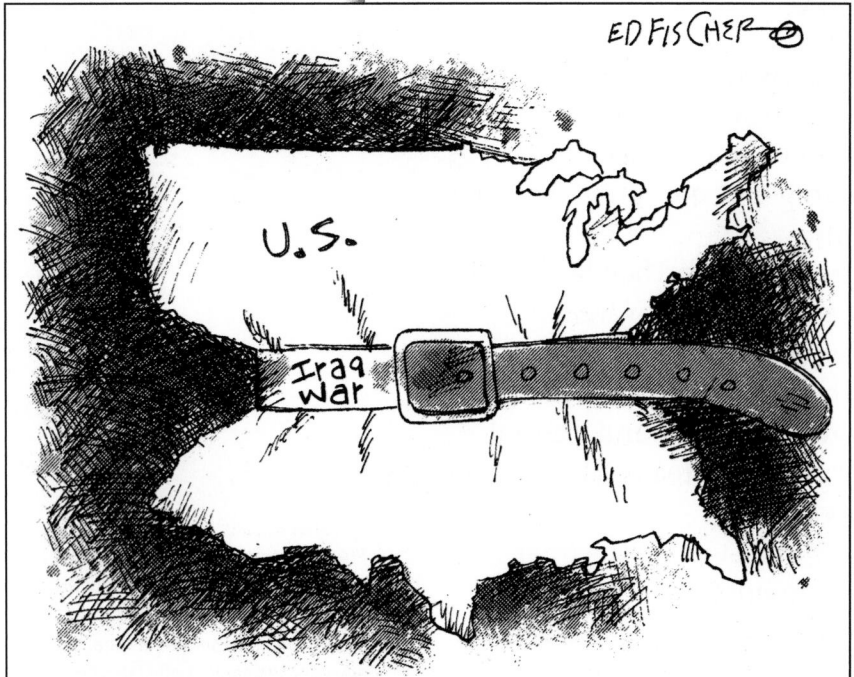

CARTOON: Fischer - Ed/Cartoonstock

If the president chooses to send troops into military conflict, such as in Iraq, it can greatly increase government spending on defense.

▶ CRITICAL THINKING

Analyzing What does this cartoon say about how the cost of a military action affects spending for other national priorities? Which branch makes decisions about defense spending?

Congress Versus the President

As you read in Lesson 2, the president is the commander in chief. Congress has certain war powers, too. Only it can declare war. It can stop the president from using the armed forces in certain ways. Finally, Congress alone can spend—or hold back—money for defense.

The Constitution does not clearly state how the legislative and the executive branches should work together in this area. As a result, Congress and the president have often competed over who controls the war powers.

One branch or the other has had more control over the war powers at different times. In the first 20 years or so after World War II, presidents had more power in this area. Congress lost much of its control. Then, near the end of the Vietnam conflict, Congress took back some of its war powers. The situation has changed again in recent years. With the war on terrorism, the balance of control has moved back again toward the presidency.

✓ PROGRESS CHECK

Identifying What executive agencies help the president in making and carrying out foreign policy?

The Tools of Foreign Policy

GUIDING QUESTION *What are the tools the president uses to carry out U.S. foreign policy?*

The president and Congress carry out foreign policy in several ways. These **methods,** or procedures, include reaching agreements with other countries and naming ambassadors. Other methods include giving foreign aid, making trade policy, and, when needed, using the military.

Reading HELPDESK

Academic Vocabulary

method a procedure or process of doing something

treaty a formal agreement between the governments of two or more countries

executive agreement an agreement between the president and the leader of another country

Treaties and Executive Agreements

Formal agreements between the governments of two or more countries are called **treaties.** Some treaties concern defense. One of the most important is the treaty that formed the North Atlantic Treaty Organization (NATO). In this pact, the United States, Canada, and many nations in Western Europe promised to defend one another if attacked.

The Senate must approve any treaty by a two-thirds vote. The president can work around the Senate by making an **executive agreement.** This is an agreement between the president and the leader of another country. Many of these agreements deal with matters like trade. Some are about having the armed forces of nations work together.

Appointing Ambassadors

The president appoints about 150 ambassadors. Each of them must be confirmed by the Senate. Ambassadors represent our nation to other nations. They are sent only to those countries that have governments whose right to exist we recognize, or accept. Sometimes the foreign policy team thinks that the government of a certain country has gained power illegally. In that case, the president can refuse to recognize it.

Foreign Aid

Foreign aid is a powerful tool to help carry out foreign policy. Foreign aid consists of money, food, military help, or other supplies given to other countries. One of this nation's greatest examples of foreign aid was the Marshall Plan. The program helped Western Europe rebuild after World War II.

In late 2004, a tsunami killed more than 130,000 people in Indonesia. In this photo, U.S. Navy personnel bring in food, water, and other aid to the stricken region. Since 1950 the United States has supported Indonesia's development. The United States considers the Southeast Asian nation important to regional stability.

▶ CRITICAL THINKING
Drawing Inferences Why do you think supporting development and democracy in foreign nations is part of U.S. national security strategies?

PHOTO: Bullit Marquez/AP Photo

Recognize Quality Sources

Search the Web for information about NAFTA. Identify at least six sources. Evaluate each source by answering questions such as Who is the author of the site? Is the information accurate? Is the site up-to-date? Does the site show bias?

trade sanction an effort to punish another nation by imposing trade barriers

embargo an agreement among a group of nations that prohibits them all from trading with a target nation

Academic Vocabulary

target selected person or thing to receive an action

International Trade

The president has the power to make economic agreements with other nations. These agreements cover what products may be traded and the rules for this trade.

Sometimes the president chooses to block trade with a nation to try to convince it to change its policies. One way to block trade is to use **trade sanctions.** These trade barriers stop or slow trade with another nation in order to punish it. One kind of sanction is an **embargo.** This is an agreement by a group of nations to stop trading with a **target** nation.

Congress plays a role in other economic areas. For instance, it sets tariffs. These are taxes on goods that are imported, or bought from other countries. Congress also must approve the treaties that allow the United States to join trade groups. The members of these groups agree to trade with one another without barriers. They include the North American Free Trade Agreement (NAFTA) and the World Trade Organization (WTO).

Military Force

As commander in chief, presidents sometimes decide they must use the armed forces to carry out a foreign policy decision. Many times they have sent troops to trouble spots around the world. This has been done even when Congress has not declared war.

The president's war powers are an important tool of foreign policy. President Bill Clinton called for attacks on bases used by terrorists in 1998. In 2003 President George W. Bush ordered American armed forces to invade Iraq and remove that nation's dictator, Saddam Hussein. In 2009 President Barack Obama increased the number of U.S. troops in Afghanistan.

✓ PROGRESS CHECK

Describing What is an executive agreement?

LESSON 3 REVIEW

Review Vocabulary

1. Write a sentence explaining how *trade sanctions* and *embargoes* are used.

2. Write a sentence using two of these terms: *foreign policy, national security, treaty.*

Answer the Guiding Questions

3. *Identifying* What are the four main goals of American foreign policy?

4. *Making Connections* What foreign policy tools does the president have that could be used to deal with international terrorism?

5. **ARGUMENT** Which goal of American foreign policy do you think is most important? Write a paragraph explaining why.

netw⊙rks

There's More Online!

☑ **GRAPHIC ORGANIZER**
Federal Bureaucracy

☑ **CHARTS**
Selected Executive Offices
of the President

The President's Cabinet

Lesson 4
How the Executive Branch Works

PHOTO: (tl) Jeff Chiu/AP Photo; (tc) Gene Blevins/LA Daily News/Corbis; (tr) NASA

ESSENTIAL QUESTION *What is required of leaders?*

IT MATTERS BECAUSE
Decisions made by people working in the executive branch affect many areas of life.

Executive Office Agencies

GUIDING QUESTION *What offices make up the Executive Office of the President?*

In 1801 President Thomas Jefferson had a tiny staff. Only a few advisers, a messenger, and a part-time secretary helped him. Today thousands of experts, advisers, secretaries, and clerks assist the president. Most of these people work in the Executive Office of the President (EOP). They are all part of what is called the president's administration.

The EOP was set up under Franklin D. Roosevelt in 1939. Its purpose was to help the president do his job. The office has grown since its beginning. Today it has nearly 2,000 employees. Its budget is around $400 million. The president's staff has come a long way.

The White House Office

The EOP is overseen by the president's chief of staff. This person takes care of the president's schedules. The chief of staff also decides who is allowed to meet with the president. The chief of staff, along with the deputy chiefs of staff and senior advisers, serve as the president's closest advisers.

Reading HELPDESK

Taking Notes: *Summarizing*

As you read, create a chart to summarize the functions of the federal agencies.

Agency Type	Function
Executive agencies	
Government corporations	
Regulatory commissions	

Content Vocabulary

- **cabinet**
- **federal bureaucracy**
- **executive agency**
- **government corporation**
- **regulatory commission**
- **political appointee**

The Executive Office of the President assists the president in both domestic and foreign matters.

▶ **CRITICAL THINKING**

1 *Making Inferences* Which unit of the EOP do you think crafts policy to combat global warming?

2 *Theorizing* Why do you think the size of the EOP has grown over the years?

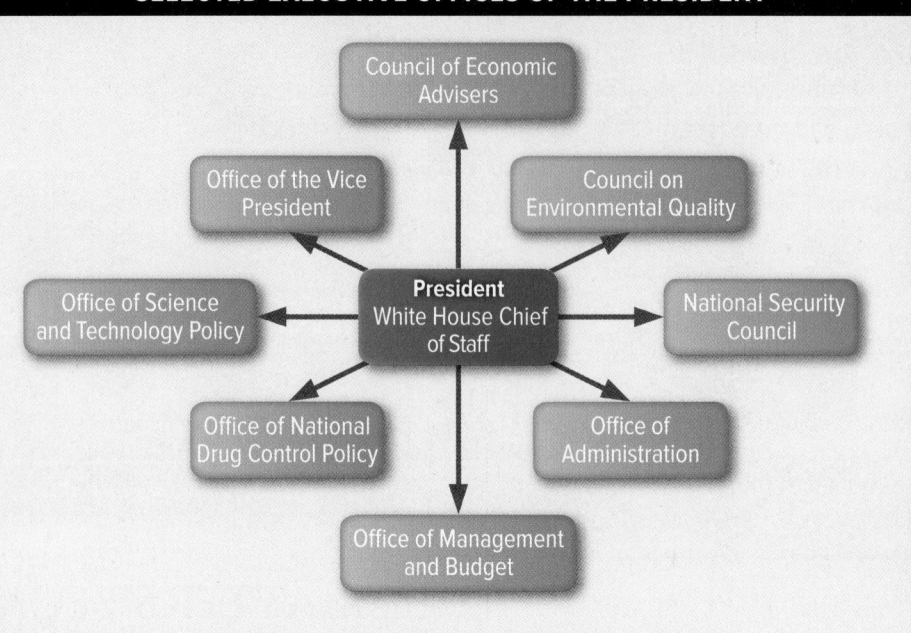

Council of Economic Advisers

Office of the Vice President

Council on Environmental Quality

Office of Science and Technology Policy

President
White House Chief of Staff

National Security Council

Office of National Drug Control Policy

Office of Administration

Office of Management and Budget

The heart of the EOP, however, is the White House Office. This group is made up of about 500 people who work directly for the president. Their many tasks include helping the president develop policy and communicate with Congress and the general public.

Office of Management and Budget

The Office of Management and Budget (OMB) prepares the federal budget. The budget shows the president's spending plans for the coming year. It also monitors, or oversees, spending in all the agencies of the executive branch. The director of the OMB works closely with the president.

National Security Council

The National Security Council (NSC) advises the president on matters of national security. The NSC includes the vice president, the secretaries of state and defense, and the chairperson of the Joint Chiefs of Staff. The Joint Chiefs of Staff are the top commanders from the four parts of the armed services. The Director of National Intelligence also serves on the NSC. Intelligence is information about the actions and plans of other governments. The National Security Advisor, appointed by the president, heads the NSC.

Reading **HELP**DESK

Content Vocabulary (cont.)

- civil service system
- spoils system
- merit system

cabinet a group of advisers to the president that includes the heads of 15 top-level executive departments

Academic Vocabulary

role the job or function of a person or thing

Council of Economic Advisers

The Council of Economic Advisers (CEA) helps the president carry out the **role,** or job, of economic leader. The president names people to the CEA, but the Senate must approve them. The CEA gives advice on economic policy. It addresses such matters as job growth, prices, and trade.

✓ PROGRESS CHECK

Identifying Which officials make up the National Security Council?

The President's Cabinet

GUIDING QUESTION *What role does the president's cabinet play in the government?*

The EOP is only a small part of the president's administration. Thousands more people work in 15 large units called departments. The heads of those departments form the group of presidential advisers known as the **cabinet**. The head of the Department of Justice is called the attorney general. All other department heads are called secretaries. As you can see from the chart, the 15 departments work in many different areas.

21ˢᵗ Century
SKILLS

Using Tables and Charts

Review the chart on the president's cabinet. How many departments were created in the past 50 years as compared to all the previous years? What conclusions can you draw from this information? Discuss your conclusions with a partner.

THE PRESIDENT'S CABINET

Department	Role
Department of State (1789)	Plans and carries out the nation's foreign policy
Department of the Treasury (1789)	Collects, borrows, spends, and prints money
Department of Defense (1789 as War Department; renamed in 1949)	Manages the armed forces
Department of Justice (1870)	Responsible for all aspects of law enforcement
Department of the Interior (1849)	Manages and protects nation's public lands and natural resources
Department of Agriculture (1889)	Assists farmers and consumers of farm products
Department of Commerce (1903)	Supervises trade, promotes U.S. business, tourism
Department of Labor (1913)	Deals with working conditions, wages of U.S. workers
Department of Health and Human Services (1953)	Works for the well-being and health of all Americans
Department of Housing and Urban Development (1965)	Deals with the special needs and problems of cities
Department of Transportation (1966)	Manages nation's highways, railroads, airlines, and sea traffic
Department of Energy (1977)	Directs overall energy plan for the nation
Department of Education (1979)	Provides advice and funding for schools
Department of Veterans Affairs (1989)	Directs services for armed forces veterans
Department of Homeland Security (2002)	Oversees America's defenses against terrorist attacks

CHART SKILLS

The president's cabinet includes the heads of the executive branch departments. The year next to the department name shows when the department was first formed.

1 *Identifying* Which cabinet departments are the oldest? The newest?

2 CRITICAL THINKING

Making Inferences What departments would be involved in a treaty about the trade of foods grown on American farms?

A Transportation Safety Administration (TSA) worker screens an airline traveler. The TSA is a division of the Department of Homeland Security. It is responsible for the safety of the nation's transportation systems.

▶ CRITICAL THINKING
Drawing Conclusions Why do you think that it is the responsibility of the federal government to oversee transportation safety?

Article II, Section 2, of the Constitution mentions that the president may require "in writing" the opinion of the heads of each of the executive departments "upon any Subject relating to the Duties of their respective Offices." It does not, however, specifically mention the cabinet. Meeting with a cabinet is tradition, or custom. The tradition began with President George Washington. He met regularly with the heads of the first four departments. These were the attorney general and the secretaries of state, war, and the treasury. Later presidents followed this example. As more executive departments were created over the years, the cabinet grew.

Cabinet Responsibilities

Cabinet members give the president advice on matters that touch the departments they lead. The secretary of agriculture, for example, works with the president on issues that have an effect on farmers. Cabinet members also carry out the president's plans within their departments. Suppose that the president wants to start new programs for job training. The secretary of labor will be given the task of putting that plan into action.

The president decides when the cabinet is to meet. The president may also ask the vice president and other top aides to join meetings of the cabinet. Meetings may be held as often as once a week or hardly at all. Many presidents have not relied heavily on their cabinets. They often have felt free to ignore cabinet advice. They expect the department heads to carry out their policies, though.

Cabinet members spend most of their time directing the activities in their departments. To hold their posts, the department heads must be approved by the Senate.

Department of Homeland Security

In 2002, President Bush signed the Homeland Security Act. That law set up the new Department of Homeland Security. The task of this department is to protect the nation from attacks by terrorists. Part of that work is to gather information about terrorists and their plans.

This was the first new department set up since 1989. That year, the Department of Veterans Affairs was formed. It runs programs for former members of the armed forces.

PHOTO: Jeff Chiu/AP Photo

Reading HELPDESK

federal bureaucracy agencies and the employees of the executive branch of government

Academic Vocabulary
specific falling into a particular category

The Vice President

For many years, presidents gave little authority to their vice presidents. That has changed, though, in recent times. Vice President Al Gore, for example, served as a close adviser to President Bill Clinton about the environment. Vice President Dick Cheney advised President George W. Bush on foreign policy. Under President Obama, Vice President Joseph Biden led a team that tried to find ways to help families have a better standard of living.

✓ PROGRESS CHECK

Stating When does the cabinet meet?

The Federal Bureaucracy

GUIDING QUESTION *What is the federal bureaucracy?*

The executive branch also has hundreds of agencies. They deal with everything from running the space program to deciding what can be used to make hot dogs. Together, the agencies and employees of the executive branch are called the **federal bureaucracy** (byu•RAH•kruh•see). About 3 million people work in the executive branch.

These workers do three basic kinds of tasks. Through these tasks, they help make government policy.

First, agencies write rules that put laws passed by Congress into practice. Laws are often written in very general terms. The agencies have to turn those guidelines into **specific** rules. That way, people and businesses can know what to do to follow the law.

21st Century SKILLS

Researching on the Internet

Visit the White House Web site. Search for information about the current vice president of the United States. Find out what specific responsibilities the current vice president has, such as issues in which he or she is very active. Write a paragraph summarizing your findings.

This fire fighter battles a wildfire in Angeles National Forest in California. The Forest Service manages 193 million acres of national forests and grasslands.

▶ CRITICAL THINKING
Making Connections What role does Congress have in operating the Forest Service?

In this 2007 photograph, space shuttle *Discovery* heads for the *International Space Station*. NASA ended its 30-year-old space shuttle program in 2011. The government plans to rely on commercial spacecraft for future missions.

▶ CRITICAL THINKING
Making Inferences What conclusions can you draw from this change in procedure?

Second, departments and agencies carry out the day-to-day activities of the federal government. Some workers deliver the mail, some collect taxes, and some take care of national parks. Others perform thousands of other services.

Third, federal agencies oversee certain activities. For example, they watch banks to make sure that they obey the rules about banking. They decide if products are safe to use. They establish rules that protect our health and the environment. Agencies cannot simply take this work on for themselves. Congress must pass a law to give them the power to do their work.

Independent Agencies

The executive branch has many independent agencies. They are called independent because they are not part of a cabinet department. These agencies can be grouped into three types: executive agencies, government corporations, and regulatory commissions.

Executive agencies are independent agencies that deal with certain specific areas within the government. The National Aeronautics and Space Administration (NASA), for example, runs the space program. The Central Intelligence Agency (CIA) provides policy makers with intelligence information. The Environmental Protection Agency (EPA) establishes and enforces regulations that protect human health and the environment.

Some agencies are **government corporations.** These are businesses that are owned by the government. Like any business, they provide goods or services and charge people to buy those goods or services. The difference is that these corporations are not supposed to make a profit. The United States Postal Service is one example. The Tennessee Valley Authority is another. It sells energy to people living in a certain part of the country.

The job of **regulatory commissions** is to protect the public. They make and enforce rules that an industry or group must follow. For instance, the Federal Communications Commission (FCC) makes rules for television and radio stations. The U.S. Consumer Product Safety Commission establishes safety standards for thousands of types of consumer products. Unlike the other two types of independent agencies, regulatory commissions do not report to the president. The president does name the people who head these commissions. He or she cannot fire them, though. Only Congress can remove them.

PHOTO: NASA

Reading **HELP**DESK

executive agency
independent agency that deals with certain specific areas within the government

government corporation
a business owned and operated by the federal government

regulatory commission
independent agency created by Congress that can make rules concerning certain activities and bring violators to court

Government Workers

The top jobs in a department or agency usually go to **political appointees.** These are people chosen by the president. Some are picked because they have experience in the work the department does. Some are named because they supported the president during the election. People in these jobs usually leave office when the president does.

About 90 percent of those who work in the federal government are civil service workers. Unlike political appointees, civil service workers usually have permanent jobs. These people might be clerks or lawyers or park rangers. They are hired through the **civil service system.** This is the practice of hiring government workers on the basis of open, competitive examinations and proven ability.

Before 1883, many federal jobs fell under the **spoils system.** In this practice, people won government jobs as a reward for political support. Each new president fired many government workers and replaced them with supporters. The idea was, "To the victor belong the spoils [jobs]."

Under the spoils system, appointees were not always qualified to perform their jobs. In response, Congress passed the Civil Service Reform Act of 1883. That law created the civil service system. It also placed limits on the number of jobs a new president could give to friends and backers.

The Office of Personnel Management (OPM) directs the civil service system today. It sets standards for federal jobs. It also gives tough tests to people who want those jobs. The civil service system is a **merit system.** Government officials hire new workers from lists of people who have passed the tests or otherwise met civil service standards.

✓ PROGRESS CHECK

Describing Which jobs go to political appointees today?

political appointee a person appointed to a federal position by the president

civil service system the practice of hiring government workers on the basis of open, competitive examinations and merit

spoils system rewarding people with government jobs on the basis of their political support

merit system hiring people into government jobs on the basis of their qualifications

LESSON 4 REVIEW

Review Vocabulary

1. What is the difference between an *executive agency* and a *regulatory commission*?

2. How are the *civil service system* and the *merit system* connected?

Answer the Guiding Questions

3. ***Explaining*** Why is the work of the Office of Management and Budget so important?

4. ***Identifying*** What are the main functions of the members of the cabinet?

5. ***Explaining*** How does a government corporation operate?

6. **ARGUMENT** Federal agencies enforce thousands of regulations that affect our lives. Some people say the government plays too large a role in society. Write a paragraph on whether you agree with this viewpoint and why.

Write your answers on a separate sheet of paper.

1 Writing Activity

EXPLORING THE ESSENTIAL QUESTION

What is required of leaders?

In this chapter you learned about the many roles, responsibilities, and duties of the president. Think about what personal characteristics and background (such as education and job experience) a person would need to be a great president. Make two lists—one of desired characteristics and another of background factors. Then use your list to poll people you know to find out which characteristic and which background factor they think is most important. Summarize your findings in a short report about your poll.

2 21st Century Skills

INFORMATION LITERACY The federal bureaucracy consists of hundreds of departments, agencies, bureaus, offices, services, boards, and commissions that affect many areas of American life. Find one that interests you and learn more about it. Visit its Web site to learn how it is organized, what its role is, how it does its job, and how its work affects Americans. Organize what you learn in a written report, an oral report, a visual aid, or a slide-show presentation for the class.

3 Being an Active Citizen

Identify a situation in your community or in the news that you feel needs greater federal involvement. Find out which agency in the federal bureaucracy has responsibility in this area. Write a letter to the head of this agency asking the agency to look into the matter.

4 Understanding Visuals

Only part of a president's power comes from the Constitution. Another part comes from having the support of the people. Presidents who lose public support find it more difficult to effectively use the powers they have. For this reason, presidential advisers keep a close watch on public opinion polls about the president. This political cartoon makes a comment about polls that measure the public's approval of the president. Examine the cartoon. Which president is being referred to? How do you know? What comment is the cartoonist making about this president's approval rating?

CARTOON: DAVE GRANLUND/PoliticalCartoons.com

REVIEW THE GUIDING QUESTIONS

Directions: Choose the best answer for each question.

1 How does a person become president of the United States?

  A. by winning the popular vote

  B. by winning enough electoral votes

  C. through the merit system

  D. through the spoils system

2 Why was the Twenty-fifth Amendment passed?

  F. to create the Electoral College

  G. to limit the president to two terms

  H. to establish the order of presidential succession if the president dies or leaves office

  I. to set conditions for when a vice president becomes president

3 Which of these powers does the Constitution give the president?

  A. appointing judges

  B. declaring war

  C. declaring laws unconstitutional

  D. suspending Congress

4 How does a president fulfill the role of economic leader?

  F. by meeting with foreign leaders

  G. by negotiating treaties

  H. by planning the federal budget

  I. by leading the armed forces

5 Which of the following best describes President Clinton's order to attack terrorist bases?

  A. embargo against terrorists

  B. military force used as a foreign policy tool

  C. executive agreement

  D. presidential power to grant amnesty

6 Which of these describes an executive agency that oversees an industry and makes sure it obeys the law?

  F. cabinet department

  G. executive agency

  H. government corporation

  I. regulatory commission

DBQ ANALYZING DOCUMENTS

Directions: Analyze the excerpt and answer the questions that follow.

President Gerald Ford made this observation about the presidency:

> *"You know, the President of the United States is not a magician who can wave a wand or sign a paper that will instantly end a war, cure a recession, or make bureaucracy disappear."*

7 **Explaining** What point was President Ford making in this remark?

A. No one can do a good job of being president.

B. The federal bureaucracy is too big.

C. The president's power is limited.

D. The president should have more power.

8 **Stating** Which sentence best states Ford's view of what people should expect of a president?

F. They should demand that the president solve major problems.

G. They should understand that the president may not be able to solve major problems.

H. They should impeach a president who does not follow campaign promises.

I. They should expect a president to accomplish little or nothing.

SHORT RESPONSE

> *"The FDA is responsible for protecting the public health by assuring the safety, efficacy [effectiveness], and security [safety] of human and veterinary drugs, biological products, medical devices, our nation's food supply, cosmetics, and products that emit radiation."*
>
> —Food and Drug Administration, "What We Do"

9 What type of independent agency do you think the Food and Drug Administration is? Why do you think so?

10 What steps do you think the Food and Drug Administration must take to carry out its work?

EXTENDED RESPONSE

11 **ARGUMENT** Based on what you have read in this chapter, what do you think are the challenges that a president faces in forming and putting into action a foreign policy? Which of those challenges do you think is the biggest? Why?

Need Extra Help?

If You've Missed Question	1	2	3	4	5	6	7	8	9	10	11
Review Lesson	1	1	2	2	3	4	2	2	4	4	2, 3, 4

The Judicial Branch

ESSENTIAL QUESTIONS • *How can governments ensure citizens are treated fairly?* • *Why do people create, structure, and change governments?*

The Story Matters...

The United States Supreme Court did not have its own building until 1935. Instead, the Court met in New York City, Philadelphia, and then in the U.S. Capitol in Washington, D.C. Finally, in 1929, Chief Justice William Howard Taft convinced Congress to approve a permanent home for the Court.

The Supreme Court building was built near the U.S. Capitol. Taft asked architect Cass Gilbert to design "a building of dignity and importance."

Some of the country's most important decisions are made in this building. Throughout U.S. history, fiercely debated issues have been resolved by the Supreme Court. These rulings often have a long-lasting and far-reaching effect on our lives.

◀ *This detail of the Supreme Court building shows part of the engraved phrase that reads in full, "Equal Justice Under Law."*

PHOTO: Kenneth Garrett/Getty Images

215

Real-Life Civics

> **EDUCATION** Supreme Court decisions about how to apply the law can affect many aspects of our daily life, even when we are students in school. In 1954, for example, the Supreme Court ordered the end of public school segregation in a landmark case called *Brown* v. *Board of Education.* In 1957 nine African American students tried to integrate the all-white Little Rock Central High School. Governor Orval Faubus, who opposed desegregation, used the Arkansas National Guard to bar the doors to the school. President Eisenhower called in federal troops to enforce the Court's decision. More recent Court rulings have addressed issues such as prayer in schools, drug-testing of students, and diversity programs in public colleges.

The African American students who integrated Little Rock Central High School needed the protection of U.S. soldiers to attend school.

Two U.S. Army military policemen guard a suspect being held at the U.S. Naval Station at Guantanamo Bay in Cuba.

PHOTOS: (l) Bettmann/CORBIS, (tr) PETER MUHLY/AFP/Getty Images

> **LEGAL RIGHTS** Supreme Court decisions can also change the behavior of the federal government. After the 2001 terrorist attacks, the United States held foreign terrorist suspects in Guantanamo Bay, Cuba. These people were denied due process under U.S. law. The families of four prisoners sued. They argued that the prisoners were protected by the Constitution, and had the right to attorneys and to appear in court. The government disagreed. It said the prisoners were not citizens and were not on American soil. In 2004 the Supreme Court ruled in the landmark case, *Rasul* v. *Bush*, that foreign prisoners were protected by the Constitution. This ruling changed the actions of the federal government.

CIVIC LITERACY

★ ★ ★ ★

Making Inferences What do these Supreme Court rulings show about the kinds of cases the Court hears?

Your Opinion Do you think any rulings by the Supreme Court have affected your life? Explain.

217

There's More Online!

☑ **GRAPHIC ORGANIZER**
Federal Courts

☑ **CHART**
Dual Court System

☑ **GAME**

Federal Courts

levels of courts: trial, appeals, Supre

s powers from U.S. Constitution and

cases involving federal law

dges appointed for life

upreme Court can hear appeals from
supreme courts

Lesson 1
Federal Courts

ESSENTIAL QUESTION *How can governments ensure citizens are treated fairly?*

IT MATTERS BECAUSE
The federal courts help keep order in society.

Role of the Federal Courts

GUIDING QUESTION *What is the role of the federal courts?*

What would society be like if people had no way to settle disputes in a fair manner? Would disputes lead to violence? Would the strongest people always win? Fortunately, in the United States, we settle disputes between people in courts.

Courts make up the judiciary, or the judicial branch of government. This branch has two main jobs. It tries to ensure that the laws are fairly enforced. It also interprets the laws.

Courts hear two types of cases: criminal cases and civil cases. In a criminal case, people accused of crimes appear in court for a trial. In a criminal trial, witnesses give evidence. A jury or a judge decides on a verdict of guilty or innocent.

Civil disputes occur between parties who feel that their rights have been harmed. In a civil case, each side presents its position in court. The court applies the law to the facts before it. Then it decides in favor of one side or the other. There are three kinds of civil disputes: between two private parties (people, companies, or organizations), between a private party and the government, and between the U.S. government and a state or local government or between state governments.

PHOTO: (tc) AP Photo/Betty Wells; (tr) PIERRE VERDY/AFP/Getty Images

Reading**HELP**DESK

Taking Notes: *Describing*

As you read, complete a graphic organizer to identify the role of each level in the federal court system.

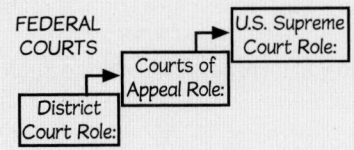

FEDERAL COURTS

District Court Role:

Courts of Appeal Role:

U.S. Supreme Court Role:

Content Vocabulary

• **dual court system**
• **jurisdiction**
• **exclusive jurisdiction**
• **concurrent jurisdiction**

Origin of the Federal Court System

From 1781 to 1789, the United States was governed by the Articles of Confederation. Under this government, there was no national court system. Each state had its own laws and its own courts. There was no way to guarantee that people would receive equal justice in all the states.

To solve these problems, the Founders decided to create a federal judiciary. Article III of the Constitution established a national Supreme Court. It also gave Congress the power to make lower federal courts if Congress saw the need for them.

Congress lost little time in creating lower federal courts. With the Judiciary Act of 1789, it established two types of lower federal courts: district courts and circuit courts. The district courts served as trial courts for distinct geographic regions. They handled minor civil and criminal cases. The circuit courts took more serious cases and heard appeals from the district courts. In 1891, Congress took trial responsibility from the circuit courts, making them exclusively courts of appeal. Over the years, the basic structure of the federal court system has remained the same. The 94 district courts at the lower level are trial courts. The 13 circuit courts in the middle are appeals courts. The Supreme Court, the court of final appeal, is at the top.

Dual Court System

The United States has a **dual court system.** Our federal courts exist alongside 50 separate state court systems. Each state has its own laws and courts. The state courts get their powers from state constitutions and laws. Federal courts get their powers from laws passed by Congress.

DUAL COURT SYSTEM

Federal Courts	State Courts
• Three levels of courts: trial, appeals, Supreme	• Three levels of courts: trial, appeals, supreme*
• Derives powers from U.S. Constitution and federal laws	• Derives powers from state constitution and state laws
• Hears cases involving federal law	• Hears cases involving state law
• Most judges appointed for life	• Most judges elected or appointed for set terms
• U.S. Supreme Court can hear appeals from state supreme courts	• State appeals courts never hear cases that originate in federal courts.

*structure and names of courts vary by state

CHART SKILLS

All 50 state courts operate independently of each other and of the federal courts.

► CRITICAL THINKING

1 *Contrasting* How do federal and state courts differ?

2 *Making Inferences* What are some advantages of a dual court system?

dual court system a court system made up of both federal and state courts

PHOTO: AP Photo/Betty Wells

The U.S. Constitution says that those accused of crimes have certain rights, including a public trial and a lawyer.

▶ **CRITICAL THINKING**
Analyzing Visuals Which rights of the accused do you see in this image?

Reading**HELP**DESK

The Goal of the Court System

The words "Equal Justice Under Law" are written on the building that houses the United States Supreme Court. Our legal system is based on this ideal. The goal of this legal system is to treat every person the same.

Under the Constitution, every person accused of breaking the law has the right to have a public trial and a lawyer. If an accused person cannot afford a lawyer, the court will name one and pay for his or her services. Each person is **presumed,** or assumed to be, innocent until proven guilty. Each person has the right to ask the courts to review his or her case if, in the person's view, the law has not been applied correctly.

The ideal of equal justice is difficult to achieve. Judges and juries are not free from their own prejudices or those of their community. Poor people do not have the money to spend on the best lawyers, as wealthy people and large companies do. Nonetheless, American courts try to uphold this ideal.

✔ **PROGRESS CHECK**

Explaining Why did the Framers of the Constitution create a federal judiciary?

Academic Vocabulary
presume to assume to be true

jurisdiction a court's authority to hear and decide cases

Federal Court Jurisdiction

GUIDING QUESTION *What kinds of cases are heard in federal courts?*

Article III of the Constitution gives federal courts **jurisdiction**— the authority to hear and decide a case—only in certain kinds of cases. Placing limits on these courts prevents them from interfering with state courts.

Federal cases must involve the Constitution, federal law, or the federal government. These courts also handle cases that involve different states or people from different states. Finally, federal courts handle cases that involve some special areas of law as well.

The Constitution and Federal Law

Suppose a person believes that a constitutional right, such as freedom of speech, has been violated. That person could sue in federal court.

Congress has passed laws that define some actions as federal crimes. Examples are kidnapping, tax evasion, and counterfeiting. Federal courts handle these cases. They also hear civil cases that involve federal laws.

Disputes Between States or Parties from Different States

Disagreements between state governments are taken to federal court. Suppose the states of Colorado and California disagree over which has a greater right to water from the Colorado River. A federal court would handle that case.

Lawsuits between citizens of different states also come under the federal courts. Suppose that someone from Maine thought that a company in another state had made a faulty product that harmed him or her. The person from Maine would sue the company in federal court.

Admiralty and Maritime Laws

Admiralty and maritime laws concern crimes, accidents, and property at sea. For example, two parties might disagree over which of them has the right to property recovered from a shipwreck. That case would be handled in federal court.

Those accused of piracy against U.S. Navy and commercial ships may be tried in federal courts. Here suspected Somali pirates are guarded by U.S. troops.

► **CRITICAL THINKING**
Drawing Conclusions Why would such crimes be tried in federal court?

PHOTO: PIERRE VERDY/AFP/Getty Images

The Federal Government

The government is not above the law. When the government is part of a legal dispute, the matter goes to federal court. For example, the government might sue a company for failing to deliver goods as promised in a contract. Or a company might sue the government for not paying for goods on time.

Cases with Foreign Governments and U.S. Diplomats

Any dispute between a foreign government and the U.S. government goes to federal court. The same is true when there is a dispute between a foreign government and an American company or citizen. Also, if American officials at work in another nation are accused of a crime, this is a federal case.

Types of Jurisdiction

For most of the areas just described, federal courts have **exclusive jurisdiction.** That is, only they have the authority to hear the cases. When state law is involved, the case is heard in a state court. Most U.S. court cases involve state law and are tried in state courts.

Sometimes, though, either a federal or a state court could hear a case. In that situation, the two courts are said to have **concurrent jurisdiction.** For example, either court may try someone accused of committing a crime that breaks both state and federal law. The same is true when citizens of different states have a dispute with a value of at least $75,000. In such a case, the person who brings the suit can choose either a federal court or a state court. The person being sued has the right to insist on the case being heard in a federal court, though.

exclusive jurisdiction authority of only federal courts to hear and decide cases

concurrent jurisdiction authority of both state and federal courts to hear and decide cases

☑ PROGRESS CHECK

Identifying What are two examples of cases where the federal courts would have exclusive jurisdiction?

LESSON 1 REVIEW

Review Vocabulary

1. How is *jurisdiction* divided in the *dual court system*?

2. What is the difference between *exclusive jurisdiction* and *concurrent jurisdiction*?

Answer the Guiding Questions

3. ***Identifying*** What are the three levels of the federal court system?

4. ***Explaining*** Where do the federal courts get their power?

5. **INFORMATIVE/EXPLANATORY** How does the Constitution define and limit the power of the federal courts?

netwⓞrks

There's More Online!

☑ **GRAPHIC ORGANIZER**
District Courts and
Courts of Appeals

☑ **MAP**
Federal Judicial Circuits

☑ **CHART**
Federal Court System

Lesson 2

The Federal Court System

PHOTO: (tcl) AP Photo/Pablo Martinez Monsivaís; (tcr) Joshua Roberts/Bloomberg via Getty Images; (tr) F. Carter Smith/Bloomberg via Getty Images

ESSENTIAL QUESTIONS • *How can governments ensure citizens are treated fairly?*
• *Why do people create, structure, and change governments?*

IT MATTERS BECAUSE
Lower federal courts handle most cases involving federal law.

The Lower Courts

GUIDING QUESTION *How are the federal courts organized?*

You have learned that district courts, the courts of appeals, and the Supreme Court make up the federal court system. Each layer in the federal court system has its own purpose and structure. At the top of the federal system is the U.S. Supreme Court. District courts and courts of appeals—the courts that are below the U.S. Supreme Court—make up the lower federal courts. What are the roles of the lower courts and federal judges?

District Courts

The U.S. district courts are the lowest level of the federal system. For most matters that reach federal court, district courts usually have **original jurisdiction**, or the authority to hear cases for the first time. There are 94 district courts. Every state has at least one of them, and some states have more.

As trial courts, district courts are responsible for determining the facts of a case. They take both criminal and civil cases. In a criminal case, a district court will decide if a person is guilty or innocent based on the evidence presented. District courts are the only federal courts in which witnesses testify and juries hear cases and reach verdicts.

Reading **HELP**DESK

Taking Notes: *Differentiating*

As you read, complete a pair of graphic organizers about each level of the lower courts to understand how they differ.

Content Vocabulary

• **original jurisdiction**	• **opinion**
• **appellate jurisdiction**	• **precedent**
• **ruling**	• **litigant**

• **tenure**
• **subpoena**

Lesson 2 **223**

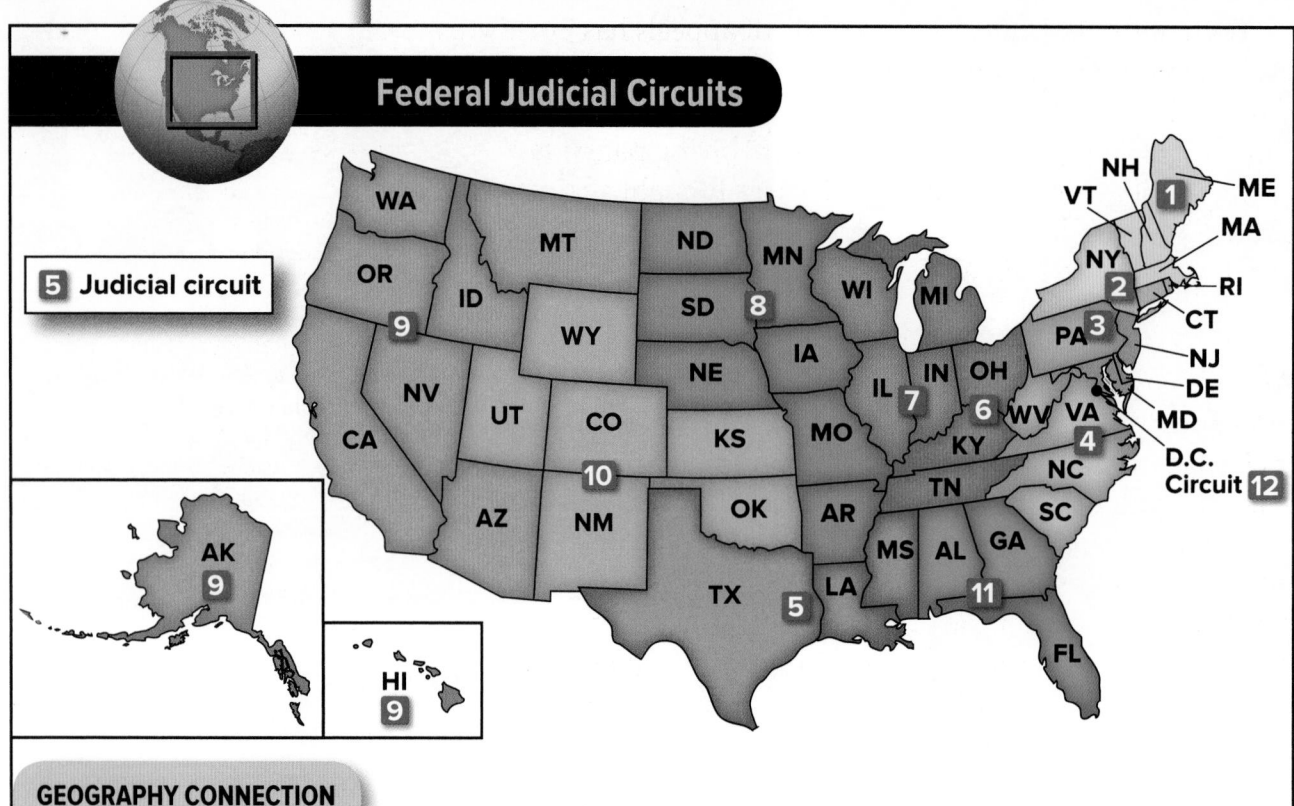

Federal Judicial Circuits

5 Judicial circuit

GEOGRAPHY CONNECTION

There are 13 circuits in the U.S. circuit courts of appeals.

1 **LOCATION** In which circuit are Alabama, Georgia, and Florida?

2 **CRITICAL THINKING** *Making Inferences* Why do you think the circuits vary in the size of the geographical area they cover?

Circuit Courts of Appeals

You have learned that the circuit courts of appeals are between the district courts and the U.S. Supreme Court in the federal system. They are also called federal appeals courts, courts of appeals, or appellate courts.

Appeals courts differ from trial courts. They do not decide on the guilt or innocence of a person in a criminal case. Nor do they decide which party should win a lawsuit. Instead, they have **appellate** (uh•PEH•luht) **jurisdiction.** This is the authority to review the fairness of a case appealed from a lower court. Appeals courts may also review the decisions of a federal regulatory agency if a party says that the agency acted unfairly.

Lawyers appeal a case when they feel that the district court judge made a mistake. The appeal is based on how the law was applied by the judge. A person found guilty might think that the judge was wrong to allow some evidence to be used. An appeal can also be based on how the judge interpreted the law.

The losing side appeals. In a criminal case, though, only an accused person who has been found guilty can appeal. If the prosecution loses, there can be no appeal.

Reading **HELP**DESK

original jurisdiction the authority of a court to hear cases for the first time

appellate jurisdiction the authority of a court to hear a case appealed from a lower court

ruling an official decision by a judge or a court that settles a case and may also establish the meaning of a law

Each of the 12 United States courts of appeals has jurisdiction over a circuit, or geographic area. In 1982 Congress created a thirteenth appeals court, the Court of Appeals for the Federal Circuit. This court hears special cases involving patent law or international trade, or other civil cases brought against the United States. This court is headquartered in Washington, D.C., but it can hear cases in all parts of the country.

Rulings

Appeals courts do not hold trials. Instead, a panel of three or more judges reviews the record of the case from the trial court. It also listens to arguments made by lawyers for both sides. Then the judges meet and make a decision by majority vote.

Their decision is not about a criminal defendant's guilt or innocence or which side should win in a civil lawsuit. The panel rules only on whether the original trial was a fair one. Their decision is known as a **ruling,** or an official decision that settles a case and helps establish the meaning of the law. The judges can decide a case in one of three ways:

- They can uphold the result of the trial, which leaves the verdict in that trial unchanged.
- They can reverse the result of the trial. The judges take this action if they think the original judge made an error in procedure or in interpreting the law.
- They can remand the case. This means sending the case back to the lower court to be tried again. The judges take this step if they think the original trial was not right in some way.

Decisions of the courts of appeals are final unless they are appealed. Those appeals are made to the U.S. Supreme Court.

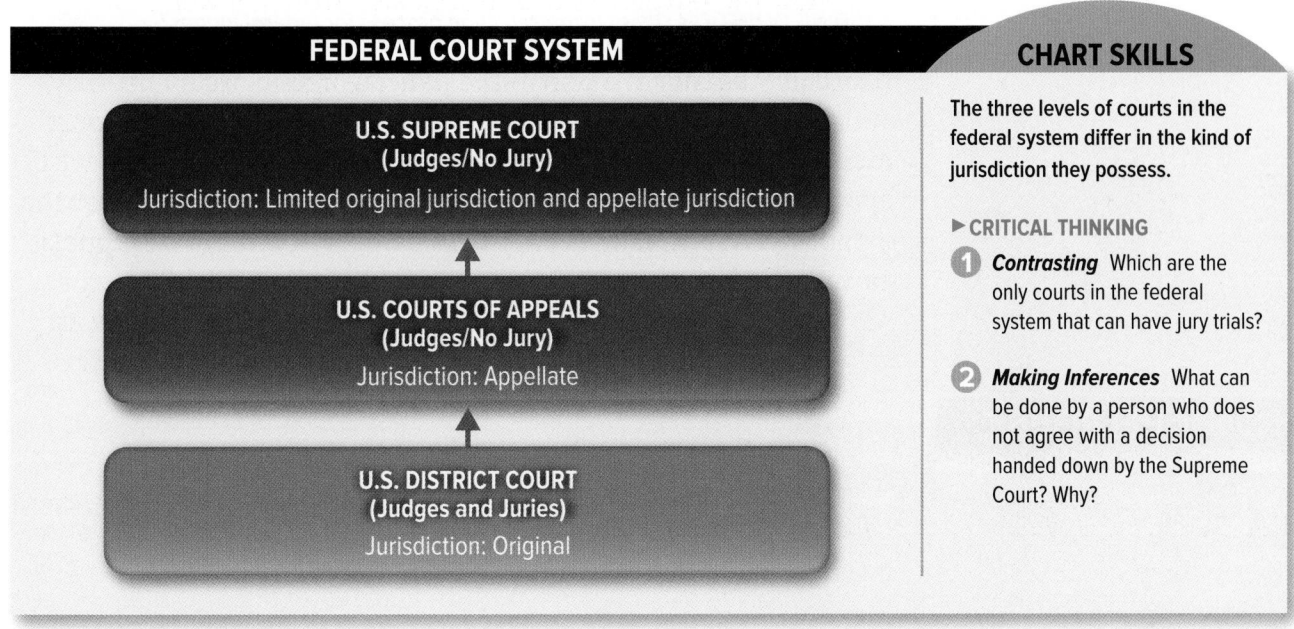

FEDERAL COURT SYSTEM

U.S. SUPREME COURT
(Judges/No Jury)
Jurisdiction: Limited original jurisdiction and appellate jurisdiction

U.S. COURTS OF APPEALS
(Judges/No Jury)
Jurisdiction: Appellate

U.S. DISTRICT COURT
(Judges and Juries)
Jurisdiction: Original

CHART SKILLS

The three levels of courts in the federal system differ in the kind of jurisdiction they possess.

▶ CRITICAL THINKING

1 *Contrasting* Which are the only courts in the federal system that can have jury trials?

2 *Making Inferences* What can be done by a person who does not agree with a decision handed down by the Supreme Court? Why?

Opinions

When an appeals court makes a ruling, one judge writes an opinion for the court. The **opinion** offers a detailed explanation of the legal thinking behind the court's decision. The opinion sets a precedent for all courts and agencies within the district. A **precedent** can be used as the basis for a decision in later, similar cases. A precedent does not have the force of law, but it is a very powerful legal argument. Judges and courts follow precedents in nearly all cases.

Principles of the Legal System

Certain judicial principles were established early in the nation's history. One is that no federal court, not even the Supreme Court, may initiate action. That is, a judge or justice may not seek out an issue and ask both sides to bring it to court. The courts must wait for **litigants**, or parties to a lawsuit, to come before them.

The importance of precedent comes from a principle of British law. This principle states that the decisions of the highest court in the jurisdiction are binding on the courts under it. For this reason, all courts in the country must follow the precedents set by the United States Supreme Court. You will read more about this precedent in Lesson 4. In addition, the judges on each court of appeals are supposed to follow decisions made by earlier courts in that circuit. District courts should follow the precedents of the circuit in which they are found.

✔ **PROGRESS CHECK**

Identifying What kinds of rulings do appeals courts make?

Federal Judges

GUIDING QUESTION *What is the selection process for federal judges?*

The chief decision makers in the judicial branch are the federal judges. They are the final authority in federal courts. More than 650 judges serve on the district courts. Each district court has at least two judges. Some district courts in areas with high populations have more than two because there are more cases to hear. Each appeals court has from 6 to 28 judges. The Supreme Court has nine judges. Supreme Court judges use the title *justice*.

All federal judges are nominated by the president. Supreme Court justice Antonin Scalia was nominated by President Ronald Reagan and has served on the high court since 1986.

▶ **CRITICAL THINKING**
Comparing What do all federal judges have in common?

PHOTO: (cl) AP Photo/Pablo Martinez Monsivais

---

opinion a detailed explanation of the legal thinking behind a court's decision in a case

precedent a ruling that is used as the basis for a judicial decision in a later, similar case

litigant one of the parties involved in a lawsuit

Academic Vocabulary

consent approval

PHOTO: Joshua Roberts/Bloomberg via Getty Images

Appointing Federal Judges

Article II, Section 2 of the Constitution says that the president appoints all federal judges. The president's appointment power is not unchecked. The president can appoint a federal judge only with the advice and **consent,** or approval, of the Senate. A simple majority in the Senate is needed to approve someone as judge.

Vacancies in the courts arise when a judge resigns, retires, or dies. Then the appointment process begins. The Constitution does not set particular qualifications that federal judges must meet. In general, presidents want to appoint judges who share their ideas about justice and the law.

When naming judges to district courts, presidents often follow a practice called senatorial courtesy. In this tradition, the president first submits the name of a candidate to the senators from the candidate's state. If one of the senators objects to the candidate, the president then typically nominates another candidate. Senatorial courtesy usually does not apply to the naming of judges to courts of appeals or the Supreme Court.

Presidents are careful to choose candidates who are likely to be approved by the Senate. Many individuals and groups offer opinions on nominees. They include Justice Department officials, the American Bar Association, and interest groups. Sometimes the Senate rejects a nominee based on doubts about his or her qualifications or legal philosophy.

The Senate must approve nominees to be federal court judges. In 2010, nominee Elena Kagan appeared at Senate confirmation hearings and was then approved as a Supreme Court justice.

▶ CRITICAL THINKING
Making Connections How does the process for federal judge appointments demonstrate checks and balances in the U.S. government?

Members of the U.S. Marshals Service, begun under George Washington in 1789, are officers of the federal courts. One of their duties is to escort convicted persons to jail.

▶ **CRITICAL THINKING**
Drawing Conclusions Why do you think the U.S. Marshals are important to the federal courts?

tenure the right to hold an office once a person is confirmed

Academic Vocabulary
preliminary something that introduces or comes before something else

subpoena an order that requires a person to appear in court

Term of Office

Once appointed, federal judges have their jobs for life. They can be removed from office only through the process of impeachment. The Framers gave federal judges this right to hold their office, or **tenure,** so they can be free from public or political pressures when they hear cases.

Other Court Officials

Judges do not work alone. They have help from clerks, secretaries, court reporters, and other workers. Each district court also has three key officials.

Magistrate judges do much of a judge's routine work. They issue court orders, such as search warrants. They hear **preliminary,** or introductory, evidence and decide if a case should be brought to trial. They decide whether people under arrest should be held in jail or released on bail. Magistrates may also serve as judges in minor cases. Magistrate judges are appointed by a majority of the federal judges in a district. Unlike district court judges, magistrate judges do not have lifetime appointments. They serve terms of eight years and can be reappointed.

Each district has a United States attorney and one or more deputies. The job of these lawyers is to prosecute people accused of breaking federal law. They also represent the government in civil cases in which the government is involved. U.S. attorneys are appointed to four-year terms by the president. They have to be approved by the Senate.

Each federal judicial district also has a United States Marshal. Marshals and their staffs make arrests, collect fines, and take convicted persons to prison. They protect jurors, keep order in federal courts, and deliver subpoenas. A **subpoena** (suh•PEE•nuh) is a court order that requires a person to appear in court.

☑ **PROGRESS CHECK**

Describing What are the duties of a magistrate judge?

LESSON 2 REVIEW

Review Vocabulary

1. What is the difference between *original* and *appellate jurisdiction*?

2. What are judicial *opinions* and *precedents*, and why are they so important?

Answer the Guiding Questions

3. *Identifying* What kinds of cases are heard by the district courts?

4. *Explaining* What role does Congress have in the appointment of federal judges?

5. **ARGUMENT** Do you agree with the practice of giving federal judges tenure? Explain your reasoning in a paragraph or two.

networks

There's More Online!

☑ **GRAPHIC ORGANIZER**
U.S. Supreme Court

☑ **POLITICAL CARTOON**
Keeping Score

☑ **VIDEO**

Lesson 3
The Supreme Court

ESSENTIAL QUESTION *How can governments ensure citizens are treated fairly?*

IT MATTERS BECAUSE
The Supreme Court decides what the Constitution means and thus what rights Americans have.

Jurisdiction and Duties

GUIDING QUESTION *What is the jurisdiction of the Supreme Court?*

The Supreme Court's main job is to decide whether laws are allowed by the U.S. Constitution. Chief Justice John G. Roberts, Jr., sees this duty as part of an effort by all Americans to keep the Constitution strong:

PRIMARY SOURCE

❝ What Daniel Webster termed, 'the miracle of our Constitution' is not something that happens in every generation. But every generation in its turn must accept the responsibility of supporting and defending the Constitution, and bearing true faith and allegiance to it. ❞

—Chief Justice John G. Roberts, Jr.

Jurisdiction

The Supreme Court has original jurisdiction in only two types of cases. One type is cases that involve disputes between two or more states. The other type is cases that involve diplomats from foreign countries. In all other instances, the Court hears cases that have been appealed from the lower courts.

Reading **HELP**DESK

Taking Notes: *Organizing*

As you read, complete a graphic organizer like the one shown by filling in details about the U.S. Supreme Court under each heading.

U.S. Supreme Court			
Jurisdiction	Duties	Powers	Limits

Content Vocabulary
- **judicial review**
- **constitutional**
- **nullify**

Lesson 3 **229**

The nine justices of the 2010–2011 session of the U.S. Supreme Court included Elena Kagan (top right) and Sonia Sotomayor (top left), both appointed by President Obama.

▶ **CRITICAL THINKING**

Evaluating Do you think that federal judges should serve for life, as stated in the Constitution? Explain your answer.

PHOTO: Chip Somodevilla/Getty Images

The Supreme Court has final authority in cases involving the Constitution, acts of Congress, and treaties with other nations. The Court's decisions are binding on all lower courts. The Supreme Court hears only a small percentage of the cases it receives. The Court chooses which ones it will handle. When the Court refuses to hear a case, the decision of the lower court remains in effect.

Duties of Justices

The Supreme Court is made up of nine justices—the chief justice and eight associate justices. The chief justice is the Court's leader. Congress sets this number and has the power to change it. The justices are important decision makers. Their rulings can affect citizens just as the acts of a president or Congress do.

The main duty of justices is to hear and rule on cases. They choose which cases to hear from among the thousands appealed to the Court each year.

Qualification of Justices

The Constitution does not name any qualifications for a Supreme Court justice. In the past, justices have always had legal training. However, there is no requirement that they must be lawyers. Before being named to the Court, many have practiced or taught law or held other public offices. More than three dozen had never been judges before joining the Court.

Because the justices interpret what the Constitution means, the Supreme Court has great power. The men and women who sit on the Court, like all federal judges, have their jobs for life.

Reading Strategy: *Making Connections*

How do Congress and the president affect the Supreme Court? Draw two boxes, each connected by an arrow to a third box. Label the two boxes "Congress" and "President." Label the third box "Supreme Court." Place notes in each of the two top boxes telling how each can check or affect the Supreme Court.

That means that any person named to the Court will likely have influence for a long time. For these reasons, nominees receive a great deal of attention.

Presidents have to choose a nominee very carefully to try to make sure he or she wins the Senate's approval. In recent years, members of Congress and the media have looked at a nominee's personal life as well as his or her professional qualifications and experience. Some nominees have had to withdraw their names.

✓ PROGRESS CHECK

Explaining What happens if the Supreme Court refuses to hear a case?

Powers and Limits

GUIDING QUESTION *What powers are given to the Supreme Court?*

Article III of the Constitution creates the judicial branch. It does not describe the branch in detail, though. Over the years, Congress has established most of the rules that govern the powers and the organization of the Supreme Court. In addition, the system of checks and balances in the Constitution puts limits on the power of the federal court system, including the Supreme Court.

American Leaders

• Sandra Day O'Connor (1930–)

When a Supreme Court vacancy opened up in 1981, President Ronald Reagan decided to fulfill his campaign promise to name the first woman justice. He chose Sandra Day O'Connor, an Arizona appeals court judge.

Unlike most Supreme Court justices, O'Connor also had broad political experience. After earning a law degree in 1952, she found that most law firms would not hire a woman—except as a legal secretary. She went into public service, had three sons, and practiced law privately. Appointed to a state senatorial vacancy in 1969, she later successfully ran for the position. She became the first woman majority leader of the Arizona state senate in 1972. O'Connor won an election for superior court judge in 1974 and was later appointed to the appeals court.

Her nomination to the Supreme Court had strong support. There was also opposition by some because she had been in favor of the Equal Rights Amendment (ERA) and refused to back an antiabortion amendment.

O'Connor retired from the Court in 2006. Her years on the Court marked her as a conservative jurist. However, she often occupied the Court's middle ground, casting the deciding vote on many controversial issues. O'Connor always insisted that it was the "power of my arguments, not my gender" that made her a powerful force on the Court.

PHOTO: Mark Wilson/Getty

Looking at Leaders

Analyzing What did Justice O'Connor mean when she said, "[the] power of my arguments, not my gender" made her a force on the Court?

▶ **CRITICAL THINKING**

Hypothesizing What does the
scoreboard in this cartoon tell you
about the typical votes on rulings of
the Court?

CARTOON: Christopher Weyant/*The New Yorker*

Judicial Review

One of the most important powers of the Supreme Court is
the power of judicial review. **Judicial review** means that the
Court can review any federal, state, or local law or action to see
whether it goes against the Constitution. A law that is
constitutional, or follows the Constitution, can stand. If the
Court decides that a law is unconstitutional, it can **nullify,** or
legally cancel, that law or action. Chief Justice John Marshall
described the great power of judicial review when he said,

PRIMARY SOURCE

❝ It is emphatically [strongly] the province [function] and duty of the judicial
department to say what the law is. Those who apply the rule to particular cases,
must of necessity expound [explain] and interpret that rule. If two laws conflict
with each other, the courts must decide on the operation of each. ❞
—Chief Justice John Marshall, *Marbury* v. *Madison* (1803)

The power of judicial review is an important check on the
legislative and executive branches of government. It prevents
them from straying too far from the Constitution. Congress and
the executive branch must follow the rulings of the Supreme
Court. In some cases, the Court decides that state laws or local
laws conflict with the Constitution. In those instances, state and
local governments must go along with the decision.

Reading**HELP**DESK

judicial review the power of the
Supreme Court to say whether any federal,
state, or local law or government action
goes against the Constitution

constitutional in accordance with
the Constitution

nullify to cancel
legally

Academic Vocabulary

challenge to object to a
decision or outcome

Marbury v. Madison

The Constitution does not give the Supreme Court the power of judicial review. The Judiciary Act of 1789 gave the Court the power of judicial review for acts of state governments. In 1803 the Court used the case of *Marbury* v. *Madison* to make clear that it had this power in regard to acts of Congress.

Justice Marshall's opinion in that case set forth three principles of judicial review:

- The Constitution is the supreme law of the land.
- If there is a conflict between the Constitution and any other law, the Constitution rules.
- The judicial branch has a duty to uphold the Constitution. Thus, it must be able to determine when a law conflicts with the Constitution and to nullify laws that do.

Limits on the Supreme Court

The system of checks and balances puts limits on the power of federal courts, including the Supreme Court. First, the Court can only hear and make rulings on the cases that come to it. The Court will not rule on a law or an action that has not been **challenged,** or objected to, on appeal. Second, all cases taken by the Court must be actual legal disputes. A person cannot simply ask the Court to decide whether a law is constitutional. Third, the Court can only take cases that involve a federal question.

Another limit is that traditionally the Court has refused to deal with political matters. The justices have thought it was best to leave these questions to be answered by the executive or legislative branch. After the 2000 presidential election, the Court heard two cases of a political nature. They both involved the recounting of votes in Florida.

Americans do not always agree with the rulings of the Supreme Court. Here citizens demonstrate against a Court ruling that determined that the recount of votes in Florida in the 2000 election violated the Fourteenth Amendment. As a result of the ruling, George W. Bush became president.

▶ CRITICAL THINKING
Evaluating Should popular opinion influence Supreme Court decisions? Explain your answer.

Enforcement, or the carrying out of the Court decisions, is an additional limitation to the Court's power. The Supreme Court has no resources to make governments do what it orders. It must depend on the executive branch and on state and local officials to follow the rules it establishes. The executive branch usually does enforce Court decisions, but that has not always been the case.

For instance, President Andrew Jackson refused to obey the decision made by the Court in *Worcester* v. *Georgia*. This 1832 case involved conflict between the state of Georgia and the Cherokee Nation. Chief Justice Marshall told the state to stop breaking treaties that the Cherokee people had signed with the federal government. Jackson refused to take any steps to make the state obey the Court's ruling. Most citizens agreed with President Jackson. As a result, there was no public pressure to force him to uphold the Court's decision.

By contrast, President Dwight Eisenhower used the full power of the federal government to enforce federal court decisions calling for the desegregation of public schools. In 1957 he sent army troops to escort nine black students into an all-white school in Little Rock, Arkansas.

If Congress disagrees with a Court ruling, it can pass a new law or change a law that the Court has found to be unconstitutional. Congress and state legislatures can also try to undo Court rulings by changing the Constitution with an amendment. In the years before the Civil War, the Supreme Court made a decision in the case *Dred Scott* v. *Sandford*. In it, the Court said that African Americans could not be U.S. citizens. The Fourteenth Amendment, approved in 1868, overturned that part of the Court's decision.

☑ PROGRESS CHECK

Synthesizing How is judicial review a part of our federal system of government?

21ˢᵗ *Century* SKILLS

Interpreting Points of View

Think about President Andrew Jackson's refusal not to enforce the Supreme Court's decision in *Worcester* v. *Georgia*. What possible points of view do you think the president may have had? Discuss the issue with a partner and offer the interpretations you come up with to the rest of the class.

LESSON 3 REVIEW

Review Vocabulary

1. How does the power of *judicial review* check the legislative and executive branches?

2. What does it mean to *nullify* a law?

Answer the Guiding Questions

3. *Identifying* In what cases does the Supreme Court have original jurisdiction? Appellate jurisdiction?

4. *Drawing Conclusions* What is the most important power of the Supreme Court? Explain.

5. **INFORMATIVE/EXPLANATORY** Think about the qualifications a Supreme Court justice should have. Then write a "help wanted" ad for a Supreme Court justice.

Marbury v. Madison

In the early 1800s, the role of the judicial branch was unclear and its influence small. How did the Supreme Court establish its power of judicial review?

President Adams spent his last night in office signing commissions, or official paperwork for appointments.

PAINTING: Liza Biganzoli/National Geographic Society Image Collection

Background of the Case

As President John Adams's term expired in 1801, Congress passed the Judiciary Act of 1789. This bill gave the outgoing president a chance to appoint 42 new justices of the peace in the District of Columbia. The Senate approved the people Adams named. However, not all the paperwork was delivered before the next president—Thomas Jefferson—was sworn in.

Jefferson wanted to stop Adams's appointments from taking place if he could. One of his first acts as president, then, was to order his secretary of state, James Madison, not to deliver the final four appointments.

William Marbury was one of the four who did not receive his appointment in time. Acting according to the terms of the Judiciary Act, he filed suit in the Supreme Court against Madison. Marbury claimed he should have received his appointment as declared by the Senate.

The Decision

The Supreme Court heard the case in 1803. Chief Justice John Marshall announced the ruling. He stated that Marbury's rights under the Judiciary Act had been violated. However, the Court further ruled that the part of the act that would have given the Supreme Court the power to enforce the delivery of Marbury's appointment was unconstitutional. Even though Marbury was ruled the winner, the Court could not force the president to give him the appointment.

Marshall wrote:

❝ It is emphatically the province [function] and duty of the judicial department to say what the law is. Those who apply the rule to particular cases, must of necessity expound [explain] and interpret the rule. ❞

Why It Matters

In *Marbury* v. *Madison*, the Supreme Court first claimed the right to declare acts of the legislative and executive branches unconstitutional. With that step, it defined itself as the final authority on what the Constitution means. By doing so, it made the judicial branch independent of and equal to the other branches.

Analyzing the Case

1. **Explaining** Why is *Marbury* v. *Madison* a landmark case?

2. **Describing** Why did the Supreme Court refuse to allow the appointment of the last judges?

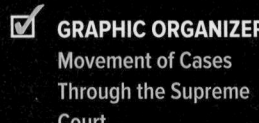
There's More Online!

☑ **GRAPHIC ORGANIZER**
Movement of Cases
Through the Supreme
Court

☑ **GRAPH**
Supreme Court Caseload

☑ **CHARTS**
Landmark Supreme Court
Decisions
Supreme Court Rulings on
Segregation

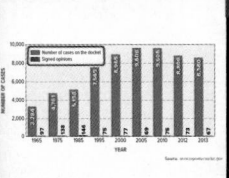

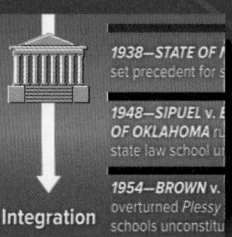

1938—STATE OF
set precedent for s

1948—SIPUEL v.
OF OKLAHOMA r
state law school u

1954—BROWN v.
overturned *Plessy*
schools unconstitu

Integration

Lesson 4
Supreme Court Procedures and Decisions

ESSENTIAL QUESTION *How can governments ensure citizens are treated fairly?*

IT MATTERS BECAUSE
The Court uses a careful process to arrive at its decisions.

Court Procedures

GUIDING QUESTION *What kinds of cases does the Supreme Court decide to hear?*

How does the highest court in the land work? The Supreme Court meets each year for about nine months. Each term begins the first Monday in October. A term is named for the year in which it begins, so the 2012 term began October 2012. Special sessions may be called to deal with urgent matters. The justices follow a set of specific procedures before they make a ruling.

How Cases Reach the Court

Nearly all cases come to the Supreme Court on appeal from a lower court. Most appeals reach the Court by a request for a **writ of certiorari** (SUHR•sheeuh•REHR•ee). This is Latin for "to make more certain." This order directs a lower court to send its records on a case to the Supreme Court for review. This happens if one of the parties in a case claims that the lower court made an error. Sometimes a lower court is not sure how to apply the law to a particular case. That court will then ask the Supreme Court to hear the case.

The Supreme Court does not have to accept all cases presented to it. It carefully chooses the cases it will hear.

PHOTO: (tc) AP Photo/D ana Verkouteran

Reading **HELP**DESK

Taking Notes: *Sequencing*

As you read, complete a flowchart to show the
steps as a case moves through the Supreme Court
after a request for a writ of certiorari is made.

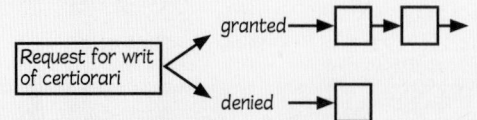

Content Vocabulary

- **writ of**   • **caseload**
  certiorari   • **brief**
- **docket**   • **stare decisis**

236 *The Judicial Branch*

Selecting Cases

Justices review possible cases and consider their merits. A case has merit if it involves a key constitutional question. Such questions often center on amendments. They may deal with issues such as freedom of speech, equal protection of the laws, and fair trials. The Court also takes cases when courts of appeal have made different decisions on the same point of law. By taking the case, the justices can settle that point of law to give guidance to the lower courts.

Supreme Court justices tend to select cases that involve legal rather than political issues. These cases affect the entire country rather than individuals or particular groups. The cases always involve a real dispute between two opposing sides. In other words, the cases must deal with real people and events.

The Court accepts a case when four of the nine justices agree to do so. Accepted cases go on the Court **docket,** or calendar of cases to be heard.

Caseload

The workload of cases in a period of time is called the **caseload.** The Supreme Court gets about 10,000 petitions, or requests, for writs of certiorari each term. It hears arguments for about 75 to 80 cases. The Court opinions for these cases set out principles that apply to the nation as well as to each specific case. Through these cases, the Court interprets the law.

✓ **PROGRESS CHECK**

Summarizing How do the justices decide the merits of a case?

21ˢᵗ Century
SKILLS

Make Connections

Create and complete a word net to show what factors the Supreme Court considers in choosing which cases to hear.

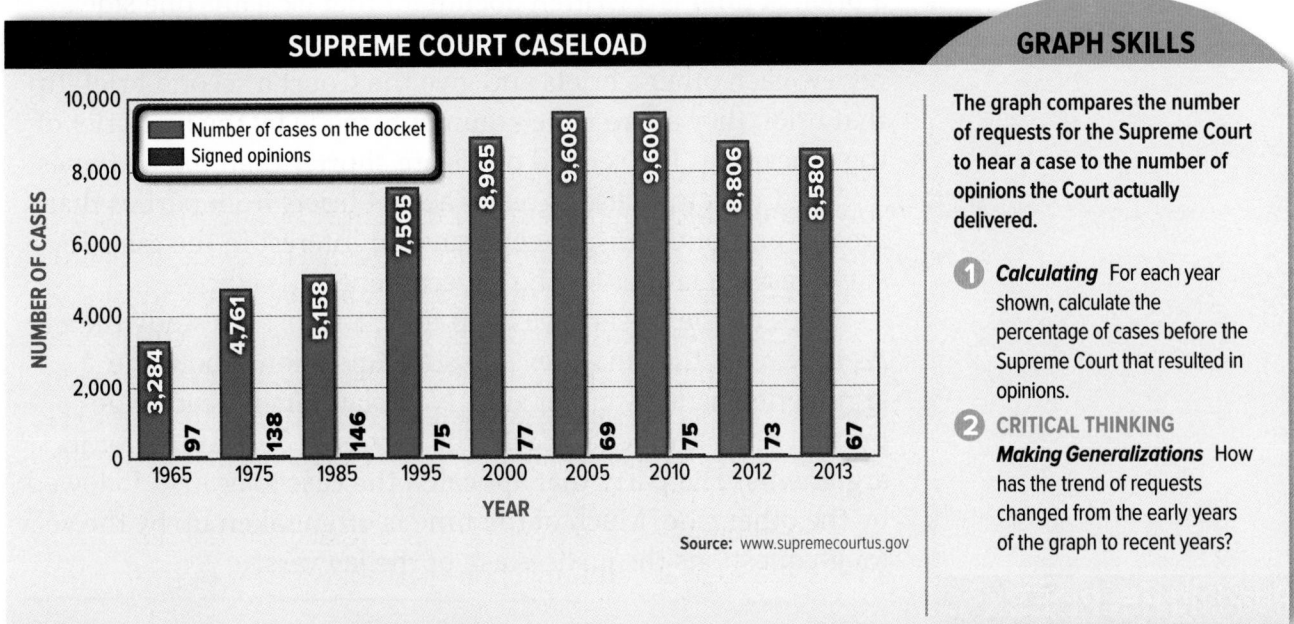

SUPREME COURT CASELOAD

(Bar graph showing Number of cases on the docket and Signed opinions by year)

Year	Number of cases on the docket	Signed opinions
1965	3,284	97
1975	4,761	138
1985	5,158	146
1995	7,565	75
2000	8,965	77
2005	9,608	69
2010	9,606	75
2012	8,806	73
2013	8,580	67

NUMBER OF CASES — YEAR

Source: www.supremecourtus.gov

GRAPH SKILLS

The graph compares the number of requests for the Supreme Court to hear a case to the number of opinions the Court actually delivered.

1 *Calculating* For each year shown, calculate the percentage of cases before the Supreme Court that resulted in opinions.

2 CRITICAL THINKING *Making Generalizations* How has the trend of requests changed from the early years of the graph to recent years?

- **concurring opinion**
- **dissenting opinion**
- **unanimous opinion**

writ of certiorari an order a higher court issues to a lower court to obtain the records of the lower court in a particular case

docket a court's calendar, showing the schedule of cases it is to hear

caseload a judge's or court's workload of cases in a period of time

► **CRITICAL THINKING**
Evaluating Why do you think the Supreme Court limits the time allowed for oral arguments?

PHOTO: AP Photo/Dana Verkouteran

How the Court's Rulings Are Made

GUIDING QUESTION *What factors affect the Court's decisions?*

The Supreme Court hears cases appealed to it by everyone from prisoners in jail to presidents. How do the justices handle these cases? How do they go about making decisions and informing the public?

Written and Oral Arguments

Once the Court takes a case, the lawyers for each side prepare a brief. A **brief** is a written document that explains one side's position on the case. The two parties also have a chance to review each other's briefs and give the Court a second brief. In that brief, they answer the arguments made by the first brief of the other side. The second briefs are shorter than the first ones.

The Court may also agree to accept briefs from parties that are not part of the dispute but have an interest in the case. In some cases, a lawyer for the government adds a brief.

Once all the briefs have been filed, the justices study them. As they read, they may develop some questions about the arguments made by either side. Next, lawyers for each side present oral arguments. Each side gets only 30 minutes for its arguments. The party that appealed the case goes first, followed by the other side. Much of the time is often taken up by the very tough questions the justices ask of the lawyers.

Reading **HELP**DESK

Reading Strategy: *Summarizing*

To summarize information, you briefly tell the main idea in your own words. On a separate sheet of paper, summarize the factors that can affect the rulings of the Supreme Court justices.

brief a written document explaining the position of one side or the other in a case

Conference

Each week during the term, the justices get together to make their first decisions about the cases they have been studying. These meetings take place in secret; no audience is present, and no meeting minutes are kept. The chief justice presides over the meeting and is the first to lay out his or her views on the case. The other justices then take turns stating their views on the case. These presentations proceed in order of seniority, beginning with the longest-serving justice. After all have had their say, the justices vote on the case. At least six justices must be present to vote on a ruling. A majority vote decides a case.

LANDMARK SUPREME COURT DECISIONS

CIVIL LIBERTIES

- **Brown v. Board of Education (1954)** overturned **Plessy v. Ferguson (1896)**, which said African Americans could be provided with "separate but equal" public facilities; began school integration
- **Reed v. Reed (1971)** held that a state law that discriminated against women was unconstitutional
- **Roe v. Wade (1973)** legalized a woman's right to an abortion under certain circumstances
- **Bush v. Gore (2000)** ruled that Florida recount of presidential votes violated Fourteenth Amendment; recount stopped and Bush became president

FIRST AMENDMENT RIGHTS

- **Brandenburg v. Ohio (1969)** expanded the protection of political speech unless it is linked to immediate lawless behavior
- **Near v. Minnesota (1931)** ruled against censorship of information, defining "prior restraint" of written material as unconstitutional
- **DeJonge v. Oregon (1937)** reinforced peaceable assembly and association protection of the First Amendment
- **Engel v. Vitale (1962)** held that a public school district's practice of starting the day with prayer violates the establishment clause
- **United States v. Eichman (1990)** struck down Federal Flag Protection Act; held that flag burning is expressive speech

FEDERAL POWER

- **Marbury v. Madison (1803)** established the Supreme Court's power of judicial review
- **McCulloch v. Maryland (1819)** ruled that in a conflict between national and state power, the national government is supreme
- **Gibbons v. Ogden (1824)** established that Congress has sole authority to regulate interstate commerce

RIGHTS OF THE ACCUSED

- **Gideon v. Wainwright (1963)** declared that a person accused of a major crime had the right to legal counsel during a trial
- **Miranda v. Arizona (1966)** ruled that at the time of arrest suspects cannot be questioned until informed of their rights
- **Hamdan v. Rumsfeld (2006)** ruled that special military courts for foreign prisoners violated U.S. military law and international laws

CHART SKILLS

A landmark Supreme Court decision is a Court ruling that marks a turning point for legal history and American society.

▶ CRITICAL THINKING

1 *Analyzing Visuals* Which case helped show that federal law was superior to state law?

2 *Making Inferences* Which First Amendment rights case would be especially welcomed by publishers of newspapers? Why?

Segregation is the policy of keeping racial groups separate. In the *Plessy* v. *Ferguson* decision, the Court accepted segregation, saying that the facilities given the races could be "separate but equal."

▶ CRITICAL THINKING

1 *Analyzing Visuals* What effect did the decision in *Gong Lum* v. *Rice* have on this policy?

2 *Making Inferences* What changing social attitudes do you think were the basis of the *Brown* decision?

Segregation

1896—PLESSY v. FERGUSON
established "separate but equal" doctrine

1927— GONG LUM v. RICE
applied "separate but equal" to public schools

1938—STATE OF MISSOURI EX REL. GAINES v. CANADA
set precedent for states to "equalize" African American schools

1948—SIPUEL v. BOARD OF REGENTS OF UNIVERSITY OF OKLAHOMA ruled race-based denial of entrance to state law school unconstitutional

1954—BROWN v. BOARD OF EDUCATION
overturned *Plessy* v. *Ferguson*, declaring segregation in public schools unconstitutional

Integration

Factors Influencing Decisions

The facts of a case and the law that applies to it are the bases for judicial decisions. Yet many factors can affect justices' decisions. These include precedents, the nation's social atmosphere, and the justices' own views.

A guiding principle for all judges is called **stare decisis** (STEHR•ee dih•SY•suhs). This Latin term means "let the decision stand." It refers to the practice of using earlier court decisions to decide cases. By following precedent, courts make the law predictable.

Yet the law must also be flexible. Social conditions, public ideas, and technology change over the years. Although the Supreme Court is protected from outside pressures, changing social conditions can affect Court rulings. As the highest U.S. court, the Supreme Court can overrule precedents. Thus, the Court may interpret the law in new ways. Note the Court's changing views of segregation, or keeping racial groups separate, tracked on the time line of rulings on segregation.

Justices have varying views of the law and the role of the courts in society. Some believe the Court should be very active. Others think it should not promote new ideas or policies. Political checks limit the extent to which courts can exercise judicial review.

Finally, justices are human beings. Each sees the world based on personal life experiences. Those views affect their decisions.

--- *Why It* ---
MATTERS

Supreme Court Decisions

The decisions of the Supreme Court have a lasting effect on all Americans. Two of the Court's landmark rulings that had an impact on American students were *Brown* v. *Board of Education*, 1954, and *Tinker* v. *Des Moines*, 1969. The first ended school segregation. The second protected freedom of speech for students at school. How do these rulings affect you?

Reading HELPDESK

stare decisis the practice of using earlier judicial rulings as a basis for deciding cases

concurring opinion a statement written by a justice who votes with the majority, but for different reasons than the others

dissenting opinion a statement written by a justice who disagrees with the majority opinion, presenting his or her own opinion

unanimous opinion a Supreme Court ruling on a case in which all justices agree on the ruling

Writing Opinions

Written opinions set a precedent for lower courts to follow. Some of the Court's landmark decisions are grouped in four categories in the chart. In major cases, the Court issues at least one written opinion. One justice is assigned to write the majority opinion. Either the chief justice or the longest-serving member of the majority assigns the writing.

The majority opinion states the facts and gives the ruling. It also explains the Court's reasoning in reaching its decision. The reasoning often draws on the precedents set by earlier decisions.

Sometimes a justice agrees with the majority decision but for different reasons. That justice may choose to write a separate statement called a **concurring opinion.** Justices who oppose the majority decision write a **dissenting opinion.** In it, they explain why they disagree with the majority. As in the majority opinion, they cite precedents to explain the basis for the different view.

The Court issues a **unanimous opinion** when all the justices agree. These decisions have special force.

After opinions are **drafted**, or written in their first form, each one is reviewed by the justices on that side of the question. Thus, the justices in the majority look at the majority opinion. Those who disagree read the dissenting opinion. The justices comment on the draft that they read. The justice who wrote the opinion must take these comments into account. If the justice who wrote the majority opinion does not take other justices' views into account, one of them might withdraw support for the majority position. Revising the draft, then, is an important task.

When the opinions are in final form, the Court announces its decision. These written opinions guide rulings in new cases before the Supreme Court and other courts around the country.

✓ PROGRESS CHECK

Identifying Main Ideas What role do changing social conditions play in Court rulings?

Academic Vocabulary

draft to write a document in its first form

LESSON 4 REVIEW

Review Vocabulary

1. Write a sentence to show how a court's *docket* and *caseload* are related.

2. How do a *concurring opinion* and a *unanimous opinion* differ?

Answer the Guiding Questions

3. *Identifying* What is the key factor in the Court's decision to hear a case?

4. *Discussing* Do you think justices can remain objective? Explain your answer.

5. **ARGUMENT** Do you agree that the Supreme Court should be allowed to reinterpret the law to meet changing social conditions? Explain your reasoning.

Write your answers on a separate sheet of paper.

1 Writing Activity

EXPLORING THE ESSENTIAL QUESTION
How can governments ensure citizens are treated fairly?

In an essay, explain how the organization of our court system helps protect our rights as citizens.

2 21st Century Skills

USING TECHNOLOGY Search the Internet or use other resources to locate a map of the nearest federal district court and circuit court of appeals for the circuit in which your community is located. Mark the locations on a state map.

3 Being an Active Citizen

Some Americans do not understand what the Supreme Court does or how it works. Write a questionnaire that includes six to ten questions about what you think are key points about the Court and its work. Ask your questions of five or six people and note their responses. Based on those answers, write a brief guide that tells the facts about the Court and clears up any misunderstandings people have.

4 Understanding Visuals

Political cartoonists use their art to express political opinions in an entertaining manner. Some subject matter is serious and some is more humorous. Examine the political cartoon shown here. Read the conversation balloon and labels. What is the cartoonist saying about the influence of the political perspective of the president on the Supreme Court?

REVIEW THE GUIDING QUESTIONS

Directions: Choose the best answer for each question.

1 What is the goal of the federal court system?
   A. to treat everyone equally
   B. to settle civil disputes
   C. to keep the streets safe
   D. to try politicians

2 Concurrent jurisdiction occurs when
   F. admiralty and maritime laws are broken.
   G. U.S. diplomats are involved.
   H. there is a disagreement between two states.
   I. a crime involves both state and federal law.

3 Giving life tenure to judges
   A. limits them to two consecutive terms.
   B. helps free judges from public pressure.
   C. is a civil right.
   D. is a form of senatorial courtesy.

4 The power of judicial review means
   F. the Court can review any federal, state, or local law to decide whether it is constitutional.
   G. Supreme Court rulings are reviewed by Congress.
   H. the Supreme Court reviews all decisions of the lower courts.
   I. the Supreme Court reviews all state laws.

5 To request a hearing, one must petition for
   A. stare decisis.
   B. a docket.
   C. a writ of certiorari.
   D. a writ of habeas corpus.

6 When all justices agree on a decision and the reasoning behind it, the Court may issue a
   F. concurring opinion.
   G. dissenting opinion.
   H. brief.
   I. unanimous opinion.

DBQ **ANALYZING DOCUMENTS**

Directions: Analyze the excerpt and answer the questions.

The following excerpt is from the 1963 Supreme Court decision in *Gideon* v. *Wainright*. The justices delivered a unanimous opinion in favor of Clarence Earl Gideon.

> *"The right of an indigent [poor] defendant in a criminal trial to have the assistance of counsel [a lawyer] is a fundamental right essential to a fair trial, and petitioner's trial and conviction without the assistance of counsel violated the Fourteenth Amendment."*
>
> —*Gideon* v. *Wainwright* (1963)

7 **Analyzing** The Supreme Court ruled in this case that which of the following is a criminal defendant's fundamental right?

A. a trial

B. a conviction

C. counsel

D. bail

8 **Identifying Central Issues** What was at stake in this case?

F. fairness of the trial process   **H.** freedom of speech

G. question of state law   **I.** abuse of power

SHORT RESPONSE

> *"The Eighth and Fourteenth Amendments forbid imposition [use] of the death penalty on offenders who were under the age of 18 when their crimes were committed. The judgment of the Missouri Supreme Court setting aside the sentence of death imposed upon Christopher Simmons is affirmed [upheld]."*
>
> —Justice Anthony Kennedy, *Roper* v. *Simmons* (2005)

9 From what court was this case appealed? Did the U.S. Supreme Court confirm, reverse, or remand the decision of that lower court?

10 The Eighth Amendment forbids "cruel and unusual punishment." Does the Court think that the death penalty is a matter of "cruel and unusual punishment" in all cases? Why or why not?

EXTENDED RESPONSE

11 **Informative/Explanatory** Compare and contrast the roles and functions of district courts, circuit courts of appeals, and the U.S. Supreme Court.

Need Extra Help?

If You've Missed Question	❶	❷	❸	❹	❺	❻	❼	❽	❾	❿	⓫
Review Lesson	1	1	2	3	4	4	4	4	3, 4	3, 4	1, 2, 3

Political Parties

ESSENTIAL QUESTION
How do citizens, both individually and collectively, influence government policy?

netw🞉rks

There's More Online about political parties.

CHAPTER 8

Lesson 1
History of Political Parties

Lesson 2
Political Parties Today

The Story Matters...

Rallies for candidates during a presidential campaign are usually loud, colorful, and exciting. Enthusiastic supporters wear pins, wave signs, and cheer their candidate's speeches. Most of these supporters belong to the candidate's political party.

Political parties play a key role in the election process. They provide a way for Americans who share similar beliefs and goals for the nation's future to express their opinions.

Political parties provide money and other resources to support the candidates who belong to their party. Although today two main parties—Democrats and Republicans—dominate, many voters identify themselves as Independents. Other smaller political parties add diversity of opinions, excitement, and complexity to American political campaigns and elections.

◀ *In 2008, supporters of Republican John McCain cheered for their candidate for president at a Colorado rally.*

PHOTO: Chip Somodeville/Getty Images

245

Real-Life Civics

> **TODAY** Americans often have strong views about government and the laws under which they live. For many years, Americans have expressed their views through their association with one of the two main political parties—the Democrats or the Republicans. Recently, however, some citizens have grown dissatisfied with politicians from both parties. They have formed a new group known as the Tea Party movement. Members of the Tea Party object to increases in taxes and government spending, and they are working to elect candidates who agree with their views. At large rallies all across the country, Tea Party members have come together to encourage change in American government.

Tea Party activists hold a "Tax Day Rally" in Boston.

On the night of December 16, 1773, American colonists disguised as Native Americans boarded three British ships in Boston Harbor. Using axes and hatchets, the colonists broke open more than 300 crates of tea and threw the contents into the harbor.

PHOTOS: (l) The Melanie Stetson Freeman/The Christian Science Monitor/Getty Images; (tt) The Bridgeman Art Library/Getty Images

LONG AGO In 1773, another group of Americans came together to protest government policies. At this original tea party—the Boston Tea Party—dissatisfied American colonists protested the British government's taxation policies. They were especially angry about a tax on tea, a favorite drink of the time. To make their feelings known, the group of colonists raided British merchant ships in Boston Harbor and dumped the ships' cargoes of tea into the water. Other protests followed, and the colonies soon found themselves fighting for their independence in the American Revolution.

CIVIC LITERACY

★ ★ ★ ★

Analyzing Why do you think the members of the Tea Party movement chose to name themselves after the historical event known as the Boston Tea Party?

Your Opinion Would you be willing to join a group whose view differed from the view of the majority? Why or why not?

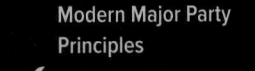

netw**o**rks

There's More Online!

☑ **GRAPHIC ORGANIZER**
Modern Major Party
Principles

☑ **CHARTS**
Evolution of American
Political Parties
Major Third-Party Candidates

☑ **TIME LINE**
Party Control of the Presidency,
1861–2013

Lesson 1

History of Political Parties

ESSENTIAL QUESTION *How do citizens, both individually and collectively, influence government policy?*

IT MATTERS BECAUSE
Political parties are one of the major ways citizens participate in the political process and influence the direction of government.

Growth of American Parties

GUIDING QUESTION *Why did political parties develop in the United States?*

Do you and your friends share opinions about the things you like and dislike? Do you discuss your feelings about school, sports, or music? Have you ever joined a group that shares your interests? In a similar way, some Americans join a political party to share ideas with others who feel as they do. A **political party** is a group of people with broad, shared interests. They join together to help the candidates they support win elections. They also work to shape government policy.

Two major parties have competed for power during most of the nation's history. For this reason, the United States is said to have a **two-party system.** The names and makeup of the two main parties have changed over time.

The First Parties

The U.S. Constitution does not mention political parties. In fact, many of the leaders who wrote the Constitution did not like the idea of political parties. They feared that parties, or "factions" as they called them, would lead to divisions that

PHOTO: (tl) Getty Images; (tc) AFP/Getty Images; (tr) Getty Images

Reading **HELP**DESK

Taking Notes: *Comparing*

As you read, complete a graphic organizer like the one shown here to identify the major political parties in the United States and their positions on a number of issues.

| Modern Major Party Principles | |
Party	Positions on Issues

Content Vocabulary
- **political party**
- **two-party system**
- **third party**
- **platform**

would weaken the new nation. Despite this, by the late 1790s two groups had formed to compete for political power. Parties arose because people had different ideas about what the government should do.

Secretary of the Treasury Alexander Hamilton and Secretary of State Thomas Jefferson were the leaders of the first parties. Hamilton thought that if the federal government was too weak, individuals' rights would be in danger. So he favored a strong national government. He also believed that a strong central government was needed to have a healthy economy. Jefferson, on the other hand, wanted to protect people's rights by limiting the power of the national government. He supported more power for the states, which were closer to the people.

Hamilton and his followers formed the Federalist Party. Jefferson and his supporters formed the Democratic-Republican Party. Starting in 1800, Jefferson's party grew stronger, while the Federalists lost support. The Federalist Party soon faded away.

EVOLUTION OF AMERICAN POLITICAL PARTIES

PARTY	DATES OF EXISTENCE	DESCRIPTION
Federalist	1790s–1820	Favored a strong central government
Democratic-Republican	1790s–1828	Formed to oppose Federalists; favored state over national government
National Republican	1825–1834	Split from Democratic-Republicans to oppose Andrew Jackson and work for strong central government
Democratic	1825–Present	Formed from Democratic-Republicans; supported Andrew Jackson; said it supported common people
Whig	1834–1854	Formed from National Republicans and others; favored internal improvements
Republican	1854–Present	Formed from Whigs and other groups; opposed spread of slavery to new territories and favored internal improvements

CHART SKILLS

For most of its existence, the United States has had a two-party system. New parties have grown out of older parties.

1 **Identifying** Which party has been active the longest?

2 CRITICAL THINKING
Making Connections How is the Republican Party connected to the National Republican Party?

political party an association of voters with broad common interests who want to influence or control decision making in government by electing the party's candidates to public office

two-party system a system of government in which two political parties compete for power

Today's Major Parties Form

By 1824, the Democratic-Republican Party was so dominant that four presidential candidates ran under the party's banner. After a close-fought election, John Quincy Adams defeated Andrew Jackson. Tensions between the two candidates and their supporters remained. Sectional differences among North, South, and West increased the tension. By 1828, the Democratic-Republican Party had split. Those who supported candidate Andrew Jackson called themselves the Democratic Party. They wanted to **stress** their ties to common people. Those who opposed Jackson called themselves National Republicans.

The National Republicans faded quickly, though. The Whig Party took their place as the main opponent of the Democrats until the 1850s. The Whigs tried to win broad support by proposing ambitious internal improvements such as roads and canals. They also tried to avoid the controversial issue of slavery.

In 1854 people who opposed slavery joined together to form a new party. They called themselves the Republican Party. Some Republicans thought slavery should be abolished in the Southern states. Others did not go that far, but they did agree that it should not spread to the territories controlled by the United States government. Democrats wanted to allow the people in each territory to decide for themselves whether to permit slavery. As the slavery issue grew more important, the Whig Party dissolved. Since the late 1850s, the Republicans and the Democrats have remained the major parties in our nation.

For about 75 years following the Civil War, the Republican Party dominated national politics. A Democrat served as president for only 16 years in that span. The Great Depression tipped the balance to the Democrats. A Democrat was president for 28 of the next 36 years. Since 1968, though, Republicans have won the presidency seven times to the Democrats' four times.

✔ **PROGRESS CHECK**

Describing How did Federalists view the power of the national government?

John C. Frémont was the Republican Party's first presidential candidate. He lost the 1856 election to James Buchanan. Abraham Lincoln was the first Republican to be elected president.

▶ CRITICAL THINKING
Explaining How did a controversial issue lead to the formation of the Republican Party?

JOHN C. FREMONT. Wm L. DAYTON.
THE REPUBLICANS CHOICE FOR PRESIDENT VICE PRESIDENT FROM 1857 TO 1861.

PHOTO: Getty Images

Reading HELPDESK

Reading Strategy: *Summarizing*

When you summarize a reading, you find the main idea of the passage and restate it in your own words. Read about how America's main political parties differ. On a separate sheet of paper, summarize the reading in one or two sentences.

Academic Vocabulary

stress to give special importance to

promote to advance a cause or idea

third party a political party that challenges the two major parties

250 *Political Parties*

Third Parties

GUIDING QUESTION *What is the importance of third parties in American politics?*

Throughout American history, smaller political parties have competed for power with the two main parties. These smaller parties are known as **third parties.**

Third parties have not had widespread support from voters. Yet they have influenced American politics in important ways. For example, third parties have often **promoted** ideas that were unpopular at first. Over time some of these ideas gained popularity and became law. The Populist Party of the 1890s called for senators to be elected directly by voters. It also wanted the workday to last only eight hours. The Progressive Party of the early 1900s pushed for changes, too. It worked to give voters a more direct role in government and more power to make laws.

In 2000 Ralph Nader ran as the presidential candidate of the Green Party, which wants policies that will favor the environment.

▶ CRITICAL THINKING
Categorizing What kind of third party is the Green Party?

Types of Third Parties

Some third parties form to promote a particular cause. These are known as single-issue political parties. For example, the Prohibition Party was formed in 1872. Its main purpose was to ban the sale of alcohol. Single-issue parties usually fade away when the issue loses importance or is adopted by a major party.

Other third parties are formed by people with a certain ideology, or set of beliefs, about government. One example is the Communist Party USA. Members believe that the government or workers should own all resources and businesses. Third parties united by an ideology can last for a long time.

Still other third parties unite around an independent leader with a strong personality. Such parties often do not last beyond the defeat of that candidate. Ross Perot was one such leader. He ran for president as an independent in 1992. Then, he founded the Reform Party when he ran again in 1996. He lost both elections and the Reform Party has grown weaker in recent years.

Third parties have a hard time competing against the two larger, more powerful parties. The names of Republican and Democratic candidates are always placed on the ballot in many states. On the other hand, third-party candidates must gather signatures from a large number of voters in order to appear on the ballot. These candidates have more hurdles to overcome. As a result, third parties often cannot raise enough money to compete effectively.

PHOTO: Getty Images

The Tea Party movement arose in 2009 to protest what it saw as the growing size of government.

▶ CRITICAL THINKING

Predicting Do you think a group such as the Tea Party movement can become a new political party? Why or why not?

Other Party Systems

Political parties exist in most countries, but two-party systems are rare. The role that political parties play differs with each nation's political system.

Many democracies have multiparty systems; that is, they have three or more parties. For example, Canada has three major parties, France has more than eight, and Israel has more than twenty. In these countries, one party rarely wins enough support to control the government. As a result, several parties must work together.

Some nations have a one-party system. In the People's Republic of China, for instance, only one party—the Communist Party—exists. As a result, only Communist Party members fill government positions. No rival candidates are allowed to run for office. Thus, elections are mainly for show. One-party systems are not democratic.

✓ PROGRESS CHECK

Identifying Name three types of third parties and explain why they form.

platform a series of statements expressing a party's principles, beliefs, and positions on election issues

Party Differences

GUIDING QUESTION *How do America's major modern political parties differ?*

Today's two major U.S. parties differ in their ideas about how much the government should be involved in the economy and in citizens' lives. Democrats tend to think that the federal government should be more directly involved in regulating the economy. They believe that the government should also help provide housing, income, education, and jobs for the poor. Republicans favor less government regulation of the economy as the best way to promote prosperity. Both parties believe that economic growth will give unemployed people a better chance to find jobs on their own.

Both parties are national parties. That means they usually field candidates in elections throughout the country. Nonetheless, each party tends to do better in some sections of the country than in others. The Democrats are particularly strong in the Northeast and on the West Coast. Republican support is very strong in the South.

Sometimes the ways in which the two major parties differ in their views on a specific topic may seem small. One reason is that both adopt some moderate views. They hope this will help them appeal to as many voters as possible. The parties may also seem similar because most Americans generally agree on many issues.

How can citizens identify the differences between the parties? They can read the platform that each party writes when it nominates a presidential candidate every four years. The **platform** is a series of statements expressing the party's core beliefs and its positions on various issues.

✓ PROGRESS CHECK

Explaining Why do the two major parties often seem similar?

Why It — MATTERS

Party Platforms

Party platforms try to appeal to as many people as possible, while at the same time drawing clear differences from other parties. What might be some important platform issues?

LESSON 1 REVIEW

Review Vocabulary

1. Why do *third parties* usually not last very long in the American *two-party system*?

2. Why do *political parties* create *platforms*? How are *platforms* useful to voters?

Answer the Guiding Questions

3. ***Explaining*** How did the first two major American political parties differ?

4. ***Analyzing*** How have third parties been important in American history?

5. ***Contrasting*** How do the two major political parties of today differ?

6. **INFORMATIVE/EXPLANATORY** Why do ideological third parties last longer than the other two kinds of third parties?

netw⊙rks

There's More Online!

☑ **GRAPHIC ORGANIZER**
Political Party Roles

☑ **CHART**
Organization of Political
Parties

☑ **POLITICAL CARTOON**
Boss Tweed

☑ **VIDEO**

Lesson 2
Political Parties Today

PHOTO: (tl) Bettmann/Corbis; (tcl) AFP/Getty Images; (tcr) AP Photo/The Daily Times, Ben Chrismant; (tr) Kerry-Edwards 2004, Inc./Sharon Farmer, photographer

ESSENTIAL QUESTION *How do citizens, both individually and collectively, influence government policy?*

IT MATTERS BECAUSE
Understanding how political parties work helps citizens as they follow campaigns and select candidates they wish to support.

Organization of Political Parties

GUIDING QUESTION *How are political parties organized?*

Have you ever been a candidate in a school election? Perhaps you helped a friend who was running for office. What did you do to try to win? Political parties also want their candidates to win. To reach this goal, major parties organize at the local, state, and national levels. These levels are only loosely joined. Party members at all levels share similar political beliefs. Therefore, they share an ultimate goal. They want to help the party win election to as many offices as possible.

National Organization and Convention

Each party has a **national committee.** It includes members from every state. The national chairperson heads this committee. Each party's national committee raises money for presidential elections. It also organizes the party's national convention.

At the national convention, delegates choose the party's candidates for president and vice president. Delegates are chosen through presidential primary elections. In some states they are chosen in a **caucus** (KAW•kuhs), or special meeting.

Reading **HELP**DESK

Taking Notes: *Identifying*

As you read, use the graphic organizer to identify the roles of political parties.

Political
Party Roles

Content Vocabulary

- **national committee**
- **caucus**
- **precinct**
- **political machine**
- **direct primary**
- **closed primary**
- **open primary**

254 *Political Parties*

In the past, conventions were suspenseful events. Delegates from around the country decided on their presidential candidate. Today, however, the identity of the candidate is already known when the convention begins. Still, the convention is an important time for building party unity. It also launches the election campaign.

The major parties also have campaign committees for the party's candidates for Congress. These committees raise money. They also give advice and support to the candidates.

State and Local Organizations

The 50 state committees work to elect party candidates to state offices. These include the offices of governor, state legislator, and others. The committees also help to elect their parties' candidates to national offices.

At the local level, parties have thousands of city, town, and county committees. The county chairperson, who runs the county committee, often has a great deal of power.

Each city or county is divided into election districts called precincts. A **precinct** (PREE•sihngt) is a geographic area that has a specific number of voters. A precinct could be an entire small town, or it might be a group of **adjacent** neighborhoods in a large city.

21ˢᵗ Century
SKILLS

Write a Research Report

Conduct research and write a report on national political conventions that made history or stirred controversy. You may wish to focus your research. For example, you can research and write about the first national political convention or the last convention at which the party's presidential nominee was actually chosen. Some notable Republican conventions include 1976 and 1980. Notable Democratic conventions include 1968 and 1972.

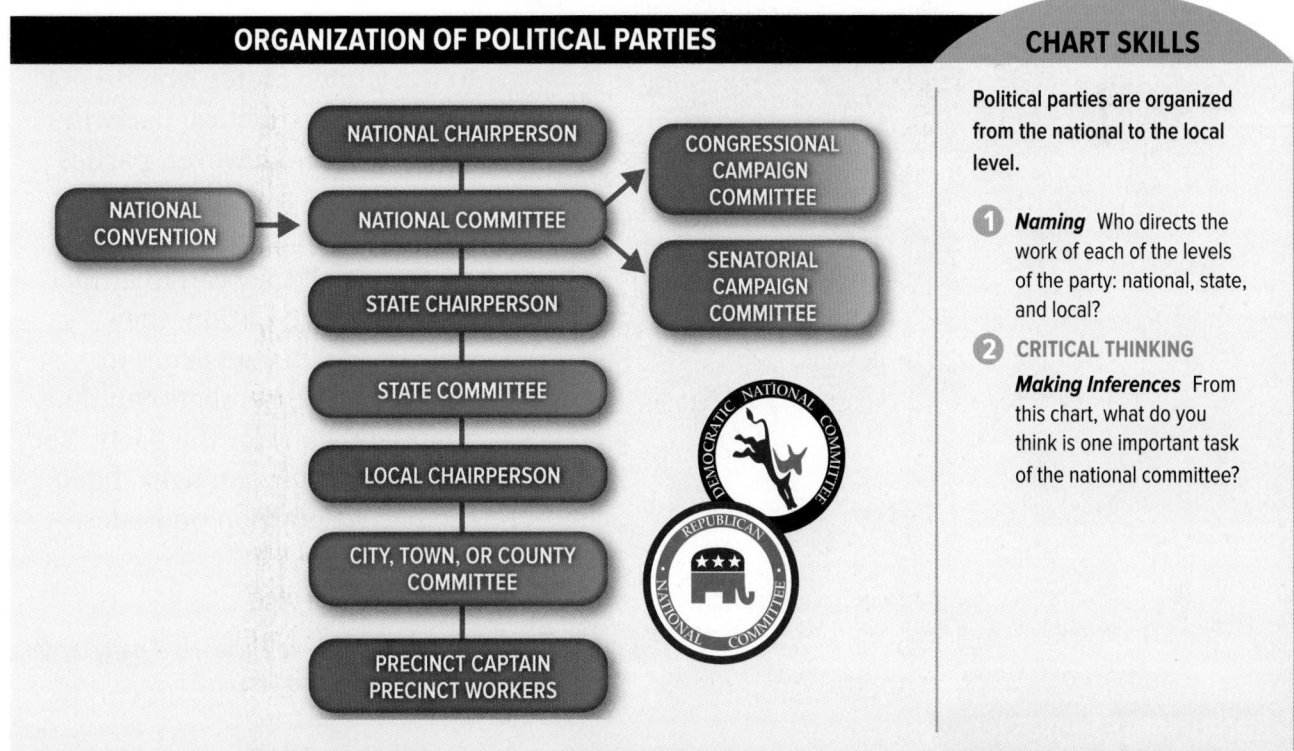

ORGANIZATION OF POLITICAL PARTIES

- NATIONAL CONVENTION
- NATIONAL CHAIRPERSON
- NATIONAL COMMITTEE
- CONGRESSIONAL CAMPAIGN COMMITTEE
- SENATORIAL CAMPAIGN COMMITTEE
- STATE CHAIRPERSON
- STATE COMMITTEE
- LOCAL CHAIRPERSON
- CITY, TOWN, OR COUNTY COMMITTEE
- PRECINCT CAPTAIN PRECINCT WORKERS

CHART SKILLS

Political parties are organized from the national to the local level.

1 **Naming** Who directs the work of each of the levels of the party: national, state, and local?

2 **CRITICAL THINKING**

Making Inferences From this chart, what do you think is one important task of the national committee?

- plurality
- majority

national committee representatives from the 50 state party organizations who run a political party

caucus a meeting of political party members to conduct party business

precinct a geographic area that contains a specific number of voters

Academic Vocabulary

adjacent located next to

Lesson 2 **255**

"Boss" Tweed ran the famous Tammany Hall political machine of New York City.

► CRITICAL THINKING
Analyzing Does the cartoonist believe Tweed can be kept in jail? Explain.

Each precinct appoints a captain. Party leaders depend on precinct captains to build the party at the local level. Precinct captains organize volunteers to distribute leaflets and register voters. They also help get voters to the polls on Election Day.

Political Machines

Sometimes a local party organization grows very powerful. Then, year after year, its candidates win every election. Such a strong organization is called a **political machine.** In the late 1800s and early 1900s, these groups ran many cities. There were few social systems in place to help the poor. The machines provided jobs and other aid to those who voted for them.

One famous political machine was New York City's Tammany Hall. Its leader was William Marcy "Boss" Tweed. He and his friends grew rich by taking illegal payments from businesses. Many in the Tweed machine ended up in prison.

Most people now agree that political machines are harmful. When one party is in power for too long, it is more likely to ignore people's needs. Machines also run the risk of public officials becoming corrupt, as happened with Tweed's machine.

Becoming Involved in a Political Party

In the United States, you do not have to join a political party in order to vote. However, parties offer citizens a great way to participate in politics. Political parties do all they can to attract members. In addition, they welcome whoever wishes to belong. Party members can do volunteer work for the party. Very active members can help shape the party's position on issues.

✓ PROGRESS CHECK

Explaining How do higher-level party leaders depend on precinct leaders?

"STONE WALLS DO NOT A PRISON MAKE."—*Old Song.*
"NO PRISON IS BIG ENOUGH TO HOLD THE BOSS". IN ON ONE SIDE, AND OUT AT THE OTHER.

PHOTO: Bettmann/Corbis

Reading HELPDESK

political machine a strong party organization that can control political appointments and deliver votes

PHOTO: AP Photo/Pablo Martinez Monsivais

Selecting Party Candidates

GUIDING QUESTION *How do political parties nominate candidates?*

In the United States, citizens can run for almost any public office in the land. Yet when it comes time to elect a candidate to office, voters often have a choice between just two candidates, one from each major party. How are candidates chosen to run in an election? One of the major jobs of political parties is to nominate, or choose, candidates for office. To do so, parties typically use the direct primary. In a **direct primary,** voters choose candidates to represent a party in a general election.

Types of Primary Elections

There are two main forms of the direct primary: closed and open. They differ in terms of which voters can take part.

Most states hold a **closed primary.** In this case, only party members can vote. For example, only Republicans can vote in the Republican Party's primary.

Some people favor the closed primary. They say that it prevents members of one party from crossing over into the other party's primary to vote for weak candidates. These weak candidates would then be easy to defeat in the general election.

Political campaigns rely on the energy and passion of campaign volunteers. Supporters of John McCain and Mitt Romney compete for attention during the 2008 presidential Republican Party primaries.

▶ CRITICAL THINKING
Evaluating Why is the primary an important process for a political party?

---

direct primary an election in which voters choose candidates to represent each political party in a general election

closed primary an election in which only the declared members of a political party are allowed to vote for that party's nominees

Others oppose the closed primary. They say that it prevents independent voters from taking part in primaries. In most states, voters who do not belong to a party cannot vote in either major party's primary. For this reason, some states have an **open primary.** In these elections, any registered voter can vote in a primary.

Winning a Primary

The candidate who wins the primary is typically the one who gets a **plurality,** or the most votes. A candidate with a plurality wins even if his or her share is less than 50 percent of all the votes cast.

In a few states, the winner must have a **majority.** This means the winning candidate must get more than 50 percent of the total votes. Sometimes, no candidate receives a majority in the primary. When this happens, the party holds a second primary called a runoff. The two candidates with the most votes take part in this primary. The winner of the runoff becomes the party's candidate in the general election.

Most offices have only one officeholder: one mayor, one representative for a district. Sometimes, though, more than one type of position is vacant in the same election. A city might have several city council members, for instance. In these cases, a party can nominate more than one candidate. It will choose the top vote-getters in the primary.

Political parties work to elect the candidates they nominate. One way they do this is by having volunteers try to persuade voters to vote for the party's candidate.

▶ CRITICAL THINKING
Making Generalizations Why is support from parties important for candidates?

PHOTO: AFP/Getty Images

Third-Party Nominees

Major political party candidates are always listed on the general election ballot. In most states, third-party candidates can also get on that ballot through the power of petition. A petition is a paper that officially asks that a person be placed on the ballot as a candidate. The candidate must then get enough qualified voters to sign the petition papers.

 **PROGRESS CHECK**

Contrasting What is the difference between an open and a closed primary?

Other Political Party Functions

GUIDING QUESTION *What other roles do political parties play?*

The main purpose of political parties in the United States is to elect candidates to office. Parties also play another important role. They help the people of the United States practice self-government. Political parties enable citizens to communicate with their government leaders and help ensure that the government remains responsive to the needs of the people. Political parties

- support candidates
- communicate with citizens
- run the government
- link different parts of government
- act as a watchdog over government

Supporting Candidates

After a political party names its candidates, it helps them try to win the general election. Parties raise money for several purposes. They use funds to pay for campaign appearances, to buy ads, and to pay workers. Party workers and volunteers register citizens to vote. On Election Day, they try to make sure that their supporters go to the polls.

Third-party candidates like Michael Badnarik, the 2004 Libertarian candidate for president, have to do many things for themselves, including handing out bumper stickers to potential supporters.

▶ **CRITICAL THINKING**
Comparing How do you think the level of support a third party can offer its candidates compares with what the major parties can offer theirs?

PHOTO: AP Photo/The Daily Times, Ben Chrisman

Reading Strategy: *Identifying*

When you read, it is useful to identify details related to a topic. Create and fill in a graphic organizer that shows how political parties use the funds they raise to help meet their goals.

Communicating with the People

Parties help citizens and candidates talk to each other. This helps government work in two ways. First, through speeches, printed material, and ads, candidates tell voters where they stand on issues. Second, candidates listen to what citizens have to say on the issues.

Sometimes people feel strongly about an issue. They may oppose a government policy. They may want new laws on a particular issue. A political movement that begins with the people is known as a grassroots movement. When a grassroots movement becomes strong enough, a political party often adopts its ideas. Sometimes these movements gain enough strength to become a third party.

Running Different Parts of Government

Political parties play a key role in running the government. Congress and most state legislatures are organized based on party membership. Leaders within the legislature work hard to make sure that all the lawmakers in their party support the party's position on any bills being discussed.

At meetings with voters, candidates listen to voters express their views on issues.

CRITICAL THINKING

Analyzing How does this activity improve self-government?

PHOTO: Kerry-Edwards 2004, Inc./Sharon Farmer, photographer

Reading **HELP**DESK

Reading Strategy: *Summarizing*

To summarize a reading, you find the main idea and restate it in your own words. Read about how political parties help people communicate. On a separate sheet of paper, summarize the reading in one or two sentences.

260 *Political Parties*

Parties play a role in the executive branch as well. The president, governors, and some mayors have the power to appoint individuals to fill certain high-level jobs. The executives usually name people who believe in their party's ideas. In this way, leaders can count on their top aides to carry out policies they support.

Linking Different Levels of Government

Political parties also help officials at different levels or branches of government work together. Suppose the mayor of Tampa, Florida, and the governor of Florida are from the same party. If so, they are likely to have similar goals and ideas. They might even have worked together on campaigns or party business in the past.

These connections can make it easier for them to join forces to address problems that affect both the city and the state. What if a majority of lawmakers belong to the same party as the chief executive? Then the legislative and executive branches are likely to work closely together to pass laws the party favors.

Acting as a Watchdog

Between elections, one political party is out of power. This is the party that lost the elections for president, governor, or congressional seats. This party then acts as a watchdog over the party in power. It tries to make sure that members of that party do not misuse or abuse their power.

The party out of power is often called the opposition party. The opposition gives voice to people who disagree with the ideas of the party in power. In this way, the opposition party hopes to attract voters. This role also forces the party in power to pay attention to the views of a wide range of people.

✓ PROGRESS CHECK

Making Generalizations How do political parties help the American people practice self-government?

Why It
MATTERS

The Importance of a Watchdog

Have you ever played a game in which one of the players gets to decide if the rules are being broken? That is what government would be like without outside watchdogs to point out wrongdoing. What is the state of politics in your area? Is one party in control and another in opposition? How does the opposition party perform its watchdog function?

LESSON 2 REVIEW

Review Vocabulary

1. How might a *precinct* be involved with a *political machine*?

2. Explain the difference between a *plurality* and a *majority* in terms of choosing a candidate for a primary.

Answer the Guiding Questions

3. ***Summarizing*** Describe the general organization of political parties, from the national to the local level.

4. ***Explaining*** What is the main method that political parties use to choose candidates for office? Who takes part in this process in most states?

5. ***Evaluating*** Other than choosing candidates for office, what do you think is a party's most important function? Why?

6. **ARGUMENT** Write a paragraph explaining why you think primaries should be either open or closed.

Write your answers on a separate sheet of paper.

1 **Writing Activity**

EXPLORING THE ESSENTIAL QUESTION

How do citizens, both individually and collectively, influence government policy?

Make a pamphlet explaining how citizens can play an active role in influencing government policy. Research different ways citizens can be involved. You might interview a party or group activist. Explain whether you think a citizen has more influence on policy by working as an individual or within a political party. Include activities citizens can perform as individuals and as part of a group.

2 **21st Century Skills**

ANALYZING Create a media presentation analyzing the positions of the Democratic and Republican parties on three issues you care about, such as education, security, or the environment. Look for information in sources such as party Web sites, newspapers, and television news shows. Review the information about each party's position on the issues you chose. Then create a media presentation with slides on each issue. Briefly state each party's view and its good or bad points. Share your slide show with the class.

3 **Being an Active Citizen**

In a small group, identify an issue in your school or community that needs attention, such as creating a community garden or a new food bank. Write a letter to the local offices of the two major political parties and one smaller party explaining the problem and your idea for a solution. Ask them for comments and suggestions. As a group, prepare a presentation comparing the party responses. Which supported your idea? Which did not? Did they offer other solutions that made sense?

4 **Understanding Visuals**

Examine this political cartoon about the government deficit. A deficit occurs when the government spends more money than it takes in. What are the two characters saying? How do the statements of the two symbols reflect party beliefs? What point is the cartoonist making? Does the cartoonist think one party is more realistic than the other?

REVIEW THE GUIDING QUESTIONS

Directions: Choose the best answer for each question.

1 What is a party platform?

A. a place where party leaders meet

B. a statement of a party's beliefs and positions

C. a method a party uses to contact followers

D. a list of a party's candidates

2 What parties became the chief rivals starting in the 1850s?

F. Democratic-Republicans and Federalists

G. Federalists and National Republicans

H. Republicans and Democrats

I. Whigs and Democrats

3 What type of third party is most likely to last a long time?

A. ideological party

B. independent party

C. single-issue party

D. leader-centered party

4 In what kind of election can any registered voter help to choose a party's candidates?

F. closed primary

G. general election

H. open primary

I. party primary

5 What is the name for a political organization so strong that its candidates win elections year after year?

A. county committee

B. political machine

C. political party

D. political monopoly

6 A key role of a political party that is out of power is to

F. select third-party candidates.

G. run the government.

H. hold a closed primary.

I. act as a watchdog over the party in power.

DBQ ANALYZING DOCUMENTS

Directions: Analyze the document and answer the questions that follow.

This is a passage from the platform of the Bull Moose Party, a third party that competed in the 1912 presidential election.

"Political parties exist to secure responsible government and to execute [carry out] the will of the people.

From these great tasks both of the old parties have turned aside. Instead of instruments to promote the general welfare, they have become the tools of corrupt interests which use them . . . to serve their selfish purposes."

7 **Identifying** The platform says that the two purposes of a political party are running the government responsibly and

A. winning elections.

B. carrying out the will of the people.

C. gaining political power.

D. collecting needed campaign funds.

8 **Drawing Conclusions** According to the platform, how had the major parties failed?

F. by taking away citizens' right to vote

G. by joining together instead of competing

H. by doing the will of corrupt interests

I. by failing to find good candidates

SHORT RESPONSE

"Democratic priorities remain clear: to provide a tax cut for working families, to promote policies that produce jobs and economic growth, and to assist millions of our fellow Americans who have lost their jobs through no fault of their own."

—Representative Nancy Pelosi (California), 2010 press release

9 According to Representative Pelosi, what are the Democratic Party's priorities?

10 Do the priorities mentioned by Pelosi agree with the Democratic Party's basic beliefs? Explain.

EXTENDED RESPONSE

11 **Informative/Explanatory** You are the chairperson of a political party. Write a short speech detailing the roles that political parties play.

Need Extra Help?

If You've Missed Question	**1**	**2**	**3**	**4**	**5**	**6**	**7**	**8**	**9**	**10**	**11**
Review Lesson	1	1	1	2	2	2	1	1	1	1	2

Voting and Elections

ESSENTIAL QUESTIONS • *What are the rights and responsibilities of citizens?*
• *Why do people create, structure, and change governments?*

netw⚬rks

There's More Online about voting and elections.

CHAPTER 9

Lesson 1
Who Can Vote?

Lesson 2
Elections and Campaigns

The Story Matters...

The right to vote is perhaps the most important privilege you will have as a citizen in a representative democracy. Elections give citizens the opportunity to choose their leaders, decide important issues, and shape their government.

Citizens can cast their ballots through the mail before Election Day. However, most people go to their local polling station at a school, a church, or even a neighbor's house.

Whether an election is held to choose a local mayor, a state governor, or the president of the United States, voting is a personal process that takes place in a small, private voting booth. The ballots are secret. Privacy and secrecy ensure that each voter can cast his or her ballot free from outside influences or pressure.

◄ *In the 2006 elections, a local car dealership served as the polling station for these voters in Glendale, California.*

PHOTO: ROBYN BECK/AFP/Getty Images

Real-Life Civics

> **NOW** Presidential candidates need to get their messages out to a vast number of people across a huge area. Modern technology has made that task easier than it used to be—but also very expensive. Candidates rely on TV and radio ads, news coverage of their campaign events, and even appearances on popular talk shows. They employ professional media consultants who help them shape their appeals to voters. They also maintain official Web sites and use social media to make their views and intentions public. In short, candidates today are likely to use all available means to reach voters. This was not always the case, however. In 1956 Adlai Stevenson, running for president against Dwight Eisenhower, dismissed television advertising as undignified. Stevenson lost.

Candidate Barack Obama appeared on *The Daily Show with Jon Stewart* in 2007 to get his message out.

In 1940, President Franklin Roosevelt used a "whistle-stop" train tour to reach voters in Glendale, California.

THEN Before radio and television provided a way to reach the nation, getting a message out to Americans often meant going to meet them in person. Presidential candidates traveled in special trains to meet voters. They often gave speeches from the back of the caboose. These "whistle-stop" tours were a way to speak to a large number of potential voters. Presidents who campaigned in this way included Woodrow Wilson, Herbert Hoover, Theodore Roosevelt, and Franklin Delano Roosevelt. Perhaps the most famous "whistle-stop" tour occurred in 1948. President Harry S. Truman traveled 30,000 miles through 28 states to rally supporters. He went on to win reelection.

PHOTOS: (l) AP Photo/Jason DeCrow, File; (tr) Bettmann/CORBIS

CIVIC LITERACY

★ ★ ★ ★

Analyzing Explain which you think would have a greater effect on a voter: a personal visit from a presidential candidate to the voter's hometown or a message from a presidential candidate on social media.

Your Opinion With so many places to gather information about presidential candidates, where would you seek the most accurate information to inform yourself before voting?

267

netw✹rks
There's More Online!

☑ **GRAPHIC ORGANIZER**
Voting Process

☑ **BIOGRAPHY**
Alice Paul

☑ **CHART**
Extending the Right to Vote

☑ **POLITICAL CARTOON**
Voter Apathy

☑ **SLIDE SHOW**
Woman Suffrage

☑ **GAMES**

Lesson 1

Who Can Vote?

ESSENTIAL QUESTION *What are the rights and responsibilities of citizens?*

IT MATTERS BECAUSE
The right to vote spread slowly to more and more people.

Qualifying to Vote

GUIDING QUESTION *What are the requirements to vote?*

For most of history, the vast majority of people never had a chance to choose their rulers. Instead, they lived under powerful rulers such as kings and queens who inherited their thrones.

Today, in the United States, it is different. Citizens have the right to vote for leaders. It is one of our most treasured rights. Casting a vote is at the core of American citizenship. For most adults, voting for the first time is a rite of passage that is as exciting as and even more important than getting a driver's license.

Expanding Suffrage

The Declaration of Independence states that "all men are created equal." Unfortunately this **principle,** or basic belief, of giving equal rights to all people has not always been achieved. In the early years of our country, **suffrage,** or the right to vote, was limited to small groups of people. A few states allowed both white and African American males to vote. Typically, however, only white, male landowners were allowed to vote. Over the years, suffrage has expanded to include more and more Americans.

PHOTO: (tl) Jim West/Alamy; (tcr) Hulton Archive/Getty Images; (tcr) U.S. Army; (tr) Rob Crandall/Alamy

Taking Notes: *Sequencing*

As you read, create a chart like the one shown to list the steps in the voting process.

The Voting Process	
1.	
2.	
3.	

Content Vocabulary

- suffrage
- register
- polling place
- ballot
- voter turnout rate
- apathy

People who were once barred from voting included white adult males who could not afford to buy property, all women, African American males, Native American males, and people under 21 years of age. Gradually, the barriers that kept these groups from voting were removed.

Over time individual states increased suffrage. However, the expansion of voting rights was largely accomplished by adding amendments to the Constitution. The first step came in 1870, after the Civil War, when the nation ratified the Fifteenth Amendment. The Fifteenth Amendment states that no person can be denied the right to vote because of race or color. Its purpose was to extend suffrage to African Americans who were recently freed from slavery. The amendment was unable to achieve that goal, however. Many Southern states passed laws to keep African Americans from exercising this right. It took nearly a century for true suffrage to be granted to African Americans.

The Nineteenth Amendment extended suffrage to all American women. For decades, women had fought for the right to vote. Some states had given them that right, but they did not enjoy the ability to vote across the entire nation. Women finally achieved that victory in 1920, when the Nineteenth Amendment was ratified. One suffragist, or person who fought for women's right to vote, later recalled:

More American women than men turn out to vote, in both presidential and nonpresidential elections.

▶ CRITICAL THINKING
Making Inferences Why do you think suffragists worked so hard to gain voting rights for women?

TEXT: Alice Paul Biography, Copyright 1972 by Alice Paul Institute, Inc. PHOTO: Jim West/Alamy

PRIMARY SOURCE

❝ I never doubted that equal rights was the right direction. Most reforms, most problems are complicated. But to me there is nothing complicated about ordinary equality. ❞

—Alice Paul, from a 1972 interview, quoted in a biography published by the Alice Paul Institute

The Twenty-sixth Amendment, ratified in 1971, lowered the voting age to 18. Before that, the voting age in most states was 21. Now, many people can vote before they graduate from high school.

Academic Vocabulary
principle basic belief

suffrage the right to vote

American Leaders

• Alice Paul, Suffragist, (1885–1977)

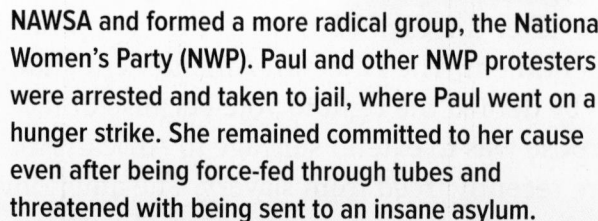

The banners asked a simple question: "Mr. President—what will you do for woman suffrage?" In 1917, a group of women who called themselves the "Silent Sentinels" carried banners with this question for President Woodrow Wilson. They were led by the fierce and determined Alice Paul.

Born in 1885 to a Quaker family, Paul was raised to believe that men and women were equal. After graduating from college, she spent time in England. While there, she saw British suffragists parading, picketing, and speaking out for their cause—gaining women the right to vote. Upon returning to the United States, Paul decided to take up the cause. She joined the National American Woman Suffrage Association (NAWSA). On March 3, 1913, Paul staged a parade for woman suffrage in Washington, D.C., on the day that Woodrow Wilson was inaugurated as president. The parade drew national attention to the issue of woman suffrage.

Paul soon left the NAWSA and formed a more radical group, the National Women's Party (NWP). Paul and other NWP protesters were arrested and taken to jail, where Paul went on a hunger strike. She remained committed to her cause even after being force-fed through tubes and threatened with being sent to an insane asylum.

Paul's persistence paid off. By the end of 1917, President Wilson finally announced his support for the Nineteenth Amendment.

Looking at Leadership

What actions did Paul take that show fierce commitment to her cause? Why do you think she felt so strongly about woman suffrage?

Voting Requirements Today

Today, many barriers to voting have been eliminated. More people than ever before can take part in government by voting. When an American citizen turns 18, he or she has the right to vote in all local, state, and national elections.

However, some groups of people are not eligible, or qualified, to vote. In most states, people who have committed serious crimes are not eligible to vote while imprisoned. Also, people who suffer certain mental illnesses may lose their eligibility. People born in other countries who have immigrated to the United States are not allowed to vote until they become citizens. Other than these exceptions, the great majority of adult American citizens are eligible to vote. This means that hundreds of millions of Americans have a part in running their own government. As Abraham Lincoln said, we have "a government of the people, by the people, for the people."

✓ PROGRESS CHECK

Specifying Which amendment to the Constitution gave suffrage to women?

PHOTO: Hulton Archive/Getty Images

Reading HELPDESK

Reading Notes: *Categorizing*

As you study the chart of acts extending the right to vote, consider the manner by which each law extends the right to vote. For example, some laws prohibit certain actions. Others set standards. Create two or more categories and arrange these laws accordingly.

Action and Impact

1870 Fifteenth Amendment
Prohibits denying a person's right to vote on the basis of race

1920 Nineteenth Amendment
Guarantees women the right to vote

1924 Congressional Act
All Native Americans given citizenship

1944 *Smith* v. *Allwright*
Supreme Court rules prohibiting African Americans from voting in primary elections is unconstitutional

1957 Civil Rights Act of 1957
Justice Department can sue to protect voting rights in various states

1960 Civil Rights Act of 1960
Introduces penalties against anybody who obstructs an individual's voting rights

1961 Twenty-third Amendment
Residents of District of Columbia given right to vote

1964 Twenty-fourth Amendment
Outlaws poll tax in national elections

1965 Voting Rights Act of 1965
Literacy tests prohibited; Federal voter registrars authorized in seven southern states

1970 Voting Rights Act Amendments of 1970
Lowers the minimum voting age to 18 in federal elections

1971 Twenty-sixth Amendment
Minimum voting age reduced to 18 for all elections

1975 Voting Rights Act Amendments of 1975
Bans literacy tests and mandates bilingual ballots in certain areas

1982 Voting Rights Act Amendment of 1982
Extends provisions of two previous voting rights act amendments

1992 Voting Rights Language Assistance Act
Extends use of bilingual ballots and voting assistance

1993 National Voter Registration Act
Makes it easier to register to vote and to maintain registration

2006 Voting Rights Act Reauthorization and Amendments Act of 2006
Prohibits use of tests or devices to deny the right to vote; requires certain jurisdictions to provide voting materials in multiple languages

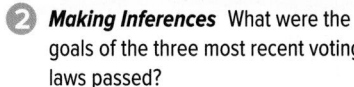

CHART SKILLS

Large groups of people gained the right to vote by constitutional amendments. Different laws passed by Congress have also affected people's right to vote and the process of voting.

▶ CRITICAL THINKING

1 *Differentiating* How was the effect of the Twenty-sixth Amendment different from that of the law passed in 1970?

2 *Making Inferences* What were the goals of the three most recent voting laws passed?

Lesson 1 **271**

These U.S. soldiers serving overseas are taking part in a voter registration drive. Ease of registration, particularly Election Day registration, increases voter turnout. States also use absentee balloting and early voting to encourage participation.

▶ CRITICAL THINKING
Making Connections Why do you think voter registration is important?

Steps in the Voting Process

GUIDING QUESTION *What steps must you follow to vote?*

Voting is not just a matter of checking a box or clicking a mouse. Voting is a process that involves three steps. These steps are registering, preparing, and casting your ballot.

Registering to Vote

Except for North Dakota, all states require citizens to register before they can vote. To **register** means to officially sign up to vote. Registering puts your name on the list of eligible voters.

How do you register to vote? First, you have to make sure to do it on time. The process is different in different states. Most states require voters to register at least 25 days before an election. Some states let voters register on Election Day.

To register, you need to fill out a form. Registration forms ask for your name, address, age, and often your political party preference. You may register as a member of a political party or as an independent voter. You will need to provide a driver's license, a birth certificate, or some other valid form of identification to prove your citizenship and age.

In many states, you can register to vote through the mail. Forms can be downloaded from the Web. You can also find forms and register at public places such as government offices, libraries, and agencies that serve people with disabilities. The National Voter Registration Act requires states to let people register when they renew their driver's licenses. Some people call this the "Motor Voter" law.

Preparing to Vote

Once you have registered, you will be able to participate in the next election. But that does not mean you are ready to vote. The second important step in the voting process is preparing to vote.

Your vote will help determine the outcome of an election. This means it will affect the lives of many people. You owe it to yourself and to your fellow citizens to prepare to vote.

A prepared voter is a voter who is informed about public issues and current events. Today, keeping up with the news is easier than ever. Web sites, television, radio, newspapers, books, and magazines are all good sources of information.

PHOTO: U.S. Army

Reading HELPDESK

register to record or enroll

polling place the location where voting is carried out

Other sources of information may include candidates' speeches, debates, and campaign literature. Campaign literature may be a combination of letters, pamphlets, and ads. They are distributed by political parties and by private groups. You will need to be alert to bias in these materials. Be careful to separate facts from opinions.

Once you inform yourself about the issues, you will need to decide where you stand. Which candidate will you support? Use the information you have gathered to help you decide. Ask yourself questions like these:

• Does the candidate stand for the things I think are important?
• Is the candidate reliable and honest?
• Does the candidate have relevant past experience?
• Will the candidate be effective in office?
• Does the candidate have a real chance of winning?

Sometimes Americans vote for candidates even though they do not have a real chance of winning the election, because they want to show their support for a certain point of view.

Casting Your Vote

Many states allow early voting. This means that citizens can vote during a set period of time before Election Day. Each state has its own rules. Some states allow early voting by mail. Others allow early voting in person at certain locations. Early voting makes it easy for people to vote.

The place you go to vote on Election Day is called a **polling place.** Polling places are usually set up in schools, community centers, fire stations, or other public buildings. Each precinct, or voting district, has one polling place.

21ˢᵗ Century
SKILLS

Write a Persuasive Paragraph

Write a persuasive paragraph aiming to convince the reader to vote for a specific candidate based on that candidate's background, positions on the issues, experience, and chances of winning. If there is an election going on, you can base your paragraph on an actual candidate that interests you. Otherwise, you can write about an "ideal" candidate.

Polling places are generally open on Election Day from early morning to early evening, though the specific times vary from state to state.

▶ CRITICAL THINKING
Identify What is the name for the voting district to which each polling place belongs?

"VOTER APATHY IS ON THE INCREASE AGAIN."   "WHO CARES?"

Apathy, or lack of interest, about political participation and voting is greater among younger Americans than among older Americans.

▶ **CRITICAL THINKING**

Assessing What do you think is a consequence of voter apathy?

When you arrive at your polling place, you will have to present some form of identification and sign in. Officials will check your name against the list of registered voters to make sure that you are eligible to vote. Once you have been approved, you wait your turn to go to the voting booth. The booth may have a curtain, or it may have simple dividers. The purpose of these barriers is to make sure that each person is able to cast his or her vote in secret.

A **ballot** is a list of the candidates' names that shows their political party and the office they are seeking. States decide what kind of ballot to use. Your ballot might be a piece of paper with check boxes that you mark with a special pen. It might be a punch card that you put into a machine. The machine punches a hole next to the candidate of your choice. Or your ballot might be a computer touch screen.

Citizens who cannot get to the polls on Election Day can vote by absentee ballot. Typically, absentee ballots are used by people who know they will be traveling on Election Day or by military personnel serving far away from home. Voters must request an absentee ballot before the election. They return their marked ballot to the election board. On or shortly after Election Day, election officials open and count the absentee ballots.

Many polling places hand out stickers that read "I voted!" Wearing the sticker is an outward display that you have fulfilled a civic responsibility. It is also a reminder to others to go vote. As President Franklin Delano Roosevelt said,

PRIMARY SOURCE

❝ The ultimate [final] rulers of our democracy are not a president and senators and congressmen and government officials, but the voters of this country. ❞

—speech at Marietta, Ohio, July 8, 1938

✔ **PROGRESS CHECK**

Summarizing What are the three steps in the voting process?

Why Your Vote Counts

GUIDING QUESTION *Why is it important to vote?*

Have you ever heard the phrase "every vote counts"? It's true. The United States is pledged to the ideal of equality. When you

CARTOON: Baloo-Rex May/Cartoon Stock

ballot the list of candidates for which you cast your vote

voter turnout rate percentage of eligible voters who actually vote

apathy a lack of interest

vote, your vote will be counted exactly the same way, and be given the same value, as everyone else's vote.

Reasons to Vote

Voting is a right and a responsibility of citizenship. When you are eligible to do so, there are important reasons why you should vote in every election. Voting gives you a chance to choose your government leaders. It also allows you to express satisfaction or dissatisfaction with the performance of the people who already hold office and want to be reelected. It gives you a voice in how your community, state, and country are run. In a speech in 1965, President Lyndon Johnson called the vote "the most powerful instrument ever devised . . . for breaking down injustice."

Citizens who vote share some characteristics. They generally have positive attitudes toward government and citizenship. Many of them believe that they have a right—and a duty—to make their voice heard.

Understanding Voter Participation

Despite the fact that voting gives people a voice and gives them power, some Americans choose not to vote. The **voter turnout rate** is the percentage of eligible voters who actually do vote. For example, if 100 people are eligible to vote in a community election and only 60 people vote, the voter turnout rate is 60 percent. Although it varies by election, the voter turnout rate in American elections is often well below 50 percent.

Why is turnout low? One reason for low voter turnout is **apathy,** or lack of interest. Studies show that many people feel they are "too busy" to vote. Another reason is that people fail to register to vote. When people move to a new address—which millions of Americans do every year—they need to register to vote. Many simply do not. People who are registered are likely to take the time to vote.

✅ **PROGRESS CHECK**

Summarizing What does the saying "every vote counts" mean?

Why It MATTERS

Your Vote Counts

Voting occurs in many areas of life in addition to political elections. What organizations are you familiar with in which voting takes place? Do you belong to a club or other group in which decisions are made through voting? What rules, if any, govern voting in those situations?

LESSON 1 REVIEW

Review Vocabulary

1. What is *suffrage*?

2. How is *apathy* related to *voter turnout rate*?

Answer the Guiding Questions

3. ***Identifying*** What are the two basic qualifications to vote in the United States?

4. ***Explaining*** If you were a voter, what would you do to become informed before an election?

5. ***Synthesizing*** How does voting affect society?

6. **NARRATIVE** Write a journal entry as if you have just cast your first vote. Describe how you felt about voting.

Landmark Supreme Court Cases

Bush v. Gore

At the end of the 2000 presidential election, Americans had what seemed to be a simple question. Who won? The answer, it turned out, would be settled by the U.S. Supreme Court.

As some Democrats demanded a revote, Florida officials reviewed disputed ballots.

PHOTO: (tr) Marta Lavandier/AP Photo

Background of the Case

The 2000 presidential election between Democratic candidate Vice President Al Gore and Republican Governor George W. Bush of Texas was a tight race. It became clear that whoever won Florida would have the 270 electoral votes needed to win. Only a few hundred votes separated the two candidates. Unfortunately, many of the paper ballots were damaged or not marked properly.

The candidates turned to the Florida courts to decide how the disputed votes should be counted. The state supreme court said that each ballot that showed a "clear indication of the intent of the voter" should be counted. The court ordered a recount, where all votes were to be counted again. Lawyers for Bush appealed the case to the U.S. Supreme Court. They argued that it would be impossible to tell a voter's intent on a mismarked ballot.

The Decision

On December 12, the Supreme Court ruled for Bush in a 5-4 decision. It said that the votes could not be counted consistently across Florida in different counties that used different methods, because not every ballot would be treated equally.

❙❙ *[W]e are presented with a situation where a state court . . . has ordered a statewide recount with minimal procedural safeguards. . . . [T]here must be at least some assurance that the . . . requirements of equal treatment and fundamental fairness are satisfied.* ❙❙

—Bush v. Gore (2010)

The Supreme Court ordered the recount to stop. The original result would stand. As a result, Bush won Florida by 537 votes. Winning Florida gave him enough electoral votes to win in the Electoral College. Bush received 271 electoral votes to Gore's 266. George W. Bush became the 43rd president of the United States.

Why It Matters

The ruling raised issues about the fairness of American elections and the powers of the Supreme Court. Many thought that the Court had overstepped its authority by making a political decision beyond its jurisdiction. Critics said that the power to settle this issue constitutionally belonged to the state of Florida, not the U.S. Supreme Court. To this day, *Bush* v. *Gore* remains one of the Court's most controversial decisions.

Analyzing the Case

1. **Explaining** What reason did the Court give for its decision?
2. **Evaluating** Do you agree with the Court's decision in this case? Why or why not?

276 *Voting and Elections*

netw⊚rks

There's More Online!

☑ **GRAPHIC ORGANIZER**
Purpose of Elections

☑ **GRAPHS**
Presidential Elections
2012 Electoral Votes

☑ **CHART**
The Electoral College Process

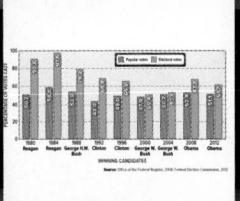
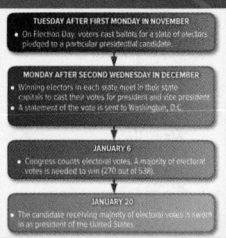

Lesson 2
Elections and Campaigns

ESSENTIAL QUESTION *Why do people create, structure, and change governments?*

IT MATTERS BECAUSE
Elections are a key way that citizens express their will.

Types of Elections

GUIDING QUESTION *Why are there different types of elections in the American political system?*

How many people do you think hold elected office in the United States? The president, the vice president, and all the members of Congress add up to 537. When you add the 50 state governors and other state and local officials, the total might surprise you. There are more than *half a million* (500,000) elected officials in the United States.

With so many elected officials, it is not surprising that elections are a large part of American life. In this lesson, you will find out how elections work. Learning about elections will prepare you for the day you take part in this exciting aspect of citizenship.

Primary and General Elections

In most states, the first step in the election process is called a primary election. These elections are usually held in the spring or summer. The purpose of the primary election is to choose one candidate from each party to run in the general election. The person who receives the most votes in each party becomes the party's candidate for an office.

PHOTO: (tl) Michael Appleton/NY Daily News Archive via Getty Images; (tr) Brooks Kraft/Corbis

Reading **HELP**DESK

Taking Notes: *Identifying*

As you read, complete a table stating the purpose of different types of elections. Add more rows as needed.

Type of Election	Purpose

Content Vocabulary

- **issue**
- **initiative**
- **referendum**
- **recall**
- **Electoral College**
- **popular vote**

People can participate in the election process in more ways than voting. People help their chosen candidate get elected by donating money, sharing information about their candidate, and showing their support at rallies like the one above.

▶ CRITICAL THINKING
Making Connections Why do you think some people become involved in a campaign early in the process?

Sometimes no person wins a majority of the votes in a primary. In some states when this happens, a runoff election is held. The person who wins the runoff moves on to the general election.

The general election is held throughout the country on the same day. These elections always take place on the first Tuesday after the first Monday in November. National elections are held in even-numbered years. All seats in the U.S. House of Representatives and about one-third of the seats in the Senate are up for election every two years. Presidential elections are held every four years. Usually state and local officials, such as state legislators, mayors, and city council members, are also elected at this time.

For most offices, the candidate who wins the most votes wins the election. Voting for the president has special rules that will be described later in the lesson. If an election is very close, the loser can demand a recount. In that case, all the votes are counted a second time. If that fails to settle the election, another election might be held. In the case of a national election, Congress may step in to settle a dispute.

Initiatives and Referendums

In many elections people vote on **issues,** or topics of public interest. Suppose a city council wants to build a new school. It might put the idea on a ballot so voters can approve or reject it.

Two special processes give voters a direct voice in governing. One is called an initiative, and the other is called a referendum. An **initiative** is a process that lets voters propose new laws or amendments to state constitutions. First, people in favor of the law must gather enough signatures to place the item on the ballot. The proposed law is called a proposition, or "prop." In the election, people vote for or against the proposition.

A **referendum** asks voters to accept or reject a law passed by a state or local legislature. Some states require voters to approve changes to the state constitution, for instance. Often, a referendum involves new taxes or tax increases.

PHOTO: Michael Appleton/NY Daily News Archive via Getty Images

Content Vocabulary (cont.)

- **winner-take-all system**
- **canvass**
- **political action committee (PAC)**

issue matter of debate or dispute

initiative a procedure by which citizens can propose new laws or state constitutional amendments

referendum a procedure by which citizens vote on state or local laws

Special Elections

Some states allow **recall** elections. In a recall, people vote on whether to remove an official from office. Like an initiative, the process begins with people signing a petition. If enough citizens ask for a recall, a special election will be held. If the majority votes to remove the official in that election, he or she must give up the office.

Sometimes an official dies in office or resigns before the term of office has ended. In those cases, a special election might be held. These elections are staged to fill a vacant office. They are called "special" because they do not take place at a regularly scheduled time.

✓ PROGRESS CHECK

Comparing What is the difference between a recall election and a special election?

Presidential Elections

GUIDING QUESTION *How are presidents elected?*

Who elects the president of the United States? If you answered "the American people" or even "registered voters," you would be wrong. Many Americans are shocked to learn that presidents are not elected directly by the people. The rules for choosing a president are different from those for filling most offices.

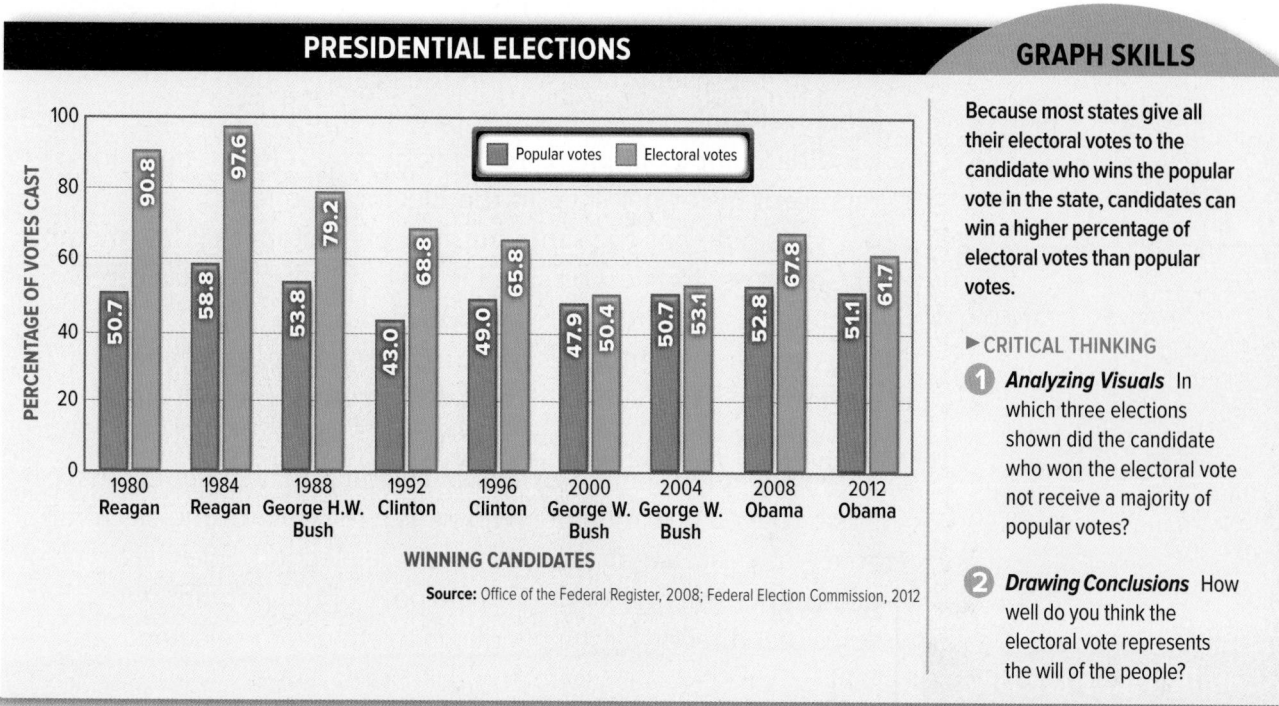

PRESIDENTIAL ELECTIONS

GRAPH SKILLS

Because most states give all their electoral votes to the candidate who wins the popular vote in the state, candidates can win a higher percentage of electoral votes than popular votes.

▶ CRITICAL THINKING

1. *Analyzing Visuals* In which three elections shown did the candidate who won the electoral vote not receive a majority of popular votes?

2. *Drawing Conclusions* How well do you think the electoral vote represents the will of the people?

Source: Office of the Federal Register, 2008; Federal Election Commission, 2012

recall a special election in which citizens can vote to remove a public official from office

Twenty-six states and the District of Columbia require their electors, by law or party pledge, to vote for their party's candidate. Even without such a requirement, electors almost always vote for their party's candidate.

▶ CRITICAL THINKING

1 *Drawing Conclusions* Why do you think some states do not require their electors to pledge to a candidate?

2 *Making Connections* About how much time passes between the time the public votes and the actual election of the president?

TUESDAY AFTER FIRST MONDAY IN NOVEMBER
- On Election Day, voters cast ballots for a slate of electors pledged to a particular presidential candidate.

MONDAY AFTER SECOND WEDNESDAY IN DECEMBER
- Winning electors in each state meet in their state capitals to cast their votes for president and vice president.
- A statement of the vote is sent to Washington, D.C.

JANUARY 6
- Congress counts electoral votes. A majority of electoral votes is needed to win (270 out of 538).

JANUARY 20
- The candidate receiving majority of electoral votes is sworn in as president of the United States.

Understanding the Electoral College

When voters cast their ballots in a presidential race, they are actually electing special representatives called electors. These electors have pledged to vote for a particular candidate. Electors represent their state in the group known as the **Electoral College.** A person voting for a Republican presidential candidate, for example, is really voting for a Republican to represent his or her state in the Electoral College.

Each state has the same number of electors as it has members of Congress. In addition, the District of Columbia has three electors. As a result, there are 538 electors in all.

After a presidential election, in December, the winning electors meet in their state capitals. They cast their electoral votes for president and vice president. They send their votes to the Senate. In January, the House and Senate meet to count these votes. The candidate who wins a majority of the electoral votes—at least 270—is the winner of the election. The electoral vote determines the president. The purpose of the **popular vote,** the votes cast directly by the people, is to choose the electors.

Reading **HELP**DESK

Electoral College a group of people named by each state legislature to select the president and vice president

popular vote the votes cast by individual voters in a presidential election, as opposed to the electoral vote

winner-take-all system a system in which the candidate who wins the popular vote in a state usually receives all of the state's electoral votes

Criticisms of the Electoral College

In most states, the winner of the popular vote in a state wins all of that state's electors. Some people criticize this **winner-take-all system.** Under this system, a candidate who loses the popular vote can still win the electoral vote and the presidency. In other words, a candidate who wins the popular vote can lose the election. This has happened four times in our nation's history, most recently in 2000.

There is another problem with the winner-take-all system. It is extremely difficult for third-party candidates to be represented in the electoral vote.

The Constitution set up the Electoral College system. When the Framers discussed how to choose the president, two different views arose. Some wanted the American people to have direct control over government. Others felt that giving the people the power to choose the president might be dangerous. The people could be too easily moved by emotions to make a wise choice, they feared. The Framers settled on a mixed system. Electors choose the president, but the popular vote chooses the electors.

Many Americans think we should elect the president by direct popular vote. Others think that a state's electoral votes should be divided among candidates according to how many popular votes they receive. No change to the Electoral College can happen without amending the Constitution.

✓ PROGRESS CHECK

Identifying When people vote for the president of the United States, for whom are they actually voting?

Running for Office

GUIDING QUESTION *How do candidates run for political office?*

National elections take place every two years. States might hold elections every two years also, as might local governments. With so many elections, it can seem that it is always campaign season.

An election campaign is a candidate's effort to win an election. Running for office is serious business. Even local races can be expensive and complicated. For a national election, the effort is staggering. In 2008, the candidates for president together raised and spent more than $1.5 billion.

PHOTO: Courtesy of Johnathan Espinoza

Jonathan Espinoza's interest in politics began at age 13, when he attended a campaign meeting for a local school board member running for reelection. Not long after this, Jonathan was asked to speak at a city event. After his speech, city council members appointed him to the city's youth commission. This group advises the city council on community sports programs and other recreational activities for teens. It also suggests laws or ordinances that might be used to address such issues as teen involvement in gangs, graffiti (also called tagging), and rising crime rates in some areas of the city.

Jonathan began regularly attending school board and city council meetings. He volunteered to campaign for a county official running for the California state senate. "I looked up the issues he supported," Jonathan said. "I felt my candidate had a good grasp of the issues that are important in our community." Jonathan went house-to-house knocking on doors, giving out campaign literature, and asking people about the issues that concerned them.

Working for the election of candidates he favors and participating in city government have taught Jonathan some valuable skills. "I have learned to listen to people, with my ears open and my mouth closed. I now know how to disagree with people and still support them and give them the right to disagree with me."

Citizenship and Teens

What did Jonathan learn by working for the election of the candidate he supported?

Candidates try to reach voters on a more personal level with public appearances. Sarah Palin greets voters during the 2008 presidential campaign.

▶ CRITICAL THINKING
Evaluating How important do you think it is for a candidate to be likable? Explain.

Running a Campaign

A campaign might involve a mom running for the local school board. It could center around a well-known politician running for president. Either way, all runs for office have some things in common. First, a candidate must meet the qualifications for office. These are standards set by law. For example, a candidate for president must be at least 35 years old, have lived in the United States for at least 14 years, and be a natural-born citizen.

Someone thinking of running for president often begins by forming an exploratory committee. The committee's job is to find out how much support the person is likely to get. If a full campaign seems worthwhile, the candidate will publicly announce that he or she is running for office. Candidates try to get a lot of media attention when they make these announcements.

Typically, several people from each party run against one another for the same office. In the end, though, usually only one candidate is chosen to run. In a presidential campaign, this choice is often made in a series of state primary elections. The results from these primaries are ratified at the party's national convention. Delegates to the convention are chosen to represent the majority vote in their state's primary election. Some states' delegates are selected by party committees or in party meetings.

National conventions are huge, televised events. They last several days. Political parties use the conventions to get as much media coverage as possible.

Once they are chosen, candidates for any office hit the campaign trail. Campaigning includes many different actions. Candidates make speeches and give interviews to the press. They appear at community events. They answer voters' questions at special meetings. They issue statements giving their positions on issues. They debate their opponents. The goal of all these actions is to convince as many people as possible to vote for them. Candidates have busy schedules. The work gets even busier the closer it gets to the election.

PHOTO: Brooks Kraft/Corbis

Reading HELPDESK

Academic Vocabulary

pursue to try to reach or attain

canvass to seek votes from voters

political action committee (PAC) political organization established by a corporation, labor union, or other special-interest group designed to support candidates by contributing money

Of course, candidates have staffs to help them. Volunteers help candidates **pursue** voters in a variety of ways. Some **canvass** neighborhoods, or go door-to-door to gather support. Some contact voters by telephone or the Internet. Candidates also hire experienced professionals. These staff members give advice on how to appeal to the most voters.

Candidates try to boost their image by getting endorsements, or public support from important people and groups. Celebrities, politicians, newspapers, unions, professional groups, and countless private groups endorse candidates.

Candidates also advertise on television, radio, and Web sites. They use newspapers, bumper stickers, yard signs, and buttons to get their names and ideas out in public. It costs vast amounts of money to stay in the public eye.

Campaign Finance

Campaigns are expensive. Local campaigns cost thousands of dollars. State campaigns cost hundreds of thousands. Congressional campaigns can cost tens of millions. A race for president requires hundreds of millions of dollars.

Where does all the money come from? Most of it comes from donations. Individuals, corporations, unions, and various private groups donate to political campaigns. **Political action committees (PACs)** are organizations set up by interest groups to collect and direct money to candidates and their campaigns.

The Federal Election Commission (FEC) regulates campaigns and how they are funded. Still, many Americans worry that campaigns have gotten too expensive. They believe that politicians will want to help the people who donated money more than they will want to be impartial, or fair, when they are in office.

☑ **PROGRESS CHECK**

Inferring Why do candidates want endorsements?

LESSON 2 REVIEW

Review Vocabulary

1. What is the difference between an *initiative* and a *referendum*?

2. In a presidential election, what is the relationship between the *popular vote* and the *Electoral College*?

Answer the Guiding Questions

3. *Inferring* How is the role of voters different in primary elections and in general elections?

4. *Synthesizing* How does a candidate for president win the office?

5. *Explaining* What role do political action committees play in political campaigns today?

6. **ARGUMENT** Study the experience of two candidates in a current or recent election. Write a paragraph explaining which you would vote for based on their experience.

Write your answers on a separate sheet of paper.

1 **Writing Activity**

EXPLORING THE ESSENTIAL QUESTION
Why do people create, structure, and change governments?

Take the role of a candidate for the local school committee. Write a short speech stating your plans for improving the school system. Pair with another student and take turns delivering your speeches. After each pair of speeches, the class will vote for its preferred candidate.

2 **21st Century Skills**

WRITE A BLOG ENTRY Use a reliable Internet site to watch a video of a debate between two candidates for national or state office. Take notes on the plans outlined by the candidates. Decide, based on those plans, which candidate you support. Write a blog entry that identifies the candidates, the office they seek, and your preferred candidate. Explain your choice.

3 **Being an Active Citizen**

Do you plan to register to vote? Do you plan to vote? You have to be 18 to vote, but it is never too early to practice. Go to your state's Web site and download a voter registration form. Complete it. Write a paragraph explaining whether it was easy or difficult to do.

4 **Understanding Visuals**

Look at the cartoon. Answer these two questions: (1) What is the message of the cartoon? (2) Do you agree with the message? Explain why or why not.

REVIEW THE GUIDING QUESTIONS

Directions: Choose the best answer for each question.

1 According to the Twenty-sixth Amendment, who can vote?
A. high school students
B. women
C. people of any race
D. 18-year-olds

2 What does the National Voter Registration Act require states to do?
F. to let people vote even if they have committed crimes
G. to let people register to vote when they renew their driver's licenses
H. to allow people to specify party affiliation when they register
I. to allow people to register to vote in presidential elections

3 Which of these would be the best source for evaluating a candidate's statements on issues?
A. the candidate's issue-based position papers
B. the Web site of the candidate's political party
C. newspaper articles analyzing the candidate's positions
D. political advertising paid for by the candidate's opponent

4 What determines how a candidate is chosen when no candidate wins a majority of votes in a primary election?
F. local laws
G. state law
H. federal law
I. the United States Constitution

5 To be elected president, a candidate *must* win
A. the electoral vote.
B. the popular vote.
C. the special election.
D. the party's nomination.

6 What is the purpose of campaign advertising?
F. to canvass voters
G. to raise money
H. to win the primary
I. to make the candidate's ideas known

DBQ **ANALYZING DOCUMENTS**

Directions: Analyze the document and answer the questions.

"The right of citizens of the United States to vote in any primary or other election for President or Vice President, for electors for President or Vice President, or for Senator or Representative in Congress, shall not be denied or abridged by the United States or any State by reason of failure to pay any poll tax or other tax."

—U.S. Constitution, Twenty-fourth Amendment, ratified in 1964

7 **Analyzing** What is the purpose of this amendment?

A. to reduce taxes

B. to protect voting rights

C. to regulate voter registration

D. to change the rules for the Electoral College

8 **Identifying** Which best describes elections the amendment affects?

F. presidential primaries

G. state and national elections

H. state and local elections

I. elections for federal office

SHORT RESPONSE

"The people are not qualified to exercise [carry out] . . . the executive department, but they are qualified to name the person who shall exercise it. With us, therefore, they choose this officer every four years."

—Thomas Jefferson, letter to a French friend (1789)

9 What is Jefferson saying about the role of "the people" in elections?

10 Do you agree with Jefferson's statement? In a few sentences, explain why or why not.

EXTENDED RESPONSE

11 **INFORMATIVE/EXPLANATORY** Candidates use many methods, including policy papers, campaign Web sites, ads, speeches, and debates, to communicate their ideas to voters. Which method would you use as a candidate? Why?

Need Extra Help?

If You've Missed Question	**1**	**2**	**3**	**4**	**5**	**6**	**7**	**8**	**9**	**10**	**11**
Review Lesson	1	1	1	2	2	2	1	1	2	2	2

Public Opinion and Government

networks

There's More Online about public opinion and government.

CHAPTER 10

ESSENTIAL QUESTION
How do citizens, both individually and collectively, influence government policy?

The Story Matters...

Sometimes they march. At other times they may stand as still as soldiers at attention. They carry big signs with bold lettering. They are union members on a picket line, gathering together to express some dissatisfaction with their job situation. The issues vary, but often include wages, working conditions, and benefits. Whatever the issue, a union's strength is in the number of its members.

Unions are special interest groups, or organizations made up of people with common interests. When they stage protests, they hope to sway public opinion. If television, newspaper, and other media coverage is positive, it can help them in negotiations with employers. Powerful unions and other interest groups can also influence lawmakers and public policy.

◄ *Members of the American Federation of State, County, and Municipal Employees union protest in California.*

PHOTO: Jim West/PhotoEdit

287

Real-Life Civics

> **INFLUENCE** How do people in government make policy decisions? How do they decide what is best for the country's citizens? As they put together plans for government actions, policy makers may seek the opinions of special interest groups.

With membership open to anybody over the age of 50, the AARP (American Association of Retired Persons) is one of the country's largest—and most powerful—interest groups. The AARP focuses on a wide variety of issues that concern many older Americans. These issues include Social Security, other retirement benefits, and health care. Among the AARP's advertised list of member benefits is "a voice in Washington and in your state." When an interest group of this size speaks, lawmakers tend to listen.

Members of the AARP attend a rally in support of a Medicare health care bill.

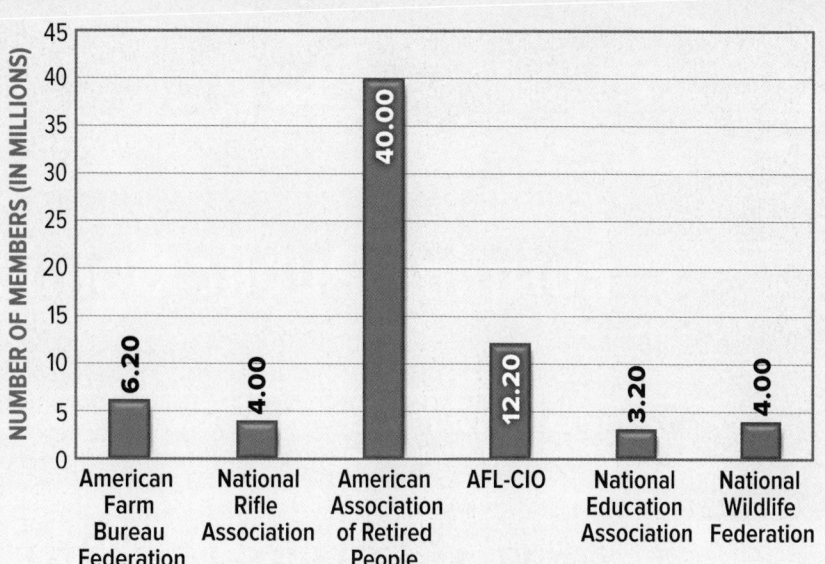

MEMBERSHIP OF SELECTED INFLUENTIAL INTEREST GROUPS

NUMBER OF MEMBERS (IN MILLIONS)

American Farm Bureau Federation: 6.20
National Rifle Association: 4.00
American Association of Retired People: 40.00
AFL-CIO: 12.20
National Education Association: 3.20
National Wildlife Federation: 4.00

INTEREST GROUP

Sources: www.fb.org/index.php?fuseaction=newsroom.newsfocus&year=2007&file=nr1206.html; www.nra.org/Aboutus.aspx; www.aarp.org/about-aarp/; www.aflcio.org/aboutus/; www.nea.org/home/1594.htm; www.nwf.org/About.aspx

The graph shows the number of Americans who are members of some of the largest interest groups in the United States.

> **STRENGTH IN NUMBERS** When lawmakers listen to the opinions of interest groups, whose voice is loudest? If influence is measured by numbers, then the groups represented in the graph have a good share of power. Interest groups play a key role in shaping policy and legislation. The interests of the groups shown on the graph are wide-ranging. The AFL-CIO, or American Federation of Labor and Congress of Industrial Organizations, focuses its attention on labor law and policy. The National Rifle Association (NRA) wants to uphold an individual's right to bear firearms. The other groups concern themselves with legislation and policy issues related to aging, wildlife conservation, education, and farming. Laws related to these and many other issues are influenced by the millions of members who belong to the country's interest groups.

CIVIC LITERACY

★★★★

Inferring Which interest group in the graph has the most members? Why might that group have such a large membership?

Your Opinion What are some issues that are important to you? Would you be willing to join interest groups related to those issues? Explain your answer.

netw⊙rks

There's More Online!

☑ **GRAPHIC ORGANIZER**
Sources of Public Opinion

☑ **POLITICAL CARTOON**
Polls

☑ **GRAPHS**
News Sources
Presenting Poll Data
What Polls Show

☑ **VIDEO**

☑ **SLIDE SHOW**
Representing a Cause

Lesson 1
Forming Public Opinion

ESSENTIAL QUESTION *How do citizens, both individually and collectively, influence government policy?*

◯ IT MATTERS BECAUSE
Public opinion affects leaders' actions, but leaders also try to shape public opinion.

Public Opinion

GUIDING QUESTION *What is public opinion?*

Have you ever been in a situation where people were making decisions that affected you? Did you ask those making the decisions to give you a chance to say what you thought about that situation? Did you speak out to let your ideas be known?

That is what many Americans do when they care deeply about political issues. In a democracy, the public—all the people in our nation—are the source of political power. By speaking out, members of the public make their views known. In doing so, they can influence the decisions that leaders make.

The Role of Public Opinion in a Democracy

The term for the views of all Americans is *public opinion*. **Public opinion** refers to the ideas and attitudes that people hold about an issue or a person.

Public opinion plays two key roles in a democracy. First, public opinion helps shape the decisions that officials make. Congressional and state legislators often travel back to their districts to meet with voters and talk about bills that are up for

PHOTO: (tl) Darrin Klimek/Getty Images; (tcl) Digital Vision/PunchStock; (tcr) DAVE GRANLUND/PoliticalCartoons.com; (tr) Grey Villet/Time Life Pictures/Getty Images

Reading **HELP**DESK

Taking Notes: *Identifying*

As you read, complete a graphic organizer by identifying three sources of public opinion.

> Sources of Public Opinion
> ☐ ☐ ☐

Content Vocabulary

- **public opinion**
- **mass media**
- **interest group**
- **public opinion poll**
- **pollster**

a vote. These officials recognize that if they are to represent the people, their votes should reflect the views of the people.

Presidents are guided by public opinion in this way too. They need to have a good sense of when the public is ready for a new idea. President Franklin D. Roosevelt once said, "I cannot go any faster than the people will let me." That statement reflects a truth about leadership in a democracy.

Second, public opinion also shapes how successful a president is in putting his or her plans into action. Presidents need the support of Congress to carry out their programs. A president is more likely to have that support if his or her plans are popular with the public. The same is true of state governors and city mayors. When these leaders have the backing of the public, lawmakers are more willing to go along with their plans.

Of course, public opinion is a complicated thing. The United States has more than 310 million people. They come from different regions and backgrounds. In fact, Americans agree on very few issues. Instead, different groups hold distinct opinions. For instance, some Americans want the government to take a larger role in the economy. Others disagree. They want a smaller, less active government. Between these two positions are many other opinions. When enough people hold an opinion, government officials listen to them.

Sources of Public Opinion

Where do opinions on public issues come from? Why do people hold such different views about these matters? Several factors may influence opinions. One is a person's background. Another is the mass media. A third is interest groups.

Personal Background

People's opinions are often based on their experiences and their situation in life. Age and **gender**—being male or female—play key roles in shaping opinions. So do race and religion. A person's job, income, and where he or she lives affect opinions too. All these personal factors work together to influence how each individual views public issues.

Americans are free to express their opinions in many different ways, from wearing a T-shirt with a message to writing a letter to a member of Congress.

▶ **CRITICAL THINKING**
Listing What are two other ways of expressing opinions that you can name?

PHOTO: Darrin Klimek/Getty Images

public opinion the ideas and attitudes that people hold about elected officials, candidates, government, and political issues

Academic Vocabulary

gender whether a person is male or female

Think about the issue of education. A mother of two school-age children who lives in a city will probably want her state to invest more money in education. An elderly person who lives in a small town will probably be less interested in seeing increased spending on schools. On the other hand, an older adult who is a teacher would have yet another point of view, even if he or she does not have school-age children.

One new medium is the microblog, a very short message posted by phone or computer to a Web site that can be accessed by anyone who belongs to the Web site's network.

▶ CRITICAL THINKING
Categorizing Is this kind of communication a private message or a type of mass medium? Explain.

Mass Media

A second factor shaping opinion is the mass media. A medium is a means of communication. *Media*, the plural, refers to many different means of communication. Cell phone text messages are a medium of communication. The **mass media** include all the various methods of communication that reach large numbers of people. These media include television, radio, Internet Web sites, newspapers, magazines, books, recordings, and movies.

The mass media influence public opinion in many ways. Television news shows and newspapers shape public opinion with the stories they publish. If they carry many stories about an issue, people may begin to view that issue as important. The opinions stated by television news commentators can affect the way people respond to issues. Newspapers also publish editorials that take a position on important issues. Editorials can encourage support for the author's point of view. The same thing is true of blogs posted on the Internet.

Interest Groups

A third source of public opinion is **interest groups.** These groups are made up of people who share a point of view about an issue. Interest groups try to influence public opinion in many ways. They work to convince other people to adopt their point of view. They also work to convince public officials to support their positions. Because they may put political pressure on leaders to act in a certain way, interest groups are sometimes called pressure groups.

PHOTO: DAVID GANNON/AFP/Getty Images

mass media a mechanism of mass communication, including television, radio, the Internet, newspapers, magazines, books, recordings, and movies

interest group a group of people who share a point of view about an issue and unite to promote their beliefs

Features of Public Opinion

Public opinion is often described in terms of three factors. They are *direction*, *intensity*, and *stability*. Each measures a different aspect of public opinion.

Direction refers to whether public opinion on a topic is positive or negative. For example, are people for or against spending more money on national defense? Are they for or against a cut in taxes? On most topics, the direction of public opinion is mixed. Still, one side can be stronger than the other.

Intensity refers to how strongly a person or group holds an opinion on an issue. Most Americans have the strongest beliefs about issues that directly affect them. For example, farmers are more interested than city dwellers in farm issues. People who use a subway train or a bus to get to work are very interested in mass transit.

When people hold a strong opinion on an issue, they pay more attention to it. They may also decide to become active on that issue. They might join an interest group or work on an election campaign. Still others might take part in public actions aimed at solving a problem.

Stability is a matter of how firmly people hold to their views. In other words, how likely are they to change their minds? Opinions tend to be very stable when they are based on strong beliefs. For example, most people's opinions about civil rights are more stable than their opinions about political candidates.

☑ **PROGRESS CHECK**

Determining Cause and Effect What factors influence public opinion?

PHOTO: (b) Julie Dermansky/Corbis; (inset) Digital Vision/PunchStock

An explosion at an oil well in the Gulf of Mexico in April 2010 started an oil spill that damaged wildlife and the local economy and lasted for months. The story dominated news coverage.

▶ **CRITICAL THINKING**
Predicting What kind of impact do you think this heavy media coverage had on the company that owned the well? Why?

Survey companies conduct polls to understand people's positions on issues and on political candidates. Newspapers often report these poll results.

► CRITICAL THINKING

Analyzing What attitude does the cartoonist have toward polling? Why do you say so?

Public Opinion Polls

GUIDING QUESTION *How is public opinion measured?*

Public opinion can affect policy, but how do political leaders learn what the public thinks about an issue? They draw on two tools: election results and measures of public opinion.

Election Results

One way to discover public opinion on an issue is by looking at election results. If voters elect a candidate, they probably agree with many of the candidate's ideas.

Election results are not always a sure way to measure public opinion, however. People vote for candidates for many reasons. Maybe they liked how a candidate looked. Perhaps they supported some, but not all, of the candidate's views. They may back a candidate because of his or her party. For these reasons, election results give only a rough sense of public opinion.

Another problem with using elections as measures of public opinion is that they happen only every few years. If leaders had to wait until the next election to know public opinions, they could spend two or more years with no sense of what people think.

Polls Measure Public Opinion

To keep in touch with public opinion more regularly, many public officials rely on polls. A **public opinion poll** is a survey

Reading HELPDESK

public opinion poll a survey in which individuals are asked to answer questions about a particular issue or person

pollster a specialist whose job is to conduct polls regularly

Academic Vocabulary

random by chance

in which individuals are asked to answer questions about a particular issue or person. Today hundreds of groups conduct such polls. Members of the media and politicians refer to poll results to check on people's attitudes.

Most presidents, for example, have a specialist whose job is to conduct polls. This **pollster** can measure how popular the president is. He or she can also find out how the public feels about programs that the president is considering. For example, a poll might ask people if they support or oppose a change in immigration laws.

Pollsters have different ways of selecting the people they survey. One way is by picking a group of people at **random,** or by chance. Pollsters may talk to about 1,500 people from all over the nation. Such a sample usually includes both men and women. It also includes people of nearly all races and ages. Finally, a random sample polls people with different incomes. A good sample is a small representation of the entire population. That way, it can present a reasonably accurate picture of public opinion as a whole. Polls conducted using random sampling are known as scientific polls.

To find out how people really feel about an issue, pollsters must word questions carefully. Poorly worded questions can lead to confused answers. Also, by changing the wording of the questions, pollsters can influence the answers they receive. For example, the question "Do you favor cutting taxes?" might produce one kind of answer from a person. "Do you favor cutting taxes if it means letting poor people go hungry?" might produce a different answer from the same person.

PHOTO: Grey Villet/Time Life Pictures/Getty Images

21st Century

SKILLS

Researching on the Internet

Want to know what people think of the job the president is doing? The Gallup organization publishes daily tracking polls showing the president's job approval rating with Americans. Go online to see the current number. What was it one month ago? Three months ago? Is there a trend you can see?

Polls can be conducted by interviewing people in person or by calling them on the phone. Pioneer pollster Louis Harris (right) often conducted his polls by going door-to-door.

► **CRITICAL THINKING**
Evaluating Which polling method do you think would most likely lead a person to agree to answer the questions? Why?

Lesson 1 **295**

Polls in which the questions are worded so as to shape a person's responses are called push polls. Push polls are strongly criticized by companies and individuals who carry out scientific polls. When looking at poll results, citizens should ask themselves whether the questions were fair and unbiased. In push polls, questions are designed to create a certain response.

Pros and Cons of Polls

Some people believe that public opinion polls are useful. They say that polls tell politicians what citizens think about issues. Polls show officials whether people approve or disapprove of the way they are doing their jobs. Officials do not have to wait for the next election to find out what is important to voters.

Those in favor of polling also point to another feature of these surveys. People's responses are often broken down by particular groups, such as how men and women or people earning different amounts of money respond to the same question. These categories help leaders know what specific groups think about an issue. That knowledge can help guide their decisions.

Other people see problems with using polls. They argue that polling makes elected officials focus on pleasing the public. They think officials should instead focus their attention on making wise decisions for the common good.

Many people also worry that polls have a strong effect on how people vote. The media carry out polls constantly during election campaigns and then report who is ahead in the race. Critics argue that these polls treat an election like a horse race. They worry that focusing on polls ignores the candidates' views on important issues. In addition, some say that polls can discourage voting. If the polls show one candidate far ahead of another, some people may decide not to bother voting.

☑ **PROGRESS CHECK**

Identifying Besides elections, what is another way to measure public opinion?

LESSON 1 REVIEW

Review Vocabulary

1. Define the terms *mass media* and *public opinion*, and explain how the mass media affect public opinion.

2. What is a *public opinion poll*, and who uses the information from one?

Answer the Guiding Questions

3. *Explaining* What are three features of public opinion? What does each describe?

4. *Describing* In polling, what are random samples? What makes a good random sample?

5. **ARGUMENT** Supporters of polling argue that it is a tool for democracy. Critics of polling think that it makes politicians reactors rather than leaders. In a paragraph, explain which opinion you agree with and why.

netw⊚rks

There's More Online!

☑ **GRAPHIC ORGANIZER**
Roles of the Media

☑ **GRAPHS**
America's Use of Mass Media
Where Americans Go to Get
News

Lesson 2
The Mass Media

ESSENTIAL QUESTION *How do citizens, both individually and collectively, influence government policy?*

IT MATTERS BECAUSE
The mass media can be an important source of information about government and public issues.

The Influence of the Media

GUIDING QUESTION *How do the media influence public opinion and government?*

How do you find out what is going on in the world? Do you listen to the radio in the morning? Do you download podcasts? Does your school have a newspaper or a news show that reports events? Do you check headlines on the Internet or watch the evening news on television? If you are like most Americans, you get your news from one or more of these forms of mass media. In the United States, the mass media play a key role in informing people about issues. They also influence government. Finally, the media link the people to elected officials.

There are two types of mass media sources. Print media include newspapers, magazines, newsletters, and books. Radio, television, and the Internet are examples of electronic media.

In using media information, you must remember an important fact. Most American media outlets are private businesses. They are run to make a profit. For that reason, media managers often decide what to publish based on what will attract the most viewers, listeners, or readers. The larger the audience, the more the media can charge advertisers. This fact shapes what the media cover.

PHOTO: (tl) Mark Wilson/Getty Images; (tc) AP Photo/Sang Tan; (tr) Kayte M. Deioma/PhotoEdit

Reading **HELP**DESK

Taking Notes: *Organizing*

As you read, create a graphic organizer to record the different roles of the media.

Roles of the Media

Content Vocabulary

- **public agenda**
- **leak**
- **watchdog**
- **prior restraint**
- **libel**

Influencing the Public Agenda

The government deals with many problems and issues. Those that receive the most time, money, and effort from government leaders make up what is often called the **public agenda.** An agenda is a set of items that a person or group wants to address.

The media can influence which problems officials regard as important. When the media focus on a problem, people begin to worry about it. Then they expect the government to deal with it.

Covering Candidates and Officials

The mass media can also influence who runs for office. Usually candidates are experienced politicians. They spend years working in their political parties. Some candidates, though, are people who were famous in another field. For instance, actor Arnold Schwarzenegger was elected governor of California in 2003. When candidates are already well-known, the media cover their campaigns with interest. In this way, the candidate benefits from the media's desire to cover their campaign.

Reporters and politicians have a complex relationship. They need each other. Reporters need information to write articles. Political leaders need media coverage to get their message out. At the same time, the two groups often clash. As one presidential assistant explained, "Politicians live—and sometimes die—by the press. The press lives by politicians."

Officials try to use the media to their advantage. They may **leak,** or secretly pass on, information to reporters. They may do this to test the public's response to a proposal before they openly **acknowledge,** or admit, that they are considering it. If the public reacts well, officials might act on the idea. If the public reacts negatively, officials can drop it. Politicians also use leaks to shape public opinion on an issue, or to gain favor with a reporter.

At the same time, reporters can present news in ways that show an official in a bad light.

The media report on the actions and statements of public officials. When other public officials—like then–California governor Arnold Schwarzenegger—visit the president, the White House press corps interviews them to learn what was discussed.

▶ **CRITICAL THINKING**
Analyzing What personal qualities do you think a good reporter needs?

PHOTO: Mark Wilson/Getty Images

Content Vocabulary (cont.)
- malice
- shield laws

public agenda issues considered most significant by government officials

leak to release secret government information by anonymous government officials to the media

They can ask officials tough questions about the positions that the officials take. Politicians sometimes try to avoid this difficulty by refusing to answer their questions. That practice, though, can result in criticism from the media.

Watchdog Role

The mass media also play a crucial **"watchdog"** role. That means they keep a close eye on government activities. Journalists write stories that expose waste and corruption at all levels of government. These kinds of stories attract a large audience. Throughout our history, the media have played this role. This has served the interests of both the media and the public by exposing wrongdoing by public officials.

Media and National Security

Americans need to stay informed. At the same time, the government must keep some secrets for national security reasons. The government can classify, or label, some information as secret. That information is then off-limits to reporters.

The government can use other methods to try to shape the news. During the first part of the war in Iraq, some journalists accompanied American troops going into battle. They reported on battles and on daily life of the troops. Some critics said that this practice allowed the government to control news reporting.

☑ PROGRESS CHECK

Categorizing What are the two broad types of mass media sources?

In the fall of 2010, a news Web site released secret documents about events in the war in Iraq that embarrassed the United States government. Until then, the documents had been secret.

▶ CRITICAL THINKING
Categorizing Which of the three roles of the media is represented by news articles that expose the actions of government officials?

PHOTO: AP Photo/Seng Tan

Academic Vocabulary
acknowledge to admit

watchdog the role played by a media organization that exposes illegal practices or waste

When you summarize, you briefly tell the main idea of a section in your own words. Read the paragraph explaining why the Framers wanted the press to be free. Then summarize it in your own words.

Protecting the Press

GUIDING QUESTION *What are the restrictions on freedom of the press?*

The Framers understood that democracy needs a free flow of information and ideas. Citizens need information to understand public issues. They need that information to be free of government control as well. So the Framers wanted the press to be independent to ensure that goal.

The Framers showed how highly they valued a free press by protecting the press from government interference. The First Amendment to the U.S. Constitution says that Congress cannot pass any law that would limit the freedom of the press. When it was written, the amendment applied to print media, which were the only forms in existence. Now, though, this protection extends to radio, TV, and the Internet as well.

Because of the First Amendment, the media are free from prior restraint. **Prior restraint** refers to government censorship of material before it is published. Generally, the government cannot censor the media that way. Reporters and editors are free to decide what they will say, even if it is unpopular. In fact, sometimes the media publish information that embarrasses the government or a politician.

Freedom Within Limits

Freedom of the press is not unlimited, though. As you have read, the government can keep some information secret. Also, no one is free to publish false information that will harm another

---

GRAPH SKILLS

The media that people use vary according to age.

▶ CRITICAL THINKING

1 *Analyzing Visuals* Which type of medium is most used by people of all age groups?

2 *Contrasting* How does media use among people 65 years old and older differ from that among people aged 18 to 24?

AMERICA'S USE OF MASS MEDIA

Source: U.S. Census Bureau: *Statistical Abstract of the United States.* 2009.

prior restraint the act of stopping information from being known by blocking it from being published

libel written untruths that are harmful to someone's reputation

malice evil intent

shield law a law that protects a reporter from revealing his or her sources

Academic Vocabulary

regulatory describing an agency that controls or governs

person's reputation. Doing so is called **libel.** Anyone who believes a written story has harmed him or her may sue the publisher for libel. Government officials rarely win libel lawsuits, however. In *New York Times Co.* v. *Sullivan* (1964), the Supreme Court ruled in a libel case. It said that public officials must prove actual **malice,** or evil intent, to win a libel suit. The official must prove that the publisher either knew the material was false or showed a reckless disregard for the truth.

The media also have some other protections. Gathering news may depend on getting facts from people who do not want to have their names made public. The press and the government have fought many battles over reporters' right to keep their sources secret. Most states have **shield laws** that protect reporters from having to reveal their sources.

Regulating the Media

The federal government does have ways to regulate the broadcast media. The airwaves available for radio and TV broadcasting are limited. The government decides who can use them. In order to receive a license that allows them to broadcast, companies must meet certain standards. For example, a portion of their programming must be devoted to covering public affairs, usually through news programs. In addition, the Federal Communications Commission (FCC) oversees broadcasters. The FCC is a **regulatory,** or managing, agency. It cannot censor broadcasts, but it can punish stations that break its rules. Fines for breaking these rules can run to several thousand dollars, so stations are careful about what people say and do on the air. For example, stations edit out words that break FCC rules.

✓ **PROGRESS CHECK**

Identifying What are two ways the federal government can manage broadcast media?

LESSON 2 REVIEW

Review Vocabulary

1. How are the *public agenda* and the media connected?

2. How might *leaks* help the media perform their role as a *watchdog*?

3. Use *prior restraint* and *libel* to explain the limits placed on the free press.

Answer the Guiding Questions

4. *Analyzing* Why do politicians and the media need each other?

5. *Describing* What are two ways freedom of the press is limited?

6. **ARGUMENT** Journalists want to be free of government limits on their work. Government officials want some control over the media. Taking the point of view of a journalist or a government official, write a paragraph to persuade others to your position on how much government should be able to restrict what the media report.

Hazelwood School District v. Kuhlmeier

The Supreme Court's 1969 ruling in Tinker v. Des Moines *found that public school students had a First Amendment right to freedom of speech in the school. Did those rights extend to freedom of the press?*

Background of the Case

Hazelwood East High School, near St. Louis, Missouri, had a school newspaper for students in its journalism classes. Before each issue, Principal Robert Reynolds reviewed the pages. While looking over an issue, Reynolds objected to two articles. One article was about three students who were pregnant. The other talked about one student's experience with parents who were getting a divorce. No students' names were used in the articles. Nevertheless, Reynolds felt readers could easily identify who the students were. For that reason, he canceled the two pages on which those articles appeared.

Kathy Kuhlmeier and two other students who worked on the newspaper did not like this decision. They sued the school. They claimed that their First Amendment rights to freedom of the press had been denied.

The Decision

Relying on the Supreme Court's decision in *Tinker* v. *Des Moines*, a lower court ruled in favor of the students. The school appealed the case to the Supreme Court. On January 8, 1988, the Supreme Court reversed this ruling. The Court drew a sharp line between individual expression—which it supported in *Tinker*—and the content of a school newspaper. Justice Byron R. White wrote:

❝ A school must be able to set high standards for the student speech that is disseminated [distributed] under its [sponsorship] . . . and may refuse to disseminate student speech that does not meet those standards. ❞

Teachers serve as advisers to the students who work on school newspapers.

Why It Matters

The *Hazelwood* decision did not, of course, take away all First Amendment rights from school newspapers. Nevertheless, supporters of free speech and student interest groups said that the *Hazelwood* decision meant censorship. The Student Press Law Center reports that a number of schools, fearing lawsuits, have done away with student newspapers. Following this decision, some schools have even blocked the publication of student yearbooks. Others have moved to stop stage performances or to censor the content of student-based Web pages.

Analyzing the Case

1. **Analyzing** Why did the students writing for the school newspaper sue the school?
2. **Concluding** How do you think the Hazelwood decision could affect a school's responsibility to educate?

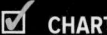

networks

There's More Online!

☑ **GRAPHIC ORGANIZER**
   Interest Groups

☑ **CHART**
   • Interest Groups Active
     in Health Care Reform Debate
   • Propaganda Techniques

☑ **POLITICAL CARTOON**
   Lobbyists

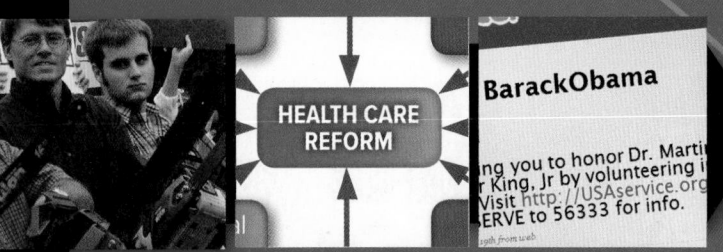

Lesson 3

Interest Groups and Lobbying

ESSENTIAL QUESTION *How do citizens, both individually and collectively, influence government policy?*

IT MATTERS BECAUSE

Interest groups are one vehicle people use to make their views known and to work for causes they believe in.

Interest Groups

GUIDING QUESTION *How do special-interest groups influence public policy?*

Have you ever gone to see your senator or representative's social media page or Web site? Have you ever e-mailed or called your representatives? Government officials want to be linked with their constituents—the people they represent. They want to hear from those people, to know what they think and why they think it. If you want the government to take action, you have many ways to contact your representatives.

As an individual, you have just one voice. That voice might not stand out when a member of Congress hears from thousands of people. How can you make your voice stronger?

One way to strengthen your voice is to join with others who agree with you on an issue. When you join together with others, you all pool your resources and increase your influence. Interest groups can be a powerful force to bring about change. An interest group is a group of people who share a point of view and unite to promote that viewpoint. The First Amendment guarantees Americans the right to assemble and to belong to interest groups. The right to petition the government makes it possible for those groups to meet with officials to promote their goals.

PHOTO: (tl) Congressional Quarterly/Getty Images; (tr) ICP-UK/Alamy

Reading **HELP**DESK

Taking Notes: *Summarizing*

As you read, use a graphic organizer to summarize the ways interest groups influence government and the ways government regulates interest groups.

Influencing Government
1.
2.
3.
4.

⇦⇨

Regulating Groups
1.
2.

Content Vocabulary

• **public-interest group**
• **nonpartisan**
• **lobbyist**

Lesson 3 **303**

The interest group Earthjustice staged this "21 Chainsaw Salute" to protest a government decision that allowed lumber companies to cut trees in national forests.

▶ CRITICAL THINKING
Categorizing What type of interest group do you think Earthjustice represents? Why?

Business and Labor Groups

Some interest groups are based on shared economic goals. For instance, the U.S. Chamber of Commerce promotes the interest of businesses. Other interest groups act for specific types of businesses. The National Automobile Dealers Association, for example, works on behalf of companies that sell cars and trucks. These groups try to sway government decisions on issues that affect their industries.

Some interest groups are formed by workers. The American Federation of Labor and Congress of Industrial Organizations (AFL-CIO) is the largest such group. It is formed by many labor unions that have joined together. Unions try to improve wages, working conditions, and benefits for their members.

Other Interest Groups

People also join together to work for the rights of people who share similar characteristics. The National Association for the Advancement of Colored People (NAACP) tries to improve the lives of African Americans. The AARP (American Association of Retired Persons) stands up for the interests of older Americans.

Other interest groups focus on particular issues. For example, the Sierra Club wants to protect nature. The National Rifle Association (NRA) looks after the interests of people who own guns.

The interest groups described so far promote only the goals of their members' interests. **Public-interest groups** work to benefit larger sections of society. They support causes that affect the lives of most Americans. One example is the League of Women Voters. This **nonpartisan** group is free from ties to any political party. Its purpose is to educate voters about candidates and issues. Other public-interest groups work for the rights of all consumers.

Reading HELPDESK

Reading Strategy: *Taking Notes*
Use a two-column chart to take notes on interest groups. In the left column, list the types. In the right column, list examples of each type.

public-interest group an organization that supports causes that affect the lives of Americans in general

nonpartisan free from party ties or bias

Interest Groups at Work

Interest groups play an important role in our country. Their main goal is to influence the decisions that leaders make. To do this, they use four main types of actions. These are being active in elections, working through the courts, working directly with lawmakers, and trying to shape public opinion. Groups can use one or more of these approaches. Many use all four.

Being Active in Elections

Many interest groups become involved in elections. They support certain candidates. For example, the Sierra Club might back candidates who favor laws to protect nature. Many interest groups have formed political action committees (PACs). In fact, most labor unions have PACs. So do many companies and trade associations.

PACs collect money from group members. They give that money to help candidates they think will support their positions on the issues they care about. They can also spend money to oppose candidates they want to see defeated. For instance, a political action committee might buy television or radio ads that criticize a candidate it knows does not share its goals.

Working Through the Courts

Many interest groups try to shape policy by bringing cases to court. For instance, an interest group for women might help a woman worker sue a company if it feels she was paid unfairly. The NAACP has used lawsuits to help end laws that treated African Americans unfairly.

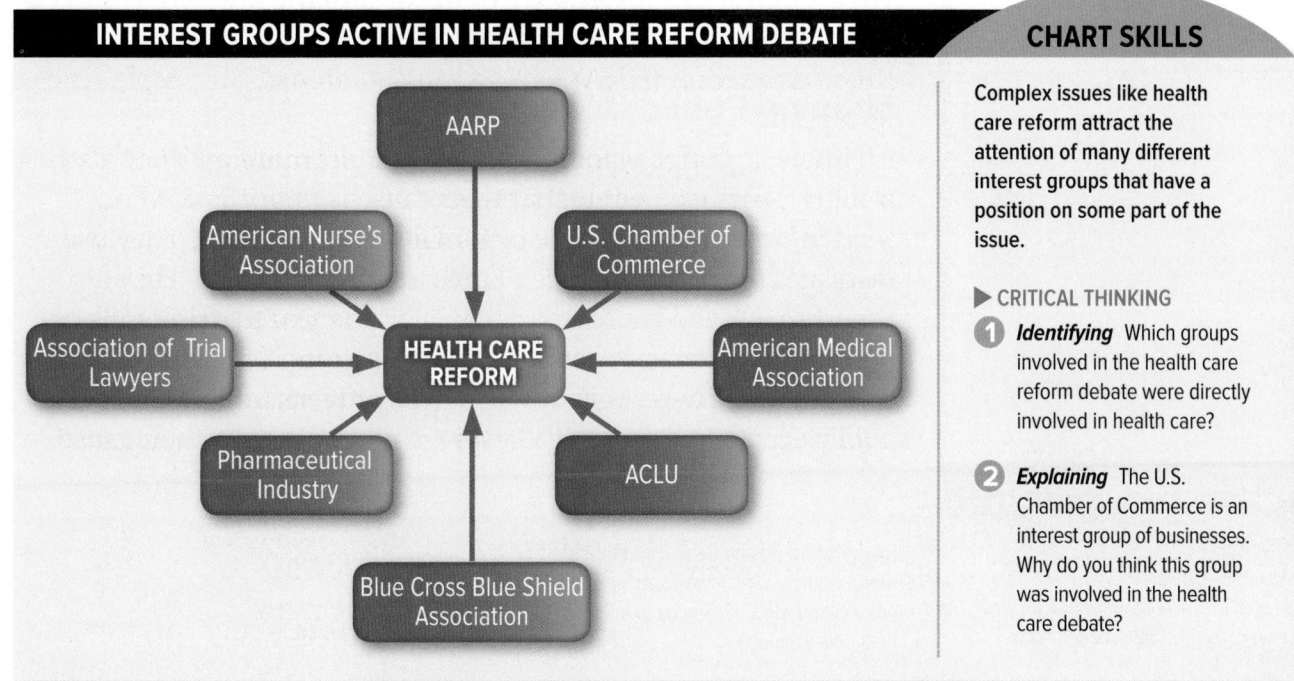

INTEREST GROUPS ACTIVE IN HEALTH CARE REFORM DEBATE

- AARP
- American Nurse's Association
- U.S. Chamber of Commerce
- Association of Trial Lawyers
- HEALTH CARE REFORM
- American Medical Association
- Pharmaceutical Industry
- ACLU
- Blue Cross Blue Shield Association

CHART SKILLS

Complex issues like health care reform attract the attention of many different interest groups that have a position on some part of the issue.

▶ CRITICAL THINKING

1 *Identifying* Which groups involved in the health care reform debate were directly involved in health care?

2 *Explaining* The U.S. Chamber of Commerce is an interest group of businesses. Why do you think this group was involved in the health care debate?

"I DON'T ACTUALLY DO EVIL ANY MORE. I LOBBY CONGRESSMEN."

SCHWADRON

This political cartoon pokes fun at the more than 12,000 people registered with the federal government as official lobbyists.

▶ CRITICAL THINKING

Analyzing Visuals What is the cartoonist's attitude toward lobbyists? How can you tell?

Directly Influencing Officials

One of the most important methods interest groups use to shape policy is lobbying. **Lobbyists** are people who represent interest groups. They contact lawmakers or other government officials directly. Lobbyists are active at all levels of government—local, state, and national.

The term *lobbyist* was first used in the 1830s. At that time, it described people who waited in the lobbies of the state capitol buildings to ask lawmakers for favors. Few lobbyists use that strategy today. Good lobbyists know whom to contact about a particular concern. They understand how the government works and are very good at public relations. They are also skilled at making friends and speaking persuasively.

The most effective lobbyists supply lawmakers with information that helps their causes. They suggest solutions to problems. Sometimes they write drafts of bills for lawmakers to consider. They may even testify before Congress about the bills. All of these activities give lawmakers a lot of information. Of course, these actions also reflect only the interest group's position on the issue. They are **biased,** in that they do not present all sides of an issue. When many different groups are involved, however, their different biases may even out.

The work of lobbyists does not end once a law is passed. Their interest groups also try to make sure the laws are enforced in ways that favor their interests.

Shaping Public Opinion

All interest groups want to influence public opinion. They also want to convince people that their cause is important. Many send information to people by e-mail or regular mail. They use messages to try to convince people to join the group. They also advertise. Maybe you have seen ads urging you to drink milk or buy American-made products. Business groups sponsor these types of ads. Interest groups also hold protests and organize public events to gain media coverage and notice for their cause.

CARTOON: Harley Schwadron/CartoonStock

lobbyist representative of an interest group who contacts lawmakers or other government officials directly to influence their policy making

Academic Vocabulary

biased favoring one view
guarantee to promise

Interest groups can provide useful, in-depth information on an issue. They may also use propaganda techniques to promote their ideas. Propaganda is presenting information in a slanted or biased way. The chart about propaganda techniques describes different methods that groups use. Understanding these will help you identify bias in the information you see.

☑ PROGRESS CHECK

Naming What tools do interest groups use to influence government and public opinion?

Regulating Interest Groups

GUIDING QUESTION *How does the government regulate interest groups?*

The Constitution **guarantees,** or promises, Americans the right to take part in interest groups. Still, both state governments and the federal government have laws about what these groups can do. Some laws limit how much money PACs may contribute to candidates. Others require lobbyists to register with officials who have the authority to oversee them. Lobbyists must also state who hired them, how much they are paid, and how they spend money related to their work. These laws are aimed at preventing lobbyists from gaining unfair influence.

PROPAGANDA TECHNIQUES

THE BANDWAGON

"Polls show our candidate is pulling ahead, and we expect to win in a landslide."

NAME-CALLING

"Candidate A is a dangerous extremist."

ENDORSEMENT

Popular beauty queen says, "I'm voting for Candidate B and so should you."

TRANSFER

Associating a patriotic symbol with a candidate.

GLITTERING GENERALITY

"Candidate B is the one who will bring us peace and prosperity."

JUST PLAIN FOLKS

"My parents were ordinary, hardworking people, and they taught me those values."

STACKED CARDS

"Candidate C has the best record on the environment."

CHART SKILLS

These propaganda techniques, or methods, are similar to those that companies use in advertising to promote their products to consumers.

▶ CRITICAL THINKING

1 *Identifying* Which of these methods would be used by a group that opposed a candidate? Why?

2 *Applying* Suppose you saw an ad for a candidate that included the phrase "She's one of us." Which technique would that represent?

Federal and state laws also require former government officials to wait for a period of time before they can become lobbyists. The delay is meant to stop these former officials from using friendships and inside knowledge to help special-interest groups. This kind of law, however, has not been successful. After waiting for a period of time, former lawmakers do become lobbyists. Because they understand how the legislature works and often still have friends among lawmakers, they can be very influential.

Interest groups have critics and defenders. Some people say that interest groups and lobbyists have too much say in government. They claim that by giving money to a campaign, special-interest groups gain power over elected officials. Many critics point to the example of Jack Abramoff. He was one of Washington's most powerful lobbyists. In 2006, Abramoff admitted that he corrupted government officials and stole millions of dollars from his lobbying clients. Some critics say that it is wrong for interest groups to have more influence than ordinary voters.

Other people defend interest groups. They say these groups help make known the wishes of large groups of people. In that way, they help make sure that the government responds to people's concerns. In this view, interest groups provide a service by letting representatives know the people's wishes.

Supporters of interest groups also say that these groups are an important part of a democracy. They provide a way for Americans to take an active role in government. By joining forces, ordinary people can pressure the government to follow the policies they believe are important.

✓ PROGRESS CHECK

Explaining Why must former government officials wait before becoming lobbyists?

LESSON 3 REVIEW

Review Vocabulary

1. How are *public-interest groups* and *nonpartisan* groups similar? How are they different?

2. How do *lobbyists* differ from political action committees (PACs)?

Answer the Guiding Questions

3. *Identifying* What are four ways that interest groups promote their viewpoints and try to influence public policy?

4. *Explaining* Why does the government regulate interest groups, despite constitutional guarantees of their right to exist? Explain the reason for one regulation to support your answer.

5. **INFORMATIVE/EXPLANATORY** You have read about political parties and about interest groups. Write a paragraph in which you compare interest groups and political parties. How are they similar? How are they different?

Issues to Debate

Are social networking sites good for democracy?

Social networking sites—like Facebook, MySpace, and Twitter—are part of daily life. Can these sites have any impact on government? Can they be tools for democracy? People are debating.

On one side are people who think that these sites will increase democracy. They argue that networking sites make it easier for people to join with others. Some even say that people can use the sites to more easily bring about profound change.

On the other side are those who dismiss social networking sites. They argue that the connections people make on these sites are not deep. As a result, they say, these connections are unlikely to have a major impact.

> **Political candidates employ Internet marketing experts to run expensive online campaigns. Besides outreach, online efforts help candidates collect valuable data.**

Yes

Those who see social networks as a revolutionary tool often point to the role of this technology in forming grass-roots movements in countries. Lecturer and writer Howard Rheingold makes the point: "Joseph Estrada was toppled as president of the Philippines in part because of text-message-organized protests, and Roh Moo-Hyun won an upset victory for president in South Korea also in part because of a last-minute text-message-based get-out-the-vote effort." Rheingold goes on to say that denying the role of these sites in elections is ignoring the facts.

—Howard Rheingold, *The New York Times*, 2010

No

Others say that clicking a symbol on a social networking site to show agreement with a cause means little. Real change, they say, requires deeper commitment. Writer Malcolm Gladwell makes this argument: "Social media are built around weak ties. Twitter is a way of following (or being followed by) people you may never have met. Facebook is a tool . . . for keeping up with the people you would not otherwise be able to stay in touch with." Gladwell says that to really bring about change, activists need discipline and dedication. That, he argues, is not likely to be developed by sending tweets or clicking a button that says "Like."

—Malcolm Gladwell, *The New Yorker*, 2010

Debating the Issue

1. **Making Connections** What political use might social networking sites have? Explain.

2. **Analyzing** Would social networking sites be better for get-out-the-vote movements than for movements of deeper social change? Why or why not?

3. **Analyzing** Do you agree with Gladwell that ties on social networking sites are weak? Why or why not?

4. **Making Inferences** How could these sites be useful in countries where the government censors the news?

Write your answers on a separate sheet of paper.

1 Writing Activity

EXPLORING THE ESSENTIAL QUESTION
How do citizens, both individually and collectively, influence government policy?

In an essay, describe three forces that influence the actions of government officials. Explain how politicians learn about public opinion and how knowing public opinion can affect their actions; how the media affect public opinion and the actions of government officials; and how interest groups influence policy. Give an example of each of these sources of influence. Conclude by stating which of the three forces you think has the most effect on the government and explaining why you think so.

2 21st Century Skills

PERSUADING Working with a small group, identify an issue you care a lot about. Think of your group as an interest group. You want to inform others about your issue and your point of view about it. Decide what message you want to put out to people. Make a video or design a Web page that gets that message out. In assembling your video or Web page, be sure to consider the audience you want to reach and how you can influence that audience.

3 Being an Active Citizen

As a class, brainstorm issues that you think are important in your community. Then, working with a small group, choose one of those issues and conduct a poll to find out where people in your area stand on that issue. Design a survey of five to ten questions about the issue. Word the questions carefully to avoid influencing answers. Have each person in your group get five people to respond to the questions. Tally your results and discuss with the class.

4 Understanding Visuals

Political cartoons use humor to make a point. Examine the political cartoon shown here. Who is the character in the cartoon? What kind of media does he represent? Summarize the cartoon's message. What does it say about how the media are changing? What does it say about the information that people obtain from media sources?

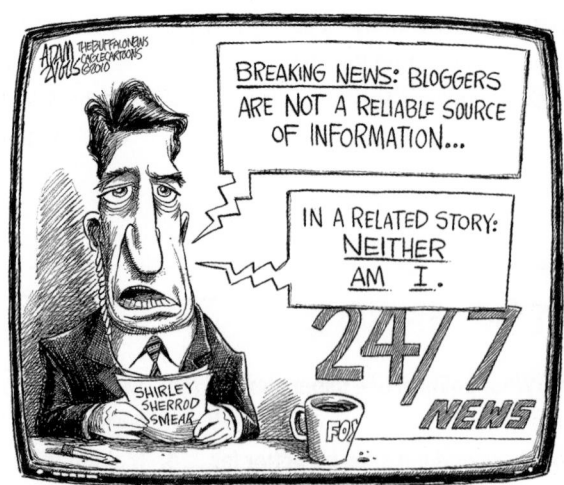

CARTOON: ADAM ZYGLIS/PoliticalCartoons.com

REVIEW THE GUIDING QUESTIONS

Directions: Choose the best answer for each question.

1 Which of the following is a source of public opinion?
- **A.** the mass media
- **B.** regulatory commissions
- **C.** surveys
- **D.** pollsters

2 In terms of opinions, *stability* refers to
- **F.** the direction of public opinion.
- **G.** whether opinion is positive or negative.
- **H.** the strength of a person's opinion.
- **I.** how firmly people believe in their views.

3 Issues that receive the most time, money, and attention from government leaders make up
- **A.** the mass media.
- **B.** public opinion.
- **C.** the public agenda.
- **D.** a public-interest group.

4 Which of the following is an example of a politician using the mass media to get his or her message out?
- **F.** leaking information
- **G.** reporting corruption
- **H.** restricting libel
- **I.** establishing prior restraint

5 What is the name for representatives of interest groups who contact public officials directly?
- **A.** propagandists
- **B.** lobbyists
- **C.** pollsters
- **D.** political action committees

6 What is an argument in favor of interest groups?
- **F.** They tell elected officials what the people want.
- **G.** They have too much influence on government.
- **H.** They encourage corruption among politicians.
- **I.** They are almost always nonpartisan.

DBQ **ANALYZING DOCUMENTS**

Directions: Analyze the excerpt and answer the questions.

The following passage comes from the Web site of an interest group called Common Cause and describes its work.

"Common Cause's work to improve ethics in Washington dates back to the first days of the organization. The group has helped make significant institutional reforms on Capitol Hill, which include creating tough Congressional ethics standards and financial disclosure laws and establishing a ban that restricts members from taking gifts, free vacation trips, and expensive meals from special interests."

—Common Cause Web site, 2010

❼ Classifying Which of the following best describes Common Cause?

A. a labor union

B. a public-interest group

C. a political action committee

D. a partisan polling organization

❽ Predicting Which of the following might Common Cause criticize?

F. partisan groups

G. political parties

H. public opinion polls

I. lobbyists

SHORT RESPONSE

"Our liberty cannot be guarded but by the freedom of the press, nor that be limited without danger of losing it."

—Thomas Jefferson, letter to John Jay, 1786

❾ What is Jefferson's point about the importance of the press to a democracy? Do you agree or disagree? Why?

❿ Think about what you have read about the roles the press plays. Which role, do you think, would be what Jefferson had in mind when he attached such importance to freedom of the press?

EXTENDED RESPONSE

⓫ Informative/Explanatory Think about the roles of the individual, the mass media, and interest groups in American government. What are the most effective ways an individual or group can participate in government? What impact do the three roles have on monitoring and influencing government? Use evidence from the chapter as support.

If You've Missed Question	❶	❷	❸	❹	❺	❻	❼	❽	❾	❿	⓫
Review Lesson	1	1	2	2	3	3	3	3	2	2	1,2,3

TEXT: "Meet the Press" Transcript for November 11, 2007, MSNBC, November 11, 2007.
TEXT: Ethics in Government, Common Cause, www.commoncause.org.

State Government

networks

There's More Online about state government.

CHAPTER 11

ESSENTIAL QUESTION
Why and how do people create, structure, and change governments?

The Story Matters...

No matter where you live in the United States, a capitol building stands in your state capital. State capitols usually house the state's legislature. Some even include courtrooms.

In Alabama, the State Capitol houses the offices of the governor and other executive branch officials. Since 1985, however, the state's lawmakers have worked in a separate building known as the State House. The state supreme court also has its own building.

These buildings make up the State Capitol Complex. Within a few square blocks, the work of state government gets done. The governor crafts a budget, legislators debate new laws, and the state supreme court decides cases.

◀ *The Alabama State Capitol building also serves as a museum of the state's history.*

PHOTO: Ilene MacDonald/Alamy

313

Real-Life Civics

▶ **ECONOMY** Governors hold an important job with a variety of duties. In her second term, Washington Governor Christine Gregoire had several goals. One top priority was to balance the state budget in difficult economic times. She worked to create jobs by making her state a good place to start and run a business. She also traveled to Japan and China in an effort to increase opportunities for exporting Washington products. These exports include aerospace industry products, paper and other wood products, food and agricultural products, and electronics. On her trade mission, Gregoire also looked for ways to attract international tourists to Washington state. Increasing both exports and tourism will help the state's economy to grow. Gregoire was elected governor in 2004 and 2008.

Governor Gregoire visits a supermarket in Shanghai, China, during a trip to explore economic opportunities for her state.

Virginia Governor Tim Kaine tours a neighborhood in Suffolk, where homes were destroyed by a tornado.

DISASTERS State governors must respond quickly to local disasters. They will visit the scene, address the public, work toward recovery, and try to prevent future tragedies. In 2008 Governor Tim Kaine of Virginia reacted after at least three tornadoes swept through the central and southeastern parts of his state. The tornadoes left a 25-mile path of destroyed houses and livelihoods in the towns of Colonial Heights, Lawrenceville, and Suffolk. More than 200 people were injured and more than 1,300 surviving homes lost power. The cost of the damage was more than $21 million. After touring the worst-hit areas and speaking with victims, Governor Kaine declared a state of emergency. Such a declaration allows the state government to bypass regular procedures and act quickly to aid the disaster's victims.

CIVIC LITERACY

★★★★

Analyzing How do the actions of Governor Gregoire and Governor Kaine show the varied responsibilities of state governors?

Your Opinion What do you think a governor hopes to achieve through a visit to a disaster site? Would you appreciate a visit from a governor during such a time? Explain.

Lesson 1
The Federal System

ESSENTIAL QUESTION *Why and how do people create, structure, and change governments?*

IT MATTERS BECAUSE
Both state and federal governments provide services to people.

Federal and State Powers

GUIDING QUESTION *How does the federal system allow the national government and state governments to share power?*

If you have ever traveled on a highway, you might have seen a road sign with a red, white, and blue shield and a number. This symbol shows that the road is an interstate highway. These roads connect major cities and are mostly paid for by the federal government. The sign might also have had an outline of a state with a number, which means that the road is a state highway.

Why would the same road be both a state and a federal highway? That happens because the United States has a federal system of government. In a **federal system,** the national government and the state governments share and divide powers. Both build highways. That is just one example of how these two levels of government do similar jobs.

In our federal system, some powers are left to the state governments and others to the federal government. Some powers are shared by both. There has been an ongoing debate about how our federal system should work. Some favor states' rights over the power of the national government. Others argue that the powers of the national government should be increased.

PHOTO: (tl) Ramin Talaie/Corbis; (tcl) Ilene MacDonald/Alamy; (tcr) Thinkstock/Getty Images; (tr) Roy Dabner/epa/Corbis

Taking Notes: *Contrasting*

As you read, fill out a chart contrasting state governments and the federal government.

State Governments and
Federal Government

Similarities	Differences

Content Vocabulary
- **federal system**
- **reserved powers**
- **concurrent powers**
- **supremacy clause**
- **grants-in-aid**

federal system the sharing of power between the central and state governments

States in the Constitution

Do you remember what kind of system the Articles of Confederation set up? Under that government, the nation was a loose union of states. The states were relatively stronger than the central government.

In writing the Constitution, the Framers created a stronger central government. However, they believed that state governments were important as well. Anti-Federalists like Patrick Henry were against giving states less power. Even James Madison, who believed in a strong central government, knew that it was important for states to keep certain powers.

As a result, the Framers created a federal system that divides powers between state and national governments. The Constitution limits the powers of states while offering states protections. For instance:

- Article IV, Section 1 says that each state must respect legal actions taken by other states. Because of this section, for example, one state accepts a driver's license given by another.
- Article IV, Section 2 promises that each state will treat the people of other states equally. For example, states cannot give people from another state tougher punishment for a crime than their own citizens would get.
- Article IV, Section 3 guarantees each state's area. The section says that land cannot be taken from any state to make a new state without its approval. It also says that two states cannot be joined into a new state unless they agree.
- Article IV, Section 4 promises each state a republican form of government. It also vows to protect that government against an enemy attack or a revolt.

21st Century SKILLS

Identifying Points of View

When you identify points of view, you think about how an issue affects different people. Write a short dialogue between an anti-Federalist, who was against giving more power to the central government, and someone who believed that a strong central government was more important than strong state governments.

Each state has control over its National Guard units. However, in times of war the federal government can call the National Guard into action to take part in federal missions. This member of the guard was called to serve in the Iraq War.

▶ CRITICAL THINKING
Making Inferences How does the National Guard demonstrate the workings of the federal system?

Lesson 1 **317**

National Government
(Expressed, Implied, and Inherent powers)

National and State Governments
(Concurrent Powers)

State Governments
(Reserved Powers)

- Regulate foreign and interstate commerce
- Coin money
- Provide an army and navy
- Declare war
- Establish federal courts below the Supreme Court
- Conduct foreign relations
- Exercise powers implied by the expressed powers

- Levy taxes
- Borrow money
- Spend for general welfare
- Establish courts
- Enact and enforce laws

- Regulate intrastate commerce
- Establish local government systems
- Administer elections
- Protect public welfare and safety

CHART SKILLS

The Constitution gives some powers to the federal government and reserves some to the states. Both levels share other powers.

1 *Identifying* Which level creates local government?

▶ **CRITICAL THINKING**

2 *Making Inferences* Why do you think the states are blocked from coining money?

Sharing and Dividing Powers

The key to federalism is the way the Constitution assigns powers. Some powers are given only to the federal government. The federal government has three kinds of power.

- *Expressed* powers are those listed in the Constitution. Most of these powers are given in Article I, Section 8.
- *Implied* powers are not listed in the Constitution but can be based on it. For instance, it says that the president is commander in chief of the armed forces. Therefore, the president may send troops in response to a serious crisis.
- *Inherent* powers are the kinds of powers a government has simply because it is a government. Buying land from another country is an example.

Reading **HELP**DESK

Reading Strategy: *Outlining*

When you outline information in a reading, you organize similar kinds of information under a common heading and include only main points. Create an outline with the following headings:

I. Sharing and Dividing Powers
  A.
  B.
  C.
  D.
  E.

II. Limits on State Powers
  A.
  B.

Reserved powers are given only to states. Reserved powers come from the Tenth Amendment. It says that all powers not given to the federal government are reserved for the states.

Some powers are held by both the national and state governments. These shared powers are called **concurrent powers**. The Constitution does not mention concurrent powers. Yet, both levels of government need such powers in order to **function**. Examples of powers that both the state and federal governments hold include the powers to tax, set up courts, and enforce and create laws. Which kind of power is building highways? If you said "concurrent power," you are right.

Limits on State Power

The Constitution does put some limits on the powers of the states. For example, states cannot declare war, issue their own money, or impose taxes on imports from other countries or states. Nor can states make treaties with another country. In addition, according to the Fourteenth Amendment, states cannot take away the rights of their citizens "without due process of law." Also, states are required to give every citizen "equal protection of the laws."

Courts have used this amendment to make the Bill of Rights apply to the states. When written, the Bill of Rights was aimed at the federal government. For instance, the First Amendment says that Congress—not the states—cannot limit freedom of religion or speech. The Framers worried that a central government that was too strong could take away people's freedoms. They did not fear the state governments.

Yet, states did take away people's rights. For example, states in the South passed laws to limit the rights of African Americans. The Fourteenth Amendment gives courts a tool to stop states from making such laws.

Another limit to state power comes from the **supremacy clause**. Article VI says that the Constitution, and all federal laws, "shall be the supreme Law of the Land." If a state law conflicts with the words of the Constitution or a federal law, the state law is thrown out.

PHOTO: Ilene MacDonald/Alamy

Education is a power reserved for the states. State colleges, like Florida State University, provide education for citizens.

▶ **CRITICAL THINKING**
Drawing Conclusions What are some advantages to having states, as opposed to the federal government, provide education to its citizens?

---

reserved powers powers that the Constitution does not give to the national government and that are kept by the states

concurrent powers powers shared by the state and federal governments

Academic Vocabulary
function to serve a purpose

supremacy clause the clause in Article VI of the Constitution that makes federal laws prevail over state laws when there is a conflict

Working Together

The federal and state governments also work together. Each year the federal government gives billions of dollars to the states in **grants-in-aid.** This money is used to meet goals set by Congress. Grants might be for education, health care, or other purposes. Some grants give specific instructions to states. Others set goals but do not detail how to reach those goals or how the money should be spent.

In recent years, states have been unhappy about certain federal decisions. At times, Congress tells states to take certain actions without giving money to pay for those actions. State officials call these laws unfunded mandates. Critics say these laws are unfair and **violate** the rights of states.

Sometimes states do not want to follow laws Congress passes. For example, many states have resisted the Real ID Act, passed in 2005. The law set tough new ID standards for granting or renewing driver's licenses. Congress said these were needed for national security reasons. Within a few years, though, the legislatures of half the states formally protested the law.

State governments work with one another, too, to achieve common goals. Missouri and Kansas, for example, agreed in 1965 to create a bi-state agency to operate the transit system for Kansas City, Missouri, and neighboring Kansas City, Kansas. New Jersey and Pennsylvania have agreed not to charge income tax to people who work in one state but live in the other. Some states in the West have formed a group to design a common energy policy. States also help one another through a legal process called extradition. In this process, a person charged with a crime who has fled to another state is returned to the state where the crime was committed.

✓ **PROGRESS CHECK**

Identifying What are two limits that the Constitution puts on the powers of state governments?

States often work together to pool resources on projects, such as public transportation, that benefit their citizens. The Port Authority of New York and New Jersey is one example. It manages some of the region's main trade and transportation networks.

▶ **CRITICAL THINKING**

Making Inferences What are some advantages to states working together toward a common purpose?

PHOTO: Sandra Baker/Alamy

The State Constitutions

GUIDING QUESTION *What characteristics do all state governments share?*

Have you visited a state besides the one in which you live? If so, you may have noticed some ways that other states' climate or geography compare to your own. But you probably did not think about how state governments compare and contrast.

Similarities in State Constitutions

Each state has its own constitution. These documents set forth the structure of the state's government. Like the U.S. Constitution, they organize government into three branches— the executive, the legislative, and the judicial. They also describe the powers of each branch.

State constitutions also include a list of the specific rights guaranteed to citizens of the state. It is not surprising that states have recorded these rights. Such lists appeared in several state constitutions before the U.S. Constitution was written. In fact, James Madison drew on state constitution lists when he wrote the Bill of Rights.

Another way state constitutions are similar is that they establish control over lower-level government. Aside from guaranteeing each state a republican form of government, the U.S. Constitution says little about state governments. State constitutions, though, give details about the form of local government within the state.

The Massachusetts state constitution, the nation's oldest, was drafted largely by John Adams. It influenced the U.S. Constitution and other state constitutions. The Massachusetts State House, or capitol, was built in 1798. Its dome served as a model for the U.S. Capitol and many state capitol buildings.

▶ **CRITICAL THINKING**
Inferring Why do you think Massachusetts provided a model for other states' constitutions?

PHOTO: (tl) Thinkstock/Getty Images; (tr) The Granger Collection

Lesson 1 **321**

Differences Among State Constitutions

State constitutions differ in some ways. Massachusetts has the oldest constitution still in use. Its framework was written in 1780. Some states had earlier written constitutions, but these were replaced with new ones.

New Hampshire's constitution, at little more than 9,000 words, is the shortest state constitution. Alabama's, at about 365,000 words, is the longest. One reason that state constitutions are so long is that they are often far more specific than the U.S. Constitution, which is more general in its wording. California's constitution, for instance, even includes a long list of the kinds of resources that cannot be taxed. For example, these tax-free items include trees younger than four years old.

Alabama's state constitution has added the most amendments—more than 800 of them. But nearly three-quarters of these amendments affect only one county in the state. The fewest amendments have been made to Rhode Island's constitution—only 10. But its current constitution has only existed since 1986.

Some state constitutions allow for the creation of a special constitutional revision commission to propose amendments. The Florida constitution requires a commission review every 20 years to see if the constitution still meets the state's needs.

State constitutions reflect differences among the state governments. You will read more about those differences in the other sections of this chapter. No state constitution can include elements that clash with the U.S. Constitution, though.

✓ PROGRESS CHECK

Comparing Why are state constitutions often longer than the U.S. Constitution?

LESSON 1 REVIEW

Review Vocabulary

1. What is the difference between *reserved powers* and *concurrent powers*?

2. Why is a *supremacy clause* needed in a *federal system*?

Answer the Guiding Questions

3. *Identifying* What are two powers that the federal and state governments share?

4. *Comparing* How are the structures of state and federal governments similar?

5. **ARGUMENT** In 2010 the National Governors' Association and the Council of Chief State School Officers presented national standards for math and English-language arts for students in kindergarten through high school. The federal government hopes states will use these standards instead of the varied state guidelines. But education is usually left to the states. Do you think a national approach is good or bad? Write a letter to your representative in Congress giving your view.

Can States Set Immigration Law?

Illegal immigration has become a growing concern in the United States. As many as 11 million people are believed to live in the country illegally. Some states have been very hard-hit. The great number of illegal immigrants has a financial impact. This is because the state must provide such services as health care and education. Arizona, with perhaps more than 450,000 illegal immigrants, is one such state. The federal government makes immigration policy. For example, it decides who can immigrate and how they can become citizens. But some state leaders think that Congress has not done enough. In 2010 Arizona passed a law that calls on police to check the immigration status of anyone they stop or arrest. It also requires immigrants to carry papers proving they are here legally. The law sparked a debate over its fairness and whether it was within the power of state government to make such a law.

Protesters of the Arizona immigration law march to the state capitol in Phoenix in July of 2010.

Yes

"The truth is the Arizona law is both reasonable and constitutional. It mirrors substantially what has been federal law in the United States for many decades. Arizona's law is designed to complement [go along with], not supplant [replace], enforcement of federal immigration laws. . . . [The] Arizona [law] states that the federal government, along with local law enforcement officers authorized by the federal government, can only determine an alien's immigration status."

—Arizona governor Jan Brewer, July 6, 2010

No

"In our constitutional system, the federal government has preeminent [supreme] authority to regulate immigration matters. This authority derives [comes] from the United States Constitution and numerous acts of Congress. . . . Although states may exercise their police power in a manner that has an incidental or indirect effect on aliens [immigrants], a state may not establish its own immigration policy or enforce state laws in a manner that interferes with the federal immigration laws. The Constitution and the federal immigration laws do not permit the development of a patchwork of state and local immigration policies throughout the country."

—U.S. Department of Justice, July 6, 2010

Debating the Issue

1. **Summarizing** What are two problems that critics say come from illegal immigration?

2. **Analyzing** What kind of power does Governor Brewer say Arizona is using with its immigration law—expressed, reserved, concurrent, or some other? Why?

3. **Making Inferences** What part of the Constitution does the Justice Department say the law is going against? Why does it make that claim?

4. **Evaluating** Which argument do you find more convincing? Why?

Lesson 2
The State Legislative Branch

ESSENTIAL QUESTION *Why and how do people create, structure, and change governments?*

IT MATTERS BECAUSE
State legislatures make laws that affect many aspects of your life such as the quality of schools, roads, and parks.

How Legislatures Function

GUIDING QUESTION *What are the functions of state legislatures?*

Did you know that in most states, the legislative branch is much like that of the federal government? Forty-nine states have a bicameral legislature, with two houses, like Congress. Each state calls its upper house the senate. The lower house is usually called the house of representatives. Nebraska is the only state with a **unicameral** (YOO•nih•KAM•ruhl), or one-house, legislature.

Legislators and Leaders

Nebraska has the smallest legislature, with only 49 senators. The largest chamber belongs to New Hampshire, with 424 members.

State senators serve four-year terms in two-thirds of the states. House members generally serve for two years. In most states, a person must be either 18 or 21 to serve in the lower house. **Minimum** ages for state senators range from 18 to 25 years old.

All states pay their legislators. Most states pay a salary, but a few pay lawmakers a daily rate while the legislature meets. Salaries range from New Hampshire's low of $200 per year to California's high of $95,000 per year.

PHOTO: (tl) AP Photo/Steven Senne; (tc) Steve Yeater/AP Photo; (tr) Ron Buskirk/Alamy

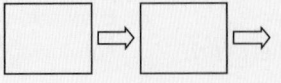

As in the United States Congress, each house in a state legislature has a presiding officer. In the lower chamber, that person is chosen by members of the body. He or she is typically called the speaker. In some states, the lieutenant governor heads the senate. Members of each party in each house choose someone to serve as their party's leader in that house. These members become the majority leader and minority leader. They play roles in setting the schedule for legislation and for planning when bills will be discussed.

Representation

The districts that members represent need to be roughly equal in population. Every 10 years, the federal government carries out a census to count all Americans. Census results are the basis for drawing district boundaries that will be used for the next 10 years. The task of working out the boundaries of legislative districts is called **redistricting** (ree•DIHS•trihkt•ihng).

In the past, many states often made little effort to draw new boundaries to reflect changes in population. As a result, rural districts often included far fewer people than those in cities. In Alabama, for instance, one state senator from a rural district represented fewer than 16,000 people. Another senator, from a city, represented more than 600,000. This huge difference made city dwellers less powerful than those people who lived in the country. Having unfair district sizes like these is called **malapportionment** (MA•luh•PAWR•shuhn•muhnt).

The United States Supreme Court put an end to this practice. In the 1962 case *Baker* v. *Carr,* citizens in Tennessee's large cities asked that the state's legislative boundaries be redrawn to better reflect population shifts from rural areas to the cities. The Court ruled that state legislative districts had to be roughly equal in terms of population. That ruling affected all states, not only Tennessee. It resulted in the redrawing of legislative boundaries throughout the country. The goal was to try to ensure that each citizen in a state has an equal voice in government.

21ˢᵗ *Century* SKILLS

Interpreting Points of View

When you interpret points of view, you think about how different people might view the same issue or idea. Before the 1962 Supreme Court ruling on *Baker* v. *Carr,* some states did not redraw districts, even when population had shifted dramatically. Write a few sentences in which you explain why some legislators might not want to change district boundaries. What reasons might they give?

Students and legislators in Massachusetts gather after a bill on college tuition limits that they supported has been defeated.

▶ **CRITICAL THINKING**
Speculating What might cause residents of a state to join together to call for a new law to be enacted?

Content Vocabulary	unicameral	Academic Vocabulary	redistricting the	malapportionment
• **legislative referendum**	having a one-house legislature	**minimum** the least quantity possible	process of redrawing legislative districts	unequal representation in state legislatures
• **popular referendum**				

State senates, like this one in California, meet to vote on bills.

▶ CRITICAL THINKING

Making Inferences Why do you think a bill must first be approved by a committee before the full chamber can vote on it?

Legislatures at Work

Lawmakers meet during a legislative **session.** A session lasts a few months, though the members can agree to extend it. Sometimes legislatures call a **special session.** This is a meeting held for a specific purpose, such as addressing a crisis. In most states, either the governor or the legislature can call these sessions. In some states, only the governor can.

State legislators do several jobs. They approve the people named by the governor to fill some state offices. They also work for the people of their district. For instance, they may help citizens by directing them to the correct state agency to solve a problem or by making an inquiry on their behalf.

The legislators' chief job though is to make laws. The steps in this process are similar to those in the process followed by Congress. Ideas for new laws may come from individual citizens, the governor, or the legislators. But a lawmaker must introduce the bill. Then it goes to a committee that reviews the bill and may revise it. If the committee members approve the bill, it goes to the full chamber for discussion and a vote. If a majority votes to pass the bill, it goes to the other house. The same process—committee and then full vote—is repeated. Once both houses approve a final version of the bill, it goes to the governor to be signed.

Reading **HELP**DESK

session a meeting of a legislative or judicial body to conduct business

special session a legislative meeting called for a specific purpose

Citizen Power

A **legislative referendum** takes place when the legislature asks voters to approve a law it has passed. In some states the people must approve actions such as borrowing money or raising taxes. In 49 states, voters must approve changes to the state constitution.

In about half the states, citizens can petition for a **popular referendum** if they dislike a law. This tool allows voters to decide if they want to repeal the law that some people object to.

✓ PROGRESS CHECK

Analyzing In which state would bills not be passed by two houses before going to the governor? Why?

State Economic Issues

GUIDING QUESTION *What economic challenges do state legislatures face?*

States always face tough choices about what services to fund. Should they repair roads or improve schools? Should they hire more state police officers or do more to maintain state parks? In all but one state, the law demands that the budget be balanced. This means that, unlike the federal government, states cannot spend more money than they collect. Nor can most states borrow money to meet regular expenses, as Congress does.

Therefore, if a state's income is less than expected, that state's government must take quick action. In many states, the governor or the legislature has the power to cut spending in order to balance the budget.

State Revenues and Spending

States **rely** on taxes as their major source of income. The main types of taxes are income taxes and sales taxes. People pay sales taxes when they purchase goods. Nearly all states have a sales tax, ranging from about 3 percent to 8 percent. Most states also tax the income that people earn from working or from other sources. Together, these taxes supply about two out of every three dollars that all states receive.

Residents enjoy the natural beauty at state parks, like Chewacla State Park in Alabama.

▶ CRITICAL THINKING
Speculating How might residents react to cuts in funding for parks? How might legislators respond?

PHOTO: Ron Buskirk/Alamy

---

legislative referendum a vote called by a legislature to seek voter approval of a law

popular referendum a question placed on a ballot by a citizen petition to decide if a law should be repealed

Academic Vocabulary

rely to depend on something or someone

States also get income from other sources. They charge fees for such things as licenses to marry, drive, and fish. They may also charge use fees. For instance, the toll that a driver pays to travel on certain roads is a use fee.

Most state spending goes to pay for services. These services include aid to local governments, benefits to the poor and disabled, health care, education, and payroll for state workers. States have other expenses as well, such as providing police protection, maintaining roads, and keeping up state parks.

Budget Crunch

Balancing the budget becomes challenging for states when they have less income. For several years starting in 2007, the U.S. economy had problems. Many businesses had to lay off workers. The national unemployment rate reached 10 percent. With so many people out of work, state income tax revenues fell. People without jobs had less money to buy products, so sales tax revenues also fell. States could not collect enough taxes to meet expenses. Many had to make deep budget cuts. Some states increased taxes to gain more revenue. But this meant that people had less money to spend to stimulate the economy.

At the same time, states faced growing demands. More people were relying on unemployment payments. Many also required help with health care and other needs. The federal government stepped in to give states extra money. But this aid could not continue indefinitely.

Some states faced huge budget shortfalls. Illinois, for example, had a budget of about $34 billion in 2011. But it was projected that Illinois would have only half of that amount in revenue in 2012. Other states were also hit hard. Some 40 states had too little revenue to meet their spending needs.

☑ **PROGRESS CHECK**

Summarizing What are the main sources of income for state governments?

LESSON 2 REVIEW

Review Vocabulary

1. In a sentence, explain how *redistricting* can affect *malapportionment*.

2. Explain the difference between a *legislative referendum* and a *popular referendum*.

Answer the Guiding Questions

3. *Explaining* What jobs do state legislators carry out?

4. *Comparing and Contrasting* Why do states face more difficult budget problems than the federal government?

5. **INFORMATIVE/EXPLANATORY** Write an essay explaining how state legislatures are similar to and different from Congress.

networks

There's More Online!

☑ **GRAPHIC ORGANIZER**
Governors' Roles

☑ **CHART**
Governors' Roles
Governors Become President

☑ **GAME**

Lesson 3
State Executive Branch

ESSENTIAL QUESTION *Why and how do people create, structure, and change governments?*

IT MATTERS BECAUSE
The executive branch carries out the laws of the state.

The Governor

GUIDING QUESTION *What are the powers and duties of a governor?*

Have you ever thought that you might like to be the governor of your state? In seven states, you can run for this office as soon as you become 18 years old. In most states, however, you will have to wait a few more years—until you are 30. Other requirements also vary widely among the states.

The Office of Governor

Most states require that a person who serves as governor be a resident of the state. Surprisingly, a handful of states do not have that requirement. Among the many states that have the requirement, the specifics vary greatly. While a candidate for governor in Missouri and Oklahoma must have lived there for at least 10 years, someone who has lived in Rhode Island for just 30 days can run for governor of that state.

Most states limit a person to no more than two terms as governor. But nearly a dozen states have no such limit. Some states, such as Virginia, allow more than one term but do not allow the terms to be consecutive. Someone who is governor for a term must sit out at least one term before being able to hold the office again. Most governors' terms are four years.

PHOTO: (tl) Gail Oskin/WireImage/Getty Images; (tc) Eric Engman/Getty Images; (tr) AP Photo/Mike Derer

Reading HELPDESK

Taking Notes: *Identifying*

As you read, fill in the concept web shown with examples of the different roles that governors fulfill. Add more connections if you need to.

Governors' Roles

Content Vocabulary

- **line-item veto**
- **commute**
- **parole**

Lesson 3 **329**

Governors, like Deval Patrick of Massachusetts, play many different roles, some of which involve other branches of the government.

1 *Identifying* Which roles of the governor involve other branches of government?

▶ **CRITICAL THINKING**

2 *Analyzing* Which role of the governor do you think is most important? Least important? Explain your reasoning.

PHOTO: Gail Oskin/WireImage/Getty Images

Chief Executive
Carries out state laws; appoints officials; prepares a budget

Commander in Chief
In charge of National Guard (state militia)

Ceremonial Leader
Greets important visitors; represents the state

Legislative Leader
Proposes legislation; approves or vetoes legislation

Judicial Leader
Offers pardons and reprieves; grants parole

Party Leader
Leads the political party in the state

The Chief Executive

Like the president, a governor has many roles. Each role comes with some powers. Two of these roles have developed through **tradition** rather than by law. For instance, a governor's ceremonial role and position as party leader are based on tradition, not on the state constitution.

A governor's main job, like that of the president, is to head the executive branch of government. In this role, he or she is responsible for making sure that the laws of the state are carried out. Also, just as the president commands the nation's armed forces, the governor is the head of the state's National Guard.

Governors often name people to fill state offices. Typically these choices are not final until the state senate has confirmed, or approved, the person. Governors also choose a person to fill a seat in the U.S. Senate if a seat should become vacant. That power comes to them from the U.S. Constitution. However, governors do not have as much control over the people in their cabinets as presidents do.

In most states, the governor also writes the state's annual budget. Typically the legislature must approve it before it goes into effect.

Reading HELPDESK

Academic Vocabulary

tradition a custom; the long-followed way of doing things

line-item veto to veto only a specific part of a bill

Academic Vocabulary

specific clearly specified, precise, or explicit

commute to reduce a criminal's sentence

parole to grant a prisoner an early release from prison, with certain restrictions

Other Roles of the Governor

Governors have certain legislative duties, too. Early each year, they deliver a "state of the state" message to the legislature and the state's citizens. In it, governors outline their goals. Then they send bills to the legislature that will help the state reach those goals. Governors can also call a special session of the legislature to respond to a crisis.

Like presidents, governors have the power to veto bills. For all but six governors, this power goes further. They can use a **line-item veto.** This means they can veto **specific** parts of a bill rather than the whole law. Lawmakers can override either of these kinds of vetoes by voting to pass the bill again.

Governors have some judicial powers as well. They can appoint judges. They can change criminal sentences. A governor may grant pardons to criminals. A pardon removes a criminal's punishment. A governor can also choose to **commute,** or reduce, someone's sentence. These rulings can be made before any punishment has been served. Governors can also grant prisoners an early release from prison. That early release is called **parole** (puh•ROHL).

Next in Line

What happens if the governor dies or for some reason leaves office before the end of a term? In 43 states, the next person in line is the lieutenant governor. In some states, candidates for governor and lieutenant governor run as a team, or on the same ticket. In other states, they run separately. They may even belong to different political parties. The next person in line steps into the governor's position with surprising frequency. Between 2000 and 2010, governors were replaced 20 times.

✓ **PROGRESS CHECK**

Evaluating What kind of check is there on the governor's power to appoint people to fill vacant offices?

PHOTO: Eric Engman/Getty Images

Lieutenant Governor Sean Parnell waves to a crowd after being sworn in as governor of Alaska. Parnell replaced Governor Sarah Palin when she resigned in 2009.

▶ **CRITICAL THINKING**
Drawing Conclusions Why do you think that most states have a lieutenant governor?

State Executive Departments

GUIDING QUESTION *What is the role of the executives who head a state's administrative departments?*

In the federal government, the executive branch has many departments and agencies. They serve a number of needs at the national level.

State governments also have a number of executive departments, agencies, and boards. Some are similar to those at the federal level, such as departments of labor, justice, and agriculture. Others are specific to state needs, including departments of health and public works and highways. Many states also have boards of welfare to help those in need.

The federal departments, agencies, and boards are headed by officials whom the president chooses and the Senate approves. At the state level, on the other hand, elected officials run many departments. These officials get their jobs without the governor playing a role. They are independent, so they might not be willing to take direction from the governor.

Major Executive Officials

Most states have five major executive officials. Each carries out important activities in the state. The titles of these officials differ from state to state.

An official for New Jersey's department of weights and measures does an inspection at a gas station.

▶ **CRITICAL THINKING**
Drawing Conclusions How does this state department help you as a consumer?

PHOTO: AP Photo/Mike Derer

Reading Strategy: *Summarizing*

When you summarize a reading, you find the most important points and restate them in your own words. Summarize the similarities and differences between the federal and state executive branches.

- The secretary of state oversees elections in the state and the recording and publishing of all laws. The office headed by this person also keeps other kinds of official records.
- The attorney general is the state's chief lawyer. He or she is the leader of the lawyers who represent the state in legal matters. These include disputes with the federal government.
- The state treasurer's main duty is to handle and keep track of the flow of money into and out of the state government.
- The state auditor's job is to review the conduct of state departments and offices. This official makes sure that work is being done honestly and efficiently. Auditors ensure that tax dollars are not misused.
- The commissioner or superintendent of education oversees the state's public school system. This person is concerned with the content that should be studied in each subject in each grade and other school-related issues.

In most states, the first three offices are filled through elections. About half the states also elect the auditor. In others, the auditor is chosen by one or both houses of the legislature or named by the governor. The head of education is elected in only about a third of the states. In the rest, the official is named by the governor or by a special group of officials.

State Cabinets

In most states, the executive department officials make up a cabinet. The cabinet meets regularly with the governor to give advice and share information. These officials from the different departments each bring special knowledge when discussing issues. The size of cabinets varies widely, from fewer than 10 members in some states to as many as 75 in New York. Some cabinets meet every week. Others meet only every one or two months.

✓ PROGRESS CHECK

Explaining What is the role of the cabinet?

LESSON 3 REVIEW

Review Vocabulary

1. Explain the difference between a veto and a *line-item veto*.

2. Describe the difference between a governor's judicial powers to *commute* and to *parole*.

Answer the Guiding Questions

3. *Identifying* What is the chief duty of a governor?

4. *Analyzing* Many executive department heads are elected in their own right, not appointed by the governor. How can that affect the governor's ability to direct them? Why?

5. **NARRATIVE** Write a journal entry describing a day in the life of a governor. Be sure to include examples of the many different roles a governor plays.

netw⊙rks
There's More Online!

☑ **GRAPHIC ORGANIZER**
  Courts

☑ **CHARTS**
  State Court Structure
  Pros and Cons of Electing Judges

☑ **TIME LINE**

☑ **GAME**

Lesson 4
State Judicial Branch

ESSENTIAL QUESTION *Why and how do people create, structure, and change governments?*

IT MATTERS BECAUSE
State courts decide many issues affecting people's lives.

The Structure of State Courts

GUIDING QUESTION *How is the state's judicial system organized?*

Have you ever watched a scene in a television show where a lawyer questions a tense witness and introduces dramatic evidence? Such courtroom dramas occur in state courts across the country.

Although each state has its own court system, all state court systems are organized in a similar fashion. Every state has two sets of courts, known as lower courts and higher courts. At each level, the courts hear cases that differ in how serious and **complex** they are.

Lower Courts

The lower courts are trial courts. In a **trial court,** a judge or a jury listens to the evidence that is presented and reaches a verdict, or decision, in favor of one party in the case or the other. Lower trial courts go by different names depending on their location. In rural areas, for example, they may be called justice courts. When they cover an entire county, they are often referred to as district courts. In cities, lower-level trial courts are often called municipal courts.

PHOTO: (tl) Design Pics Inc./Alamy; (tc) AP Photo/Rogelio Solis - File; (tr) AP Photo/Chronicle-Telegram - Bruce Bishop

Reading **HELP**DESK

Taking Notes: *Categorizing*

As you read, fill in a chart like the one shown with examples of types of courts in each category.

	Lower Level	Higher Level
Trial		
Appellate		

Content Vocabulary

- **trial court**
- **misdemeanor**
- **civil case**
- **plaintiff**
- **defendant**
- **appellate court**
- **felony**

Lower-level courts may handle criminal cases and civil cases. In a criminal case, a person is accused of committing a crime. A trial is held to determine whether the person is guilty or innocent. If the accused person is found guilty, he or she is punished.

Crimes handled in the lowest level of courts are simple ones. For example, they may be traffic violations or misdemeanors. **Misdemeanors** (MIHS•dih•MEE•nuhrz) are the least serious crimes, such as theft of a small sum of money or trespassing. Usually, misdemeanors are punished by a fine or a short stay in a local jail rather than in a prison. These cases are often decided by a judge instead of a jury.

Lower-level courts also hear civil cases. In **civil cases,** two parties are involved in a dispute in which one claims to have been harmed in some way by the other. The person who claims to have been harmed is the **plaintiff.** The person said to have caused the harm is the **defendant.**

An example of a civil suit is an argument between two neighbors over the line that divides their property. Many civil cases have to do with contracts, or business agreements. Often in these cases, one party says that another party did not carry out the actions promised in the contract. The civil cases that are heard in lower-level courts involve small sums of money.

Higher Courts

The higher courts are the second level of state courts. They can be either trial courts or appellate courts. In an **appellate** (uh•PEH•luht) **court,** the party who has lost the case in a lower court appeals the decision. To appeal means to ask a judge to review and reverse the earlier case. The party who appeals might think that legal errors were made during the trial and that these errors had an effect on the outcome of the court's decision. The appellate court decides whether errors in applying the law were made.

In lower-level courts, a judge, and not a jury, often makes a decision about a defendant's guilt or innocence.

▶ **CRITICAL THINKING**
Making Inferences Why might cases be decided in this way?

PHOTO: Design Pics Inc./Alamy

Academic Vocabulary

complex complicated or intricate

trial court type of court in which a judge or a jury listens to the evidence and reaches a verdict, or decision, in favor of one party or another in the case

misdemeanor the least serious type of crime

civil case court case in which one party in a dispute claims to have been harmed in some way by the other

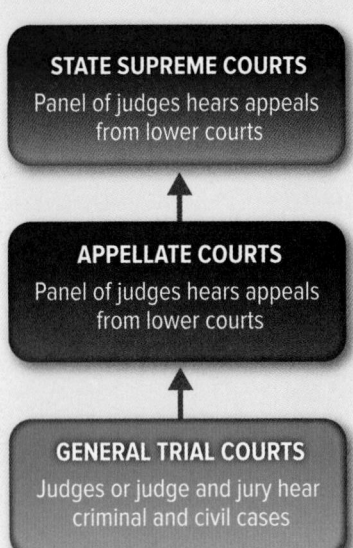

STATE SUPREME COURTS
Panel of judges hears appeals
from lower courts

APPELLATE COURTS
Panel of judges hears appeals
from lower courts

GENERAL TRIAL COURTS
Judges or judge and jury hear
criminal and civil cases

LOWER COURTS

Justice Courts—rural and
small towns

Magistrate Courts—larger
towns, smaller cities

Municipal Courts: traffic,
juvenile, misdemeanors
—larger cities

CHART SKILLS

The diagram shows the
different levels of state courts
and some names of courts at
each level.

▶ CRITICAL THINKING

1 *Identifying* How many
levels of courts are shown
in the diagram?

2 *Analyzing* Why is the
state supreme court called
the "court of last resort" for
state law?

Higher-level trial courts handle more serious crimes called **felonies** (FEH·luh·neez). Some examples of felonies include assault, robbery, kidnapping, and murder. Trials in these courts do not always involve juries. The accused person can choose to have the judge, and not a jury, determine guilt or innocence.

Higher trial courts also handle civil cases that are more serious than the civil cases handled in lower courts. They may involve huge sums of money. Civil cases may also be decided either by a jury or by a judge.

Forty-one states have two levels of appellate courts. The exceptions are generally states with small populations, such as Delaware and Montana. The first line of appeal is in an intermediate appellate court. This court is often called the court of appeals. Usually a group of judges hears a case. They study the information given by both sides and compare the case to past cases that were similar. Then they agree on a decision. They may decide to let the earlier court ruling stand, or they may choose to overturn it.

Courts in one state are not bound by the rulings of another state's courts. However, a court may consult the ruling of another state's courts if it feels the decision relates to the case it is hearing.

State Supreme Court

Each state also has a supreme court at the top level of its court system. The state supreme court hears appeals from the intermediate appellate courts. State supreme courts generally issue, or give out, written explanations of their rulings. These decisions guide judges as they try cases in the future. In most states, these courts take both civil and criminal cases. Oklahoma and Texas, however, have separate courts for civil appeals and criminal appeals.

State supreme courts are called "courts of last resort," but that is not entirely true. In state law, they are the final word. However, someone who loses an appeal in the state supreme court may believe that the ruling violated his or her rights under the U.S. Constitution. If so, that person can appeal the case to the U.S. Supreme Court. The Court may or may not choose to hear the case.

✓ PROGRESS CHECK

Explaining What is the role of state supreme courts?

plaintiff the person in a
civil case who claims to
have been harmed

defendant the person in a
civil case who is said to have
caused the harm

appellate court type of court in which a
party who lost a case in a lower court asks
judges to review that decision and reverse it

felony type of crime more
serious than a misdemeanor

Staffing the Courts

GUIDING QUESTION *What are the usual methods for selecting judges?*

If you were to appear in a court, what qualities would you want the judge to have? To be effective, judges must know the law. They should be free of **bias** so they can judge fairly. They are also expected to be independent—to avoid being swayed by political pressure.

Yet judges in the United States serve in a representative democracy. In such a system, the people generally vote to select those who hold government office. Can the general public be counted on to choose judges wisely? Will they have enough information about the experience, knowledge, and character of judges to make good decisions?

Choosing Judges for Trial Courts

With the various levels of trial courts, it is not surprising that judges for these courts are chosen in many different ways. Some judges are selected by governors, state legislators, the state supreme court, or city officials. Other judges are elected by voters. Some states use a combination of processes depending on whether it is a judge's first term or a later term. In this mixed approach, an elected official chooses a judge for his or her first term on the bench. When that term ends, if the judge seeks a new term, he or she has to stand for election by the people.

Even election systems differ. Some elections are nonpartisan, which means that candidates are not linked to any political party. Other election systems allow judges to have a party identity.

The terms of office for judges also vary. Among the high-level trial judges, the term is usually from six to eight years. But a term can be as few as four years or as many as ten.

Judges elected by the people often use campaign signs, like these at the Neshoba County Fair in Philadelphia, Mississippi.

▶ CRITICAL THINKING

Formulating Questions What questions might voters ask a judge who is running for election in your area?

PHOTO: AP Photo/Rogelio Solis - File

Academic Vocabulary

bias good or bad feelings about a person or group that affects judgment

Choosing Judges for Appellate Courts

In the appellate courts, states are almost evenly split in how they select judges. About half of the states elect judges. In the other half, the governor chooses judges. In some of those states, the appointments must be confirmed by the state legislature or another governmental body.

In 41 states, the judges for the state supreme courts serve for terms of six, eight, or ten years. The rest have terms that are longer or shorter. Some states give longer terms to the chief justice. In other states, the position of chief justice rotates among all the justices on the court. In this case, each justice serves as chief for only two or three years.

Once their term is done, judges have to be approved again to continue to serve on the bench. Forty-one states require that judges be approved by popular vote. In the other states, either the governor or the legislature makes the decision. About half of the states require that judges retire after they have reached a certain age. In most of these states, the retirement age ranges from 70 to 75. Other states have no set age at which judges must retire.

Although judges can be removed from office by impeachment, this process can take a long time. Most states also have boards to look into complaints about judges. If the board finds that a judge has acted improperly, it can make a recommendation to the state supreme court. The court has the power to suspend or remove the judge.

 **PROGRESS CHECK**

Summarizing What are the most common ways to select appellate judges?

LESSON 4 REVIEW

Review Vocabulary

1. What roles do the *plaintiff* and the *defendant* play in a civil case?

2. What is the difference between a *misdemeanor* and a *felony*?

Answer the Guiding Questions

3. ***Summarizing*** What happens in a lower or trial court?

4. ***Comparing and Contrasting*** Describe how states choose judges for trial courts and for appellate courts.

5. **ARGUMENT** Identify the method for choosing appellate court judges that you think is best. Write down reasons for your choice. Then take the role of a state senator and write a speech proposing that your state adopt that method. Support your stand with reasons.

In re Gault

In the case in re Gault, the Supreme Court considered whether the way a juvenile defendant was treated violated his constitutional right to due process.

A juvenile defendant and his attorney

Background of the Case

Over time, states developed a separate court system for juveniles—people under 18 years old. The system did not follow normal procedures in criminal law. Instead, some rules were changed to protect young people. Other rules were designed to move cases involving young people quickly.

Gerald Gault was arrested early in 1964 and put on probation. If a person on probation commits another crime, the punishment is usually harsher. During his probation, Gault, then 15, was arrested again. At two different hearings, he was not given a lawyer. He confessed to the crime, though he was never told of his right not to respond to questioning. The court sentenced him to six years in a state youth detention center. For the same crime, an adult would have been sentenced to no more than a $50 fine and two months in jail.

Gault's parents appealed to the U.S. Supreme Court. They said that because officials took Gault's confession without telling him of his right to a lawyer, his due process rights, guaranteed by the Fourteenth Amendment, had been violated.

The Decision

In an 8–1 decision, the Court ruled that the procedures the state used violated Gault's due process rights. The justices said that officials failed to follow due process by not telling Gault's parents of his hearing and not telling Gault he had the right to a lawyer. Another due process failure was not telling Gault of his right to remain silent. That right protects a person accused of a crime from making statements that could be used against him in a court of law. The Court said

that the state cannot ignore the rights of juveniles. Justice Abe Fortas wrote:

◀◀ [T]he question is whether . . . an admission by the juvenile may be used against him in the absence of clear . . . evidence that the admission was made with knowledge that he was not obliged to speak and would not be penalized for remaining silent. . . . We conclude that the constitutional privilege against self-incrimination is applicable in the case of juveniles as it is with respect to adults. ▶▶
—Justice Abe Fortas, *In re Gault*, 1967

Why It Matters

The decision extended due process protection to juveniles. Juvenile courts still struggle to balance juveniles' rights with the desire to treat them differently from adults in order to protect them.

Analyzing the Case

1. **Comparing** Explain the differences in how the police would have treated Gault if he were an adult and not a juvenile offender.

2. **Evaluating** Does the Court's decision make it impossible to treat juvenile and adult cases differently? Why or why not?

PHOTO: AP Photo/Chronicle-Telegram - Bruce Bishop

Write your answers on a separate sheet of paper.

1 Writing Activity

EXPLORING THE ESSENTIAL QUESTION

Why and how do people create, structure, and change governments?

Find out what rules your state uses for a legislative referendum. Then write a brief oral presentation describing why and how this process is used. You may use visual aids with your presentation.

2 21st Century Skills

CREATING A DATABASE State governments now provide a wealth of information on the Internet. Focusing on one house of the legislature, one executive agency, or one type of court, create a database of your state's resources on the Web. In your database, include URLs and brief descriptions of the content on each page. Also include an evaluation of how easy it is to find information on each page and how helpful you find each page to be.

3 Being an Active Citizen

Find the names of the one or two state legislators who represent the district in which you live. Use the Internet or other resources to discover what issues they are most concerned about. Choose one of these issues that might affect you and your family. Write a letter to one of your representatives expressing your views on the issue. Explain why it matters to you. Give reasons to support your opinions.

4 Understanding Visuals

ANALYZING A POLITICAL CARTOON This political cartoon was drawn in the midst of an economic downturn, when states faced a serious budget crunch. What view does the cartoonist have of the problem and the solution?

REVIEW THE GUIDING QUESTIONS
Directions: Choose the best answer for each question.

1 What kind of power is a state government's power to tax?

A. concurrent

B. expressed

C. reserved

D. supreme

2 What principle is used to create state legislative districts?

F. They should be roughly equal in area.

G. They should split the state into urban and rural districts.

H. They should be similar in population.

I. They should follow natural land and water features.

3 Why do states have budget difficulties that the federal government does not have?

A. No one is willing to loan money to the states.

B. People expect more from state government.

C. States are smaller and have less revenue.

D. States must balance their budget without borrowing money.

4 What power do some governors have that a president does not have?

F. appoint people to office

G. command armed forces

H. line-item veto

I. set plans for legislation

5 Which state official oversees the collecting and counting of votes?

A. attorney general

B. secretary of state

C. state auditor

D. state treasurer

6 Which court would handle the first appeal of a case tried in a higher-level state trial court?

F. district court

G. intermediate appellate court

H. municipal court

I. state supreme court

DBQ **ANALYZING DOCUMENTS**

Directions: Analyze the excerpt and answer the questions that follow.

Alabama Governor Bob Riley said the following in a speech to the state legislature in 2010.

"The second part of our recovery plan is a tax credit for new jobs in counties with the highest unemployment. . . . These proposals will create jobs immediately . . . when jobs are needed the most and where they are needed most."

7 **Analyzing** Which of his roles as governor was Riley exercising when he proposed this plan?

A. chief executive   **C.** legislative leader
B. judicial leader   **D.** party leader

8 **Synthesizing** Based on what you have read in your textbook, what has to happen for Riley's plan to take effect?

F. The legislature must pass a law, and he must sign it.
G. The state courts must end their blocking of the law.
H. The state treasurer must release the money to the legislature.
I. The U.S. Congress must pass a law giving Alabama the money.

SHORT RESPONSE

Article III, Section 3, of Florida's constitution discusses legislative sessions.
"(c) **Special Sessions** *(1) The governor, by proclamation stating the purpose, may convene [bring together] the legislature in special session during which only such legislative business may be transacted as is within the purview [aim] of the proclamation. . . . (d)* **Length of Sessions** *A regular session of the legislature shall not exceed sixty consecutive days."*

9 What is the length of a regular session of the legislature? Why do you think this constitution provides a maximum number of days?

10 Why do you think this constitution limits the work of special sessions to only the issues raised by the governor in calling that session?

EXTENDED RESPONSE

11 **Informative/Explanatory** Write a paragraph explaining the duties of the legislature during its session. Include a description of a special session.

Need Extra Help?

If You've Missed Question	**1**	**2**	**3**	**4**	**5**	**6**	**7**	**8**	**9**	**10**	**11**
Review Lesson	1	2	2	3	3	4	2	1, 2	2	1, 2, 3	2, 3

Local Government

networks

There's More Online about local government.

ESSENTIAL QUESTION
Why do people create, structure, and change governments?

The Story Matters...

Many towns across the United States have town hall buildings like this one in Sandwich, Massachusetts. Local people and visitors are welcome to come to the town government offices located here. Sandwich residents gather at another, larger location for an annual town meeting where they discuss and vote on a variety of important issues.

The practice of holding town meetings to discuss local issues goes back to the American colonies. American colonists in the 1700s often met in local inns or taverns to discuss political matters. In some New England towns, people gathered in a central pasture or a commons in the town center. The tradition of governing through town meetings continues in many small American communities today.

◀ *This town hall in Sandwich, Massachusetts, houses the government of the historic community that dates back to the 1600s.*

PHOTO: Barry Winiker/Getty Images

Real-Life Civics

> **RECREATION** An important responsibility of local governments is to provide recreational services for residents. These often include recreation centers, athletic programs, libraries, cultural events, and parks.

One such local park is San Francisco's Golden Gate Park. Here, visitors can stroll in beautiful gardens, listen to a free concert, rent a boat on the lake, or play a round of golf on the park's golf course. Children can explore a state-of-the-art playground, ride on a carousel, visit the horse stables, or play soccer on the park's sports fields. Shaped much like Central Park in New York City, Golden Gate Park extends over more than 1,000 acres. Plans for the park were first drawn up in 1870. Over many years, land once covered by sand dunes was transformed into a park that 13 million visitors a year enjoy.

▷ A man sits at the top of a long slide with his children at Children's Playground in San Francisco's Golden Gate Park.

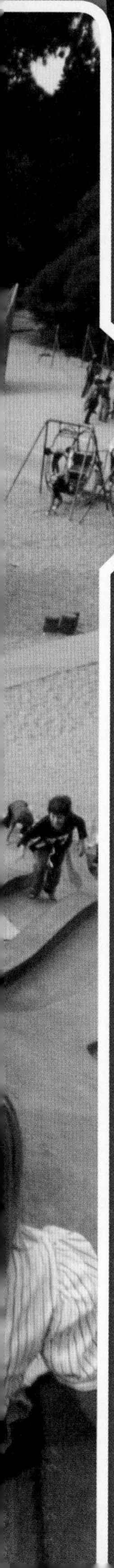

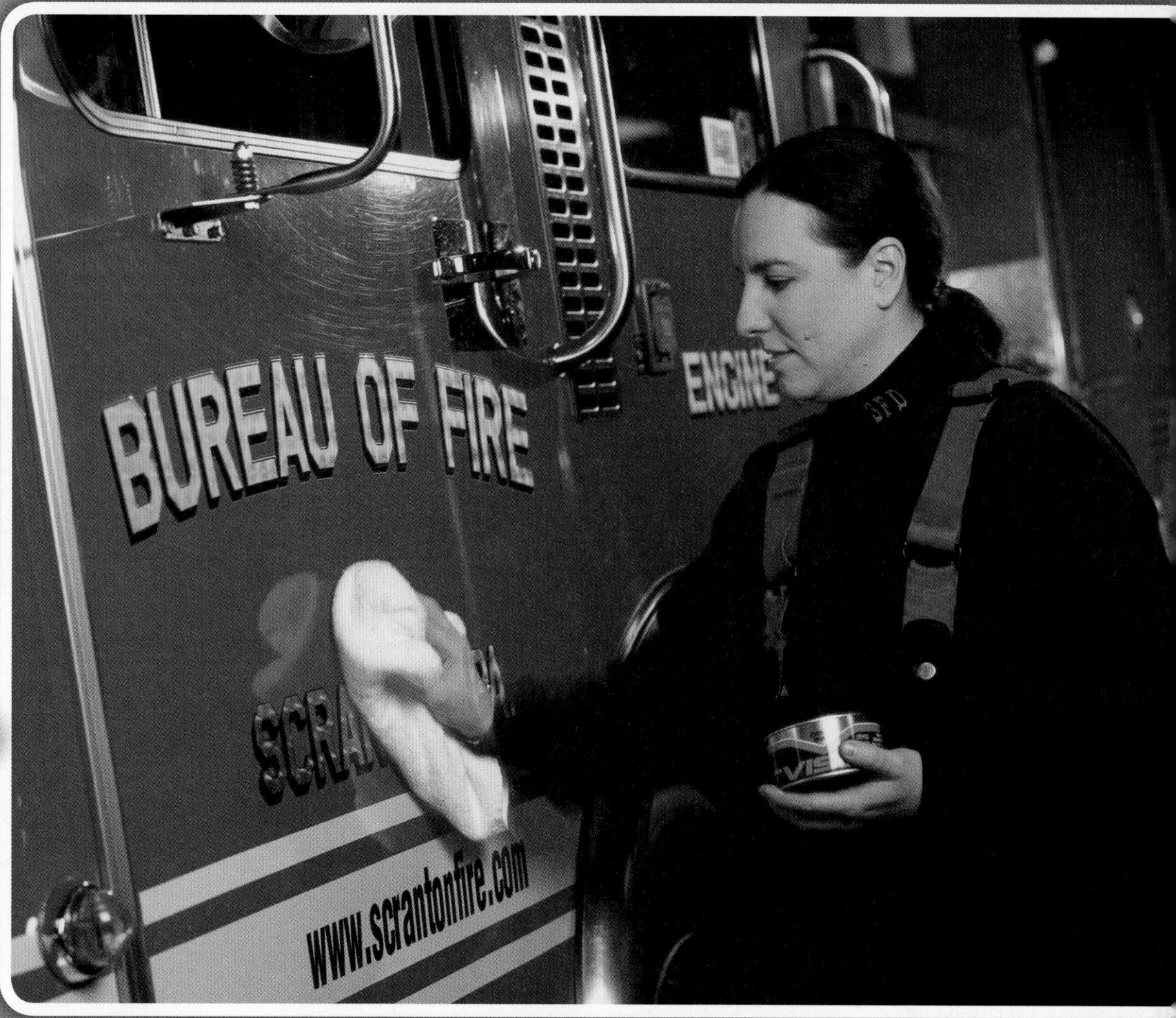

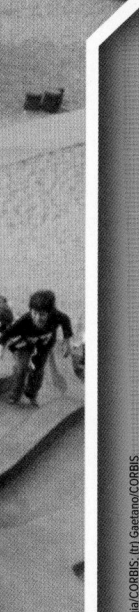

A firefighter polishes the door of a fire truck in Scranton, Pennsylvania.

SAFETY Local governments provide vital services that are often taken for granted by citizens. Most people rarely notice that the highway they drive on is newly paved. While everyone expects a quick response in an emergency, few consider how police officers, firefighters, and emergency vehicles are always available. Many such essential local services have been in place for more than a century. For example, the fire department of Scranton, Pennsylvania, began before the Civil War as a volunteer fire department. A 1901 Scranton city ordinance made it a "paid" city service. It and hundreds of other local fire departments across the country make it their business to save lives and property.

PHOTO: (l) Lowell Georgia/CORBIS, (tr) Gaetano/CORBIS

CIVIC LITERACY

★★★★

Analyzing If your local government had to make budget cuts, which services do you think residents could do without? Which services do you think are essential? Explain.

Your Opinion If you could design a park or recreation center for your community, what features might you include based on the needs of local residents?

netw🌐rks

There's More Online!

☑ **GRAPHIC ORGANIZER**
Forms of City Government

☑ **CHART**
Strong-Mayor and
Weak-Mayor Government

☑ **CHART**
Council-Manager and
Commission Governments

Lesson 1

City Governments

ESSENTIAL QUESTION *Why do people create, structure, and change governments?*

IT MATTERS BECAUSE

Most Americans live in cities and towns. Their local government has a direct influence on their daily lives.

How City Governments Are Created

GUIDING QUESTION *How are local governments created, funded, and organized?*

Do you live in a city? If you do not, it is likely that you will sometime in your life. Today more than 80 percent of Americans live in cities or urban areas.

Local governments are closer to the people than are other units of government. They provide services such as road maintenance, police and fire protection, and schools. Though local governments are important to people, they are not fully independent. The powers they have come from a higher level of government. In the United States, state constitutions usually set up the powers and duties of local governments.

Paying for Local Government

Where do local governments get the money to pay for the services they provide? Grants from the state and federal governments make up about 40 percent of local governments' income. More than 25 percent comes from taxes on land and buildings. Other taxes, such as sales taxes, make up about 10 percent of their budget. The rest comes from fees and fines for things such as parking, dog licenses, and traffic violations.

PHOTO: (tl) Craig Cozart/Getty Images; (tc) Ted Soqui/Corbis; (tr) Library of Congress

Reading HELPDESK

Taking Notes: *Identifying*
As you read, complete a graphic organizer listing the basic forms of city government.

Forms of City Government

Content Vocabulary

- **incorporate**
- **city charter**
- **home rule**
- **ordinance**
- **at-large election**
- **special district**
- **metropolitan area**
- **suburb**

346 *Local Government*

Becoming a City

A city is officially called a municipality. Most states define a municipality as an **incorporated** place—a local area with an organized government that provides services to residents. An area incorporates when the people ask the state legislature for a **city charter** and the state grants it. The charter gives power to a local government. An area must meet certain standards in order to get a charter. For example, it may need to have a certain number of people living within it. A city charter is like a constitution. It describes the type of city government, its structure, and its powers.

Some states give home rule to their cities. Under **home rule,** cities have the power to write their own charters. As a result, they can choose their own type of government. Home rule allows cities to act with less interference from the state. Still, these laws do limit city governments' freedom of action.

☑ PROGRESS CHECK

Summarizing How are city governments created?

The Mayor-Council Form

GUIDING QUESTION *How does the mayor-council form of government operate?*

Do you know how your local government is set up? Every city charter describes the type of government the community will have. Most urban areas in the United States use one of three basic forms of government. These are the mayor-council form, the commission form, and the council-manager form.

Until the early 1900s, most American cities had a mayor-council form of government. It is still a common form of city government today. In fact, it is the form of government favored by the nation's largest cities.

The Division of Power

Like the national government, the mayor-council form is based on the separation of powers. Executive power belongs to a mayor. Legislative power belongs to a city council. Voters elect both the mayor and the members of the council.

21ˢᵗ *Century*
SKILLS

Analyze News Media

Scan a copy of your local newspaper from 25 years ago, 50 years ago, and 75 years ago. Make a note of the issues that were important to your community at those times. In what ways has your community changed? In what ways has it remained the same? You may look for copies of old newspapers at your local library or historical society.

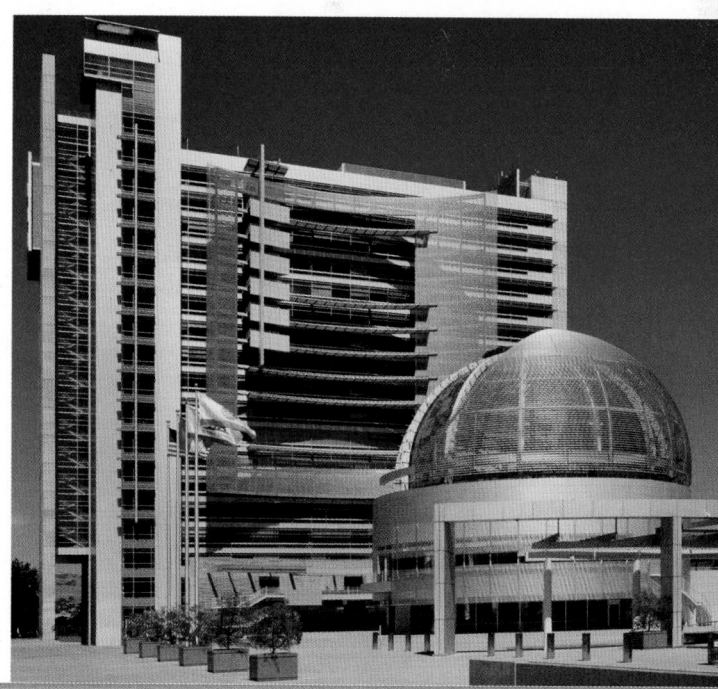

A city hall is the seat of government for a community. The rotunda outside of the San Jose, California, city hall was designed to be used for special occasions and formal events, such as the annual State of the City Address.

▶ CRITICAL THINKING
Identifying Central Issues Why do you think it is important for residents to have access to local government?

incorporate to receive a state charter officially recognizing the government of a locality

city charter a document granting power to a local government

home rule allows cities to write their own charters, choose their own type of government, and manage their own affairs

Understand how your school is governed. Find out how many members serve on the school board, how they are selected, how long they serve, and what their qualifications are. What are the duties of the school board? What is the role of the superintendent of schools?

There is an old saying: "You can't fight city hall." But, in fact, people do confront their local leaders during council meetings or in other public forums. Councils, for example, devote a portion of their meetings to comments from the public.

▶ **CRITICAL THINKING**
Making Connections How does citizen participation aid local government?

The mayor is similar to a state governor or the president. He or she is the chief executive of the city government. The mayor oversees the running of various city departments. Often the mayor appoints the people who head these departments and other offices. Major departments usually include public works, the police and fire departments, and the transportation department.

The council acts as the city's legislature. It passes city laws, which are usually called **ordinances.** The council also approves the city's budget.

Most city councils have fewer than 10 members. These members usually serve four-year terms. Cities have different plans for organizing council members. Some cities are divided into voting districts called wards. Each ward elects a representative to the city council. In other cities, council members are elected at-large. In an **at-large election,** council members are elected by voters in the entire city rather than in individual wards. Some cities mix these two systems. Some council members are chosen by ward, and others are elected by voters at-large.

Strong Mayors and Weak Mayors

There are two main types of mayor-council government. What sets them apart is how much power the charter gives to the mayor. These two types are the strong-mayor system and the weak-mayor system.

Today, most large cities have a strong-mayor system. Under this system, the mayor has strong executive powers. The mayor carries out the day-to-day activities of the city, much like a governor carries out the affairs of a state. A strong mayor's administrative powers can include appointing various city officials and writing the city's budget. A strong mayor typically has the power to veto, or cancel, laws passed by the city council.

Strong mayors tend to **dominate,** or have great influence over, the cities they lead. This influence partly comes from the great authority granted to strong mayors by their city charters. Two other factors also play a part in giving these mayors so much influence.

PHOTO: Ted Soqui/Corbis

Reading **HELP**DESK

ordinance a law, usually of a city or county

at-large election an election for an area as a whole; for example, statewide

Academic Vocabulary

dominate to have great influence over
reluctant unwilling

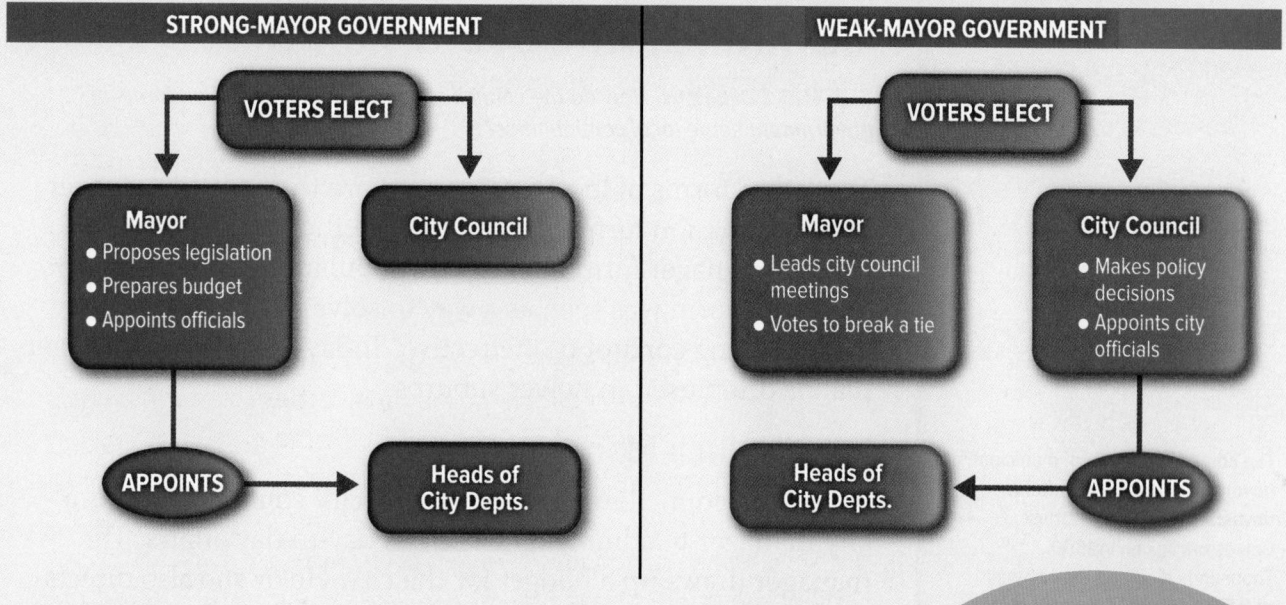

| STRONG-MAYOR GOVERNMENT | WEAK-MAYOR GOVERNMENT |

VOTERS ELECT

Mayor
- Proposes legislation
- Prepares budget
- Appoints officials

City Council

APPOINTS → **Heads of City Depts.**

VOTERS ELECT

Mayor
- Leads city council meetings
- Votes to break a tie

City Council
- Makes policy decisions
- Appoints city officials

Heads of City Depts. ← **APPOINTS**

CHART SKILLS

With both mayor-council forms of government, the ultimate source of power is the people.

▶ CRITICAL THINKING

1 **Contrasting** Who controls city departments under a strong-mayor government? Who controls those departments under a weak mayor?

2 **Making Inferences** Do you think the mayor in a weak- mayor system prepares the city budget? Why or why not?

First, in most cities, council members hold their positions part-time while mayors work full-time. This means that mayors have more time to spend on matters of government. Mayors also tend to have large staffs. That means they have more resources to draw on. As a result, they can become more involved in more issues.

Second, in large cities, council members are usually elected by wards. As a result, they usually focus on issues that are important to the part of town they represent, rather than the entire city. By contrast, strong mayors represent the whole community.

The strong-mayor system was developed in response to the inefficiencies of the weak-mayor system. Under a weak-mayor system, the mayor's power is limited. The council, not the mayor, names department heads and makes most policy decisions. The mayor usually directs council meetings but votes only in case of a tie. The weak-mayor system dates from the nation's earliest days. Former colonists were tired of the injustices done to them by British officials. As a result, they were **reluctant** to grant any official too much power.

The success of the mayor-council form of government depends largely on the person who serves as mayor. In the strong-mayor system, a politically skillful mayor can provide effective leadership. Under the weak-mayor plan, many people share responsibilities. Thus, success depends upon the mayor and council working well together.

☑ PROGRESS CHECK

Making Inferences Why would successful government be less likely under a weak-mayor plan?

Council-Manager and Commission Governments

GUIDING QUESTION *How do the council-manager and commission forms of government serve local communities?*

Two other forms of local government are the council-manager and commission forms. Both started in the early 1900s. The council-manager form is still quite popular. When it began in 1912, this form was seen as a way to solve the problem of city leaders being corrupt or ineffective. Today the council-manager plan is often used in newer suburbs.

The Council-Manager Form

Under the council-manager form, the city council appoints a city manager to administer the city's day-to-day affairs. The manager draws up a budget for the city. He or she also directs city departments. The manager handles all issues that affect city workers. The manager reports to the council. City council members can fire the manager if a majority of them choose to do so. Most city managers have special training in areas such as managing money and city planning.

In many smaller cities with managers, council members gain their seats through at-large elections. Some people believe this system makes it possible for council members to look out for the interests of the whole city and not just their neighborhood.

The Commission Form

The commission form was first used a few years before the council-manager form. Only a small number of cities still use it. A commission government does not divide legislative and executive powers. Instead, the government is split into several separate departments. Each of those departments handles a different set of tasks. Examples include police, fire, finance, and health.

The heads of these departments are called commissioners. Each is elected by the city's voters. In their roles as department heads, they have the executive power. That is, they run the daily activities of the department under them.

The commission form of municipal government developed after a devastating hurricane struck Galveston, Texas, in 1900. Thousands died and the city was nearly destroyed. City leaders decided that a commission system was the best way to handle the emergency.

▶ **CRITICAL THINKING**
Analyzing In what way or ways does the council-manager form of government improve upon the commission form?

PHOTO: Library of Congress

Reading HELPDESK

Reading Strategy: *Activating Prior Knowledge*

Before you read, scan the lesson and make a list of the headings and vocabulary terms. Next to each, write a brief note describing what you already know about the topic.

special district a unit of government that deals with a specific function, such as education, water supply, or transportation

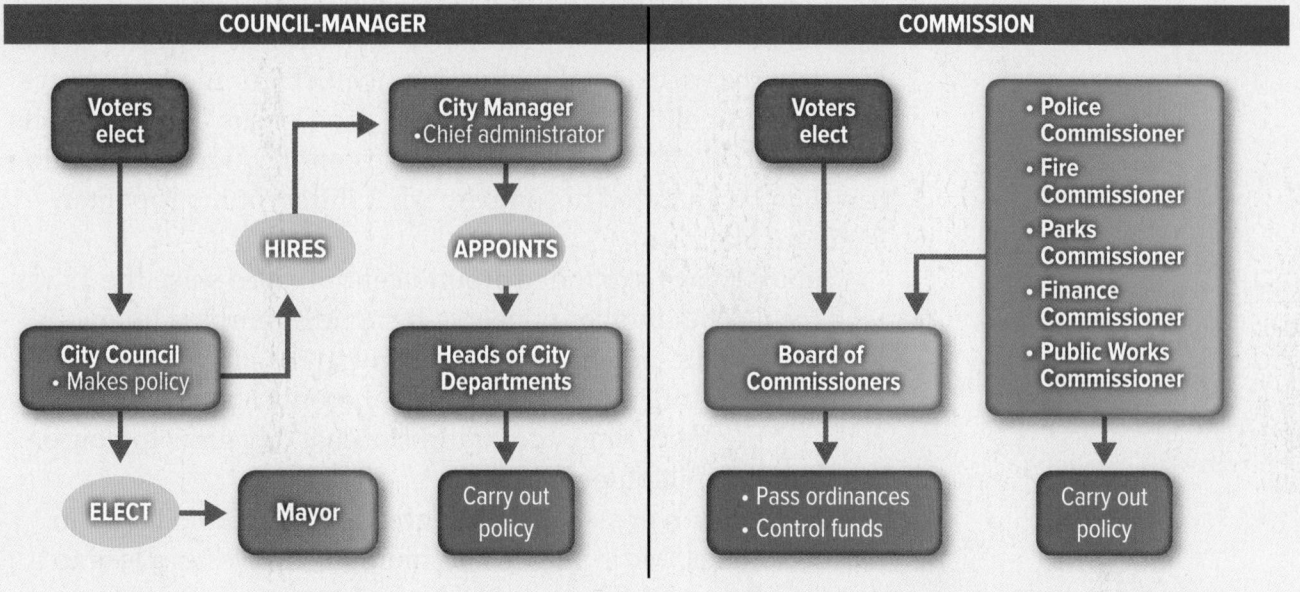

COUNCIL-MANAGER

Voters elect → City Manager • Chief administrator

HIRES

City Council • Makes policy

APPOINTS

Heads of City Departments

ELECT → Mayor

Carry out policy

COMMISSION

Voters elect → Board of Commissioners

• Police Commissioner
• Fire Commissioner
• Parks Commissioner
• Finance Commissioner
• Public Works Commissioner

• Pass ordinances
• Control funds

Carry out policy

Commissioners meet regularly as a body called a commission. They choose one commissioner as chairperson. The person in this position leads the commission meetings. He or she has no additional power, however. The commission acts as a legislature by passing ordinances and making policy decisions.

Many cities have discovered the limitations of the commission form of government. With no clear leadership, a commission is often unable to set and meet goals. Each commissioner is likely to focus on his or her own department and not the city as a whole. Commissioners may compete for a larger share of the city budget. Nearly all cities that once used a commission form of government have changed to a council-manager or mayor-council form of government. Even Galveston, Texas, which created the commission form, now has a council-manager system.

Other Units of Government

Two other important types of municipal government are the special district and the metropolitan area. The **special district** is a unit of government that is formed to handle a specific task. This task may be education, water supply, or transportation. A local school district is the most common example of a special district. A board or commission runs the district. Its members might be elected or appointed.

CHART SKILLS

The commission and council-manager forms of local government have been in use since the early 1900s.

▶ CRITICAL THINKING

1 *Analyzing Visuals* How does the way department heads are chosen in the council-manager form of government differ from the way they are chosen in the commission form?

2 *Comparing* How are the commissioners similar to department heads?

A **metropolitan area** is formed by a large city and its suburbs. **Suburbs** are the communities near or around cities. A metropolitan area may also include small towns that lie outside the suburbs but that are influenced by the larger city. The U.S. Census Bureau has a name for areas that include a central city and suburbs with a total population of 50,000 or more. They are called Metropolitan Statistical Areas. The Census Bureau collects data about all of these areas across the country. That information can then be analyzed to compare what different metropolitan areas are like.

Suburbs have expanded around central cities since the 1950s. As a result, the number of people living in suburbs is often greater than the number of those living in the city. For example, Detroit had 2 million people in 1950 and only about 910,000 in 2009. At the same time, the suburbs of that city grew to house more than 4 million people.

Metropolitan areas have been growing larger and larger in recent decades. More people and more businesses can lead to more challenges. More people mean more cars. This can cause traffic jams and other problems. Larger numbers of people can lead to more crime. Issues may arise over land use. Pollution can be a problem too. These challenges can become worse if different cities and towns try to address them separately. If different governments take different approaches, they may cause problems for one another. The communities in some metropolitan areas, therefore, have decided to face some of their challenges together. They have created councils that bring together city and suburban officials. These councils are able to make area-wide decisions concerning population growth and municipal services such as mass transit.

metropolitan area a large city and its suburbs

suburb a community that is near a larger city

✓ **PROGRESS CHECK**

Contrasting How does a council-manager government differ from a commission government?

LESSON 1 REVIEW

Review Vocabulary

1. How are the terms *incorporate*, *city charter*, and *home rule* related?

2. Write a sentence explaining how the terms *metropolitan area* and *suburb* are related.

Answer the Guiding Questions

3. *Specifying* What is a city charter, and what is its purpose?

4. *Contrasting* What is the difference between a strong-mayor system and a weak-mayor system?

5. *Analyzing* What advantage does a city manager have over a mayor in running city government?

6. **ARGUMENT** Suppose that your unincorporated community has decided to become a municipality. Write an entry for your blog page explaining which type of city government you favor forming and why.

Plessy v. Ferguson

After the Civil War, African Americans and some others around the nation asked a question that touched on basic rights. Why, they wondered, do African Americans not receive equal treatment under the law?

Segregated entryway to a restaurant, 1948

Background of the Case

In the late 1800s, many Southern states passed laws that required African Americans and whites to use separate services. The practice of separating people based on their race is called segregation.

In Louisiana, segregation laws required African American train passengers to ride in separate cars from white passengers. A group of African Americans believed this law went against the Constitution. They wanted to challenge it, hoping that the courts would agree with them and strike down the law. In 1892, they asked an African American named Homer Plessy to help them test the law.

Plessy was only one-eighth African American and could pass as a white person. The law, however, applied to all people of African American heritage.

Plessy boarded a train in New Orleans. He sat in a car reserved for whites. When Plessy refused to leave, he was arrested. Judge John Ferguson found Plessy guilty.

Plessy appealed to the Louisiana Supreme Court. That court said his conviction was valid. Plessy then appealed that decision to the United States Supreme Court.

The Decision

Plessy's lawyer argued that the Constitution guaranteed that all Americans would receive equal treatment under the law. He said that the Louisiana law went against the Constitution by treating Plessy differently.

In a 7-1 vote, the Court ruled that separate facilities for blacks and whites were not unconstitutional, as long as the facilities were of equal quality.

Justice Henry Brown wrote the Court's decision. He wrote, "A legal distinction [difference] between the white and colored races . . . has no tendency to destroy the legal equality of the two races." Justice John Marshall Harlan disagreed. His dissenting opinion said, "Our Constitution is color-blind. . . . In respect of civil rights, all citizens are equal before the law."

Why It Matters

The *Plessy* decision said that segregation laws were legal. As a result, these laws continued for many years. In 1954, the ruling in *Brown* v. *Board of Education* finally helped to end segregation in the United States.

Analyzing the Case

1. **Summarizing** What did people hope to gain by challenging the railway-car law?

2. **Explaining** Why did the Supreme Court rule against Plessy?

3. **Drawing Conclusions** What effect do you think the *Plessy* decision had on towns and cities across the nation?

PHOTO: Joseph Schwartz/CORBIS

netw⊕rks
There's More Online!

☑ **GRAPHIC ORGANIZER**
Elected County Officials

☑ **CHART**
Organization of County
Government

☑ **GAME**

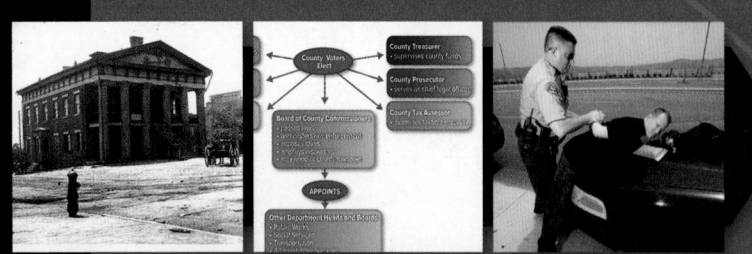

Lesson 2
County Governments

ESSENTIAL QUESTION *Why do people create, structure, and change governments?*

IT MATTERS BECAUSE
Like city governments, county governments affect people's everyday lives. However, county governments provide different services and meet different needs.

How County Governments Are Organized

GUIDING QUESTION *How is county government organized?*

Have you ever had to call 911 for help? Have you ever had to buy a license for a dog or to go fishing? In most states, these needs are handled by county government. The **county** is normally a state's largest territorial and political unit. The U.S. Census Bureau recognizes more than 3,000 counties or divisions like counties in the nation.

County Characteristics

The first county in what is now the United States was formed in Virginia in 1634. Massachusetts and Pennsylvania also had counties in colonial times. Today, all states except Connecticut and Rhode Island are comprised of counties. Texas has 254 counties. Delaware and Hawaii have only 3 each. Two states do not even use the word *county*. In Alaska, they are called boroughs. In Louisiana, they are known as parishes.

PHOTO: (tl) Wallace G. Levison/Time Life Pictures/Getty Images; (tr) Drive Images/Alamy

Reading **HELP**DESK

Taking Notes: *Identifying*
As you read, use a graphic organizer to identify the county officials elected by voters.

Sheriff
Elected County Officials

Content Vocabulary
• **county**
• **county seat**

county normally the largest territorial and political subdivision of a state

354 *Local Government*

Counties come in many sizes. Los Angeles County, California, has about 10 million residents. Only 45 people live in Loving County, Texas, though. San Bernardino County, California, has more land area than the states of Vermont and New Hampshire combined.

County Seats

During the 1800s, the county courthouse was the center of county government. Trials took place there. So did other government activities. The courthouse was also home to government records. The town where a county courthouse is located is called a **county seat.** County seats often became a center for the network of county roads.

As states in the Midwest and South mapped out counties, officials thought about the importance of county seats. They wanted to be sure that all people in the state would be able to have county services. They believed that people who lived in the farthest corners of a county should be able to travel to the county seat and back by horse and buggy in the same day. That is why states in those areas have so many fairly small counties.

☑ PROGRESS CHECK

Explaining How were county seats originally chosen?

The Functions of County Government

GUIDING QUESTION *What functions do county governments perform?*

County government has changed in recent years. In some areas, cities now provide many services that counties once did. On the other hand, many counties have taken on duties that city governments once handled. These duties range from providing sewer and water service to mass transit systems.

county seat a town where the county courthouse is located

21ˢᵗ *Century* SKILLS

Analyzing Historical Maps

Go online to find a political map of your state before it achieved statehood. Compare it to a political map of your state today. Have the state, county, or town boundaries changed? How?

In the more sparsely settled regions, counties were especially important units of government. This 1900 photograph of a county courthouse shows the typical horse-drawn transportation of the day.

▶ CRITICAL THINKING

Making Inferences What factors besides transportation might help determine the location of the county seat?

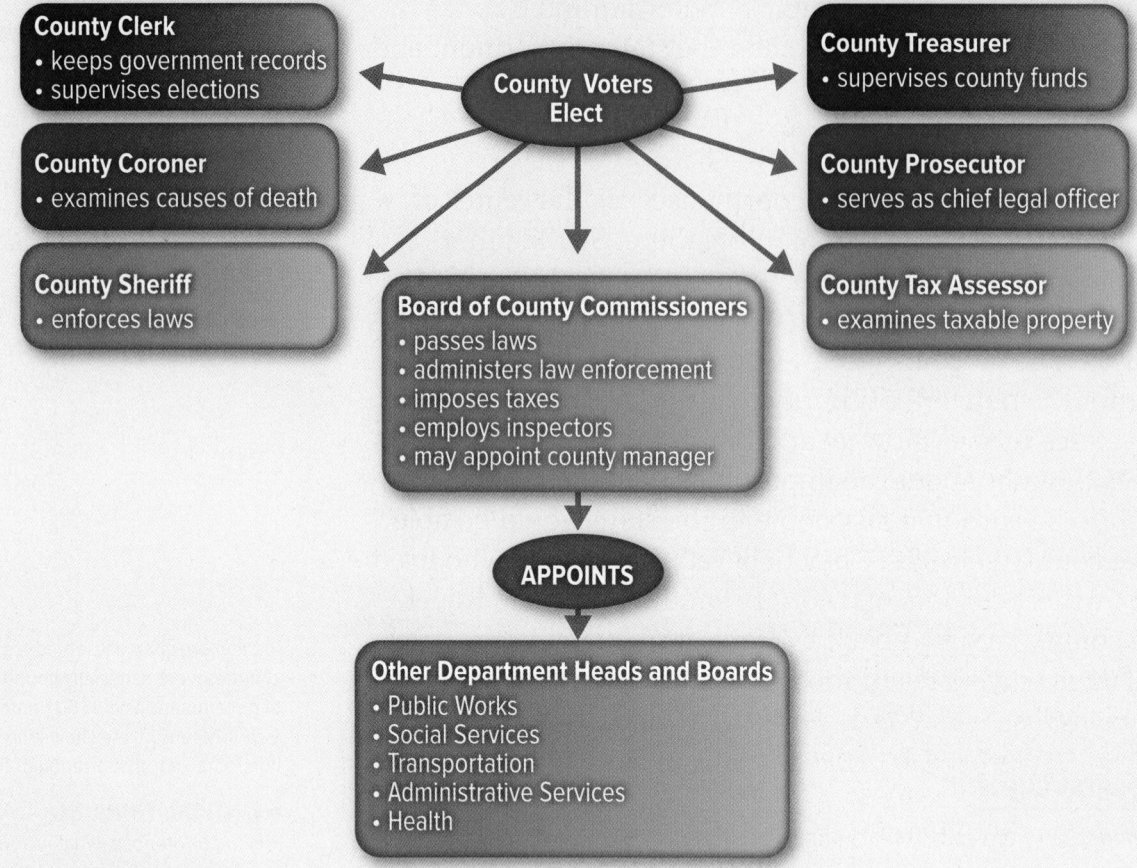

County Clerk
• keeps government records
• supervises elections

County Voters Elect

County Treasurer
• supervises county funds

County Coroner
• examines causes of death

County Prosecutor
• serves as chief legal officer

County Sheriff
• enforces laws

Board of County Commissioners
• passes laws
• administers law enforcement
• imposes taxes
• employs inspectors
• may appoint county manager

County Tax Assessor
• examines taxable property

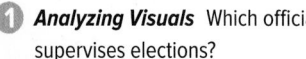

APPOINTS

Other Department Heads and Boards
• Public Works
• Social Services
• Transportation
• Administrative Services
• Health

CHART SKILLS

County governments have several officials who may be elected by voters or appointed by elected officials.

▶ CRITICAL THINKING

1 *Analyzing Visuals* Which official supervises elections?

2 *Making Inferences* What county officials would be involved in the investigation of a murder and the arrest and trial of someone accused of the crime?

Who Runs a County?

Most counties are run by a board of elected officials called commissioners or supervisors. Typically, three to five commissioners serve on a county board. They usually serve four-year terms. The board acts as the county's legislature. It passes ordinances, or laws, and sets the county's budget for the year. It also **levies** taxes and may enforce the laws. In addition to commissioners or supervisors, other officials play a role in county government.

Reading **HELP**DESK

Academic Vocabulary

levy to demand and collect a tax or other payment

Forms of County Government

County governments are organized in a few different ways. The basic form is the strong commission. The two other forms are the commission-manager and commission–elected executive types. These forms have come into more use in recent years.

In the strong commission form, the county board acts as both legislature and executive authority. Board members pass laws and also see to carrying out the laws. They work alongside other county officials to do some of this executive work. They also oversee the work of people they name to particular offices. The chart on the organization of county government shows examples of these departments.

The people who serve on county boards have a great variety of backgrounds. They come from many different jobs. They may not have experience in government. To help them, many states now run training programs for board members. Most board members work part-time. They have to be ready to respond to emergencies, though. Many meetings are at night, so county residents who work in other jobs can attend.

As public needs have grown, many counties have changed the role of the county board. In these counties, the board operates only as a legislature. Counties use one of two methods to handle the executive power. First is the commission-manager form of government. In this method, the board names someone as county manager. This official acts much like a city manager. Second is the commission–elected executive type. In this approach, counties create a new office called the county executive. This official, like the members of the board, is elected.

Whether appointed or elected, the county manager or executive carries out the laws for the county. He or she manages county government. He or she also appoints top officials. The county board works alongside this leader.

Sheriffs, DAs, and More

Sheriffs are elected officials. They typically serve two to four years. The sheriff is the county's chief officer for enforcing the law. The sheriff's department enforces court orders and runs the county jail. In some counties, the sheriff's department shares duties with one or more police departments. Because counties were often the first governments formed by American settlers, sheriffs have played a leading role in local law enforcement.

Sheriffs maintain the county courthouse and jail, deliver summonses, transport prisoners, and enforce criminal law. Their jurisdictions often overlap those of local law enforcement.

▶ CRITICAL THINKING
Making Connections Why do you think both sheriffs and local police are needed?

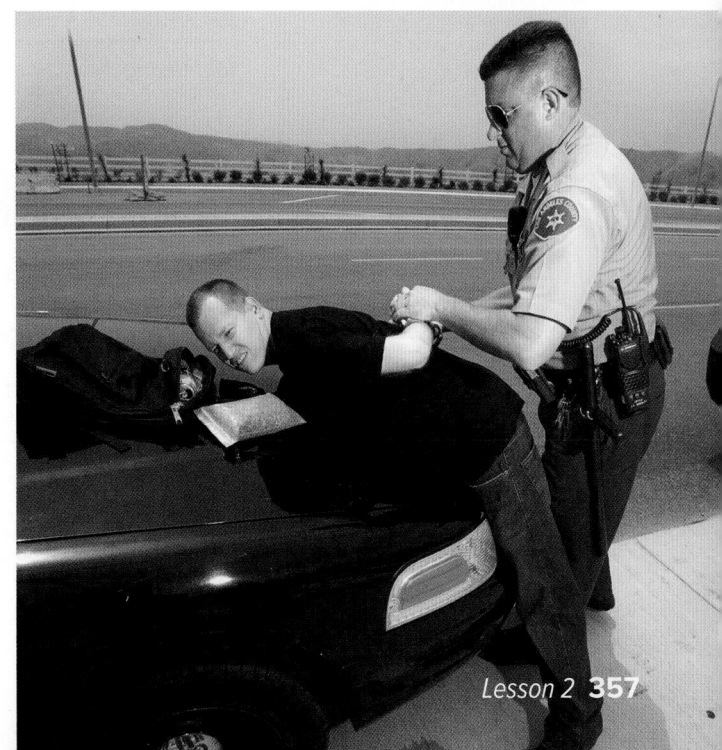

Other county duties are handled by officials who may be appointed or elected. Bringing criminals to justice is the role of the district attorney (DA), called the county prosecutor in some counties. In most counties, the district attorney is elected by voters. The district attorney investigates crimes and brings charges against those suspected of breaking the law. He or she then works to prove in court that the accused persons are guilty.

Three county officials handle the county's finances. The assessor looks at all taxable property within the county. He or she **estimates,** or sets a rough value on, how much it is worth. The tax placed on each property is based on the assessor's estimate. The county treasurer is in charge of the county's funds. He or she collects taxes and pays the county's bills. An auditor makes sure that the county spends its money according to state and local law.

A county clerk keeps official government records. Some county clerks' offices maintain public records such as birth, marriage, and death certificates. They also conduct elections.

The county coroner works closely with the police. This official is called on to look into any death that might not be natural. A coroner does not necessarily have any special medical training. In some counties, the duties of the coroner fall to the sheriff's office or the justice of the peace, a low court official. Other counties have replaced the coroner with the medical examiner system. This system uses trained scientists to investigate deaths caused by injury, violence, or unknown causes.

More than 2 million people work for counties across the country. The number of county workers has grown in recent years. That growth reflects the increase in tasks that county governments have taken on.

✓ PROGRESS CHECK

Identifying What body governs most counties in the United States?

LESSON 2 REVIEW

Review Vocabulary

1. Explain what a *county* is.

2. What is a *county seat*? Explain the relationship between a *county* and a *county seat*.

Answer the Guiding Questions

3. *Comparing* How do counties vary across the country?

4. *Explaining* List three of the elected officials in a county. What services does each provide for the county?

5. **INFORMATIVE/EXPLANATORY** Write a brief description of how counties originated in the United States and how they have changed over time.

networks

There's More Online!

☑ **GRAPHIC ORGANIZER**
Forms of Government

☑ **CHART**
Dividing the Land into Townships

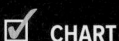

Lesson 3

Towns, Townships, and Villages

ESSENTIAL QUESTION *Why do people create, structure, and change governments?*

IT MATTERS BECAUSE

American democracy began in towns. The town meetings held in the New England colonies allowed community members to take part in their government. Town meetings are still held today.

Towns and Town Meetings

GUIDING QUESTION *How and why did town governments and meetings develop?*

Think about a meeting that you attended recently. Was it well organized? Was something accomplished? Read on to find out how meetings like those you may attend are an important part of local government in some parts of the country. In fact, they are the foundation of local government in some areas.

In 1654 a group of men in Sudbury, Massachusetts, gathered to discuss how to divide the land. The town has changed in many ways since that day. But one thing has not changed. The people of Sudbury still meet to discuss issues.

Towns, Townships, and Counties

Most states are divided into counties. Counties, too, are often divided into smaller political units. In the New England states, political units that are smaller than cities and larger than villages are called **towns.** In many other states, especially in the Midwest, counties are divided into areas called **townships.** Townships can have several smaller communities within them.

PHOTO: (tl) Toby Talbot/AP Images; (tc) The Granger Collection - NYC; (tr) Nathan Benn/Alamy

---

Reading **HELP**DESK

Taking Notes: *Identifying*

As you read, name the different forms of government below the county level by completing a graphic organizer.

Forms of Government

Content Vocabulary

- **town**
- **township**
- **town meeting**
- **village**

town political unit that is larger than a village and smaller than a city

Voters in Woodbury, Vermont, turn in their ballots in a town meeting. The citizens of Woodbury have a long history of participation in local government. Since 1806 the people of Woodbury have used town meetings to help shape their community.

▶ CRITICAL THINKING
Identifying Central Issues Why are town meetings unable to handle the day-to-day affairs of a town?

The United States Census Bureau identifies 20 states that have towns or townships. Like county and city governments, town and township governments receive their powers from the state.

The governments of towns and townships relate to county government in different ways across the nation. The differences tend to appear in different regions. In New England, town governments handle most of the government duties of most small communities. In this part of the country, counties are mainly judicial districts. That is, they are set up mainly as areas to organize the local court system.

In the mid-Atlantic states and in the Midwest, township government is important. In these states, county and township governments share powers. States in the South and the West often have no townships. In these regions, county governments tend to be more important.

New England Town Meetings

New England town government is one of the oldest forms of democracy in the United States. **Town meetings** allow community members to voice their feelings on matters ranging from local issues to world events.

In early town meetings, citizens—rather than elected representatives—made the important decisions. Town meetings, therefore, are a form of direct democracy. They are called direct democracy because the people are directly involved in governing themselves. This differs from the representative democracy common throughout most of the United States. In a representative democracy, of course, voters elect people to public office. Those officials are the ones who pass the laws and see that they are carried out.

Town meetings are still important in some New England towns. Town meetings are held once a year. Residents come to the meeting to discuss local ordinances, taxes, and budgets. The majority of registered voters at the meeting decide these issues.

PHOTO: Toby Talbot/AP Images

Reading HELPDESK

township a subdivision of a county that has its own government

town meeting a gathering of local citizens to discuss and vote on important issues

Academic Vocabulary

complex having many parts connected together

similar almost the same

They determine how the town government will act over the course of the next year—until the next town meeting.

There are limits to the effectiveness of town meetings, though. Because they occur only once a year, they are useful only for making broad decisions. They are not a good way to deal with the everyday details of government. So each New England town elects a group of officials called selectmen to run local government. *Selectman*, a very old title, now applies to women as well as to men. Towns may also elect executives such as a clerk and a treasurer.

As New England towns grew larger over the years, their governments became more **complex.** As a result, direct democracy did not work as well as it had in the past. In response, some New England towns replaced the traditional town meetings with representative town meetings. In these meetings, only town meeting representatives may vote. Town meeting representatives are elected by the town's voters in annual town elections. Other towns have ended the meetings altogether. Instead, they have a town council that runs the local government.

✓ **PROGRESS CHECK**

Defining What are town meetings?

Townships and Villages

GUIDING QUESTION *How are township and village governments organized?*

Towns and township governments in New York, New Jersey, and Pennsylvania are **similar** to New England town governments. These local governments typically serve densely populated urban areas. Townships in states such as Indiana, Kansas, Nebraska, and Ohio are more rural in nature.

21st Century
SKILLS

Conduct Research

Conduct research to find out more about town meetings that are held today. Choose a place governed by a town meeting and write a short report that tells where and when the meeting takes place, who participates, and what kinds of specific issues are discussed.

Thomas Jefferson proposed a system for surveying, or measuring, the land west of the thirteen colonies. Surveying began shortly after the American Revolution.

▶ **CRITICAL THINKING**

Making Predictions What role do you think surveying played in the development of local government?

Small towns and villages can still be found throughout the country. This Vermont town has held its meetings in the same meetinghouse every year since 1801.

▶ CRITICAL THINKING
Making Connections What type of government do you think this New England town has?

Townships

As the United States expanded westward, it gained new land. Congress conducted surveys of the land. A survey is a study and measurement of an area of land. For purposes of description, surveyors divided the land into equal square blocks. Each block was usually six miles wide and six miles long. These blocks are known as congressional, or survey, townships. These measurements helped the government distribute land to settlers.

Settlers moved into these new areas. They set up local governments, also called townships. Sometimes people use the term *civil township* to distinguish them from congressional townships. A typical township is 36 square miles. Many of these townships follow the original congressional survey lines. Unlike congressional townships, civil townships are units of government.

Most townships elect a small body of officials. This body is known as a township committee, board of supervisors, or board of trustees. This group has lawmaking powers. It usually holds regular meetings that citizens may attend. In this way, the people of the township have a voice in their government.

Townships have become less important as cities and counties have taken over many township duties. Counties and townships may work together to provide local services.

Village Government

The **village** is the smallest unit of local government. Villages almost always lie within the borders of townships or counties. Communities with small populations often have no need for their own government. County or township governments handle most of their needs.

In some communities, people may grow unhappy with the services the county provides. For example, people might want to set up their own school system, or the community might

PHOTO: Nathan Benn/Alamy

village smallest unit of local government

want to organize as a village. A community cannot simply decide to form a village government, however. You may recall that a community has to ask the state for the right to incorporate as a city. In the same way, a small community needs the state's permission to set up a village government. When the state legislature passes a law, the community can form a village government.

The government of most villages is made up of a small board of trustees. This board is elected by the voters. The village board has the power to collect taxes. It may spend this money on projects that benefit the community, such as taking care of streets, sewer and water systems, or libraries.

Some villages also elect an executive. The title of this official may be chief burgess, president of the board, or mayor. Like many cities, a large village might hire a city manager who has training in particular skills.

Becoming a village has many benefits. The people of the village usually receive better services than they had before. A community also has an improved standing when it becomes a village. This step can make the community more attractive to visitors and to possible new residents and businesses. It also gives the people of the village more control over local affairs than they had before they formed a village government.

Becoming a village does have a major drawback, however. The residents of the village might have to pay higher taxes to support this extra layer of government. The people in many village communities believe that this cost is worth it for the other benefits they enjoy.

☑ PROGRESS CHECK

Explaining What is an advantage of setting up a village government?

Why It
MATTERS

Addressing Local Concerns

Sometimes communities establish villages to address local concerns. In a similar way, students can form committees to serve certain functions. For example, students can form committees to organize dances or other events. Find out the rules for forming and serving on a committee in your school.

LESSON 3 REVIEW

Review Vocabulary

1. What is a *town meeting,* and in what part of the nation are they typically held?

2. What is a *village*? What is its relationship to a *township*?

Answer the Guiding Questions

3. *Describing* How did town government develop in the United States?

4. *Summarizing* How are townships governed?

5. **ARGUMENT** Suppose you are living in a small community that has no government. Some residents want to convert the community into a village. Write a letter to the editor of the local newspaper to convince the newspaper's readers to support or oppose this plan.

Write your answers on a separate sheet of paper.

1 Writing Activity

EXPLORING THE ESSENTIAL QUESTION
Why do people create, structure, and change governments?

In this chapter, you learned about various forms of government for counties, cities, towns, and villages. Imagine that your school will incorporate as a county, city, town, or village. Which of these forms of government would you choose for it? Write an essay that states your choice and explains why you chose that form and why you rejected the others.

2 21st Century Skills

MEDIA LITERACY Follow events in your community and the activities of your local government for one week. Use the coverage on local television or in local newspapers and information on the Internet as resources. At the end of the week, answer these questions: What is my local government doing well? In what areas could local officials be doing better? Provide at least three examples to defend your argument. Express your analysis in a blog.

3 Being an Active Citizen

Conduct research to find out about the organization and operation of your local government. With a group of classmates, create a chart to show how your local government is organized. The chart should include each elected and appointed office or department in your local government and show how it is connected to the others. Along with the chart, include an information sheet that states the purpose of each office or department, the services it provides, and the name of the official in charge of it.

4 Understanding Visuals

Cities and towns often hold meetings where residents can speak before the mayor or city council. Study this photo of one such meeting. Then write a paragraph explaining what is going on in this scene. Explain whether this illustrates direct democracy or representative democracy.

PHOTO: AP Photo/James A. Finley

REVIEW THE GUIDING QUESTIONS

Directions: Choose the best answer for each question.

1 In which form of city government does the city council appoint the department heads?

   A. commission form

   B. strong-mayor system

   C. weak-mayor system

   D. council-manager form

2 Which document establishes the power and duties of most local governments?

   F. home rule law

   G. city charter

   H. state constitution

   I. the U.S. Constitution

3 Which county official enforces court orders?

   A. assessor

   B. coroner

   C. district attorney

   D. sheriff

4 What is the largest political unit in most states?

   F. a metropolitan area

   G. a county

   H. a township

   I. a special district

5 Which type of government handles the needs of most small communities in New England?

   A. state

   B. county

   C. township

   D. town

6 What is the smallest unit of local government?

   F. township

   G. special district

   H. village

   I. board or commission

DBQ **ANALYZING DOCUMENTS**

Directions: Analyze the table and answer the questions that follow.

7 **Identifying** Which of the counties shown on this table has the most employees?

A. Los Angeles

B. Dade

C. Cook

D. Harris

8 **Calculating** How many more employees does Los Angeles County have compared to the county with the next-highest number of workers?

F. more than two times

G. more than three times

H. more than five times

I. more than ten times

EMPLOYEES IN COUNTY GOVERNMENT, 2007	
Los Angeles, California	105,700
Dade, Florida	47,800
Fairfax, Virginia	43,900
Du Page, Illinois	42,200
Ventura, California	34,100
Hamilton, Ohio	29,700
Middlesex, New Jersey	29,000
Cook, Illinois	25,700
Macomb, Michigan	23,800
Harris, Texas	23,700
San Diego, California	23,700

Source: U.S. Bureau of the Census, *Statistical Abstract of the United States*, 2010

SHORT RESPONSE

The following passage is from the 2010 State of the City address by the mayor of Palm Bay, Florida.

"The City is embarking on two major brick and mortar projects—the construction of a new Fire Station . . . and a new City Hall Annex that will serve to house our operations that are currently in rented space. . . . Bringing these services to City Hall will allow us the ability to provide more comprehensive services to our citizens at a lower cost."

—Mayor John J. Mazziotti, January 21, 2010

9 According to this passage, what benefits and service improvements does this city plan to provide to the people who live there?

10 From the information in this document, identify the form of local government that exists in Palm Bay. What clues in the passage led you to reach this conclusion?

EXTENDED RESPONSE

11 **Argument** Some writers say that local government is the most important because it is closest to the people. Do you agree or disagree with that idea? Why or why not?

Need Extra Help?

If You've Missed Question	1	2	3	4	5	6	7	8	9	10	11
Review Lesson	1	1	2	2	3	3	2	2	1	1	1, 3

Dealing With Community Issues

ESSENTIAL QUESTION
How do citizens, both individually and collectively, influence government policy?

◄ *Workers attempt to capture oil washed onto the beach in Port Fourchon, Louisiana, after the Gulf of Mexico oil spill in 2010.*
PHOTO: Joe Raedle/Getty Images

netw⊙rks
There's More Online about dealing with community issues.

CHAPTER 13

The Story Matters...

On April 20, 2010, an offshore oil drilling rig exploded in the Gulf of Mexico. Eleven oil workers died and many were injured in the explosion. Two days later, the rig sank. Oil gushed out of the underwater well, fouling the waters of the Gulf.

Government, community leaders, and volunteers rushed to respond. The leaking oil threatened seabirds and other marine wildlife. The disaster also hurt the nearby fishing communities that made their living from the waters of the Gulf. People tried to contain the spill and keep the oil from spreading farther. Others worked to clean beaches or tend to sickened wildlife. By the time the well was capped, millions of gallons of oil had polluted the coastal waters. The disaster had a terrible impact on the area.

Real-Life Civics

COMMUNITY PLANNING Every day we take advantage of community services. Whenever we use water, head to schools and libraries, stroll on sidewalks and through parks, or drive on roads, we enjoy what communities have to offer. It takes resources—like good people and money to run a city or town. It also requires smart planning.

Problems big and small must be addressed. How will fire and emergency services be handled? What should be done about garbage removal? Where will the community's water supply come from and will there be enough of it? How will wastewater be treated? Members of the community along with government officials play a role in answering these questions.

Water treatment facilities remove harmful wastes and chemicals from the water, making it safe for residents to use.

People opposed to a suggested nuclear waste dump took their concerns to the California state capital in Sacramento.

VOICING CONCERNS Clean drinking water, good schools, and a safe environment are goals we can all agree on. However, not everyone sees eye to eye on how communities should reach these goals. Sometimes, community goals appear to conflict. Building a nuclear power plant might provide the reasonably priced energy that a community needs, but it also creates harmful waste that must be disposed of. It is the job of community members and leaders to solve such difficult problems. In Ward Valley, California, residents protested for 113 days before convincing officials to relocate a nuclear waste site away from their community.

CIVIC LITERACY

★ ★ ★ ★

Analyzing Think about an event or a project you have planned. Use what you know about successful planning to describe the value of effective community planning.

Your Opinion What changes would you like to make to your community?

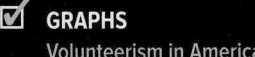
netw⊙rks

There's More Online!

☑ **GRAPHIC ORGANIZER**
Planning Commission

☑ **GRAPHS**
Volunteerism in America

☑ **VIDEO**

Lesson 1

How a Community Handles Issues

ESSENTIAL QUESTION *How do citizens, both individually and collectively, influence government policy?*

IT MATTERS BECAUSE
People who live together in communities cooperate to solve problems and make plans.

Shaping Public Policy

GUIDING QUESTION *How does public policy work to serve the needs of the community?*

Do you think going to school should make you sick? A group of families in Sugar Hill, Georgia, did not think so. These families found out that a new school would be built between two garbage landfills. They formed a group called Community Awareness Regarding Education and Safety (CARES) to try to get the decision changed. They began to study risks to the health of schoolchildren that might result from building the school in that location.

CARES set up committees to do research and to contact the media. The school did open. However, CARES **convinced,** or persuaded, the school board to test for poisonous materials in the building. Mindy Clark, a CARES founder, explained, "We're going to fight. We know too much to walk away."

Mindy Clark and CARES worked to change a **policy.** A policy is a course of action that a group takes to address an issue. All organizations have policies. Most businesses, for example, have policies about the rules to follow when hiring, promoting, or firing employees.

PHOTO: (tl) Courtesy of Austen Pearce; (tc) Doug Menuez/Getty Images; (tr) Lance Iversen/San Francisco Chronicle/Corbis

Taking Notes: *Analyzing*

As you read, complete a graphic organizer like the one shown by identifying the people who might serve on a community planning commission.

Planning Commission

Content Vocabulary

- policy
- public policy
- planning commission

- short-term plan
- long-term plan
- infrastructure

Public policy is about the government response to solving problems or resolving issues in the community. Public policy may deal with a specific issue. For example, the decision to build or not build a particular road is a public policy decision. Public policy also deals with much broader issues, such as health care and the environment. A public policy is not necessarily a law. It may not even be written down.

Public Policy Origins

Where do ideas for public policy begin? They may come from the government. Political parties, interest groups, or the media may suggest them. Another source of policy ideas, especially at the local level, is private citizens. As Mindy Clark and CARES show, often one person or group can have a great effect on government policies.

☑ PROGRESS CHECK

Defining What is public policy?

teen citizens   in action

Growing a Community

Austen Pearce
Maricopa, Arizona

Austen Pearce has been volunteering at the local food bank for a while. He noticed that whenever local farmers came in to donate fresh fruit and vegetables, the families waiting for food always seemed a little happier. Austen started looking for a way to provide more fresh produce for needy families. He remembered reading a book about community flower gardens. "I thought," he says, "instead of a flower garden, why not a vegetable garden? "

Austen wrote to the mayor describing his idea. The mayor agreed. A local farmer donated an acre of land, and a master gardener agreed to teach Austen gardening. Together they planned the garden and began the planting.

Many Maricopa residents helped. The owner of a local hardware store donated some plants. Volunteers planted cantaloupes, watermelons, tomatoes, squash, okra, and peppers. Members of local church groups helped weed and water the plants.

For the past two years, the garden has produced over 7,000 pounds of fresh produce each year. This food helps to feed around 200 families. The garden has also had one unexpected benefit. "It has," says Austen, "increased community involvement by giving others in the community a chance to give back."

Citizenship and Teens

Who benefited from Austen's garden? Why do you think so?

PHOTO: (tr, bl) Courtesy of Austen Pearce

_____
• **resource**
• **master plan**

Academic Vocabulary

convince to persuade or win over

policy a guiding course of action

public policy the government response to solving problems or resolving issues in the community

Planning for the Future

GUIDING QUESTION *How do community leaders make public policy decisions?*

Have you ever had to decide between two things you wanted to do or buy? What kinds of things did you think about before you made your decision? In the same way, communities have to make decisions about what actions to take. The decisions that community leaders make can affect many people. As a result, they have to make these decisions very carefully.

Many people whose job it is to make public policy look at what may happen in the future. Then they plan for the future outcomes that they think are most likely to happen. Many local governments use planning commissions to do this work. A **planning commission** is a group that gives advice about future needs. Its goal is to prepare for and guide the growth of the community in the future.

A planning commission may include many different people. Examples are government leaders, business leaders, and people who live in the community. It may also include **professionals,** or workers with much education and high-level skills. For instance, architects and traffic experts would have knowledge that could help a planning commission plan for the future.

Businesses that wish to build new office or shopping complexes may need to get the approval of a community's planning commission before they can proceed.

▶ **CRITICAL THINKING**
Explaining Why would that approval be necessary?

Short-Term and Long-Term Plans

Local governments and their planning commissions make both short-term and long-term plans. A **short-term plan** is a policy meant to be carried out over the next few years. For example, giving a company a permit to build apartments is a short-term plan. A **long-term plan** is a broader policy meant to serve as a guide over the next 10, 20, or even 50 years. To make long-term plans, a planning commission makes educated guesses about a community's future needs.

PHOTO: Doug Menuez/Getty Images

Reading**HELP**DESK

planning commission an advisory group to a community

Academic Vocabulary

professional worker with much education and high-level skills

short-term plan a government policy being carried out over the next few years

long-term plan a government plan for policy that can span 10 to 50 years

PHOTO: Lance Iversen/San Francisco Chronicle/Corbis

For example, suppose that the population of a community is growing. This growth is expected to continue into the future. Having more and more people living in the area raises questions for local government. What demands will this larger number of people put on the town's **infrastructure**—its system of roads, bridges, water, and sewers?

Think about road systems. If more people live in the community, there will probably be more traffic. After all, those people will need to go from their homes to work and to stores to buy food and other goods. Will that new level of traffic be too much for the town's current system of roads? Should the town build new highways? Or should it rely on mass transit to carry people around? This kind of transportation uses buses, trains, and other vehicles to move large numbers of people around a town. Whatever choice town leaders make, where will they find the money to pay for that solution?

Priorities and Resources

The answers to these questions about planning usually depend on two things—priorities and resources. Priorities are the goals a community thinks are most important or most urgent. In setting priorities, a community must decide what it values most. For example, is it more important to have a thriving business center or a peaceful place to live?

Improved roadways are just one example of infrastructure improvements that communities need when they grow.

▶ CRITICAL THINKING
Making Inferences What other infrastructure improvements would a growing community need?

infrastructure a community's system of roads, bridges, water, and sewers

Think about several goals that you think your community should have. List at least five goals. Then prioritize the goals by writing a number from one through five next to each. Use the number one for the highest priority goal and five for the lowest. Write a paragraph explaining why you ranked the goals as you did.

A community must set its goals and rank them in order of importance. Suppose a local government gets a large portion of its revenues from income and sales taxes. It may decide that its top goal is to attract new businesses. New businesses provide people with jobs and spending money. When people have more money, they shop more. With more revenue, town leaders can pursue other goals. They might also want to improve services or preserve open spaces, such as parks and playgrounds. They might want to make the town's schools better. Town leaders need to compare the importance of all these goals to one another and rank them from most to least important.

After a community sets its priorities, it must determine what resources it has and how to use them. **Resources** are the money, people, and materials at hand to reach the community's goals. Suppose, for example, that the town decides it wants to improve mass transit. Is there enough money to buy new buses? How much will it need to spend every year to pay for bus drivers and to keep the buses running? The town will have to find ways to increase its resources to cover those higher costs.

Creating a Master Plan

After determining priorities and resources, a planning commission makes specific decisions about the community's future. It usually spells these out in a **master plan.** This plan states a set of goals. It also explains how the government will carry out these goals to meet changing needs over time. If the local government accepts the plan, it becomes public policy. The government then is responsible for carrying the policy out.

resource the money, people, and materials available to accomplish a community's goals

master plan a plan that states a set of goals and explains how the government will carry them out to meet changing needs over time

✔ PROGRESS CHECK

Analyzing What factors should a community consider when setting priorities? Why?

LESSON 1 REVIEW

Review Vocabulary

1. What is *infrastructure*?

2. What is the difference between a *short-term plan* and a *long-term plan*?

Answer the Guiding Questions

3. *Identifying* What are two examples of public policies that deal with specific issues?

4. *Explaining* How can government leaders, business leaders, citizens, and professionals each contribute to the work of a planning commission?

5. *Making Inferences* What can communities do to increase the resources that may be needed to carry out a plan?

6. **INFORMATIVE/EXPLANATORY** Imagine you are a community leader creating a master plan for a city park. You want to plan for new attractions, like ball fields and playgrounds. You also want to ensure that the park retains its natural beauty. How do you balance the two goals? Describe your plan in one or two paragraphs.

networks

There's More Online!

☑ **GRAPHIC ORGANIZER**
Education Issues

☑ **GRAPHS**
Sources of School
Funding
Violent and Property Crime Rates,
2004–2013
Amounts of School Funding

☑ **POLITICAL CARTOON**
Education Funding

☑ **VIDEO**

Lesson 2
Education and Social Issues

ESSENTIAL QUESTION *How do citizens, both individually and collectively, influence government policy?*

IT MATTERS BECAUSE

Education, crime, and social problems have a big effect on the lives of everyone in a community.

Why It
MATTERS

Education Pays

The more education a person has, the more income he or she is likely to earn. In 2008, a head of household with a high school diploma had a median income of $39,962. That same year, a head of household with a bachelor's degree from a college or university had a median income of $78,290. How does that compare to the earnings of the high school graduate?

Public Education

GUIDING QUESTION *How do public schools handle financial and social challenges?*

The U.S. Constitution sets forth the powers and duties of the federal government. It does not mention education. As a result, public education has always been under the general control of the states. In colonial times, some local governments took the lead. They began offering free public education to children. The practice spread until it reached almost all of the United States after the Civil War.

As public education grew, local school districts raised most of the money for schools. They also decided how students would be taught. In 1816, Indiana set up the first modern public school system. Today in most states, local communities still run elementary and secondary schools. In doing so, they follow rules set by state governments.

Today about 50 million students attend the nation's public elementary and secondary schools. Nearly 6 million other students go to private schools. About 1.5 million are home schooled. Home schooled students do not attend school. Instead, the student's parents or guardians teach him or her in the home.

PHOTO: (tl) CORBIS; (tc) Kevin Winter/Getty Images; (tr) 2010 John Cole, and Politicalcartoons.com

Reading**HELP**DESK

Taking Notes: *Summarizing*

As you read, complete a graphic organizer like the one shown by listing four challenges that schools face.

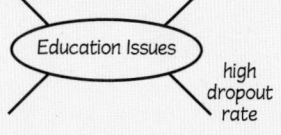

Education Issues

high dropout rate

Content Vocabulary

- charter schools
- tuition voucher
- community policing

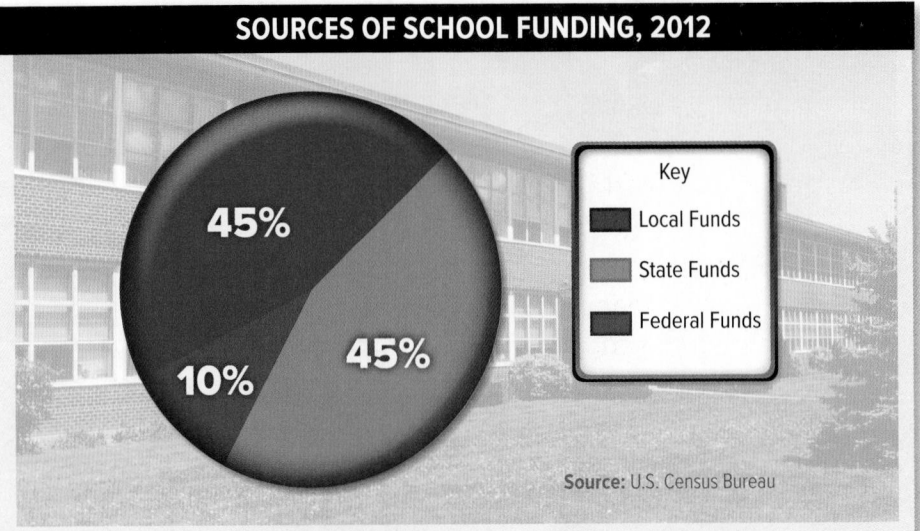

SOURCES OF SCHOOL FUNDING, 2012

All three levels of government provide money for public schools.

► CRITICAL THINKING

1 *Identifying* What share of school funds comes from the federal government?

2 *Predicting* What would happen to school systems if state funding were to be cut? Why?

45%

45%

10%

Key
■ Local Funds
■ State Funds
■ Federal Funds

Source: U.S. Census Bureau

The Federal Government's Role

Though local districts run public schools, the federal government plays an important role in education. It provides about 8 percent of school funding. In return, it requires local schools to follow certain rules. One such rule tells schools how to meet the needs of students with disabilities.

In recent years, the federal government's role in public education has grown. In 2001 President George W. Bush signed the No Child Left Behind Act. To get a share of the $26.5 billion the law provided, states had to test all students in grades three through eight in reading, science, and math. Bush hoped this law would set higher performance standards for schools that were not doing well. In 2009, President Barack Obama signed a law creating a $4.35 billion Race to the Top Fund. To win a share of the money, states had to make progress in meeting four goals: adopting standards for student success, using technology to track students' work, rewarding creative teachers, and turning around struggling schools.

The federal government's increasing role in education has caused strong disagreement. Some critics claim that the federal government is going beyond its constitutional limits.

Challenges: Financial and Social

The biggest education issue facing the states is to make sure that all students equally receive high-quality schooling. Today, school districts in wealthy areas receive much more money

PHOTO: imageshop/PunchStock

Reading HELP DESK

Reading Strategy: *Distinguishing Fact from Opinion*

Read the material on competency tests. Identify statements of fact and statements that reflect opinions.

than those in poorer areas. This difference occurs because many districts depend on property taxes for a large share of the money used for schools. The value of property differs greatly from one place to another, however. As a result, a town with higher property values gets more tax revenue than a town where property is worth less. Many states supply money to schools in poorer areas to try to narrow the gap in funding.

To try to raise money, some schools have tried new approaches such as teaming with companies for help. For example, soft drink vending machines have been placed in some schools. The schools receive a share of the proceeds. Critics say that this solution is not a good one. They say it promotes products high in sugar, which are not healthful for children.

Schools face many social problems too. These include low test scores, high dropout rates, and crime and violence on school property. Solving these problems requires a wide range of actions. Many of these solutions must take place outside the schools because the problems are rooted in broader social issues. These issues include poverty, broken families, drug and alcohol use, and crime.

Testing

Many people claim that student performance can be improved by using competency tests. These tests measure students' abilities in different subjects. The federal government requires tests in reading, math, and science. Some states also require students to take competency tests. Students must pass these tests in order to be promoted to the next grade or to receive a high school diploma at the end of the 12th grade.

Competency tests have three main purposes:

- They provide measures of students' learning that can be used to compare performance over time.
- They indicate each student's strengths and weaknesses.
- They show how well teachers, schools, and even entire districts are educating children.

Supporters of competency testing say that these tests make schools and teachers responsible for what takes place in the classroom. However, many teachers' organizations oppose such testing. They argue that it forces teachers to spend valuable classroom time teaching students how to pass tests. As a result, critics say, teachers are less able to help students fully understand the subject matter.

One goal of the Race to the Top Fund was to encourage states to develop ways of assessing students' knowledge that went beyond what was tested in traditional multiple-choice tests.

▶ CRITICAL THINKING
Analyzing What kinds of skills might not be easy to test with multiple-choice tests?

PHOTO: CORBIS

Alternatives to Public Schools

States are trying different solutions to improve schools. One method is to test new ways of organizing schools. About 40 states now allow **charter schools** to be set up. These schools receive state funding. However, they do not have to meet many of the state **regulations,** or rules, for public schools.

Opponents say that charter schools are likely to enroll many of the better students. They say this is not good because it means that "problem" students are left behind in the public schools. Supporters say there is no evidence that charter schools have this effect. They also say that charter schools are good because they offer **alternatives,** or other choices, for schooling.

Another educational choice is for cities and states to give parents **tuition vouchers.** These are like coupons issued by the government to parents or guardians to pay for their children to attend private schools. Several states have tried using vouchers in recent years.

Teachers' unions oppose vouchers. They believe that vouchers draw education funds out of the public school system and put them into private schools. Other opponents say that vouchers violate the First Amendment because they can be used to pay for instruction at religious schools. The Supreme Court has ruled that it is constitutional to use vouchers for

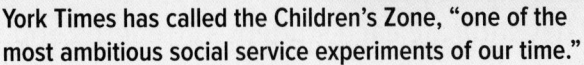

American Leader

• Geoffrey Canada, Educational Activist

New York City's Harlem neighborhood is a vibrant community troubled by poverty, crime, and poor schools. Geoffrey Canada, a graduate of Bowdoin College and the Harvard School of Education, is work-ing to change that. His plan is the Children's Zone, a 100-block area that aims to give children an enriching environment. It includes parent education that begins when babies are born and free social, educational, and medical services for children living in the area.

Located within the Children's Zone is Canada's charter school, the Promise Academy, which boasts a ratio of one adult for every six students, a modern science lab, and a cafeteria that serves healthy food in order to fight obesity. Canada, who grew up in poverty, promises parents: "If your child comes to this school, we will guarantee that we will get your child into college."

About one-third of the money for the Children's Zone comes from the government. The rest is from private donations. The New York Times has called the Children's Zone, "one of the most ambitious social service experiments of our time."

Looking at Leadership

Why might Canada believe it is important to educate parents of young babies in Harlem?

PHOTO: Kevin Winter/Getty Images; TEXT: Geoffrey Canada. The Harlem Children's Zone, Inc.

Reading**HELP**DESK

charter school a type of school that receives state funding but is excused from meeting many public school regulations

Academic Vocabulary
regulation a rule
alternative other choice

tuition voucher a certificate issued by the government providing money for education payments, allowing families the option of sending students to private schools

these schools. However, the funds must go directly to the parents or guardians, and not directly to the schools, in order to be allowed. Also, the funds cannot be used to promote the religious goals of the school.

Some school districts have tried to bring in private companies to run schools. These businesses promise to improve the quality of education. They also agree to provide schooling at lower cost. At the same time, they make a profit for themselves.

✅ **PROGRESS CHECK**

Identifying Cause and Effect What is the reason for the spending gap between wealthy and poor school districts?

When governments face tight budgets, they may have to cut spending in areas that they would like to fund more fully, such as education.

▶ **CRITICAL THINKING**
Analyzing Visuals What is the attitude of the cartoonist to education funding cuts? Explain why you think so.

Crime and Social Problems

GUIDING QUESTION *What can governments do about crime and social problems?*

The United States has about 2.3 million criminals in prison, more than any other nation in the world. This is true both in terms of the total number of prisoners and the percentage of the country's population.

Poverty and Crime

Crime rates are usually highest in large cities. There, poverty and crime often go hand in hand. Many of the poorest people in inner cities drop out of school early. They spend much of their time on the streets. Crime often becomes the only way of life they know.

Police Departments

America's large cities have more police officers than all of the nation's other law enforcement units combined. Urban police, then, are a major crime-fighting force in the nation.

More than 3,000 county sheriffs, along with their deputies, enforce the law in rural areas. In addition, every state has a law enforcement agency known as the highway patrol or state police. The main job of these agencies is highway safety. In addition, they often play an important role in investigating crimes and capturing suspects.

Enforcing the law is the primary task of police departments. However, uniformed police officers also work to keep the peace. Their job includes handling neighborhood disputes and providing services such as directing traffic.

VIOLENT AND PROPERTY CRIME RATES, 2004–2013

VIOLENT CRIME

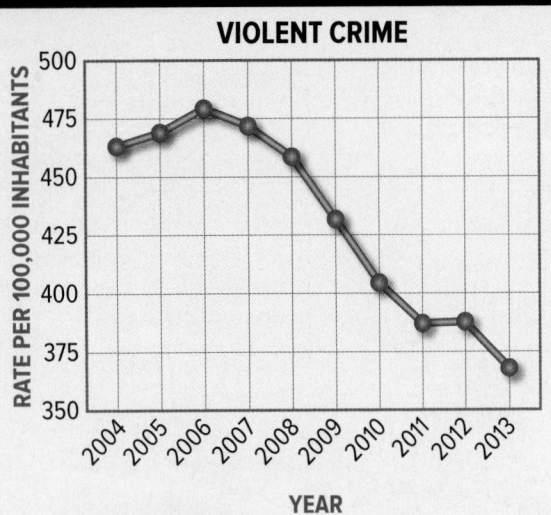

PROPERTY CRIME

Source: U.S. Federal Bureau of Investigation, *Crime in the United States*, 2013.

GRAPH SKILLS

Violent crimes are those that include causing the death of another person, physical attacks on another person, and robbery. Property crime means taking a person's property but without any attack on the person.

▶ CRITICAL THINKING

1 *Analyzing* What has happened to the rate of both types of crime since 2004?

2 *Synthesizing* These statistics do not show the actual number of crimes committed. What do they show?

Crime rates have been falling in recent years. Much of this change is a result of a type of police work called **community policing.** Under this program, police play a visible and active role in neighborhoods. They walk or ride bicycles around the community. This helps them get to know the people who live there. The program also gets ordinary citizens to take part in neighborhood watch groups. These groups aim to prevent crime. People in the group agree to watch the behavior of all people in the neighborhood. If they see any suspicious activity, they quickly report it to the police. The police can then arrive on the scene to investigate.

Social Programs

The government provides welfare programs. Their purpose is to give financial help to Americans who suffer from ill health, old age, poverty, and physical disabilities. Government officials have long struggled over how best to lessen poverty and pass on money to those in need.

Critics of welfare claim that it harms self-respect among poor people. They say it can also lead people to become dependent

ReadingHELPDESK

community policing local police force visibly keeping the peace and patrolling neighborhoods

on the help rather than taking responsibility for their own lives. Supporters of welfare say that it is the only way many poor families can avoid hunger and homelessness. Supporters argue that society as a whole has a responsibility to help those who are less well off.

After years of debate, in 1996 Congress changed the way financial help was given to poor people. The new plan created a program called Temporary Assistance for Needy Families (TANF). Under TANF, the states have more power to develop and run their own programs than they did under the previous system. The federal government gives money to the states to pass on as welfare payments. Each state then decides who can receive welfare and how much money each person gets. State plans have to meet certain federal rules, however. For example, a person can receive welfare for only five years during his or her lifetime. States also have to provide job training programs for the poor to help them leave welfare.

The number of people on welfare dropped sharply after TANF became law. In 1995 about 14.2 million people received welfare payments. By 2010 there were slightly more than 4 million people who received TANF payments each month.

Opponents of the law claim that its success came mostly from the booming economy of the late 1990s. At that time, more workers were needed. People on welfare had no difficulty finding jobs. After 2008, the economy slumped. On the other hand, the number of people receiving welfare is still less than in the past. Some observers say that this is a problem. They argue that hard times have now left many Americans both without jobs *and* without the welfare payments.

☑ **PROGRESS CHECK**

Explaining What is the basic purpose of welfare programs?

— *21ˢᵗ Century* —
SKILLS

Articulating Ideas

The text presents the arguments of those who favor and who oppose welfare programs. Review those arguments. Then write a paragraph stating your own opinion on the issue and explaining why you think as you do.

LESSON 2 REVIEW

Review Vocabulary

1. What is a *charter school?*

2. What are tuition vouchers and why do critics believe that they violate the First Amendment?

3. What is *community policing* and why has it been successful?

Answer the Guiding Questions

4. *Explaining* Why is funding a problem for some public school systems?

5. *Identifying* How does the government attempt to combat poverty through Temporary Assistance for Needy Families (TANF)?

6. **ARGUMENT** Alternatives to public schools include charter schools, tuition vouchers, and even schools that are run by private businesses. Write a letter to the editor expressing whether or not you think that these options are good solutions for meeting the educational challenges public schools face. Provide support for your opinion.

netw☉rks
There's More Online!

☑ **GRAPHIC ORGANIZER**
  Sources of Pollution

☑ **VIDEO**

☑ **CHART**
  Recycling

Lesson 3
Environmental Issues

ESSENTIAL QUESTION *How do citizens, both individually and collectively, influence government policy?*

IT MATTERS BECAUSE
Protecting the environment provides people with a safe and clean place to live.

Environmental Concerns

GUIDING QUESTION *Why is it important to protect and preserve the environment?*

Matt Bell lives near the Cincinnati–Northern Kentucky Airport. The stream behind his home, he explained, "used to be crystal clear." Now the stream is filled with a thick white haze. No animals or plants can live in it. This problem was caused by the runoff from the nearby airport of fluid used to take ice off the wings of planes. Hundreds of planes a day take off from the busy transportation center. In the winter, these planes must have ice removed with a special chemical. This chemical has found its way into the creek behind Matt Bell's home. No one disagrees that airplanes need to be deiced. Could it be done without damaging the stream, though?

What Is Environmentalism?

We pay a high price for living in an industrial society. Every time we turn on a light or throw out trash, we may harm our environment. Many people around the world have adopted **environmentalism,** the movement concerned with protecting our environment. Often it is up to local communities to handle environmental problems.

Reading**HELP**DESK

Taking Notes: *Identifying*

As you read, complete a graphic organizer like the one shown by identifying four sources of air and water pollution.

Sources of Pollution

Content Vocabulary

- **environmentalism**
- **solid waste**
- **landfill**

- **NIMBY**
- **toxic**

- **recycling**
- **conservation**

Until the 1970s, state and local authorities, or people in power, paid little attention to the environment. That approach led to problems. Pollution, the dirtying of air and water with chemicals, increased. As a result, in 1970 Congress passed the Clean Air Act and set up the Environmental Protection Agency (EPA). The EPA has taken the lead in setting federal goals and standards for the environment. Meanwhile, many states have set up programs to check air and water quality.

Waste Disposal

One environmental problem is getting rid of **solid waste,** or garbage. Americans **generate,** or produce, about 250 million tons of solid waste each year. **Landfills,** or places where waste can be dumped, are filling up fast. That means more space is needed to hold trash. Another problem with landfills is that rainwater seeping through the trash damages water supplies. Officials have had to close some landfills as a result.

The search for new landfill sites is often difficult. No one wants a garbage dump in his or her general area. Indeed, there is a name for this way of thinking, or **attitude.** The name is **NIMBY,** which stands for "not in my backyard." Opposition from citizens' groups has blocked the use of possible landfill sites.

Some solid waste is burned in huge incinerators. This burning causes other kinds of problems, however. **Toxic,** or poisonous, smoke from burning causes air pollution. New ways to remove pollutants from smoke are being developed. The devices now available to do this are costly, though.

Recycling

Another way of getting rid of waste is by **recycling.** This means reusing old materials to make new ones. These materials include paper, metal cans, plastic and glass bottles, and plastic bags. Many Americans recycle materials in their homes, schools, and workplaces.

Landfills have to meet various rules and regulations to prevent damaging substances from seeping into the ground and to keep insects or other pests from living off food scraps that have been thrown out.

► CRITICAL THINKING
Analyzing Why would water leaking out of a landfill be a problem?

PHOTO: Paul Sancya/AP Images

environmentalism movement concerned with protecting the environment

solid waste the technical name for garbage

landfill a place where garbage is dumped

Academic Vocabulary

generate to produce

attitude a feeling or way of thinking

This strange looking boat is the *Plastiki*, made from 12,500 plastic bottles. It was built to dramatize the need to recycle. In the spring and summer of 2010, *Plastiki* sailed from San Francisco to Sydney, Australia. The builders' mission was to "beat waste."

▶ CRITICAL THINKING

Analyzing Do you think building this boat will inspire people to recycle? Why or why not?

Paper is the number one material we throw away. For every 100 pounds (45 kg) of trash, about 31 pounds (14 kg) is paper. When paper is recycled, it saves forests and reduces air and water pollution. Unfortunately, not all waste can be recycled. In addition, many people do not take part in recycling efforts.

Conservation

Another approach to helping the environment is conservation. **Conservation** means preserving and protecting natural resources. There are many ways to promote conservation. Some stores offer customers money back when they return shopping bags or use their own bags. Laws encourage and sometimes require businesses to reduce the amount of packaging they use for their products.

People can conserve electricity by buying energy-saving appliances and turning off unnecessary lights. They can conserve oil and natural gas by adjusting thermostats, using more efficient furnaces, and reducing heat loss in their homes. Similarly, private citizens in many areas are greatly reducing their use of water. Conservation is becoming a way of life for more and more Americans.

✓ PROGRESS CHECK

Applying What are some ways to practice conservation?

PHOTO: ROBERT GALBRAITH/Reuters/Corbis

Reading**HELP**DESK

NIMBY an acronym that stands for "not in my backyard"; attitude of opposing landfills near one's home

toxic poisonous or deadly

recycling reusing old materials to make new ones

conservation the careful preservation and protection of natural resources

Protecting the Air, Water, and Land

GUIDING QUESTION *How do local governments control pollution and deal with waste?*

How much pollution do you create? Much air, water, and land pollution comes from industrial sources. However, individuals are responsible for pollution as well.

Pollution from Industry

Water pollution comes mostly from factories. They produce many kinds of chemical waste. For many years, some factories pumped this waste directly into rivers and streams. Others buried it. As a result, the waste was able to seep into underground supplies of water. Factory smokestacks released many poisonous gases into the air.

Today, the federal government has done much to lower industrial pollution in the air and water. Federal rules limit the amounts and kinds of waste that factories may release. However, lack of funds often keeps many of these rules from being strictly enforced.

Pollution from Individuals

Pollution from factories is much easier to control than pollution caused by individuals. In most cities, cars and trucks cause the worst air pollution. To reduce it, the federal government required the removal of lead from gasoline. It also ordered automakers to develop more efficient engines. The auto industry also was told to give cars devices that remove pollutants from exhaust.

Another way to reduce air pollution is to persuade people to drive less. Many local governments are building mass transit systems so that more people will use buses and trains. They also encourage drivers to carpool by creating carpool lanes.

A serious threat to the quality of air inside buildings is smoking. Smoke is harmful to people's lungs. As a result, many cities and counties have passed no-smoking ordinances. Almost all states ban smoking in public buildings.

Many automakers are now manufacturing electric-powered cars. These cars run on a battery and do not pollute. Some cars are hybrids. They can run on gasoline if the battery loses power.

Why It Matters box

Why It MATTERS

Air Pollution and Health

Pollution is not just a problem for the environment. Air pollution can also have an impact on people's lives. Asthma is a condition that makes it difficult for sufferers to breathe. Those who have asthma can have serious problems breathing on days when air pollution is high.

Many of the nation's power plants generate electricity by burning coal. This burning releases harmful chemicals into the air, which winds can carry.

▶ **CRITICAL THINKING**
Making Inferences Why is this pollution a national, and not a local, problem?

Hazardous Waste

Hazardous waste is a major danger. Perhaps the most serious form is radioactive waste from nuclear power plants. This waste takes many, many years to become safe. Hazardous waste also includes runoff from pesticides. Farmers and gardeners spray these chemicals on plants to kill insects. This practice can be a problem when the chemicals enter the water supply. Hazardous waste also includes motor oil, auto engine coolant, and batteries that have been improperly thrown away.

In the past, toxic waste was often put in metal containers. These containers were covered in concrete and then dumped into the ocean. Federal laws passed during the 1970s and 1980s banned this and other ocean dumping practices. Today, the only way to get rid of hazardous waste is by leaving it at places specially set aside for its disposal. However, those land disposal sites are filling up fast.

No method of getting rid of hazardous waste is completely safe. Leaks can occur. Sometimes entire communities are affected. In 1978 the town of Love Canal, New York, had to be abandoned. Many of the town's people, especially children, had serious health problems after coming in contact with leaking toxic waste.

Grassroots Efforts and New Laws

Beginning in the 1960s, citizens formed groups to do something about protecting the environment. The Sierra Club, the Audubon Society, and the Wilderness Society became widely known. These organizations worked to protect the environment and conserve natural resources.

Many communities and businesses responded to the work of these groups. One approach they have taken is to work for sustainable development. This phrase refers to efforts that build economic growth but do not harm the environment. City planners are trying to reduce the spread of cities. They are also increasing green spaces such as parks and open land. Builders are designing

Many Americans choose to ride a bicycle or walk to work.

▶ CRITICAL THINKING
Analyzing How do these actions reduce pollution?

PHOTO: Erik Isakson/Getty Images

ReadingHELPDESK

Reading Strategy: *Explaining*

Sustainable development means promoting economic growth while protecting the environment. The text gives many examples of actions thought to promote sustainable development. Choose one of those actions and explain how it promotes the goals of sustainable development.

buildings so that they will use less energy to heat and cool them. Steps include windows that prevent outside air from leaking into the building and also block inside air from leaking out. As a result, having these windows means the heating and cooling system of the building has less work to do.

Businesses have taken other steps to protect the environment as well. Companies in the forestry industry, for instance, plant young trees after they cut down older trees. Taking this step means there will still be tree roots to hold the soil. If this step was not taken, rainfall could wash the soil away.

More and more private citizens have also come to support protecting the environment. As a result, the federal government took action. The National Environmental Policy Act was signed into law in 1970. It created the Environmental Protection Agency (EPA). The EPA took on the job of setting and enforcing pollution standards. It also helped state and local governments work together to lower pollution.

The Clean Air Act of 1970 set standards for smoke from factories and exhaust from cars. These rules set specific limits to the amount of pollution that can be released into the air. In following years, Congress passed two more laws to protect the environment. The Clean Water Act (1972) put limits on the dumping of pollutants into the nation's lakes and rivers. The Endangered Species Act (1973) set up ways to save animal species that were under threat of dying out completely.

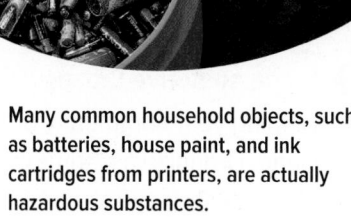

Many common household objects, such as batteries, house paint, and ink cartridges from printers, are actually hazardous substances.

▶ CRITICAL THINKING
Explaining Why should these objects not be thrown into ordinary trash?

PHOTO: Picture Contact BV/Alamy

 PROGRESS CHECK

Identifying What have individual citizens done to protect the environment?

LESSON 3 REVIEW

Review Vocabulary

1. What does *NIMBY* stand for? What attitude does it represent?

2. What are *environmentalism* and *conservation*? Why is someone who believes in environmentalism likely to practice conservation?

Answer the Guiding Questions

3. *Inferring* How does recycling paper help the environment?

4. *Explaining* Why is it important to protect the environment?

5. *Summarizing* Why is hazardous waste a serious problem? How have governments attempted to control it?

6. **ARGUMENT** Which of the environmental issues discussed do you think is most critical today? Write a paragraph that identifies and explains your choice.

Write your answers on a separate sheet of paper.

1 Writing Activity

EXPLORING THE ESSENTIAL QUESTION
How do citizens, both individually and collectively, influence government policy?

Public policies are the actions the government takes in response to issues or problems that affect the entire community. Make a list of several examples of public policy regarding education. Then choose one policy. Identify the problem or issue it is meant to address and the action the government has taken. Then explain what might happen if there were *no* government response.

2 21st Century Skills

CREATE A PUBLIC SERVICE ANNOUNCEMENT Many communities are using neighborhood watch programs to help reduce crime. Create a public service announcement to encourage people in a community to take part in one of these programs.

3 Being an Active Citizen

Helping your community protect the environment can be as simple as keeping it clean. Organize a cleanup day for your school, a local park, or other community property. Pick a date and time, publicize it with posters and through other means, and invite volunteers to lend a hand.

4 Understanding Visuals

Communities across the country must dispose of solid waste. Recycling reduces the amount of waste that must be handled. Study the graph below. Then explain which materials can be recycled, and how much solid waste can be recycled.

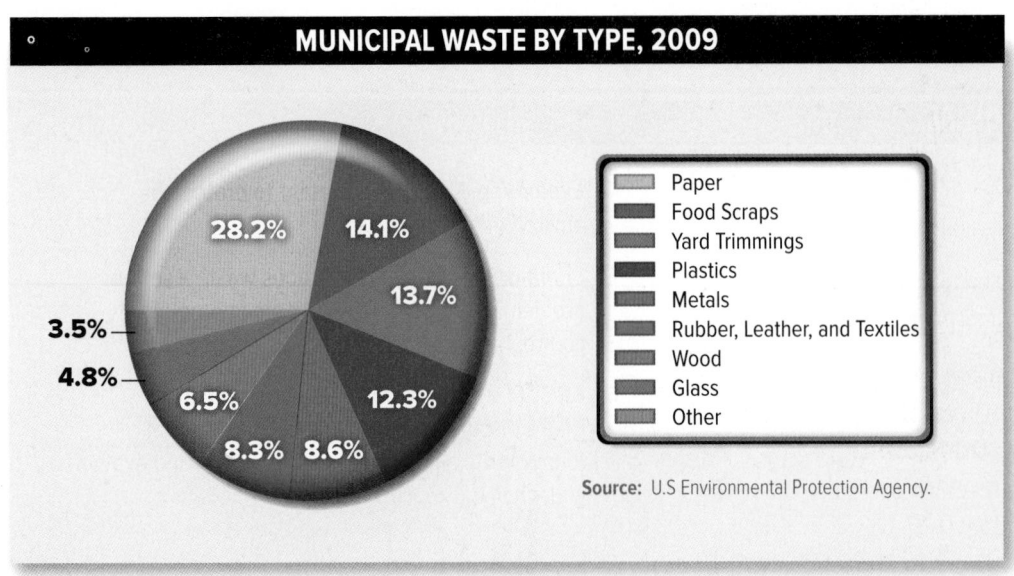

MUNICIPAL WASTE BY TYPE, 2009

28.2% 14.1% 13.7% 3.5% 4.8% 6.5% 12.3% 8.3% 8.6%

- Paper
- Food Scraps
- Yard Trimmings
- Plastics
- Metals
- Rubber, Leather, and Textiles
- Wood
- Glass
- Other

Source: U.S Environmental Protection Agency.

REVIEW THE GUIDING QUESTIONS

Directions: Choose the best answer for each question.

1 The money, people, and materials available to accomplish a community's plan are its
   A. policies.
   B. resources.
   C. priorities.
   D. infrastructure.

2 Granting a company a permit to build apartments is an example of a
   F. master plan.
   G. public policy.
   H. long-term plan.
   I. short-term plan.

3 What is one criticism of charter schools?
   A. Charter schools have high dropout rates.
   B. Charter schools only enroll problem students.
   C. Charter schools take funds from public schools.
   D. Charter schools produce poor academic performance.

4 Which program sets a five-year lifetime limit on receiving welfare?
   F. Race to the Top
   G. No Child Left Behind
   H. Temporary Assistance to Needy Families
   I. community policing

5 Which is the most environmentally friendly way to handle solid waste?
   A. recycle it
   B. take it to a landfill
   C. burn it
   D. conserve it

6 How can cities reduce air pollution?
   F. by improving public transportation
   G. by dumping toxic waste in the ocean
   H. by eliminating runoff from pesticides
   I. by requiring the use of lead in gasoline

DBQ **ANALYZING DOCUMENTS**

Directions: Analyze the excerpt and answer the questions that follow.

Americans [produce] about 250 million tons of trash [each year] and [recycle] 83 million tons of this material, equivalent to a 33.2 percent recycling rate. On average, we [recycle] 1.5 pounds of our individual waste generation of 4.5 pounds produced per person per day.

—"Municipal Solid Waste Generation, Recycling, and
Disposal in the United States," Environmental Protection Agency (2008)

7 **Drawing Conclusions** From this passage, "recycling rate" means

A. pounds of trash per person per day

B. percentage of trash that is recycled

C. quantity of trash in tons

D. number of Americans who recycle

8 **Identifying** Which statement does the passage support?

F. "The United States produces more trash than other countries."

G. "The United States has a high recycling rate."

H. "The United States produces hundreds of millions of tons of trash."

I. "The United States is increasing the amount of trash it recycles."

SHORT RESPONSE

"Providing a high-quality education for all children is critical to America's economic future. Our nation's economic competitiveness and the path to the American Dream depend on providing every child with an education that will enable them to succeed in a global economy that is predicated [based] on knowledge and innovation."

—White House Education Issue Brief (2010)

9 Why does the White House brief say that education is related to the nation's economic future?

10 Does this passage support a stronger role for the federal government in education? Why or why not?

EXTENDED RESPONSE

11 **Argument** Suppose you are the mayor of a city. As mayor, you must address such issues as education, economic growth, crime, preserving the environment, and providing services for the poor. Write a paragraph identifying which area you would give the highest priority to and explaining why.

Need Extra Help?

If You've Missed Question	**1**	**2**	**3**	**4**	**5**	**6**	**7**	**8**	**9**	**10**	**11**
Review Lesson	1	1	2	2	3	3	3	3	2	2	1, 2, 3

Citizens and the Law

ESSENTIAL QUESTION
How do laws protect individual rights?

The Story Matters...

A car moves swiftly down the highway. Is it going faster than the posted speed limit? Suddenly, blue lights flash and a siren wails. From out of nowhere, a police cruiser appears. It catches up to the speeding car. The officer waves the car over to the side of the road.

If you have witnessed a police officer ticketing a driver, then you have seen law enforcement in action. Such encounters are among the most obvious ways that citizens see public laws and regulations at work. Drivers need to understand and obey the laws regarding speed limits and roadway safety. Laws made by the government require drivers to pass tests to get their licenses. The government also regulates the placement of traffic signs along the roadside. Driving laws, along with the other types of laws that citizens follow every day, are necessary. They allow people to live together in a peaceful, orderly society.

◄ *If a driver gets a ticket for violating a traffic law, he or she may face a fine, traffic school, higher insurance payments, or even a suspended driver's license.*

PHOTO: Blend Images/SuperStock

391

Real-Life Civics

> ## PURPOSE OF LAWS
Laws are created to keep citizens safe and to maintain order in society. This sign reminds beachgoers that certain activities are against the law on this stretch of sand. It also tells the public that these rules will be strictly enforced. Most of the restrictions are related to safety. Glass containers may easily break, exposing bare feet to sharp shards of glass. Tether lines on surfboards help to protect surfers and nearby swimmers from injury. Drinking alcohol and then swimming is also dangerous behavior. While this list may seem long, each rule has a purpose. The same is true of all our laws. However, laws can sometimes become outdated. Then they may lose the support of the citizens they affect. When that happens, laws can be changed.

This sign alerts the public to the activities that are not allowed on a particular beach in Florida.

PROHIBITED ON THE BEACH

- NO DOGS ALLOWED 9 A.M. – 5 P.M
- NO ALCOHOLIC BEVERAGES
- NO GLASS CONTAINERS
- NO LITTERING
- NO SURFBOARDS WITHOUT TETHER LINES

STRICTLY ENFORCED

PHOTOS: (l) Derrick Alderman/Alamy; (tr) AP Photo/Hillery Smith Garrison

Citizens against gun violence gather for the Million Mom March held on the National Mall in Washington, D.C.

CHANGING LAWS

On Mother's Day, May 14, 2000, many thousands of people gathered on the National Mall in Washington, D.C. They carried signs, posters, and banners protesting what they believed was a lack of meaningful U.S. gun control laws. Called the Million Mom March, the demonstration actually included women and men from around the country. Their goal was to prevent gun violence by changing current laws or making new laws. Supporters of causes like this one march in the hope that Congress will take action. Rallies are not the only way to change our laws. In fact, it takes great commitment and support from both citizens and lawmakers to alter or create a law. It can happen—but it does take time.

CIVIC LITERACY

★ ★ ★ ★

Analyzing In what ways are the beach regulations and the laws being addressed in the gun control rally related? What does this tell you about the general purpose of our laws?

Your Opinion Describe two laws that affect your life. Would you like to change these laws? Why or why not?

393

Lesson 1
Sources and Types of Law

ESSENTIAL QUESTION *How do laws protect individual rights?*

⊙ IT MATTERS BECAUSE
Laws protect public safety and keep order in society.

Why We Have Laws

GUIDING QUESTION *What is the purpose of laws?*

Have you ever wondered why certain laws exist? Why, for example, do many states require children to wear bicycle helmets? More injuries from bicycling than any other sport send children aged 5 to 14 to hospital emergency rooms. Using a bicycle helmet greatly reduces the risk of head injury. As you can see, helmet laws are meant to protect you from getting hurt. Laws affect nearly everything we do—the food we eat, how we drive our cars, how we buy and sell things, and so much more.

Keeping the Peace

Laws are sets of rules that help people get along. People, organizations, and governments deal better with one another when they follow the same rules. Laws establish which actions a society permits and which it does not. They set the rules for working out civil disagreements over money, property, and contracts.

Laws also help keep the peace and prevent criminal acts. The police and the courts enforce the law. If you break the law, you can expect to be punished. Laws set punishments to discourage **potential** criminals.

Reading**HELP**DESK

Taking Notes: *Identifying*

As you read, complete a graphic organizer identifying characteristics of a good law.

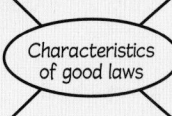

Characteristics
of good laws

Content Vocabulary

- **common law**
- **precedent**
- **statute**
- **lawsuit**
- **constitutional law**
- **case law**
- **administrative law**

What Makes a Law a Good Law?

Some laws are better than others. Good laws share certain characteristics. Such laws are

- fair
- reasonable
- understandable
- enforceable

A fair law gives equal treatment to all people who are in similar situations. Thus, a rule that says only tall people are allowed to ride on a public bus and short people must walk would not be fair.

Good laws are not only fair, but also reasonable. In England in the 1700s, if you stole a loaf of bread you might have had your hand cut off. In some ancient cultures, crimes such as stealing or causing a public disturbance were punishable by death. Today we view such harsh punishments as unreasonable because the punishment does not seem appropriate. That is, it does not fit the crime.

Moreover, good laws are understandable. If a law is not easy to understand, people might disobey it without realizing they are doing so. Of course, ignorance of a law is no excuse for breaking that law. Still, if laws are too complicated, people might break them unintentionally.

Finally, good laws are enforceable by local communities, state authorities, or federal authorities. People tend to obey laws they understand and believe to be reasonable and fair. The government's ability to enforce a law often depends on the people's willingness to obey it.

✓ **PROGRESS CHECK**

Making Connections How do laws help people live together peacefully?

Some states have laws that require young bicyclists to wear helmets, but others do not.

▶ **CRITICAL THINKING**
Speculating Why do you think this is so?

Academic Vocabulary

potential capable of being or becoming

Development of the Legal System

GUIDING QUESTION *What early legal systems influenced the laws we live by today?*

The writers of the U.S. Constitution based the nation's system of laws on ideas, traditions, and laws passed down from generation to generation. Some of these ideas date back thousands of years.

Scholars believe that some kind of law existed in even the earliest human societies. It is thought that prehistoric people used unwritten rules of behavior. These rules helped them avoid or cope with social conflict. The earliest laws were probably passed orally from one generation to the next. Over time, people began to write down their laws.

Code of Hammurabi

The earliest example of a written **code** of law was developed in Babylonia, an ancient Middle Eastern empire. In about 1760 B.C., the legal decisions of King Hammurabi (HA•muh•RAH•bee) were collected and carved into a large stone pillar. They were written in the Akkadian language in wedge-shaped script called cuneiform. The code included laws related to the family, marriage and adoption, slavery, and agricultural and business practices. It also set prices for goods and services. By today's standards, the Code of Hammurabi laid down very severe penalties.

Hammurabi (standing) receives the blessing of Shamash, the god of justice. The Code of Hammurabi was carved into the stone pillar in cuneiform (inset).

▶ CRITICAL THINKING

Analyzing Visuals Why do you think this scene is at the top of the monument? Why is it significant?

PRIMARY SOURCE

❝ If fire break[s] out in a house, and some one . . . take[s] the property of the master of the house, he shall be thrown into that self-same fire. ❞

—Code of Hammurabi, c. 1760 B.C.

Israelite Law

The Israelites were another ancient people who lived near the eastern Mediterranean coast. They followed a different set of written laws. These laws forbade acts such as murder and theft. Under our modern laws, these acts are also crimes.

Reading HELP DESK

Reading Strategy: *Paraphrasing*

When you paraphrase, you restate a particular sentence or sentences in your own words. Paraphrase the quote from the Code of Hammurabi.

Academic Vocabulary

code an organized statement of a body of law

Roman Law

The most important laws that developed in the Western world came from ancient Rome. The first code of Roman law was published in 450 B.C. Over centuries, the Roman senate adopted a great many laws. Roman judges wrote commentaries on them, which often became part of the law. As the Roman Empire grew, its laws spread to parts of Europe, Africa, and Asia.

In A.D. 527, Justinian I became ruler of the Eastern Roman Empire, also known as the Byzantine (BIH•zehn•TEEN) Empire. By that time, law in the empire was in a state of confusion. In A.D. 533, Justinian simplified Roman law into an orderly body of rules. This set of laws, called the Justinian Code, became the basis of law for the Byzantine Empire. It also became part of the laws of the Roman Catholic Church, known as canon law. Although canon law dealt with church rules and regulations, it influenced legal procedures outside the church.

Napoleonic Code

The Justinian Code eventually shaped the laws of many European countries, such as France. In 1804 the French emperor Napoleon Bonaparte carried out a major reform of France's laws. As the ancient Romans had done, Napoleon brought his unified law code, or Napoleonic Code, to the lands he controlled. In addition, many other places in Europe and South America based their laws on the Napoleonic Code.

In 1825 the state of Louisiana wrote a set of laws based on the Napoleonic Code. The Louisiana Territory had been under French rule before the United States bought it in 1803. Although they have been revised over the years, the laws of Louisiana still bear their Napoleonic origins.

Justinian I (center) helped organize the laws of the vast Byzantine Empire over which he ruled.

▶ CRITICAL THINKING
Making Connections Why is it important for the United States to have a unified code of laws?

21ˢᵗ Century
SKILLS

Interpret Points of View

Although Justinian I and Napoleon Bonaparte lived more than 1,200 years apart, each is known for creating a law code. Write a dialogue between Justinian I and Napoleon in which they discuss the reasons they created their respective codes.

Even today, English barristers, or lawyers, and judges wear robes and wigs during criminal cases, a tradition that dates back hundreds of years.

▶ **CRITICAL THINKING**
Identifying Central Issues How did the tradition of common law come about in England?

English Common Law

The most important influence on the American legal system is English law. The English system of **common law** is based on court decisions rather than on a legal code. The system involves analyzing how a previous judge applied a law and then applying it in the same manner.

Common law developed after 1066. At that time, conquerors from northern France, the Normans, took control of England. They set up a new royal family. The English kings began to send judges into the countryside. The judges held trials to carry out the law. Judges decided a new case by following **precedent,** or the rulings set forth earlier in similar cases. Precedents are legal opinions that become part of the common law. In this way, laws became unified, or common to all regions.

The English blended Roman law and canon law into the body of common law. The law came to incorporate basic principles of individual rights. These principles include the idea that a person should be considered innocent until proven guilty.

Because it is based on the decisions of judges, common law is considered judge-made law. It was the main source of laws in England for hundreds of years. Over time, the English Parliament gained the power to create laws as well. Laws created by legislative bodies such as Parliament are known as **statutes.** Although statutes passed by Parliament came to play an increasing role in the legal system, common law remained the foundation of English law.

When English settlers came to North America in the 1600s and 1700s, they brought with them their traditions of common law and individual rights. Both became key parts of the basic laws of the new nation, the United States. They continue to play a key role in the U.S. judicial system today.

☑ **PROGRESS CHECK**

Making Connections How are Roman law, the Justinian Code, and the Napoleonic Code related?

PHOTO: Doug Menuez/Getty Images

ReadingHELPDESK

common law a system of law based on precedent and customs

precedent a ruling that is used as the basis for a judicial decision in a later, similar case

statute a law written by a legislative branch of government

Types of Laws

GUIDING QUESTION *What types of laws exist in the American legal system?*

If you watch the local television news or read the newspaper, you have probably seen stories about crimes. Criminal laws prohibit, or ban, such acts as theft or drunk driving. Other kinds of laws deal with disputes between people (or groups of people) or between the government and its citizens. These are known as civil laws. Another branch of laws is called public laws. These regulate how individuals deal with the government. They also regulate the organization and conduct of the government. You learned about public laws earlier.

Criminal and civil laws directly affect all Americans. These laws help maintain a peaceful and orderly society. People who break these laws are likely to find themselves in a courtroom.

Criminal Law

Criminal laws seek to protect public safety. Crimes are graded as either felonies or misdemeanors. Murder, robbery, and other serious crimes are felonies. Felonies have serious consequences for the victim and the criminal. Misdemeanors are lesser offenses, such as vandalism or stealing low-cost items. Typically, misdemeanors carry a fine or a jail sentence of less than one year.

Crimes against property are the most common type of crime. They do not involve force or the threat of force against the victim. These include crimes in which property is destroyed, damaged, or stolen. Stealing a bike, shoplifting, identity theft, and setting fires are examples of crimes against property.

21st Century SKILLS

Compare and Contrast

Create a two-column graphic organizer to help you compare and contrast civil and criminal law.

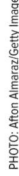

Graffiti is a violation of criminal law. It is a form of property crime. Here a map at Coney Island in New York has been vandalized.

▶ CRITICAL THINKING

Analyzing Why do you think it is a crime to write graffiti?

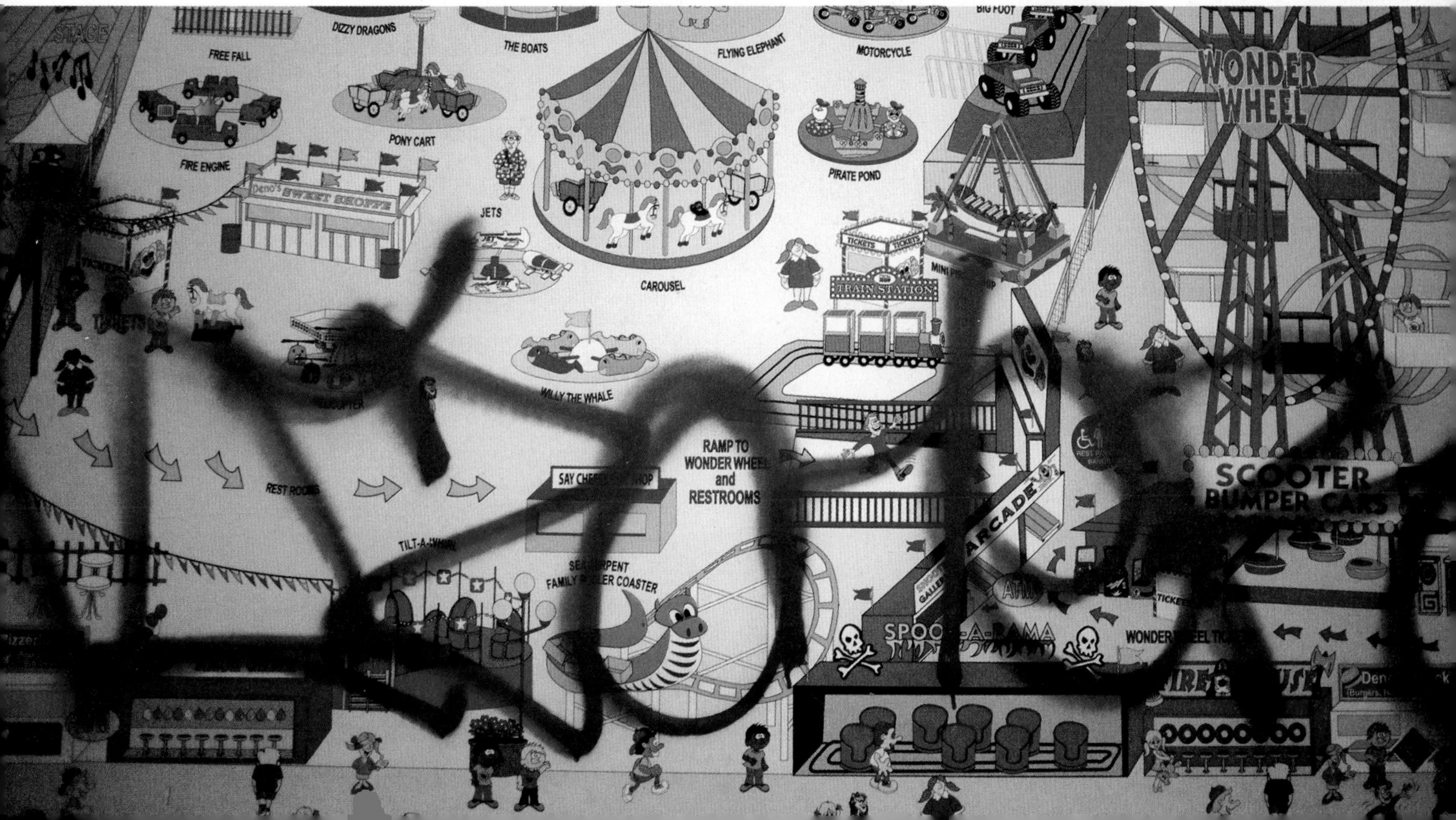

PHOTO: Afton Almaraz/Getty Images

Student Government

Laws in our country are in place to maintain a peaceful and orderly society. Just like these laws, school rules ensure the safety and security of students. Make a list of some of the rules in your school. Add a few rules that you think should also be on the list and explain why.

In addition to following the laws of the United States, those in the military must conform to another set of laws.

▶ **CRITICAL THINKING**

Assessing Why do you think it is important that the armed forces have their own set of laws?

Civil Law

Civil laws do not concern society at large or criminal offenses. Rather, they are about disputes between people or groups. A civil case may be a disagreement over a broken contract. For example, suppose you order something from a mail-order catalog and charge it to your credit card. The mail-order company has, in effect, made a contract with you. If you do not receive the item, the company has broken the contract. You can then take the company to court to get your money back.

A civil case brought before a court is called a **lawsuit.** This is a legal action to seek a remedy for harm that has been done. People who think they have been wronged take action by filing a lawsuit. The government cannot bring such a case.

Military Law

Military law is a set of statutes that apply to those serving in the armed forces of the United States. These laws also apply to civilians who work for the military. People subject to these statutes also have to follow the civil laws. Military laws concern such acts as disobeying or showing disrespect to superior officers, physically striking superior officers, desertion, and mutiny. People accused of serious offenses may end up at a court-martial. This is a court, made up of officers, that tries those accused of breaking military laws.

Sources of Law

Laws that govern our lives and protect our rights come from many sources. These include

- the U.S. Constitution
- state constitutions
- statutes
- case law
- administrative agencies

PHOTO: Chung Sung-Jun/GettyImages

ReadingHELPDESK

lawsuit a legal action in which a person or group sues to collect damages for some harm that is done

constitutional law branch of law dealing with the formation, construction, and interpretation of constitutions

case law a law established by judicial decisions instead of by legislative action

administrative law rules and regulations set by government agencies

The U.S. Constitution is the most important source of law in the United States. It is the supreme, or highest, law of the nation. Although each state has its own state constitution, no state or local law may conflict with the U.S. Constitution.

Constitutional law deals with the structure and meaning of constitutions. Constitutional cases decide the limits of the government's power and the rights of the individual.

A statute is a law written by a legislative branch of government. The U.S. Congress, state legislatures, and local legislatures write thousands of statutes. Statutes regulate our behavior in many ways. They set speed limits, minimum wages, and rules for food inspection, to name a few. Statutes are also the source of many of the rights and privileges we take for granted, such as the right to a free public education.

Case Law

As you have read, judicial precedent plays an important role in our justice system. Often, especially in civil cases, a judge decides the outcome of a case. Judicial decisions carry the weight of law. Sometimes a case cannot be decided by existing statutes. In such situations, judges look to precedent to make a decision. Law established by judicial decision is called **case law.**

Administrative Law

Administrative law refers to the rules and regulations that the executive branch makes to carry out its job. The federal and state constitutions give legislatures the power to create administrative agencies. Many agency rules and regulations carry the weight of law. For example, the Federal Aviation Administration might issue an order requiring airlines to install a new type of safety device. Such a regulation would be an administrative law.

✓ **PROGRESS CHECK**

Identifying What is the most important source of law in the United States?

LESSON 1 REVIEW

Review Vocabulary

1. How are *common law* and *precedent* related?

2. What is a *statute*?

3. What is the difference between *case law* and *administrative law*?

Answer the Guiding Questions

4. *Explaining* What are some reasons that society needs laws?

5. *Making Connections* What role did English common law have in the United States?

6. *Identifying* What is the difference between civil and criminal laws?

7. **INFORMATIVE/EXPLANATORY** How have the systems of law dating from ancient Rome influenced the U.S. legal system?

Miranda v. Arizona

The *Miranda* decision strengthened the rights of people accused of crimes and dramatically impacted police procedure for dealing with those in their custody.

Ernesto Miranda (right) speaks with his attorney.

Background of the Case

Starting at a young age, Ernesto Miranda made a career out of car theft, armed robbery, assault, and other serious offenses. In 1963 he was arrested in Arizona on suspicion of armed robbery. While in police custody, he confessed to the robbery, as well as to kidnapping and rape. His written confession included a preprinted statement. The statement indicated that he knew of his right to remain silent. At trial, Miranda's signed confession convinced the jury that he was guilty.

Miranda appealed the decision. His lawyer argued that Miranda was unaware of his right against self-incrimination and his right to have a lawyer present during interrogation. The lawyer also claimed that Miranda was tricked into confession. He asked that the confession obtained while in police custody be inadmissible, or not used as evidence in court.

The Decision

The Supreme Court ruled in Miranda's favor. The Court based its decision on several factors. It noted that police interrogations by their very nature put severe emotional pressure on a suspect. Without support of counsel and a full understanding of their rights, suspects can be pressured and tricked into making incriminating statements. The Court also held that individuals cannot fully practice their Fifth Amendment rights if they do not understand the consequences of waiving those rights.

The Court outlined a set of procedures police must follow in order to ensure that individuals can exercise their Fifth Amendmen rights. It held that unless these procedures are followed, the state cannot prove that a suspect was aware of his or her rights.

Why It Matters

The Miranda decision caused a major change in police procedure. When police question individuals in their custody, they must first fully inform them of their Fifth Amendment rights. This procedure is known as the Miranda Warnings. The Court instructed the police to inform individuals in their custody that

1. they have the right to remain silent.
2. anything they say can be used against them in court.
3. they have the right to consult with a lawyer and to have the lawyer present during interrogation.
4. if they cannot afford a lawyer, one will be appointed to represent them.

Analyzing the Case

1. **Identifying the Main Idea** On what basis did Miranda appeal his conviction?
2. **Inferring** Why do you think it is important for individuals in police custody to have a lawyer present during questioning?

PHOTO: Bettmann/Corbis

networks

There's More Online!

☑ **GRAPHIC ORGANIZER**
Protecting Rights of the Accused

☑ **CHART**
Constitutional Rights of the Accused

☑ **GAME**

☑ **TIME LINE**
Equal Protection

Lesson 2

The American Legal System

ESSENTIAL QUESTION *How do laws protect individual rights?*

IT MATTERS BECAUSE

Under the American system of justice, the U.S. Constitution protects the rights of individuals.

Basic Legal Rights

GUIDING QUESTION *What basic legal rights are provided to all Americans?*

In many American schools, school officials or police officers sometimes search students' lockers, book bags, and other belongings. They cannot, however, look through students' things whenever they wish. This is because you are protected from such unreasonable searches by the U.S. Constitution. The Constitution establishes this and many other important rights concerning individuals and the law.

Protections Against Unlawful Imprisonment

One of the most important protections, found in Article I, is the **writ of habeas corpus.** *Habeas corpus* (HAY•bee•uhs KAWR•puhs) is a Latin phrase that roughly means "you should have the body." This odd phrase refers to the practice of bringing a prisoner ("the body") before a judge to justify his or her imprisonment. In the United States, a prisoner has the right to ask for a writ of habeas corpus. The writ is a court order. It requires a prison official to bring the prisoner before a judge. The judge will then decide whether the accused was lawfully imprisoned. Habeas corpus safeguards individuals against being kept in jail unlawfully.

Reading **HELP**DESK

Taking Notes: *Identifying*

As you read, complete a graphic organizer to show what the government *cannot* do and *must* do to protect the rights of the accused.

Protecting Rights of the Accused	
Cannot	Must

Content Vocabulary

- writ of habeas corpus
- bill of attainder
- ex post facto law
- due process
- search warrant
- exclusionary rule

Lady Justice symbolizes impartiality and equal protection under the law. Blindfolded, she judges guilt or innocence with the scales in her left hand and fights evil with the sword in her right hand.

▶ CRITICAL THINKING
Explaining What does Lady Justice's blindfold symbolize?

Article I also forbids the government from issuing bills of attainder and ex post facto laws. A **bill of attainder** is a law that punishes a person accused of a crime without a trial or a fair hearing in court. An **ex post facto law** is a law that would allow a person to be punished for an action that was not against the law when it was committed. *Ex post facto* means "after the fact."

Administration of Justice

The Constitution also makes sure that the government respects our individual rights as it carries out the law. After the Civil War, the Fourteenth Amendment granted civil rights to formerly enslaved people. This amendment requires the states to treat all people equally under the law. It bans unequal treatment based on factors such as gender, race, and religion. Since the 1950s, the amendment has been used to challenge policies that discriminate against minorities and women.

The Fourteenth Amendment also strengthens the Fifth Amendment right of due process. **Due process** means that the government may not take our lives, liberty, or property without following legal procedure. For example, a person accused of a crime must have the opportunity for a trial by jury.

☑ PROGRESS CHECK

Explaining How does the Constitution protect you from unlawful imprisonment?

The Rights of the Accused

GUIDING QUESTION *What legal protections does the U.S. Constitution offer a citizen who is accused of a crime?*

Have you ever seen a movie in which police officers read suspects their rights? This reading gives suspects the protection of the U.S. Constitution.

The Constitution makes sure that people accused of crimes receive fair treatment. They must also have every chance to defend themselves. The rights it grants are based upon the **presumption** of innocence. A person is believed to be innocent until proven guilty in a court of law.

Fourth Amendment Rights

The Fourth Amendment protects citizens against "unreasonable searches and seizures." It gives Americans the right to be

PHOTO: Getty Images

Reading **HELP** DESK

Content Vocabulary (cont.)
- **Miranda Warning**
- **double jeopardy**
- **bail**

404 *Citizens and the Law*

writ of habeas corpus
a court order that requires police to bring a prisoner to court to explain why the person is being held

bill of attainder
a law that punishes a person accused of a crime without a trial or a fair hearing in court

ex post facto law a law that would allow a person to be punished for an action that was not against the law when it was committed

secure in their homes and property. No police officer or other government agent can search your home or take your property without probable cause, or a valid reason. If law officers want to search your home for evidence of a crime, they must first get a search warrant. A **search warrant** is a judge's authorization for a search. It describes the exact place to be searched and what objects may be seized, or taken. Police must show the judge that they have probable cause to obtain a search warrant.

If police find evidence of a crime through an illegal search, the evidence may not be used in court. The 1961 Supreme Court case *Mapp* v. *Ohio* ruled that illegally obtained evidence will be excluded, or barred, from a state court trial. Such evidence had already been banned from a federal court trial. This rule is known as the **exclusionary rule.** In other words, evidence gained in a way that violates the Fourth Amendment may not be used in a trial.

Fifth Amendment Rights

The Fifth Amendment states that no person can be forced "to be a witness against himself" in a criminal case. It protects individuals against self-incrimination. This means that individuals do not have to answer questions that might show they were involved in a crime.

Before the 1960s, police often pressured suspects to confess to a crime before they saw a lawyer or appeared in court. This practice ended in 1966 with the Supreme Court case *Miranda* v. *Arizona*. The Court ruled that police must inform suspects of their right to refuse to answer police questions.

Drug searches such as this one at a school seek to prevent potential harm caused by drug use. At the same time, protecting people's rights is always important. In this search, lockers are being swabbed for traces of drugs. If traces are found, they represent probable cause for a search.

▶ **CRITICAL THINKING**
Inferring How is the probable cause requirement in the Fourth Amendment a reflection of the presumption of innocence?

PHOTO: Scott Lituchy/Star Ledger/Corbis

| **due process** following established legal procedures | Academic Vocabulary **presumption** an attitude or belief based on likelihood | **search warrant** a court order allowing law-enforcement officers to search a suspect's home or business and take specific items as evidence | **exclusionary rule** a rule that evidence gained by police in a way that violates the Fourth Amendment may not be used in a trial |

CONSTITUTIONAL RIGHTS OF THE ACCUSED

The Constitution protects the rights of people accused of crimes in many different ways.

► CRITICAL THINKING

1 **Describing** What protections does the Fifth Amendment guarantee?

2 **Analyzing** How does due process of law limit what government can do?

Source	Rights
Article I	• habeas corpus • protects against bills of attainder • protects against ex post facto laws
Fourth Amendment	• protects against unreasonable searches and seizures
Fifth Amendment	• guarantees due process • protects against self-incrimination • protects against double jeopardy • provides for grand juries in the case of federal crimes
Sixth Amendment	• guarantees the right to counsel • guarantees the right to know the accusations • guarantees the right to a speedy public trial • guarantees the right to confront witnesses • guarantees the right to be tried by an impartial jury
Eighth Amendment	• forbids cruel and unusual punishments • prohibits excessive bail
Fourteenth Amendment	• requires the states to treat all people equally under the law • guarantees due process

The case began in 1963, when Arizona resident Ernesto Miranda was convicted, or found guilty, on charges of kidnapping and other serious crimes. His conviction was based on a confession he had made while in police custody. Miranda appealed his conviction. He claimed that he did not know that he had the right to remain silent and to have a lawyer with him while the police questioned him.

The Arizona Supreme Court rejected Miranda's appeal. Miranda next appealed his conviction to the U.S. Supreme Court. The nation's highest court agreed to hear his appeal. In a landmark 5–4 decision, the court ruled in Miranda's favor. They threw out his conviction and ordered that he be given a new trial. In the new trial, the prosecution would not be allowed to present Miranda's confession as evidence. Despite his new trial, Miranda was found guilty.

The Court's decision, however, had a far-reaching effect. It required police nationwide to follow certain new procedures. These procedures are designed to protect a suspect's Fifth Amendment rights. They are also designed to ensure that any confession the police obtain can be used in court. Before they

Reading**HELP**DESK

Reading Strategy: *Making Connections*

When you make connections, you state how one idea connects to another in your own words. Read what Ernesto Miranda claimed again. Read the bulleted text that identifies Miranda rights. Write a paragraph explaining how the Miranda case led to the Miranda Warning.

can question a person in their custody, police must now issue what is known as a **Miranda Warning.** The Miranda Warning informs suspects that

- they have the right to remain silent
- anything they say may be used against them as evidence
- they have the right to an attorney; if they cannot afford one, the court will provide one

The Fifth Amendment also protects the accused from **double jeopardy.** *Jeopardy* means "to be put at risk of criminal penalty." A person who is tried for a crime and found not guilty may not be tried again for the same crime.

The Fifth Amendment entitles people accused of serious federal crimes to be brought before a grand jury. A grand jury is a group of 12 to 23 citizens that hears evidence presented by a prosecutor. It decides whether the government has enough evidence to bring a suspect to trial. If the grand jury finds enough evidence to justify a trial, it indicts, or formally charges, the suspect. In some states, a preliminary hearing is used instead of a grand jury indictment.

Sixth Amendment Rights

The Sixth Amendment grants the accused the right to be defended by a lawyer. In the 1963 Supreme Court case *Gideon* v. *Wainwright*, the Court said that the amendment means that if a defendant cannot afford a lawyer, the state must provide one. Before this ruling, the federal government provided lawyers for poor defendants in federal cases. Some states, though, provided a lawyer only for crimes punishable by death. As you have read, the Supreme Court in the *Miranda* decision felt that a lawyer was necessary to protect a suspect against self-incrimination.

The accused have the right to know the accusations against them. They can question witnesses against them in court. They have the right to be tried by an impartial, or fair, jury. The jury is made up of people who know no one in the case and who do not have an opinion about it. Jurors are usually chosen from the area where the crime was committed.

Miranda warning? No, this is just a routine traffic stop. You don't get *Mirandized* until <u>after</u> you finish incriminating yourself.

This cartoon refers to *Berghuis* v. *Thompkins*, a 2010 case in which the Supreme Court ruled that if a suspect is silent, this can be a waiver of Miranda rights. A suspect must clearly state that he or she is invoking Miranda protections.

▶ CRITICAL THINKING
Analyzing Based on what the police officer says to the motorist, what do you think the cartoonist's opinion is of the Supreme Court's ruling?

Miranda Warning list of rights police must inform persons of before questioning, including the right against self-incrimination and the right to counsel

double jeopardy putting someone on trial for a crime for which he or she was previously acquitted

The Sixth Amendment also guarantees the right to a speedy and public trial. This protects defendants from being held in jail for an unreasonably long time. It also means that trials should not be closed to the public or the news media.

Today, many cases do not go to trial. Instead, the prosecutor and the defendant agree to a plea bargain. A plea bargain is an agreement in which the defendant pleads guilty to a reduced charge. In return, the defendant receives a lighter sentence than he or she would get if found guilty of the original charge.

Eighth Amendment Rights

The Eighth Amendment outlaws excessive, or extreme, penalties. It forbids "cruel and unusual punishments." A punishment may not be out of **proportion** to the crime. For example, a life sentence for shoplifting would be excessive.

Some people believe that the death penalty is cruel and unusual. In 1972 the Supreme Court ruled in *Furman* v. *Georgia* that the death penalty as then carried out was unconstitutional. The justices did not say that the death penalty itself was cruel and unusual. Instead, they found that it was being applied unequally. It unfairly targeted African Americans and the poor. Such unequal application of the law is a violation of the Fourteenth Amendment. After the *Furman* decision, states revised their death penalty laws to meet the Court's guidelines.

The Eighth Amendment also prohibits excessive bail. **Bail** is a sum of money that serves as a security deposit. An arrested person can pay a court to be let out of jail while awaiting trial. When the defendant shows up for trial, the money is returned. In setting the amount of the bail, the judge looks at the seriousness of the crime, the criminal record of the accused, and the ability of the accused to pay bail.

✓ PROGRESS CHECK

Explaining Explain why illegally obtained evidence cannot be used in court.

LESSON 2 REVIEW

Review Vocabulary

1. How does the Constitution's Article I ban on *ex post facto laws* protect people?

2. What does the *exclusionary rule* prevent? How does the use of *search warrants* support this rule?

3. What is the purpose of the *Miranda Warning*?

4. What do courts expect an accused person will do in return for *bail*?

Answer the Guiding Questions

5. ***Making Inferences*** How would a bill of attainder threaten a person's freedom? Provide an example.

6. ***Finding the Main Idea*** How do Fourth Amendment rights keep Americans secure in their homes?

7. **ARGUMENT** Is the death penalty cruel and unusual punishment, and therefore a violation of the Eighth Amendment? Describe your reasoning in an essay.

Issues to Debate

Can schools punish students for off-campus Internet speech?

In 1969, the Supreme Court ruled in *Tinker* v. *Des Moines* that on-campus student speech is protected by the First Amendment. In the ruling, this protection is limited. It does not extend to speech that significantly disrupts class work or school order. Nor may the speech harm the rights of others. Today, many students use technology to communicate through the Internet. Blogs, social networking sites, and other Internet-based communications blur the line between off-campus and on-campus speech. Can schools punish students for Internet speech that is created off campus?

> Computers have become a common feature in many classrooms.

Yes

In 2007, two Pennsylvania middle school students created a fake profile of their principal on a social networking site. The school claimed that the fake profile violated school policies and suspended the students. The parents of one student sued the school district superintendent. They claimed that the school district cannot punish a student for out-of-school conduct that is not disruptive. The court ruled that the fake profile violated the principal's rights. The profile was against both school policy and the law.

❝[T]he line between on-campus and off-campus speech is blurred. . . . As technology allows such access [to the Internet in school], it requires school administrators to be more concerned about speech created off campus—which almost inevitably leaks onto campus—than they would have been in years past.❞

—Judge James M. Munley, U.S. District Court,
J.S. v. *Blue Mountain School District* **(2008)**

No

In 2007, Florida high school student Katherine Evans created an online group attacking one of her teachers. On the social networking site, she asked others to express their "feelings of hatred" for the teacher. After two days, she deleted the group. Two months later, the school principal learned of the group and suspended Evans. Evans filed suit, claiming the principal had violated her right to free speech. In 2010, a federal district court denied the principal's efforts to have the case dismissed.

❝This is an important victory both for Ms. Evans and Internet free speech because it upholds the principle that the right to freedom of speech and expression in America does not depend on the technology used to convey opinions and ideas.❞

—Maria Kayanan, Associate Legal Director,
ACLU of Florida

Debating the Issue

1. **Identifying the Main Idea** How does the Internet affect school speech?

2. **Describing** What does the judge say has changed for school administrators because of greater student access to the Internet?

3. **Analyzing** What serious element did the case about the fake profile involve that the case about the online group did not?

4. **Drawing Conclusions** Do you think freedom of speech on the Internet should be limited? Explain.

Write your answers on a separate piece of paper.

1 **Writing Activity**

EXPLORING THE ESSENTIAL QUESTION
How do laws protect individual rights?

In this chapter, you learned how our laws protect us from illegal imprisonment and protect our right to be treated fairly by the government if we are accused of a crime. Review the protections you have read about. Which one do you think is most important to citizens? Explain the reasons for your choice, and give some possible consequences if we did not enjoy this protection.

2 **21st Century Skills**

DRAWING INFERENCES AND CONCLUSIONS The Supreme Court's decision in *Miranda* v. *Arizona* greatly affected the rights of the accused and the procedures used by police. Use the Internet to research the limits of the *Miranda* decision. Use the information you find to create a list of frequently asked questions (FAQs) about the *Miranda* decision. Present your FAQs and their answers to the class.

3 **Being an Active Citizen**

Our federal, state, and local legislatures pass laws that affect those they govern. In our legal system, ignorance of the law is no excuse. Your school community also has rules. Help students in your school and in your classroom understand the rules. Interview your principal and your teacher to find out what rules students are expected to follow. Create a chart showing the rules for your school and class. Make the chart clear and engaging. Post it in a visible place in the classroom.

4 **Understanding Visuals**

After the *Furman* decision in 1972, the death penalty was suspended. Some states eliminated the death penalty altogether. Most, however, rewrote their laws to comply with the Court's findings. Based on the information in the map, what generalizations can you make about the death penalty in the United States? Find your state on the map. Does your state allow the death penalty? From examining the map, write a paragraph to summarize what you know about the death penalty in the nation and your state.

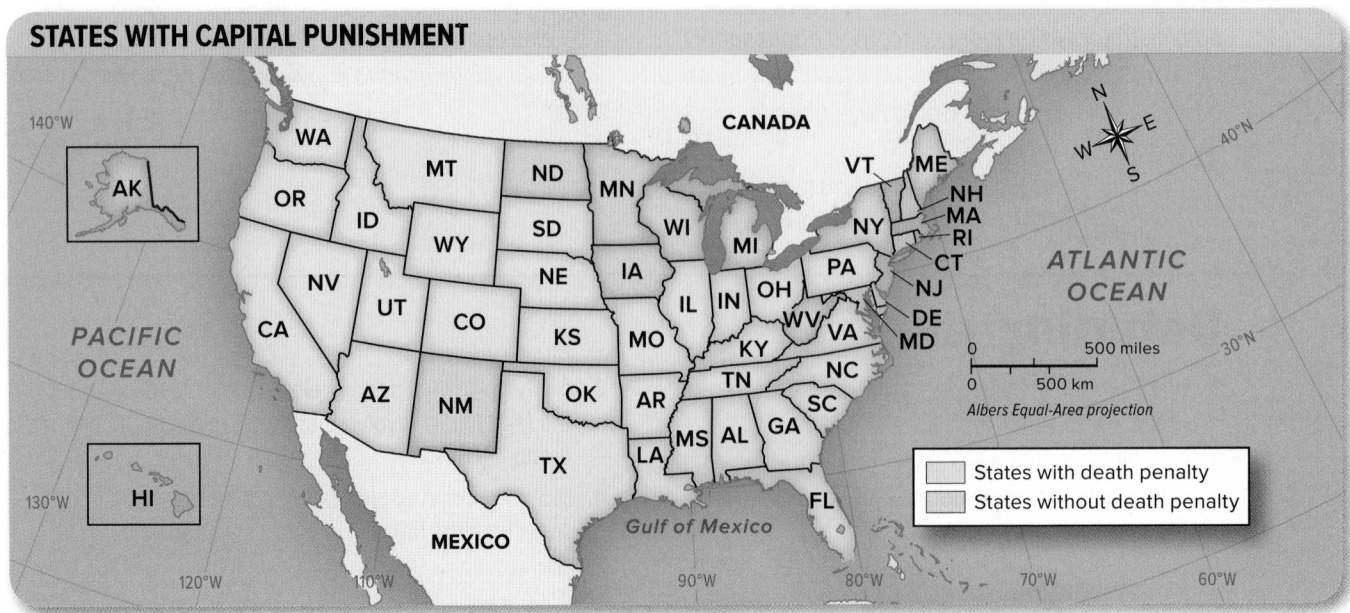

STATES WITH CAPITAL PUNISHMENT

REVIEW THE GUIDING QUESTIONS

Directions: Choose the best answer for each question.

1 What is the most important influence on the American legal system?

A. Roman law

B. the Justinian Code

C. English common law

D. the Napoleonic Code

2 In addition to criminal law, what type of law are all Americans most directly affected by?

F. military law

G. civil law

H. public law

I. administrative law

3 At what point are criminal defendants no longer presumed to be innocent?

A. once the trial starts

B. once bail is put up

C. once proven guilty

D. once a search warrant is obtained

4 Under the Fourteenth Amendment, all individuals are entitled to what legal protection?

F. due process

G. double jeopardy

H. free counsel

I. indictment

5 What happens if a criminal defendant cannot afford a lawyer?

A. He or she automatically loses the case.

B. The court appoints a grand jury to investigate.

C. The court will provide a defense lawyer.

D. The defendant is released without trial.

6 Which of the following must the police have in order to obtain a search warrant from a judge?

F. bail

G. a Miranda Warning

H. habeas corpus

I. probable cause

DBQ **ANALYZING DOCUMENTS**

Directions: Analyze the excerpt and answer the questions that follow.

The Supreme Court's decision in the *Miranda* case clarified the rights of those accused of crimes.

"The warning of the right to remain silent must be accompanied by the explanation that anything said can and will be used against the individual in court. This warning is needed in order to make him aware not only of the privilege, but also of the consequences of forgoing [waiving] it."

—Supreme Court decision, *Miranda* v. *Arizona* (1966)

7 **Identifying the Main Idea** According to the Court, the consequences of waiving, or giving up, the right to be silent must be understood in order to

A. stop talking.

C. appear in court.

B. confess.

D. fully use the right.

8 **Identifying** If an individual waives his or her right to silence,

F. he or she will go to jail without bail.

G. the court will appoint a lawyer.

H. anything he or she says can be used in court.

I. he or she must confess to the crime.

SHORT RESPONSE

"If any one steal cattle . . , if it belong to a god or to the court, the thief shall pay thirtyfold therefor; if they belonged to a freed man of the king he shall pay tenfold; if the thief has nothing with which to pay he shall be put to death."

—Code of Hammurabi, c. 1760 B.C.

9 In the Code, why is more than one fine set for stealing livestock?

10 Explain how this section of the Code of Hammurabi violates the individual rights we enjoy under the U.S. Constitution.

EXTENDED RESPONSE

11 **Informative/Explanatory** You have learned about many kinds of laws in the United States. Write a paragraph about the legal system. Briefly describe criminal, civil, constitutional, and military laws.

Need Extra Help?

If You've Missed Question	**1**	**2**	**3**	**4**	**5**	**6**	**7**	**8**	**9**	**10**	**11**
Review Lesson	1	1	2	2	2	2	2	2	1	1	1, 2

Civil and Criminal Law

netw⊕rks

There's More Online about civil and criminal law.

CHAPTER 15

ESSENTIAL QUESTIONS • *Why does conflict develop?*
• *How can governments ensure citizens are treated fairly?*

The Story Matters...

What do you get when you purchase a movie ticket? The ticket allows you to watch a film on a big screen and listen to the dialogue and the music on a quality sound system. You can sit in a comfortable seat. You can share the experience with other moviegoers—all of whom have purchased tickets just as you did. The man in the photo, however, is not just watching a movie in this theater. He is secretly recording the film. He is also breaking the law.

The sale of illegally made copies of movies, also known as pirated or bootlegged videos, is a big problem for the entertainment industry. The money that is lost to such pirating amounts to billions of dollars yearly. The penalty for any crime depends on how the crime is classified under the law. Federal law considers movie pirating to be the theft of someone's property. People convicted of this crime face fines and imprisonment.

◄ *This man may face a large fine as well as imprisonment if he is convicted of illegally recording a film.*

PHOTO: Dan Bannister/Getty Images

Real-Life Civics

> **PRISONS** Prisons are usually scary-looking places. In this California prison, barbed wire tops high metal fences. Guard towers loom over grim-looking walls. To visitors, the prison seems to say: Keep out! But those locked inside are clearly meant to stay there—until they have served their time for the crimes they have committed.

Society runs prisons where criminals serve sentences. All criminal acts, both minor and serious, have a range of consequences. Victims of crimes may suffer harm to their body or mind, or the loss of money or property. The courts decide on the kind of punishment that people who break criminal laws will get. Those who are found guilty of minor acts may get fines or short prison sentences. The more serious the crime, the tougher the sentence will be.

Prisons often use fences, electronic sensors, razor wire, and cameras to prevent escape.

Convicted criminals sometimes do supervised community service to repay society.

PHOTOS: (l) AP Photo/Rich Pedroncelli, File; (tr) Roger Bamber/Alamy

> **COMMUNITY SERVICE** Convicted criminals sometimes do community service as part of a prison sentence or in place of time spent in prison. Some prisons use work programs to try to change a convict's behavior. Inmates perform community service outside prison, such as painting public buildings or picking up litter along highways. These jobs help inmates to repay society and prepare them to reenter the world outside prison. For some minor or nonviolent crimes, a judge may sentence a convicted person to pay a fine and do community service instead of serving time in prison. The person spends a certain number of hours doing supervised tasks similar to those in prison work programs.

CIVIC LITERACY

★ ★ ★ ★

Classifying What different types of punishment may a person be subject to if a court decides he or she is guilty?

Your Opinion Do you think community service is a reasonable punishment for those who have been convicted of minor crimes? Explain your answer.

networks

There's More Online!

☑ **GRAPHIC ORGANIZER**
Steps in a Civil Lawsuit

☑ **CHART**
Civil Cases

Lesson 1
Civil Law

IT MATTERS BECAUSE

Civil law makes it possible for people to settle disputes in an orderly way.

Types of Civil Law

GUIDING QUESTION *What is civil law?*

If you watch crime shows on television, you have an idea of what criminal law involves. Criminal law deals with people who have been accused of acts that harm society. If identified, the suspects are arrested and tried for those acts. If found guilty, they are punished.

Another type of law does not involve crimes against society. Instead, it involves disputes. Those disputes might be between two or more individuals, a person and a company, two or more companies, or a person or a company and the government. This type of law is called civil law. These disputes arise when people think they have been harmed by someone else's actions.

Like criminal law, civil law can involve a court case. In a criminal trial, the government prosecutes a person accused of a crime. In civil law, the court case stems from a lawsuit. Most lawsuits fall into one of the four branches of civil law. Those branches are contract law, property law, family law, and personal injury law. Each deals with particular kinds of legal disputes.

PHOTO: (tl) Fuse/Getty Images; (tc) jazzminebeaulieu/Getty Images

Reading**HELP**DESK

Taking Notes: *Sequencing*

As you read, complete a diagram like this one to show the steps in a civil lawsuit.

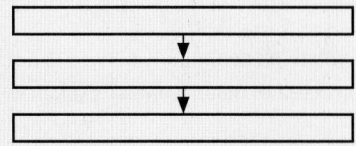

Content Vocabulary

- **contract**
- **tort**
- **negligence**
- **plaintiff**
- **defendant**
- **complaint**
- **damages**
- **summons**
- **discovery**

Contract Law

A **contract** is an agreement between two or more parties to exchange something of value. If one party to a contract fails to keep his or her promise, the other party can sue him or her. In that suit, the second party claims to have been injured in some way by the failure of the other to follow the contract.

You might think that a contract has to be written, but many everyday actions result in contracts without signing any papers. For example, when a server at a restaurant takes your order for food, a contract is formed. Each party has promised the other something of value. The restaurant has promised food. You have promised to pay for the meal.

The contract between you and the restaurant is an example of an oral, or spoken, contract. Many contracts, of course, are written. In fact, some contracts must be written. For example, a contract for the sale of anything worth more than $500 cannot be enforced unless it is in writing. Written contracts can be complex. Parties to contracts should review them carefully before signing them.

Property Law

Property law includes rules that must be followed in buying and selling land or a building. An owner must have papers proving that he or she has the right to sell or transfer the property.

Property law also covers the way property is cared for and used. For instance, there are laws requiring owners who rent out their property to keep it in good repair for the renter's use.

Why It MATTERS

Keeping Order

One of the key responsibilities of government is to maintain order. Having a body of civil law to resolve disputes is one way it does so. Think of the kinds of issues that are faced in civil law. They include disputes over contracts, about property rights, between family members, or over claims that one person is responsible for injuring another. Write a paragraph explaining what might happen in these kinds of disputes without a legal process to handle them.

PHOTO: Fuse/Getty Images

Buying a home makes a person, or a couple, a property owner. It is a complex process with many legal papers that need to be signed.

▶ **CRITICAL THINKING**
Speculating If you were buying property, would you hire a lawyer to help you with the process? Why or why not?

Reading Strategy: *Organizing*

Take notes on the types of civil law by making a chart with a column that defines each type and another column that has examples of types of cases.

contract a set of promises between agreeing parties that is enforceable by law

Home owners may be liable for a visitor's injury based on negligence if the visitor slips on snow or ice, falls, and suffers an injury.

▶ CRITICAL THINKING
Drawing Conclusions Why is it a good idea for home owners to clean snow and ice off their property after a storm?

At the same time, renters have a responsibility to take care of the property while they use it. Disputes can arise over these responsibilities. For example, it is the owner's responsibility to repair a leaky roof on a rented house. But what if the renter does not tell the owner about a leak until major damage has occurred? Who should pay for the repairs then? If the owner and renter cannot agree, a court must decide.

Family Law

Another area of civil law involves rules applied to family relationships. This area involves matters such as birth, adoption, marriage, divorce, and death.

How a divorcing couple divides the property they once owned together is a matter of civil law. So is the question of how the former spouses will divide the right to take care of any children they have. Deaths sometimes lead to property disputes. For example, people might disagree about what goods each should receive when a family member dies. Disagreements over these issues often end up in court.

Personal Injury

The fourth branch of civil law involves wrongful actions that cause injury to another person or damage to his or her property. These cases are called **torts.** Suppose someone throws a ball that breaks a window and broken glass flying from the window cuts another person. The injured person could sue the one who threw the ball to make him or her pay for the injury.

There are two types of torts. An intentional tort is a deliberate act that results in harm. Throwing the ball at the window might qualify as this type of tort. The other type is called **negligence** (NEH•glih•JUHNTS). Negligence is careless or reckless behavior. It occurs when someone does something that a reasonable person would not have done. Playing ball close to a window could be seen as negligence. Negligence also exists when a person *fails* to do something that a reasonable person would have done. Disagreement over whether or not an action is reasonable can lead to a lawsuit.

☑ PROGRESS CHECK

Summarizing Why do people file lawsuits?

PHOTO: jazzminebeaullieu/Getty Images

tort a wrongful act, other than breaking a contract, for which an injured party has the right to sue

negligence a lack of proper care and attention

plaintiff the person who files a lawsuit

defendant the person who is being sued

complaint a formal notice that a lawsuit has been brought

The Legal Process in Civil Cases

GUIDING QUESTION *What legal procedures are followed in civil lawsuits?*

As you have seen, many disputes end up in lawsuits. Each lawsuit involves at least two parties. The person who files a lawsuit is the **plaintiff.** The person being sued is the **defendant.**

The process begins when the plaintiff's lawyer files a **complaint** with the court. The complaint states the wrong that the plaintiff says the defendant committed and how the plaintiff was harmed. A complaint may ask the court to order the defendant to pay the plaintiff a sum of money, called **damages,** to repay the plaintiff for the loss. It may ask the court to order the plaintiff to take a certain action, such as honoring a contract.

When a complaint is filed, the court sends out a **summons.** This document tells the defendant that he or she is being sued. It also says when and where the defendant must appear in court.

Before the Trial

The defendant's lawyer may **respond** to, or answer, the complaint by filing an answer to the charges. In the next step, the lawyers on each side build their cases. They check the facts, question possible witnesses, and gather evidence about the dispute. This process is called **discovery.**

Sometimes the parties agree to the terms to settle a suit. This agreement is called a settlement. The parties might agree on a sum of money the defendant will pay the plaintiff. In return, the plaintiff agrees to drop the lawsuit. The parties might also agree that the defendant will act to fulfill the terms of a contract.

Settlements can take place at any time in the process, including after a trial has begun. A high percentage of civil cases are settled rather than being decided by a trial. Settling a case avoids the substantial expense of a trial.

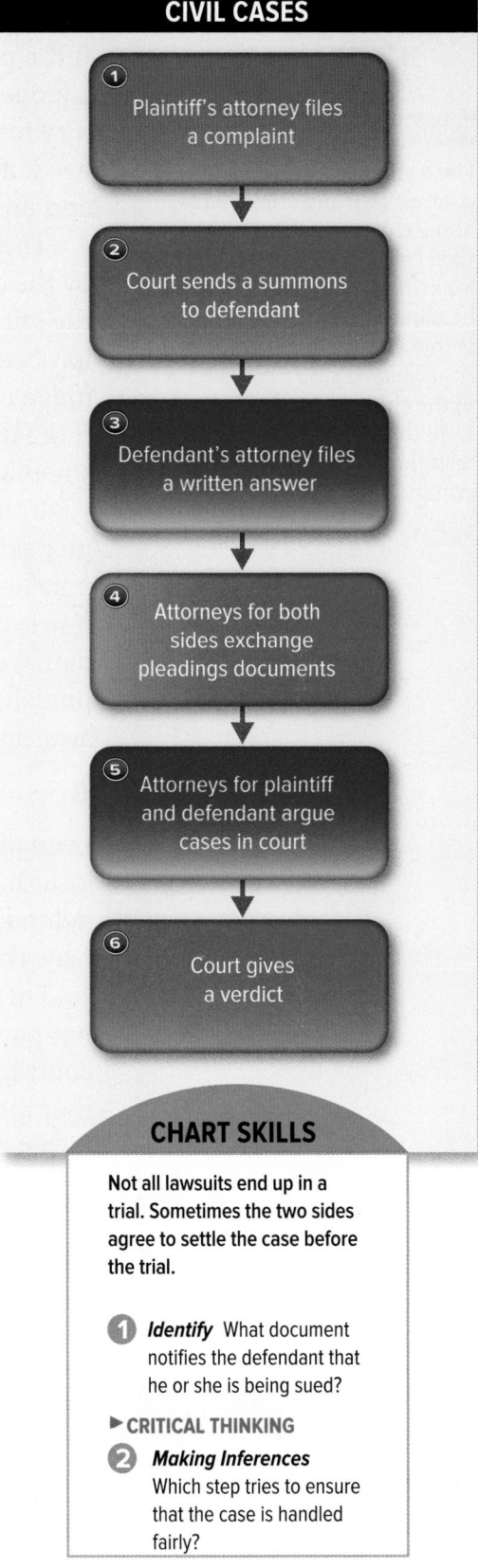

CIVIL CASES

1. Plaintiff's attorney files a complaint
2. Court sends a summons to defendant
3. Defendant's attorney files a written answer
4. Attorneys for both sides exchange pleadings documents
5. Attorneys for plaintiff and defendant argue cases in court
6. Court gives a verdict

CHART SKILLS

Not all lawsuits end up in a trial. Sometimes the two sides agree to settle the case before the trial.

1. **Identify** What document notifies the defendant that he or she is being sued?

► **CRITICAL THINKING**

2. **Making Inferences** Which step tries to ensure that the case is handled fairly?

---

damages money ordered by a court to be paid for injuries or losses suffered

summons a notice directing someone to appear in court to answer a complaint or a charge

Academic Vocabulary

respond to give a spoken or written answer

discovery a process by which lawyers have the opportunity to check facts and gather evidence before a trial

Compare and Contrast

Use a chart to compare and contrast civil and criminal law. Make column headings for *Civil Law* and *Criminal Law*. Make rows with these headings: *Cause of dispute; Person on trial; Person making complaint; Possible outcomes*. Fill in the chart with information from this lesson and as you read the next lesson on criminal law.

The Trial

If the parties do not settle, the suit continues to trial. Most likely, a judge will decide the case. However, either side can ask for a jury to hear the case and decide who wins. Even when a jury is used, a judge presides over the case. He or she maintains order and ensures that both sides are treated equally under the law.

The plaintiff presents his or her evidence first, followed by the defendant. Lawyers for each side have a chance to question the witnesses offered by the other side. When all the evidence has been presented, both sides summarize their case. Finally, the judge or jury issues a verdict, or decision, in favor of one party. If the defendant wins, the plaintiff gets nothing. In fact, he or she might have to pay the court costs.

If the plaintiff wins and damages are involved, the judge or jury sets the amount of damages the defendant must pay. This may be less money than the plaintiff requested. In some cases, however, the judge or jury might award the plaintiff punitive damages. This is additional money the defendant must pay to punish him or her for bad conduct. Punitive damages are often awarded for intentional torts.

Appeals and Other Actions

Even after the verdict is given, a case might not be over. The loser has the right to appeal the case to a higher court. A defendant who lost may ask to have the verdict overturned or to have the amount of damages reduced.

Further action also might be needed if the defendant does not pay damages. In such cases, the plaintiff must go back to court to obtain a court order to force payment. A judge can order that the money be deducted from the defendant's paycheck by his or her employer. The judge can also order that property owned by the defendant be seized and sold to pay the plaintiff.

✓ PROGRESS CHECK

Defining What are damages?

LESSON 1 REVIEW

Review Vocabulary

1. Write a sentence or two about civil law that explains the meaning of *tort* and *negligence*.

2. Explain the meaning of *plaintiff* and *defendant* by describing their roles in a lawsuit.

3. Write a sentence that explains the connection between a *complaint* and a *summons*.

Answer the Guiding Questions

4. *Identifying* What are the four main categories of civil law?

5. *Hypothesizing* How could the discovery process lead to a settlement in a civil case?

6. **ARGUMENT** In your opinion, should civil cases be tried before a jury? Explain why or why not.

networks

There's More Online!

☑ **GRAPHIC ORGANIZER**
Steps in a Criminal Case

☑ **INFOGRAPHIC**
U.S. Regional Crime Rates

☑ **CHARTS**
Steps in a Criminal Case
Sentencing Options

☑ **GAME**

Lesson 2
Criminal Law

ESSENTIAL QUESTIONS • *Why does conflict develop?*
• *How can governments ensure citizens are treated fairly?*

IT MATTERS BECAUSE

When you are an adult, you will probably be called at some time to serve on a jury. When that time comes, knowing about criminal law will make you a better juror.

Crime and Punishment

GUIDING QUESTION *What does criminal law involve?*

Have you ever done something at home for which you were punished? What kind of punishment did you receive? You may have thought that the punishment was harsh. That punishment was probably minimal compared to those given to persons convicted of crimes. Those guilty of serious crimes can be sentenced to many years in prison—even the rest of their lives.

A **crime** is any act that harms people or society and that breaks a criminal law. Shoplifting, purposely setting a fire, stealing a car, and murder are crimes. Crimes are seen as actions that harm society because they violate the social order.

Each state has a **penal** (PEE•nuhl) **code.** This document lists the state's criminal laws and the punishments that can be given to those found guilty of each crime. The federal government also has a penal code. Robbing a bank or carrying out an act of terrorism is a federal crime, for instance. Most crimes, though, break state laws. For that reason, most criminal cases are tried in state courts, and most inmates are in state prisons.

PHOTO: (tl) Spencer Grant/Alamy; (tc) David R. Frazier/Photolibrary - Inc.; (tr) AP Images

Reading **HELP**DESK

Taking Notes: *Sequencing*

As you read, create a diagram showing what takes place in a criminal case after an arrest is made.

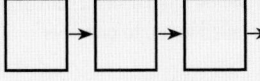

Content Vocabulary

- crime
- penal code
- misdemeanor
- felony
- sentence
- prosecution
- plea bargaining
- cross-examination

Property crime 1960.4
Violent crime 335.1

Property crime 2,560.4
Violent crime 333.4

Property crime 3,094.8
Violent crime 403.5

Property crime 2,885.4
Violent crime 367.4

0   500 1,000 1,500 2,000 2,500 3,000 3,500
CRIMES PER 100,000 INHABITANTS

Source: Federal Bureau of Investigation, Crime in the United States, 2013

Northeast   Midwest   South   West

INFOGRAPHIC

Local, state, and federal law- enforcement personnel compare crime rates in different areas to understand trends and to see what kind of police response is needed.

▶ **CRITICAL THINKING**

1 *Analyzing Visuals* Which region of the country has the highest rate of property crime? Of violent crime?

2 *Applying* What are two examples of violent crimes?

Types of Crime

There are two broad categories of crimes based on how serious they are. **Misdemeanors** (MIHS•dih•MEE•nuhrz) are minor crimes for which a person can be fined a small sum of money or jailed for up to a year. Simple assault—threatening to physically attack someone or trying to carry out such an attack—is a misdemeanor. So is theft of something worth less than $100.

More serious crimes are called felonies. **Felonies** are crimes that are punishable by more than one year in prison. Examples are kidnapping and most types of assault. Homicide—killing another person—is the most serious felony. Homicides come in various types. Involuntary manslaughter happens when someone is killed but not intentionally. Murder is intended. Murder may result in the most extreme punishment: death.

Some crimes can be either a misdemeanor or a felony. As you have read, theft of something worth less than $100 is usually a misdemeanor. Stealing something worth more than that amount is typically a felony. Vandalism is the crime of damaging someone else's property on purpose. Like theft, this crime can be a misdemeanor or a felony. It depends on the amount of damage done.

Reading**HELP**DESK

crime an act that breaks a law and causes harm to people or to society in general

penal code a state's written criminal laws

misdemeanor minor crime for which a person can be fined a small sum of money or jailed for up to one year

felony more serious crime such as murder, rape, kidnapping, or robbery

Crimes can also be grouped as being against property or against people. Theft and vandalism are crimes against property. Assault and murder are crimes against people. Crimes against people are seen as more serious because they cause direct harm to a person. The difference between theft and robbery is an **illustration,** or example, of the way these two types of crime are seen. Stealing something from a store is theft. It may be a misdemeanor. Taking something from a person by force or threat is robbery. That crime is almost always a felony. Crimes against people are also called violent crimes.

Punishment for Crimes

In general, the more serious the crime is, the harsher the punishment. Most criminal laws set minimum and maximum penalties for each type of crime. This gives a judge some leeway in deciding each case because the circumstances of each case will differ. Judges may give different **sentences,** or punishments, for the same crime because of the different circumstances in the two cases.

Some prisoners become eligible for parole, or early release, after serving part of their sentence. If parole is **granted,** or allowed, the person must regularly report to a parole officer for the remainder of the sentence.

The Purposes of Punishment

Prison sentences have several purposes. One is simply to punish the person so he or she can pay back society. A second function is to protect society by locking up a dangerous person. Third, punishment serves as a warning to keep other people from committing crimes. Finally, punishment can help criminals change their behavior. Prisoners may take part in counseling, job training, and educational programs to help them gain skills they need to become responsible members of society after they are released.

✓ **PROGRESS CHECK**

Classifying What are the two ways of classifying crimes?

PHOTO: Spencer Grant/Alamy

In some prisons, prisoners who have not completed their education can take classes and earn a diploma.

▶ **CRITICAL THINKING**

Analyzing What is the purpose of providing programs like schooling and counseling for prisoners?

sentence the punishment given to someone found guilty of committing a crime

Academic Vocabulary

illustration an example that helps make something clear

grant to allow

Police take the fingerprints of each person they arrest. Each person has a unique set of fingerprints that do not change over his or her lifetime.

▶ **CRITICAL THINKING**
Making Inferences How might police use fingerprints in investigating a crime like a robbery?

Criminal Case Procedure

GUIDING QUESTION *What are the legal procedures in a criminal law case?*

At each step in a criminal case, the rights of the person suspected or accused of a crime are protected by the Bill of Rights. The government must follow the rules of due process to treat a suspect fairly. In criminal cases, the government is the plaintiff. It is called the **prosecution.** In this role, the government starts the legal process against the defendant.

Arrest and Booking

Criminal cases begin when police believe a crime has been committed. The police must gather enough evidence to convince a judge to order the arrest of the person they believe committed the crime. The judge then issues an arrest warrant. The warrant lists the suspect's name and the crime. When the police make an arrest, they must advise the accused of his or her right to remain silent and the right to have an attorney.

The suspect is then taken to the police station for booking. Booking involves making a record of the arrest. The suspect is usually photographed and fingerprinted during this process.

The Preliminary Hearing

A short time after booking, the police must bring the suspect before a judge to be charged. At this stage, the prosecution must show the judge that they have probable cause—a good reason—for believing that the accused committed the crime. If so, the process continues. The judge explains the charges to the suspect. If the suspect cannot afford a lawyer, the judge appoints one. A defense lawyer's job is to speak on behalf of the accused person.

If the crime is a misdemeanor, the suspect enters a plea at this time. If the plea is guilty, the judge sentences him or her. If the suspect pleads not guilty, the judge sets a date for a trial.

If the crime is a felony, the suspect enters no plea at this point. Instead, the judge sets a date for a hearing to learn more about the case. The judge then either sends the accused back to jail or releases him or her. The judge may require the suspect to post bail, which means leaving a sum of money with the court until the trial. The judge may choose to release the person on his or her own recognizance, or control. In this case, the suspect promises in writing to appear in court.

PHOTO: David R. Frazier/Photolibrary - Inc.

prosecution the government in its role as the party who starts the legal proceedings against someone accused of a crime

plea bargaining the process in which a defendant agrees to plead guilty to a less serious crime in order to receive a lighter sentence

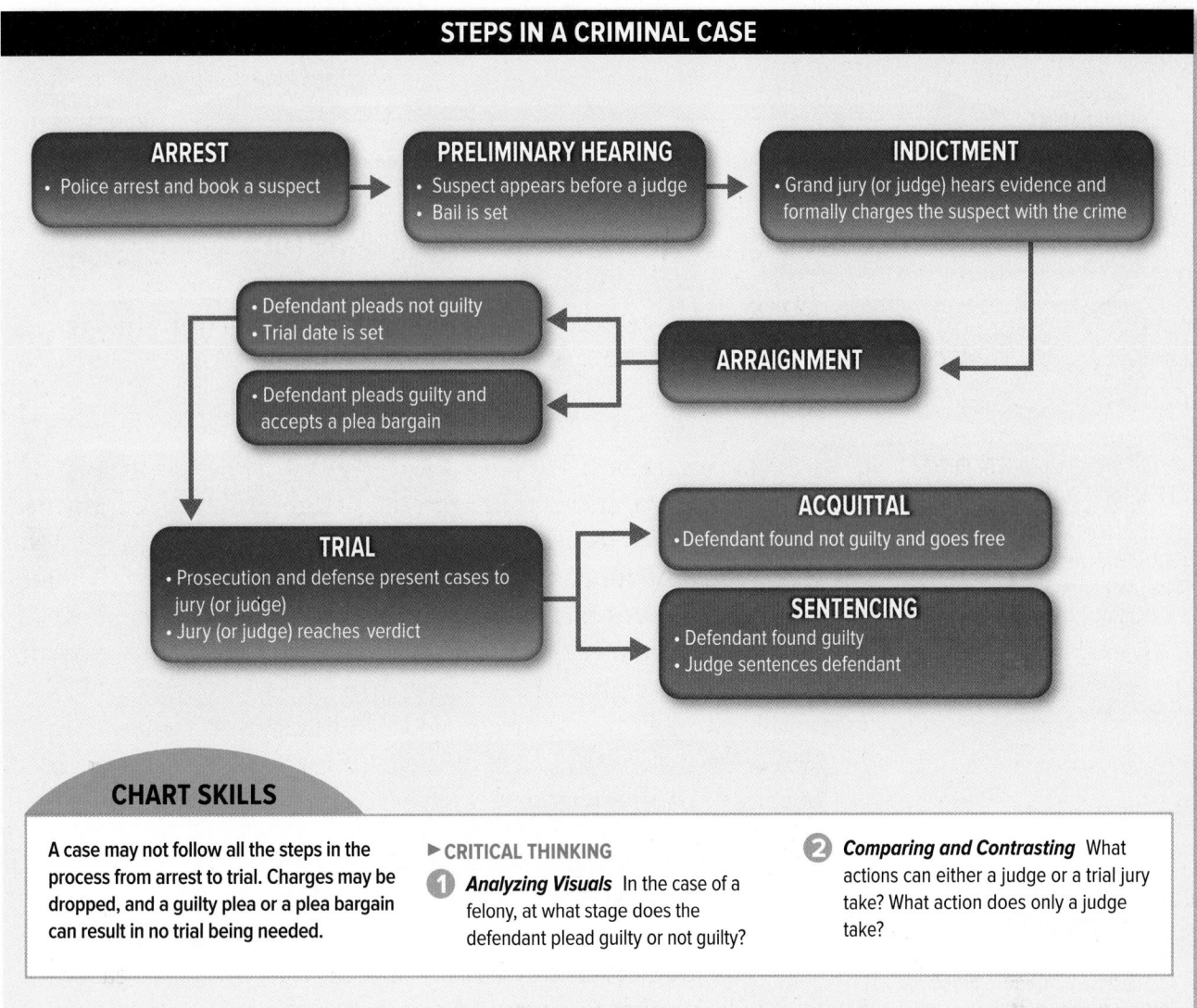

STEPS IN A CRIMINAL CASE

ARREST
• Police arrest and book a suspect

PRELIMINARY HEARING
• Suspect appears before a judge
• Bail is set

INDICTMENT
• Grand jury (or judge) hears evidence and formally charges the suspect with the crime

ARRAIGNMENT

• Defendant pleads not guilty
• Trial date is set

• Defendant pleads guilty and accepts a plea bargain

TRIAL
• Prosecution and defense present cases to jury (or judge)
• Jury (or judge) reaches verdict

ACQUITTAL
• Defendant found not guilty and goes free

SENTENCING
• Defendant found guilty
• Judge sentences defendant

CHART SKILLS

A case may not follow all the steps in the process from arrest to trial. Charges may be dropped, and a guilty plea or a plea bargain can result in no trial being needed.

▶ CRITICAL THINKING

1 *Analyzing Visuals* In the case of a felony, at what stage does the defendant plead guilty or not guilty?

2 *Comparing and Contrasting* What actions can either a judge or a trial jury take? What action does only a judge take?

Indictment, Arraignment, and Pleas

The next step is to indict the accused, or charge him or her with the crime. In many states, a grand jury must take this step. Other states allow judges to do so. The judge may think the evidence against the accused is not strong enough to bring charges. If so, he or she will dismiss the case.

If the case is not dismissed, arraignment follows. With a felony, the accused pleads guilty or not guilty at this point. A guilty plea ends the case. The judge will issue a sentence. If the defendant pleads not guilty, the judge sets a date for the trial.

The prosecution and defense lawyers may discuss **plea bargaining**. In plea bargaining, the prosecution agrees to charge the defendant with a less serious crime in return for a plea of guilty. If the two sides reach an agreement, a trial is not needed.

Plea bargaining saves the government the time and expense of a trial. For the defendant, it usually means a lighter sentence than if he or she were to be convicted of the original crime. Most criminal cases end through plea bargaining.

SEVERE PUNISHMENT ←————————————————————→ MILDER PUNISHMENT

EXECUTION
- Convicted person is sentenced to die; this form of punishment is not permitted in some states.

IMPRISONMENT
- Convicted person is sentenced to jail or prison.

WORK RELEASE
- Convicted person works in the community, but returns to jail at night or on weekends.

HOUSE ARREST
- Sentence is served at home; the person must wear an electronic device that allows authorities to track his or her location.

PROBATION
- Convicted person is released, but monitored by a probation officer.

SUSPENDED SENTENCE
- Sentence does not have to be served unless the person gets into more trouble with the law.

FINE
- Convicted person pays the government a sum of money set by the court.

RESTITUTION
- Convicted person pays back or makes up for whatever loss was suffered by the victim of the crime or the victim's family.

COMMUNITY SERVICE
- Convicted person completes a certain number of hours of unpaid, supervised work that benefits the local community.

CHART SKILLS

These sentences are organized from least to most severe. All these sentencing options are not necessarily available for each crime.

▶ CRITICAL THINKING

1. *Analyzing Visuals* Which sentences involve monetary punishments?

2. *Making Inferences* What do you think would happen to someone who broke the terms of probation? Why?

The Trial

Defendants in felony cases have a right to a jury trial. However, most choose to be tried by the judge. If the defendant asks for a jury trial, the first step is to choose the jurors.

As the trial begins, the lawyers for each side make opening statements outlining their cases. The prosecution presents its case, followed by the defense. Each side offers evidence and calls witnesses. Witnesses give their testimony by answering the questions from each side. After each witness testifies, the other side is allowed to ask questions. This second set of questions is called **cross-examination.**

After both sides have presented their case, each makes a closing statement. Then the judge instructs the jury, if there is one, by explaining how the law applies to the case.

Reading HELP DESK

Reading Strategy: *Activating Prior Knowledge*

Note the order in which the two sides present their arguments. Think about the order followed in a civil trial. How is the sequence in the two kinds of trials related?

cross-examination the questioning of a witness at a trial or hearing to check or discredit the witness's testimony

The Verdict, Sentencing, and Appeals

If a jury is used, the members of the jury then go to a room to review the evidence and arguments given by the two sides in the case. These deliberations, or discussions, are secret. The jury does not have a time limit for reaching a verdict. Jurors can discuss the case as long as they need to.

When they are ready, the jurors vote on whether the defendant is guilty or not guilty. American law is based on the idea that a person is innocent until proven guilty. To find the accused guilty, the jury must be convinced beyond a reasonable doubt that the accused committed the crime. In nearly all states, the vote must be unanimous. That is, every member of the jury must agree. In a federal district court, the jury's decision must also be unanimous for a conviction. If a jury cannot reach a verdict, even after many votes, the judge will declare a mistrial. A mistrial means no decision—the accused person is found neither guilty nor innocent. The prosecution must then decide whether to try the defendant again.

If the defendant is found not guilty, he or she is set free. This outcome is called an acquittal. If the verdict is guilty, the judge sets a court date for sentencing. If the crime is a serious one, the judge may hold a hearing on the defendant's background. The defendant's family history, any previous criminal record, and other factors may influence the judge in sentencing. Victims of the crime may be allowed to make statements at a sentencing hearing. The judge can take these statements into account as well.

People found guilty of felonies often appeal the verdict to a higher court. The appeals court does not try the case again, however. It only decides whether the defendant's rights were violated or if the judge made errors during the trial.

☑ **PROGRESS CHECK**

Explaining Why are most criminal cases settled without going to trial?

LESSON 2 REVIEW

Review Vocabulary

1. Use the following terms in a few sentences about criminal law: *crime*, *penal code*, and *sentence*.

2. What are the differences between *misdemeanors* and *felonies*?

Answer the Guiding Questions

3. *Explaining* Why are some actions defined as crimes?

4. *Sequencing* What six steps occur in a criminal case between arrest of a suspect and sentencing?

5. **ARGUMENT** Plea bargaining is controversial. Some say it is needed for the justice system to work. Others say it allows criminals to avoid punishment. Choose one side of this debate. Write a paragraph to persuade readers to see your point of view.

Gideon v. Wainwright

Today we take for granted that every defendant, rich or poor, will have a lawyer. But this was not always true. It took an inmate's appeal to the U.S. Supreme Court to ensure this right for all Americans.

Clarence Earl Gideon

Background of the Case

The Sixth Amendment to the Constitution says that a person accused of a crime has the right to "the assistance of counsel [a lawyer] for his defence." What if a defendant is too poor to afford a lawyer? In 1938, the Supreme Court had ruled that in federal trials, the government had to provide a defense lawyer for those defendants. Just four years later, however, the Supreme Court refused to apply this right to cases in state courts. The Court said each state could make its own rules.

In 1961, Clarence Earl Gideon was arrested for breaking into a pool hall in Florida. Gideon could not afford a lawyer. At his trial, he asked the judge to name one for him. The judge refused. The judge was following Florida law. It required the state to provide lawyers only in death penalty cases. Since Gideon did not face the death penalty, that rule did not apply.

Gideon was not well educated and had no training in the law. He did not do a good job of defending himself at his trial. He was found guilty and sentenced to five years in prison.

From his cell, Gideon handwrote an appeal to the U.S. Supreme Court. In it, he argued that a person's Sixth Amendment right to an attorney should not depend on being able to afford one. The Court agreed to hear the appeal.

The Decision

In March 1963, the Supreme Court issued its ruling in *Gideon* v. *Wainwright*. (Louie Wainwright was the head of Florida state prisons.) All nine justices agreed. Justice Hugo Black was the author of the Court's decision.

❝[A]ny person haled [forced] into court, who is too poor to hire a lawyer, cannot be assured a fair trial unless counsel is provided for him.❞

Justice Black went on to explain how important lawyers are:

❝That government hires lawyers to prosecute, and defendants who have money hire lawyers to defend are the strongest indications . . . that lawyers in criminal courts are necessities, not luxuries.❞

The Court ordered that Gideon be tried again, this time with a lawyer appointed to help him. In the second trial, Gideon was acquitted.

Why It Matters

As a result of Gideon, states had to provide poor defendants with a lawyer in all cases. Robert F. Kennedy, who had been attorney general of the United States, once summed up the importance of the case. Because Clarence Earl Gideon wrote his letter to the Supreme Court, Kennedy said, "the whole course of American legal history has been changed."

Analyzing the Case

1. **Identifying** What protection did the *Gideon* case guarantee?
2. **Evaluating** Do you agree with Robert F. Kennedy's view of the case? Why or why not?

netw@rks
There's More Online!

☑ **GRAPHIC ORGANIZER**
Juvenile Justice System

☑ **GRAPH**
Dropout Rates and the Risk of Going to Prison for a Crime
Juvenile Crime

☑ **CHART**
Juvenile Cases

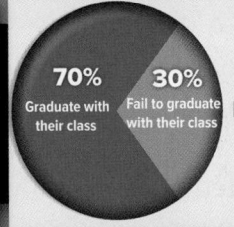
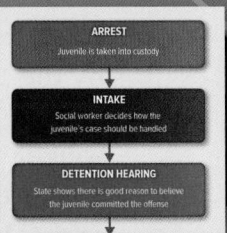

70% Graduate with their class	**30%** Fail to graduate with their class

ARREST
Juvenile is taken into custody

INTAKE
Social worker decides how the juvenile's case should be handled

DETENTION HEARING
State shows there is good reason to believe the juvenile committed the offense

Lesson 3
The Juvenile Justice System

ESSENTIAL QUESTION *How can governments ensure citizens are treated fairly?*

IT MATTERS BECAUSE

The juvenile justice system is structured differently from the adult system. This system handles cases of crimes committed by juveniles and also neglect of juveniles.

Juvenile Justice

GUIDING QUESTION *How has treatment of young criminal offenders changed?*

Do you know that at one time children who committed crimes were treated like adults? They were jailed along with adults. Long prison terms were common. So were beatings by guards.

Beginnings of a Juvenile Justice System

In the mid-1800s, some people began to believe that family failure was the reason juveniles committed crimes. They said that the parents of these children had failed to teach them proper values. The reformers called for a special court that would take over the parents' job. Instead of punishing these children as adults, this court would help them learn right from wrong. The first juvenile court with this aim was set up in Cook County (Chicago), Illinois, in 1899.

Many people supported the goal of trying to **rehabilitate** (REE•uh•BIH•luh•TAYT), or correct, a young offender's behavior. However, they also had strong feelings that children should be punished for crimes. The debate over these two aims of the juvenile justice system continues today.

PHOTO: (tl) Mikael Karlsson/Arresting Images

Reading **HELP**DESK

Taking Notes: *Explaining*

As you read, complete a chart like this one to help you understand the juvenile justice system. Add more rows as needed.

Step	Description
Custody	
Intake	

Content Vocabulary

- **rehabilitate**
- **juvenile delinquent**
- **delinquent offender**
- **status offender**
- **custody**

Changes to the System

By the 1960s, many people thought the juvenile justice system needed to be changed. They thought too much **emphasis,** or weight, was placed on punishment. In some cases, children were treated more harshly than adults who committed the same crime. In a series of decisions, the U.S. Supreme Court ruled that children have some of the same legal rights that adults have:

- the right to be told of the charges against them
- the right to an attorney
- the right to cross-examine witnesses against them
- the right to remain silent when being questioned

The Court also ruled that "guilty beyond a reasonable doubt"—the standard in adult cases—should apply to juvenile cases too.

By the 1990s, public opinion was swinging back the other way. Juvenile crime rates were rising rapidly. Public calls for law and order grew louder. As a result, state legislatures passed laws requiring harsher penalties for both juveniles and adults. Thus, many states changed their laws to make it easier for young offenders to be tried in adult courts.

Juvenile Justice Today

Every state has its own special set of laws for handling **juvenile delinquents** (JOO•vuh•NEYE•uhl dee•LIHN•kwuhnts)—the name given to young people who commit crimes. Most states consider anyone under age 18 to be a juvenile. However, some states set the age as low as 16. Anyone over the cutoff age who commits a crime will be tried as an adult in the criminal justice system. Those below that age are treated as juveniles in the justice system.

In addition, a juvenile charged with a felony such as murder can be tried as an adult in most states. Some states automatically transfer a young offender to adult court under certain conditions. In other states, the decision about where to try a juvenile is left up to the judge or the prosecutor.

Some juvenile offenders are sent to camps, where they have group sessions and other kinds of help to try to lead them away from criminal activity.

► CRITICAL THINKING
Categorizing Which goal of the juvenile criminal justice system does this approach reflect? Why do you think so?

PHOTO: Mikael Karlsson/Arresting Images

Reading**HELP**DESK

Content Vocabulary (cont.)

- **detention hearing**
- **adjudication hearing**
- **disposition hearing**

rehabilitate to correct a person's behavior

Academic Vocabulary

emphasis weight or stress

juvenile delinquent a child or teenager who commits a serious crime or repeatedly breaks the law

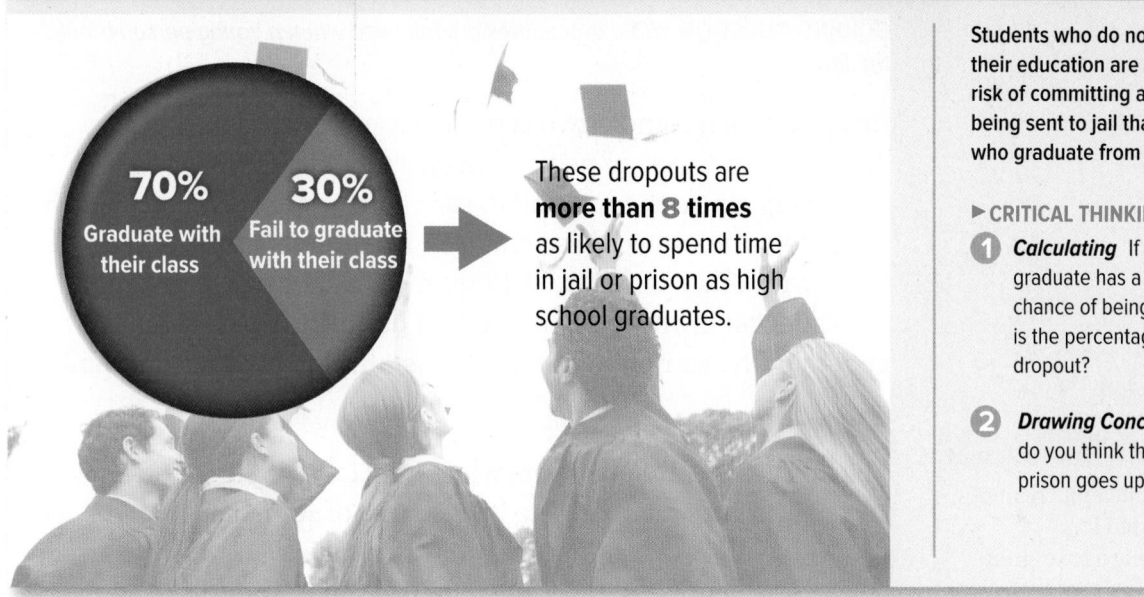

70% Graduate with their class

30% Fail to graduate with their class

These dropouts are **more than 8 times** as likely to spend time in jail or prison as high school graduates.

Students who do not complete their education are at greater risk of committing a crime and being sent to jail than students who graduate from high school.

▶ **CRITICAL THINKING**

① ***Calculating*** If a high school graduate has a one percent chance of being jailed, what is the percentage for a dropout?

② ***Drawing Conclusions*** Why do you think the risk of prison goes up in this way?

Juvenile Offenders

Children and teens currently commit many crimes each year. Some crimes are **minor,** or comparatively less important, such as shoplifting or vandalism. Others crimes, though, are serious. Some young people commit armed robbery and even murder. Studies show that children who live in poverty are more likely to get into trouble with the law. So are those who are abused, neglected, or suffer emotional or mental problems. But these factors alone do not explain why certain young people commit crimes. Many children who face these challenges never have trouble with the law. Many children or juveniles who do not have such challenges do commit crimes.

The justice system sees juveniles who commit crimes as one of two types. **Delinquent offenders** are young people who have committed acts that would be crimes if committed by adults. **Status offenders** are those who have committed acts that would *not* be crimes if done by adults. Such offenses include running away from home or skipping school. Status offenders are considered beyond the control of their parents or guardians. For this reason, the court will supervise them.

☑ **PROGRESS CHECK**

Identifying What adult rights has the Supreme Court extended to juvenile offenders?

PHOTO: Fancy Photography/Veer

Academic Vocabulary

minor of comparatively less importance

delinquent offender a youth who has committed an offense that is punishable by criminal processes

status offender a youth charged with being beyond the control of his or her legal guardian

The Juvenile Court System

GUIDING QUESTION *What procedures are followed when a young person breaks the law?*

Juvenile courts handle two types of cases—neglect and delinquency. Cases of neglect involve young people whose caregivers abuse them or fail to care for them. A juvenile court has the power to remove these children from their homes and place them with other families. Delinquency cases involve juveniles who commit crimes. The process of handling these cases is generally the same, though in each state it may differ in detail.

The Intake Process

The police have broad powers when they take a young person into custody. To take **custody** is to take charge of someone in an official way. If the offense is minor, the police can give the youth a warning and release him or her to a parent or caregiver. They also have the option of referring the case to a social service agency. They may

CHART SKILLS | JUVENILE CASES

The process for juvenile cases is somewhat similar to that for adults.

▶ CRITICAL THINKING

1. **Identify** What happens during the intake stage?

2. **Compare and Contrast** How is the adjudication hearing different from an adult's trial?

ARREST
Juvenile is taken into custody

INTAKE
Social worker decides how the juvenile's case should be handled

DETENTION HEARING
State shows there is good reason to believe the juvenile committed the offense

ADJUDICATION HEARING
Similar to an adult trial, but closed to public

DISPOSITION HEARING
Similar to sentencing hearing in an adult case

Reading **HELP**DESK

custody taking charge of someone in an official way

detention hearing a juvenile court process that is much like a preliminary hearing in adult criminal law

adjudication hearing the procedure used to determine the facts in a juvenile case

disposition hearing the final settlement and sentencing in a juvenile case

take this step if the youth needs counseling or drug treatment. If the offense is serious or the youth has a prior record, the police may turn him or her over to the juvenile court.

Once a youth is in the juvenile court system, a social worker carries out a review called intake to decide how the case should be handled. About a third of the cases leave the juvenile justice system at this point. Some are dismissed, and some are moved to adult court. Other cases go through what is called diversion. This means that the youth will receive counseling, drug treatment, or other services but will not go to court.

The Hearing Process

Those who remain in the system after intake face up to three hearings. The **detention hearing** is like the preliminary hearing for adults. The state must show that there is good reason to believe the youth committed the crime.

The **adjudication** (uh•joo•dih•KAY•shuhn) **hearing** is like an adult trial. However, it is closed to the public and usually does not include a jury. At this hearing, the attorney for the youth presents evidence, calls witnesses, and cross-examines witnesses for the state. At the end, the judge finds the youth to be innocent or "delinquent." That is like a guilty verdict.

Delinquent youths face a **disposition hearing.** This is like the sentencing hearing for adults. The judge may give the youth probation. If so, the youth is released and allowed to remain free as long as he or she meets conditions set by the judge for a period of time. If the youth completes that time with no more trouble, the charges will be dropped and removed from his or her record. If the crime was serious, the youth may be sent to an institution for young offenders. Most delinquents who are sent to an institution serve from one to three years. In some states, they can be held until age 18 or 21.

✓ PROGRESS CHECK

Comparing What steps in the juvenile court system are similar to a trial and to a sentencing hearing in the adult court system?

LESSON 3 REVIEW

Review Vocabulary

1. Explain the difference between a *delinquent offender* and a *status offender*.

2. Use the terms *rehabilitate* and *juvenile delinquent* in a sentence that shows your understanding of the juvenile justice system.

Answer the Guiding Questions

3. *Summarizing* How has the treatment of juveniles changed over time?

4. *Identifying* What options exist for treating juvenile offenders besides locking them up?

5. **ARGUMENT** Should young people ever be tried as adults? Explain why or why not.

Write your answers on a separate sheet of paper.

1 Writing Activity

EXPLORING THE ESSENTIAL QUESTIONS

Why does conflict develop?

How can governments ensure citizens are treated fairly?

In this chapter, you learned about the law and how it is enforced through the civil, criminal, and juvenile court systems. Explain in a two- or three-paragraph essay how these systems protect individuals and society, safeguard people's rights, and ensure that all people are treated fairly.

2 21st Century Skills

DEBATE SKILLS Suppose your state legislature is considering passage of a mandatory sentencing law. The bill removes from judges the power to decide the sentence for persons convicted of armed robbery. Instead, it would set a specific punishment for that crime, regardless of the circumstances of the particular case. Think about reasons for and against the new law. Then take the role of a member of the state legislature. Prepare a one-minute statement in favor of the bill. Then prepare a one-minute statement opposing it.

3 Being an Active Citizen

As a class, hold a mock trial. Choose students to serve as judge, defendant, prosecutor, and defense attorney, and 12 to be jurors. The defendant is accused of shoplifting several items from a clothing store. One student should act as the store owner and be witness for the prosecution. One should act as a friend of the accused and be a witness for the defense. Have the prosecutor-student review the details of the crime with his or her witness. The defense attorney-student should review the defense case with the defendant and his or her witness. Stage the trial, and then have the jury deliver a verdict. Discuss the experience as a class.

4 Visual Literacy

Study the photo to the right and determine what is going on in this scene. Write a paragraph describing what you think is taking place.

REVIEW THE GUIDING QUESTIONS

Directions: Choose the best answer for each question.

1 Which of these situations might lead to a lawsuit for negligence?

   A. Divorcing parents argue over custody of their children.

   B. Neighbors disagree over the boundary between their land.

   C. A worker is killed after his employer fails to repair a piece of equipment.

   D. A professional football player quits the team a year before his contract expires.

2 Which term is used to refer to a person being sued in a dispute over a contract?

   F. plaintiff

   G. defendant

   H. status offender

   I. delinquent offender

3 Which document spells out what actions are crimes and what punishments go with each one?

   A. a penal code

   B. an arrest warrant

   C. a summons

   D. a complaint

4 During a criminal case, when does a person accused of a felony enter a plea of guilty or not guilty?

   F. during booking

   G. at the preliminary hearing

   H. at arraignment

   I. during intake

5 In what situation can a juvenile be tried as an adult in most states?

   A. if the juvenile is over age 14

   B. if the juvenile is over age 15

   C. if the juvenile has a criminal record

   D. if the crime is a felony

6 What is a major goal of the juvenile justice system?

   F. to correct offenders' behavior

   G. to solve the underlying social problems causing the behavior

   H. to get repeat offenders off the streets

   I. to keep offenders in school

DBQ ANALYZING DOCUMENTS

Directions: Analyze the table and answer the questions that follow.

7 **Comparing** Which type of crime received the longest sentences in both years?

A. assault

B. robbery

C. tax law violations

D. murder

8 **Making Generalizations** Which statement is supported by the data in this table?

F. Sentencing guidelines began in 2000.

G. Sentences grew longer after 2000.

H. Sentences became shorter in 2005.

I. Mandatory sentencing laws were in effect in 2000 but not in 2005.

AVERAGE PRISON SENTENCE, SELECTED FELONY CRIMES, 2000 AND 2005

Type of Offense	Average Sentence: 2000 (months)	Average Sentence: 2005 (months)
Murder	94.2	136.8
Assault	33.0	49.5
Robbery	93.0	101.6
Fraud	23.5	26.2
Drug offenses	75.5	85.8
Tax law violations	18.5	23.4

Source: U.S. Census Bureau, *Statistical Abstract of the United States*, 2010, Table 324

SHORT RESPONSE

Florida recently considered making changes to its juvenile justice system. An editorial in a Florida paper explained why:

"Walter McNeil, secretary of the Department of Juvenile Justice, . . . said [the system] . . . has come to depend too heavily on 'incarceration.' . . . What he meant was that the system has resorted primarily to locking juvenile offenders up. All too often it means putting young people who . . . made a mistake, but are salvageable, in with young criminals headed for the adult justice system."

—*Pensacola News Journal*, November 13, 2007

9 According to McNeil, what aim of the juvenile justice system has Florida been emphasizing?

10 What negative result could arise from placing juvenile offenders with those who have committed many crimes?

EXTENDED RESPONSE

11 **Informative/Explanatory** The U.S. Constitution bans "cruel and unusual punishments." Yet the federal government and many states execute some murderers. Using what you have learned about the criminal justice system, write a paragraph analyzing why the death penalty is still in use.

TEXT: Fixing Juvenile Justice System Can Help to Repair Broken Lives, Pensacola News Journal November 13, 2007.

Need Extra Help?

If You've Missed Question	1	2	3	4	5	6	7	8	9	10	11
Review Lesson	1	1	2	2	3	3	2	2	3	3	2

Introduction to Economics

ESSENTIAL QUESTIONS · *Why and how do people make economic choices?*
· *How do economic systems influence societies?*

The Story Matters...

There is much to do before a hurricane hits . . . and much to purchase. People worry that the effects of the hurricane will lead to scarce supplies of food, gas, and other necessities. So they hurry to markets to stock up on items such as bread, milk, water, and canned food.

Lines also form at gas stations. Gasoline will be needed not only to fuel cars and trucks, but also to run generators in case of a power outage. The person in this photo is selling extra gallons of gasoline to her customer.

Because people stock up, they often buy out available supplies of goods or gas. If the effects of the storm prevent more goods from reaching the area, there may be shortages.Then people may have to pay more, or do without for a while.

◄ *A gas station attendant fills up a customer's extra gas tanks in anticipation of a hurricane.*

PHOTO: AP Photo/Chris Brandis

Real-Life Civics

▶ **RESOURCES AND PEOPLE** What sort of natural resource is shown in this photo? What products might be made from this natural resource? The logs, of course, are the resource. Workers use saws to cut down trees and turn them into logs. Drivers use trucks to move the logs out of the forest. Later, a worker will grade the logs for quality and measure them to determine their volume and value. Then the logs will become products, such as lumber for building projects or wood pulp for paper products. The natural resources—the logs—and the people involved in their processing are both important parts of an economy.

A worker measures logs stacked for processing. On a log deck like the one shown, logs may be graded for quality and measured to determine volume. ▷

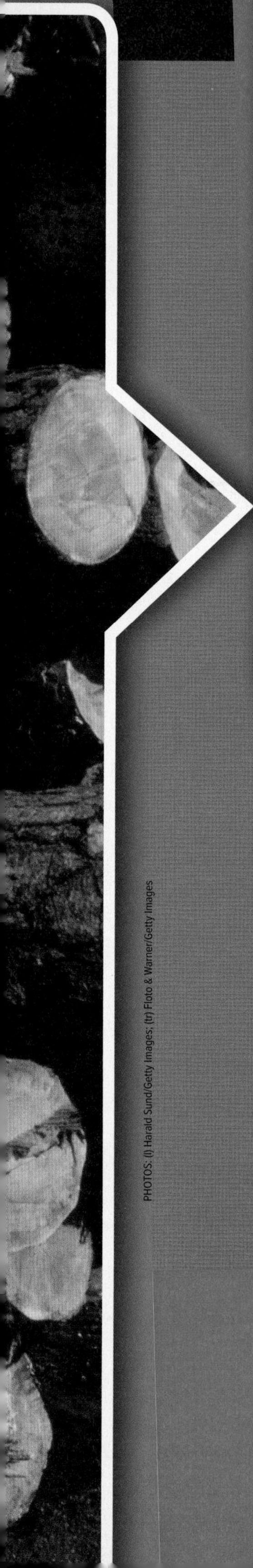

At this American auto factory, robotic machines do many of the production tasks. People are needed to run and maintain the machines and the assembly line.

TOOLS Besides natural resources and people, tools are needed to make a product. Therefore, tools play an important role in the economy. Some tools, such as hammers, paintbrushes, and sewing needles, are simple and have been in use for a very long time. Other tools are much more complex. Robotics is an example of the most recent and advanced tools used in factories today. Look at the robotic machines in this American automobile factory. They are making frames for cars and trucks and doing other tasks in producing vehicles. Since the 1980s, robots have played a major role in the automobile industry. They are fast and strong and can perform tasks that would be dangerous for people.

PHOTOS: (l) Harald Sund/Getty Images; (tr) Floto & Warner/Getty Images

CIVIC LITERACY

★ ★ ★ ★

Comparing Create a list of what is needed to make products in the lumber industry and the automobile industry. What do these industries have in common?

Your Opinion How important do you think people are to an economy? Explain your answer.

netw⊙rks

There's More Online!

☑ **GRAPHIC ORGANIZER**
The Three Kinds of Resources

☑ **POLITICAL CARTOON**
Saving Money

☑ **CHART**
Choices All Societies Face

☑ **VIDEO**

☑ **GAME**

Lesson 1

What Is Economics?

ESSENTIAL QUESTIONS • *Why and how do people make economic choices?*
• *How do economic systems influence societies?*

IT MATTERS BECAUSE

As someone who uses goods and services and will someday be a worker, you are part of the American economic system.

Our Wants and Resources

GUIDING QUESTION *What is scarcity, and how does it affect economic choices?*

After an hour of shopping, Jayna found a dress she liked. Then, as she walked toward the cash register, a pullover caught her eye. It was her favorite color, and she liked it immediately.

Jayna had a problem, though. The sweater cost as much as the dress she had already picked out. She did not have enough money to buy both. What should she do?

Jayna faced a common problem. She had to decide how to use her limited amount of money to satisfy her wants. **Wants** are desires that people have that can be met by getting a product or a service. Jayna had to make a choice between competing wants.

Unlimited Wants

If Jayna is like the rest of us, her wants are not limited to just two items. If you think about all the things you want, the list is probably so long that we could say your wants are unlimited.

Wants fall into two groups. The first is *goods* and includes things that we can touch or hold. The second is *services* and includes work that is done for us. Services include the health

PHOTO: (tl) Image Source/Getty Images; (tcl) Glow Images; (tcr) CORBIS (tr) Bloomberg via Getty Images

Reading **HELP**DESK

Taking Notes: *Comparing*

As you read, fill out a graphic organizer comparing the three kinds of resources.

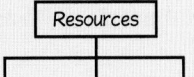

Content Vocabulary

- want
- economics
- resource
- scarcity
- economic system
- traditional economy
- market economy
- command economy
- mixed market economy

care provided by a doctor, the haircut by a hairstylist, or advice about money provided by a banker.

Limited Resources

If resources are limited, and if wants are unlimited, then we have to make choices. **Economics** is the study of how people choose to use their limited resources to satisfy their unlimited wants. **Resources** are all the things that can be used in making products or services that people want. Economists talk about three types of resources:

- *Natural resources* include a nation's land and all of the materials nature provides that can be used to make goods or services. Good soil for growing crops, trees for cutting lumber, and iron for making steel are natural resources.
- *Labor* includes workers and their abilities. The more workers a society has, the more it can produce. Workers' knowledge and skills are important, too. The more workers know and the better their skills are, the higher the quality of goods and services they produce.
- *Capital,* which includes buildings and tools, is the third type of resource. Businesses build factories to manufacture goods. Equipment such as computers can help work go more quickly. Trucks or trains are used to move goods around. Capital resources make work more productive.

The Basic Economic Problem

Jayna is not the only one who has the problem of satisfying her competing wants. This is the type of economic problem that everyone—from individuals to cities, states, and countries—faces every day.

Scarcity occurs whenever we do not have enough resources to produce all of the things we would like to have. In fact, no country has all of the resources it needs, or would like to have. Because of this, *scarcity is the basic economic problem.* The topic of economics looks at how we go about dealing with this basic economic problem.

☑ **PROGRESS CHECK**

Identifying What is the basic economic problem faced by people and nations alike?

PHOTO: Image Source/Getty Images

A woman is signing for a package that has been delivered to her home.

▶ **CRITICAL THINKING**
Analyzing Visuals What main good and main service do you see in this picture?

---

want desire individuals and nations have that can be met by getting a good or a service

economics the study of how individuals and nations make choices about ways to use scarce resources to fulfill their needs and wants

resource a thing that can be used—natural resources, labor, capital—to make goods or services

scarcity the situation of not having enough resources to satisfy all one's wants

With so many wants to satisfy, saving money is not always an easy economic choice to make.

▶ **CRITICAL THINKING**

Drawing Conclusions Why does the father joke that his child is so good at economics that he deserves a Nobel Prize?

Societies and Economic Choices

GUIDING QUESTION *What determines how societies make economic choices?*

Just as **individuals** make economic choices, so do entire countries. Scarcity is an economic problem in every nation. Will a society use its limited resources for education or for health care? Will a nation focus on helping businesses grow so they can create more jobs? Or will it spend money on training people for new jobs? Will it spend money on defense or on cleaning up the environment?

Three Basic Economic Questions

Scarcity of resources forces societies to make economic choices. These choices must answer three questions: What goods and services will be produced? How will they be produced? Who will consume, or use, them?

Each country or society has to decide *what* goods and services it will produce to meet its people's needs and wants. In making these decisions, societies consider the natural, human, and capital resources they have. A nation with plenty

Reading **HELP**DESK

Reading Strategy: *Summarizing*

When you summarize, you restate the main idea of a passage in your own words. Read the passage about the three basic economic questions. On a separate sheet of paper, write three sentences summarizing your reading.

Academic Vocabulary

individual a person

distribute to deliver

of land, fertile soil, and a long growing season is likely to use its land to grow crops. A country that has large reserves of oil might decide to produce oil.

After deciding what to produce, members of a society must decide *how* to produce these goods and services. Should they encourage businesses to build factories for large-scale manufacturing of products such as automobiles or shoes? Or should they promote small businesses and individual craftsmanship instead?

After goods and services are produced, a society must decide *who* gets the goods and services. Societies have different ways of **distributing** goods. The choices they make for distributing goods affect how the goods are consumed. For example, should new housing units be reserved for low-income people, or should they be rented to anyone who can afford them? Should new cars be given to public officials, or should they be sold to the highest bidder?

The resources of a nation are not the only reason societies answer the three basic questions differently. What a society values, or thinks is most important, also has a big influence. Some societies value individual freedom the most. Others think that economic equality is most important. Different answers to the three basic questions help a society promote the ideas its people believe are most important. The important thing to remember is that all societies face the same three problems of deciding *what* to produce, *how* to produce, and *for whom* to produce.

Societies can use many different resources for production. Land (left) is a natural resource required for the production of crops. Workers (center) checking the quality of microchips are an example of labor, or human resources. A crane (right) is a capital resource. Without cranes, international shipping and trade would be much slower and more expensive.

▶ CRITICAL THINKING
Categorizing Give examples of natural resources, labor resources, and capital resources used in growing corn. Describe what each one is for.

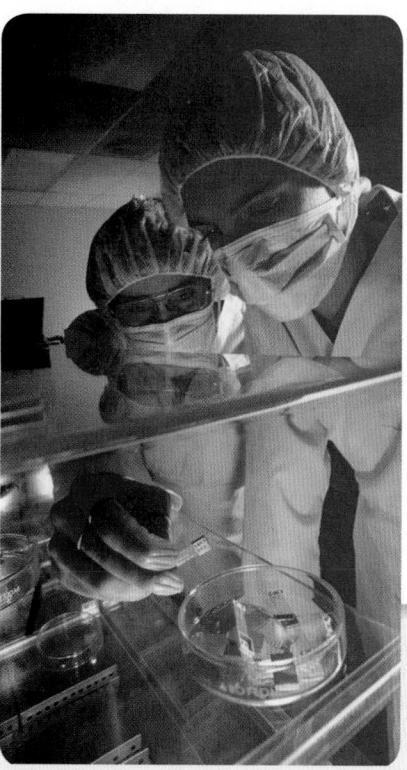

CHOICES ALL SOCIETIES FACE

Societies face the same economic problem that individuals do.

1 *Identifying* What are the three basic economic questions that societies face?

2 *Explaining* Why do societies have to make economic choices?

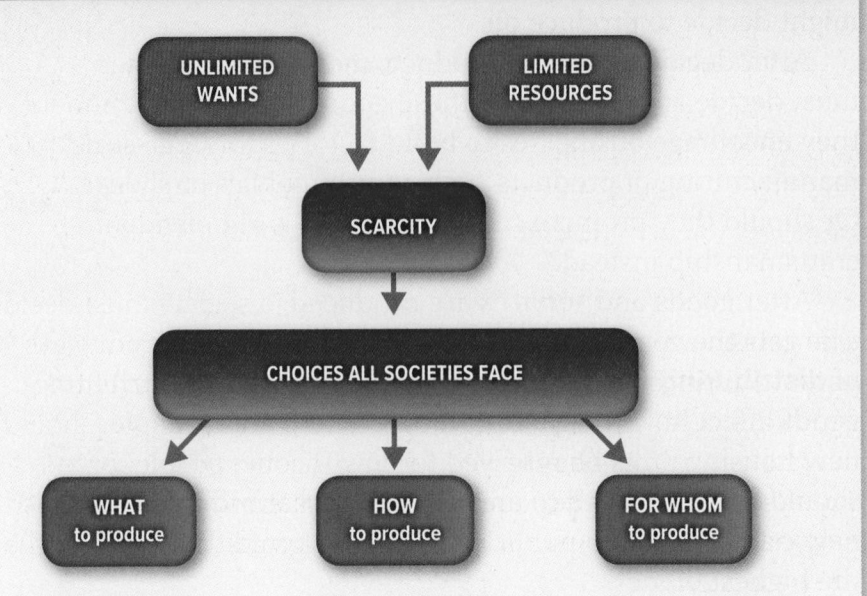

Economic Systems

Societies make economic choices or decisions in different ways. Each country has its own **economic system,** or way of producing the things people need and want. The way that a society decides the three basic economic questions determines the type of economic system the society has.

In a **traditional economy,** the economic questions are answered on the basis of habit or custom, or the way things have always been done. For example, if you were born into a family of farmers, you would grow up to be a farmer. You would also farm in the same way your parents and grandparents did. These economies generally are not very productive. They are not likely to change much over time. This means they will not adopt new and better ways of producing goods.

In a **market economy,** individuals and businesses own the resources used to produce goods and services. They answer the three economic questions on the basis of profit and price. Each person and each business makes choices based on a desire to find the most profit from using their resources. They then sell the things they produce. They use the money they receive to buy other things they want. Prices play an important role in the market economy. You will learn more about the role of prices later in this chapter.

Reading **HELP**DESK

economic system a nation's way of producing things its people want and need

traditional economy an economic system in which the decisions of what, how, and for whom to produce are based on custom or habit

market economy an economic system in which individuals and businesses own all resources and make economic decisions on the basis of price

In a **command economy**, planners who work for the government answer the economic questions. They decide what will be produced, for example whether the society will produce machines or consumer goods. They also decide how these goods will be produced and to whom they will be made available. Individuals and businesses in a command economy do not have much say in how the economy works. Government planners *command* the actions that producers must follow.

The American Economy

The United States is based on a market economy. In a market economy, businesses are free to compete for profit with little interference from the government. Individuals and businesses can choose how to use their resources. They choose what to produce and how to produce it. Individuals and businesses use prices to determine who will receive the goods and services that are produced.

The United States does not have a pure market system, though. The government does play a role in the economy. It oversees the way markets work to make sure that businesses act fairly and honestly. This helps markets function smoothly by making sure buyers and sellers can trust each other. The government also makes rules for how workers are to be treated. For example, the government requires that a minimum wage be paid to most workers. The government also provides some services, such as education, national defense, and disaster relief. The economy also has elements of a traditional economy. For example, many people decide to work in the same job as a parent. Because our economy has some elements of all three types of economies (traditional, market, and command), the United States has a **mixed market economy.**

 PROGRESS CHECK

Defining What determines the kind of economy a nation has?

21st Century SKILLS

Make Connections

Before reading the section titled "The American Economy," think about what you have read about the three types of economic systems. Which do you think is the American economic system? Why do you think so?

command economy an economic system in which the government makes the major economic decisions

mixed market economy a market economy that has elements of command and tradition

LESSON 1 REVIEW

Review the Vocabulary

1. What are *resources,* and what are the three kinds that economists have identified?

2. What is an *economic system*?

3. Why is the U.S. economy called a *mixed market economy*?

Answer the Guiding Questions

4. *Making Connections* How do resources and wants create scarcity?

5. *Explaining* What are the differences among traditional, command, and market economies?

6. **NARRATIVE** Write a short story about a student your age who has to make an economic choice. In your story, reveal how plentiful wants conflict with scarce resources.

networks

There's More Online!

☑ **GRAPHIC ORGANIZER**
Benefit-Cost Analysis

☑ **CHART**
Marginal Cost and Revenue
for Joe's Seafood Depot

☑ **GRAPH**
Marginal Analysis for Joe's
Seafood Depot
The Law of Diminishing Returns

☑ **GAMES**

Lesson 2

Economic Decisions

ESSENTIAL QUESTIONS • *Why and how do people make economic choices?*
• *How do economic systems influence societies?*

IT MATTERS BECAUSE

You make economic decisions every day, and you will do so all your life.

Trade-Offs

GUIDING QUESTION *Why are trade-offs important in making economic decisions?*

Have you ever had to make a choice between two things you really wanted to buy? If so, you have had some practice with economic decision making. Perhaps you had to choose between buying a video game and going to a movie with your friends. To make a good decision, you had to consider the benefits and the costs of each choice. In fact, you already think about many of your choices in the same way that economists do.

Making Trade-Offs

Making a **trade-off** is giving up one alternative good or service for another. If you choose to buy a pair of running shoes, you are exchanging your money for the opportunity to own the running shoes rather than something else that might cost the same amount.

A trade-off does not only apply to decisions involving money. For example, you might need to decide whether to go to a friend's party or study for an important test. In this case, you would have to make a trade-off with your time. What will you give up—time with friends or studying time?

PHOTO: (tl) Burke/Triolo Productions/Getty Images; (tc) BananaStock/PunchStock

Reading**HELP**DESK

Taking Notes: *Sequencing*

As you read, use a flowchart to describe the steps of a benefit-cost analysis.

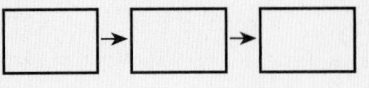

Content Vocabulary

- **trade-off**
- **opportunity cost**
- **fixed cost**
- **variable cost**
- **total cost**
- **marginal cost**

446 *Introduction to Economics*

Businesses also make trade-offs. A company might have to decide whether to invest in research for new products or spend money on advertising to increase sales of existing products. Managers might need to choose whether to give big bonuses to a few workers or small raises to all workers.

Governments face trade-offs, too. If they spend money to build schools, they might not have enough money to build roads or pay for national defense.

Opportunity Costs

When faced with a trade-off, people eventually choose one **option,** or alternative, over all others. For example, you decide to buy a pair of running shoes and give up the chance to buy something else. Or, you choose to study and give up the opportunity to spend time with your friends.

Opportunity cost is the cost of the next-best use of your money or time when you choose to do one thing rather than another. Economists use the term *opportunity cost* very specifically. The term is reserved only for the next-most-attractive alternative. Other options rejected earlier in the decision-making process are not considered opportunity costs.

The choices made by businesses and societies also have opportunity costs. Suppose your city has narrowed its choices to spending money on park improvements or fixing city sidewalks. If it decides to spend money on the park, the opportunity cost would be the sidewalks that would not be fixed. If Congress votes to increase spending on early childhood education rather than on food programs, the opportunity cost is the support not given to the food programs.

Economic decisions involve using any resource. Choosing to watch a television show one evening will not cost you any money. However, that choice has an opportunity cost. The cost is the time you could have spent doing other things, such as listening to music or visiting your friends.

Businesses also face opportunity costs that do not involve money. For example, some companies may often require employees to spend time learning new computer programs.

Why It MATTERS

Identifying Opportunity Cost

When you make a decision about what to do, consider what you are giving up: the opportunity to do something else. On a sheet of paper, write the two things you would most like to do when you next have free time. Assume you will not have enough time to do both. Label your favorite *Choice 1.* Label the other *Choice 2: cost.* Choice 2 is the opportunity cost of doing Choice 1.

Decisions, decisions. Opportunity costs are everywhere—even at yard sales!

▶ **CRITICAL THINKING**
Analyzing Visuals What is a possible opportunity cost for the woman who is buying the roller skates? Explain your answer.

- revenue
- marginal revenue
- benefit-cost analysis

trade-off the alternative you face when you decide to do one thing rather than another

Academic Vocabulary
option an alternative or choice

opportunity cost the cost of the next-best use of time or money when choosing to do one thing or another

The opportunity cost of that decision is the loss of the employees' work while they are being trained. Why would a company make such a decision? The company might believe the training will help workers be more productive in the long run. Good decisions involve weighing all possible options.

You might think you can avoid opportunity cost. For example, suppose you want to watch two television shows that air at the same time. You could choose to see one television show today and record the other one to watch later. On that day in the future, though, you will still face the need to make a choice. When you sit down to watch the show you recorded, you will have to give up some other activity that you also want to do.

☑ PROGRESS CHECK

Explaining What is a trade-off in an economic decision?

Measuring Costs and Revenues

GUIDING QUESTION *How do costs and revenues influence economic decision making?*

To understand how businesses make economic decisions, it is useful to look at the kinds of decisions a business typically makes. Let us look at the example of Joe's Seafood Depot. Joe's Seafood Depot has been making and selling seafood for 10 years. Joe wonders if his business would be better off if it were open longer every day.

Assessing Costs

Joe must first figure out the additional cost of staying open longer. To make these calculations, Joe has to take into account different kinds of costs.

Some of Joe's expenses are fixed costs. **Fixed costs** are expenses that do not change no matter how much a business produces. Rent is a good example of a fixed cost. Insurance is another. Joe will pay the same rent and insurance for his building whether his seafood restaurant is open eight hours a day, as it is now, or longer. Because fixed costs will not change if he stays open longer, Joe will ignore these costs.

Another kind of cost **varies,** or changes, depending on how much a business produces. These expenses are **variable costs.** Labor is a variable cost. Joe will have higher payroll costs if the Seafood Depot is open longer. This is because employees will be

Food costs vary depending on how many customers come in and what they order. The two dishes in the photo probably did not cost the same to make or buy, for example.

▶ **CRITICAL THINKING**
Analyzing Visuals What other example of variable costs can you see in this photo?

PHOTO: BananaStock/PunchStock

Reading **HELP**DESK

fixed cost an expense that does not change no matter how much a business produces	**Academic Vocabulary** **vary** to change	**variable cost** an expense that changes depending on how much a business produces

MARGINAL COST AND REVENUE FOR JOE'S SEAFOOD DEPOT

Added Hours	Marginal Cost	Marginal Revenue
1	$30	$70
2	$30	$60
3	$30	$50
4	$30	$40
5	$30	$30
6	$30	$20

These schedules show the marginal cost and revenue if Joe keeps his restaurant open from one to six hours longer each day.

► CRITICAL THINKING

1 *Identifying* In the first hour, how much greater is marginal revenue than marginal cost?

2 *Drawing Conclusions* What do you think causes marginal revenue to go down steadily from hour to hour?

working more hours. Supplies are another variable cost. If the Seafood Depot is open more hours and sells more seafood, Joe will have to spend more on ingredients.

Joe could combine both fixed and variable costs to find his **total cost.** He is now open a total of eight hours per day and has fixed costs of $300. Because his variable costs are $160, his total costs are $460, the sum of his total and his variable costs. His total cost will be higher if his restaurant is open longer, but the higher costs will all be due to the increase in his variable cost.

When businesses face a decision, they typically think about increasing or decreasing activities in small units. They look at their **marginal cost,** which is the increase in expenses caused by producing another unit of something. The additional unit Joe is considering is staying open for another hour of business. Staying open longer will not increase his fixed costs. Those expenses will stay the same regardless of how long he is open. However, his total cost will go up because his variable cost will rise since he will have to hire workers for an extra hour.

The chart shows that Joe expects to have a marginal cost of $30 for every additional hour he stays open.

Different Types of Revenues

Joe's **revenue**—the money a business receives from selling its goods or services—is the sum of all the money Joe receives from his customers. However, when it comes to making business decisions, another type of revenue is more useful to consider.

Why It
MATTERS

Making Decisions

Business owners base their decisions in large part on how these choices affect their profits. They avoid decisions that cause them to lose money. How can you use similar thinking in making your own decisions?

---

total cost the combination of all fixed and variable costs

marginal cost the additional or extra opportunity cost associated with each increase of one unit of sales

revenue the money a business receives from selling its goods or services

This graph shows what happens to Joe's marginal revenue as he stays open for additional hours.

▶ CRITICAL THINKING

1 *Making Connections* What is the source for the information in this graph?

2 *Evaluating* What is the added cost of staying open for four more hours, and what is the benefit?

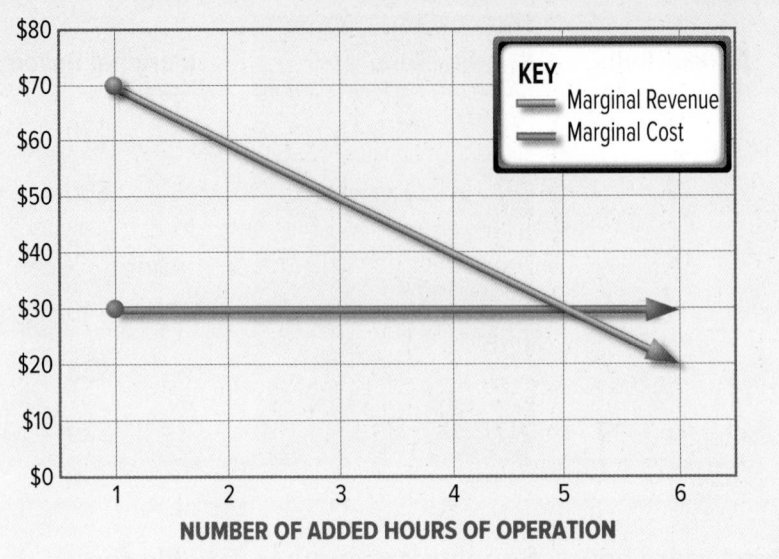

To compare his options, Joe will estimate his **marginal revenue.** Marginal revenue is the additional income received from each increase of one unit in sales. In this example, marginal revenue will be the added income Joe receives from each additional hour that his restaurant is open.

Marginal Analysis

Marginal analysis compares the additional benefit of doing something with the additional cost of doing it. If the additional benefit is greater than the additional cost, the rule is to do it. If the cost is greater than the benefit, the rule is not to do it.

Joe's Seafood Depot could use marginal analysis to help decide how many more hours to remain open. The graph shows that the marginal revenue of staying open one more hour is $70 and the marginal cost is only $30. Because the marginal benefit is greater than the marginal cost, Joe's will stay open at least one more hour. The marginal benefit remains greater than the marginal cost for the second, third, and fourth hours as well. As a result, Joe's will stay open for at least an additional four hours and maybe even a fifth hour.

When doing marginal analysis, the rule is to continue doing something until the marginal cost is equal to the marginal revenue. In Joe's case, the two are equal at five extra hours. The fifth hour of extra revenue exactly offsets his additional cost.

Reading**HELP**DESK

marginal revenue the additional income received from each increase of one unit of sales

benefit-cost analysis economic model that compares the marginal costs and marginal benefits of a decision

Benefit-Cost Analysis

Benefit-cost analysis compares the size of the benefit with the size of the cost by dividing the two. This type of analysis helps businesses choose among two, three, or more projects.

For example, suppose a business must choose between investments A and B. If A is expected to generate $100 in revenue at a cost of $80, the benefit-cost ratio is 1.25. We get the number 1.25 by dividing $100 by $80. If project B is expected to generate $150, and if it costs $90, it will have a benefit-cost ratio of 1.67. The business would then choose the one with the higher benefit-cost number, or project B.

Marginal analysis is useful when making one decision at a time, such as Joe's decision about how many more hours to stay open. When choosing between two or more alternatives, however, benefit-cost analysis can be more useful.

Thinking Like an Economist

The decisions most people face cannot always be evaluated in terms of money. Yet even those decisions can be analyzed with marginal analysis. For example, suppose you are deciding how long a nap to take. The marginal benefit will be the greatest during the first hour of sleep and then less and less. A line graph of this marginal benefit would look like Joe's graph of marginal revenue. It would slope downward the longer the nap got.

There would also be a cost: the opportunity cost of other things you could not do. The marginal cost of the first hour of sleep would likely be small. But the longer you slept, the greater the marginal cost would be.

Eventually, falling marginal benefits would exactly equal the increasing marginal costs. Even if you are not aware of it, marginal analysis applies to almost everything we do. This is what it means to "think like an economist."

☑ **PROGRESS CHECK**

Summarizing What two things are compared in a marginal analysis?

21st Century
SKILLS

Analyze Visuals

What if Joe's marginal cost was $40 per additional hour? Would it make sense for him to keep the restaurant open longer? For how many hours?

LESSON 2 REVIEW

Review the Vocabulary

1. Explain *opportunity cost* in making an economic decision.

2. Give an example of a *fixed cost* and a *variable cost*.

3. What is the difference between a business's *total cost* and its *revenue*?

4. What are *marginal costs* and *marginal revenues*?

Answer the Guiding Questions

5. ***Describing*** Describe a typical economic decision. What is the trade-off? What is the opportunity cost?

6. ***Analyzing*** Why is it useful for individuals to do a benefit-cost analysis?

7. **ARGUMENT** Write a public service announcement that explains the benefits of identifying opportunity costs when making decisions.

networks

There's More Online!

☑ **GRAPHIC ORGANIZER**
Changes to Demand and Supply

☑ **INFOGRAPHIC**
Demand and Supply for Oil

☑ **GRAPHS**
Change in Demand for Video Games Supply Curve

☑ **SLIDE SHOW**

☑ **VIDEO**

Lesson 3
Demand and Supply in a Market Economy

ESSENTIAL QUESTIONS • *Why and how do people make economic choices?*
• *How do economic systems influence societies?*

IT MATTERS BECAUSE

Demand and supply work together to set the prices of the goods and services you buy and use.

Demand and Supply Make Markets

GUIDING QUESTION *How do demand and supply affect prices?*

Suppose you go to a store sale. You see a sign on a rack that says "Take 25 percent off the price of these shirts." Or the sign might say "$5 off selected shirts." However it is phrased, the sign tells you that the price of the shirts has changed.

Where do prices come from? What do they tell us? Why do they change? Are prices important? As you will see, there is a lot to learn about something as seemingly simple as a price.

In a command economy, government officials set prices for most goods. They decide what to manufacture and the amount that various goods—such as shirts, bread, and cars—will cost.

In a market economy like the United States, however, prices are set by a kind of interaction. This interaction is the effect that two forces—demand and supply—have on each other. These forces result from the desires of two groups. **Consumers** are the people who buy goods and services. **Producers** are the people or businesses that provide goods and services.

PHOTO: (tl) Getty Images; (tcl) Daniel Dillon/Alamy; (tcr) Blend Images/Getty Images; (tr) Getty Images

Reading HELP DESK

Taking Notes: *Describing*

As you read, complete a chart describing the factors that cause demand and supply to change.

Demand change	Supply change

Content Vocabulary

- consumer
- producer
- demand
- supply
- market
- competition
- equilibrium price
- surplus
- shortage

Demand and Supply

In economics, **demand** is the amount of a good or service that people (consumers) are willing and able to buy at various prices during a given time period. This definition mentions four parts:

- *Amount*—Demand measures how much of a good or service consumers are willing to buy over a range of possible prices. So the demand for a certain music CD refers to the quantities that consumers would buy at prices such as $10, $15, and $20.
- *Willing to buy*—Consumers must be willing to buy a good or service or there is no demand.
- *Able to buy*—Consumers must have the ability to buy the good or service. Consumers who want a certain good but do not have the money to buy it do not affect the demand for that item.
- *Price*—The quantity that consumers are willing and able to buy is associated with a particular price, be it high or low.

We will see that these price-and-quantity relationships can be expressed in either a chart or a graph.

Supply is the amount of a good or service that producers are willing and able to sell at various prices during a given time period. As the price of a good or service goes up, producers tend to supply more. As the price goes down, they tend to supply less.

Markets and Competition

The quantity of a particular item that is demanded or supplied at each price can be shown in a schedule. The information on a schedule can then be drawn as a line on a graph. The graph includes a *demand curve* and a *supply curve*.

Look at the following graph of Demand and Supply for Oil. Note that each point on the demand curve shows the amount demanded at a particular price. Likewise, each point on the supply curve shows the quantity supplied at a particular price. The line showing demand slopes down to the right. That is because people tend to demand more when the price is low and less when the price is high. The slope of the supply curve goes in the opposite direction. That is because producers tend to supply more when the price is high and less when the price is low.

PHOTO: Getty Images

Take the role of this T-shirt seller. Suppose it costs you $5 to buy a T-shirt and print a slogan on it. Would you want to sell more T-shirts at $6 or at $10?

▶ CRITICAL THINKING

Analyzing Assume the seller in the photo wants to sell as many shirts as he can before the end of the day. What is one thing he could do to increase demand for his shirts?

consumer a person who buys goods and services

producer a person or business that provides goods and services

demand the amount of a good or service that consumers are willing and able to buy over a range of prices

supply the amount of a good or service that producers are willing and able to sell over a range of prices

DEMAND AND SUPPLY FOR OIL

The price of crude oil is set by demand and supply. Crude oil is used to make gasoline, heating oil, jet fuel, and other products. Its price affects the whole economy.

1 *Explaining* Why is the demand for oil much lower at a price of $50 per barrel than the supply at that price?

▶ **CRITICAL THINKING**

2 *Analyzing Visuals* What would cause the equilibrium price for crude oil to go up?

Demand Schedule for Crude Oil	
Price Per Barrel	**Quantity Demanded**
$10	50
$20	40
$30	30
$40	20
$50	10

Supply Schedule for Crude Oil	
Price Per Barrel	**Quantity Supplied**
$10	10
$20	20
$30	30
$40	40
$50	50

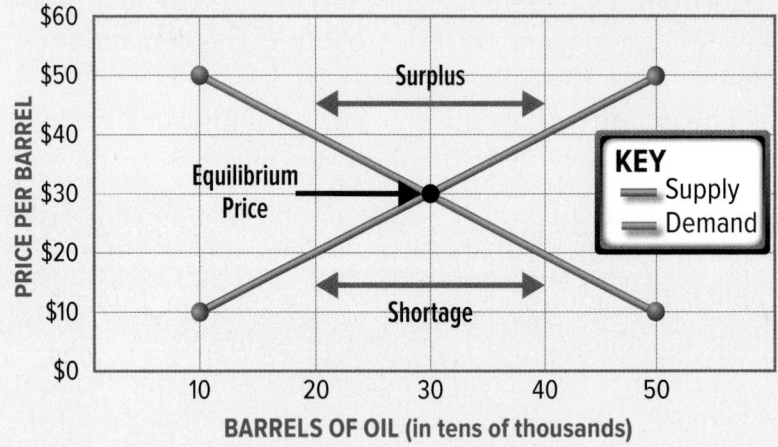

The demand and supply curves together show a *market*. A **market** is a place where buyers and sellers of the same good or service come together. It can be at a specific location, like a farmers' market. A market can also exist on the Internet.

To be efficient, markets must have many competing buyers and sellers. This **competition,** or struggle among sellers to attract buyers, keeps a product's price at or near a certain level. Too few sellers may keep a price above the level that would be set by competition. That is why U.S. law bans monopolies.

How Prices Are Set

Markets are vital to the U.S. economy. They allow us to choose how we spend our money. In a market economy, people buy what they want instead of what government thinks they should have. In addition, markets are efficient. When they operate freely, they set their own prices. Markets also help prevent the production of too many, or too few, goods and services.

Reading**HELP**DESK

market a location or an arrangement that allows buyers and sellers to get together and buy or sell a certain product

competition efforts by different businesses to sell the same good or service

equilibrium price the price set for a good or service in the marketplace, where demand and supply are perfectly balanced

surplus situation in which the amount of a good or service supplied by producers is greater than the amount demanded by consumers

How does a market set a price? Look at the graph again. Note that the supply and demand curves meet at one point. That point is the price the marketplace sets for the good or service. It is called the **equilibrium** (EE•kwuh•LIH•bree•uhm) **price**. Here, demand and supply are balanced. The equilibrium price in the graph is $30. At this price, consumers want to buy the same amount of a good or service that producers are willing to offer.

If the price were higher, producers would be willing to produce more. But consumers would not be willing or able to buy more. This would result in a **surplus,** in which the amount supplied by producers is greater than the amount demanded by consumers. A surplus tends to cause prices to fall.

If the price were lower than the equilibrium price, there would be a **shortage.** This occurs when the quantity demanded is greater than the quantity supplied. A shortage will cause the price to rise. If gasoline were in short supply, prices would go up. The forces applied by surpluses and shortages keep a price at its equilibrium level. Thus, a market finds its own price, while in a command economy government officials set prices.

Finally, markets support our democratic political system, in which citizens vote for candidates they choose. When you shop, your dollars are like votes for the goods or services you want. If consumers "vote" with their dollars for a product, producers will make more of it. So, spending your dollars is like voting for the products you want.

Factors Affecting Demand

Several factors affect demand, causing the demand curve to move left or right. A movement in either direction causes the equilibrium price to change.

One factor that affects demand is the number of consumers. Look at the Change in Demand for Video Games graph. If more consumers enter the market, they buy more of the product at each and every price. The demand curve shifts to the right. If consumers leave the market, then fewer people are available to buy the video games. This change causes the demand curve to move left, shown in the bottom graph.

Another factor is a change in consumer income. If people earn more, they may buy more video games at each price. This causes demand to go up. The demand curve moves to the right, and the equilibrium price rises.

shortage situation in which the supply of the good or service available is less than the demand for it

Why It MATTERS

Demand Is Your Economic Voice

Demand is the consumers' voice, the way all individuals can influence the market. If you think a good or service is priced too high, you may not have to buy it at that price. You can choose to buy a substitute, buy from another seller, or go without the good. What will a seller have to do if enough consumers make those choices? Why?

Many rental car companies such as the ones shown compete for people's business. This helps keep the price of renting a car low.

▶ CRITICAL THINKING
Determining Cause and Effect What would happen to the price of renting a car if competition decreased, and how would this affect the supply of cars for rent?

Many factors could affect demand for video games. The top demand graph shows demand going up. The bottom demand graph shows demand going down.

▶ **CRITICAL THINKING**

1 *Determining Cause and Effect* What economic situation would cause consumers' incomes to go down, and what would happen to the video game demand curve?

2 *Making Inferences* Demand for video games has increased because of a change in consumer preferences. What, therefore, happens to the demand curve?

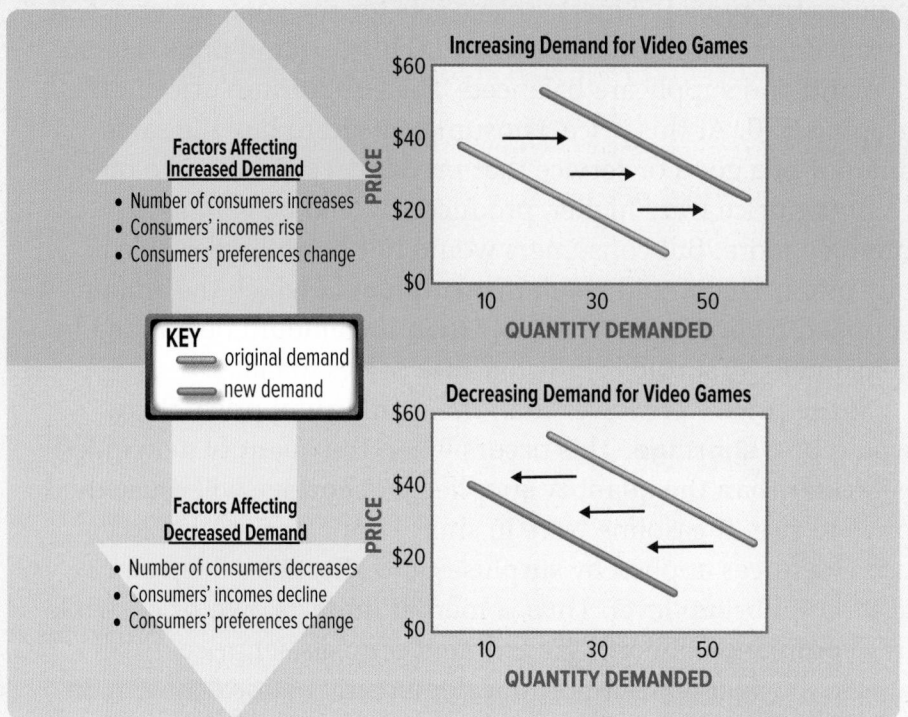

Factors Affecting Increased Demand
- Number of consumers increases
- Consumers' incomes rise
- Consumers' preferences change

KEY
— original demand
— new demand

Factors Affecting Decreased Demand
- Number of consumers decreases
- Consumers' incomes decline
- Consumers' preferences change

On the other hand, if people earn less, they do not buy as many games at every possible price. Then the demand curve shifts left, and the equilibrium price decreases.

The third factor that affects demand is a change in consumer preferences. This is a change in consumers' like or dislike for a product. If scientists discovered that a certain organic compound was good for our health, consumers would buy more of it. This would shift the product's demand curve to the right. But if we learned that it was harmful, people would buy less of it. This would shift the demand curve to the left.

Factors Affecting Supply

Several factors affect supply. The two key factors are the number of suppliers and the costs of production.

As the number of suppliers increases, the available quantity of a good or service increases. Then, more of the item is produced at all prices, and the supply curve moves to the right. If some suppliers leave the market, the supply curve shifts to the left. When there are fewer suppliers, price tends to go up. Consumers have fewer choices, so producers can charge more.

Reading**HELP**DESK

Reading Strategy: *Making Generalizations*

When you make a statement that applies to different facts, you are making a generalization. Read the passage about prices and the three economic questions. On a separate sheet of paper, write a generalization about the relationship between price and the three economic questions.

Anything that affects the cost of production also influences supply. As the cost of producing a good or service goes up, producers supply less. This shifts the supply curve to the left. Or, if producers find ways to make a good or service more cheaply, they are willing to supply more of it at all prices. This moves the supply curve to the right. New technology may drive down production costs. Computers, for instance, make workers more efficient. A new manufacturing process can reduce waste. This cuts production costs. Lower costs lead to more supply.

✓ PROGRESS CHECK

Identifying What three changes will cause demand to rise?

The Economic Role of Prices

GUIDING QUESTION *How do prices help consumers and businesses make economic decisions?*

In a market economy, prices drive the markets for goods and services. A market is any setting where goods and services are exchanged for money. It can even exist on the Web. A Web site is part of that market if goods and services are sold on the site.

In this type of economy, consumers and producers use prices to help make economic decisions. Prices also measure value. They send signals to both consumers and producers.

Prices and the Economic Questions

All economic systems answer three basic questions: *what* to produce, *how* to produce, and *for whom* to produce. In a market economy, prices help answer these questions.

Everyone needs groceries. The price of a main dish item might affect what you eat for dinner on a particular day. Prices are always changing.

▶ CRITICAL THINKING
Explaining How do prices help producers figure out what products consumers are willing and able to buy?

PHOTO: Blend Images/Getty Images

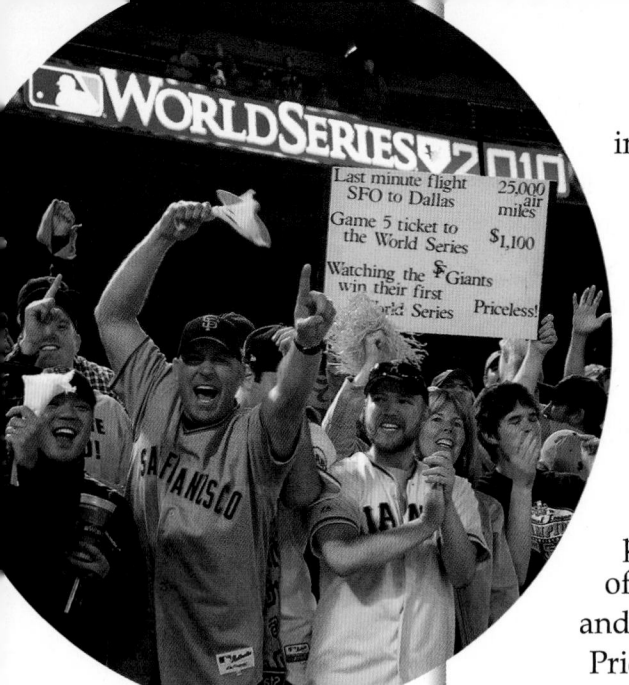

For these happy San Francisco Giants baseball fans, watching their team win the World Series is an experience beyond price. As you can see from the sign, they were willing to pay a lot to be in the right place at the right time.

▶ CRITICAL THINKING

Hypothesizing What does the $1,100 price of a Game 5 World Series ticket tell you about its value? How would consumers respond if all baseball tickets cost $1,100, and what would producers do?

Prices help determine what to produce by influencing the decisions of producers. If consumer demand for a product is high, demand drives up the price of that product. Businesses react by trying to increase the production of that product to meet the demand. Or, if consumer demand for a product is low, the price of the product falls and businesses produce less of it. Why are no large-screen black-and-white televisions produced? The reason is that consumers do not want them and would not buy them. People want to see television programs in color. To meet that demand, producers of large-screen televisions focus on improving picture and color quality.

Prices also affect how goods and services are produced. For example, cars built by hand would be far too expensive. Instead, automakers use mass production to lower the price. This method lets them produce cars at a price consumers can pay.

Prices also decide for whom goods and services are produced. Products are made for consumers who can and will buy them at a particular price.

Prices as Measures of Value

Every good and service in a market economy has a price. The price sets the value of each good or service on any particular day. Consumers and producers then use the prices to value goods and services. If a T-shirt costs $10 and a pair of jeans costs $25, then a pair of jeans is worth two and a half T-shirts.

Prices as Signals

Prices send signals to consumers and producers. If consumers think an item is priced too high, they will not buy it. Suppose a bakery charges $5 for a bagel. If nearby bakeries charge less, consumers will not buy the $5 bagel. The lack of demand sends a signal to that bakery owner that the price should be lower.

The reverse is also true. When consumers cannot find a good or service at the low price they want to pay, they must recognize that no producer is willing to supply it to them at that price. Consumers will have to **adapt,** or change, their expectations about what they have to pay to get that good or service, or they will have to go without it. For example, students might want to pay only $250 for a powerful laptop computer.

ReadingHELPDESK

Academic Vocabulary

adapt to change in response to new circumstances

interaction effect of two or more things on each other

However, if producers do not offer powerful laptops for less than $450, the students will have to accept the higher price and adapt to it, or go without laptops.

Prices in a Command System

You have been reading about how prices work in a market economy like that of the United States. However, some nations have other economic systems. In a command economy, government officials answer the three basic economic questions. They decide what to produce, how to produce it, and for whom to produce it. Government officials also set prices on most goods and services.

In a command economy, then, the price is not something that consumers and producers work out through the **interaction** of demand and supply. Instead, prices are set by the government based on its idea of the relative value of goods and services.

Even in some command economies, though, price may answer the third economic question: for whom goods and services are produced. For example, Cuba has a command economy. For nearly 50 years, Cuba paid all workers the same wage, whether they were doctors, teachers, or farmers. Cuban officials did this to give everyone the same buying power, but the policy did nothing to increase production. Recently, the government realized that its system was not working. Leaders decided to allow the most productive workers and managers to earn more money. As a result, these workers were able to consume more even though this policy did nothing to increase production.

☑ **PROGRESS CHECK**

Comparing Are prices more changeable in a market economy or in a command economy? Why?

LESSON 3 REVIEW

Review the Vocabulary

1. Explain the role of *consumers* and *producers* in a market economy.

2. Explain the four parts of the definition of *demand*.

3. How does *competition* among too few sellers affect price?

Answer the Guiding Questions

4. *Analyzing* When a store has a sale, it cuts the prices on the goods it sells. Is that more likely to happen when there is a surplus or when there is a shortage? Explain.

5. *Summarizing* What are three functions of prices in a market economy?

6. **INFORMATIVE/EXPLANATORY** New products are often expensive, and then they become less expensive over time. Use the factors that affect supply and demand to explain why this happens. First explain what makes new products have higher prices. Then explain why the same products are sold at lower prices over time.

Write your answers on a separate piece of paper.

1 **Writing Activity**

EXPLORING THE ESSENTIAL QUESTIONS
Why and how do people make economic choices?
How do economic systems influence societies?

Suppose you are the marketing manager of a video game company. The company's creative team has two ideas for new video games. One game is for younger children and the other game is for teens. They cost about the same amount of money to develop. Write a report to the company president explaining why the company can afford to invest in only one of these games, identifying the one you think is a better choice and explaining why you think so. In your report, use economic ideas you have read about.

2 **21st Century Skills**

CREATE A NEW PRODUCT Invent a good or service you think would appeal to students your age. Write a report explaining how supply and demand would affect the price of this product or service.

3 **Being an Active Citizen**

Consumers can take advantage of competition to save money. Identify a product or service that people buy regularly and that is widely sold either in your community or via the Internet. Research the price of the good or service at six businesses that offer it. Prepare a chart comparing the prices that different sellers have set for the good or service. Then make a graph showing how much a consumer can save in a year by buying the good or service at the lowest price. Share your findings with friends and family and your class.

4 **Understanding Visuals**

The graph shows a demand curve for a package of five recordable CD-ROMs. Explain what factors could produce the changes in quantity demanded that would move the demand curve to the left or to the right.

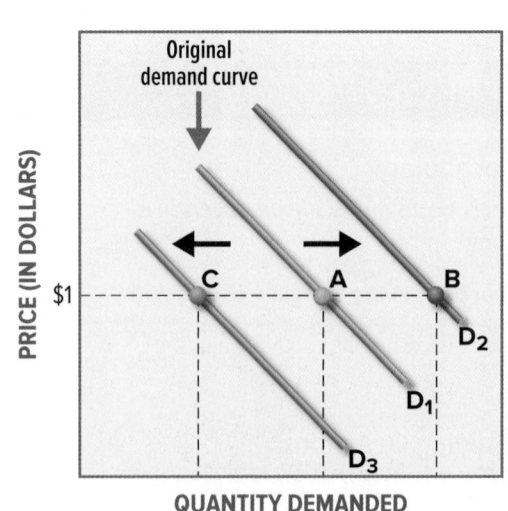

REVIEW THE GUIDING QUESTIONS

Directions: Choose the best answer for each question.

1 Machines, energy, and skills are examples of
   A. labor.
   B. resources.
   C. wants.
   D. capital.

2 In what type of economy does the government answer the three basic economic questions?
   F. command economy
   G. market economy
   H. money economy
   I. traditional economy

3 Which type of cost is labor?
   A. fixed cost
   B. marginal cost
   C. total cost
   D. variable cost

4 Which statement best explains why businesses do marginal analysis?
   F. to compute total costs
   G. to measure total revenues
   H. to decide how much to produce
   I. to decide which is best among several investments

5 What situation may occur when a price is below its equilibrium level?
   A. opportunity cost
   B. shortage
   C. surplus
   D. trade-off

6 What is the best definition of a market?
   F. any store
   G. any Web site that sells something
   H. any situation in which goods and services are exchanged
   I. any communication between individuals

DBQ **ANALYZING DOCUMENTS**

Directions: Analyze the graph and answer the questions that follow.

7 **Making Generalizations** Which statement best describes the price of gasoline between 1980 and 1995?

  A. The price steadily declined.

  B. The price steadily increased.

  C. The price never exceeded $2.00 per gallon.

  D. The price went up and down many times.

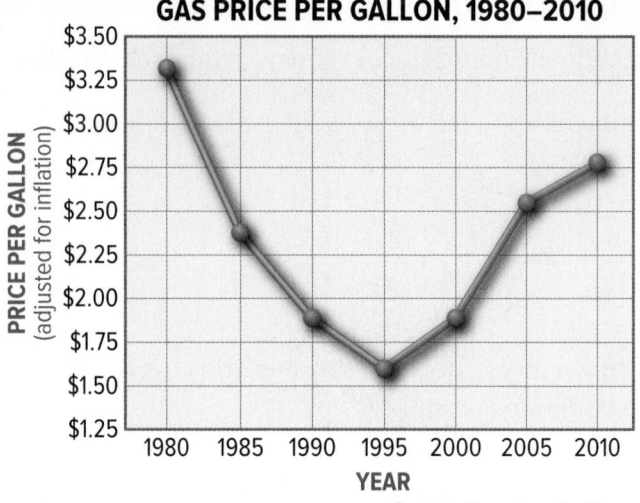

GAS PRICE PER GALLON, 1980–2010

Source: Department of Energy.

8 **Drawing Conclusions** What economic reason might explain the steep jump in the price of gas beginning in 1995?

  F. revenue

  G. trade-off

  H. surplus

  I. shortage

SHORT RESPONSE

"The market price of every particular commodity [good] is regulated [controlled] by the proportion [interaction] between the quantity, which is actually brought to market, and the demand of those who are willing to pay the natural price of the commodity."

—Adam Smith, *The Wealth of Nations*, 1776

9 What kind of economic system is Smith describing? How does this economic system promote freedom?

10 Why do consumers in the situation Smith describes face trade-offs?

EXTENDED RESPONSE

11 **Informative/Exploratory** Opportunity cost plays a role in every economic decision. Explain the meaning of this term. Then give an example of a choice you have made and analyze the opportunity cost of this decision.

Need Extra Help?

If You've Missed Question	1	2	3	4	5	6	7	8	9	10	11
Review Lesson	1	1	2	2	3	3	3	3	1	2	2

The American Economy

ESSENTIAL QUESTION
Why and how do people make economic choices?

◀ *A construction worker frames a new home in Carrollton, Texas.*

PHOTO: AP Photo/LM Otero

networks

There's More Online about the American economy.

CHAPTER 17

Lesson 1
Gross Domestic Product

Lesson 2
Economic Flow and Economic Growth

Lesson 3
Capitalism and Free Enterprise

The Story Matters...

Home building is a major industry in the United States. The U.S. Census Bureau says there were 112.6 million occupied housing units in the nation between 2005 and 2009. Two-thirds were owner occupied. That means there were more than 75 million homeowners in the United States.

The right to own private property is central to our democratic principles. The Constitution guarantees that no citizen will be deprived of "life, liberty, or property" without due process of law. Moreover, property ownership is a vital part of the U.S. economic system. It gives citizens a reason to work hard and save their money. Owning a home gives people pride and a sense of belonging. It is also considered a worthwhile investment since homes often go up in value with the passage of time.

Real-Life Civics

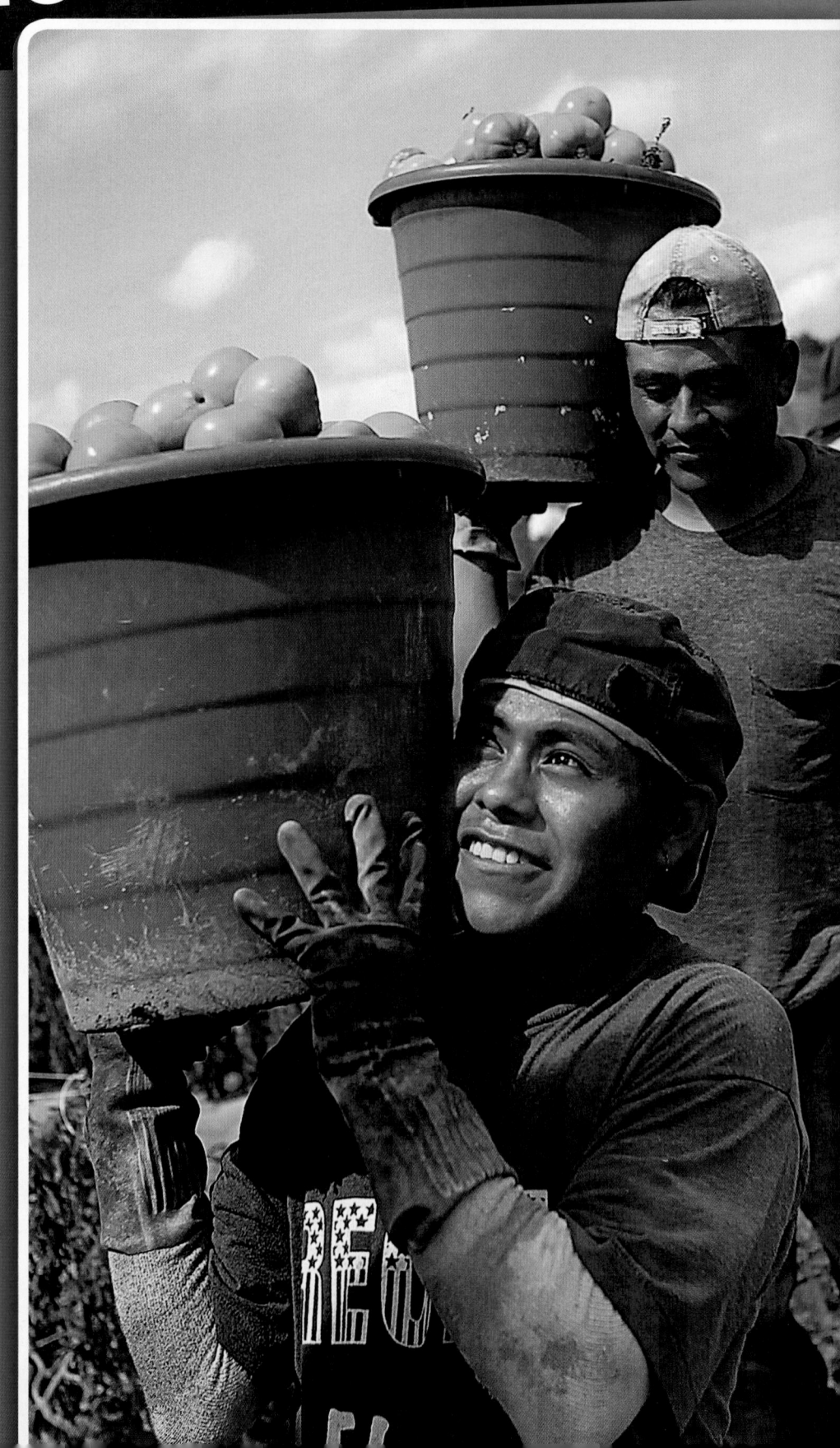

▷ **PRODUCTS** The United States produces more than $2 billion worth of fresh and processed tomatoes every year. More than two-thirds of the tomatoes come from Florida and California. Each of these states devotes 30,000 to 40,000 acres of land to tomato crops. Some tomatoes are sold fresh and others are processed into familiar products such as ketchup, tomato sauce, and canned soup.

Tomatoes make up only a tiny percentage of all the goods produced in the United States each year. The total U.S. goods and services in 2010 were valued at $15 trillion. This output makes the United States the single largest national economy in the world.

▷ Workers carry buckets of tomatoes from a tomato field in Homestead, Florida.

A hairstylist works on his customer's hair at his salon in Arlington, Virginia.

PHOTOS: (l) Joe Raedle/Getty Images; (tr) AP Photo/Jacquelyn Martin

> **SERVICES** In 2008 there were more than 800,000 barbers, hairdressers, and other personal-appearance workers employed in the United States. Barbers and hairdressers shampoo, cut, style, and color hair to enhance a customer's appearance. Other personal-appearance workers provide facials and other skin treatments. Such businesses are just one type of service provider in the United States. Service providers are people paid to do something of value for a customer. Other service providers include teachers, engineers, performers, lawyers, accountants, and health care providers. Each of these workers contributes to the United States economy.

CIVIC LITERACY

★ ★ ★ ★

Analyzing How are a personal-appearance worker who cuts and styles hair and a factory worker who makes personal-appearance products such as shampoo or skin cream alike and different in economic terms?

Your Opinion Think of a service that you or your family has recently purchased and explain how you think the service provider contributed to the U.S. economy.

465

networks
There's More Online!

☑ **GRAPHIC ORGANIZER**
Factors of Production

☑ **GRAPH**
U.S. Gross Domestic Product,
1960–2010

☑ **SLIDE SHOW**
Factors of Production

☑ **GAME**

Lesson 1

Gross Domestic Product

ESSENTIAL QUESTION *Why and how do people make economic choices?*

IT MATTERS BECAUSE
The success of the U.S. economy affects the quality of life for everyone who lives here.

Why GDP Is Important

GUIDING QUESTION *Why is Gross Domestic Product important to a nation?*

You can see the busy U.S. economy all around you. Farmers raise crops, and factories produce many kinds of goods. Employees stock goods on store shelves. Shoppers crowd the stores to buy those products. A **product** may be either a good or a service. Goods are something you can touch, like bicycles, cell phones, books, pens, and clothes. Products also include services, or work done for someone for pay. Repairing a car, giving a haircut, and babysitting a child are examples of services.

GDP Measures Total Output

All this economic activity is reflected in the **Gross Domestic Product (GDP).** GDP is the total market value of all final products produced in a country during a single year. What is the GDP of the United States? In 2010, the annual **output,** or amount produced, in the United States totaled about 15 *trillion* dollars. The United States is the world's single largest national economy. In fact, U.S. output is about one-fifth of all the goods and services produced in the world. In 2010 China had the second-largest economy, with about $9 trillion.

PHOTO: (tl) Dynamic Graphics/Jupiter Images; (tc) Ryan McVay/Getty Images; (tr) Alex Segre/Alamy

ReadingHELPDESK

Taking Notes: *Identifying*

As you read the lesson, complete a diagram identifying the four factors of production.

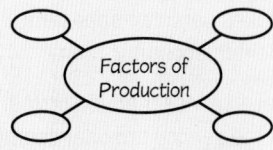

Factors of Production

Content Vocabulary

- **product**
- **Gross Domestic Product (GDP)**
- **entrepreneur**
- **GDP per capita**
- **standard of living**

GDP Represents Income

Making goods and providing services create income for people in the economy. This is another reason why measuring GDP is important. GDP is a way to measure the nation's income. It includes purchases made by consumers, businesses, and the government. The workers who make a bicycle, for example, are paid for their labor. In fact, making the bicycle produces labor for other workers, too. The workers who gather the resources used to make the metal, the paint, the seats, and the tires also earn wages. So do the people who design the bike and the machine operators who make the parts. All this labor—and more—is needed to produce the bicycle.

Factors of Production

You learned about the three types of resources used to make goods and provide services—natural resources, labor, and capital. Together with entrepreneurs, these are considered the four factors of production. **Entrepreneurs** (AHN•truh•pruh•NUHRZ) are risk-taking people who start and run businesses. These people bring together the other factors of production to create businesses. The people who formed the company that makes the bicycles are entrepreneurs. So is the woman who opens a shop to sell bicycles. They take risks. They invest money in companies that might or might not succeed. They take the risk in the hope of a reward: a business that earns money.

Labor is not the only factor of production that earns income when a bicycle is produced. So do the other factors of production. Remember that land includes forests, soil, and mineral deposits. The natural resources that go into a bicycle—the metal used in the frame and the rubber used in the tires—must be paid for. As a result, this factor of production brings income to the companies that own those resources. The same is true of capital. The wrenches, machinery, buildings, and other tools used to make the bicycle also must be bought. They, too, generate income for the companies and workers that make and sell them.

✔ **PROGRESS CHECK**

Explaining Why does GDP represent income for all factors of production?

PHOTO: Dynamic Graphics/Jupiter Images

Well over 100 million bicycles are produced in the world each year. That figure is double the number of cars produced.

▶ **CRITICAL THINKING**

Formulating Questions Ask four questions relating to the four factors of production of a bicycle. Identify each factor of production.

---

product anything that is produced; goods and services

Gross Domestic Product (GDP) total market value of all final goods and services produced in a country during a single year

Academic Vocabulary

output amount produced

entrepreneur a risk-taking person who starts a new business, introduces a new product, or improves a management technique

Measuring GDP

GUIDING QUESTION *Why is GDP difficult to measure?*

Because so many different goods and services are produced during a year, measuring GDP is difficult. This is true for any economy, not just one the size of the U.S. economy. To calculate this and other measurements, the government uses thousands of highly skilled economists and government workers.

A simple example shows how economists calculate the GDP of a nation. Suppose a tiny country has an economy that produces only three goods: bicycles, computers, and watches. The country makes ten of each of these products in a year. Suppose the price of each bicycle is $200, the price of each computer is $1,500, and the price of each watch is $100. To find the GDP of this imaginary economy, we multiply the price of each good sold by the quantity produced. Then the three results are adde66005d. The total amount, or GDP, for this nation, then, would be $18,000 ($2,000 worth of bikes, $15,000 worth of computers, and $1,000 worth of watches).

Economists do this sort of math to find the GDPs of real countries. However, we need to know some additional information about GDP.

GRAPH SKILLS

U.S. GROSS DOMESTIC PRODUCT, 1960–2010

GDP, the total market value of all final products produced in the country during a single year, has increased over time in the United States. The United States now has the largest GDP of any nation in the world.

1 *Stating* How much did the economy grow between 1990 and 2000?

▶ CRITICAL THINKING

2 *Analyzing* Which decade shown on the graph enjoyed the greatest growth?

Source: Office of Management and Budget

Reading HELPDESK

Reading Strategy: *Defining*

To help get a better understanding of GDP, define each of the words in this term: *gross*, *domestic*, and *product*. Choose the definition that best fits the concept.

Academic Vocabulary

transfer to move ownership of something

GDP Only Includes Final Products

Not all economic activities are included in GDP. GDP reflects only the market value, or price, of *final* goods and services produced and sold. A final good or service is one that is sold to its final user. A bicycle sold to you is a final good. Intermediate goods are ones that go into making a final good. The parts used to make the bicycle are intermediate goods. Intermediate goods are not counted in GDP because the final price of the bike includes the value of the parts.

Products such as bicycles, clothing, and haircuts are called consumer goods and services. These are goods we consume. Economists use the word *consume* to mean "use as a customer." But what about the goods businesses use—such as machines or office supplies—to make consumer goods? These are called producer goods. They are also known as investment goods or capital goods. These, too, are included in calculating GDP.

What GDP Does Not Include

GDP does not include every kind of activity in the economy. It includes only final goods and services produced and sold in the market. It does not include intermediate goods and services. The value of used goods is also not counted. This is because the value of these products was counted when they were first sold. **Transferring** them, or moving ownership to a new owner, creates no new production. Thus, that sale is not included a second time in the GDP.

This woman is shopping for some new clothes (left). Americans spend more than $314 billion on clothes and accessories each year. They also spend $85 billion on furniture. This store (inset) is offering used furniture for sale.

▶ CRITICAL THINKING
Differentiating Describe these two stores in relation to GDP.

Economists use GDP per capita so they can compare economies regardless of size. It is similar to the use of averages to compare the performances of athletes. How do you decide which of two basketball players is better at scoring points if they have not played the same number of games? If you calculate the number of points each scores per game, you can make the comparison.

GDP per capita Gross Domestic Product on a per-person basis; GDP divided by population

standard of living the material well-being of an individual, a group, or a nation as measured by how well its needs and wants are satisfied

GDP does not include work that family members do around the home. For example, it does not include the value of the cooking or cleaning a parent does. It also does not cover chores you do, even if you are paid to do them.

GDP Per Capita

GDP tells how large a country's economy is. But when we compare the output of countries, **GDP per capita** is a better measure. *Per capita* means "for each person." GDP per capita is calculated by dividing the country's GDP by its population. The result states GDP in terms of each person in the country. That makes it easier to compare the output of two countries.

China, for example, has the second-largest economy in the world. China's population is so large, however, that more than 100 other countries have a larger GDP per capita. In a relatively wealthy country like the United States, GDP per capita is in the tens of thousands of dollars. In the poorest countries, GDP per capita is just a few hundred dollars.

The Standard of Living

The **standard of living** is the quality of life of the people living in a country. GDP, however, is not a measure of the standard of living. This is because GDP is an aggregate, or a total, number. When we look at GDP, we do not know what was produced, how it was produced, or for whom the production was intended. A country with a GDP that goes to a very few rich people might have a lower standard of living than a country of equal size that produces its goods and services for everyone.

How production takes place is also important. China has a very productive economy but is also a big polluter. If a country does not take steps to reduce its pollution, it could have a lower standard of living than another country.

✓ PROGRESS CHECK

Comparing What is the difference between GDP and GDP per capita?

LESSON 1 REVIEW

Review Vocabulary

1. What is a *product*?

2. Why does an *entrepreneur* need natural resources, labor, and capital?

Answer the Guiding Questions

3. *Describing* What is Gross Domestic Product (GDP), and what does it represent?

4. *Analyzing* Why is GDP not necessarily an accurate measure of a nation's standard of living?

5. **INFORMATIVE/EXPLANATORY** Write a short song or jingle that explains why and how entrepreneurs do what they do.

networks
There's More Online!

☑ **GRAPHIC ORGANIZER**
Economic Sectors

☑ **CHART**
Circular Flow of Economic Activity

☑ **GRAPH**
Consumer Expenditures

☑ **VIDEO**

Lesson 2
Economic Flow and Economic Growth

ESSENTIAL QUESTION *Why and how do people make economic choices?*

IT MATTERS BECAUSE
People of all ages and from every part of the country contribute to the U.S. economy.

The Circular Flow Model

GUIDING QUESTION *Why do resources, goods, and services flow in a circular pattern in a market system?*

How can you understand what goes on in a country's economy? Economists like to use models to show how things work. A model is a graph or diagram used to explain something. Demand and supply curves are models. In this lesson we will study another one, the **circular flow model.** This model shows how resources, goods and services, and money flow between businesses and consumers. The model has a circular shape because the flows it shows have no beginning or end. For example, you might have a job in a bookstore. You use the income you earn to purchase a book. The bookstore uses that money to pay your wages, and so on. As you can see, the money flows in a circular pattern.

The circular flow model has four parts. Two parts are markets where buying and selling take place. Two parts are **sectors,** or categories, that stand for the two main groups of participants in the markets. These are the people and businesses that are active in the economy. We will start by looking at the two markets.

PHOTO: (tl) Ariel Skelley/Getty Images; (tc) Ross Harrison Koty/Getty Images; (tr) Digital Vision/PunchStock

Reading **HELP**DESK

Taking Notes: *Identifying*

As you read the lesson, complete a diagram identifying the four sectors of the economy.

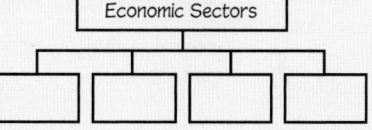

Economic Sectors

Content Vocabulary

- circular flow model
- factor market
- product market
- economic growth
- productivity
- specialization

The Factor and the Product Markets

The first market is the **factor market.** This is where factors of production are bought and sold. When people go to work, they sell their labor in the factor market. Capital resources like machines and tools are also bought and sold in the factor market, as are natural resources like oil and timber.

The **product market** is where goods and services are offered for sale. You can think of this market as one big store where all products and services are sold. All exchanges of goods and services take place in the product market.

The Consumer Sector and Business Sector

Economists think of the buyers in the economy as being divided into four groups called sectors. To keep the diagram simple, the circular flow model shown here has only two sectors: the consumer sector and the business sector. The two sectors not shown are the government sector and the foreign sector. After you have learned how the first two sectors operate, these other sectors will be discussed.

Consumers take part in both the factor and the product markets. When consumers go to work, they sell their labor in the factor market. When they get paid, they take that money to the product market, where they buy goods and services. To earn more income, they return to the factor market and sell their labor again.

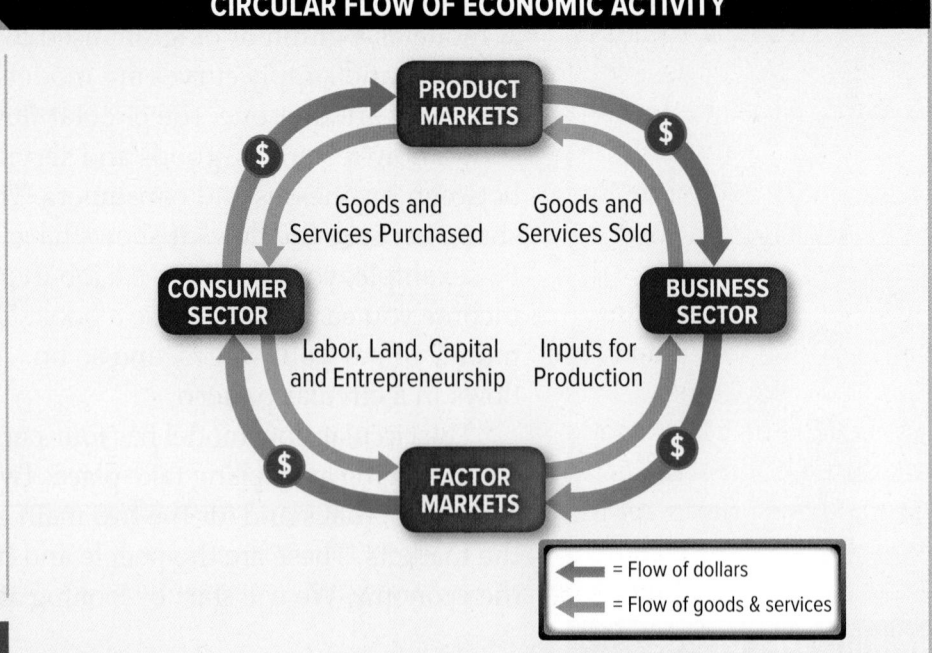

CHART SKILLS

This simple model of the circular flow of economic activity shows how the business and consumer sectors interact in the factor market and the product market.

▶ CRITICAL THINKING

1 *Analyzing Visuals* What happens in the product market?

2 *Explaining* How do consumers get the income they need to buy products?

CIRCULAR FLOW OF ECONOMIC ACTIVITY

PRODUCT MARKETS

Goods and Services Purchased

Goods and Services Sold

CONSUMER SECTOR

BUSINESS SECTOR

Labor, Land, Capital and Entrepreneurship

Inputs for Production

FACTOR MARKETS

= Flow of dollars
= Flow of goods & services

Reading**HELP**DESK

Content Vocabulary (cont.)

- **division of labor**
- **human capital**

circular flow model a model showing how goods, services, and money flow among sectors and markets in the American economy

Academic Vocabulary

sector a category, or a part of a whole

factor market a market where productive resources are bought and sold

By doing their weekly grocery shopping, this family is participating in the product market. The average American family spends more than 12 percent of its income on food.

▶ CRITICAL THINKING
Finding the Main Idea This family is acting as what sector of the economy?

The business sector represents all the companies that produce goods and services. This sector is also active in both markets. Businesses sell goods and services in the product market. They use the money they receive from these sales to buy land, labor, and capital in the factor market.

The Circular Flow

If you look at the whole diagram, you can see that the loop representing money always flows in the clockwise direction. Starting with the consumer sector, money flows through the product market to the business sector. Money then flows through the factor market back to the consumer sector. The loop representing goods, services, and factors of production flows in the opposite direction.

The key feature of the model is to show that money flows in one direction while the products and productive resources flow in the opposite direction. This is precisely what happens in real life. For example, suppose you purchase a bottle of water from a vending machine. You put the money in, and the water bottle comes out. The money and the product you buy flow in opposite directions.

The circular flow model also shows something else. It shows that markets link the consumer and business sectors. You probably will never set foot in the factory that makes some of your favorite products. However, you still interact with that factory when you buy its products at the store.

Why It
MATTERS

You Are Part of the Consumer Sector

You and everyone in your family play a part in the circular flow. You are part of the consumer sector. When you have a job, you are selling your labor in the factor markets. Whenever you buy a good or service, you make that purchase in the product markets.

product market a market where goods and services are for sale

Reading Strategy: *Paraphrasing*

Describe in your own words the circular flow of economic activity. Use real-life examples of each sector you describe.

PHOTO: Ross Harrison Koty/Getty Images

The government is a big spender. This single military fighter costs more than $15 million.

▶ CRITICAL THINKING

Making Connections How does the factor market connect the consumer sector and the government sector?

The Government and Foreign Sectors

The simplified circular flow model does not show the government and foreign sectors. Both of these sectors are important, but adding them to the model would make it more difficult to understand.

The government sector is **comprised,** or made up, of units of the federal, state, and local governments. These units go to the product market to buy goods and services, just as people in the consumer sector do. Sometimes the government sells goods and services to earn income. For example, state universities charge tuition. Such charges are not enough to fund the government, though. Instead, governments use taxes and borrowing to get the money they need to operate.

The foreign sector is made up of all the people and businesses in other countries. They act in both U.S. markets. Businesses in other countries buy raw materials in U.S. factor markets. They also sell their goods and services to consumers in U.S. product markets.

In recent years, about 15 percent of the goods and services we in the United States buy have come from foreign countries. Also, about 13 percent of the things we produce are sold outside the United States.

✓ PROGRESS CHECK

Applying Where and how have you participated in the product market?

Academic Vocabulary

comprise to be made up of

economic growth the increase in a country's total output of goods and services over time

productivity the degree to which resources are being used efficiently to produce goods and services

474 *The American Economy*

Promoting Economic Growth

GUIDING QUESTION *How can nations create and promote economic growth?*

The United States has experienced a clear upward trend in GDP over the past 50 years. This reflects our nation's steady economic growth. **Economic growth** is the increase in a country's total output of goods and services over time. Whenever GDP goes up from one year to the next, it means the economy has grown. Government and business leaders work hard to promote economic growth. Why? Because when the economy grows, the nation's wealth increases. This also helps improve the standard of living.

Two things are needed for economic growth. The first is additional resources. The second is increased productivity.

Additional Produtive Resources

As you know, the four factors of production are used to make goods and provide services. If a country were to run out of these factors, increasing production would be much more difficult and perhaps impossible. This would cause economic growth to slow or even to stop.

One key resource, land, is in limited supply. Only so much oil is under the ground, and it may run out someday. There is only so much timber to be cut, so it is important to plant new trees regularly. Also, our country has a limited amount of freshwater, so it is important to use it wisely and keep it clean. When we work to save or preserve our trees, fields, streams, and other natural resources, we are helping lay a foundation for future economic growth.

Economic growth also needs a growing population or one that is becoming more productive. This takes us to the next requirement for growth—productivity.

Increasing Productivity

Productivity is a measure of how efficiently resources are used to create products. Productivity goes up when more products are made with the same amount of factors of production in the same amount of time. Productivity goes down if fewer products are created using the same amount of the factors of production or more time. Suppose a factory that has made 1,000 computers each week begins to make 1,100 a week with the same number of workers. In that case, its productivity has increased.

The automobile assembly line is a good example of the division of labor. Each worker stays in one place and performs a single task to assemble, or put to together, a car. The car is assembled piece by piece as it moves down the line. The use of the assembly line in manufacturing led to a rise in productivity and a reduction in costs.

▶ **CRITICAL THINKING**
Drawing Conclusions How do you think the use of assembly lines in manufacturing affected the country's economic growth?

Write a Research Report

Automaker Henry Ford pioneered the use of assembly lines in automobile manufacturing in 1913. Research the ways in which the assembly line changed how Americans made and bought cars. In your report, include details on how these changes affected autoworkers.

specialization when people, businesses, regions, and/or nations concentrate on goods and services that they can produce better than anyone else

division of labor the breaking down of a job into separate, smaller tasks to be performed individually

human capital the sum of people's knowledge and skills that can be used to create products

Over the years, there have been two key changes in how products are made. These are specialization and the division of labor. Both improve productivity. **Specialization** occurs when people, businesses, regions, or countries concentrate on goods or services that they can produce more efficiently than anyone else. For example, a region that has a mild climate and fertile land will specialize in farming. A person who has good mechanical skills might specialize in car repair. By specializing, each becomes more efficient—or productive.

Specialization by people leads to another development that increases productivity: division of labor. **Division of labor** means breaking down a job into separate, smaller tasks that are done by different workers. This improves productivity—which increases economic growth.

Businesses always strive to be more productive because their goal is to make more money. They may increase productivity in different ways. One way is to improve production methods. For example, a factory might invent a new process that results in less waste of a costly resource. Businesses can also use new and better information technology. Computers, for example, let one person do work that was once performed by several people.

Production can also be improved by using higher-quality factors of production. This is especially true of one factor of production: labor. When economists talk about the quality of labor, they use the term *human capital*. **Human capital** refers to the knowledge, skills, and experience that workers can draw on to create products. How can we improve human capital? Three key factors are education, training, and experience. As workers gain more of these, the quality of their work improves and they become more productive. As you know, greater productivity leads to economic growth and a higher standard of living.

☑ **PROGRESS CHECK**

Synthesizing How do people benefit from economic growth?

LESSON 2 REVIEW

Review Vocabulary
1. What is the difference between a *factor market* and a *product market*?

2. What do the terms *specialization* and *division of labor* mean? How is each related to *productivity*?

Answer the Guiding Questions
3. *Identifying* What roles does government play in the circular flow model?

4. *Analyzing* How do you think specialization is related to differences in GDP between one country and another?

5. **INFORMATIVE/EXPLANATORY** Suppose you manufactured a product that required a scarce natural resource that was rising in cost. Describe how increased productivity might help you avoid passing on rising costs to your consumers in the form of higher prices.

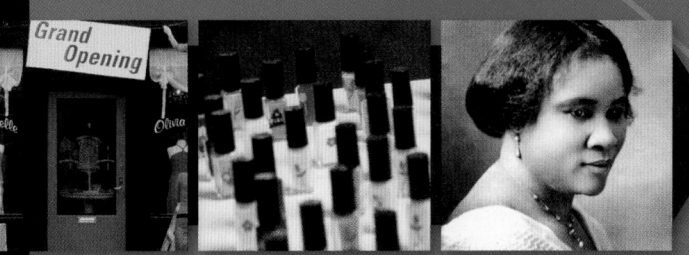

networks
There's More Online!

☑ **GRAPHIC ORGANIZER**
Capitalism

☑ **BIOGRAPHY**
C.J. Walker

☑ **VIDEO**

Lesson 3
Capitalism and Free Enterprise

ESSENTIAL QUESTION *Why and how do people make economic choices?*

IT MATTERS BECAUSE
Each of us enjoys the freedom to choose a job and decide how to use our money under the economic system called capitalism.

Capitalism in the United States

GUIDING QUESTION *What makes capitalism a successful economic system?*

The American market economy is huge. It accounts for about one-fifth of all the economic activity in the world. How did the United States become such an economic powerhouse?

One answer is in the way in which American citizens go about satisfying their basic economic wants. We engage in producing, buying, and selling goods and services in very productive ways. In the United States, citizens—not the government—make most of the economic decisions. This kind of economic system is called capitalism. In **capitalism,** private citizens own and decide how to use the factors of production in order to make money. Our system is also called a free enterprise economy. In a **free enterprise** system, individuals and groups have the freedom to start businesses with little government interference.

Six unique features of the free enterprise system contribute to the economic health of the United States and some other countries. These features are (1) economic freedom; (2) markets; (3) voluntary exchanges; (4) the profit motive; (5) competition; and (6) private property rights.

Reading**HELP**DESK

Taking Notes: *Organizing*

As you read the lesson, complete a web diagram by identifying the features of capitalism. Provide an example of each.

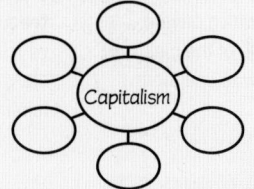

Capitalism

Content Vocabulary

- **capitalism**
- **free enterprise**
- **voluntary exchange**
- **profit**
- **profit motive**
- **competition**

Small businesses like this one produce about half of the nonfarm GDP in the private sector (that is, not including farming and government spending).

▶ **CRITICAL THINKING**
Making Connections How do you think the economy would be affected if people were not allowed to start their own businesses?

Economic Freedom

In the United States, we place a high value on the freedom to make our own economic decisions. People are free to buy and sell the factors of production—land, labor, and capital. Americans are free to become entrepreneurs and choose what type of goods or services to offer. They may also choose where to locate their business, whom they hire, and how they want to run the business.

Workers have the freedom to sell their labor. Americans can decide on what jobs they will do. In addition, they are free to save, invest, or spend the money they earn. Moreover, they can choose how to save their money, where to invest it, and what goods and services to buy with it.

The freedoms given to Americans and their businesses give the United States economy an important advantage over more restricted economies. These freedoms allow the marketplace to adapt quickly to changing economic conditions. As a result, the economy is more efficient and productive.

Markets

As you read earlier, buyers and sellers exchange goods and services for money in markets. Two forces are at work in these exchanges: demand and supply. Who decides what is supplied and what is demanded? The buyers and sellers themselves—individuals and businesses—make these decisions. The government does not tell producers what to make or consumers what to purchase. Consumers demand products, and businesses supply them.

Markets are not perfect. Some types of goods, such as public defense or a highway system, are not easily bought and sold in markets. Problems can arise from markets, too. Over time, though, markets have proven to be the best way to bring buyers and sellers together. Markets encourage competition, as you will read soon. But markets have another advantage as well. Markets also establish prices, and therefore do not need the involvement of government.

Reading**HELP**DESK

Content Vocabulary (cont.)
- **private property rights**
- **laissez-faire economics**

capitalism a system in which private citizens own most, if not all, of the means of production and decide how to use them within legislated limits

free enterprise economic system in which individuals and businesses are allowed to compete for profit with a minimum of government interference

Voluntary Exchange

The activity that takes place in the markets is known to economists as voluntary exchange. **Voluntary exchange** is the act of buyers and sellers freely and willingly choosing to take part in marketplace transactions. These transactions are the buying and selling of goods and services. The buying and selling of any factors of production is a transaction as well. In these exchanges, both the buyer and the seller give something up—money or a product. Both exchange what they have for something else that they want—a product or money. When these exchanges take place voluntarily, or willingly, both the buyer and the seller benefit. If they did not benefit, the exchange would not have happened in the first place.

The Profit Motive

You can understand what would make a person want to buy something in a market. The reason is simple: The consumer wants that good or service. But why would someone want to make or supply that product? The equally simple answer is that he or she wants money.

In a capitalist economy, people risk their savings by investing in businesses. Investing in a business is risky because the business might not succeed. On the other hand, if the business succeeds and grows, investors can earn great rewards.

People take risks in the hope of making a profit. **Profit** is the amount of money left over from the sale of goods or services after all the costs of production have been paid. The **profit motive** is the desire to earn money by creating and selling goods and services. This motive drives the U.S. economy. It is a major reason why capitalism is a successful economic system.

The profit motive pushes people to think of new or improved goods and services. It leads people to imagine new, more productive ways of making and supplying those goods and services. The new businesses that Americans start help the U.S. economy grow and prosper.

PHOTO: Jim McHugh/Corbis Outline

This young woman created a line of nail polish when she was just a teenager. Millions of young people throughout the world learn about entrepreneurship through education programs such as Junior Achievement.

▶ **CRITICAL THINKING**
Finding the Main Idea What role does entrepreneurship have in a market-based economy?

---

voluntary exchange the act of buyers and sellers freely and willingly engaging in market transactions

profit the money a business receives for its products or services over and above its costs

profit motive the driving force that encourages individuals and organizations to improve their material well-being

Competition

Starting a business does not ensure success. Businesses compete with one another. In fact, capitalism thrives on **competition**— the struggle among businesses with similar products to attract consumers. The most efficient producers sell goods at lower prices. Lower prices attract buyers. If other producers cannot improve their productivity or offer a better-quality product, they might be forced out of business. Competition leads to greater efficiency, higher-quality products, and more satisfied customers.

Private Property Rights

Under capitalism, people and businesses have **private property rights.** This means they have the freedom to own and use their property as they wish. They can even choose to **dispose** of, or get rid of, that property. Private property rights give Americans the **incentive,** or drive, to work, save, and invest. That is the case because we can keep any gains that we earn. Private property has another important benefit; people tend to take better care of things they own.

☑ PROGRESS CHECK

Explaining Why do people risk their money to start businesses?

AMERICAN ENTREPRENEURS

• C. J. Walker, Beauty Products Entrepreneur

The woman known as C. J. Walker was born Sarah Breedlove in 1867 to parents who were emancipated slaves. She was poor and had little formal education, but she became one of the first woman millionaires in this country.

With an initial investment of $1.50 in savings, Walker developed a line of beauty products for black women. Thousands of Walker saleswomen sold the popular products door-to-door. Her business earned $500,000 per year, an income she grew further by investing in real estate.

C. J. Walker attributed her success to hard work and a willingness to take chances. "I . . . came from the cotton fields of the South. From there I was promoted to the washtub. From there I was promoted to the cook kitchen. And from there I promoted myself into the business of manufacturing hair goods and preparations."

Walker became a well-known philanthropist in the African American community. She used her wealth to fund scholarships and to support artists and writers. She gave to civil rights organizations, including the NAACP.

PHOTO: Michael Ochs Archives/Getty Images

Looking at Leadership

How does Walker's story serve as an example of entrepreneurship?

The Origins of U.S. Capitalism

GUIDING QUESTION *How is the history of capitalism associated with the Founders?*

In 1776 Adam Smith, a Scottish philosopher and economist, published a book titled *The Wealth of Nations*. The book is still important today. In fact, Smith is considered to be the father of modern economics. In his book, Smith argues that the best way for society to advance is for people to work for their own self-interest, or their own well-being.

Businesses want to make money. That desire will lead them to make products that people need and want. People will give their money to the businesses that supply those needs and wants. In a similar fashion, people compete to sell their labor and employers compete to purchase it. The result is an efficient use of resources and a stable society.

In addition, Smith argued that all of this happens naturally, "as if by an invisible hand." In other words, market exchanges work best with little government interference.

From the writings of Smith and others came the idea of **laissez-faire** (LEH•SAY•FEHR) **economics.** *Laissez-faire*, a French term, means "to let alone." According to this philosophy, government should not interfere in the marketplace. Instead, it should limit itself to those actions needed to make sure that competition is allowed to take place.

When the United States was formed, many of the Founders were influenced by *The Wealth of Nations*. James Madison read it, and Alexander Hamilton borrowed from it in his writings. Thomas Jefferson wrote, "In political economy [economics], I think Smith's *Wealth of Nations* is the best book."

☑ PROGRESS CHECK

Explaining What role did Adam Smith believe government should play in the marketplace?

Why It MATTERS

Competition in Your Life

Have you ever competed with other students for placement on a team, a role in a school production, or to represent your school in some other way? Do you think this competition resulted in a better team or production? Explain.

laissez-faire economics belief that government should not interfere in the marketplace

LESSON 3 REVIEW

Vocabulary

1. What are the key features of *capitalism* and *free enterprise* in the U.S. economy?

2. What are *private property rights*? How are you affected by them?

Answer the Guiding Questions

3. *Determining* Under capitalism, who decides *what* gets produced and *who* uses the goods and services?

4. *Drawing Conclusions* How did the writings of Adam Smith influence the economy of the United States?

5. **INFORMATIVE/EXPLANATORY** Adam Smith said that people work for their own self-interest. Write a paragraph describing this idea and whether you agree with it. Use examples of particular jobs to support your opinion.

CHAPTER 17 Activities

Write your answers on a separate sheet of paper.

1 **Writing Activity**

EXPLORING THE ESSENTIAL QUESTION

Why and how do people make economic choices?

Every person who lives in the United States contributes to and is affected by the capitalist system. Write an essay to explain how you take part in our economy. Use these questions as a guide: How does your role as a consumer contribute to GDP? Where do you fit in the circular flow model of the economy? How are you affected by the competition of businesses? What economic freedoms and private property rights do you enjoy?

2 **21st Century Skills**

CREATE A NEW PRODUCT Have you ever heard of "Yankee ingenuity"? How about "American inventiveness"? Americans are famous for creating, inventing, and innovating. The entrepreneurial spirit runs deep in this country. Does it within you? Have you ever wanted to invent something? Here's your chance. A trick to inventing is to think of problems people face and then try to come up with a solution. Make a list of common problems and brainstorm solutions. When you come up with an invention, make a poster that advertises its features.

3 **Being an Active Citizen**

Every community in the United States is home to entrepreneurs. With the help of your teacher or another adult, locate a local entrepreneur and contact him or her. Prepare for and conduct a brief interview with your subject. Focus your questions on how the American economic system made the entrepreneur's business possible. Then type up your questions and the responses to post on a bulletin board about local entrepreneurs.

4 **Understanding Visuals**

A market is a place where buyers and sellers exchange products and money. Markets are "capitalism in action." Study the photograph of a farmers' market. Identify in the photograph evidence of each of the following features of capitalism: economic freedom, markets, voluntary exchanges, the profit motive, competition, and private property rights.

PHOTO: Zane Williams/Getty Images

REVIEW THE GUIDING QUESTIONS
Directions: Choose the best answer for each question.

1 Which list correctly names three of the four factors of production?
   A. productivity, specialization, and efficiency
   B. goods, services, and entrepreneurs
   C. supply, demand, and scarcity
   D. natural resources, labor, and entrepreneurs

2 What is the name for the total market value of all the final goods and services produced in a country in one year?
   F. GDP
   G. income
   H. productivity
   I. resources

3 GDP per capita measures
   A. GDP per year.
   B. the total market value of a country's production.
   C. GDP per person.
   D. a nation's standard of living.

4 Entrepreneurs are driven to start and invest in business because of
   F. the cost of production.
   G. the division of labor.
   H. economic interdependence.
   I. the profit motive.

5 In a capitalist economy, competition is allowed to prosper with a minimum of
   A. government interference.
   B. voluntary exchange.
   C. specialization.
   D. division of labor.

6 Adam Smith stated that an "invisible hand"
   F. created modern economic theory.
   G. leads to the efficient use of resources.
   H. was a danger to economic success.
   I. was the power of government in the economy.

DBQ **ANALYZING DOCUMENTS**

Directions: Analyze the table and answer the questions that follow.

7 **Drawing Conclusions** What conclusion can be reached on the basis of these data?

A. The United States has the highest per capita GDP in the world.

B. The United States has the highest per capita GDP of these five countries.

C. Many other countries have a higher per capita GDP than the United States.

D. China is the most populous country in the world.

8 **Analyzing Visuals** Which of these nations has the lowest per capita GDP?

F. Japan

G. China

H. Germany

I. India

COMPARING SELECTED NATIONAL ECONOMIES, 2013

Country	GDP (in trillions)	GDP per Capita
USA	$16.7	$52,800
China	$13.4	$9,800
India	$5.0	$4,000
Japan	$4.7	$37,100
Germany	$3.2	$39,500

Source: CIA, *The World Factbook.*

SHORT RESPONSE

"Every individual . . . neither intends to promote the public interest, nor knows how much he is promoting it . . . he intends only his own gain. . . . By pursuing his own interest, he frequently promotes that of the society more effectually [effectively] than when he really intends to promote it."

—Adam Smith, *The Wealth of Nations* (1776)

9 Write a one- or two-sentence summary of Smith's statement.

10 How does Smith's statement support laissez-faire economics?

EXTENDED RESPONSE

11 **Argument** Do you think individuals can promote the well-being of society by promoting their own well-being? Explain your answer.

Need Extra Help?

If You've Missed Question	**1**	**2**	**3**	**4**	**5**	**6**	**7**	**8**	**9**	**10**	**11**
Review Lesson	1	1	2	2	3	3	1	1	3	3	1, 2, 3

Personal Finance

ESSENTIAL QUESTION
Why and how do people make economic choices?

The Story Matters...

Americans of all ages like to shop. Children and adults alike are interested in new products and services. Whether it is the latest electronic gadget, the newest fashion, the most recent movie, the biggest television, or the most energy-efficient car—somebody will want to buy it.

With so many purchase options available, consumers must spend—and save—wisely. For example, an average family of four in the United States may spend about 4 percent of its income on clothing. So if a family earns $40,000 in a year, family members might spend $1,600 on their clothes. That family also has to consider what it spends on food, a place to live, and many other basic expenses. Learning how to make smart decisions about how to spend and save your money will help you reach your financial goals.

◄ *A teenager sorts through the latest fashions at a department store in New York City.*

PHOTO: Jemal Countess/Getty Images

485

Real-Life Civics

▶ SPENDING WITH CARE

Before buying an expensive product such as a car or a home, most people have to plan ahead and save money. Many Americans pay a part of the price for a large purchase and borrow the rest of the money from a bank. It may take five years to pay off a car loan, and as many as 30 years to pay off a mortgage, or loan, for a home.

With so much at stake, consumers have to carefully consider what they choose to buy. There are many other major economic decisions that consumers may make. These include such expenses as attending college, moving to a new location, or taking a trip. All require planning. When you make informed choices, you can be confident that you are spending your money wisely.

▷ A salesperson shows a car to an interested buyer.

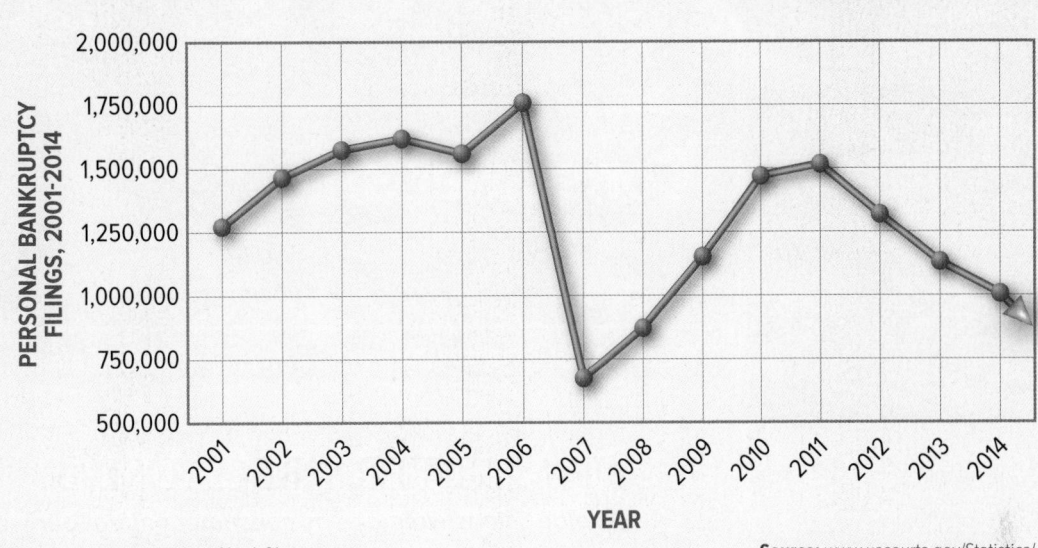

PERSONAL BANKRUPTCY FILINGS, 2001–2014 FISCAL YEARS*

PERSONAL BANKRUPTCY FILINGS, 2001-2014

YEAR

*year ending on March 31

Source: www.uscourts.gov/Statistics/

This line graph shows changes in the number of personal bankruptcies between 2001 and 2014.

MONEY TROUBLES Life rarely goes completely according to plan. Unexpected events, such as a poor economy or personal health problems, can bring on job loss. Weeks, months, or even years without steady work can lead to missed payments on loans for homes, cars, or other items. When people do not have the money to pay what they owe, they may be forced to declare personal bankruptcy. Bankruptcy is the state of being unable to pay one's debts. Many factors can lead to bankruptcy. We cannot protect ourselves against all emergencies. We can, however, do our best to build a financial cushion, by putting some income into savings.

CIVIC LITERACY
★ ★ ★ ★

Describing Describe the trend in bankruptcy filings between 2001 and 2014.

Generalizing How can a lack of financial planning lead people to spend more than they can afford?

Your Opinion Describe your relationship with money. Are you more comfortable spending money or saving it? Why?

netw⊚rks

There's More Online!

☑ **GRAPHIC ORGANIZER**
Smart Buying Strategies

☑ **INFOGRAPHIC**
Tips on Being a Successful
Consumer

☑ **CHART**
Are You an Impulse Buyer?

☑ **VIDEO**

Lesson 1

Consumerism

ESSENTIAL QUESTION *Why and how do people make economic choices?*

IT MATTERS BECAUSE

*The decisions we make as consumers affect our well-being and
our financial goals.*

Consumer Rights

GUIDING QUESTION *What rights do you have as a consumer?*

Have you ever been tempted by an advertisement for some
dazzling new product? How can you know for certain that the
ad is telling the truth about the product? How do you know
the product is safe or even that it works the way that it is
advertised?

As a consumer, you have certain rights. Many of these rights
have been secured by the efforts of consumerism. **Consumerism**
is a movement to educate buyers about the purchases they make
and to demand better, safer products from manufacturers.

Starting in the late 1800s, the government began passing
legislation to protect consumer interests. In 1906 Congress
passed the Federal Food and Drugs Act, which established
the agency now known as the Food and Drug Administration
(FDA). The FDA protects consumers by overseeing the safety
of food, drugs, and medical devices. In 1914 the government
set up the Federal Trade Commission (FTC). The FTC is the
nation's consumer protection agency. It works to prevent fraud,
deception, and unfair business practices.

PHOTO: (tl) Digital Vision/Getty Images; (tcl) Caspar Benson/Getty Images; (tcr) Tim Boyle/Bloomberg via Getty Images; (tr) Jeff Greenberg/Alamy

Reading**HELP**DESK

Taking Notes: *Identifying*

As you read, use a web diagram
to identify ways to be a smart
consumer.

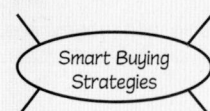

Smart Buying
Strategies

Content Vocabulary

- **consumerism**
- **redress**
- **comparison shopping**

- **generic
good**
- **warranty**

- **impulse buying**
- **disposable income**
- **discretionary income**

In 1962 President John F. Kennedy delivered a special message to Congress. The president noted that the variety of food and medicine available to consumers had greatly increased. He also observed that technological advances had made home appliances more complex. At the same time, he said, advertisements for these products had grown more persuasive.

Kennedy pointed out that the average person could not be sure of quality and safety claims made for the thousands of products on the market.

Kennedy saw consumer protections as key not only to health and safety, but also to economic success.

PRIMARY SOURCE

❝ If consumers are offered inferior products, if prices are exorbitant [too high], if drugs are unsafe or worthless, if the consumer is unable to choose on an informed basis, then his dollar is wasted, his health and safety may be threatened, and the national interest suffers. ❞

—President John F. Kennedy, 1962

Consumers face a wide variety of products and choices today.

▶ CRITICAL THINKING
Making Connections What does the consumer in the image have the right to do before making his purchase?

To protect consumers, the president proposed that four basic consumer rights be recognized. This set of rights became known as the consumer bill of rights:

1. *The right to safety:* Consumers have the right to safe products that will not harm their health or their lives.

2. *The right to be informed:* Consumers have the right to be protected against dishonest or very misleading information. They have the right to be given the facts needed to make informed choices.

3. *The right to choose:* Consumers have the right to choose from a variety of products and services at competitive prices.

4. *The right to be heard:* Consumers have the right to have their interests considered when laws are being written.

consumerism a movement to educate buyers about the purchases they make and to demand better and safer products from manufacturers

► **CRITICAL THINKING**
Drawing Conclusions Why might companies want to test products and publicize the results of their tests before selling goods?

Over time, people found that those four basic consumer rights did not provide enough protections. So consumer advocacy groups had additional consumer rights recognized:

5. *The right to* **redress**, *or remedy:* Consumers have the right to have problems corrected and to receive compensation, or payment, for false claims, poorly made goods, and poor services.

6. *The right to environmental health:* Consumers have the right not to suffer harmful air, water, and earth conditions because of human economic activity. They also have the right to work in healthy and safe environments.

7. *The right to service:* Consumers have the right to be treated respectfully and to have their questions and concerns addressed. Consumers also have the right to refuse service.

8. *The right to consumer education:* Consumers have the right to information and training that helps them realize the rights listed above.

In 1912 the Better Business Bureau (BBB) formed to help protect consumer rights. Today, the BBB is a private organization that has more than 100 branches nationwide. It rates companies and service providers according to consumer standards. The BBB also provides information to help educate consumers and reviews consumer complaints about companies.

✓ **PROGRESS CHECK**

Finding the Main Idea What rights do consumers have?

Reading**HELP**DESK

redress payment for a wrong or loss

comparison shopping the process of comparing competing products and prices in order to find the best value

generic good an item that does not have a brand name but is basically similar to a more expensive, well-known product

PHOTO: Caspar Benson/Getty Images

Consumer Responsibilities

GUIDING QUESTION *What responsibilities do you have as a consumer?*

With every right come certain responsibilities. With the right to vote, for example, comes the responsibility of staying informed. In the same way, our rights as consumers require some responsibilities on our part. Remember, as a consumer, you have the right to voice your complaints. You also have a responsibility to exercise your rights.

Be an Informed Consumer

Many consumer responsibilities might also be described as smart buying strategies. Smart consumers gather as much information as they can about what they want to buy before opening their wallets. Consumer magazines and Web sites often provide trustworthy information about product quality. Many of these sources also report on other consumers' experiences.

Advertising can help consumers learn about goods and services. However, consumers must be cautious of advertising that appeals to emotions. Ads may try to persuade people to buy things they do not really need. Some ads use questionable techniques to convince consumers to buy certain products.

Once you know what product you want, you must decide where to buy it. It is important to compare a product's price at different stores or companies. This process is known as **comparison shopping.** To comparison shop, read newspaper advertisements and store flyers, and visit different stores. Use comparison-shopping Web sites to make quick comparisons. You might also consider a generic substitute. A **generic good** is one that does not have a brand name but is similar to a more expensive, well-known product.

TIPS ON BEING A SUCCESSFUL CONSUMER

- Gather information on product quality
- Evaluate advertisments
- Comparison shop
- Consider generic products
- Consider used items
- Report problems promptly

PHOTO: Tim Boyle/Bloomberg via Getty Images

INFOGRAPHIC

A successful consumer shops carefully and thoughtfully to make his or her money go as far as possible.

▶ CRITICAL THINKING

1. *Analyzing Visuals* What is meant by the phrase "successful consumer"?

2. *Making Inferences* What do all of these tips require consumers to do?

Most stores have customer service counters to handle returns or requests for redress when an item is faulty.

► **CRITICAL THINKING**

Making Decisions What are some things you might consider when deciding whether or not to purchase an additional warranty beyond what the manufacturer supplies?

Handle Problems Appropriately

If a product or service is faulty, it is the responsibility of the consumer to obtain redress. If you buy a faulty product or service, report the problem immediately. Do not try to fix a product yourself. Many products can be safely repaired only by qualified technicians. In addition, home repair may cancel a product's warranty. A **warranty** is a manufacturer's or a seller's promise to repair or replace a faulty product within a certain time period. Most warranties require you to have the original sales slip, so put it in a safe place.

If you need redress, contact the seller or manufacturer. State the problem and offer a fair solution. Keep an accurate record of your efforts to obtain redress, including names of the people with whom you spoke or to whom you wrote. Give each person reasonable time to solve the problem before contacting another source. Be courteous. If you cannot settle your complaint with the seller, report it to your state's consumer protection agency.

Consumers have a right to expect honesty from producers and sellers. In turn, producers and sellers have a right to expect honesty from consumers. For example, suppose you purchase a camera and you drop it and break it on the way home. You should not go back to the store and tell the seller that the camera is faulty. That would be dishonest. You have a responsibility to provide the seller with the whole truth as you know it.

 **PROGRESS CHECK**

Specifying What are some ways to be an informed consumer?

Reading **HELP**DESK

Reading Strategy: *Making Connections*

When you make connections, you think about how what you have read applies to your life. If you purchased a product and then discovered that it was faulty when you got home, how would that make you feel? What steps would you take to fix the situation?

warranty the promise made by a manufacturer or a seller to repair or replace a product within a certain time period if it is faulty

Making Purchasing Decisions

GUIDING QUESTION *What steps can you take to be a successful consumer?*

Have you ever regretted spending money on something? On the other hand, maybe you wished you had bought an item when it was on sale. No matter the size of your income, spending it requires decision making. Wise consumers **distinguish,** or look for differences, among competing wants. Being a wise consumer means considering the effects of purchasing decisions.

Avoid Impulse Buying

To act on impulse means to act on emotion, without thinking about the effects of the action. **Impulse buying,** then, is an unplanned, often emotional decision to buy. Impulse buying can ruin a budget. Even thoughtful consumers can fall prey to impulse buying.

You can control impulse spending in several ways. Before you go shopping, make a list of the things you need. When you are shopping, purchase only the items on your list. If you see a tempting item, take a break. Leave the store, walk around, and decide whether you really need the item. Better yet, wait a day. The impulse may pass once you give the purchase more thought.

If you decide that you really need the item, then comparison shop. You may find a better price somewhere else. Also, be careful with online buying. It is all too easy to charge things online. The same is true when making any purchase with a credit card. Try to pay with cash, and save your credit card purchases for emergencies.

ARE YOU AN IMPULSE BUYER?

- Do you buy things you do not need or do not want?

- Does buying things make you feel better?

- Do you quickly lose interest in items you have bought?

- Do you often borrow money from friends because you have spent yours?

CHART SKILLS

Impulse buying can have negative consequences for consumers.

▶ CRITICAL THINKING

1. *Analyzing Visuals* What are the questions in the chart designed to help you do?

2. *Problem Solving* If you are an impulse buyer, what steps can you take to avoid this problem?

Academic Vocabulary

distinguish to see a difference in; to separate into categories

impulse buying an unplanned, often emotional, decision to buy

disposable income income left after all taxes on it have been paid

discretionary income income left after taxes on it have been paid and that you can choose to spend

Prioritize Your Wants

How much income do you have to spend? Economists define **disposable income** as the money that remains after you have paid your taxes. It is also called **discretionary income** because you can choose how to spend it.

All wants are not the same, however. Some wants, like food, clothing, and shelter, are needed for basic survival. Even among these wants, however, you have to make choices. Should your family eat out at an expensive restaurant or cook a low-cost meal at home? Obviously, wants such as those you need to survive are more important than others, such as a new bicycle or a DVD player. When spending money, you must choose among competing wants. Part of being a wise consumer is knowing that you have to prioritize, or rank, your wants from the most to the least important.

Think About Opportunity Cost

Making a consumer decision involves an opportunity cost. You may recall that opportunity cost refers to the next-best alternative choice—the one you did not make. Suppose a friend purchased athletic shoes that just came out on the market and you want to buy a pair as well. Before you do, ask yourself, "What can't I buy or do if I buy these shoes?" In other words, decide whether the shoes are worth what you could purchase instead.

It is important to consider what your economic goals are when you make buying decisions. The buying decisions that you make help reveal what kind of a decision maker you are and how committed, or dedicated, you are to keeping your financial goals.

☑ **PROGRESS CHECK**

Specifying What is an example of opportunity cost?

LESSON 1 REVIEW

Review Vocabulary

1. What is *comparison shopping*?

2. What is an advantage of buying a *generic good*?

Answer the Guiding Questions

3. *Finding the Main Idea* Why do consumers need a bill of rights?

4. *Explaining* What should you do if you purchase a faulty product? Why?

5. *Explaining* What are some ways to avoid impulse buying?

6. **ARGUMENT** Suppose you are saving your money to buy concert tickets to see your favorite band. While browsing in the stores at your local mall, you see a poster for this band. You already have several posters, but not this particular one. Write a persuasive essay to talk yourself out of making this impulse buy.

netw⊕rks

There's More Online!

☑ **GRAPHIC ORGANIZER**
Sources of Credit

☑ **CHARTS**
Positive and Negative Balances
Monthly Budget
Credit Card Bill

☑ **INFOGRAPHIC**
Methods of Payment by U.S.
Consumers

Lesson 2
Budgeting Your Money

ESSENTIAL QUESTION *Why and how do people make economic choices?*

IT MATTERS BECAUSE
Making and following a budget can help you organize your finances.

Using a Personal Budget

GUIDING QUESTION *How can making a personal budget lead to financial responsibility?*

Have you ever stayed home when your friends went out because you had no money to go? Learning more about budgets can help you have enough money to do the things that you would really like to do.

The best way to manage your money is to make a **budget.** A budget is a careful record that tracks all the money you earn and spend. A budget tells you exactly where your money comes from and where it goes. A budget is also a tool. It can help you cut down on impulse spending and save money for things you really want.

Budgeting Basics

The basic parts of a budget are the same whether you are a preparing an individual budget or the federal government's budget. The three parts of a budget are income, expenses, and the balance. Income is the money you earn, or any other money that you receive, such as a gift. **Expenses** are ways in which you spend money. The **balance** is the amount of money you have left over after you subtract your expenses from your income.

Reading **HELP** DESK

Taking Notes: *Identifying*

As you read, complete a graphic organizer like the one shown by identifying common sources of credit.

Sources of Credit

Content Vocabulary

- budget
- expense
- balance
- deficit
- credit
- interest
- loan
- borrower
- annual percentage rate (APR)

A budget helps consumers understand how much money they earn and how much money they spend.

▶ CRITICAL THINKING

1 *Analyzing Visuals* Which examples show a surplus, and which show a deficit?

2 *Making Inferences* What can the people with the deficit do to correct the problem?

		Income	Expenses	Balance
Positive	**Example A**	$100	$80	$20
	Example B	$100	$20	$80
Negative	**Example C**	$100	$120	-$20
	Example D	$100	$180	-$80

If you have more income than expenses, you have a surplus. In a budget, a surplus is a positive balance. If you have more expenses than income, you have a **deficit.** A deficit is a negative balance. Your goal is to keep a positive balance. This will give you a surplus that you can set aside for emergency expenses. You can also use a surplus to make a larger contribution to your savings account.

Making a Budget

Making and organizing a personal budget is not difficult. Anyone who knows the basics of addition, subtraction, multiplication, and division can do it. Follow these steps to develop a budget:

1. Make a list of everything you spend for two weeks. Include entertainment, clothing, food, personal items, gifts, transportation, donations, and savings. You could even have a category for miscellaneous expenses, or expenses that do not fit in any other category. This category might include expenses such as pet care or those that arise as a result of an unexpected event, such as repair for an electronic device. You also might want to budget for impulse items. But it is important to record *everything* you spend.

2. For the same time period, record all of the money you take in and its source. Sources might be your allowance, job earnings, borrowed money, or gifts.

ReadingHELPDESK

budget a plan for making and spending money

expense money spent on goods and services

balance amount of money left over after subtracting expenses from income; money still owed on a credit card or bank loan

deficit a negative balance

Academic Vocabulary

data factual information used for reasoning

3. After you have recorded your **data,** or information, analyze it. At the end of two weeks, did you have a surplus, a deficit, or a balanced budget? A balanced budget is one in which income equals expenses.

4. If you had a deficit, review your spending to see where your money went. Consider ways to spend less, or earn more, during the next two weeks.

5. If you had a balanced budget, decide whether you want to increase savings, have more emergency money, or increase spending. Then look for ways to cut spending or increase earnings.

6. If you had a surplus, you can increase spending, or you can save the extra money.

☑ PROGRESS CHECK

Explaining What is a balanced budget?

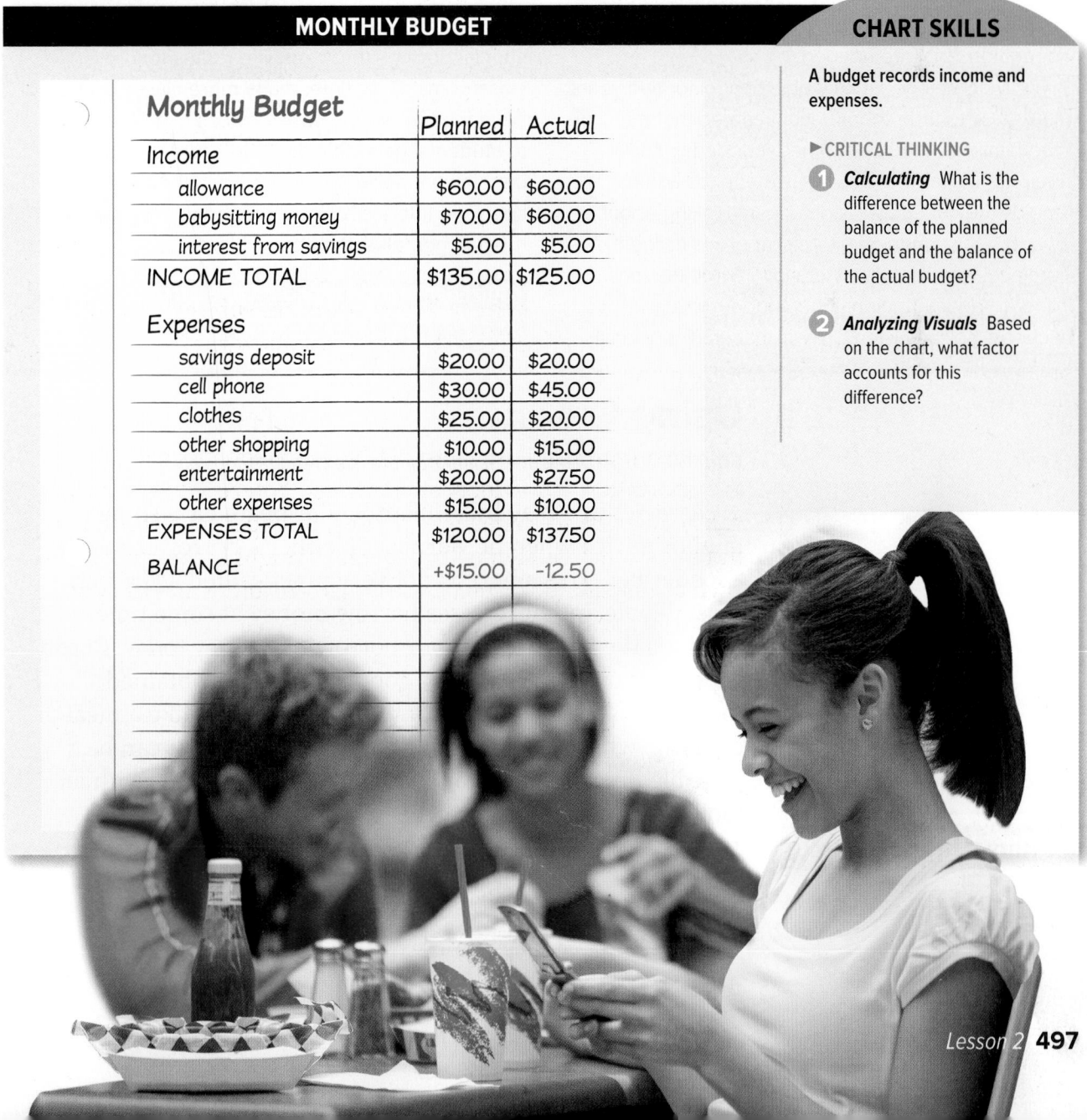

MONTHLY BUDGET			CHART SKILLS

Monthly Budget	Planned	Actual
Income		
allowance	$60.00	$60.00
babysitting money	$70.00	$60.00
interest from savings	$5.00	$5.00
INCOME TOTAL	$135.00	$125.00
Expenses		
savings deposit	$20.00	$20.00
cell phone	$30.00	$45.00
clothes	$25.00	$20.00
other shopping	$10.00	$15.00
entertainment	$20.00	$27.50
other expenses	$15.00	$10.00
EXPENSES TOTAL	$120.00	$137.50
BALANCE	+$15.00	-12.50

A budget records income and expenses.

▶ CRITICAL THINKING

❶ ***Calculating*** What is the difference between the balance of the planned budget and the balance of the actual budget?

❷ ***Analyzing Visuals*** Based on the chart, what factor accounts for this difference?

teen citizens in action

When Jacob Stern says, "Listen up," he is not just telling people to pay attention. He's talking about the project he started at age 12 to help children with hearing disabilities. For the past two years, he has worked to raise money for an elementary school called the Debbie School at the University of Miami. This school has classes for hearing-impaired children.

Jacob's interest in helping children with hearing disabilities began with his concern for his brother Oliver, who was born deaf. "After nine years and many surgeries," said Jacob, "Oliver's hearing was restored, but many families cannot afford the costly operations that are needed."

Oliver attended the Debbie School for two years. On a visit to the school, Jacob learned that many of the families with children there needed financial help to pay for the hearing aid batteries and ear molds they needed. Jacob began thinking about ways to raise money for the school. He called his project Listen Up! First, he and his brother went door-to-door in their neighborhood and at their schools, selling Listen Up! wristbands. Then, family

and friends became interested in the project, agreeing to donate money to the Debbie School instead of giving him gifts for his bar mitzvah, a religious ceremony for Jewish boys at age 13.

With the help of these groups, Jacob raised $25,000 for the Debbie School. With some of this money, the school has so far bought

The Debbie School recognized Jacob for his contribution.

special devices that work like radios for six classrooms. Over time, many more classrooms will have them as well. These devices can be attached to students' hearing aids. When students tune to a certain channel, they can clearly hear the teacher speaking into a special microphone. Now when the teacher talks, they can all listen up.

Citizenship and Teens

How is scarcity related to Jacob's Listen Up! project?

Using Credit

GUIDING QUESTION *Why is it important to use credit responsibly?*

A character in a play by William Shakespeare gave some famous advice when he warned, "Neither a borrower nor a lender be." This advice is not very practical today. In fact, most people and businesses borrow money at some time. Credit is the key tool used for borrowing money today. **Credit** is permission to pay later for goods or services obtained today. With credit, you can buy something now, like a meal or clothing, while promising to pay for it later. Credit can be a valuable item in your financial toolbox. However, as with all tools, you have to use it correctly.

PHOTO: (tr, cr) Courtesy of Jacob Stern

Reading**HELP**DESK

credit permission to pay later for goods or services obtained today

Academic Vocabulary
fee the cost of a service

interest the payment that people or institutions receive when they lend money or allow someone else to use their money

loan money lent at interest

Credit Basics

Understanding how credit works in our society requires knowing some important terms.

- A lender is a person or an institution that gives someone money temporarily and for a **fee,** or cost.
- The fee charged for borrowing money is called **interest.**
- The money lent at interest is called a **loan.** The recipient of a loan is a **borrower.**
- The **annual percentage rate (APR)** is the annual cost of credit expressed as a percentage of the amount borrowed.
- A credit rating is an estimate of a borrower's ability to repay a loan. It is based on the borrower's previous credit experiences, financial situation, job history, and other information.
- Collateral is property, such as a house, a car, or another valuable item, that a borrower pledges as security for a loan. If a borrower fails to repay a loan, the lender can seize the collateral as payment.

Sources of Credit

One source of credit that you may use is a retail store credit card. These cards are likely to have preapproved credit lines, or amounts, of $250, $500, or $1,000. These cards can be used to buy anything in the store up to the preapproved amount. You then must pay a certain portion of the purchase back every month. These payments include interest on the amount you owe.

Banks, credit unions, savings and loan associations, and finance companies offer credit to adult consumers who have a good credit rating. A bank is an institution that provides financial services, such as checking accounts and car and home loans. A credit union is like a bank but is formed by a group with a common bond. For example, a credit union may exist for all workers at a given company. The money that workers save is then lent out to other members.

A finance company specializes in making loans to individuals. Unlike banks, finance companies do not accept deposits from individuals. They are also less regulated than banks, and they charge a much higher rate of interest.

Stores that sell relatively expensive merchandise, such as clothing, electronics, appliances, and furniture, offer credit.

Consumers can apply to banks and other institutions for credit cards.

▶ **CRITICAL THINKING**
Drawing Conclusions Why do you think lenders send out offers for credit cards to people's homes?

PHOTO: (cr) Photodisc/Getty Images; (br) Jerry Arcieri/Corbis

borrower the recipient of a loan	**annual percentage rate (APR)** the annual cost of credit expressed as a percentage of the amount borrowed

In recent years, the number of teenagers who have credit cards has skyrocketed. More and more are finding themselves in debt even before they graduate from high school. Do some research to find out why so many teenagers are in debt. Write a few sentences explaining why this is so and why other teens should take extra caution before applying for that first credit card.

This credit helps customers make purchases. Stores usually offer low credit limits. A credit limit is the maximum amount a borrower may charge.

Large credit purchases, such as a car, usually require the buyer to make a down payment. This means that the buyer must pay a part of the purchase price when making the purchase. The remaining balance is then divided into equal monthly payments.

Credit Cards

Perhaps the most common type of credit in use today is the credit card. Banks, credit card companies, and stores issue credit cards. A credit card allows consumers to pay for goods and services using borrowed money, up to a preset limit.

When you apply for a credit card, the lender checks your credit rating. The lender then decides what you can afford to pay back, based on that rating, and assigns a dollar limit. Some lenders do not charge interest if you pay off your full credit balance each month. However, you will be charged an additional fee if your monthly payment is late. Late payments can result in even higher interest rates. High interest charges on unpaid balances add up quickly.

CHART SKILLS

Consumers who use credit cards receive a bill and must make payments each month.

▶ CRITICAL THINKING

1. **Analyzing Visuals** What information does this bill show?

2. **Calculating** Did the owner of this credit card pay off his balance in full? How can you tell? Will he most likely have to pay interest?

CREDIT CARD BILL

GLOBAL CREDIT

Doe, John

Statement Summary

Current summary information as of: Jan. 5, 2012

current balance	$ 130.50

Account Summary

Credit limit $1000
credit available ....$ 869

For Bonus Award information, select your previous statement summary

previous statement balance		$163.67
payments and credit	−	141.04
purchase and miscellaneous charges	+	107.87
cash advance	+	0.00
balance transfers	+	0.00
current balance	=	$130.50

Transactions (since your last statement)

Dec. 10, 2011	Joe's Grille Jacksonville, FL	$28.35
Dec. 10, 2011	Jacksonville Lanes Jacksonville, FL	$12.55
Dec. 11, 2011	Groceries Galore Jacksonville, FL	$27.97
Dec. 14, 2011	Pete's Pet Supplies Orange Park, FL	$25.10

Reading HELP DESK

Reading Strategy: *Making Inferences*

Making inferences means using clues from the text to gain a deeper understanding. The text discusses late fees, interest rates, and the interest cost of paying only the minimum balance. What does this tell you about how to handle credit card payments?

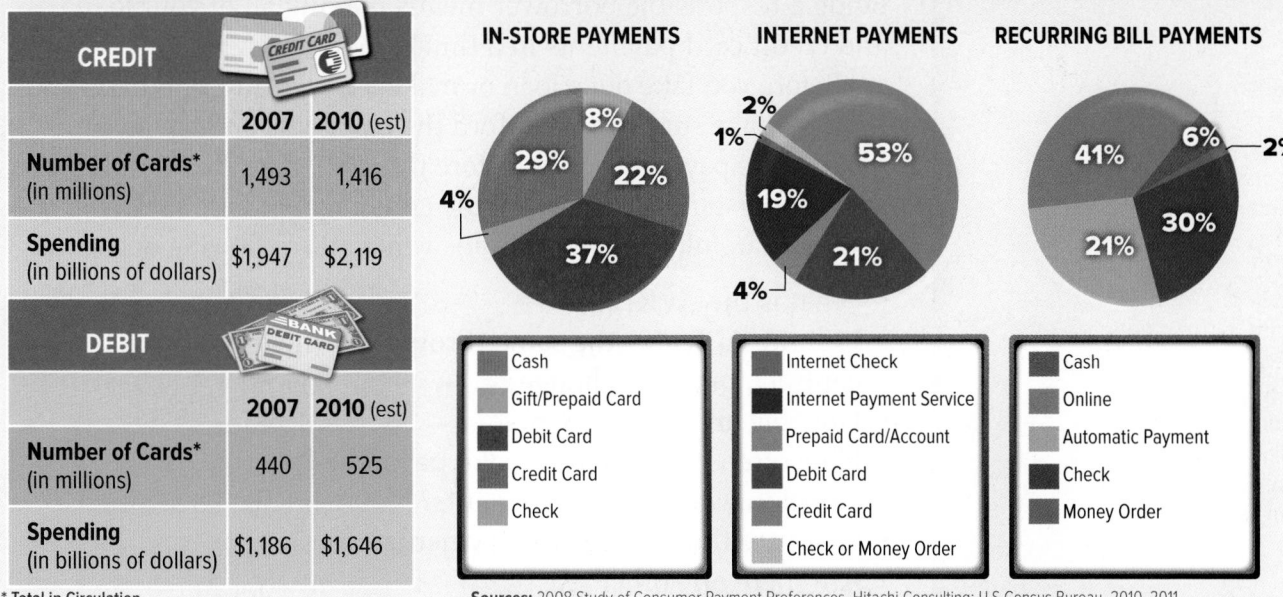

CREDIT		
	2007	**2010** (est)
Number of Cards* (in millions)	1,493	1,416
Spending (in billions of dollars)	$1,947	$2,119

DEBIT		
	2007	**2010** (est)
Number of Cards* (in millions)	440	525
Spending (in billions of dollars)	$1,186	$1,646

* Total in Circulation

IN-STORE PAYMENTS

8% • 29% • 22% • 4% • 37%

- Cash
- Gift/Prepaid Card
- Debit Card
- Credit Card
- Check

INTERNET PAYMENTS

2% • 1% • 53% • 19% • 21% • 4%

- Internet Check
- Internet Payment Service
- Prepaid Card/Account
- Debit Card
- Credit Card
- Check or Money Order

RECURRING BILL PAYMENTS

6% • 2% • 41% • 30% • 21%

- Cash
- Online
- Automatic Payment
- Check
- Money Order

Sources: 2008 Study of Consumer Payment Preferences, Hitachi Consulting; U.S Census Bureau, 2010, 2011

Here is an eye-opening example: Say you buy an item that costs $2,000 with a credit card that charges 18 percent interest. If you pay off the entire bill immediately, you pay $0 in interest. However, you may choose to pay only the minimum payment, which is usually 4 percent of the amount owed. It will then take you more than 10 years to pay for the item. By that time, you will have paid $1,142 in interest. That means that the $2,000 item will have cost you $3,142.

Benefits and Drawbacks of Credit

Americans use credit to make many purchases. Used wisely, credit can be a valuable tool for consumers. It allows you to obtain something you want without waiting until you can save the entire purchase price. Credit is especially important if you want to buy an expensive item like a car or a home. This is because it is difficult to save enough money to cover the purchase price of these items.

Making monthly payments on time can teach you financial discipline. Analyzing your financial situation to see if you can afford to use credit for a purchase is an important life skill.

However, credit also carries serious dangers. In a recent year, Americans carried a whopping $2.4 trillion in debt. Many people get into financial trouble by borrowing more than they are able to repay. Consumers who make only the minimum monthly payment soon find that they have a perpetual debt. This means that their debt goes on forever, often at a high interest rate. An unexpected job loss or a serious medical problem can lead unlucky or careless consumers into financial ruin.

INFOGRAPHIC

The three graphs show how often different methods of payment are used to make a purchase in a store or over the Internet or to make regular bill payments.

▶ CRITICAL THINKING

1 *Analyzing Visuals* How frequently is cash used for these three types of actions?

2 *Drawing Conclusions* Why do you think cash is not used for Internet payments?

Your Responsibilities as a Borrower

Being a responsible borrower means making all of your loan and credit card payments in a timely manner.

Before you take out a loan or make a credit card purchase, you need to make sure you can afford the payments and are able to make those payments on or before their due date. To do this, you must understand all aspects of the credit agreement. Look over the contract carefully and find the answers to the following questions:

- What is the APR?
- Will the APR stay the same throughout the duration of the contract, or will it change?
- How big are the payments?
- How often will I have to make payments?
- How long will I make payments?
- What are the fees for late payments?
- Are there any other fees?

After you know all the costs involved, you should review your budget carefully. Calculate your existing expenses, and add up your sources of income. Compare the two sums and calculate whether you have enough income to cover the additional expense of the credit card or loan payment. If not, then you should not take out the loan or make the purchase.

To go ahead with the purchase, you must adjust your budget by making cuts to other expenses or finding other sources of income. The cuts or the increase in income should be equal to or greater than what you need to pay for the loan or credit payment you will be making.

Another important thing to consider is how long your income will support credit payments. If your earnings are likely to decrease in the near future, then you might not want to take on the additional expense of a new payment.

✓ PROGRESS CHECK

Drawing Conclusions What might happen if a lender gives you more credit than you are able to repay?

LESSON 2 REVIEW

Review Vocabulary

1. What is the purpose of a *budget*?

2. Use the terms *borrower* and *loan* in a sentence.

3. How does *interest* relate to *credit*?

4. Write two sentences using the terms *expenses*, *balance*, and *deficit*.

Answer the Guiding Questions

5. ***Analyzing*** How can you use your budget data?

6. ***Drawing Conclusions*** How can you protect your credit rating?

7. **ARGUMENT** Write a radio script for a short public service announcement to convince others to make and follow a budget.

Lesson 3
Saving and Investing

ESSENTIAL QUESTION *Why and how do people make economic choices?*

⊙ IT MATTERS BECAUSE
Saving part of your income is the key to meeting many of your short-term and long-term financial goals.

Saving Money

GUIDING QUESTION *Why is it important to save part of your income?*

Have you ever heard the saying "Pay yourself first"? This does not mean that you should cash your paycheck and go on a spending spree. It means that savings should be the first expense in your budget. You owe it to yourself to save money for your future.

Reasons to Save Money

Everyone has long-term goals: what you want to do, where you want to live, how you want to spend your time. One way to help you reach your long-term spending goals is to save. To save means to set aside income for a while so that you have it to use later. Savings is the part of your income that you do not spend. You might already be saving some of your income for a future purpose, such as buying a car or continuing your education.

There are many good reasons to save. Most people need to save money for down payments. They must pay this money in advance before making major purchases. Buying a home or a car often requires a down payment.

PHOTO: (tc) Robert Clay/Alamy CARTOON: (tr) Jonny Hawkins, and Cartoonstock.com

Reading**HELP**DESK

Taking Notes: *Assessing*

As you read, complete a graphic organizer like the one shown. Place types of savings plans along the continuum according to how they rank from lower risk to higher risk.

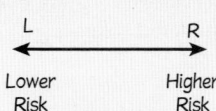

Lower
Risk

Higher
Risk

Content Vocabulary

- **principal**
- **maturity**
- **penalty**
- **return**
- **stock**
- **dividend**
- **bond**
- **mutual fund**

Lesson 3 **503**

People also save to pay for luxuries like vacations or high-definition TVs. They may save to pay for a college education or to have extra money in case of emergencies. Repairs to cars, home furnaces, and other major appliances can be expensive. So, too, can unexpected medical bills.

The whole economy benefits when you save income. Banks pay you interest on your savings deposits, which makes your savings grow. Then they use your money to make loans to other customers. Your money gets reinvested, or put back, into the local economy. That investment helps the economy grow.

Savings Accounts Versus Checking Accounts

No matter how you do it, it is important to save some of your money. You can open a savings account at a bank or a credit union. Your savings earn interest, which is added automatically to the principal. The **principal** is the amount that you deposited initially. Savings accounts are safe, but they pay less in interest than might be earned from other investments.

If you want frequent **access** to your account for paying bills or making purchases, you can open a checking account. Just as with a savings account, you make deposits into a checking account. Keep in mind, however, that some checking accounts offer little or no interest earnings on the account balance.

GRAPH SKILLS

The savings rate is the share of disposable income that has been saved. Remember that disposable income is the money left after taxes have been paid.

▶ CRITICAL THINKING

1 *Analyzing Visuals* During which decade was the ratio of personal savings to disposable income the highest? The lowest?

2 *Making Generalizations* Describe the overall trend in the ratio of savings over the course of the five decades shown.

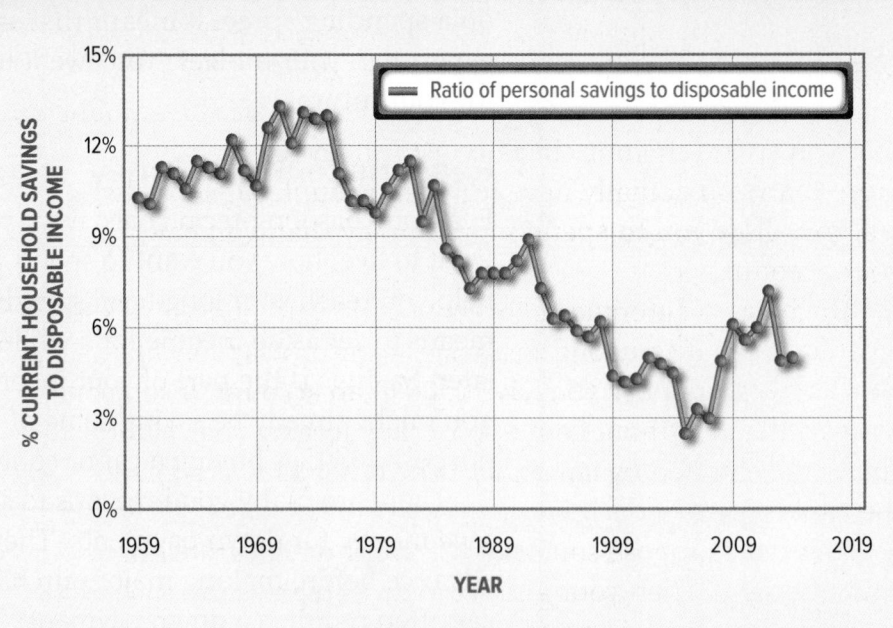

SAVINGS RATES, 1959–2014

Ratio of personal savings to disposable income

% CURRENT HOUSEHOLD SAVINGS TO DISPOSABLE INCOME

YEAR

Source: U.S. Department of Commerce: Bureau of Economic Analysis.

Reading**HELP**DESK

principal amount of initial deposit on which interest is earned

Academic Vocabulary

access the freedom to make use of something

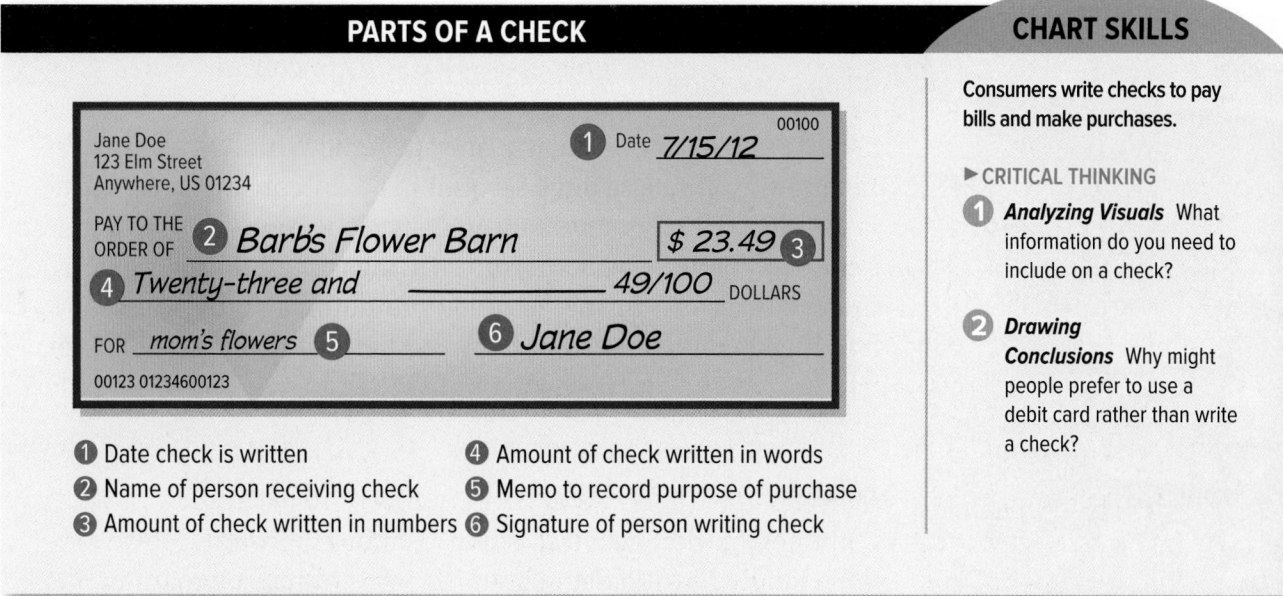

► CRITICAL THINKING

1 *Analyzing Visuals* What information do you need to include on a check?

2 *Drawing Conclusions* Why might people prefer to use a debit card rather than write a check?

1 Date check is written
2 Name of person receiving check
3 Amount of check written in numbers
4 Amount of check written in words
5 Memo to record purpose of purchase
6 Signature of person writing check

Checks are commonly used to pay bills and make purchases. When you write a check, the bank pays out of the funds in your checking account. You must be careful not to "bounce" a check. Bouncing a check means writing a check for an amount greater than the amount of money in your account. Keep a careful record of each check that you write to avoid bouncing checks. Banks often add a steep charge for every bounced check.

Many banks offer debit cards. A debit card looks like a credit card but works much like a check. When you make a purchase with your debit card, the money comes directly from your checking account so that you do not have to write a paper check. However, you still need to record the amount that you spend in your check register to avoid spending more than you actually have in your account. Most banks will not allow you to spend more money than you have in your account.

The biggest difference between a debit card and a check is what happens if someone steals your card or your checkbook. For example, suppose you have $500 in an account. If someone writes a check without your approval by forging your name, your loss is limited by law to $50. The other $450 is a loss to the bank.

However, suppose someone uses your debit card without your approval. Then your loss could go as high as the $500. This is because the bank is not responsible for the misuse of your debit card. For this reason, it is important to keep your debit card safe and secure.

✓ PROGRESS CHECK

Applying For what sorts of emergencies might a person need savings?

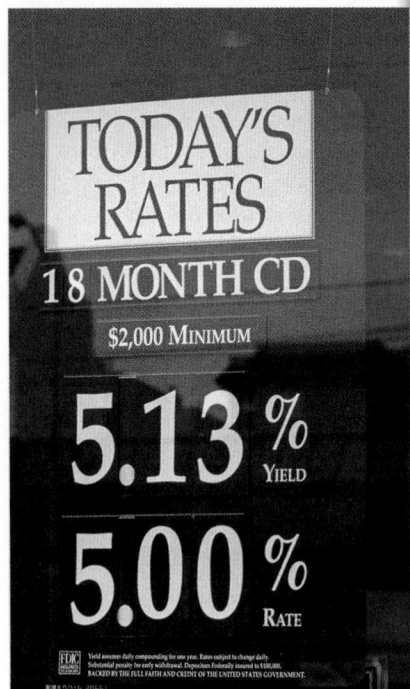

Certificates of deposit offer consumers set interest rates.

▶ CRITICAL THINKING
Analzying Visuals What are the terms for investing in this CD?

Savings Plans

GUIDING QUESTION *What types of savings plans exist?*

When people think of saving, they generally think of putting their money into a savings account in a bank or similar financial institution. The money is safe and easy to access. As an added benefit, the money you put into a savings account grows from the interest it earns. The more money you put in a savings account, and the longer you keep it there, the more interest you will earn. While savings accounts are a popular way to save, there are other ways, too.

Money Market Accounts

A money market account is like a savings account. However, you usually have to deposit larger sums of money to open one of these accounts than are needed to open a savings account. One benefit of this type of account is that it pays a higher rate of interest than a savings account. Also, many financial institutions let depositors write checks to draw on the funds in their money market account. This feature provides easy access to the money in the account.

Certificates of Deposit

Depositors may also use certificates of deposit (CDs) to save. CDs are a kind of time deposit. You agree to deposit a sum of money with a financial institution for a certain amount of time, usually several months or years. In return, the institution guarantees you a set rate of interest. The interest is added to your principal when the CD reaches **maturity.** Maturity is the preset time at which your CD is payable.

A CD almost always offers a higher rate of interest than a regular savings account or a money market account. CDs have less flexibility than those other accounts, though. You cannot make partial withdrawals as you can with regular savings or a money market account. If you really need it, you can withdraw all of the money in the CD. There is a cost in doing so before the CD reaches maturity, however. You forfeit some of the interest you would have earned. The interest you lose is called a **penalty,** or a fee for withdrawing funds early. In general, longer-term CDs pay a higher rate of interest as a reward for holding your money for a longer period of time.

PHOTO: Robert Clay/Alamy

Reading**HELP**DESK

maturity the preset time at which you may withdraw funds from a CD

penalty a fee for early withdrawal of funds

return the profit earned by an investor

stock shares of a company held by an investor

Factors to Consider When You Save

Saving money involves a trade-off. The more you save today, the more you can buy a year from now, 10 years from now, or 30 years from now. However, by saving part of your income, you have less to spend today. Deciding how much to save depends on your answers to several questions:

- How much do you spend on your everyday expenses?
- What are your reasons for saving?
- How much interest can your savings earn?
- How much income do you earn now?
- How much income do you expect to earn in the future?

If you expect to make a much higher income tomorrow, you have less reason to save a large percentage of your income. It is a good idea, however, to have some type of savings plan.

✔ PROGRESS CHECK

Identifying Which type of account is more flexible, a checking account or a CD?

Stocks and Bonds

GUIDING QUESTION *How do investments in stocks and bonds promote long-term financial goals?*

Have you and your friends pooled, or combined, your money to buy something that you could all use? This is the idea behind many key investment practices. Savings accounts, money market deposit accounts, and CDs are useful tools if you want to save. However, their **return,** or the interest payments earned by the investor, is usually low. Investments, like stocks and bonds, tend to have a higher return over time. However, stocks and bonds carry some risk.

Stocks

Stock represents ownership of a company. When you buy stock, you become a part owner in a company. Someone who owns stock is called a shareholder, or a stockholder. For example, if you own five shares of stock in a company that has sold 500 shares to investors, then you own 5/500, or 1 percent, of the business.

If the company does well, the value of your share usually goes up. If the company does not do well, your share may be worth less than you paid for it. You can sell your stock if you need the money for something else. If you sell it for more than you paid for it, you make a profit. If you sell it for less, you lose money.

Buying stock is a popular way to invest money.

► **CRITICAL THINKING**
Interpreting Point of View What message is this cartoonist sending about investing in stocks? Explain.

SAVING AND INVESTING TOOLS

	DEFINITION	ADVANTAGES	DISADVANTAGES
Bank Savings Account	deposit account that earns interest	earns interest, some flexiblity	low rate of return, limited number of withdrawals
Checking Account	account mainly used for check writing	allows frequent withdrawals	no interest or very low interest
Certificates of Deposit (CDs)	deposit account with minimum time of deposit, fixed interest rate	higher rate of interest than savings or checking accounts	no partial withdrawals, small penalty if closed out early
Money Market Accounts	high-interest savings account	higher rate of interest than CDs	limited transactions, large balances usually required
Stocks	shares of ownership in a company	variable rate of return, potential for high profits	with potential high profits comes risk of high losses
Corporate Bonds	certificates of agreement between the borrower and lender	higher rate of interest than savings or CDs, low risk	usually only high denominations available
U.S. Savings Bonds	type of bond issued by the U.S. government	low risk, easily purchased, available in low denominations	lose some interest if cashed in before agreed term of bond
Mutual Funds	investment fund that buys stock and bonds of other companies	reliable share prices and rates of return	carry some risk

CHART SKILLS

Consumers have many choices when it comes to saving and investing their money.

▶ CRITICAL THINKING

1 *Analyzing Visuals* Which tools offer high rates of interest?

2 *Explaining* Why are no partial withdrawals a potential disadvantage?

Some companies pay shareholders dividends. A **dividend** is a portion of a company's earnings paid to shareholders based on the number of shares they hold. Dividends are paid at set times, such as every quarter, or three months. Dividends can increase your profit from owning stock. Stocks generally earn a higher return than other investments because they carry more risk. Because of that risk, however, there is no guarantee that you will make money on a stock investment. In fact, if a company goes out of business, you lose your entire investment.

Bonds

Companies and governments sell bonds as a way to borrow money from investors. **Bonds** are certificates of agreement between borrowers and lenders. When you buy a bond, you lend your money to a company or the government for a specific period of time, such as 5, 10, or 20 years. Unlike stocks, buying a bond does not make a bondholder part owner of the company or the government that issued the bond.

Most bonds are in large amounts, such as $100,000 and up. Companies sell bonds to raise money for new equipment, research, and other expenses. Companies pay bondholders a fixed rate of interest over a specific period. Because of this, bonds also carry some risk. The company could become unable to pay interest or to make final repayment of the principal.

Federal, state, and local governments also borrow money to pay for expenses. The United States issues savings bonds in amounts of $25 and $50, as well as other types of bonds valued at thousands more. U.S. government bonds are considered among the safest of all investments.

Mutual Funds

Many investors find it easier and safer to invest in stocks and bonds using mutual funds. **Mutual** (MYOO•chuh•wuhl) **funds** are companies that sell stock in themselves and pool the money to purchase a wide selection of individual stocks and bonds in other companies. In a mutual fund, financial experts choose which stocks or bonds to purchase. Your return is based on the experts' choice of investments.

Mutual funds are less risky than investments in individual stocks and bonds. The funds usually own several hundred, or even thousand, different stocks and bonds. Spreading the investment among many stocks or bonds limits the loss if one individual stock or bond performs poorly.

Investors can keep daily track of their stocks, bonds, and mutual funds by watching their values on the Internet. An index, such as the Dow Jones Industrial Average (DJIA) or the Standard and Poor's (S&P) 500, keeps track of most stock prices, not just the select few that an investor may own.

☑ PROGRESS CHECK

Explaining How does a mutual fund help reduce risk?

── *21st Century* ──
SKILLS

Interpreting Points of View

Write a dialogue between someone who believes that investing in stocks is the best way to make money and someone who believes that investing in mutual funds is the best way to make money.

LESSON 3 REVIEW

Review Vocabulary

1. What happens when your CD reaches *maturity*?

2. How does a *bond* differ from a *stock*?

Answer the Guiding Questions

3. *Finding the Main Idea* How do financial institutions use savings to help the economy?

4. *Describing* What advantage does a money market deposit account or a CD have over a savings account?

5. *Explaining* What are the advantages and disadvantages of stocks?

6. **INFORMATIVE/EXPLANATORY** Describe your short-term and long-term financial goals. What steps should you take to achieve them? In your essay, be specific about which financial tools you would use to achieve each type of goal, and why.

Write your answers on a separate sheet of paper.

1 **Writing Activity**

EXPLORING THE ESSENTIAL QUESTION
Why and how do people make economic choices?

Think about the different types of economic choices that people make. List three to four examples of choices that people make about spending and saving their money. Describe how such economic choices affect individuals' financial futures.

2 **21st Century Skills**

MAKE A BUDGET Prepare a family budget. Assume a sum for monthly income and regular savings. Include these expenses: housing, food, leisure, communications, and miscellaneous. The federal government also has to prepare budgets each year. Write a paragraph comparing the process it has to follow to the process you followed.

3 **Being an Active Citizen**

Help your friends and family to be responsible consumers. Make a checklist of the signs that show a person is an impulse buyer. Then come up with a list of ways to counteract the impulse to buy an item. Before going on a shopping trip with friends or family, go over your list with them. When you are out shopping, help your friends and family to resist impulse buys by using the tips you learned in this chapter.

4 **Understanding Visuals**

Your credit rating affects how willing lenders are to give you credit. If you need a credit card, an auto loan, or a loan to buy a home or pay for school, you must have an excellent credit rating. Study the circle graph. What are the three most important factors that help determine your creditworthiness? What habits can you adopt to help maintain good credit?

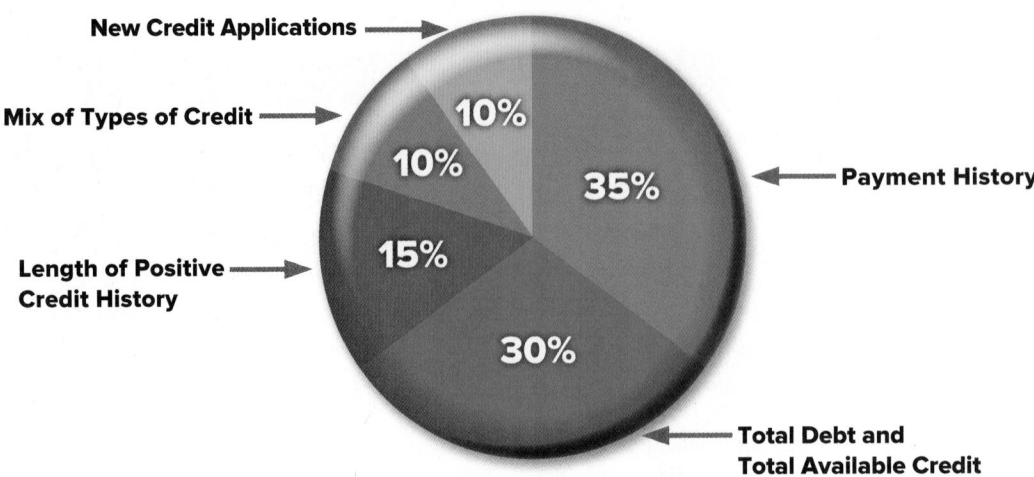

FACTORS OF A CREDIT RATING

New Credit Applications — 10%

Mix of Types of Credit — 10%

Length of Positive Credit History — 15%

30%

35% — Payment History

Total Debt and Total Available Credit

Source: www.creditrepair.org/credit-score-calculation/

REVIEW THE GUIDING QUESTIONS

Directions: Choose the best answer for each question.

1 What is the role of the Federal Trade Commission (FTC)?

   A. to make sure that stocks are traded fairly

   B. to prevent fraud and unfair business practices

   C. to oversee trade with foreign nations

   D. to encourage people to trade for goods instead of buying them

2 What motivates people to comparison shop?

   F. the enjoyment of visiting different stores

   G. the push to find the most impressive product

   H. the desire to have the latest technology

   I. the desire to get the most for their money

3 Which statement explains why people benefit from making a budget?

   A. Competition holds prices down.

   B. Surpluses are less desirable than deficits.

   C. People have scarce resources and must make choices.

   D. The government allows freedom of choice.

4 What is an advantage of using credit?

   F. Making regular monthly payments can teach financial discipline.

   G. Having the ability to buy anything means you can satisfy all your wants and needs.

   H. Using credit to buy goods is less costly than paying cash.

   I. Using credit can lead to increased savings.

5 How do individual savings help the economy as a whole?

   A. By lending the money, financial institutions help the economy grow.

   B. The money is available in case a national emergency occurs.

   C. The money grows, increasing the national wealth.

   D. Governments borrow the money by selling bonds.

6 What is the chief reason people buy stocks even though they are a risky investment?

   F. They want to own part of a company.

   G. Stocks offer the chance of a higher return than other investments.

   H. Stocks are more difficult to sell than bonds.

   I. Stocks are less risky than mutual funds.

DBQ ANALYZING DOCUMENTS

Directions: Analyze the excerpt and answer the questions that follow.

"When you pay your bills, write a check to yourself. Decide on a realistic amount. Deposit the money into a savings, investment, or retirement account. Then, pay your other bills as usual. If you find that you don't have enough money to cover all your expenses, write down the amount you are short and look for ways to trim your budget."

—"Managing Your Money: Savings," Federal Trade Commission

7 Drawing Conclusions From this passage, you can conclude that
A. you cannot follow a budget.
B. you must pay your bills by check.
C. your expenses should not exceed your income.
D. a mutual fund is a better investment than a savings account.

8 Summarizing Which statement best summarizes the passage?
F. Saving and investing your money is important.
G. Saving money is difficult.
H. It is important to trim your budget.
I. Paying all of your bills is not realistic.

SHORT RESPONSE

"[Credit card] issuers are still withholding important information. Companies are failing to disclose [tell about] penalty interest charges, which could double or even triple the interest rate for cardholders who fall two months behind. Time and again, the credit card industry has demonstrated [shown] its disdain [lack of respect] for its customers. The Fed [Federal Reserve Board] needs to press these companies to live up to the law."

—"The Customer Always Comes Last." Editorial, *The New York Times*, August 24, 2010

9 What does the editorial accuse credit card companies of doing?

10 According to the editorial, what does the Federal Reserve Board need to do?

EXTENDED RESPONSE

11 Informative/Explanatory What rights and responsibilities do consumers have? Provide examples of both with regard to making purchases and saving and investing money.

Need Extra Help?

If You've Missed Question	1	2	3	4	5	6	7	8	9	10	11
Review Lesson	1	1	1	2	3	3	2	2	1	1	1, 3

Business in America

ESSENTIAL QUESTIONS • Why and how do people make economic choices?
• How do economic systems influence societies?

networks

There's More Online about business in America.

CHAPTER 19

Lesson 1
How Businesses Are Organized

Lesson 2
Labor

Lesson 3
Roles and Responsibilities of Businesses

The Story Matters...

How would you like to wake up before dawn each morning, put in a full day of work making breads, pies, cakes, and cookies, and then work some more after the bakery has closed for the day? Owning a bakery—or any other small business—means hard work and long hours. Yet many Americans enjoy earning a living in this way. Still more dream of becoming business owners themselves.

Owning a business is one way to earn money. Like any other job, it has its risks and its rewards. Many people would rather work as someone else's employee. They may earn less, but they may also work fewer hours with less financial risk. They may also prefer having the freedom to move more easily from one job to another.

◀ *Owners of small businesses, such as this New Mexico bakery owner, have a lot of control over how they run their businesses. They also have many responsibilities.*

PHOTO: Michael Ventura/Alamy

513

Real-Life Civics

▶ **THEN** During World War II, when this photo was taken, many Americans worked in the defense industry. In factories across the nation, workers made ships, airplanes, tanks, uniforms, weapons, and other goods to support the war effort. U.S. factories also created essential products such as steel, food, clothing, automobiles, printed materials, and paper. In fact, in the 1940s, about one in three Americans worked at a manufacturing job.

Beginning in the late 1900s, the number of Americans working in factories greatly decreased. This was mainly due to technologies that enabled machines to do manufacturing tasks faster and cheaper than people could. In addition, in recent decades, many manufacturers have built factories in other countries where workers are paid less.

▷ Shipbuilders leave their Beaumont, Texas, job site in 1943.

At this Louisiana car wash, workers provide services such as washing, drying, and waxing vehicles.

PHOTO: (l) John Vachon/Anthony Potter Collection/Getty Images; (tr) Mario Villafuerte/Bloomberg via Getty Images

▶ NOW Compared to companies in the 1940s, far more American businesses today focus on providing services than on manufacturing goods. A service is work performed using special skills or knowledge that is of value to someone else. A car wash, such as the one shown in the photo, provides one kind of service. Other service industries include education, child care, health care, food preparation, business consulting, beauty care, and social services. Whether in manufacturing goods or providing services, Americans perform a wide range of jobs in a variety of settings. They work for companies large and small, or in their own businesses.

CIVIC LITERACY
★ ★ ★ ★

Contrasting How do the types of jobs many U.S. workers have today differ from the work that was available to Americans in the 1940s?

Your Opinion Which type of job would you find more appealing—a job in a factory or a job providing a service? Why?

515

netw⚬rks

There's More Online!

☑ **GRAPHIC ORGANIZER**
Types of Businesses

☑ **INFOGRAPHIC**
Forms of Business
Organization

☑ **CHART**
How a Corporation Is Organized

☑ **GRAPH**
Sole Proprietorships

☑ **GAME**

Lesson 1
How Businesses Are Organized

ESSENTIAL QUESTION *Why and how do people make economic choices?*

IT MATTERS BECAUSE
The three main types of businesses—proprietorships, partnerships, and corporations—play an important part in the nation's economy and in the daily life of nearly every American.

Sole Proprietorships

GUIDING QUESTION *What are the advantages and disadvantages of a sole proprietorship?*

Have you ever made money by mowing lawns or by babysitting? If you have, you had a small business. Each business has to be organized based on who owns the company and who provides the money to keep it running. Your lawn-mowing or babysitting business probably took a simple form. You were probably a sole proprietor.

A **sole proprietorship** (pruh•PREYE•uh•tuhr•SHIP)—also called simply a proprietorship—is a business owned by one person. Most businesses in this form are small businesses. Usually they serve the area in which they are located. You see these businesses every day. Dry cleaners, auto repair shops, beauty shops, and local restaurants often take this form. The sole proprietorship is the most common form of business organization.

Sole proprietors are their own bosses. They decide what products or services they will sell. They decide what hours the business will be open. They make decisions without having

Reading**HELP**DESK

Taking Notes: *Contrasting*

As you read, list the advantages and disadvantages of sole proprietorships, partnerships, and corporations.

Business	Advantages	Disadvantages
Sole Proprietorship		
Partnership		
Corporation		

Content Vocabulary

- **sole proprietorship**
- **financial capital**
- **liability**
- **partnership**
- **corporation**
- **charter**

to **consult,** or check with, other owners. As the only owner, a sole proprietor receives all the profits from the business.

Sole proprietorships have some disadvantages, too. First, the owner may find it difficult to raise **financial** (fuh•NAN•shuhl) **capital.** This is the money needed to run a business or expand it. Unless the business is run from the owner's home, he or she must buy or rent the place from which it operates. The owner might also have to buy equipment and supplies. If the business does not make enough money, the owner will have to use his or her personal money to meet these costs.

Second, sole proprietors have no limits on their **liability** (LEYE•uh•BIH•luh•tee), or legal responsibility, for the business. This can be a problem if the business cannot pay its debts or loses a lawsuit. Then the owner's personal property—such as a home or car—may have to be sold to pay the business's debts.

Third, sole proprietors might have trouble hiring skilled workers. Workers might prefer to take a job with a large company that has better benefits, such as health insurance.

Among sole proprietorships, the most popular types of businesses are professional, legal, and technical services; construction companies; and retailers.

► **CRITICAL THINKING**
Categorizing Which business type is shown in the photograph?

✓ PROGRESS CHECK

Describing In a sole proprietorship, who receives all profits?

Partnerships

GUIDING QUESTION *What are the advantages and disadvantages of a partnership?*
Suppose you are making so much money mowing lawns that you have little time for anything else. You could hire a helper. You have another option, too. You could find someone who could provide the extra help and use his or her own equipment in return for a share of the business. In this case, your business is no longer a sole proprietorship. It is now a **partnership**—a business that two or more people own and operate together.

As with your lawn-mowing business, partnerships often start as sole proprietorships. In some cases, a single owner cannot raise enough money to expand the business. In other cases, the owner may have enough financial capital but not have all the skills needed to run the business well. In either case, the owner may seek a partner with the money or skills that the business needs to grow.

- **board of directors**
- **franchise**
- **nonprofit organization**

sole proprietorship a business owned and operated by a single person

Academic Vocabulary

consult to seek information or advice from a person or resource

financial capital the money used to run or expand a business

Lesson 1 **517**

Sole proprietorships depend on the business skills of only one owner. If the entrepreneur is careless about record-keeping or good at making a product but not at marketing it, the business can fail. Partnerships benefit from drawing on the skills of more than one person. On the other hand, the partners need to work together for the business to succeed. Problems among the partners can doom the business. Which of these two business forms do you think is most likely to contribute to success? Write a paragraph stating and explaining your choice.

How Partnerships Are Structured

A partnership is formed when two or more people sign a legal agreement called articles of partnership. This document states what role each partner will play in the business. It tells how much money each will contribute. It **clarifies,** or explains, how each partner will share in the profit or loss of the business. The document also says how each partner can be removed or how new partners can be added. Finally, it describes how the partnership can be ended if the partners decide to do so.

Two kinds of partnerships can be formed. The most common form is called a general partnership. In this type, all partners are called general partners. They all own a share of the business and are all responsible for some of its management and debts.

The second type is a limited partnership. In this form, some owners are limited partners and some are general partners. Limited partners own a share of the business. However, they have no direct involvement in running or managing it. Instead, they usually just provide money the business needs to operate. The general partners run the business.

Limited partnerships are also called limited liability partnerships. This is because limited partners have less liability than general partners. They are liable only for the amount of money they invested in the business. The initials *LLP* after a business's name show that it is a limited liability partnership.

INFOGRAPHIC — FORMS OF BUSINESS ORGANIZATION

Partnerships and proprietorships together account for less than one fifth of total sales.

▶ CRITICAL THINKING

1. *Analyzing Visuals* What percentage of all businesses are sole proprietorships? What percentage of businesses are partnerships?

2. *Making Inferences* Why do you think there is such a large difference between the number of proprietorships and their share of all sales?

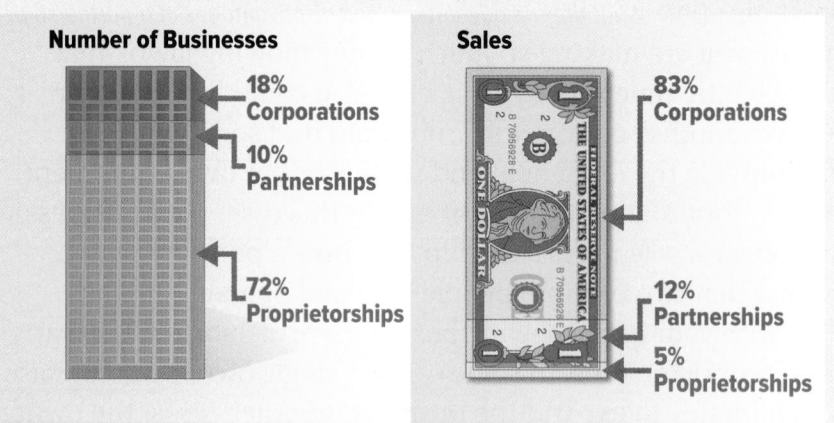

Number of Businesses
18% Corporations
10% Partnerships
72% Proprietorships

Sales
83% Corporations
12% Partnerships
5% Proprietorships

Source: IRS, Statistics of Income Division, November 2009

Reading**HELP**DESK

liability the legal responsibility for something, such as an action or a debt

partnership a business owned by two or more people

Academic Vocabulary

clarify to explain; to make something more understandable

Partnerships can be any size. Some can be as small as two partners, with no employees. In some fields, such as medicine or law, a small firm of four or five partners may be just the right size for the market it serves. Other partnerships, such as major law or accounting firms, may be huge businesses. In these companies, there may be hundreds of partners providing services in many different locations across the United States.

Advantages of Partnerships

The biggest advantage that partnerships have over sole proprietorships is that they can raise more money. Businesses use money to grow and to hire more employees. A partnership has more than one owner, so it usually has more capital to work with than a sole proprietorship does. It is also easier for a partnership to borrow money from a bank. The current partners can also add new partners to provide additional funds. Sometimes the new partners will be limited partners.

Another advantage of partnerships is that each partner often brings special talents to the business. For example, one partner in an insurance agency may be good at selling polices to new customers. The other partner may be better at providing services to people who already have policies. This business will probably be more successful as a partnership than it would be if just one person owned and operated it.

Disadvantages of Partnerships

The main drawback of a general partnership is the same as that of a sole proprietorship. Each partner has unlimited liability. He or she is fully responsible for all the debts of the business.

What does this mean? Suppose that you are in a lawn-mowing business with two partners. Each of you would get one-third of the business profits. But suppose that one of your partners buys an expensive new mower at the end of the season as your business income drops. Or suppose that one of the business's customers gets hurt by your equipment or the mower throws a stone through a car windshield. The business could be sued. If neither the business nor your partners have enough money to cover the debt or the damages, you would have to pay 100 percent of the cost out of your personal funds.

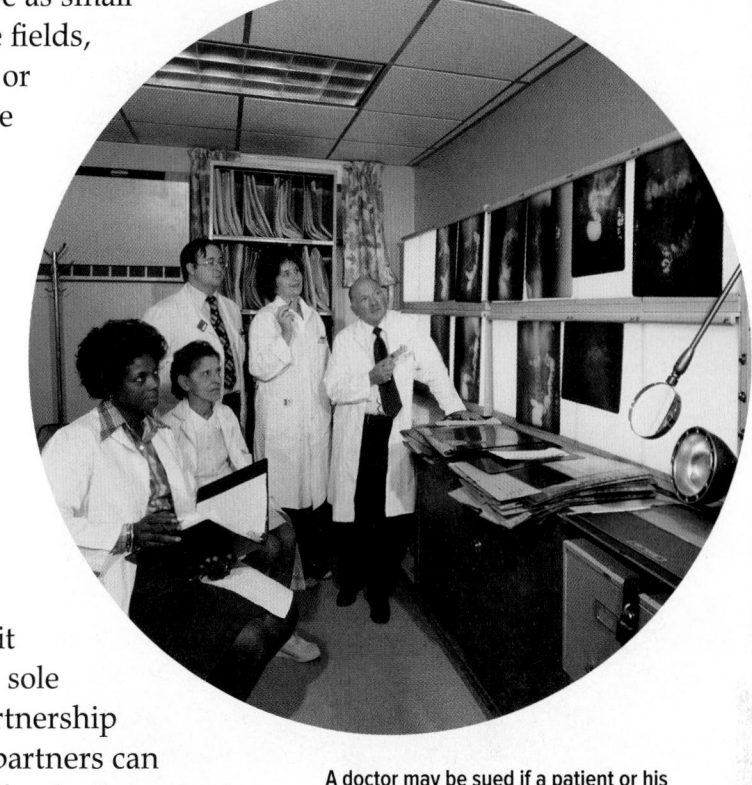

A doctor may be sued if a patient or his or her family thinks the patient was injured by the doctor's actions. For this reason, many medical practices use limited liability partnerships.

▶ CRITICAL THINKING
Making Connections What disadvantage of partnerships does this type of business solve?

✓ PROGRESS CHECK

What are the two types of partnership?

Corporations

GUIDING QUESTION *How is a corporation structured, and what are its advantages and disadvantages?*

The third major form of business is very different from either a sole proprietorship or a partnership. This third form is the corporation. A **corporation** is a business that is owned by a group of people and operates under a license. A corporation is the most complicated form of business. You can tell that a business is a corporation if the abbreviation *Inc.* follows the company's name. *Inc.* stands for "incorporated."

A corporation is legally recognized by state governments as a body that is separate from the people who own it. Under the law, a corporation has the rights and responsibilities that an individual has. Like a real person, a corporation can enter into contracts, sue and be sued, own property, and pay taxes.

General Motors (GM) is a major American corporation. Though headquartered in Detroit, Michigan, GM does business in more than 120 countries.

▶ **CRITICAL THINKING**
Identifying What document spells out how much stock a corporation can sell?

The Corporate Structure

The state where the corporation is formed grants the company a **charter.** This document gives a group of people permission to form a corporation. People invest in the corporation by buying shares of ownership. Those shares are represented by documents called stocks. Those who own the shares are called shareholders or stockholders. The charter of the corporation states exactly how much stock the corporation can sell. The corporation sells this stock to raise money so it can do business.

The charter requires a corporation to hold a meeting of stockholders every year. At this meeting, the stockholders elect a **board of directors** to represent them. Normally, for each share of stock owned, a stockholder is entitled to cast one vote for each position on the board of directors. The board of directors meets during the year to make major decisions about the corporation. It also hires a president and other managers to run the company on a daily basis. Stockholders are not involved in the day-to-day operation of the company.

PHOTO: Bloomberg via Getty Images

ReadingHELPDESK

corporation a type of business organization owned by many people but treated by law as though it were a person

charter a government document granting permission to organize a corporation

board of directors the people elected by the shareholders of a corporation to act on their behalf

The Corporation's Advantages

The corporation's biggest advantage is the ease of raising financial capital. It can raise huge amounts of money by selling stock. It can also borrow money by selling bonds, which are certificates of agreement between a borrower and a lender. It can then use that money to expand operations, open up businesses in new locations, or buy new equipment. It can also raise money to research new products. This ease of raising money is one reason that the corporation is the most common form of business for large companies.

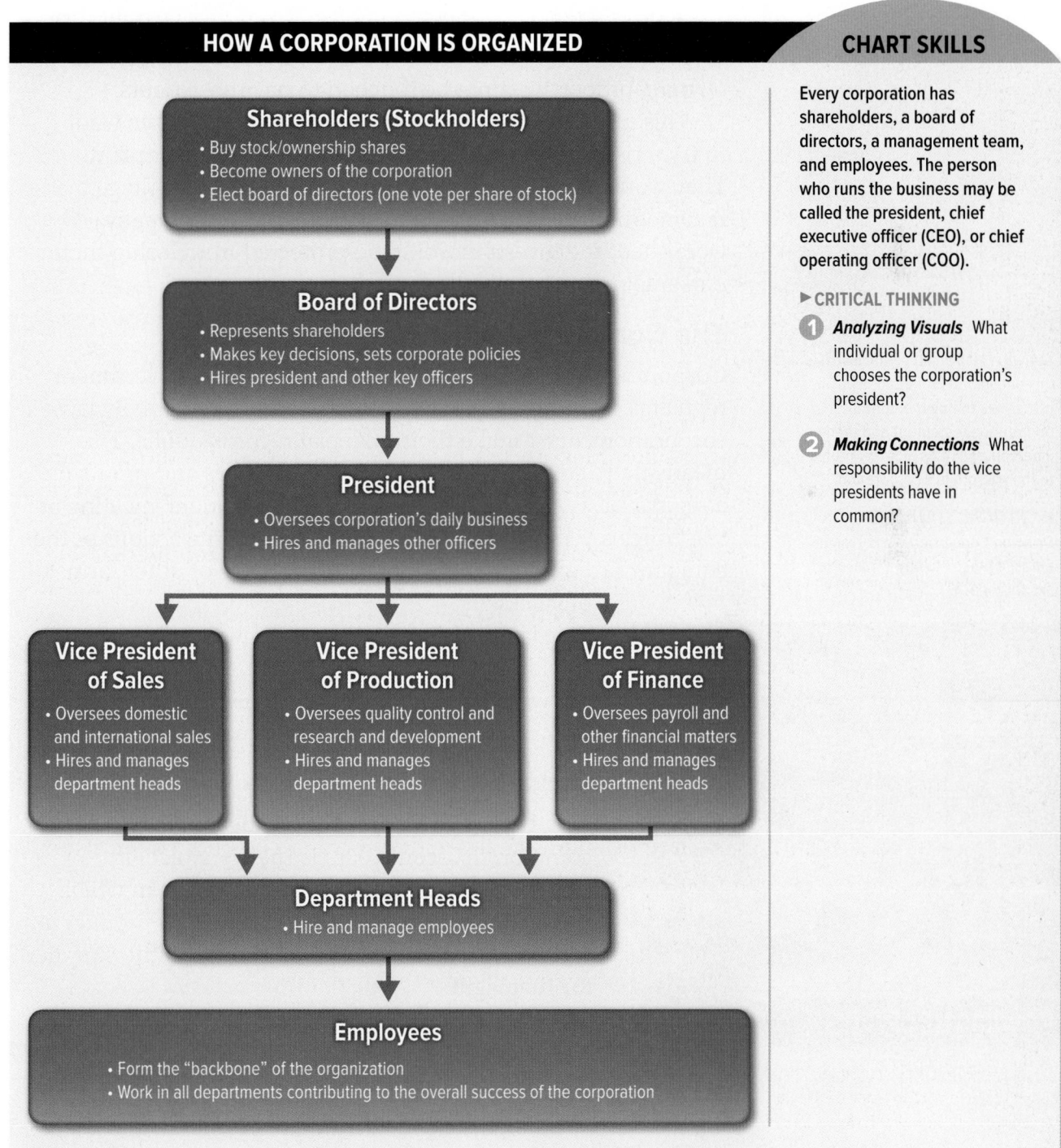

HOW A CORPORATION IS ORGANIZED

Shareholders (Stockholders)
- Buy stock/ownership shares
- Become owners of the corporation
- Elect board of directors (one vote per share of stock)

Board of Directors
- Represents shareholders
- Makes key decisions, sets corporate policies
- Hires president and other key officers

President
- Oversees corporation's daily business
- Hires and manages other officers

Vice President of Sales
- Oversees domestic and international sales
- Hires and manages department heads

Vice President of Production
- Oversees quality control and research and development
- Hires and manages department heads

Vice President of Finance
- Oversees payroll and other financial matters
- Hires and manages department heads

Department Heads
- Hire and manage employees

Employees
- Form the "backbone" of the organization
- Work in all departments contributing to the overall success of the corporation

CHART SKILLS

Every corporation has shareholders, a board of directors, a management team, and employees. The person who runs the business may be called the president, chief executive officer (CEO), or chief operating officer (COO).

▶ CRITICAL THINKING

1 *Analyzing Visuals* What individual or group chooses the corporation's president?

2 *Making Connections* What responsibility do the vice presidents have in common?

Some corporations are huge. The yearly earnings of these corporations are larger than the economies of most of the world's countries. For example, if Wal-Mart were a country, it would have an economy larger than all but 21 countries.

Another advantage is that ownership can easily be transferred. As a result, the corporation can have a long life. Proprietorships and partnerships may end when an owner resigns or dies. When a stockholder no longer wants to own part of a corporation, he or she simply sells the stock to someone else. When a stockholder dies, his or her family receives the stock.

A third advantage of the corporation is limited liability. The corporation is responsible for its debts, not the owners. The owners' property cannot be touched to pay those debts.

This advantage is important. Suppose some people want to try a risky business, like building a nuclear power plant. They would form a corporation because of this advantage. If something were to go terribly wrong and the company were sued, the investors would be protected from losing their personal property to settle the case.

The Corporation's Disadvantages

Corporations also have some disadvantages. The government regulates them more than any other form of business. By law, corporations must make their financial records public. This means they have to release reports on expenses and profits on a regular basis. They must also hold a stockholders' meeting at least once a year. All of these rules mean that the actions of the company are watched more closely than those of other forms of business.

Major corporations have millions of stockholders. If some of them are unhappy about the way the company is run, it is hard for them to unite and get the managers to make changes.

Other Forms of Business

One type of business that has become very common in recent years is the **franchise** (FRAN•CHYZ). A franchise is a business in which the owner is the only seller of a certain product in a certain area. The owner pays a fee to the supplier for that right.

To own a McDonald's franchise like this one in San Francisco, a business owner has to buy the right to operate the restaurant and then pay a percentage of its monthly profits to the McDonald's corporation.

▶ **CRITICAL THINKING**
Drawing Conclusions What might attract a person to buy a franchise like this one?

Reading**HELP**DESK

PHOTO: The McGraw-Hill Companies • Inc./John Flournoy

franchise a company that has permission to sell the supplier's goods or services in a particular area in exchange for a sum of money

nonprofit organization a business that does not intend to make a profit for the goods and services it provides

The owner also gives that supplier a share of the profits. Fast-food restaurants and hotels that are part of nationally known chains are often franchises.

The franchise owner benefits because there is no competition from another nearby seller of the same product. The supplier also helps the franchise owner run the business. The biggest disadvantage is that the franchise owner does not have complete control over the business. The national company often has many rules the franchise owner must follow. For example, the franchise owner usually cannot sell products other than those of the supplier.

All of the businesses you have read about so far have a common aim. They are organized to make a profit. However, there is another type of business organization called a **nonprofit organization.** These organizations provide goods and services without trying to make a profit. Many different types of organizations are nonprofit. For example, public schools, public hospitals, labor unions, Boy Scouts, and Girl Scouts are nonprofit organizations.

Cooperatives are another type of nonprofit organization. This is a business group formed by people who want to carry on an economic activity that benefits all of its members. There are different kinds of cooperatives. A consumer cooperative buys goods in large amounts. Members then get those goods at low prices. Service cooperatives provide members with services such as insurance or loans. Producer cooperatives help members sell their products. For example, farmers' cooperatives help members sell their crops and livestock to large central markets where they can get better prices.

☑ PROGRESS CHECK

Identifying Who owns a corporation?

LESSON 1 REVIEW

Review Vocabulary

1. What is *liability*? How are a *sole proprietorship* and a *general partnership* alike when it comes to liability?

2. What is *financial capital*? How does a *corporation* raise financial capital?

Answer the Guiding Questions

3. *Summarizing* What benefits, challenges, and risks does the owner of a sole proprietorship face?

4. *Describing* What advantages does a limited partnership have over a general partnership?

5. *Analyzing* Why are most of the nation's large companies corporations?

6. **ARGUMENT** If you owned a business, would you rather be a sole proprietor or a partner in a partnership? Write a paragraph explaining why you would prefer one form of business organization over the other.

networks
There's More Online!

☑ **GRAPHIC ORGANIZER**
Collective Bargaining
Goals

☑ **GRAPHS**
Labor Union Trends
Union Membership by State

☑ **MAP**
Right-to-Work States

☑ **CHART**
Notable Strikes in U.S. History

☑ **BIOGRAPHY**
César Estrada Chávez

Lesson 2
Labor

ESSENTIAL QUESTION *Why and how do people make economic choices?*

IT MATTERS BECAUSE
The relationship between labor and management affects the nation's economic and political life.

Organized Labor

GUIDING QUESTION *What is the role of organized labor in the U.S. economy?*

In the past 40 years or so, the country's labor force has changed greatly. The labor force is the number of people 16 years or older who have jobs or are looking for work. Since 1970, the size of the labor force has nearly doubled.

In those years, the number of workers belonging to labor unions has fallen. A **labor union** is an organization of workers that seeks to improve the wages and working conditions of its members. In the early 1970s, about one of every four workers belonged to a union. Today only one worker in eight is a union member. One reason for the decline in union membership is the shift from manufacturing jobs to service jobs. Traditionally, fewer workers in service jobs have been union members. Also, many employers have kept their workplaces union free.

Unions still play an important role in the United States, however. Workers in many important jobs and industries belong to unions. Large numbers of coal miners, airline pilots, and truck drivers are union members. Unions have also seen gains in the public service sector, where teachers and government employees work.

Reading HELPDESK

Taking Notes: *Organizing*

As you read this lesson, complete a graphic organizer showing the goals of collective bargaining.

Collective
Bargaining Goals

Content Vocabulary

- **labor union**
- **right-to-work laws**
- **collective bargaining**

- **strike**
- **picketing**
- **lockout**

- **injunction**
- **mediation**
- **arbitration**

Types of Unions

There are two types of unions. A union whose members all work at the same craft or trade is called a *trade union*. Examples are the unions formed by bakers and by printers. A union that brings together skilled and unskilled workers from the same industry is called an *industrial union*. An industrial union might have electricians, carpenters, and laborers who work together to manufacture a product. An example is the United Auto Workers (UAW).

Unions have changed over time. In the past, they were formed mostly by industrial workers. Today, even actors and professional athletes have unions. Another change is the growth in the number of government workers who are union members. In fact, more government workers belong to unions than do workers for companies. About 1.6 million of these workers belong to the American Federation of State, County, and Municipal Employees (AFSCME). AFSCME is the largest union in the nation. Prison guards, garbage collectors, and school nurses are part of this union. Some government workers, like police officers and firefighters, have their own unions.

21st Century SKILLS

Compare and Contrast

Make a Venn diagram in which you compare and contrast characteristics of labor unions today and years ago. Place any characteristics that are true of unions both then and now in the area where the ovals overlap.

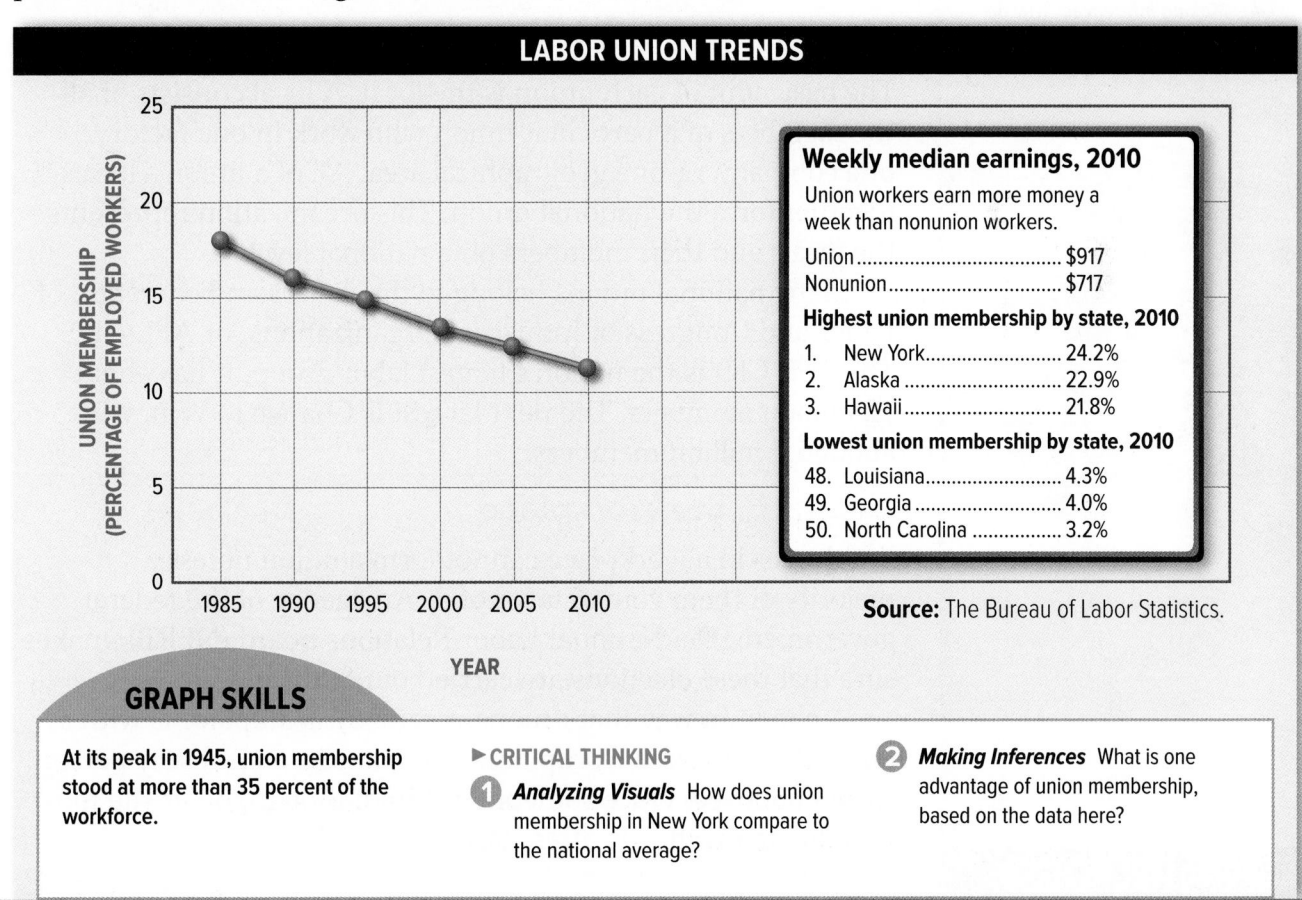

LABOR UNION TRENDS

Weekly median earnings, 2010

Union workers earn more money a week than nonunion workers.

Union $917
Nonunion $717

Highest union membership by state, 2010

1. New York........................... 24.2%
2. Alaska 22.9%
3. Hawaii.............................. 21.8%

Lowest union membership by state, 2010

48. Louisiana.......................... 4.3%
49. Georgia 4.0%
50. North Carolina 3.2%

Source: The Bureau of Labor Statistics.

GRAPH SKILLS

At its peak in 1945, union membership stood at more than 35 percent of the workforce.

▶ CRITICAL THINKING

1. *Analyzing Visuals* How does union membership in New York compare to the national average?

2. *Making Inferences* What is one advantage of union membership, based on the data here?

Reading Strategy: *Taking Notes*

Take notes on labor unions by writing questions you have about unions and then reading to find the answers.

labor union association of workers organized to improve wages and working conditions

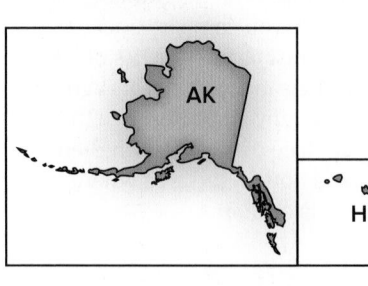

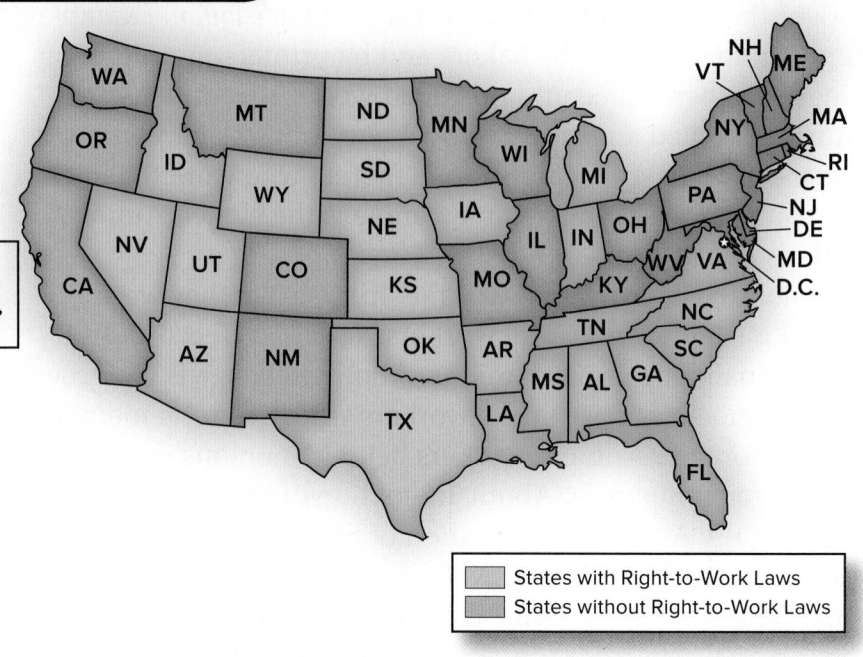

States with Right-to-Work Laws
States without Right-to-Work Laws

GEOGRAPHY CONNECTION

Right-to-work laws were made possible by a federal law passed in 1947.

1 REGIONS In what regions of the country are right-to-work states found?

▶ CRITICAL THINKING

2 *Making Inferences* Why do you think companies would prefer right-to-work laws?

Union Organization

The basic unit of each union is the local. A local consists of all the members of a particular union who work in one factory, one company, or one geographical area. All of a union's locals together form the national union. This organization represents the locals and their members on a national level.

Many national unions belong to the American Federation of Labor and Congress of Industrial Organizations, or AFL-CIO. The AFL-CIO is the nation's largest labor group. It has about 12 million members. The next-largest is Change to Win, with about 5.5 million members.

Unions in the Workplace

Employees in a workplace cannot form a union unless a majority of them vote in favor of it. An agency of the federal government, the National Labor Relations Board (NLRB), makes sure that these elections are carried out fairly and honestly.

A common way that unions organize a workplace is with a *union shop*. In these workplaces, companies can hire any person as an employee. Once someone is hired, though, he or she must join the union shortly after starting to work.

Reading**HELP**DESK

right-to-work laws state laws forbidding unions from forcing workers to join

Academic Vocabulary
circumstance situation

collective bargaining process by which unions and employers negotiate the conditions of employment

Many companies do not like the union shop. In some states, companies have convinced state governments to outlaw these arrangements. Nearly half the states have **right-to-work laws,** which ban union shops.

Other states have what is called a *modified union shop*. In this **circumstance,** or situation, a worker does not have to join a union. If workers do join the union, however, they must remain in the union as long as they hold their job. Some workplaces are *agency shops*. In an agency shop, workers who do not join the union still must pay a fee to the union for representing them.

✔ PROGRESS CHECK

Contrasting How does a trade union differ from an industrial union?

Labor Negotiations

GUIDING QUESTION *How do labor and management work out agreements?*

When a company's workers have a union, the union and the company carry out **collective bargaining** (kuh•LEK•tihv BAHR•guhn•ihng). In this process, officials from the union and the company meet to discuss the workers' contract. The contract sets the terms for working at the company. These talks often focus on wages and benefits. Benefits include health insurance, sick days, and holidays. Contracts also cover rules for workers to follow and working conditions, such as breaks for meals during the workday.

With most contracts, the two sides reach agreement during bargaining. Sometimes, though, negotiations break down. If that happens, unions and employers each have methods they can use to pressure the other side to accept their position.

PHOTO: (inset) Jim West/Alamy; (bl) Jeff Kowalsky/epa/Corbis

Labor negotiations can sometimes be difficult. At left, UAW and GM representatives reach an agreement that satisfies both sides. At right, an AFL-CIO meeting honors members for their contributions to the labor movement.

▶ **CRITICAL THINKING**
Defining What is the process of negotiating a union contract called?

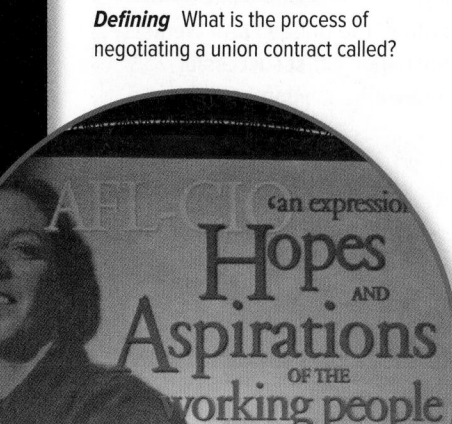

PHOTO: Arthur Schatz/Time Life Pictures/Getty Images

César Chávez knew the suffering of farmworkers. He had labored in the fields since the age of 10, when his family lost their Arizona farm during the Great Depression. Like thousands of other farmers, the Chávez family became migrant workers, constantly moving to be near work. Chávez attended some 65 schools before dropping out at the end of eighth grade.

After serving in World War II, Chávez worked for a group that was trying to win rights for Mexican Americans. However, he could not forget the migrant workers. In 1962, with the help of his wife, Helen Fabela Chávez, he began work on his dream of organizing a union for farmworkers.

In 1965, Chávez launched La Huelga—"the strike"—in which he battled the power of grape growers in California's San Joaquin Valley. Chávez asked Americans to boycott grapes until growers signed union contracts. Some 17 million Americans did, and industry profits tumbled. "For the first time," Chávez said, "the farmworker got some power." The power came in the form of the United Farm Workers, the nation's first successful farmworkers union.

Looking at Leadership

What tools did Chávez use to win recognition for his union?

Labor's Tools

Labor unions have several tools to try to advance their cause. One method unions use is to call a **strike.** In a strike, all union members refuse to work. This action is designed to shut down the company or the industry in which the workers labor. The idea is that without employees, one company—or all companies in the industry—will be forced to meet the union's demands. If they do not, the company or companies lose money every day that the workers refuse to work.

Striking workers usually stand in public view carrying signs stating that they are on strike. This tactic is called **picketing.** The goals are to embarrass the company and to build public support for the strike. Strikers also hope to discourage other workers from crossing the picket line to work at the company.

Another tool of labor is to put economic pressure on the company. The union may ask people to boycott the company, or refuse to do business with it.

Strikes can cause problems for workers, too. They can drag on for months. If so, strikers may become discouraged. Some might want to go back to work. This can put pressure on the union to give in on some of its demands. Sometimes a strike will end without workers gaining anything they wanted. In most cases, however, strikes are settled when the company and the union work out an agreement.

Employers' Tools

Employers also have ways to try to pressure unions. Their strongest tool is the **lockout.** In a lockout, the employer does not let workers enter the workplace. The employer hopes that the loss of income will force workers to accept company terms. During the lockout, the company often hires replacement workers so it can continue its business. That way, the locked-out workers suffer, but the company does not.

Companies may try to stop union actions by asking for an **injunction** (ihn•JUHNGK•shuhn). An injunction is a legal order from a court to prevent some activity. The company may ask the court to limit picketing or to prevent or stop a strike. Companies used injunctions more often in the late 1800s and early 1900s, during the start of the labor movement. They also used these court orders to try to stop unions from organizing their workers.

Reading HELP DESK

strike when workers deliberately stop working in order to force an employer to give in to their demands

picketing a union tactic in which striking workers walk with signs that express their grievances

lockout when management closes a workplace to prevent union members from working

injunction a court order to stop some kind of action

Outside Help

Unions may also seek injunctions. If issued against an employer, the injunction may order the employer not to lock out its workers. In certain industries that are considered important to the economy or national security, the government can seek an injunction. In 2002, for example, talks between the organizations that operate ports on the West Coast and dockworkers dragged on for five months. During this time, the port operators locked out the workers. President George W. Bush asked for an injunction to end the lockout. He said that keeping the ports open was important to military operations. A judge agreed and granted the injunction. The court order ended the lockout.

When the parties cannot agree on a contract, they have other **options,** or choices. They can try **mediation** (mee•dee•AY•shuhn). In this approach, they bring in a third party who tries to help them reach an agreement. They can also choose **arbitration** (ahr•buh•TRAY•shuhn). With this method, the third party listens to both sides and then decides how to settle the dispute. Both parties agree in advance to accept the third party's decision.

If a strike threatens the nation's welfare, the government can step in. Federal law allows the president to order a cooling-off period. During this time, the workers must return to work. Meanwhile, the union and the employer must try to reach an agreement. The cooling-off period lasts 80 days. If there is no agreement after that time, the workers have the right to go back on strike.

In an extreme situation, the government can temporarily take over a company or an industry. In 1946 the government seized coal mines when a strike threatened to shut off the nation's coal supply.

✓ PROGRESS CHECK

Contrasting What is the difference between a strike and a lockout?

Academic Vocabulary

option something that is chosen; a choice

mediation situation in which union and company officials bring in a third party to try to help them reach an agreement

arbitration situation in which union and company officials submit the issues they cannot agree on to a neutral third party for a final decision

LESSON 2 REVIEW

Review Vocabulary

1. What do the terms *strike* and *picketing* mean, and how are they related?

2. Compare and contrast the terms *mediation* and *arbitration*.

Answer the Guiding Questions

3. ***Explaining*** What role do unions play in the United States today?

4. ***Identifying*** What are the main areas of negotiation between unions and employers in reaching collective bargaining agreements?

5. **INFORMATIVE/EXPLANATORY** If you were an adult worker, would you join a labor union? Write a paragraph that explains the pros and cons of joining a union.

Issues to Debate

Does Outsourcing Jobs to Other Countries Hurt America?

How would you feel if you had a good job, and then your company closed and moved its operations to another country? Such an action is called outsourcing jobs. Outsourcing is a hotly debated issue, because it brings about plant closings and job losses in the United States. Who supports outsourcing? Many business leaders like the idea. They say that it helps American businesses be more competitive in world markets because they can cut costs. Others argue that outsourcing weakens the economy by taking away jobs. Which argument is correct? Does outsourcing hurt the American economy?

Workers in China make clothing for export. In 2009 China's total exports to the world topped $1.2 trillion.

Yes

Gary Pisano is a professor at the Harvard Business School. He warns that the United States is losing the ability to manufacture many of the products it invented. He says, "The prevailing view of the last 25 years is that the U.S. can thrive as a center of innovation and leave the manufacturing of the products it invents and designs to others. Nothing could be further from the truth. . . . Unless you know how to manufacture a product, you often cannot design it. . . . Knowledge about manufacturing helps you design products and get them to market quickly. . . . Unless business executives . . . in the U.S. recognize the importance of manufacturing and grow wiser about outsourcing . . . the country's economy will continue to decline."

—Professor Gary Pisano, October 1, 2009

No

David Yoffie, another Harvard Business School professor, disagrees. He believes that "the future of U.S. competitiveness . . . may depend more on the transition to services than trying to retain the country's manufacturing base." Yoffie compares two companies to prove his point. "HP [Hewlett-Packard] has become the world's leading computer company by focusing on sales . . . of computers made at very low cost in Taiwan and China. In comparison, archrival Dell, which was widely celebrated 10 years ago as one of the world's best manufacturers, is now saddled with high cost [U.S.] factories and is struggling to compete. . . . [The] U.S. has been moving towards a service economy for the last 100 years. In the long run, services will become the core of the U.S. tech world as well."

—Professor David Yoffie, October 5, 2009

Debating the Issue

1. **Defining** What is outsourcing?
2. **Identifying** What kind of jobs do both writers agree are on the decline in the United States?
3. **Differentiating** What does each writer think about the outsourcing of manufacturing jobs? Explain why each writer thinks that way.
4. **Making Decisions** Which writer's point of view on outsourcing do you agree with? Explain why.

networks

There's More Online!

☑ **GRAPHIC ORGANIZER**
Responsibilities of
Businesses

☑ **CHART**
Corporate Aid

Lesson 3

Roles and Responsibilities of Businesses

ESSENTIAL QUESTION *How do economic systems influence societies?*

IT MATTERS BECAUSE

All of society benefits when businesses provide safe, good-quality products to consumers and give fair treatment to employees.

The Social Responsibility of Businesses

GUIDING QUESTION *In what ways do businesses help their communities?*

Does your school benefit from help given by a business? That might seem like an unusual question, but businesses help schools in many ways. For example, do you play on a sports team? Is that team sponsored by a local business? Has your school club ever held a car wash at the parking lot of a local business? Does a store in the area sell school supplies at a discount? Businesses help their communities in many ways.

Businesses play several important roles in society. As producers, they supply the food, clothing, and shelter we use to meet basic needs. They also produce many things that make life more enjoyable and comfortable. Along with being producers, they also have a **social responsibility.** This is the obligation to pursue goals that benefit society as well as themselves.

Have you ever eaten a White Castle hamburger? That fast-food chain was founded by a family named the Ingrams. The Ingrams have given more than $22 million to support education.

Reading **HELP**DESK

Taking Notes: *Organizing*

As you read this lesson, identify responsibilities of businesses to consumers and to employees.

Responsibilities of Businesses	
To Consumers	To Employees

Content Vocabulary

• **social responsibility**
• **foundation**
• **transparency**

social responsibility the obligation businesses have to pursue goals that benefit society as well as themselves

They donate this money through the family's **foundation,** an institution created to promote the public good.

People who have enjoyed success in business, such as the Ingrams, can be very generous. Bill Gates, the founder of Microsoft Corporation, has given away some $23 billion. His foundation aids a wide variety of causes in the United States and around the world. For instance, his foundation has made a $100 million gift to the Tampa, Florida, public schools. It has also given more than $250 million to fight disease in Africa, Asia, and South America.

In addition, many corporations have set up their own foundations. These groups give money to support causes they believe are important. The Wal-Mart Foundation has plans to give away more than $2 billion by 2015 to help people in the United States who face hunger.

Corporations give away about $14 billion each year. Some provide free goods or services. For example, many drug companies give their products to people who need the medicines but cannot afford to pay for them. Apple and GAP give part of their profits to a fund that fights infectious diseases in 144 countries. American Express has long been involved in helping disaster victims. The company gives money to relief agencies. These agencies use that money to provide food, clothing, and shelter for the victims. Another American Express program helps groups that are trying to preserve important historical sites or natural areas.

It is not only the biggest American companies that give. About 75 percent of small companies also give money. Some support groups in their area. Others give to causes they believe in. You have seen examples of how some help schools. Some law firms or accountants provide free services to poor people or to nonprofit groups. One small business owner spoke for many business owners when explaining the reason for taking these steps: "I feel that I have an obligation to give back to the community from which I draw [an income]."

☑ **PROGRESS CHECK**

Explaining What are some of the good causes that American companies have donated to?

Tide laundry detergent has a truck that carries enough washers and dryers to do 300 loads of laundry a day. It sends the truck to areas that have been hit by natural disasters to help provide clean clothes to people in distress.

▶ **CRITICAL THINKING**

Making Inferences How can this kind of action help a business?

Reading**HELP**DESK

foundation an organization established by a company or an individual to provide money for a particular purpose, especially for charity or research

PHOTO: (t) Shawn Thew/epa/Corbis; (inset) Transtock Inc./Alamy

Other Business Responsibilities

GUIDING QUESTION *How do businesses carry out their responsibilities to their consumers, owners, and employees?*

As they carry out their many activities, businesses have different responsibilities to the groups they interact with. Laws require businesses to meet certain responsibilities. Business owners and managers may face serious problems or even legal action if they do not follow those laws. They also may suffer from a loss of reputation, or standing, which might result in a loss of business.

Responsibilities to Consumers

Businesses have important responsibilities to their customers, the people who buy their goods and services. First, businesses must sell products that are safe and that work properly. Services must be reliable. A new video game should run without flaws. An auto mechanic should change a car's oil correctly. Many companies guarantee their products and services for a period of time. They replace or redo those that do not work as they should. Second, businesses also have the responsibility to tell the truth in their advertising. Third, businesses should treat all customers fairly.

In recent years, the Consumer Product Safety Commission has ordered the recall of many toys painted with dangerous lead paint. It has also recalled millions of riding toys because of a fire hazard.

▶ **CRITICAL THINKING**
Making Connections What incentives do businesses have to meet their responsibilities to consumers?

Reading Strategy: *Organizing Information*

Read the passage titled "Responsibilities to Consumers." Then organize the information you have read in a web diagram showing three key responsibilities that businesses have to their consumers.

Google, the Internet company, has features in its offices to try to make the workplace enjoyable, comfortable, and healthy for employees. Workers can use company-provided bicycles and scooters to move from one building to another. Game rooms give employees a chance to relax and release tension from work.

▶ CRITICAL THINKING
Making Inferences How can a company benefit from taking these steps?

Responsibilities to Owners

Another responsibility is to the stockholders, who are the owners of the business. This is especially **crucial**, or important, for corporations. In this case, the people who own the company are not the same people who actually run it. To protect stockholders, corporations have to release financial reports on a regular basis. **Revealing**, or making public, this information is called **transparency.** The information is published to give investors full and accurate information. People can analyze the facts before they choose to invest money in the company.

Sometimes the managers of a corporation are not honest in these reports. The government can then prosecute them for breaking the law. The scandal involving the bankrupt energy company Enron showed the problems that arise when these reports are not truthful. The company claimed to earn millions in profits, but its financial statements were false. When the company went out of business, it owed billions of dollars. Thousands of workers lost their jobs. After that and other illegal business activities became known, Congress passed a law requiring a company's principal officers to sign a statement promising that financial statements are correct and honest.

PHOTO: Stephen Brashear/Getty Images

Academic Vocabulary

crucial very important, especially for its effect on something

reveal to make something known

transparency the process of making business deals or conditions more visible to everyone

Responsibilities to Employees

Finally, businesses have responsibilities to their workers. They are required to maintain a safe workplace. They must also treat all workers fairly and without discrimination. That is, they cannot treat employees differently because of race, religion, gender, age, or disability. Doing so is against the law. Companies cannot pay different wages to men and women who do the same work, for instance. Nor can they fire workers because they reach an older age. Such decisions must be based on the quality of the work the employees perform.

Many businesses try to help workers by providing benefits or services. For instance, many companies help employees with the costs of trade school or college. Some pay for programs to help workers stop smoking. Some provide child care or fitness centers for workers.

Health insurance is a benefit that many companies have traditionally given to their workers. However, as health insurance costs increased, many businesses grew worried about the cost of this benefit. Some stopped providing it. Others shifted more of the cost of this insurance to their workers. In 2010 Congress passed a law requiring businesses to provide health insurance. Some parts of the law are designed to place limits on increases in the cost of health care and health insurance. The law also gives tax credits to small businesses when they buy health insurance. These limits and credits were meant to make the cost of the benefit easier to meet.

Helping workers in these ways benefits the employer as well as the worker. For example, a worker who is in good health misses less work than one who is not. That worker also has more energy and can be more productive on the job.

☑ PROGRESS CHECK

Explaining Why is it important for corporations to publish financial information regularly?

21st Century SKILLS

Summarizing

The Equal Employment Opportunity Commission (EEOC) is a part of the federal government. Its job is to ensure that job applicants and workers are not discriminated against. Go to the Web site of the EEOC to learn its powers and how it works to uphold the law. Write a summary of what you find.

LESSON 3 REVIEW

Review Vocabulary

1. What is *social responsibility*, and how do businesses show it?

2. What is *transparency*, and why is it important to business owners?

Answer the Guiding Questions

3. **Summarizing** How does the government push businesses to act responsibly?

4. **Making Connections** Should businesses' responsibilities to consumers, owners, and employees be considered a social benefit? Why or why not?

5. **ARGUMENT** A business has responsibilities to its customers, its employees, its owners, and its local community. Which of these responsibilities do you think is most important? Explain your point of view in a paragraph.

Write your answers on a separate sheet of paper.

1 Writing Activity

EXPLORING THE ESSENTIAL QUESTIONS
Why and how do people make economic choices?
How do economic systems influence societies?

Business and labor have roles and responsibilities that connect them with each other and with society. Explain in an essay what business and labor contribute to society, and describe how they cooperate and sometimes come in conflict with each other.

2 21st Century Skills

MAKE AN ARGUMENT With a small group of classmates, research a recent or historical labor dispute that took place in your community or state. Engage in a collective bargaining session to see if you can resolve the issues in the dispute. Half of your group should represent the workers. The other half should represent management. Work together with your group members to present the position of your side in the dispute and to respond to the other side's position. Bargain in front of the class and try to reach an agreement.

3 Being an Active Citizen

Identify a local business or large corporation whose activities have benefited your community. What incentives do you think motivated this business to operate in your community? What incentives do you think motivate members of your community to interact with that business? Using this business as an example, create a poster or prepare a media presentation showing why and how individuals, households, and businesses interact.

4 Visual Literacy

What examples of an employer's responsibility to its workers can you identify in this photo? Write a paragraph about one of the following topics: (1) why it is important for businesses to provide benefits to employees; (2) why employers should ensure a safe workplace; or (3) why employers must not treat workers differently because of race, religion, gender, age, or disability.

PHOTO: Adam Gault/Getty Images

REVIEW THE GUIDING QUESTIONS

Directions: Choose the best answer for each question.

1 What is the most common form of business in the United States?

A. corporation

B. franchise

C. partnership

D. sole proprietorship

2 Which type of business has the greatest ability to raise financial capital?

F. a corporation

G. a franchise

H. a limited partnership

I. a sole proprietorship

3 In negotiations over wages and benefits, mediation is used when

A. a lockout has been called.

B. the government orders it.

C. the parties cannot reach an agreement on their own.

D. a strike has been called.

4 Which group accounts for most union members today?

F. employees of corporations

G. government workers

H. professional athletes

I. industrial workers

5 The government sometimes ensures that businesses behave responsibly by

A. forcing them to give to charities.

B. passing certain laws.

C. collective bargaining.

D. limiting liability.

6 Which of these is a responsibility a business has to its consumers?

F. fair treatment of employees

G. honest advertising

H. publishing financial information

I. giving to charities

DBQ ANALYZING DOCUMENTS

Directions: Analyze the excerpt and answer the questions that follow.

"The more that managers raise their vision and look 5, 10, 20 years out, the more issues they see that affect their business. In this context, it makes sense to invest in Pre-K youth development programs."

—Stephen Jordan, U.S. Chamber of Commerce, April 26, 2010

7 **Summarizing** Which statement best summarizes the point of view expressed in this passage?

A. Business leaders should focus only on short-term profits.

B. Business leaders need to look carefully at the past.

C. As businesses think longer term, they become more socially responsible.

D. Investing in youth programs will make companies quick profits.

8 **Making Inferences** How might investing in youth development programs be good for business in the long run?

F. Children buy a lot of products.

G. Well-educated children might grow up to be better workers.

H. Businesses benefit when the larger community is suffering.

I. Investing in these programs will ensure that businesses last longer.

SHORT RESPONSE

"Both the free press and free unions depend upon the right of free speech and freedom of association, which in this country are enshrined [preserved] in the First Amendment to the Constitution. The right to organize unions is the First Amendment for workers."

—Bob King, President, United Auto Workers, August 2010

9 In what ways do unions depend on freedom of speech and of association?

10 Do you agree with King's interpretation that the First Amendment applies to organizing unions? Why or why not?

EXTENDED RESPONSE

11 **Argument** Many small businesses fail. Should government provide assistance to such businesses, or should it continue to let the free market determine who survives in the marketplace? Write two paragraphs stating your response and the reasons for it.

TEXT: Is Corporate Citizenship a Movement? by Stephen Jordan. Copyright © 2010 by BCLC Blog.com.

Need Extra Help?

If You've Missed Question	**1**	**2**	**3**	**4**	**5**	**6**	**7**	**8**	**9**	**10**	**11**
Review Lesson	1	1	2	2	3	3	3	3	2	2	1, 3

Government's Role in the Economy

networks

There's More Online about government's role in the economy.

CHAPTER 20

ESSENTIAL QUESTION
How does government influence the economy and economic institutions?

The Story Matters...

The noise on the floor of the New York Stock Exchange (NYSE) can be deafening. Competition is fierce as traders clamor to buy and sell company shares. All the commotion at the NYSE helps the American government, and the American people, understand how the economy is doing. Rising stock prices and sales are usually signs of a healthy American economy.

Government plays a role in our economy's health, but many people disagree on how big that role should be. Rules regulate businesses to protect consumers. Government rules also help maintain healthy competition. With the right rules and regulations, our government hopes for a market in which investors feel comfortable and the national economy thrives.

◀ *Traders on the floor of the New York Stock Exchange buy and sell ownership shares of public companies.*

PHOTO: Jin Lee/Bloomberg via Getty Images

539

Real-Life Civics

▶ **THEN** Americans often have mixed feelings about what role government ought to play in our lives. When the economy is suffering, however, people are usually willing to put their doubts aside. In the 1930s, at the peak of the Great Depression, more than 25 percent of workers were unemployed. President Franklin Roosevelt set up a number of programs to put Americans back to work and help the economy. One such program was the Civilian Conservation Corps (CCC).

The CCC hired young men to improve conditions in rural areas and conservation lands across the country. The workers planted trees, built flood barriers, and maintained roads. The CCC left a legacy of public improvements, including the River Walk in San Antonio, Texas, and the first four parks in Florida's state park system.

In this 1940 photo, a Civilian Conservation Corps (CCC) worker helps bring electricity to a rural area. ▷

A construction crew works at a job site in Arizona's Coronado National Forest. The project was funded as part of a federal stimulus package to improve the nation's economy.

▶ NOW In 2008, the worst economic downturn since the 1930s struck the nation. President Barack Obama responded by signing a law that many hoped would boost the nation's flagging economy—and its spirits. The law, referred to as the economic stimulus package, provided $787 billion in new spending, tax cuts, and aid programs. By paying for goods and services, such as construction labor and materials, the government pumped money into the economy. As with President Roosevelt's programs in the 1930s, President Obama's stimulus package was seen by some Americans as giving government too active a role in the economy. Others felt that the stimulus did not go far enough.

PHOTO: (l) AP Photos; (tr) Norma Jean Gargasz/Alamy

CIVIC LITERACY

★ ★ ★ ★

Summarizing In what ways were government actions regarding the economy similar during the Great Depression and in 2008?

Your Opinion If you had been unemployed in the 1930s, would you have liked a job with the CCC? Why or why not?

541

netw⊙rks
There's More Online!

☑ **GRAPHIC ORGANIZER**
Benefits to
Consumers

☑ **POLITICAL CARTOON**
Pollution

☑ **CHART**
Selected U.S. Government
Regulatory Agencies

☑ **GAME**

"And this little warning light flashes when the outside air becomes too polluted to breathe."

Lesson 1
Government Involvement in the Economy

ESSENTIAL QUESTION *How does government influence the economy and economic institutions?*

IT MATTERS BECAUSE

Consumers benefit when the government promotes competition and responsible actions by businesses.

Providing Public Goods

GUIDING QUESTION *What goods does government provide?*

What products and services are available in your community without paying a fee? Do you walk on sidewalks or enjoy a local park? Do you have the protection of the police and the help of firefighters when needed? You do not have to pay for these things each time you use them. They are there for all to use. These products and services are different from those you pay for in stores and use for your own enjoyment.

Private and Public Goods

Businesses produce **private goods**, products that people must buy in order to use or own them. A person who does not pay for a private good is barred from owning or using it. If you do not buy a shirt, you cannot wear it—unless someone else buys it for you. In addition, private goods can be used by only one person. If you buy a shirt, no one else can buy that same shirt. Others can buy one like it, but not the exact shirt you bought. Similarly, if you eat a meal, no one else can eat it. Clothes, food, books, and cars are examples of private goods.

PHOTO: (tl) Rudi Von Briel/Corbis; (tcr) Mike Baldwin/CartoonStock.com; (tcr) Justin Sullivan/Getty Images; (tr) AP Photo/Charles Rex Arbogast

ReadingHELPDESK

Taking Notes: *Identifying*

As you read, identify ways the government's role in the economy benefits consumers.

Benefits to Consumers

Content Vocabulary

- private good
- public good
- externality
- monopoly
- antitrust law
- merger
- natural monopoly
- recall

Unlike private goods, **public goods** can be consumed by more than one person. For, example, your community sidewalks are public goods. If you walk on a sidewalk, that does not prevent others from walking on it as well. Police protection and national defense are also public goods. A community—not just one person—enjoys the protection of the police. Similarly, the entire nation is made safer by the armed forces.

Public goods are important to a number of people—even an entire community or nation. Yet businesses do not like to produce and sell them. Why is that? The reason is simple. It is difficult to charge everyone who might benefit from using public goods. For instance, how could someone figure out what to charge you for your use of a sidewalk or for your share of the protection offered by the police? Because it is hard to assign the costs of these goods, government takes on the responsibility for providing public goods. It pays for these goods through taxes and other fees it collects.

Externalities

Economic activities of all sorts produce side effects called **externalities** (EHK•STUHR•NAH•luh•teez). These are either positive or negative side effects of an action that **affect,** or impact, an uninvolved third person.

Public goods often produce *positive* externalities. That is, they benefit more people than those who use the goods. Everyone—not just drivers—benefits from having good roads. Good roads make it faster and cheaper to transport goods. That means those goods can be sold at lower prices. As a result, all consumers benefit. A lower price is one positive externality that comes from having good roads.

Externalities can be negative, too. *Negative* externalities result when an action has harmful side effects. For example, a car provides transportation. However, its exhaust pollutes the air. Even people without cars may suffer from air pollution's negative effects, such as breathing problems.

PHOTO: Rudi Von Briel/Corbis

About 25 million people visit New York City's Central Park every year. They walk, run, skate, and bike on its paths; enjoy its green spaces and woods; and go to the theater and the zoo. This park, like others across the country, is funded by taxes collected and then distributed by an arm of the government.

▶ **CRITICAL THINKING**
Analyzing Identify a positive economic externality that large public parks create in cities.

private good an economic good that, when consumed by one person, cannot be used by another

public good an economic good that is used collectively, such as a highway and national defense

externality an economic side effect that affects an uninvolved third party

Academic Vocabulary

affect to impact; to have an effect on

© Mike Baldwin / Cornered

SALES

"And this little warning light flashes when the outside air becomes too polluted to breathe."

PHOTO: Mike Baldwin/CartoonStock.com

The negative externality of pollution is easy to ignore from inside a vehicle. From the outside, it is hard to miss.

► CRITICAL THINKING

Explaining The government imposes a "gas guzzler" tax on vehicles that do not meet minimum standards for fuel use. How does this tax discourage the negative externality of pollution?

One of the roles of government is to encourage positive externalities and discourage negative ones. For instance, the government provides schooling to children because education usually leads to positive externalities. A well-educated workforce is more productive. As another example, to reduce pollution, the federal government has regulated car exhaust since the 1970s.

☑ PROGRESS CHECK

Explaining How does government pay for public goods?

Maintaining Competition

GUIDING QUESTION *How does government encourage or increase competition among businesses?*

Have you ever played the board game *Monopoly*®? To win, a player tries to take control of all the properties in the game and to bankrupt the other players. In other words, the winner becomes a monopoly. A **monopoly** (muh•NAH•pah•lee) is the sole provider of a good or service.

Markets work best when large numbers of buyers and sellers participate. If a monopoly gains control of a market, it does not have to compete with other companies for buyers. It can charge any price it wants. Consumers suffer because they are forced to pay that price instead of being able to shop for a better one. To prevent this problem, one of the goals of the U.S. government has long been to encourage competition in the marketplace so that monopolies do not form.

Antitrust Laws

To protect competition, the government uses antitrust laws. A trust is a combination of businesses that threatens competition. The government's goal in passing **antitrust** (AN•tee•TRUHST) **laws** is to control monopoly power and to preserve and promote competition.

Reading**HELP**DESK

monopoly a sole provider for a good or service

antitrust law legislation to prevent monopolies from forming and to preserve and promote competition

merger a combination of two or more companies to form a single business

natural monopoly a market situation in which the costs of production are minimized by having a single firm produce the product

In 1890 the government passed its first antitrust law, the Sherman Antitrust Act. This law banned monopolies and other forms of business that prevent competition. In 1911 the government used the law to break up the Standard Oil Company. That company had a monopoly on oil. In the 1980s the government used the act to break up American Telephone and Telegraph (AT&T). This action ended a monopoly on phone service and created more competition.

In 1914 Congress passed the Clayton Antitrust Act. This law made the Sherman Act stronger and clearer. The Clayton Act banned a number of business practices that hurt competition. For example, a person could no longer be a member of the board of directors of two competing companies. The law also gave the government power over some mergers.

Mergers

Sometimes two or more companies combine, or merge, to form a single business. That joining is called a **merger** (MUHR•juhr). In some instances a merger threatens competition and can then lead to higher prices. In that case, the government can use the Clayton Act to block the merger. The Federal Trade Commission (FTC) has the power to enforce this law. It can look at any merger that may violate antitrust laws. It also has the power to take the actions it finds necessary to maintain competition. For example, in 2007 a company called Whole Foods bought Wild Oats. Both companies ran supermarkets that sold natural foods. The FTC thought the merger would reduce competition. So it ordered Whole Foods to sell some of its stores. Whole Foods also had to make some other changes to restore competition.

Natural Monopolies

At times it makes sense to let a single business produce a good or service. For example, it might be better to have one company, instead of two or three, build electric power lines for a town or city. In these cases, we have a **natural monopoly.** With this kind of monopoly, a single business can produce and distribute a product better and more cheaply than several companies could.

Of course, natural monopolies have great power. They can choose to raise prices whenever they wish. For this reason, the government usually regulates these companies.

PHOTO: Justin Sullivan/Getty Images

When Whole Foods buys another grocery store chain, it grows and has one less competitor in the market.

▶ CRITICAL THINKING
Determining Cause and Effect Why does the government regulate mergers?

SELECTED U.S. GOVERNMENT REGULATORY AGENCIES

DEPARTMENT OR AGENCY	PURPOSE
Consumer Product Safety Commission (CPSC)	Protects the public from risks of serious injury or death from consumer products
Environmental Protection Agency (EPA)	Protects human health and the natural environment (air, water, and land)
Federal Trade Commission (FTC)	Promotes and protects consumer interests and competition in the marketplace
Food and Drug Administration (FDA)	Makes sure food, drugs, and cosmetics are truthfully labeled and safe for consumers
Occupational Safety and Health Administration (OSHA)	Makes sure workers have a safe and healthful workplace

CHART SKILLS

These are just a few of the federal government agencies that regulate businesses.

▶ CRITICAL THINKING

1. **Differentiating** Which regulatory agency has the power to make sure that competition exists in the marketplace?

2. **Making Generalizations** What are two other goals of government regulation?

That is, a government agency closely watches the companies that have a natural monopoly. The agency has to approve any increase in prices.

Sometimes a local government can choose a different approach. It may become the owner of the natural monopoly instead. This is often the case with such basic services as water and sewers.

In recent years, many governments decided to put an end to certain natural monopolies. They intended to bring back, or **restore,** competition. For example, about half of the states have ended the monopoly of companies that make electric power. This policy of ending regulation is called deregulation. The new approach has not always led to lower prices, though. As a result, many states are now backing away from deregulation of natural monopolies.

☑ PROGRESS CHECK

Summarizing Why does government promote competition?

Reading HELPDESK

Reading Strategy: *Paraphrasing*

When you paraphrase, you put what you have read into your own words. Read the section on natural monopolies. On a separate sheet of paper, paraphrase the last paragraph.

Academic Vocabulary

restore to bring back

recall action that causes an unsafe product to be removed from store shelves

Protecting Consumer Health and Safety

GUIDING QUESTION *How does government regulate business?*

The government also plays a major role in protecting the health and safety of the public. For example, the Food and Drug Administration (FDA) makes sure that foods, drugs, medical equipment, and cosmetics are safe. It also makes sure that companies tell the truth on product labels and in ads.

The FDA can act quickly if a problem arises. In the spring of 2010, health officials became concerned about a large increase in the number of cases of salmonella. The illness, which comes from eating contaminated food, is serious and can lead to death. The FDA traced the problem to eggs. To prevent the spread of the disease, the FDA ordered hundreds of millions of eggs removed from stores and destroyed. The FDA also created new safety rules for companies that produce eggs.

The Centers for Disease Control and Prevention (CDC) also tries to improve health. The CDC does this work in many ways. It checks air quality and distributes the flu vaccine, for example.

The goal of the Consumer Product Safety Commission (CPSC) is to protect consumers from injury. It oversees thousands of products, from toys to tools. The CPSC looks for problems in the design of a product or how it is used that can create unnecessary danger. If the CPSC finds that a product is unsafe, it will issue a **recall**. A recall means the unsafe product is removed from store shelves. For those who bought the product, the manufacturer must change the product to make it safe, offer a substitute product, or return the customer's money.

✓ PROGRESS CHECK

Identifying What is the role of the FDA?

LESSON 1 REVIEW

Review Vocabulary

1. What is an *externality*? Provide an example of an externality, as well as its source, and identify it as positive or negative.

2. Explain what a *merger* is. How can it lead to a *monopoly*?

Answer the Guiding Questions

3. *Explaining* Why do businesses not provide public goods?

4. *Describing* How do antitrust laws help maintain competition?

5. *Finding the Main Idea* How does government regulation protect the health and safety of consumers?

6. **INFORMATIVE/EXPLANATORY** Identify a public good and a private good that you use regularly. Describe each good, and identify the characteristics that make the public good public and the private good private.

Issues to Debate

Is increasing the minimum wage good for the economy?

The minimum wage is the lowest hourly rate of pay that employers may pay their workers. This lower limit is set by law. Congress first set the minimum wage in 1938. At the time, the wage was 25 cents. Initially, the law applied only to those employees whose work was part of interstate commerce, or buying and selling products across state lines. Later, Congress changed the law and made it cover most workers. Congress has also raised the rate many times. The current rate, $7.25, took effect in 2009.

The minimum wage has been in place for more than 70 years. Still, the debate over it continues. Critics say that the minimum wage discourages businesses from hiring workers. Supporters disagree.

> **Many food service workers, especially those working in fast-food restaurants, start out earning the minimum wage.**

Yes

Those who back the minimum wage say that little evidence supports the idea that it forces businesses to fire large numbers of workers. In fact, they say, some business owners find that a higher minimum wage can help them keep good employees. Keeping employees is less expensive than training new ones. In addition, raising the minimum wage gives consumers more money that they can use to buy products. This would have a positive effect on the economy as a whole. Kai Filion of the Economic Policy Institute is one supporter of the wage increase. He argues that raising the minimum wage actually creates jobs:

"Each increase provides financial relief directly to minimum wage workers and their families and helps stimulate the economy . . . thus creating jobs for other Americans."

—Kai Filion, Economic Policy Institute, 2009

No

Critics say the minimum wage hurts people with the least education and job experience. These are the workers who have minimum-wage jobs. But by forcing employers to pay these workers a certain amount, the law keeps business owners from hiring. Teens, critics say, are especially hard-hit by this law. James Sherk of the Heritage Foundation argues that a higher minimum wage hurts workers in the long run:

"Few Americans work for the minimum wage very long. They are entry-level jobs that offer inexperienced workers on-the-job training in essential work skills. . . . As minimum-wage workers become more productive, they earn higher wages. Two-thirds of minimum-wage workers earn a raise within a year. A higher minimum wage doesn't just price some unskilled workers out of a job today. It prevents them from gaining the skills that would allow them to earn more in the future."

—James Sherk, Heritage Foundation, 2009

Debating the Issue

1. **Defining** What is a minimum wage?

2. **Identifying Central Issues** In what ways might raising the minimum wage affect employment?

3. **Recalling** How might higher wages be good for businesses?

4. **Summarizing** How might a higher minimum wage hurt low-wage workers?

"You go without me. I'm feeling
a little down today."

Lesson 2
Measuring the Economy

ESSENTIAL QUESTION *How does government influence the economy and
economic institutions?*

IT MATTERS BECAUSE
*Tracking the growth of the economy helps the government craft
appropriate economic policies.*

Economic Performance

GUIDING QUESTION *Why is it important to measure an economy's performance?*

As you know, prices are the signals that help individuals,
businesses, and the government make economic decisions.
Prices are a key feature of a market economy, but they can also
be troublesome. Here is one way. Think about Gross Domestic
Product (GDP). If a country has a bigger GDP in one year than
it had the year before, does that mean its economy grew? Not
necessarily. This is only true if the growth is due to increased
output and *not* the result of higher prices. If rising prices caused
GDP to go up—because the same amount of goods is worth
more the increase in GDP is misleading. To avoid being misled
by rising prices, economists use a measure called real GDP.

Real GDP

Real GDP is GDP after the distortions caused by price increases
have been removed. Real GDP is essentially the same thing as GDP
in an economy where prices do not change. Because of this, real
GDP is a better measure of an economy's performance over time.

Reading**HELP**DESK

Taking Notes: *Categorizing*
As you read, identify indicators of
economic expansion and contraction.

Expansion	Contraction

Content Vocabulary

- **real GDP**
- **business cycle**
- **recession**

- **depression**
- **unemployment rate**
- **fixed income**

- **inflation**
- **bear market**
- **bull market**

Phases of economic expansion and contraction shape the business cycle.

▶ **CRITICAL THINKING**

1 *Analyzing Visuals* What is the growing phase of the business cycle called? What happens to real GDP in this period?

2 *Synthesize* How realistic is this illustration of the business cycle? Why?

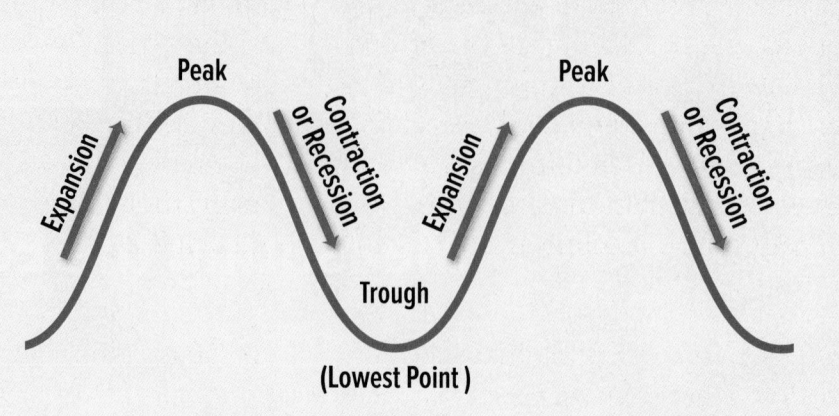

Peak

Contraction or Recession

Expansion

Peak

Contraction or Recession

Expansion

Trough

(Lowest Point)

Having a measure like real GDP is important. Business leaders want to know how the economy is doing so that they can make plans for the future. Government leaders want to know if their economic policies are working or need to be changed. Growth in real GDP **indicates,** or signals, a healthy economy. A healthy economy is one that grows, generates good jobs, and provides economic opportunity for everyone.

Business Cycles

The U.S. economy has not grown at a steady rate over time. Instead, it goes through alternating periods of growth and decline that we call the **business cycle.** The graph shows a simplified version of the business cycle. In the real world, business cycles are not as regular as the graph shows.

Every business cycle includes two distinct points—peaks and troughs. At the peak, real GDP reaches its highest point and then starts to turn down. Real GDP will eventually stop going down and then start to rise again. The point where real GDP reaches its lowest level and starts to climb again is the trough. A full business cycle lasts from one peak to the next.

The first part of the business cycle is the period when real GDP goes down, or is in a contraction. The economy is in a **recession** (rih•SEH•shuhn) if real GDP goes down for six months or more. Most recessions last less than a year.

Reading **HELP**DESK

real GDP
GDP after adjustments for inflation

business cycle
alternating periods of economic growth and decline

recession a period of declining economic activity lasting six or more months

depression state of the economy with high unemployment, severely depressed real GDP, and general economic hardship

Academic Vocabulary

indicate to signal

enormous very large

There can be exceptions, though. A recession started in December of 2007 and lasted until June of 2009. This 18-month recession was the longest since the 1930s.

Eventually real GDP will start to grow again. When that happens, the second part of the business cycle, the expansion, starts. An expansion is the period from the trough to the peak. Expansions tend to be longer than declines. Most recent expansions have lasted from six to ten years. The new peak can be even higher than the previous peak. Eventually, though, real GDP will start to decline again, starting a new business cycle.

The Great Depression

A recession may turn into a depression if real GDP continues to go down rather than turning back up. A **depression** is a period of severe economic decline. The United States had a major depression that started in 1929 and reached a trough in 1933. The fall in real GDP was so **enormous** that it took until 1939 for output to get back to the level where it had been in 1929. This long slowdown is called the Great Depression.

Most economists think real GDP fell by half from 1929 to 1933. One in four workers lost their jobs. About one-quarter of banks went out of business. Many stocks became worthless.

Most economists think that something as serious as the Great Depression cannot happen again. Laws were passed to prevent the kinds of actions that worsened the situation in the 1930s. We also better understand how the economy works and how to keep it healthy now. The government plays a larger role in the economy than it did in the 1930s. It usually takes steps to try to fix economic problems.

✔ **PROGRESS CHECK**

Identifying What does a peak on a business cycle graph mean?

PHOTO: Spencer Platt/Getty Images

21st Century SKILLS

Use and Cite Online Information

Find a government or education Web site that tells about the Great Depression. On a separate sheet of paper, write three facts that are not in your textbook. Record information about the Web site you used that tells others where you found these facts.

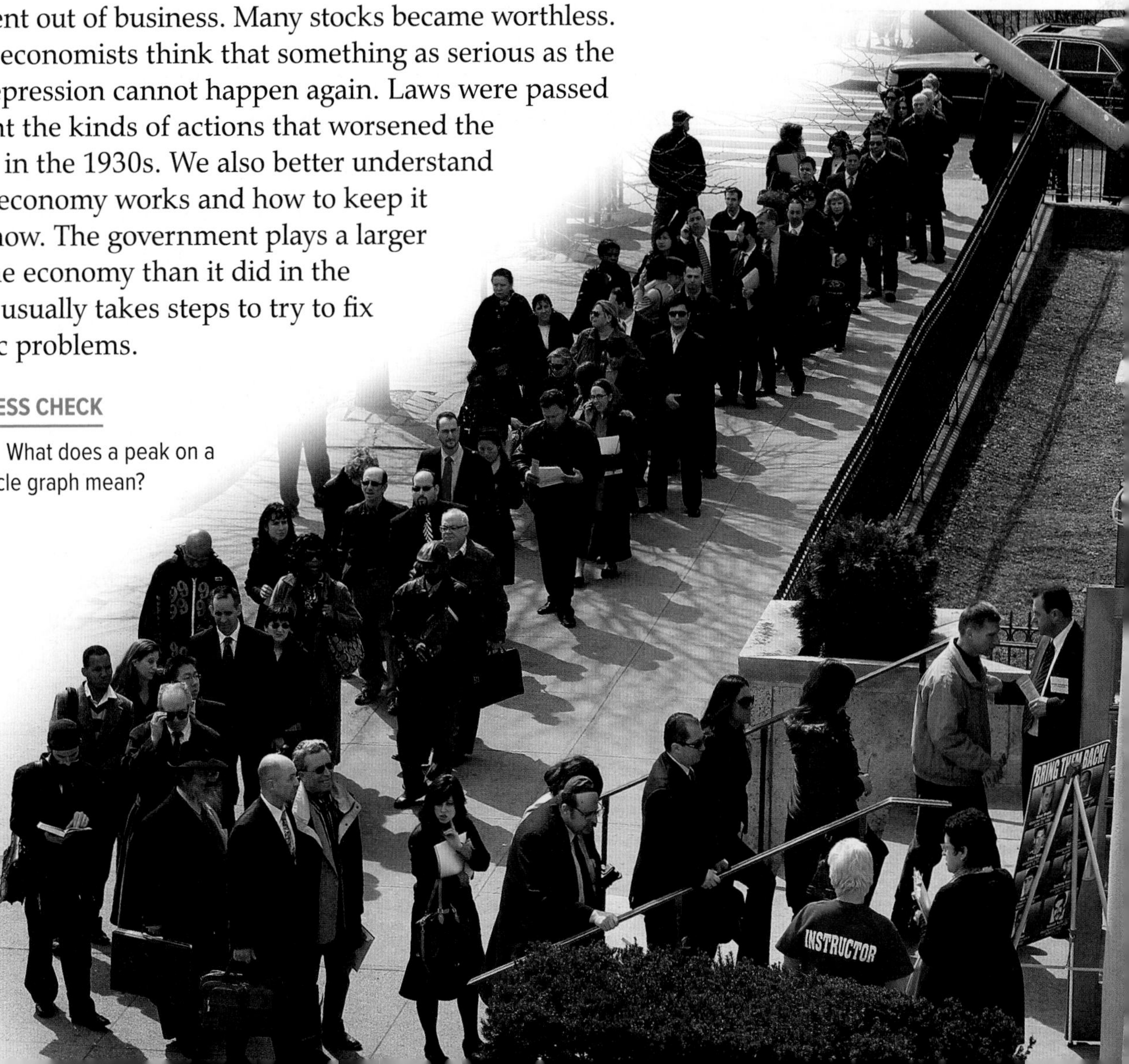

Though the recession of 2007–2009 had officially ended, this job fair in Brooklyn, New York, still attracted hundreds of job seekers in March 2010.

▶ **CRITICAL THINKING**
Determining Cause and Effect Why does a decline in the business cycle cause unemployment?

This chart shows the topsy-turvy history of the U.S. economy since 1880.

► **CRITICAL THINKING**

1 *Analyzing Visuals* What does a downward slope in the red line show? What about an upward slope?

2 *Synthesizing* Does a downward or an upward slope indicate falling consumer demand? Why?

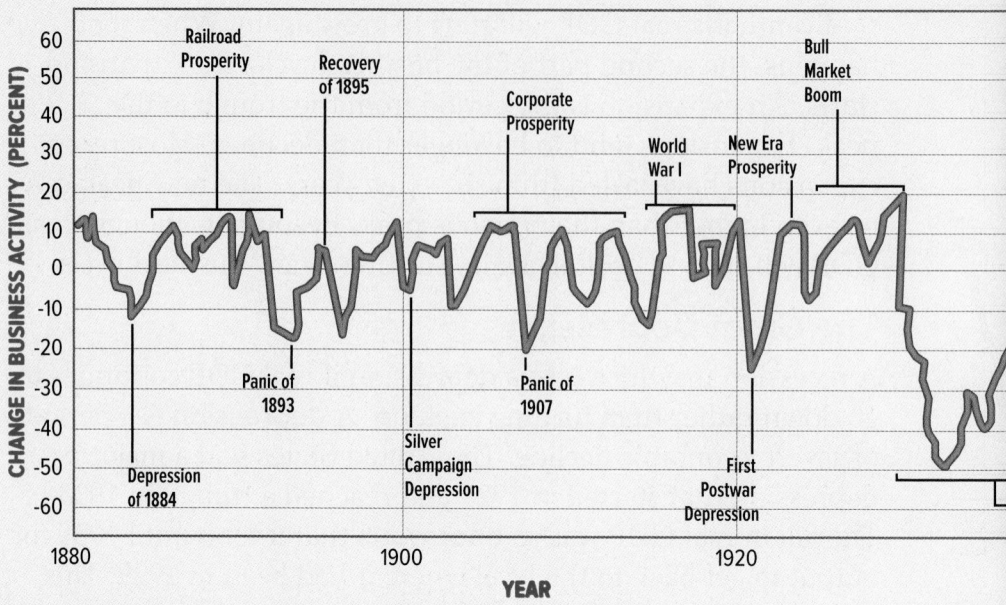

Business activity increased greatly during World War II.

Other Measures of Performance

GUIDING QUESTION *What are other signs of an economy's health?*

Suppose someone were to ask you to describe your economic situation. Before answering, you might think about whether you get an allowance, have money to buy the clothes or music you want, and have money saved for a class trip. Adults think about their economic health in a similar way. Nations have economic health, too. To judge that health, economists look at certain signs called economic indicators. One key indicator is employment. Another is how stable, or unchanging, prices are.

Employment and Unemployment

A major indicator of the health of an economy is the percentage of workers who have or do not have jobs. To get an accurate picture of the job situation, economists look at the civilian labor force. *Civilian* means "people outside the military." The civilian labor force includes all civilians 16 years old or older who are either working or are looking for work. In the United States,

PHOTO: K.J. Historical/Corbis

unemployment rate the percentage of people in the civilian labor force who are not working but are looking for jobs

fixed income an income that remains the same each month and does not have the potential to go up when prices are going up

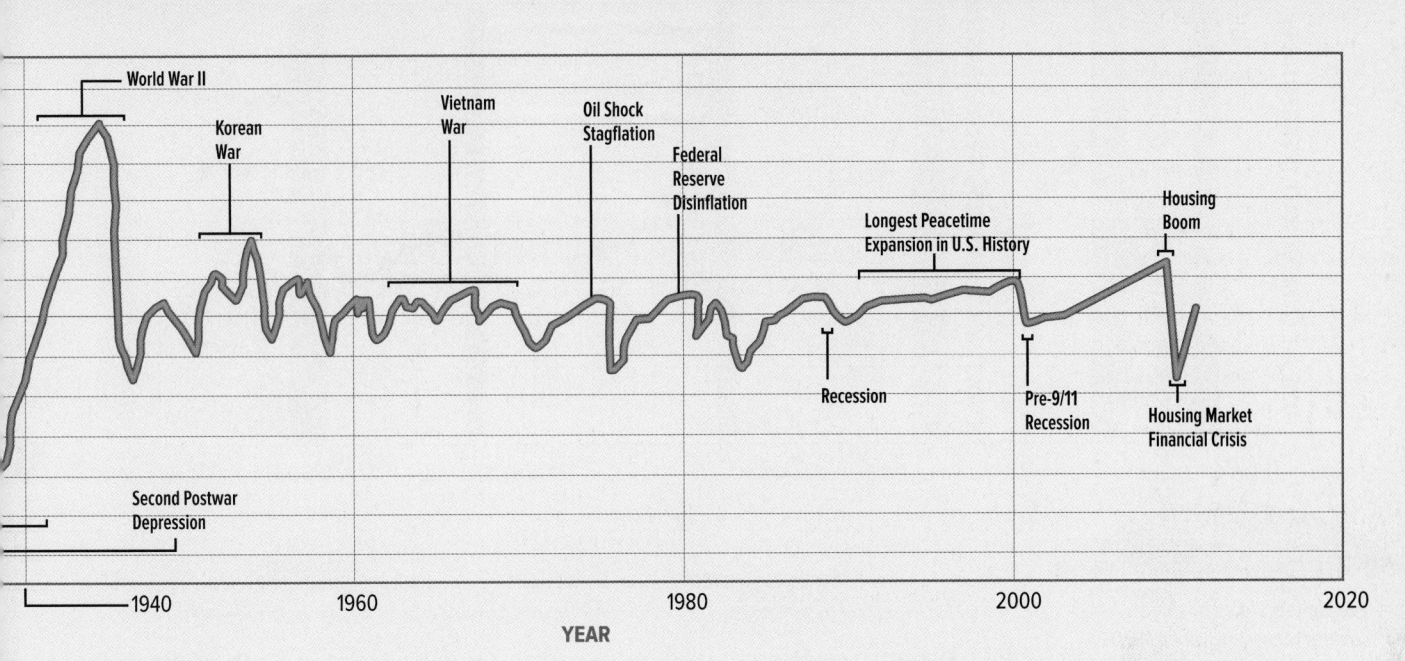

Source: National Bureau of Economic Research; *American Business Activity from 1790 to Today*, 67th ed., Ameritrust Co., January 1996, plus author's projections.

about half of all people belong to the civilian labor force. Most people in the civilian labor force fall into one of two categories: those who have jobs and those who do not.

The **unemployment** (UHN•ehm•PLOY•muhnt) **rate** is the percentage of people in the civilian labor force who are not working but are looking for jobs. In a healthy economy, the unemployment rate is low, usually around 5 percent. A high unemployment rate, closer to 9 or 10 percent, signals trouble in the economy.

The government tracks the unemployment rate every month. The rate usually changes only a little from one month to the next. It might go up or down by as little as one- or two-tenths of a percent. This may not seem like much, but a one-tenth-of-a-percent change means that 150,000 people are affected.

Recessions are difficult for people who are unemployed. Businesses want to be sure that the economy is rising before they hire workers. For this reason, the unemployment rate does not usually start to go down until well after recovery has begun.

Price Stability

Another important sign of an economy's health is the general level of prices. If prices remain stable, or steady, consumers and businesses can better plan for the future. This is especially important for people who are retired and live on a fixed income. A **fixed income** remains the same each month and does not have the potential to increase when prices go up.

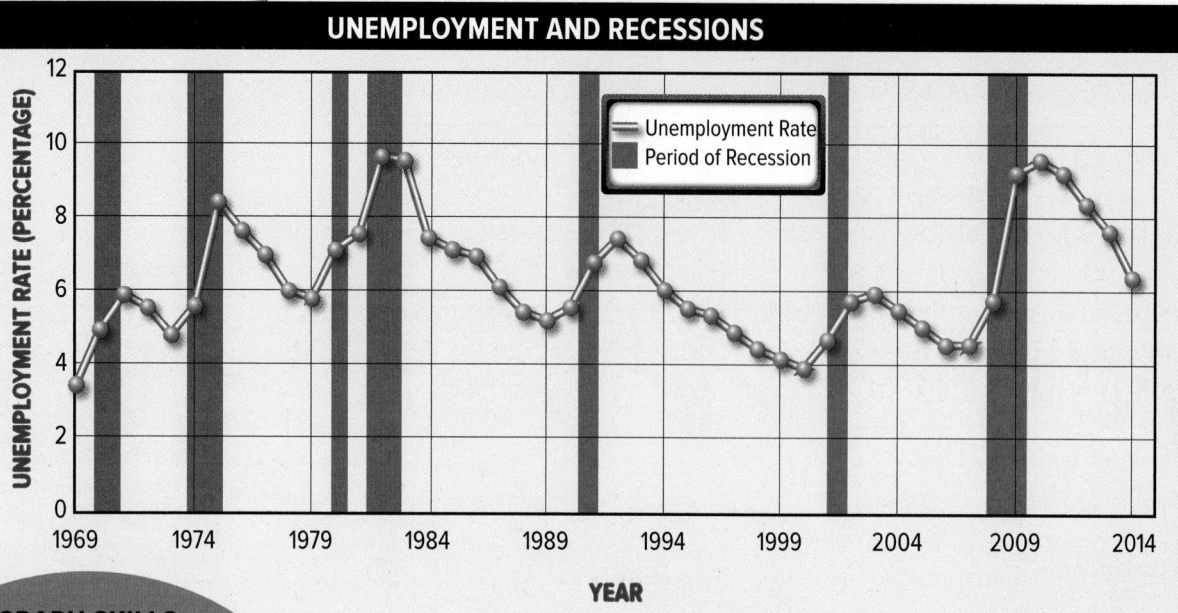

UNEMPLOYMENT AND RECESSIONS

UNEMPLOYMENT RATE (PERCENTAGE)

Legend:
- Unemployment Rate
- Period of Recession

YEAR

Source: National Bureau of Economic Research; Bureau of Labor Statistics

GRAPH SKILLS

The United States has had several recessions since 1970.

▶ **CRITICAL THINKING**

❶ *Analyzing Visuals* What do the red areas of the graph represent?

❷ *Determining Cause and Effect* Why does unemployment go up in a recession?

When prices remain stable, money has the same purchasing power, or value. When prices go up, money loses some of its purchasing power. For example, suppose an ice-cream cone that costs a dollar doubles in price to two dollars. The higher price means that your dollar buys less. You need to spend twice as many dollars to buy the same ice-cream cone.

An increase in the price of one good does not affect purchasing power much. If most prices rise, though, the situation is different. Economists have a name for a long-term increase in the general level of prices. They call it **inflation** (ihn•FLAY•shuhn). Inflation hurts the economy because it reduces everyone's purchasing power. When prices in general are going up, the value, or purchasing power, of money goes down. Rising inflation is a sign of economic trouble.

Because inflation is so serious, the government tracks it each month. It checks the prices of about 400 products that consumers commonly buy. The prices of these 400 products make up a measure called the consumer price index (CPI). Typically, the prices of some items in the CPI go up every month, and the prices of others go down. If the overall level of the CPI goes up, inflation is taking place.

✔ PROGRESS CHECK

Explaining What does inflation do to purchasing power? Why?

Reading HELPDESK

inflation a long-term increase in the general level of prices

Economic Indicators

GUIDING QUESTION *How is the stock market a measure of the economy's performance?*

Measures of performance like real GDP, unemployment, and the CPI tell us how we are doing now. Economists also study statistics to tell us where we are headed in the future.

One set of statistics is a stock index such as the Dow Jones Industrial Average or the Standard & Poor's 500. Another closely watched indicator, the Leading Economic Index, shows where the economy is likely to go in the next 6 to 12 months.

Stock Indexes

The price of any company's stock is set by supply and demand. Supply is the number of stocks available. Demand is the number of stocks investors want to buy. Changes in a company's profits or release of a new product can change the demand for its stock. Changes in demand will change the price of a stock.

Changes in the value of a single stock do not tell us much about the economy. The changes in *all* stock prices do, however. Stock indexes tell us how all stock prices are changing. Indexes give a sense of how healthy the whole stock market is.

Two common stock indexes are the Dow Jones Industrial Average (DJIA) and the Standard and Poor's (S&P) 500. The DJIA tracks prices of 30 stocks. These include companies such as Coca-Cola, McDonald's, Walt Disney, and Wal-Mart. The S&P 500 index tracks the total market value of 500 stocks.

21ˢᵗ *Century* SKILLS

Analyzing Information

The text states that the performance of one company's stock says little about the state of the economy. Changes in the prices of many stocks do give information about the economy's health, though. Why is that? Write a paragraph explaining why that is true.

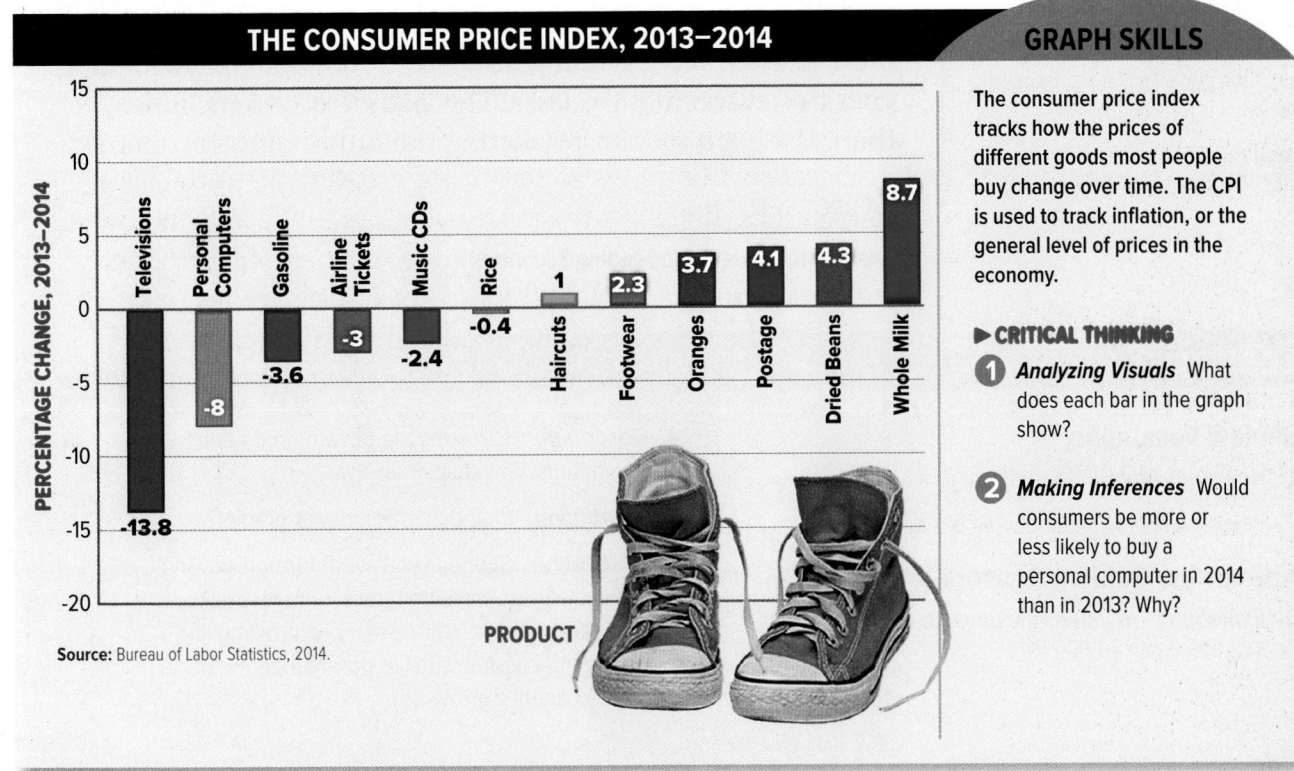

THE CONSUMER PRICE INDEX, 2013–2014

Percentage Change, 2013–2014

- Televisions: -13.8
- Personal Computers: -8
- Gasoline: -3.6
- Airline Tickets: -3
- Music CDs: -2.4
- Rice: -0.4
- Haircuts: 1
- Footwear: 2.3
- Oranges: 3.7
- Postage: 4.1
- Dried Beans: 4.3
- Whole Milk: 8.7

PRODUCT

Source: Bureau of Labor Statistics, 2014.

GRAPH SKILLS

The consumer price index tracks how the prices of different goods most people buy change over time. The CPI is used to track inflation, or the general level of prices in the economy.

▶ **CRITICAL THINKING**

1. *Analyzing Visuals* What does each bar in the graph show?

2. *Making Inferences* Would consumers be more or less likely to buy a personal computer in 2014 than in 2013? Why?

"You go without me. I'm feeling a little down today."

In the world of the stock market, optimists are called bulls and pessimists are called bears.

▶ CRITICAL THINKING

Differentiating If investors are "bullish" about a stock, what do they think will happen to the stock's price?

bear market period during which stock prices decline for a substantial period

bull market period during which stock prices steadily increase

Stock prices are good economic indicators. Indexes like the DJIA and the S&P 500 reveal investors' expectations about the future. They often tell us where the economy is headed. If investors are gloomy, they will hesitate to invest or might even sell some of their stocks. As a result, stock prices may fall.

When stock indexes are going down and investors do not have much confidence, the stock market is called a "bear market." A bear market is usually a sign that real GDP will stall or even go into recession. If investors feel good about the economy and expect it to be strong in the future, they are more likely to buy stocks. These purchases will drive stock prices up. Rising prices mean rising stock indexes. A rising stock market fueled by confident investors is called a "bull market." Bull markets are a good sign that real GDP will grow.

The Leading Economic Index®

Another measure used to forecast changes in economic growth is the Leading Economic Index. This index combines ten sets of data. The idea is that, since no single indicator works all of the time, combining many indicators is more accurate. The S&P 500 stock index is in this index. Other data include the number of hours worked in manufacturing and the number of building permits issued in the previous month.

The index is called leading because it generally points to the direction in which real GDP is headed. For example, if the leading index goes down, real GDP usually goes down a few months later. If the leading index goes up, real GDP usually goes up several months later. The leading economic index, then, is a good tool for predicting the future of the economy.

 PROGRESS CHECK

Explaining What is the Leading Economic Index?

PHOTO: Dave Carpenter, and CartoonStock

LESSON 2 REVIEW

Review Vocabulary

1. How does *real GDP* differ from *GDP*?

2. What is a *recession*, and what is a *depression*?

Answer the Guiding Questions

3. ***Explaining*** Why does the government measure economic performance?

4. ***Describing*** How does the government keep track of inflation? Why does it do so?

5. ***Identifying*** What do stock indexes predict?

6. **NARRATIVE** Suppose you lived through a swing in the business cycle from recession to peak economic growth. Write a story contrasting life during a recession with life during a period of peak economic growth.

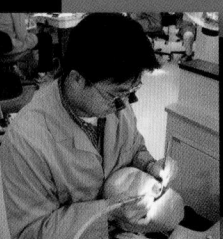

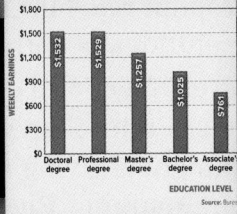

Lesson 3

The Government and Income Inequality

ESSENTIAL QUESTION *How does government influence the economy and economic institutions?*

IT MATTERS BECAUSE
Income inequality hurts individuals and the economy as a whole.

Income Inequality

GUIDING QUESTION *What factors influence income?*

The United States is often described as a wealthy country. However, not all Americans are wealthy. Some people have high incomes, but others are quite poor. Income levels vary for many reasons. Education level, family wealth, and discrimination each play a role.

Education

Education is a key to income. This is why the government wants Americans to graduate from high school and go on to higher learning. Every day, however, more than 7,000 students drop out of high school. In 2010 President Barack Obama said,

PRIMARY SOURCE

❝ [T]he success of every American will be tied more closely than ever before to the level of education that they achieve. The jobs will go to the people with the knowledge and the skills to do them—it's that simple. In this kind of knowledge economy, giving up on your education and dropping out of school means not only giving up on your future, but it's also giving up on your family's future and giving up on your country's future. ❞

—President Barack Obama, 2010

Reading**HELP**DESK

Taking Notes: *Organizing*

As you read, identify factors that influence how much income people can earn.

Factors Affecting Income	
Factor	Details

Content Vocabulary

- welfare
- Temporary Assistance for Needy Families (TANF)
- workfare
- compensation

The dropout rate hurts the nation's ability to compete economically. People without a high school diploma tend to receive lower wages and experience higher unemployment and imprisonment rates than graduates. To try to fix this problem, the government is giving money to states and towns for dropout prevention programs. Recently, the federal government has turned its efforts toward schools with the highest dropout rates.

The level of education a person **attains,** or achieves, has a great influence on his or her income. Education gives people the skills they need to get higher-paying jobs. Look at the graph of weekly earnings. Notice that a person with a bachelor's degree can earn nearly twice as much as a person who has only a high school diploma. People with the most advanced degrees earn the most and have the lowest rates of unemployment.

For these reasons, the federal government encourages people to go to college. Some programs help students from low-income families and those with disabilities prepare for college. The government also offers low-cost loans and grants that help make college more affordable.

Family Wealth

People who are born into wealth have certain advantages. A person from a family with money has better access to education. As you just read, the more education a person has, the greater his or her **potential,** or possible, income. Wealthy parents are often able to set their children up in family businesses where they can earn good incomes. Finally, such people usually leave their wealth to their children when they die.

Discrimination

Discrimination limits how much some people can earn. Unfair practices in hiring and promoting people hurt women and members of minority groups. Many of these people are prevented from getting top-paying jobs. This treatment has an impact on the economy as a whole. Women generally earn less than men. According to some estimates, if this pay gap were closed, the nation's GDP could increase by 9 percent.

Several laws aim to end discrimination. The Equal Pay Act of 1963 requires that men and women be given equal pay for equal work. This means that jobs that have the same level of skill and responsibility must pay the

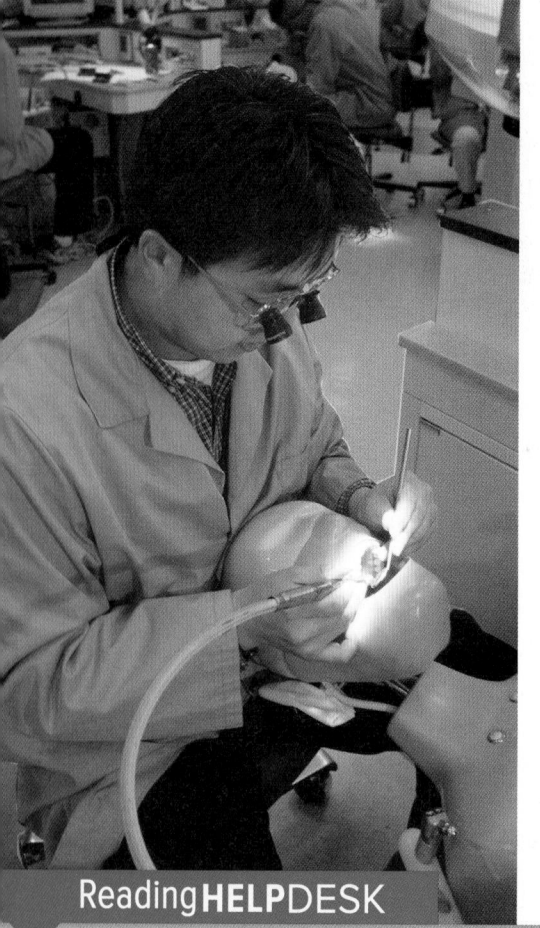

Dentistry is one of the highest-paid occupations in the United States. To become a dentist, a person must first graduate from college and then attend a dental school for at least four years.

▶ CRITICAL THINKING

Drawing Conclusions What is the relationship between the education and skills of dentists and the amount they earn?

Reading**HELP**DESK

PHOTO: Jim Sugar/CORBIS

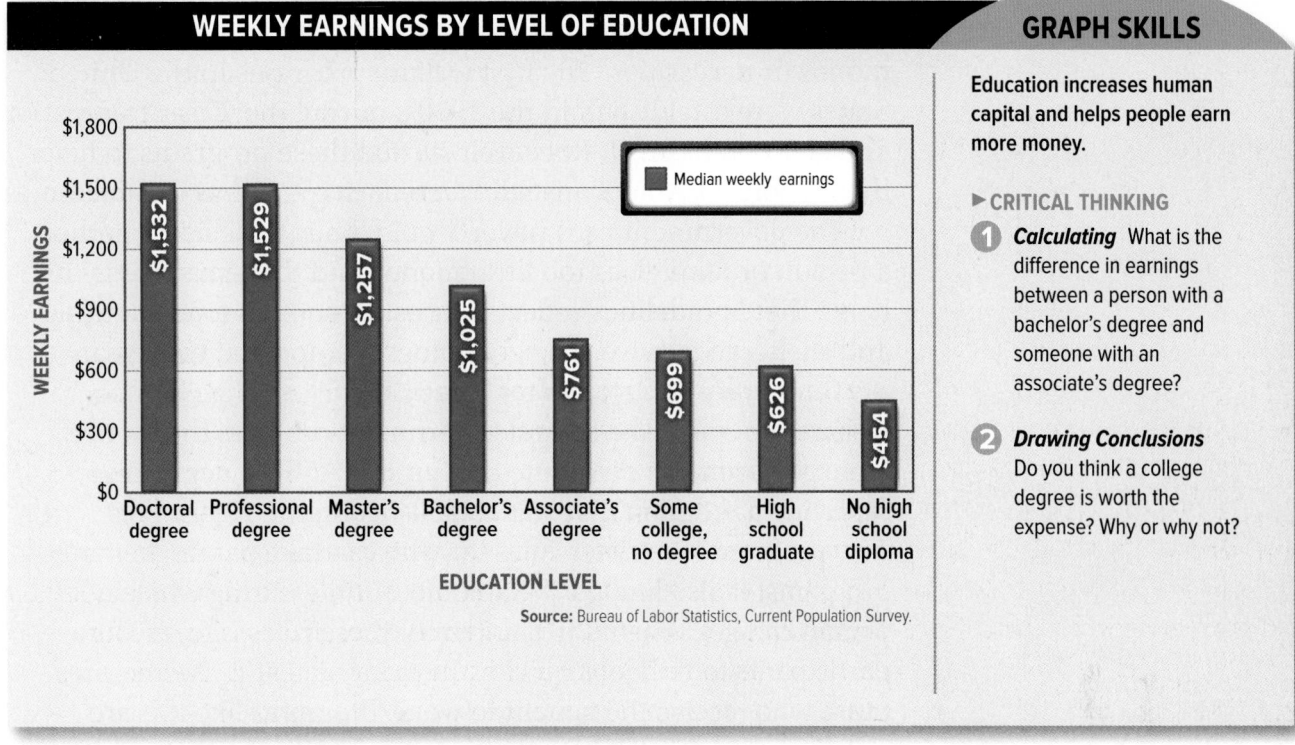

GRAPH SKILLS

WEEKLY EARNINGS

Doctoral degree	$1,532
Professional degree	$1,529
Master's degree	$1,257
Bachelor's degree	$1,025
Associate's degree	$761
Some college, no degree	$699
High school graduate	$626
No high school diploma	$454

■ Median weekly earnings

EDUCATION LEVEL

Source: Bureau of Labor Statistics, Current Population Survey.

Education increases human capital and helps people earn more money.

▶ CRITICAL THINKING

❶ *Calculating* What is the difference in earnings between a person with a bachelor's degree and someone with an associate's degree?

❷ *Drawing Conclusions* Do you think a college degree is worth the expense? Why or why not?

same. The Civil Rights Act of 1964 bans discrimination based on gender, race, color, religion, and national origin. The Equal Employment Opportunity Act of 1972 gave the government more power to enforce this law. The Americans with Disabilities Act of 1990 gave job protection to people who have physical and mental disabilities. The Lilly Ledbetter Fair Pay Act of 2009 allows workers who suffer unfair treatment because of their gender to sue employers. The government has also encouraged companies to practice affirmative action. Such a policy is meant to increase the number of minorities and women at work. This effort helps to make up for past actions that held back people in these groups.

✓ **PROGRESS CHECK**

Explaining How does education affect income?

Poverty

GUIDING QUESTION *In what ways does government help those in poverty?*

While many Americans are well off, many others are poor. In a recent year, more than 40 million people lived in poverty. This means they did not earn enough income to pay for basic needs such as food, clothing, and shelter. Tough economic times can add to these numbers. The recession that began in 2007 caused a sharp increase in the number of people living in poverty. In 2009 about 4 million more Americans found themselves in need. This means that about 44 million people, or one in seven U.S. residents, lived in poverty in 2009.

21ˢᵗ Century
SKILLS

Information Literacy: Use a Time Line

Make a time line that covers the period from 1960 to 2010. Place each of the five antidiscrimination laws described on this page in the correct place on your time line.

To aid struggling families, the federal government provides welfare. **Welfare** is aid given to those in need in the form of money or necessities. The first welfare programs in the United States were established in the 1930s, during the Great Depression. President Franklin D. Roosevelt started these programs to help the millions of Americans who were facing tough economic times.

The government uses poverty guidelines to decide whether a person or family has too little money and therefore needs this help. These guidelines reflect the cost of enough food, clothing, and shelter to survive. The guidelines are updated each year. **Temporary Assistance for Needy Families (TANF)** is one welfare program. The federal government provides the money. State governments distribute the funds. TANF began in 1996, replacing a program that was established in the 1930s. This new program set stricter rules for who can take part in welfare programs. It also limited the amount of time during which a person can get benefits. The intent of these rules is to encourage participants to find jobs quickly. In many states, TANF requires those who receive the benefit to work. Programs like this are called **workfare** (WUHRK•FAYR) programs. Work activities often take the form of community service. Those getting the aid may be required to attend job training or education programs.

The government also pays some benefits to workers in special cases. One program is unemployment insurance. This program pays compensation to workers who become unemployed through no fault of their own. **Compensation** (KAHM•puhn•SAY•shuhn) is payment to make up for lost wages. If these workers cannot find new jobs, they are usually eligible for unemployment checks for a limited period of time. Workers who are injured on the job may receive workers' compensation benefits, including lost wages and medical care.

☑ PROGRESS CHECK

Explaining What is the purpose of poverty guidelines?

welfare aid given to the poor in the form of money or necessities

Temporary Assistance for Needy Families (TANF) welfare program paid for by the federal government and administered by the individual states

workfare programs that require welfare recipients to exchange some of their labor for benefits

compensation payment to unemployed or injured workers to make up for lost wages

LESSON 3 REVIEW

Review Vocabulary

1. What is the purpose of *welfare*?

2. How is *workfare* different from *welfare*?

3. What is *compensation*? Under what circumstances does someone receive compensation?

Answer the Guiding Questions

4. *Identifying* What are some reasons for income inequality in the United States?

5. *Describing* How does TANF differ from earlier, similar welfare programs?

6. **ARGUMENT** Write a brief essay aimed at students who are thinking about dropping out of high school. Use what you learned in this lesson to convince them to stay in school. Remind them that dropping out has serious economic consequences, and explain what they are.

Brown v. Board of Education of Topeka, Kansas

In the 1950s, African Americans challenged the "separate but equal" principle that supported segregation in public schools.

Background of the Case

In 1950 in Topeka, Kansas, Oliver Brown wanted to send his eight-year-old daughter to a nearby elementary school. Because of segregation laws, Linda Brown could not go to that school. That school was for white students only. Linda was African American. Instead, she had to attend school farther from home. Since the late 1800s, courts had seen segregation as lawful as long as blacks and whites were treated equally. Brown and some other African American parents challenged this idea of "separate but equal." With the help of the National Association for the Advancement of Colored People (NAACP), a civil rights group, they sued Topeka's board of education.

Linda Brown

The Decision

The Supreme Court ruled that school segregation violated the Fourteenth Amendment. That amendment said all people should have equal protection under the law. In its decision, the Court said that segregated schools were not equal. Chief Justice Earl Warren ended the opinion thusly:

❝ *In these days, it is doubtful that any child may reasonably be expected to succeed in life if he is denied the opportunity of an education.*

We come then to the question presented: Does segregation of children in public schools solely on the basis of race . . . deprive [deny] the children of the minority group of equal educational opportunities? We believe that it does. ❞
　　　　　　　　　　—Chief Justice Earl Warren

Why It Matters

The Supreme Court's decision in *Brown v. Board of Education of Topeka, Kansas* applied only to segregation in schools. Even so, it struck down the concept at the core of segregation laws that applied in other areas: separate but equal. The road to actual desegregation was long and hard. The *Brown v. Board of Education of Topeka, Kansas* decision, however, is widely seen as the first step along the path to full desegregation.

Analyzing the Case

1. **Identifying the Main Idea** How did school segregation violate the Fourteenth Amendment?
2. **Explaining** Why is desegregation important to education?

Write your answers on a separate sheet of paper.

1 Writing Activity

EXPLORING THE ESSENTIAL QUESTION
How does government influence the economy and economic institutions?

Describe the ways in which the government tracks the health of the economy. What are the signs of economic growth? Explain how the government helps individuals in times of economic contraction or downturn.

2 21st Century Skills

FOLLOW THE STOCK MARKET Visit the Web site of the New York Stock Exchange. Locate the "Indices" tab in the daily "Market Activity" section. Find the market summary for the Dow Jones Industrial Average and the S&P 500. For one week, keep track of both indexes. Plot the daily progress of these indexes on a graph. At the end of the week, decide whether these indexes are forecasting a good or bad period for the economy. Write a paragraph explaining your decision. Include your graphs along with your paragraph.

3 Being an Active Citizen

Citizens, like the government, can help others who are experiencing economic hard times. Citizens' groups or religious organizations in your community may have programs to help struggling families. Many charities need volunteers' time, not just contributions of money. For example, you can volunteer to work in a food bank for a few hours a week or you can start a canned food drive in your community. Check your local newspaper, Web sites, and houses of worship for other ways you can help. Create a database of at least five community groups that help people. Include information about the services the groups provide and the help they need.

4 Understanding Visuals

This graph shows poverty in the United States in two ways. The number of people in poverty is the total number of individuals who meet the government's definition of being poor. The poverty rate is the percentage of the whole population that is poor. Between 1959 and 2009, when was the number of people in poverty lowest? When was it highest? Now check to see when the poverty rate was lowest. When was it highest? What effect would the growing number of poor people have on government spending? Why would it have that effect?

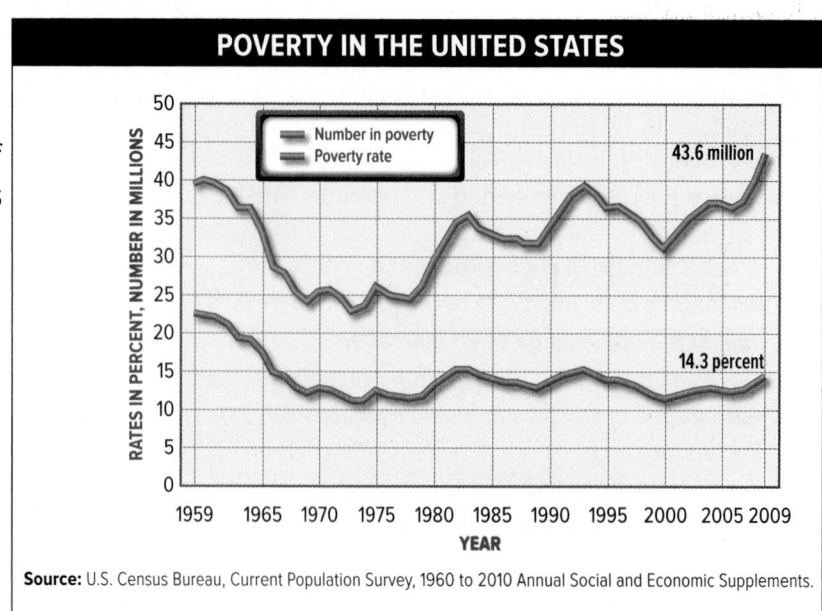

POVERTY IN THE UNITED STATES

RATES IN PERCENT, NUMBER IN MILLIONS

- Number in poverty
- Poverty rate

43.6 million

14.3 percent

YEAR

Source: U.S. Census Bureau, Current Population Survey, 1960 to 2010 Annual Social and Economic Supplements.

REVIEW THE GUIDING QUESTIONS

Directions: Choose the best answer for each question.

1 Which of these is a negative externality of increased sales of bottled water?

A. People have to dispose of more empty water bottles.

B. More people drink healthier beverages.

C. Companies increase advertising for brands of bottled water.

D. More bottled water sales decreases demand for public water.

2 What law was the government's first effort to prevent monopolies?

F. the Federal Trade Commission Act

G. the Sherman Antitrust Act

H. the Clayton Antitrust Act

I. the Federal Anti-monopoly Act

3 Which best explains why businesses would fire or lay off workers in a recession?

A. because taxes increase during a recession

B. because to earn profits in a recession they must cut costs

C. because government regulation is too costly

D. because rising prices make workers too costly

4 What would be the probable effect of inflation on consumers' demand for expensive luxury goods?

F. Demand would go up because people can afford more goods.

G. Demand would go up because luxuries are in greater supply.

H. Demand would go down because necessities cost more.

I. Demand would go down because the unemployment rate declines.

5 Which of these explains why bear markets are linked to recessions?

A. Investors buy stocks knowing that a period of growth will soon follow.

B. Investors are eager to buy stocks in new companies.

C. Investors have little confidence in the economy.

D. Investors believe that the economy is growing again.

6 What is one goal of the TANF program?

F. to encourage poor people to get a job

G. to encourage poor people to get an education

H. to help workers who lost their job through no fault of their own

I. to help workers who lost income due to injury suffered on the job

DBQ **ANALYZING DOCUMENTS**

Directions: Analyze the excerpt and answer the questions that follow.

"With the economy strong, the [welfare] reforms succeeded in moving many people off the rolls and employment rose. Today, there are few jobs available for people. . . . Welfare programs should be expanding."

—"No Welfare, No Work," editorial, *The New York Times*, February 9, 2009

7 **Inferring** According to the editorial, welfare reform

A. failed to move people off welfare and into jobs.

B. helped move people off welfare and into jobs.

C. increased unemployment.

D. expanded poverty levels.

8 **Identifying** According to the editorial, welfare should be expanded because

F. there are no jobs.

G. employment rose.

H. the economy is strong.

I. welfare reforms succeeded.

SHORT RESPONSE

"Let this session of Congress be known as the session which . . . declared all-out war on human poverty and unemployment in these United States; . . . recognized the health needs of our older citizens; . . . helped to build more homes, more schools, more libraries, and more hospitals than any single session of Congress in the history of our Republic."

—President Lyndon B. Johnson
Annual Message to the Congress on the State of the Union, January 8, 1964

9 Based on this statement, how did President Johnson view the role of the federal government in combating poverty and aiding society?

10 How might a speech like President Johnson's, delivered before Congress and televised live to the American people, influence government policy toward social inequality and income distribution?

EXTENDED RESPONSE

11 **Informative/Explanatory** According to the chapter, promoting competition is a key goal of the government. What steps does it take to try to build competition? What other steps might it take? Why might those steps work?

Need Extra Help?

If You've Missed Question	❶	❷	❸	❹	❺	❻	❼	❽	❾	❿	⓫
Review Lesson	1	1	2	2	2	3	3	3	3	3	1

The Government and Banking

ESSENTIAL QUESTION
How does government influence the economy and economic institutions?

networks

There's More Online about the government and banking.

CHAPTER 21

The Story Matters...

The U.S. Constitution gives Congress the power to coin money. As a result, we have a uniform system of currency. To keep money safe, the government also oversees banking.

The first United States Mint was established in Philadelphia in 1792. It made coins out of gold, silver, and copper. At the time, coin making required intense physical labor and horses to run some of the machinery. Because of the manual process, many coins had imperfections.

Today's U.S. Mint has two locations—Philadelphia and Denver. Both use automated machines to produce coins. The modern coin-making process, with less manual labor, ensures that few coins have imperfections. Today's coins are made of nickel, copper, and zinc.

◀ *This worker at the U.S. Mint in Philadelphia, Pennsylvania, transfers one-cent blanks before they are made into pennies.*

PHOTO: Stephen Hilger/Getty Images

565

Real-Life Civics

▶ MONEY AND BANKING

Money is a medium of exchange. That is, when you make a purchase, money is what you give up in order to get whatever you buy. In the country's early years, coins were the main form of money. Today, paper money is in far greater use.

Is currency—whether metal or paper—going out of style, though? Today, consumers do not have to carry either coins or cash. They can make a purchase simply by swiping a plastic bank card through a card reader. That card reader is tied electronically to the nation's banking system. In an instant, the amount of the purchase is subtracted automatically from the consumer's bank account—as long as the consumer has enough money in the account. Of course, the consumer can always reach into his or her wallet and pull out some cash instead.

People sometimes store large amounts of cash in a bank safe deposit box. ▷

The prices of goods and services, such as a gallon of gas, are given in dollars and cents.

> **MEASURE OF VALUE** In addition to being a medium of exchange, money is a way of assigning a value to a good or service. Look at the sign in the photograph. The price for regular gas is posted at the top; the price for plus, or premium, gas is posted at the bottom. Because the price of premium gas is higher than that of regular, we understand that it has more value or worth. Suppose you were buying a ticket to a concert by one of your favorite singers. Which would probably get you a seat closer to the stage, the $75 or the $150 ticket? The higher-priced ticket should put you in a better location at the concert. By paying attention to the signals set by prices, we use money to measure value.

CIVIC LITERACY

★ ★ ★ ★

Analyzing Based on what you have read, what is one way that people use banks?

Your Opinion Do you think we will continue to use paper money and coins in the future? Would you prefer to use a bank card for all your purchases? Why or why not?

Lesson 1

Money

ESSENTIAL QUESTION *How does government influence the economy and economic institutions?*

IT MATTERS BECAUSE

Money is used to make economic transactions.

All About Money

GUIDING QUESTION *What gives money value?*

Suppose you were selling a bicycle. Would you accept a four-ton stone in payment for it? You might, if you lived on the Pacific island of Yap. For centuries, the people of Yap used huge stone disks as money. How could they do that? Money is anything that a group of people accepts as a means of exchange. A wide variety of things, from cheese to shells to beads to gold and silver coins, have been used as money. People use money because it makes life easier for everyone.

Functions of Money

Money has three main functions. First, money serves as a *medium of exchange*. A **medium** is a means of doing something. People exchange, or trade, money for goods and services. If we did not have money, we would have to **barter,** or trade for something of equal worth. For example, a person might want to exchange a music CD for a pair of theater tickets. While this might sound like a simple task, the exchange might never take place. This is because the person with the music CD might never find anybody willing to trade theater tickets for the CD.

PHOTO: (tl) Mark Wilson/Getty Images; (tc) Rick Wilking/Reuters/Corbis; (tr) Jules Frazier/Getty Images

Reading**HELP**DESK

Taking Notes: *Categorizing*

As you read, use a chart like the one shown to fill in details about each feature of money.

Feature	Details
Function	
Trait	
Form	

Content Vocabulary

- **barter**
- **coin**
- **currency**
- **electronic money**
- **deposit**
- **commercial bank**
- **savings and loan association (S&L)**
- **credit union**

Second, money is a *store of value*. As a result, we can hold money as a form of wealth until we find something we want to buy with it. The person with the music CD does not have to wait for someone who is willing to trade for it. Instead, he or she can sell the CD and hold the money until it is needed later.

Third, money serves as a *measure of value*. Money is like a measuring stick that can be used to assign value to a good or service. When somebody says that something costs $10, we know exactly what that means.

Characteristics of Money

In order for an object to serve as money, it must have four characteristics, or features:

- *Portable.* Money must be easy to carry around so that people have it available when they want to buy something.
- *Divisible.* Money must be easy to divide into smaller amounts. That way it can be used for large and small purchases.
- *Durable.* Pieces of money should be hardy enough to stay in use for a period of time.
- *Limited Supply.* To be used as money, an object must be in limited supply. If money were easy to make, everyone would make it. The money would then become worthless. That is why making fake money—or counterfeiting—is a crime.

Forms of Money

In the United States, money comes in three forms: coins, paper bills, and electronic money. **Coins** are pieces of metal that are used as money. Examples of coins include pennies, nickels, dimes, and even some dollars. Paper bills are flat, rectangular pieces of high-quality paper used as money. Coins and paper bills make up the **currency** of the United States.

Electronic money is money in the form of a computer entry at a bank or other financial institution. Electronic money does not exist in any physical form. An example would be the money you have in a checking or savings account.

✓ PROGRESS CHECK

Summarizing What are the three functions of money?

Why It MATTERS

Bartering

Have you ever traded with someone? Perhaps you and a friend swapped baseball cards, game cards, comic books, snacks, or bracelets. Describe your transaction. How did it differ from using money?

U.S. paper money is designed and printed by the Bureau of Engraving and Printing (BEP), which has operations in Washington, D.C., and Fort Worth, Texas. The BEP prints 26 million bills each day—about $974 million. Here a worker inspects a sheet of uncut currency before it is separated into bills.

► CRITICAL THINKING

Making Inferences Why is it important for the government to produce fresh paper currency?

	Academic Vocabulary	**barter** to trade a good or service for another good or service	**coin** metallic form of money, such as a penny	**currency** money, both coins and paper bills
• **deposit insurance**	**medium** a way to carry out an action			

Paper money has several special features that help prevent criminals from making counterfeit money.

▶ **CRITICAL THINKING**

1 *Identifying* Which features shown will be useful for preventing counterfeiting?

2 *Explaining* Why would a government want to prevent counterfeiting?

Federal Reserve indicators

Microprinting

Portrait

Serial Number

Color-shifting ink

Security thread

Watermark

PHOTO: Michael Houghton · StudiOhio

Direct Deposit

Many Americans receive their wages by direct deposit. There is an advantage to this method. Workers who receive paychecks and deposit them may have to wait a few days before the funds are available to use. Direct deposit funds tend to be available the same day.

Financial Institutions

GUIDING QUESTION *What do financial institutions do?*

When most people receive their pay, they put the money into a financial institution, such as a bank. Businesses also use financial institutions as a place to deposit the money they receive from selling goods or services. The money that customers put into a financial institution is called a **deposit.** Electronic money can also be used for deposits. Some employers deposit pay directly into workers' bank accounts. The **funds,** or money, in the employer's account go down, and the money in the workers' accounts goes up.

Financial institutions put these deposits to work. They lend some of the money to individuals and businesses that need funds. For example, people borrow money to buy cars or houses or for other purposes. Businesses borrow to expand operations or buy new equipment. Banks charge interest and collect other fees on these loans. That is how they earn money. They also pay interest on the deposits they accept. The institutions try to make a profit by charging a higher rate on their loans and paying a lower rate on their deposits.

Types of Financial Institutions

Consumers and businesses choose from among several types of financial institutions. The three main types are commercial banks, savings and loan associations (S&Ls), and credit unions.

Reading**HELP**DESK

electronic money money in the form of a computer entry at a bank or other financial institution

deposit the money that customers put into a financial institution

Academic Vocabulary

funds money

Commercial banks offer full financial services to consumers and businesses. They accept deposits, provide checking accounts, make loans, and offer other banking services. They are the largest and the most important part of the financial system.

Another popular institution is the **savings and loan association (S&L)**. Historically, S&Ls loaned money to people who were buying homes. Today most S&Ls offer many of the same services as commercial banks. Most of their customers are individuals rather than businesses, however.

A **credit union** is a nonprofit cooperative that accepts deposits, makes loans, and provides some financial services. Credit unions are often formed by people who work in the same industry, work for the same company, or belong to the same labor union. Because credit unions are cooperatives, they are owned by the depositors. They tend to charge lower interest rates on loans, but lend money only to members.

Protecting Deposits

The money you deposit in a financial institution is safe from loss. It is protected by a **deposit insurance** program. The program protects deposits up to a certain amount if the institution goes out of business. The program that covers commercial banks and S&Ls is the Federal Deposit Insurance Corporation (FDIC). The program for credit unions is the National Credit Union Share Insurance Fund (NCUSIF). Both programs cover deposits of up to $250,000 for one person on all accounts within the same institution.

Businesses put their cash in deposit bags such as this one (left) when depositing their day's earnings. Business accounts, just as personal accounts, are insured by the FDIC. All insured banks must post this official FDIC sign at each teller station (right).

▶ **CRITICAL THINKING**

Making Connections How does federal deposit insurance help maintain people's confidence in the banking system?

PHOTO: (bl) Jules Frazier/Getty Images; (br) Rick Wilking/Reuters/Corbis

commercial bank a financial institution that offers full banking services to individuals and businesses

savings and loan association (S&L) financial institution that traditionally loaned money to people buying homes

credit union nonprofit service cooperative that accepts deposits, makes loans, and provides other financial services to members

deposit insurance government-backed program that protects bank deposits up to a certain amount if a bank fails

21ˢᵗ Century
SKILLS

Question

Selecting the right institution is an important part of handling your money responsibly. Prepare a list of questions you think would help you select the best place to deposit your savings.

Why is deposit insurance needed? Financial institutions do not keep on hand all the money that comes in from depositors. They lend much of it to other customers. If the institution goes out of business, then depositors would not get all their money back. Deposit insurance prevents that. It pays depositors everything they had in their accounts at the time of the failure.

The government first insured deposits in 1933. The action was taken as a result of the Great Depression. At the time, many banks were failing because panicky depositors all tried to withdraw their funds at the same time. When the banks went out of business, people lost most of their deposits. The government started the FDIC to restore confidence in the safety of deposits. It worked, and there have been no other panics since then. Today, people feel confident about their deposits.

Regulating Financial Institutions

Financial institutions are secure for another reason. A number of different state and federal agencies regulate, or oversee, the way they do business. To go into business, a financial institution must get a document called a charter. Charters may be given by either a state or the federal government. First, the government reviews the finances of the institution to make sure it has enough money to do business. Officials also look at the people who will run the business. They want to make sure they have the skills to use depositors' money wisely.

After a charter is issued, government officials watch how the business is run. They make sure the institution stays in good financial condition. They also make sure the institution follows all relevant laws. These efforts are made to protect the money that depositors entrust to the institution.

✓ **PROGRESS CHECK**

Identifying What are the three main types of financial institutions?

LESSON 1 REVIEW

Review Vocabulary

1. What does it mean to *barter*? How does money make bartering unnecessary?

2. How are *commercial banks, savings and loan associations,* and *credit unions* different?

Answer the Guiding Questions

3. *Finding the Main Idea* How does money act as both a medium of exchange and a store of value?

4. *Explaining* What is the role of financial institutions?

5. **INFORMATIVE/EXPLANATORY** Write a public service announcement (PSA) explaining why financial institutions are safe places for depositors to put their money. Make your PSA lively but informative.

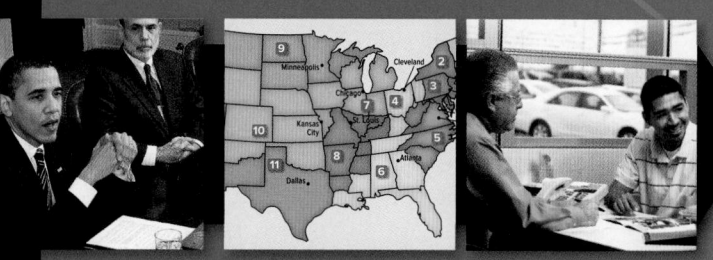

networks

There's More Online!

☑ **GRAPHIC ORGANIZER**
Fed Functions

☑ **INFOGRAPHICS**
The Federal Reserve System
Monetary Policy and Interest
Rates

☑ **GAME**

Lesson 2
The Federal Reserve System

ESSENTIAL QUESTION *How does government influence the economy and economic institutions?*

IT MATTERS BECAUSE
Your economic well-being is influenced by the Federal Reserve System.

The Fed's Structure

GUIDING QUESTION *What is the structure of the Federal Reserve System?*

In the early 1900s, the United States suffered several recessions. During these hard times, banks were unable to make new loans. This crisis hurt even the largest and strongest banks. Most people thought conditions would be better if the nation had a central bank. A **central bank** is a bankers' bank. Banks can go to it to borrow money when times are difficult.

Although a central bank was needed, the government did not have enough money to finance one. As a result, it decided to require all banks with a national charter to contribute funds to build the new central bank. In return, they would receive some stock in that central bank. The result was the 1913 creation of the Federal Reserve System, or "the Fed" as it is often called. This was the first true central bank for the United States.

Today, the Fed has a number of very important responsibilities. It manages our currency, regulates commercial banks, serves as the government's bank, and conducts certain policies to keep the economy healthy and strong. To understand how it does all these things, we first need to see how the Fed is organized.

Reading**HELP**DESK

Taking Notes: *Identifying*

As you read, use the graphic organizer shown to identify the functions of the Federal Reserve System.

Content Vocabulary

- **central bank**
- **Federal Open Market Committee (FOMC)**
- **monetary policy**
- **open market operations (OMO)**

The Board of Governors

At the top of the Fed is the seven-member Board of Governors. Each member is nominated by the president and must be confirmed by the Senate. Since the members serve for 14 years, they are fairly free of influence from elected officials. This enables them to make decisions that are in the best interest of the economy. The Board typically meets every other week.

The chairman of the Board of Governors of the Federal Reserve, Ben Bernanke (center), advises the president on economic policy. The Fed chair has great influence over the economy.

▶ CRITICAL THINKING

Drawing Conclusions What makes the chairman of the Fed so powerful?

District Banks

The Federal Reserve System has 12 districts, each with a district bank. These banks are also called Federal Reserve Banks. Each bank carries out Fed policy and oversees banking within its district. Each district bank is run by nine directors. Any profits earned by these banks are paid to the U.S. Treasury.

The Federal Open Market Committee

The **Federal Open Market Committee (FOMC)** influences the whole economy by making changes to the supply of money. The next section explains why and how the fed makes changes to the money supply.

Advisory Councils

The Board of Governors receives advice from three advisory councils. One gives advice on consumer borrowing. The second advises on matters relating to the banking system. The third works with the Board of Governors on matters related to savings and loan institutions.

Member Banks

About 2,900 commercial banks belong to the Federal Reserve System. Most of these banks are national banks, which means they have their charter from the national government. The rest are state banks. State banks have the option to join or not.

✓ PROGRESS CHECK

Identifying How many district banks are in the Fed?

PHOTO: Chip Somodevilla/Getty Images

Reading**HELP**DESK

- **discount rate**
- **reserve requirement**

central bank an institution that lends money to other banks; also, the place where the government does its banking business

Federal Open Market Committee (FOMC)
the most powerful committee of the Fed, which makes decisions that affect the economy as a whole by manipulating the money supply

Federal Reserve Districts

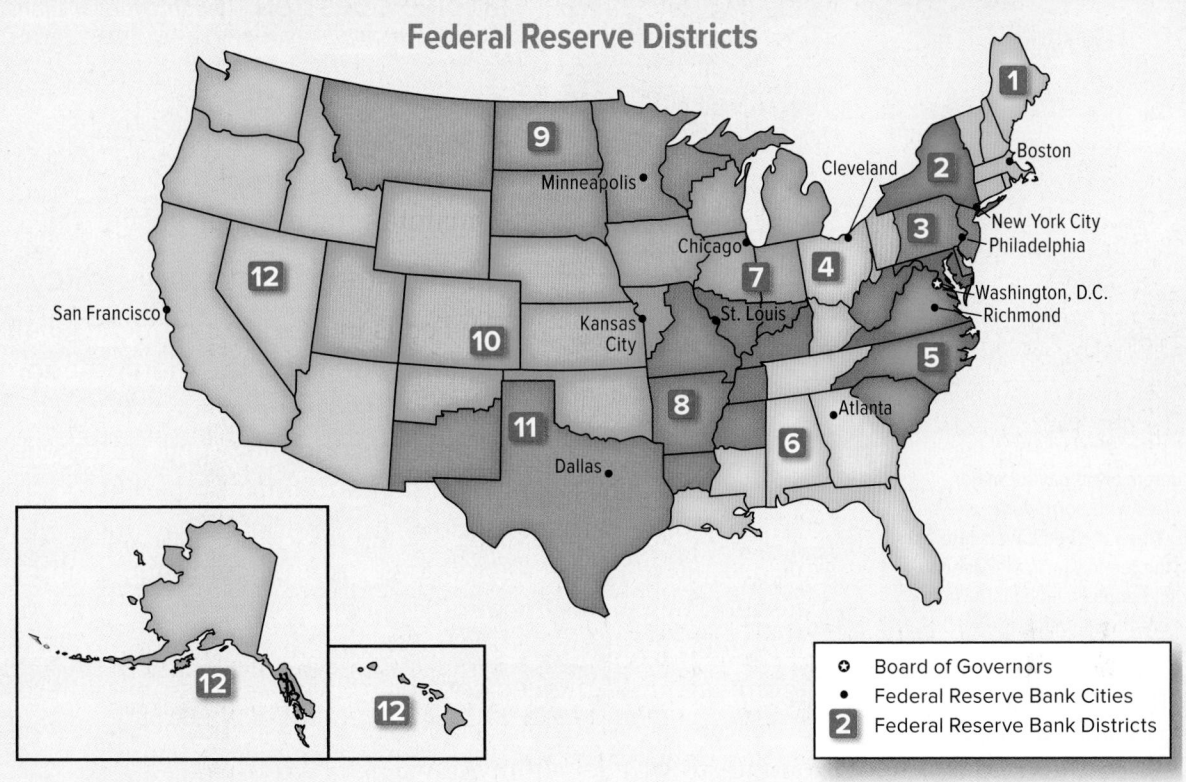

- ✪ Board of Governors
- • Federal Reserve Bank Cities
- 2 Federal Reserve Bank Districts

Organization

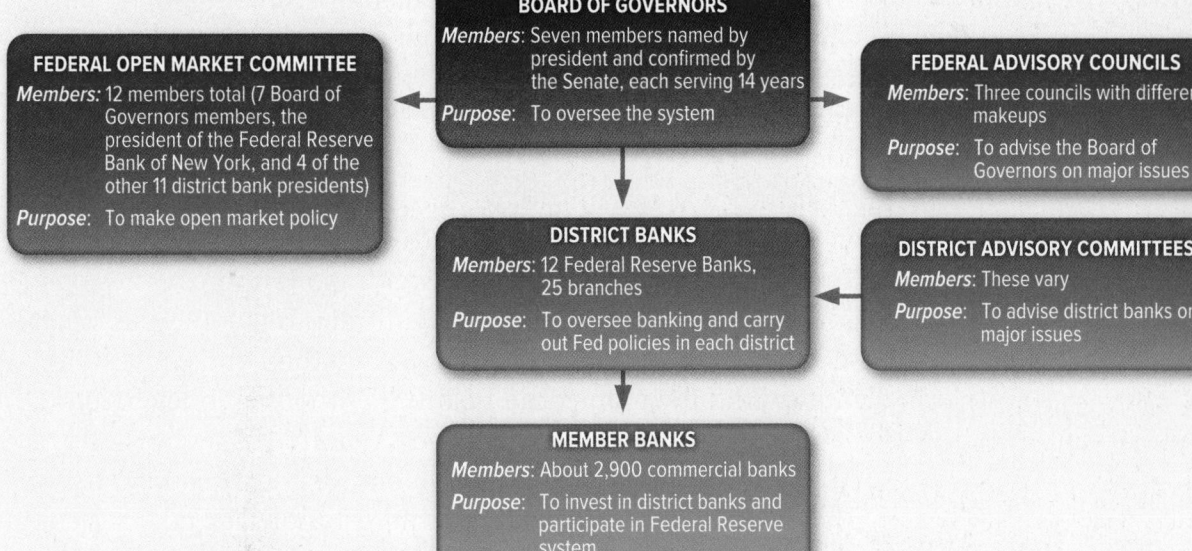

FEDERAL OPEN MARKET COMMITTEE

Members: 12 members total (7 Board of Governors members, the president of the Federal Reserve Bank of New York, and 4 of the other 11 district bank presidents)

Purpose: To make open market policy

BOARD OF GOVERNORS

Members: Seven members named by president and confirmed by the Senate, each serving 14 years

Purpose: To oversee the system

FEDERAL ADVISORY COUNCILS

Members: Three councils with different makeups

Purpose: To advise the Board of Governors on major issues

DISTRICT BANKS

Members: 12 Federal Reserve Banks, 25 branches

Purpose: To oversee banking and carry out Fed policies in each district

DISTRICT ADVISORY COMMITTEES

Members: These vary

Purpose: To advise district banks on major issues

MEMBER BANKS

Members: About 2,900 commercial banks

Purpose: To invest in district banks and participate in Federal Reserve system

INFOGRAPHIC

The Federal Reserve System has a complex structure. Each part carries out specific functions.

► CRITICAL THINKING

1 *Analyzing Visuals* Which group is the most powerful part of the Fed?

2 *Making Inferences* How does the term of each member of the Board of Governors help make the Board independent of political influence?

Consumers often pay for major purchases with borrowed money, or credit. When the Fed lowers interest rates, the fee for borrowing money is lower. People will be more likely to use credit to purchase big-ticket items, such as a car.

► **CRITICAL THINKING**
Finding the Main Idea How does the Fed lower interest rates?

What the Fed Does

GUIDING QUESTION *What are the functions of the Federal Reserve System?*

The Fed has several functions. One of its most important is to manage the nation's money supply. That role is key to maintaining a strong economy.

Conducting Monetary Policy

The Fed is in charge of monetary policy. **Monetary policy** is the **manipulation,** or changing, of the money supply to stimulate economic growth and keep prices stable. The supply and demand for money sets the price of money. The price of money is the cost of borrowing, or the interest rate. If the Fed expands the supply of money, interest rates go down. This encourages people to borrow more and buy more goods and services. This stimulates the economy and gets it going again. If the Fed contracts the money supply, interest rates go up. People will borrow less and spend less. This will tend to slow the economy down.

Using the Tools of Monetary Policy

The Fed uses three tools to control the money supply. The first and the most important is called open market operations. **Open market operations (OMO)** refers to the FOMC's actions to buy or sell government bonds and Treasury bills. Investors lend money to the government by buying these bonds and bills.

If the FOMC wants to expand the money supply, it buys government bonds back. That gives banks more money to lend to customers. With more lending going on, interest rates will go down. If the FOMC wants to contract the money supply, it sells some of the bonds it holds. To buy the bonds, investors must withdraw money from banks. With less money to lend, the banks will raise interest rates and economic growth will slow.

The second tool of monetary policy is the discount rate. The **discount rate** is the rate of interest that the Fed charges to financial institutions when they borrow money from the Federal Reserve. If the Fed wants to expand the money supply, it lowers the discount rate. The reduced rate encourages banks to borrow

Reading**HELP**DESK

monetary policy manipulation of the money supply to affect the cost of credit, economic growth, and price stability

Academic Vocabulary

manipulate to make changes to something to produce a desired effect

open market operations (OMO) the purchase or sale of U.S. government bonds and Treasury bills

from the Fed. With the banks holding more money, the money supply grows. If the Fed wants to contract the money supply, it raises the discount rate. A higher rate discourages borrowing.

The third tool of monetary policy is the reserve requirement. The **reserve requirement** is the portion of a new deposit that a financial institution cannot lend out. For example, suppose someone deposits $100. If the reserve requirement is 40 percent, the bank must keep 40 percent of that $100, or $40, as a reserve. The reserve is held either in the bank or at a Federal Reserve district bank. The institution can lend the remaining $60.

If the Fed wants to change the size of the money supply, all it has to do is change the size of this reserve requirement. To expand the money supply, the Fed could lower the reserve requirement. That makes more money available to be lent. Changing the reserve from 40 percent to 10 percent would require the bank to set aside only $10. A 10 percent reserve allows a bank to lend $90 of a $100 deposit. If the Fed wanted to contract the money supply, it could raise the reserve requirement to 50 percent. Since the reserve requirement applies to all banks, it is a powerful tool.

─── *21ˢᵗ Century* ───
SKILLS

Calculating Percentages

To find a percentage, you divide the share of an amount by the total amount. Suppose a bank, following the reserve requirement, holds in reserve $125 of a $1,000 deposit. What percentage is the reserve requirement at that time?

MONETARY POLICY AND INTEREST RATES

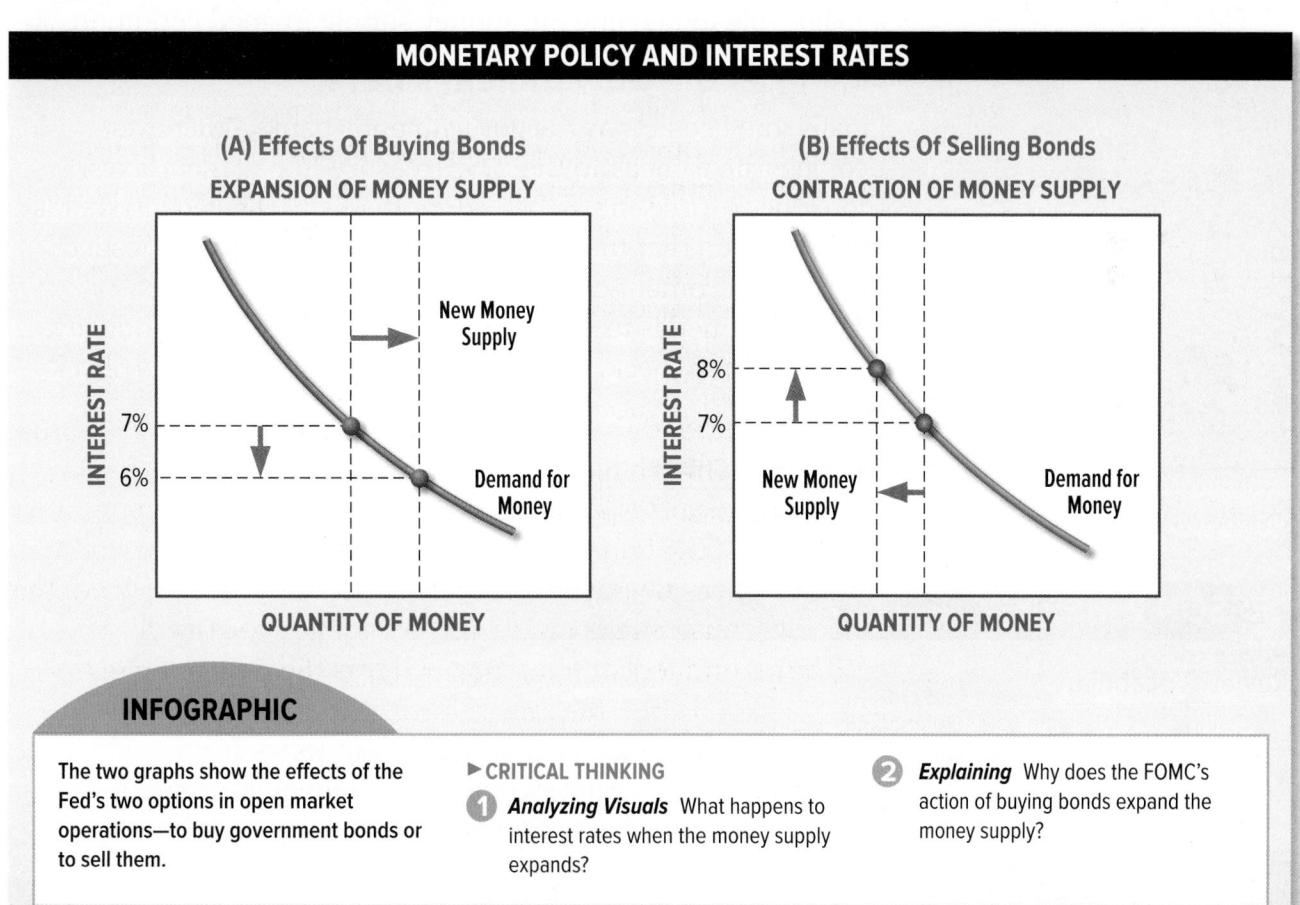

(A) Effects Of Buying Bonds
EXPANSION OF MONEY SUPPLY

(B) Effects Of Selling Bonds
CONTRACTION OF MONEY SUPPLY

INFOGRAPHIC

The two graphs show the effects of the Fed's two options in open market operations—to buy government bonds or to sell them.

▶ CRITICAL THINKING

1. *Analyzing Visuals* What happens to interest rates when the money supply expands?

2. *Explaining* Why does the FOMC's action of buying bonds expand the money supply?

discount rate the interest rate that the Fed charges on its loans to financial institutions

reserve requirement the percentage of a deposit that banks have to set aside as cash in their own vaults or as deposits in their Federal Reserve district bank

Reread the first paragraph under the heading "Regulating the Financial System." Write a sentence explaining how consumers benefit from the Fed's rules.

Regulating the Financial System

Based on laws passed by Congress, the Fed writes rules that all lenders must follow. For example, most of the forms that people have to sign when they take out a car loan were designed by the Fed. These forms require lenders to clearly spell out the terms of the loan. The Fed also writes rules that prevent lenders from using deceptive practices in making loans.

The Fed writes other rules that member banks must follow. These involve everything from ways that banks must report their reserve requirements to how they make loans to bank officers. The Fed also has the power to approve mergers between member banks.

Maintaining the Currency

The Bureau of Engraving and Printing has the duty of printing paper money. Once the money is printed, the bureau sends it to the Fed for safekeeping and to be **distributed**. The Fed is also responsible for pulling old money out of use. Whenever paper money becomes tattered and worn, it is sent to the Fed. The Fed exchanges the old bills for newer currency. Thus, the Fed plays a major role in keeping our money supply in good condition.

Acting as the Government's Bank

Finally, the Fed acts as the government's bank. Whenever people write a check to the U.S. Treasury to pay their taxes, those checks are sent to the Fed for deposit. The Fed also holds other revenue that the government receives until it is needed.

The government can write checks on these deposits whenever it needs to make a purchase or other payment. Any federal agency check, such as a monthly Social Security check, is taken out of an account at the Fed.

Academic Vocabulary

distribute to give out

☑ PROGRESS CHECK

Summarizing Why does the Fed regulate monetary policy?

LESSON 2 REVIEW

Review Vocabulary

1. Identify the central bank of the United States and describe the role of a *central bank*.

2. What is *monetary policy*? How are *open market operations*, the *discount rate*, and the *reserve requirement* related to monetary policy?

Answer the Guiding Questions

3. *Explaining* Explain how the parts of the Federal Reserve System are related to one another.

4. *Identifying* What are the roles of the district banks?

5. **INFORMATIVE/EXPLANATORY** Write an article for an online student resource that explains the four functions of the Federal Reserve System and its role in the nation's economy.

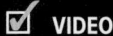

networks

There's More Online!

☑ **GRAPHIC ORGANIZER**
Financial Industry

☑ **VIDEO**

☑ **AUDIO**
Franklin Roosevelt on the Bank Crisis

Lesson 3

Banks and Banking

ESSENTIAL QUESTION *How does government influence the economy and economic institutions?*

IT MATTERS BECAUSE
Banks are an important part of the nation's economy, and people entrust banks with their money.

Banks in the Economy

GUIDING QUESTION *What purpose do banks serve in the economy?*

Financial institutions like banks accept deposits and then lend the money to others to use. In this lesson, you will look at these activities more closely.

Taking Deposits

Banks have several types of accounts. People use savings accounts, certificates of deposit (CDs), and money market accounts to save money. Checking accounts are used to pay bills, buy goods and services, and meet other expenses.

Most **savings accounts** pay interest on deposits and allow people to make withdrawals. Banks pay interest on savings accounts to encourage people to keep their money in the bank. Banks want to be able to use the funds to make loans.

A **certificate of deposit (CD)** is a type of account that pays higher interest than a savings account but has a fixed period of time. You must leave the money in the bank for that time, such as six months or a year. If you take your money out of the CD before that time, you pay a penalty. That penalty comes in the form of a lower rate of interest.

PHOTO: (tl) Brand X Pictures/Punchstock; (tc) Danita Delimont/Alamy; (tr) Bettmann/CORBIS

Reading**HELP**DESK

Taking Notes: *Cause and Effect*

As you read, use a diagram to track causes and effects of conditions in the financial industry. Add rows as needed.

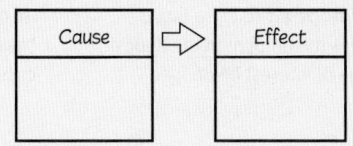

Cause	⇨	Effect

Content Vocabulary

- savings account
- certificate of deposit (CD)
- money market account
- checking account

Another type of account is a **money market account.** These accounts pay interest, but they also allow people to write checks. Some banks restrict the number of withdrawals that people can make from a money market account within a **period,** or stretch, of time. Some banks require customers to have a minimum balance for these accounts.

Money deposited in a **checking account** can be withdrawn at any time by writing a check or by using a debit card. People use checking accounts to pay their bills and make purchases. Some checking accounts pay interest, but the rates tend to be lower than on other types of accounts.

Making Loans

As you have read, banks must keep some of each deposit as a reserve. The rest can be lent to consumers or businesses. People borrow money for many different reasons. Borrowing money can make it possible for some people to purchase a car or a home, pay for house repairs, or pay college tuition. Businesses use loans to expand operations, to make new products, or to meet a payroll. Before the loan is final, a lending officer at the bank and the borrower discuss the amount to be borrowed, the interest rate, and when the loan must be repaid.

New Ways of Banking

New technology has introduced new forms of banking. Banking by telephone, cell phone, automated teller machine (ATM), and computer let people do their banking without setting foot inside a bank branch. Online banking allows people to use the Internet to check their balances and to see all transactions that have taken place. With many online services, depositors can move money between accounts and pay bills. More and more people are using cell phones for these activities. Some banks are even testing ways for people to make purchases with a swipe of their cell phones rather than by check or credit card.

☑ **PROGRESS CHECK**

Contrasting What are the different ways that savings and checking accounts are used?

Today, people can choose from a variety of ways to do their banking. Many banking transactions can be made using an ATM, a computer, or a smartphone.

▶ CRITICAL THINKING
Finding the Main Idea How has technology changed the way people make bank transactions?

PHOTO: Brand X Pictures/Punchstock

ReadingHELPDESK

savings account an account that pays interest on deposits but allows customers to withdraw money at any time

certificate of deposit (CD) a timed deposit that states the amount of the deposit, maturity, and rate of interest being paid

money market account a type of savings account that pays interest but also allows customers to write checks against the account

How Banking Has Changed

GUIDING QUESTION *How has banking become safer, faster, and more efficient over the years?*

Online and cell phone banking are not the only ways banking has changed. The banking industry is very different today than it was when the nation was founded. A number of financial crises led to new laws that changed banking in many ways.

The Earliest Banks

The first banks were chartered by states. Early in the nation's history, some leaders thought the country needed a national bank. In 1791 Congress created the First Bank of the United States to hold the government's money and make its payments. The bank also loaned money to the government and businesses. The bank had a charter for only 20 years, though.

The First Bank of the United States was allowed to go out of business when its charter ran out. Then, during the War of 1812, the government discovered it had no place to go to borrow money. As a result, leaders created another bank. This bank, the Second Bank of the United States, lasted from 1816 to 1836.

From the 1830s to the 1860s, states took over the job of supervising privately owned banks. This control was inadequate, though. Banks at that time made loans by issuing their own paper currency. These private banks printed too many bank notes, leading to a greatly increased money supply and inflation. Demand arose for uniform paper currency that was acceptable anywhere without risk.

By 1860, more than 1,500 state banks issued their own paper currency.

▶ **CRITICAL THINKING**
Making Connections Why did the national government start offering national bank charters?

National Banks

In 1863 the Union government passed the National Bank Act. The law helped bring order to the banking industry. It made it possible for banks to get a national charter. National banks were better funded than state banks. A government official called the Comptroller of the Currency regulated them. The banks issued a uniform currency backed by U.S. government bonds. National banks were safer than state banks, but did not have enough flexibility to deal with business cycles. As a result, more banking reform was needed by the turn of the century.

Reading Strategy: *Sequencing*
As you read the text, draw a simple time line to track the changes in the U.S. banking system over time. When you read, look for word clues such as *first*, *next*, and *then*.

Academic Vocabulary
period a stretch of time

checking account an account from which deposited money can be withdrawn at any time by writing a check

About 30 percent of banks failed in the United States during the banking crisis of 1930–1933. Depositors, fearing a loss of their money, rushed to their banks to withdraw cash. Such a rush to withdraw deposits is known as a run on a bank. Bank runs often caused banks to fail.

▶ CRITICAL THINKING

Making Connections Why did banks not have enough money to meet the demand for withdrawals?

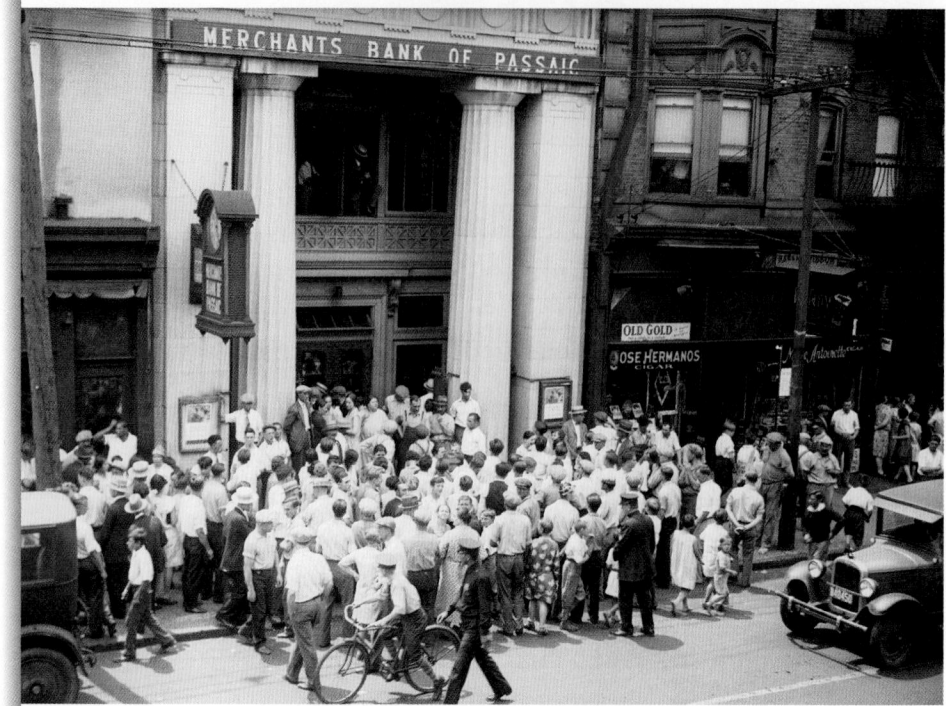

Why It —
MATTERS

Protecting Your Money

Think about the ways you handle your spending money. Do you know how much money you have? Do you know where it is? Do you make sure it is safe? Keeping your money safe is important, whether by never leaving your wallet or bag unattended or by choosing your bank wisely. Think of some ways you could keep better track of your money and keep it more secure.

The Federal Reserve System

The banking system still had problems, though. The national banks did not have enough flexibility to get through an economic downturn, or a slowing of business and economic activity. As a result, more changes were needed. In 1913 Congress created the Federal Reserve System. At first, the new system was not perfect. Each of the 12 district banks followed its own monetary policy. Some district banks tried to expand the economy in their region. Others followed different policies in their areas. As a result, the 12 banks did not work together. This problem made the Fed unable to take strong steps to end the Great Depression.

The Great Depression, 1929–1933

During the Great Depression, one out of four workers could not find a job. Many businesses closed. Thousands of banks failed when panicky depositors all tried to withdraw their money. Because banks did not have enough cash, they could not give people their money. Banks closed their doors. This caused more panic, and even more banks failed.

In response, President Franklin Delano Roosevelt ordered all banks closed for four days. He assured people that banks would reopen after they had been checked by a government official and found to be healthy. Congress then passed the Banking Act of 1933. This law created the deposit insurance program. It also gave the Fed more power to regulate banks. Another law passed in 1935 gave the Fed more powers to regulate banks. The Board of Governors was also given more authority over the district banks. This allowed the Fed to act in a united way.

The S&L Crisis

The next crisis came in the 1980s. It mainly affected savings and loan institutions. For years, the S&L industry had grown. Most S&Ls did not have enough capital, or cash and securities, to help them in a crisis, however. Congress passed legislation that allowed S&Ls to compete with banks. When the S&Ls made the riskier types of loans that banks made, hundreds failed. The insurance fund for S&L deposits failed, too. This threatened to bankrupt thousands of individual savers.

Congress responded in 1989 with a new law. It moved deposit insurance for S&Ls to the FDIC. It also set up a method for checking on the health of S&Ls and closed those that were not in good condition. The S&Ls were now under the control of the banking industry. After this crisis many of the historical differences between S&Ls and commercial banks faded.

Credit Crisis of 2008

In December 2007, the nation faced a severe financial crisis. For years, some banks and other businesses had made home loans to borrowers who were not able to repay them. Many lending companies suffered huge losses. Some went out of business. A credit crunch developed. This meant lending, which keeps the economy moving, slowed greatly. The economy came close to collapse. Shoppers stopped buying products, and many companies went bankrupt. Millions of people lost their jobs.

In the fall of 2008, the Fed loaned more than $2.5 trillion to financial institutions. The Treasury Department also loaned money to troubled companies. These actions helped prevent what some feared would have been a collapse of the entire financial system. However, the serious economic slowdown had done much damage. The economy grew very slowly after that.

✓ PROGRESS CHECK

Making Generalizations How did the changes after the S&L crisis make the banking industry safer?

― 21ˢᵗ Century ―
SKILLS

Distinguishing Fact from Opinion

Use the Internet or the library to find an article about the credit crisis of 2008. Determine if the article relies more on fact or opinion to make its case. Remember that a fact is a real event or thing. Facts can be verified, or checked. An opinion is a belief or a judgment. It expresses what someone thinks or feels.

LESSON 3 REVIEW

Review Vocabulary

1. How are *savings accounts, certificates of deposit,* and *money market accounts* different from one another?

2. How are *checking accounts* different from these other accounts?

Answer the Guiding Questions

3. ***Synthesizing*** What role do banks play in the economy?

4. ***Drawing Conclusions*** What problem was found with the national banks created under the National Banking Act?

5. **ARGUMENT** Write an article explaining why you think it was a good or a bad idea for the government to borrow money from the Fed during the financial crisis of 2008.

Write your answers on a separate sheet of paper.

1 Writing Activity

EXPLORING THE ESSENTIAL QUESTION

How does government influence the economy and economic institutions?

The government has several policies aimed at keeping the banking system healthy and safe. Write a brief description of each of these policies.

2 21st Century Skills

CREATE AND GIVE A PRESENTATION Prepare a brief presentation that explains the role of banks in the U.S. economy. Include information on how banks affect the decisions of consumers and businesses. Also include the impact of government actions on banks. Review and edit your presentation. Then deliver it to the class. Use visual aids.

3 Being an Active Citizen

Many banks take active roles in their communities. They give to charities, help nonprofit organizations do their work, and take part in community actions such as cleanup efforts. Find a bank that is contributing in some way to building your community. Do research, either by talking to bank personnel or by conducting research on the Internet, to learn more about the bank's activities. Then create a data sheet about the project and the bank's role. Add your data sheet to those of other students in the class to make a community projects binder.

4 Understanding Visuals

ANALYZING POLITICAL CARTOONS The financial crisis of 2008 prompted the government to lend billions of dollars to banks, other financial companies, and Wall Street firms. Some people believed that these steps were necessary to save the financial system. Some criticized this substantial government aid as a bailout to the rich that would not help consumers. Study the political cartoon. What attitude does the cartoonist have toward these policies? Why do you think so?

BACK TOGETHER AGAIN

REVIEW THE GUIDING QUESTIONS

Directions: Choose the best answer for each question.

1 Which of these is a function of money?

A. to signal power

B. to carry out barters

C. to simplify the exchange of goods and services

D. to show a person's importance

2 Which type of financial institution offers full services to consumers and businesses?

F. commercial bank

G. credit union

H. Federal Reserve district bank

I. savings and loan association

3 Which part of the Fed buys and sells bonds to change the money supply?

A. district banks

B. Federal Open Market Committee

C. Federal Reserve Bank of New York

D. member banks

4 When the Fed writes lending rules for banks, it is acting as a

F. government banker.

G. money supplier.

H. regulator.

I. watchdog of the financial system's health.

5 Which type of account is likely to pay the lowest interest?

A. checking

B. savings

C. money market

D. certificate of deposit (CD)

6 The government began offering deposit insurance to

F. encourage people to open checking accounts.

G. promote credit unions.

H. build the popularity of banking.

I. reassure people that deposits were safe.

DBQ **ANALYZING DOCUMENTS**

Directions: Analyze the chart and answer the questions that follow.

Account Owner	Type of Account	Account Balance
Carlos Garcia	savings	$50,000
Carlos Garcia	checking	$25,000
Carlos Garcia	CD	$250,000
Carlos Garcia	business checking	$25,000
Total		$350,000

7 **Calculating** Assuming that all of the accounts are held in the same bank, how much of Carlos's balance in the bank is not insured by the FDIC?

A. $0

B. $25,000

C. $50,000

D. $100,000

8 **Problem Solving** What should Carlos do to have all his balances insured?

F. He does not have to do anything; they are already all insured.

G. He should ask the FDIC for an exception to the rule.

H. He should move the uninsured amount to another bank.

I. He should purchase extra deposit insurance.

SHORT RESPONSE

"[T]he pace of recovery in output and employment has slowed in recent months. Household spending is increasing gradually, but remains constrained [limited] by high unemployment, modest income growth . . . and tight credit. Business spending on equipment and software is rising; however, . . . employers remain reluctant to add to payrolls. . . . Bank lending has continued to contract [decrease]."

—Federal Reserve Board, press release, August 10, 2010

9 Is the Fed report describing a period of economic growth or economic difficulty? What details support that conclusion?

10 Based on the report, on what issues would you expect the Fed to focus its policy? Why?

EXTENDED RESPONSE

11 **Informative/Explanatory** What do you think is the proper role of government in relation to banking? Why?

Need Extra Help?

If You've Missed Question	1	2	3	4	5	6	7	8	9	10	11
Review Lesson	1	1	2	2	3	3	1	1	2	2	1, 2, 3

Financing the Government

ESSENTIAL QUESTION
How does government influence the economy and economic institutions?

Lesson 1
The Federal Budget: Revenues and Expenditures

Lesson 2
Fiscal Policy

The Story Matters...

Have you ever been on a boat in rough waters? Have you seen a movie about a ship in a storm? If so, then you might appreciate the work of the United States Coast Guard. The Coast Guard has many jobs, but is best known for its search-and-rescue operations at sea. When ships are in distress—often during bad weather—they call the Coast Guard. Coast Guard rescue helicopters and ships respond as quickly as they can. Members of the Coast Guard have special training in how to rescue people from sinking boats or icy waters.

Who pays for the rescue equipment and training? In 2010, the Coast Guard received more than $10 billion from the federal government to fund its operations for the year. With these funds, the Coast Guard buys boats, helicopters, and other equipment. It also pays its highly skilled employees. When people get in trouble at sea, they depend on the Coast Guard to come to their aid.

◀ *A Coast Guard helicopter crew practices a rescue from the ship* National Geographic Endeavour.

PHOTO: Jim Richardson/Getty Images

Real-Life Civics

▶ SPENDING SHUTDOWN

Can a country ever just shut down? Not really, but when the government cannot agree upon a national budget, shutdowns and closings can occur. Late in 1995, parts of the federal government shut down. Many federal offices and departments closed. Museums and monuments run by the government, such as the Lincoln Memorial, were closed to visitors. Only federal workers who were essential to the country's safety, such as members of the armed forces, stayed on the job. At the root of this crisis was a disagreement between the president and members of Congress about how to spend the U.S. government's money. The budget crisis of 1995 made Americans more aware of how complicated financing the government can be.

During the federal shutdown in 1995, barricades blocked visitors from entering the Lincoln Memorial. Thousands of tourists usually visit the Memorial each day.

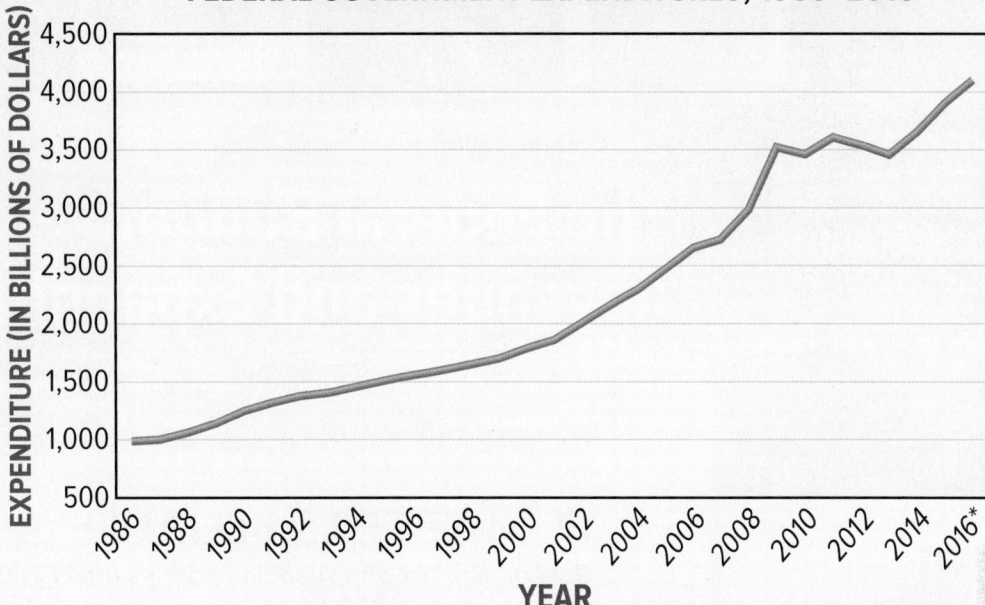

FEDERAL GOVERNMENT EXPENDITURES, 1986–2016

EXPENDITURE (IN BILLIONS OF DOLLARS)

4,500
4,000
3,500
3,000
2,500
2,000
1,500
1,000
500

1986 1988 1990 1992 1994 1996 1998 2000 2002 2004 2006 2008 2010 2012 2014 2016*

YEAR

Source: White House Office of Management and Budget; *figures given are estimates for 2016

The blue line shows how much the federal government has spent each year during the period shown on the graph.

> **SPENDING TRENDS** By 2014, spending by the federal government alone reached a total of more than $3.5 trillion. Just over 50 years earlier, in 1960, the federal government had spent less than $100 billion—less than 3 percent of its 2014 spending. Today, the U.S. government participates actively in many more programs and services than it did in 1960. This explains much of the increase in the total amount the government spends. Another reason for the rise in spending is inflation, or the rise in prices over time. Directly or indirectly, all Americans benefit from programs funded by the government. As taxpayers, we are also the source of the money that supports government spending. Therefore, it is important to understand how government budgets and finances work.

PHOTO: AP Photo/Charles Tasnadi

CIVIC LITERACY

★ ★ ★ ★

Analyzing Describe in general the changes in government spending over the time span shown in the graph. What are two factors that account for these changes?

Your Opinion Think about your own or your family's budget. Why is it sometimes difficult to make ends meet? Do you think the government has similar problems? Explain your answer.

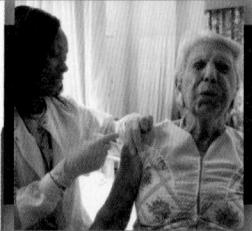

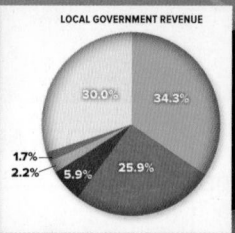

STEP 2
House and Senate pass
budget resolutions that
outline spending and taxes

LOCAL GOVERNMENT REVENUE

Lesson 1
The Federal Budget: Revenues and Expenditures

ESSENTIAL QUESTION *How does government influence the economy and economic institutions?*

IT MATTERS BECAUSE
Government tax and spending policies affect you.

Understanding the Federal Budget

GUIDING QUESTION *How does the federal budget reflect choices?*

Do you know how to make a personal budget? First, you figure out what your income is for a period of time, such as a month. Then, you estimate your savings and expenses for that month. You must think about regular expenses, such as weekly food costs. You also have to account for occasional costs—such as a birthday present for a parent. If expenses **exceed,**or are greater than, income, then you need to cut costs or find a way to earn more income.

The Budget Process

The federal government also has a budget. The federal budget covers a period called a **fiscal** (FIHS•kuhl) **year.** A fiscal year is any 12-month period chosen for keeping accounts. The fiscal year of the federal government begins October 1 and ends September 30 of the next year. Fiscal year 2015 begins October 1, 2014, and ends September 30, 2015.

The diagram of the federal budget process shows the steps in making a federal budget. This process is complex because of the size of the budget and the number of parties involved.

PHOTO: (tc) William Perlman/Star Ledger/Corbis

ReadingHELPDESK

Taking Notes: Categorizing

As you read, create a concept web linking related concepts, such as *taxes* and *revenues*.

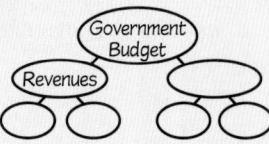

Government Budget

Revenues

Content Vocabulary

- fiscal year
- mandatory spending
- discretionary spending
- appropriations bill
- intergovernmental revenue
- sales tax

The process starts when the president **transmits,** or sends, a budget message to Congress. This message states how much the president wants to spend on each federal program. The message must be sent no later than the first Monday in February.

Next, key members of Congress agree on a *budget resolution*. This is Congress's plan for revenue and for spending on broad categories such as health. The budget has two different kinds of spending: mandatory and discretionary. **Mandatory spending** is set by laws outside the budget process. One example is Social Security, which makes payments to retirees. Mandatory spending is generally fixed from year to year. **Discretionary** (dis•KREH•shuh•NEHR•ee) **spending** involves spending choices made and approved each year. It includes items such as national defense and highways and can differ from year to year.

Next, Congress must set spending on each program for the coming year. That process starts when committees in the House write appropriations bills. An **appropriations** (uh•proh•pree•AY•shuhnz) **bill** gives official approval for the government to spend money. All appropriations bills start in the House but must be approved by both houses. After the Senate and House pass each bill, it is sent to the president. The president can either sign it into law or veto it. If the bill is vetoed, Congress can rewrite the bill or override the veto.

Sometimes Congress does not pass the budget in time. It then approves a *continuing resolution*. This law sets spending for the coming year at the same level as the year before.

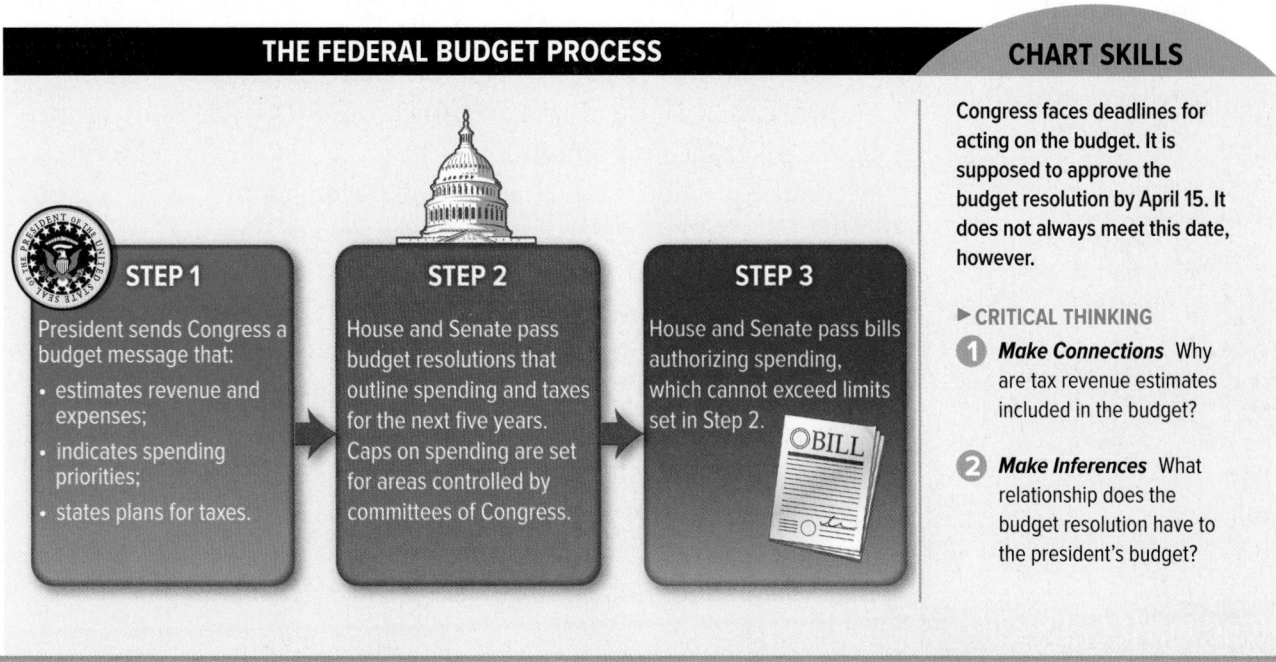

THE FEDERAL BUDGET PROCESS

STEP 1
President sends Congress a budget message that:
- estimates revenue and expenses;
- indicates spending priorities;
- states plans for taxes.

STEP 2
House and Senate pass budget resolutions that outline spending and taxes for the next five years. Caps on spending are set for areas controlled by committees of Congress.

STEP 3
House and Senate pass bills authorizing spending, which cannot exceed limits set in Step 2.
BILL

CHART SKILLS

Congress faces deadlines for acting on the budget. It is supposed to approve the budget resolution by April 15. It does not always meet this date, however.

► CRITICAL THINKING

1 *Make Connections* Why are tax revenue estimates included in the budget?

2 *Make Inferences* What relationship does the budget resolution have to the president's budget?

- **entitlement program**
- **subsidize**
- **property tax**

fiscal year any 12-month period chosen for keeping accounts

mandatory spending the federal spending required by law that continues without the need for congressional approval each year

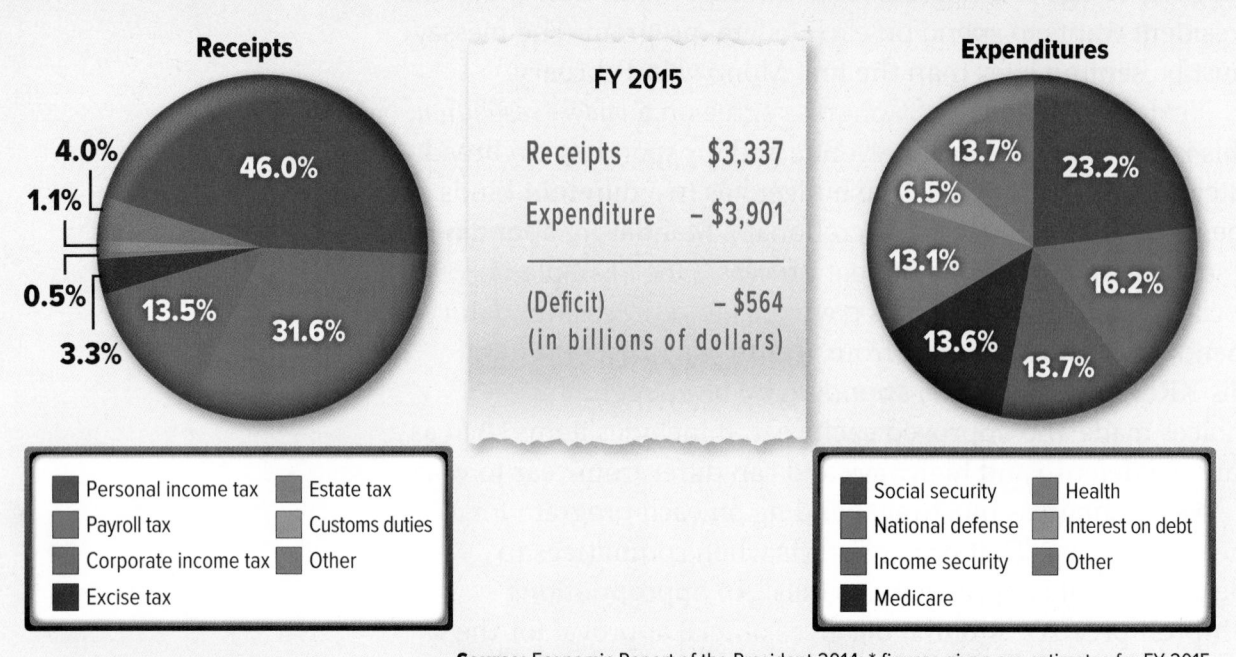

THE FEDERAL BUDGET, FY 2015*

Receipts

4.0%
1.1%
0.5%
13.5%
3.3%
46.0%
31.6%

FY 2015

Receipts	$3,337
Expenditure	– $3,901
(Deficit)	– $564

(in billions of dollars)

Expenditures

13.7%
6.5%
13.1%
13.6%
23.2%
16.2%
13.7%

- Personal income tax
- Payroll tax
- Corporate income tax
- Excise tax
- Estate tax
- Customs duties
- Other

- Social security
- National defense
- Income security
- Medicare
- Health
- Interest on debt
- Other

Source: Economic Report of the President 2014; * figures given are estimates for FY 2015

INFOGRAPHIC

Federal spending for Fiscal Year 2015 was about $564 billion higher than revenues for that year. You will learn more about this in Lesson 2.

► CRITICAL THINKING

1 *Make Predictions* What happens to federal revenue when many people lose their jobs? Why?

2 *Categorize* What are the two largest spending categories? Which is mandatory and which is discretionary?

Revenues

The federal budget is made up of two main parts—revenues and expenditures. Revenue is the money a government collects to fund its spending.

The biggest source of federal revenue is the personal income tax. This tax is paid by all people who earn income above a certain amount. The second-largest share of revenue is from payroll taxes. These are taken from workers' paychecks to fund social insurance programs such as Social Security and Medicare. Medicare provides some health care coverage for people age 65 and older. The third-largest source of revenue comes from the tax that corporations pay on their profits.

Taxes fall into three categories: progressive, proportional, and regressive. With a *progressive tax*, the tax rate goes up as income goes up. The federal income tax is a progressive tax. A *proportional tax* has a constant tax rate, regardless of income. The tax for Medicare is proportional because it is the same rate for all wage earners. A *regressive tax* takes a smaller percentage of your income as the amount you earn goes up. The sales tax is an example of a regressive tax.

Reading**HELP**DESK

discretionary spending the spending for federal programs that must receive approval each year

appropriations bill the legislation that sets spending on particular programs for the coming year

Academic Vocabulary

exceed to be greater than

transmit to send a document or a message

Expenditures

The circle graph of federal expenditures shows federal spending for Fiscal Year 2015. Social Security is the largest category. Spending in this area will likely increase in the future as the population ages and more people retire. National defense spending is close behind. Income security ranks third. It includes unemployment benefits, welfare, and retirement benefits for some government workers and other groups.

The fourth category is Medicare. This area is also likely to rise as the population ages. The fifth-largest category is health. This includes health care and long-term care for low-income people of all ages as well as those with disabilities.

The sixth category is interest on borrowed money. When the federal government borrows, it must pay interest on the debt, just like any consumer who takes out a loan. As government borrowing goes up, so does the interest it owes. "Other" includes programs in education, veteran benefits, and highway costs. Spending in the "other" category is discretionary spending.

How the Budget Process Changed Over Time

When the federal government began, it had fewer sources of revenue and spent less than government today. The budget process was very informal, with little overall planning.

Over time, federal spending increased. As a result, the budget process had to be improved. Congress passed a law in 1921 that made the process more formal. For the first time, the president was required to send a budget to Congress each year. In 1974 Congress passed another law to improve the budget process. It required Congress to set up committees to focus on the budget. It also set up the Congressional Budget Office (CBO). That office has the job of tracking spending and revenue measures and making reports to Congress.

The budget process still faces difficulties today, however. Members of Congress often add spending for pet projects to major bills. These add-ons can increase overall spending.

✓ **PROGRESS CHECK**

Comparing and Contrasting How is making the federal budget similar to and different from making a personal budget?

Elderly people have much of their health care costs covered by the Medicare program.

▶ **CRITICAL THINKING**
Making Connections What source of revenue pays for this program?

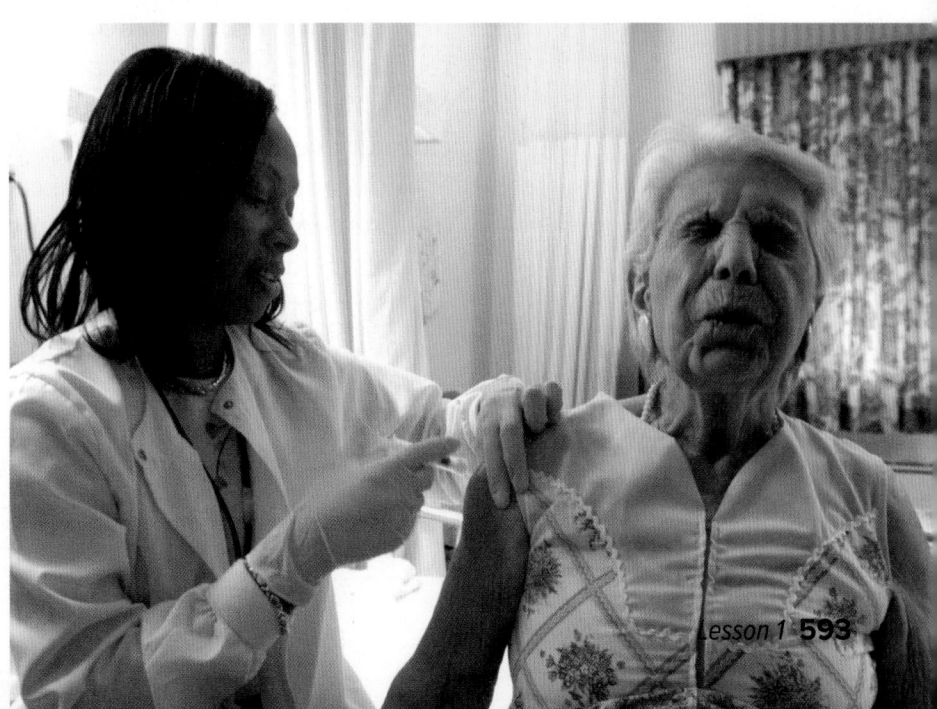

Budgeting for State and Local Governments

GUIDING QUESTION *How do state and local revenues and expenditures differ from those of the federal government?*

State and local governments also prepare budgets. The governments of all states except Vermont cannot, by law, spend more than they receive in revenue. Local governments also have to limit spending so it does not exceed revenues.

State Governments

The circle graphs of state government revenue and spending are for all states combined. **Intergovernmental revenue** is the largest source of state income. This refers to funds that one level of government receives from another level of government. States receive this money from the federal government.

Sales taxes are the states' second-most-important source of revenue. A **sales tax** is paid when someone buys a good or service. All but five states have sales taxes. Tax rates range from 2.9 percent to 7 percent. A 3 percent sales tax on clothing means that a person spending $100 on clothes pays another $3 in taxes. Sales taxes can be regressive and hurt the poor, however. As a result, many states do not tax essential goods, such as food and medicine. Some states also declare sales tax holidays. During these periods, purchases of school supplies are not taxed.

All but five states have a personal income tax. In some states this tax is proportional, with all taxpayers paying a flat rate. In others it is progressive, with high incomes taxed at higher rates.

The single biggest area of state spending is public welfare. This refers to programs meant to help those people with little money to maintain basic health and living conditions. Most of this spending goes to states' share of funding of **entitlement programs.** These are called "entitlements" because the requirements for benefits are set by law. An example is the Medicaid program. This program helps poor people get health care services.

Education is another large category of state spending. Some of this spending goes to local governments to help fund public schools. Some of it is used to **subsidize** (SUHB•suh•DEYEZ), or pay part of the cost of, students' state college education. This subsidy helps make state colleges more affordable.

Reading**HELP**DESK

intergovernmental revenue the funds that one level of government receives from another level of government

sales tax a tax paid by consumers at the time they buy goods or services

entitlement program a government program that makes payments to people who must meet certain requirements in order to help them meet minimum health, nutrition, and income needs

subsidize to aid or support a person, business, institution, or undertaking with money or tax breaks

STATE GOVERNMENT REVENUE

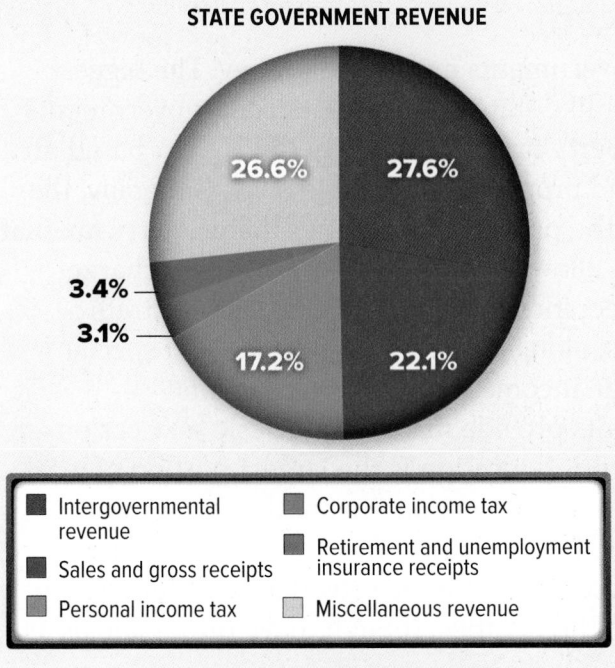

- 27.6%
- 26.6%
- 3.4%
- 3.1%
- 17.2%
- 22.1%

- ■ Intergovernmental revenue
- ■ Sales and gross receipts
- ■ Personal income tax
- ■ Corporate income tax
- ■ Retirement and unemployment insurance receipts
- ■ Miscellaneous revenue

STATE GOVERNMENT EXPENSES

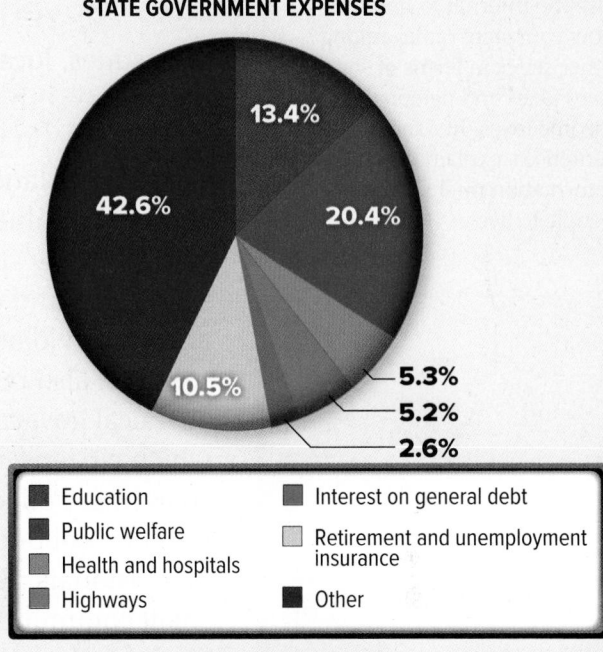

- 13.4%
- 42.6%
- 20.4%
- 10.5%
- 5.3%
- 5.2%
- 2.6%

- ■ Education
- ■ Public welfare
- ■ Health and hospitals
- ■ Highways
- ■ Interest on general debt
- ■ Retirement and unemployment insurance
- ■ Other

LOCAL GOVERNMENT REVENUE

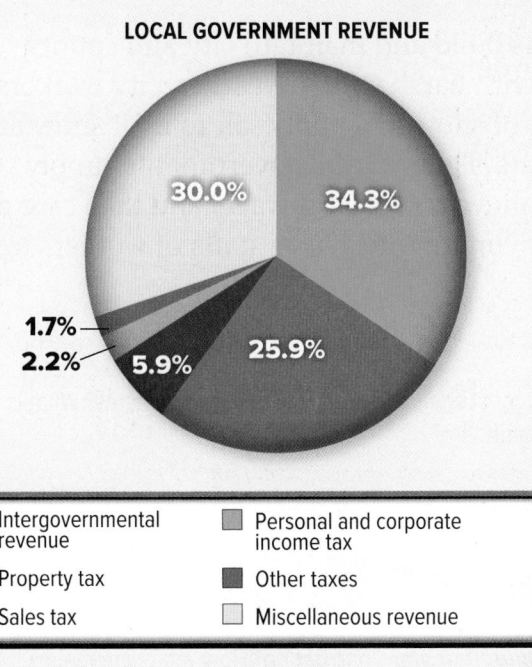

- 30.0%
- 34.3%
- 1.7%
- 2.2%
- 5.9%
- 25.9%

- ■ Intergovernmental revenue
- ■ Property tax
- ■ Sales tax
- ■ Personal and corporate income tax
- ■ Other taxes
- ■ Miscellaneous revenue

LOCAL GOVERNMENT EXPENSES

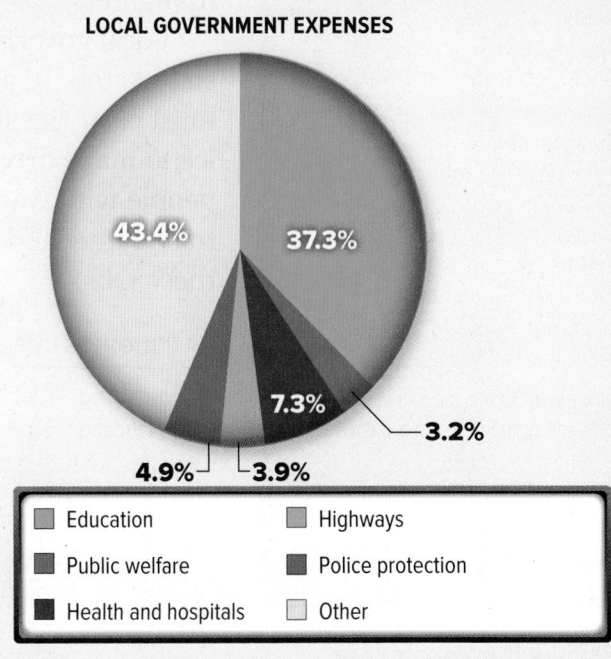

- 43.4%
- 37.3%
- 7.3%
- 3.2%
- 4.9%
- 3.9%

- ■ Education
- ■ Public welfare
- ■ Health and hospitals
- ■ Highways
- ■ Police protection
- ■ Other

Source: U.S. Bureau of the Census, Statistical Abstract of the United States

INFOGRAPHIC SKILLS

The federal government provides money to state governments. State governments, in turn, provide funds for local governments.

▶ CRITICAL THINKING

1 Comparing What is one specific tax that local government collects and state government does not?

2 Making Inferences Which level of government, state or local, would be hurt more by an end to intergovernmental revenue? Why?

"Other" refers to additional state spending in all other areas. This includes insurance payments to retired state employees andspending in such areas as state police, prisons, and parks.

Local Governments

Like states, local governments must raise money. The biggest difference is that, unlike state governments, local governments rely heavily on property taxes. A **property tax** is a tax based on the value of land and property that people own. Generally, the higher the value of the property, the higher the property tax that is paid. Many states allow their local governments to charge sales taxes and collect income taxes as well. Fines for traffic and other violations, along with fees for permits and special services, also provide income for local governments.

Local governments provide many of the basic services on which citizens depend. Education is the largest portion of local spending. Police and fire protection are another important part of local budgets. Police services are always provided by professionals. Fire protection can be provided by volunteers in small communities. Larger cities, though, have professionals as firefighters.

Local governments build and maintain city and county streets, too. In areas with harsh winter weather, city workers must clear the streets of snow and apply salt to melt snow and ice to make driving safe. Finally, local governments supply people with water, remove and treat sewage, and take care of trash removal. Larger communities have staffs of workers to do these jobs.

✓ PROGRESS CHECK

property tax a tax on the value of land and property that people own

Summarizing What is the biggest spending area for state governments? What is the largest local government expenditure?

LESSON 1 REVIEW

Review the Vocabulary

1. What is a *fiscal year*? How is it related to a budget?

2. What is the difference between *mandatory* and *discretionary spending*?

3. What is *intergovernmental revenue*? How does it *subsidize* lower levels of government?

Answer the Guiding Questions

4. ***Analyzing*** What kinds of choices are involved in making the federal budget?

5. ***Comparing and Contrasting*** How are tax revenues spent differently by state, local, and federal governments?

6. **INFORMATIVE/EXPLANATORY** Write a paragraph explaining the process by which the federal government prepares a budget and makes spending decisions. Include all steps through appropriations.

networks

There's More Online!

☑ **GRAPHIC ORGANIZER**
Federal Deficit

☑ **INFOGRAPHIC**
The Deficits and the Debt

☑ **POLITICAL CARTOON**
Lower Taxes vs. Reduced Deficits

☑ **VIDEO**

☑ **GAMES**

Lesson 2
Fiscal Policy

ESSENTIAL QUESTION *How does government influence the economy and economic institutions?*

⟲ IT MATTERS BECAUSE
Government spending is an important part of the economy, with lasting effects for all citizens.

Surpluses and Deficits

GUIDING QUESTION *What do governments do when the budget does not balance?*

Making a government budget is one thing. Following it is another. A budget, after all, is based on what officials **predict,** or forecast, will happen in the future. The unexpected can happen, however. An international conflict may break out, which may result in increased spending for defense. If heavy rains strike the Great Plains and cause massive flooding, the federal government will face the cost of helping the people who have homes that are damaged or destroyed.

Government officials know that disasters can happen and build funds into the budget to cover them. But what if more or bigger disasters than expected occur? What if a disaster is so terrible that it uses the government's entire disaster relief fund? What does the government do when, later that year, another crisis strikes?

Revenue forecasts can also go wrong. For example, if the economy slows, some workers will lose their jobs. In that case, income tax revenue will be lower than expected.

Reading**HELP**DESK

Taking Notes: *Cause and Effect*

As you read, complete a chart to identify the causes and effects of a federal deficit.

Content Vocabulary

- **balanced budget**
- **budget surplus**
- **budget deficit**
- **debt**
- **fiscal policy**
- **automatic stabilizer**

Balanced—or Unbalanced

Most governments strive to have a **balanced budget,** in which revenues and spending for the year equal each other. As you read in Lesson 1, every state except Vermont has to have a balanced budget. States can borrow money to invest in long-term projects but not to fund regular programs.

Most states save money during good times so that they have a cushion when revenues fall. States can save money in years in which they have a budget surplus. A **budget surplus** occurs when a government collects more money than it spends. In another year, if revenues fall, then states can use the reserves they saved to balance the budget. Of course, they also have the option to cut spending.

The federal government is different. It is allowed to have a **budget deficit,** or spend more than it collects in revenues in a fiscal year. To make up the difference, the federal government borrows money by selling bonds or Treasury bills. A government bond is a contract in which the government promises to repay borrowed money with interest at a specific time in the future. Most government bonds are repaid in 10 to 30 years. The government also sells Treasury bills, or T-bills. It promises to repay these in one year or less.

Deficit Becomes Debt

Budget deficits create debt because the government is borrowing money to cover some of its spending. **Debt** is money that has been borrowed and not yet paid back. Each year that the federal government runs a deficit, its total debt goes up. The line graph here shows the level of federal debt in recent years. It illustrates that the federal debt has been rising steadily for many years. If the federal government runs a surplus one year, it can use the extra money to pay down the debt. A budget surplus, then, can cause the federal debt to become smaller.

Some of the federal budget is used to fund education. This money may support programs for teachers and their students.

▶ **CRITICAL THINKING**
Making Connections How would cuts in spending on education affect you?

PHOTO: Hill Street Studios/Matthew Palmer/Blend Images LLC

UNITED STATES DEFICITS AND SURPLUSES

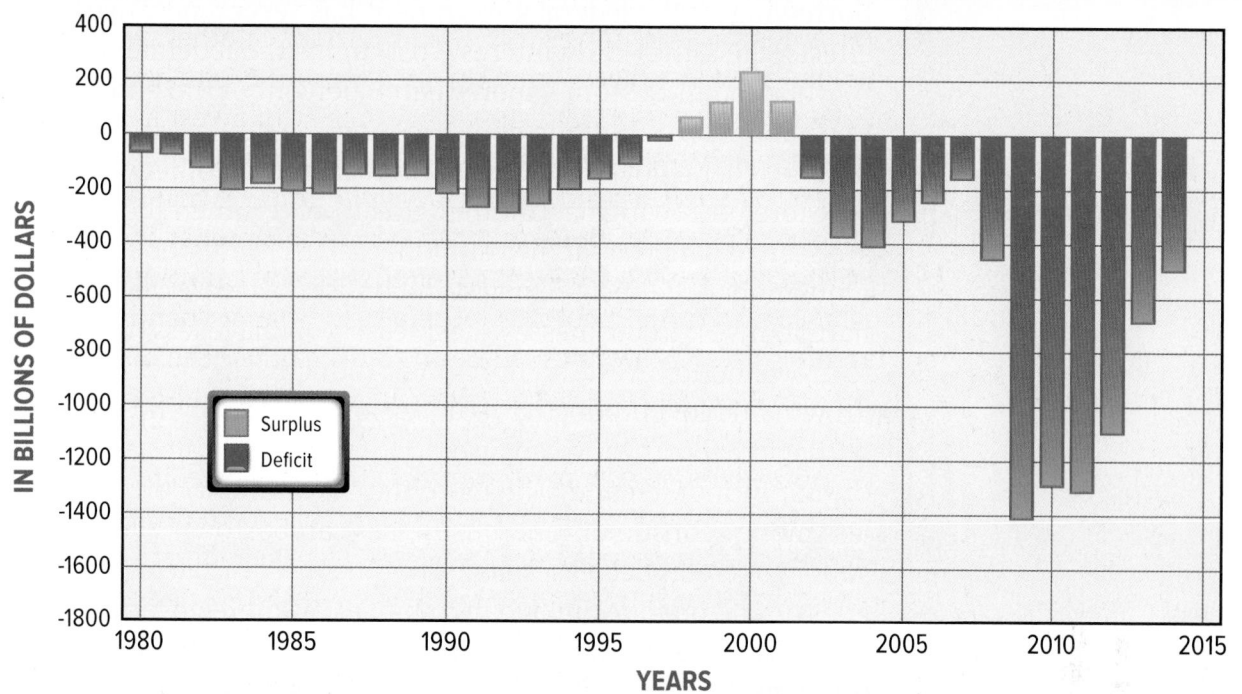

UNITED STATES NATIONAL DEBT

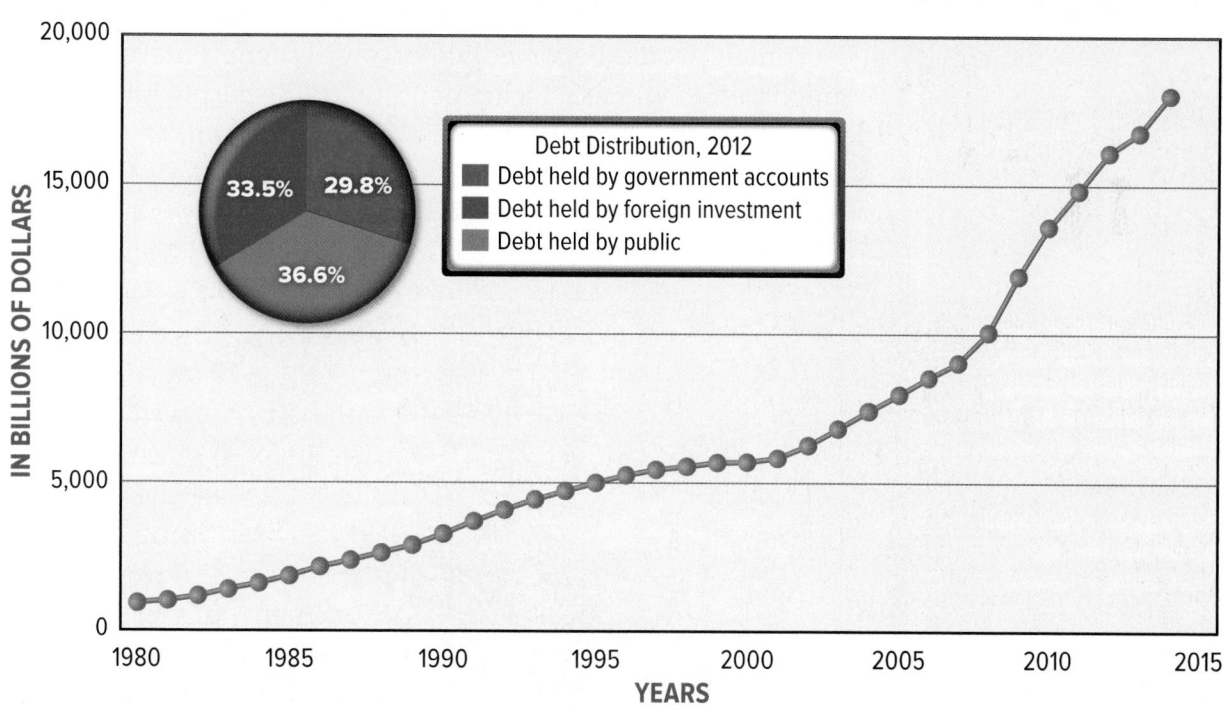

Debt Distribution, 2012
- Debt held by government accounts
- Debt held by foreign investment
- Debt held by public

33.5%   29.8%

36.6%

Source: White House Office of Management and Budget; Congressional Budget Office; U.S. Department of the Treasury; U.S. Government Accountability Office

INFOGRAPHIC SKILLS

Over the years, the federal government has relied on borrowing to cover spending. As a result, the federal debt has increased rapidly.

▶ CRITICAL THINKING

1 **Analyzing Visuals** In which years did the federal government have a budget surplus?

2 **Making Inferences** How did the federal government respond, in terms of spending, to the recession that began in 2007 and worsened in 2008? How can you tell?

Impact of Deficits and the Federal Debt

Borrowing by the federal government has several negative effects. First, the yearly interest cost drains the federal budget. As you read in Lesson 1, more than 6 percent of the budget goes to paying interest. As the debt rises and the interest cost goes up, the federal government has less to spend on other programs.

More borrowing has another effect. Government bonds are seen as safe ways to invest money, so they are popular. The more money that people invest in bonds, however, the less they have to invest in businesses. Businesses will have less money to grow and to invest in improving productivity. Slow business growth and low productivity cause slow economic growth.

Federal borrowing can also drive up interest rates as a result of supply and demand. The more the government borrows, the less money consumers and businesses can borrow. When the supply of credit decreases, its price—the interest rate on loans— goes up. If you take out a loan to buy a car, more government borrowing could result in the loan costing more than it would otherwise.

A recent report by the Congressional Research Service points out another problem. If a high level of debt continues for a long time, investors could lose confidence in the government. The government would be forced to borrow at higher interest rates. It might also be forced to cut spending or to sharply raise taxes.

✓ PROGRESS CHECK

Making Generalizations For the most part, has the federal government had a balanced budget, a surplus, or a deficit over the last two decades?

Politicians often pledge to both cut taxes and cut the deficit. Cutting taxes without reducing spending increases the deficit, so the first pledge works against the second.

▶ **CRITICAL THINKING**
Analyzing Visuals In the cartoon, why does the train have two locomotives pulling in opposite directions?

Reading**HELP**DESK

Academic Vocabulary

achieve to reach

fiscal policy how the government uses taxes and spending to reach economic goals

PHOTO: (tl) Bettmann/CORBIS; (inset) Andre Jenny/Alamy

During the Great Depression, WPA workers (left) built roads. Such projects were designed to stimulate the economy. Florida's Daytona Beach Bandshell (above) was also a WPA project. It is still used today to host concerts and weddings.

▶ CRITICAL THINKING

Making Inferences What were two ways that WPA projects helped the country during the Depression?

Managing the Economy

GUIDING QUESTION *How does the government try to influence the economy?*

For much of U.S. history, the government had a limited economic role. It left most matters to consumers and businesses. Then, in the 1930s, the government's economic role changed.

Franklin Roosevelt became president in 1933. The Great Depression had been going on for nearly four years, and millions of people were suffering. Roosevelt decided that the nation could not wait any longer for the economy to recover. The government had to act. Roosevelt started new government programs to put people back to work. These programs paid people to build schools, post offices, bridges, parks, and more. The new programs helped the economy. Later, when America entered World War II, the economy grew even stronger as people produced supplies for the military.

After the war, the economy began to focus on consumer goods. To make sure the nation did not fall back into depression, the government's economic role grew again. In the late 1940s, Congress passed a law that set the first official economic goals. The three goals were to keep people working, to keep producing goods, and to keep consumers buying goods and services.

Two policies aimed to **achieve,** or reach, these goals. One is a monetary policy handled by the Federal Reserve System. The other is **fiscal policy**. This refers to how the government uses taxes and spending to reach economic goals. The government spending by President Roosevelt is an example of fiscal policy.

A White House Council director meets with a worker at Detroit Edison in Michigan. The government awarded an $83 million grant to this company. It will create jobs by making energy-efficient electric meters for homes. The grant was part of the American Reinvestment and Recovery Act of 2009.

▶ CRITICAL THINKING

Making Inferences Why might it be hard for Congress to agree on what programs to fund?

Using Fiscal Policy to Achieve Goals

The idea behind fiscal policy is simple. If the economy slows down or enters a recession, the government can take certain steps to help the economy grow and become healthy again. Such steps could include increasing spending, cutting taxes, or a combination of the two. Using fiscal policy to boost growth is called stimulating the economy.

By boosting spending, the government creates demand for goods and services. That increase in demand could convince businesses to produce more and perhaps to hire back workers they had laid off. Cutting taxes puts more money in people's pockets. That also can lead to increased demand.

Problems with Fiscal Policy

Fiscal policy comes with problems, however. Some leaders believe that deficit spending hurts the economy. In 2009 President Barack Obama wanted to boost the economy by increasing spending. Critics protested about the increases to the federal debt.

Even when leaders agree to pursue a stimulus program, they may disagree on how much to spend or on which programs should be funded. Supporters of the 2009 bill argued for some time over these questions, resulting in a delay in putting the programs into effect.

Fiscal policy can also be slow to take effect. It can sometimes take months for Congress and the president to agree on a spending plan. Then, still more time is needed to put the plan into action. By the time the money is spent, the state of the economy may have changed.

Another problem is the difficulty in judging if a stimulus has worked. After the 2009 stimulus package, unemployment was held lower than in some earlier recessions. As a result, many economists agreed that the stimulus package saved jobs. They could not identify exactly how many jobs were saved, though.

Finally, the effects of fiscal policy are not entirely predictable. The economy is huge and complex. Any action might not be

Reading HELP DESK

Reading Strategy: *Summarizing*

To summarize, you find the main idea of a passage and restate it, reducing the number of details. Read about the problems with fiscal policy. On a separate sheet of paper, summarize the reading in one or two sentences.

automatic stabilizer any economic feature that works to increase or preserve income without additional government action

strong enough to have the desired effect or effects, or it might have unexpected effects—perhaps even negative ones.

Automatic Stabilizers

For these reasons, the government likes to use programs called **automatic stabilizers.** These programs work to increase or preserve income without the need for the government to take additional action. Since automatic stabilizers increase income, they can boost demand and spur economic growth. The two most important stabilizers are unemployment insurance and the progressive income tax system. A big advantage of both is that they are always in place. As a result, they begin to work automatically whenever the economy starts to slow down.

Think about how unemployment insurance works. In a recession, millions of people lose their jobs. When they are unemployed, they become eligible to receive unemployment insurance payments. Using these insurance payments, unemployed workers can then pay their bills and meet their basic needs, such as food and shelter, until they are rehired or find a new job.

Because the federal income tax is progressive, it also works as a stabilizer. When people work less or even lose their jobs, their income goes down. The less income people earn, the less they pay in taxes. They are taxed at a lower rate and can keep a larger percentage of their income. This partly offsets the loss of income. When the economy recovers and they go back to work, they begin to make more money. Then, when they can better afford it, they are again taxed at a higher rate. That, in turn, helps lower the deficit caused by the recession.

✓ **PROGRESS CHECK**

Analyzing Cause and Effect Under what conditions does the government use fiscal policy? Why?

Why It MATTERS

Government Spending

When Congress works on a stimulus package, your local representative often works to get federal funding for programs in your area. Think of a local program or project that you think would benefit your community. Then write a few lines to your member of Congress explaining why you think your community should get federal funding for it.

LESSON 2 REVIEW

Review Vocabulary

1. What are the differences among a *balanced budget,* a *budget deficit,* and a *budget surplus*?

2. How are *budget deficits* related to *debt*?

3. How are *automatic stabilizers* related to *fiscal policy?*

Answer the Guiding Questions

4. *Contrasting* How do state and federal governments react to an unbalanced budget?

5. *Synthesizing* What policy can Congress and the president use to influence the economy? How effective is it?

6. **ARGUMENT** As a member of Congress, you must consider a bill sent by the president cutting income taxes in the hope of stimulating the economy during a tough recession. Write a short speech for or against the president's plan. Give reasons for your position.

Write your answers on a separate sheet of paper.

1 **Writing Activity**

EXPLORING THE ESSENTIAL QUESTION
How does government influence the economy and economic institutions?

As the U.S. economy has expanded into the largest in the world, both its revenues and expenditures have grown to amounts totalling trillions of dollars. As a result, the process for creating a federal budget has become more complex. Write a description of how the process for making the federal budget has changed since the early 1900s. Describe how the process works today.

2 **21st Century Skills**

USE BAR AND CIRCLE GRAPHS Use the Internet or resources in a library to learn how your state obtains and spends its revenue. Find the data to construct two circle graphs like the ones shown in Lesson 1. Include additional categories for revenues and expenditures, if appropriate. Write a paragraph comparing the data for your state to the data for all states given in this chapter.

3 **Being an Active Citizen**

Find out when your local school board will meet to discuss the school system's budget for the upcoming year. If possible, attend the meeting, listen to the discussion, and contribute your own ideas. Then write a summary of the meeting. If you cannot attend, read a report of the meeting, and write a summary of it.

4 **Understanding Visuals**

ANALYZING VISUALS What do you see in this photograph? What natural occurrence might have caused this situation? Write a paragraph to explain how such an event might turn a national budget surplus into a budget deficit and, eventually, a debt. Discuss how the federal government responds to emergencies and disasters that strike states unexpectedly.

PHOTO: Justin Sullivan/Getty Images

REVIEW THE GUIDING QUESTIONS

Directions: Choose the best answer for each question.

❶ How does Congress actually determine spending during the year?
A. through the president's budget plan
B. by a joint budget resolution
C. with appropriations bills
D. by passing a constitutional amendment

❷ Why is interest on the debt an important part of federal spending each year?
F. It is required by the Constitution.
G. It is an obligation that results from past borrowing.
H. Congress pays citizens for their savings.
I. Congress uses it to set aside money for the future.

❸ What is the single largest source of revenue for local governments?
A. income tax
B. intergovernmental revenue
C. property tax
D. sales tax

❹ What do most state and local governments do when they face a budget deficit?
F. cut spending
G. increase spending
H. cut taxes
I. borrow money

❺ What causes growth in the federal debt?
A. payment of federal bonds
B. increase in federal taxes
C. federal borrowing
D. budget surpluses

❻ Why does the federal government sometimes use fiscal policy?
F. to control the money supply
G. to withhold funds from states
H. to add to the federal debt
I. to stimulate the economy in bad times

DBQ ANALYZING DOCUMENTS

Directions: Analyze the excerpt and answer the questions that follow.

In his Economic Report of 2010, President Barack Obama said:

"A key part of the rebalancing that must occur as the economy returns to full employment and beyond involves taming the federal budget deficit."

7 **Analyzing Primary Sources** What long-term problem does this statement address?

A. state budget shortfalls

B. tax increases

C. rising Social Security costs

D. growing federal debt

8 **Determining Cause and Effect** What action would most likely be used to address this problem?

F. selling government bonds

G. cutting federal spending

H. making interest payments

I. increasing federal spending

SHORT RESPONSE

*"The budget resolution is supposed to be passed by April 15, but it often takes longer. Occasionally, Congress does not pass a budget resolution.
If that happens, the previous year's resolution, which is a multi-year plan, stays in effect."*

—Congressional Research Service, "Introduction to the Federal Budget Process" (2008)

9 Why does Congress set deadlines for the steps in the budget process? Why are they sometimes missed?

10 Each year's budget resolution covers spending for five years. What might be the purpose of that requirement?

EXTENDED RESPONSE

11 **Argument** If you were a state governor, would you want your state to have the power to borrow money to balance the budget, as the federal government does? Why or why not?

Need Extra Help?

If You've Missed Question	**1**	**2**	**3**	**4**	**5**	**6**	**7**	**8**	**9**	**10**	**11**
Review Lesson	1	1	1	2	2	2	2	2	1	1	1, 2

International Trade and Economic Systems

ESSENTIAL QUESTIONS · *Why do people trade?*
· *Why and how do people make economic choices?*

netw⊛rks

There's More Online about international trade and economic systems.

CHAPTER 23

Lesson 1
Why and How Nations Trade

Lesson 2
Economic Systems and Development

The Story Matters...

Evidence of international trade is hard to miss in the port of Hong Kong. With the bird's-eye view shown in this photo, one can see colorful cargo containers stacked high. Hong Kong is the seventh busiest port in the world. About 230.1 million tons of cargo move in and out of the port each year. The world's busiest port, Shanghai in China, moves about 443 million tons in a year. Hong Kong's international trade has fed its economy, making it one of the world's leading financial centers. In recent years, Hong Kong has had growing competition from port cities in southern China.

China took back control of Hong Kong in 1997, after more than 150 years of British rule. However, the Chinese government has allowed people in Hong Kong more freedom than it gives to people in China. So the city continues to attract international business with its low taxes and free trade.

◄ *Cargo containers stacked to look like small skyscrapers fill the busy port of Hong Kong.*

PHOTO: Iain Masterton/Alamy

607

Real-Life Civics

BORDER TRADE What determines the amount of trade between two countries? Sometimes it is simply location. Mexico and the United States share a border, leading to a large volume of trade. Each day, thousands of vehicles carry farm and manufactured goods between the two nations. Traded goods range from electronics and car parts to vegetables and fruits. This trade has a value of more than one billion dollars per day. The United States is Mexico's largest trading partner. Mexico is the third-largest trading partner of the United States, after Canada and China. The United States has trade agreements, such as the North American Free Trade Agreement (NAFTA), with Mexico and other nations. Some Americans disagree about whether these agreements help or harm the U.S. economy.

Cargo trucks line up for inspection by the California Highway Patrol at the border between the United States and Mexico.

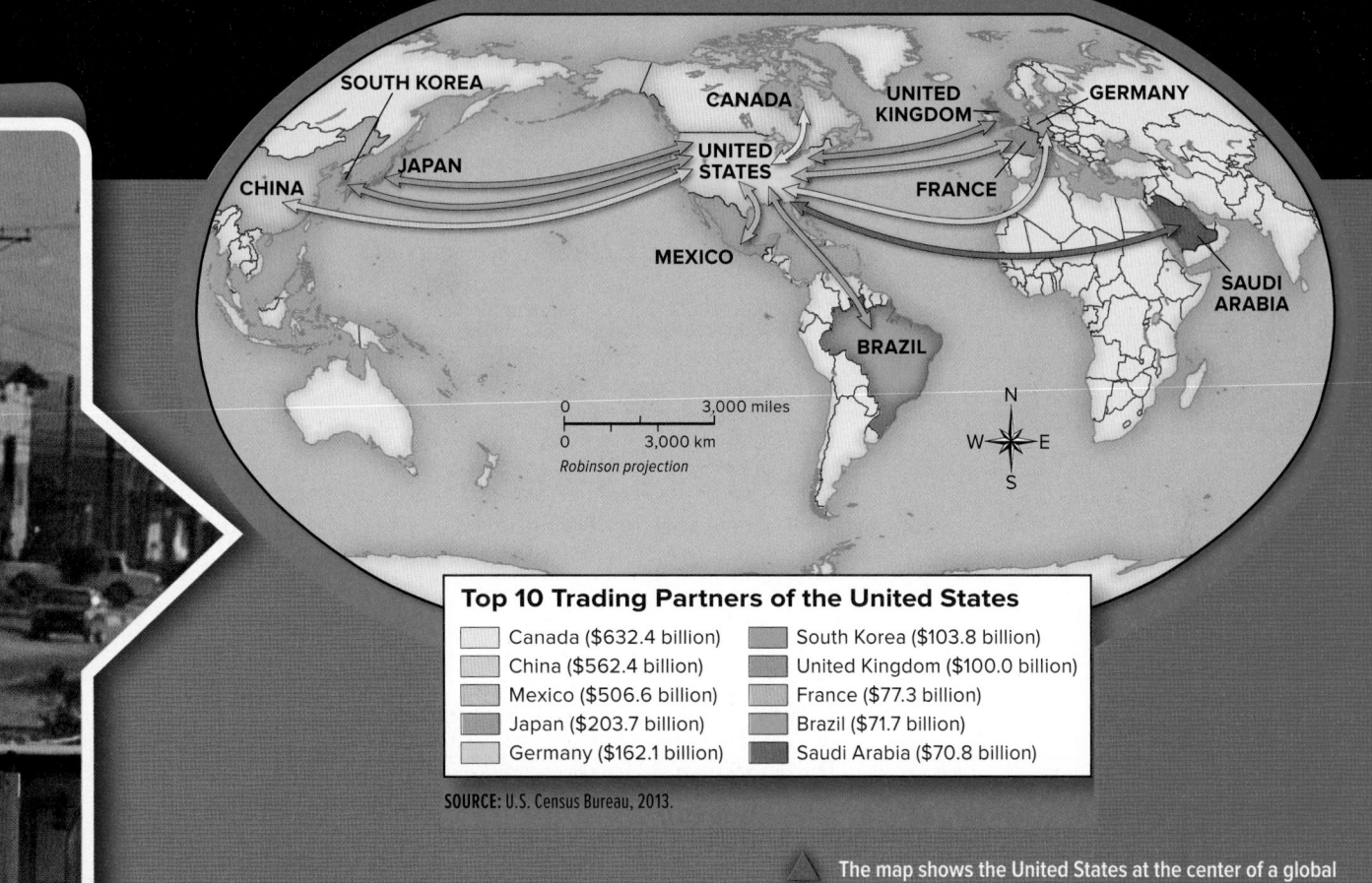

Top 10 Trading Partners of the United States

Canada ($632.4 billion)	South Korea ($103.8 billion)
China ($562.4 billion)	United Kingdom ($100.0 billion)
Mexico ($506.6 billion)	France ($77.3 billion)
Japan ($203.7 billion)	Brazil ($71.7 billion)
Germany ($162.1 billion)	Saudi Arabia ($70.8 billion)

SOURCE: U.S. Census Bureau, 2013.

The map shows the United States at the center of a global trading system with its ten major partners.

> **WORLD TRADE** Economies around the world rely on international trade. In the United States, businesses of all sizes can influence trade with other countries. A small grocery store in New York City might specialize in selling gourmet foods from France. Halfway around the world, workers in an office in India answer service calls for the products of a company in Dallas. Young people in London, England, may be buying the clothes of a new American designer—clothes that are made in Taiwan, off the southeastern coast of mainland China. When countries rely heavily on one another, good trade rules and relations become vital. For countries that share borders, such as the United States with Canada and Mexico, the effects of trade are even more visible.

CIVIC LITERACY
★ ★ ★ ★

Inferring Which country is the top trading partner of the United States? What might be one reason that the United States trades so much with this nation?

Your Opinion Do you know of any goods in your home that come from another country? How do you think U.S. trade with other countries affects your life?

PHOTO: Steve Starr/CORBIS

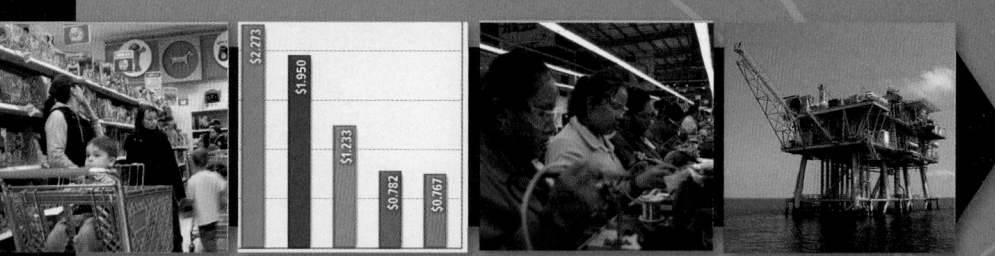

networks

There's More Online!

☑ **GRAPHIC ORGANIZER**
Free Trade

☑ **INFOGRAPHIC**
Imports and Exports,
Selected Nations

☑ **GRAPH**
U.S. Imported Consumer Goods

☑ **VIDEO**

Lesson 1
Why and How Nations Trade

ESSENTIAL QUESTION *Why do people trade?*

IT MATTERS BECAUSE

National, state, and local economies depend in large part on international trade.

Trade Between Nations

GUIDING QUESTION *Why do nations trade with one another?*

How is it that you can enjoy fresh summer fruit year-round? Why do Americans import cars from Japan or Korea, even though we can produce them at home? Why does the United States produce more than half of the world's corn?

Individual nations do not always have the necessary resources to make the products their people need and want. To solve this problem of scarcity, nations trade with one another. They trade food, manufactured goods, services, and even raw materials. Nations **import,** or bring into the country, goods produced in other nations. They **export,** or sell to other nations, goods they produce.

The main reason countries trade is because of **comparative advantage.** Comparative advantage is the ability to produce something at a lower opportunity cost than another country can. A simple example will explain how this works.

Suppose that two countries could produce only two goods, bicycles and bread. In each country, the opportunity cost of making bicycles is the bread it cannot produce while

PHOTO: (tl) Najlah Feanny/Corbis; (tcr) SUNNews.com; (tr) Guillen Photography/Alamy

Taking Notes: *Analyzing*

As you read, complete a graphic organizer listing positive and negative aspects of free trade.

Free Trade	
Positive	Negative

Content Vocabulary

- import
- export
- comparative advantage
- protectionism
- tariff
- quota

its resources are being used to make bicycles. Suppose that Country *A* could produce one bicycle or 10 units of bread while Country *B* could produce one bicycle or 15 units of bread. Country *A* thus has a lower opportunity cost. As a result, it has the comparative advantage in producing bicycles.

A country's factors of production—natural resources, labor, capital, and entrepreneurs—often determine its comparative advantage. For example, China's vast population gives it a large labor force. Many of the people in China are unskilled workers who earn low wages. As a result, China has a comparative advantage in manufacturing goods that need a lot of labor to produce. Nations with large areas of farm and ranch land—like Brazil and the United States—have a comparative advantage in farm exports. Brazil is the world's largest exporter of beef.

Some less advanced economies specialize in a single export. These economies are known as single-resource economies. Reliance on a single export, however, makes a nation's economy vulnerable to price changes in the marketplace. Diversified economies, which export a variety of products, are better able to respond to market changes.

Managing Trade

When you shop, how important to you is the price of an item? To most people, it is very important. Because many consumers want low prices, many of the nation's stores line their shelves with products from nations with low labor costs, such as China. China can produce many goods more cheaply than the United States can. Consumers benefit when they buy these less costly products. When they do, however, they take business away from domestic companies, or companies operating in the United States. This can hurt those companies, leading them to cut production and lay off their workers.

PHOTO: Najlah Feanny/Corbis

Many large retailers import a large share of the products they sell, many of them from China. One reason they do so is to keep prices low.

▶ CRITICAL THINKING
Analyze What comparative advantage does China have?

- free trade
- balance of trade
- exchange rate

import to buy goods from another country

export to sell goods to other countries

comparative advantage a country's ability to produce a good more efficiently than other countries can

Lesson 1 **611**

Trade barriers raise prices for consumers. Many workers, though, believe that having barriers to protect industries will save their jobs. Members of Congress sometimes face votes on whether or not to pass trade barriers or to enter into free trade agreements. As a citizen, you will have to evaluate these plans and let members of Congress know what you think about them.

Trade Barriers

Countries with industries that are hurt in this way by foreign trade often resort to protectionism. **Protectionism** is the use of tactics that make imported goods more expensive than domestic goods. Governments try to protect home industries in three ways: with tariffs, import quotas, or subsidies.

A **tariff** is a tax on imports. The goal is to make the price of imported goods higher than the price of those goods produced at home. For example, in the past few years, several U.S. tire manufacturers stopped making tires. They could not compete with cheap tires made in China. To help the U.S. tire industry, President Barack Obama placed a tariff on Chinese tires. The tariff added 35 percent to the cost of tires made in China.

People may want a product so badly that higher prices do not stop them from buying it. In this case, a country can block trade by using a **quota.** An import quota limits the amount of a particular good that enters a country. For example, the United States has a long history of putting quotas on sugar imports. These limits help keep prices higher for domestic producers.

Another way governments protect domestic industries is with subsidies. A subsidy is a payment or other benefit given by government to help a domestic producer. The United States and many European nations pay subsidies to farmers. These payments help farmers keep their prices competitive.

These methods to limit imports have a major drawback. In exchange for protecting jobs, they raise prices on goods.

Free Trade Agreements

Almost all economists agree that the total cost of trade barriers is higher than their benefits. For this reason, most countries now try to reduce trade barriers, a policy known as **free trade.** To increase trade, countries often join together with a few key trading partners to set up areas of free trade.

In 1994 the United States, Canada, and Mexico joined together to create the largest free trade zone in the world. In the North American Free Trade Agreement (NAFTA), the three countries agreed to remove most trade barriers. Since then, trade among the three nations has more than tripled. This increase in trade has brought lower prices and a greater variety of goods to consumers in all three countries. However, many companies hurt by these imports lost sales and had to close factories. As a result, thousands of jobs have been lost.

Reading**HELP**DESK

protectionism the use of tactics that make imported goods more expensive than domestic goods

tariff a tax on an imported good

quota a limit on the amount of foreign goods imported into a country

free trade the lack of trade restrictions among countries

IMPORTS AND EXPORTS, SELECTED NATIONS

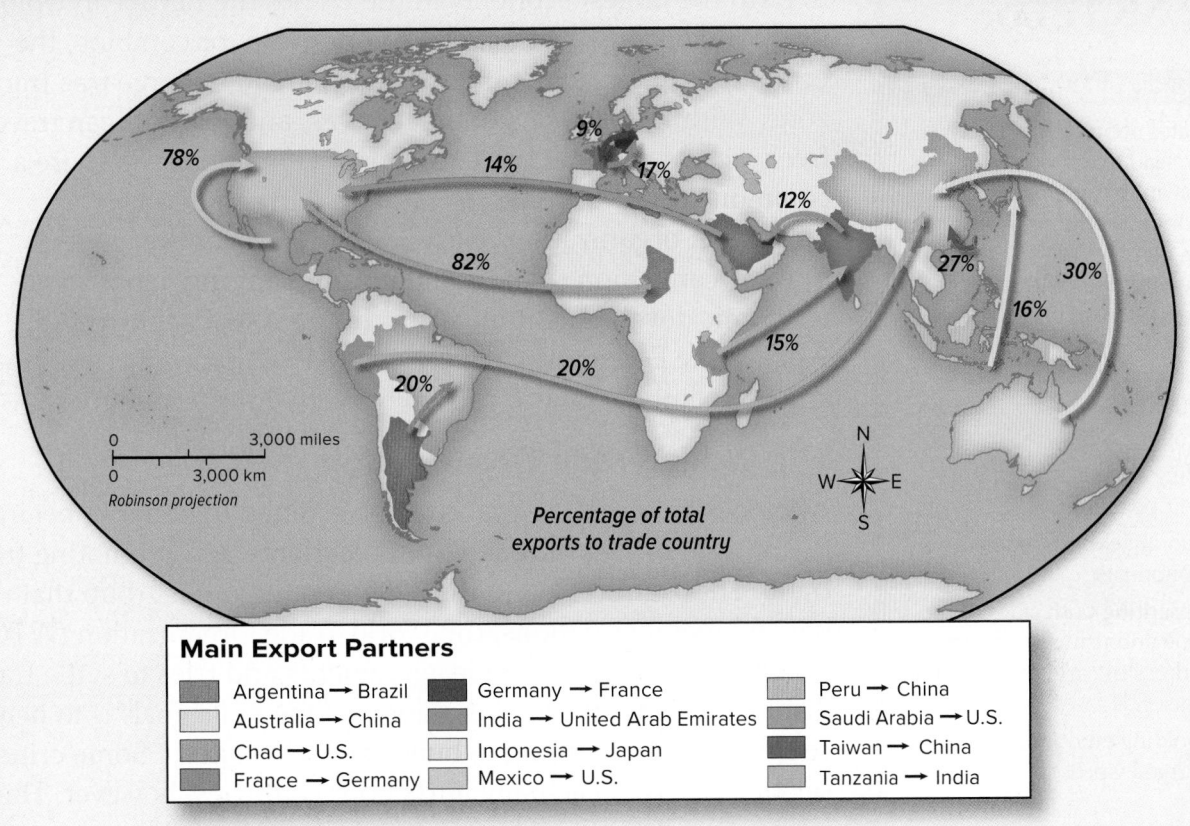

Percentage of total exports to trade country

0 — 3,000 miles
0 — 3,000 km
Robinson projection

Main Export Partners

- Argentina → Brazil
- Australia → China
- Chad → U.S.
- France → Germany
- Germany → France
- India → United Arab Emirates
- Indonesia → Japan
- Mexico → U.S.
- Peru → China
- Saudi Arabia → U.S.
- Taiwan → China
- Tanzania → India

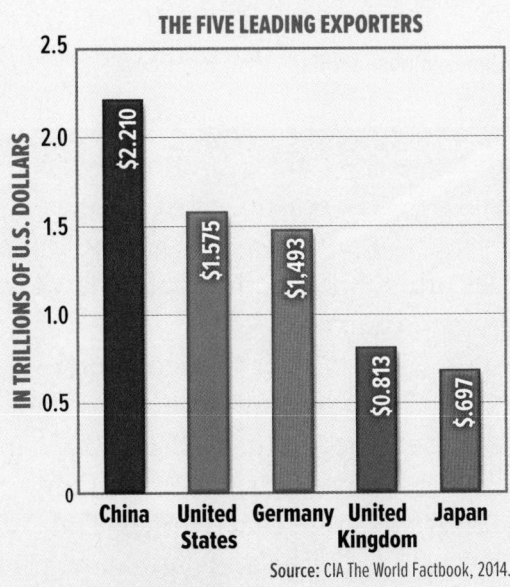

THE FIVE LEADING EXPORTERS

IN TRILLIONS OF U.S. DOLLARS

- China $2.210
- United States $1.575
- Germany $1.493
- United Kingdom $0.813
- Japan $.697

Source: CIA The World Factbook, 2014.

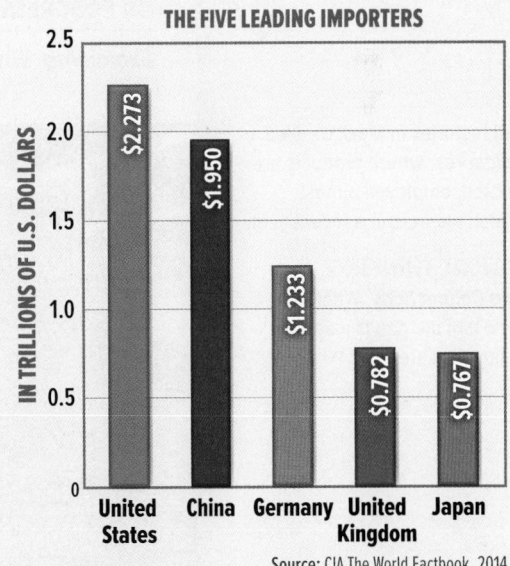

THE FIVE LEADING IMPORTERS

IN TRILLIONS OF U.S. DOLLARS

- United States $2.273
- China $1.950
- Germany $1.233
- United Kingdom $0.782
- Japan $0.767

Source: CIA The World Factbook, 2014.

INFOGRAPHIC

The map shows the major destination of exports from a few nations. The percentage figure is the share of all the exports that go to the nation's destination.

1 LOCATION Which two nations are the main export partners of the largest number of nations shown?

2 CRITICAL THINKING
Drawing Conclusions Which nation exports more than the United States?

Debates about economic issues often lead to strong arguments. Some are based on facts and reasoning; some are based more on emotion. When evaluating the statements of writers or speakers, look for signs that they are basing their ideas on reason rather than emotion. These signs include the following:

- Using statistics to support their positions
- Quoting experts, such as economists
- Presenting both sides of the issue and using reason to address the arguments of the other side
- Avoiding emotionally charged words

Special factories in Mexico called *maquiladoras*, where products are assembled, employed almost 1.8 million workers in a recent year.

▶ **CRITICAL THINKING**
Making Connections Where do you think most of the goods made in these factories are sold? Why?

The benefits of free trade encouraged 28 European nations to form the largest economy in the world, the European Union (EU). The purpose of the EU is to **integrate**, or combine, the economies of all its members. The EU creates a large free trade zone. Within this area, goods, services, and workers can travel freely across national borders. Most EU nations even share a common currency called the euro, making trade easier.

Similar organizations exist in other parts of the world. The African Union (AU) promotes unity among nations and economic development in Africa. In the Asia-Pacific region, Asia-Pacific Economic Cooperation (APEC) promotes free trade among members. It also tries to build nations' economies.

The World Trade Organization

After World War II, several countries joined together to begin the process of restoring the world economy and promoting free trade. These efforts led to the 1995 founding of a group that now has 160 member nations, the World Trade Organization (WTO).

The WTO oversees trade agreements and tries to settle trade disputes among its member nations. One of its goals is to help countries that are trying to build their economies. Some critics say that the WTO actually hurts poor countries, however. They charge that its policies favor big corporations and hurt workers, the environment, and poor countries.

✓ **PROGRESS CHECK**

Explaining Why do nations sometimes impose tariffs?

PHOTO: SUN/Newscom

Reading Strategy: *Organizing*

Organize information on the World Trade Organization by taking notes under three headings: *Description, Purpose,* and *Criticisms.* Write details from the text under the appropriate heading.

Academic Vocabulary

integrate to combine multiple components into a functioning whole

AMERICAN ENTREPRENEURS

• Walter Elias Disney, cofounder of The Walt Disney

Walt Disney once said that curiosity and courage were keys to success. In creating what became one of the world's largest companies, he showed both.

Walter Elias Disney was born in Chicago in 1901. As a boy, he loved to draw. In his early twenties, Disney started a company to make short films. The business failed, but Disney tried again. Moving to Hollywood, he began making short cartoons. Curious about adding sound to film, Disney made a short cartoon featuring a new character—Mickey Mouse. Audiences loved it. Over the next few years, Disney enjoyed growing success making short cartoons.

Meanwhile, Disney had his staff work on a bold new project—a full-length cartoon. Critics doubted that audiences would accept one, but Disney tried.

His first attempt—*Snow White and the Seven Dwarfs* (1937)—attracted large audiences.

In 1954 he started the first of two shows using a new medium, television. That same year, he opened a new kind of amusement park, Disneyland. More than a decade later, Disney built an even bigger park in Florida called Disney World. Though it opened after his death, it was a fitting tribute to a man of vision and courage.

Epcot, a theme park in Walt Disney World, attracts 10 million visitors each year.

Succeeding in Business

Describe how Disney showed curiosity and courage in business.

Balance of Trade

GUIDING QUESTION *How does a nation's trade balance affect its economy?*

A country may sell more or fewer goods and services to another country than it buys from that country. The difference between the value of a nation's imports and the value of its exports is the **balance of trade.** That balance can be positive or negative.

Positive Balance of Trade

When the value of a nation's exports is greater than the value of its imports, it has a positive balance of trade. If a country's exports are worth $100 billion and its imports are worth $70 billion, the country has a positive balance of trade of $30 billion.

A positive balance of trade is called a *trade surplus*. A country that has a trade surplus for a long period of time will find that the value of its currency goes up in international currency markets. Currencies are bought and sold just like goods and services. As a result, the value of a currency, like the value of a good or service, can go up or down.

balance of trade the difference between the value of a nation's imports and its exports

Negative Balance of Trade

When a nation imports more than it exports, it has a *negative* balance of trade. Suppose a country exports $70 billion in goods and imports $100 billion. If so, it has a negative balance of trade of $30 billion. This is called a *trade deficit*.

If trade deficits happen year after year, they hurt a nation in two ways. First, low demand for domestic goods will slow production of those goods at home. That can lead to job losses. Second, a country with ongoing trade deficits will see the value of its currency fall.

Role of Currency and Exchange Rates

Nations like to use their own currency to carry out trade. American companies want to use the dollar. Japanese companies use Japan's currency, which is called the yen. The two currencies differ in value, however. Their value in relation to each other is set by supply and demand. The value of one currency in terms of another is its **exchange rate.**

Suppose the United States wants to import goods from Japan. Japan wants to be paid in its own currency. As a result, the United States must sell dollars and buy yen. This makes more dollars available in the markets where currencies are bought and sold. The higher supply of dollars in these markets drives down the value of the dollar. In this way, excessive imports hurt a nation by lowering the value of its currency.

The lower currency value might not be completely bad. It should help the country increase its exports. The reason is simple. Because its currency is worth less, the prices of its goods go down. That makes them more attractive to other countries. The reverse is also true. If a country has an ongoing trade surplus, the value of its currency will rise.

exchange rate the value of a nation's currency in relation to another nation's currency

 PROGRESS CHECK

Defining What is the exchange rate?

LESSON 1 REVIEW

Review Vocabulary

1. What is the difference between an *import* and an *export*?

2. What is the *balance of trade*, and how does it go from negative to positive?

Answer the Guiding Questions

3. *Identifying the Main Idea* What role do trade organizations play in trade?

4. *Explaining* How does a trade surplus affect the value of a nation's currency?

5. **ARGUMENT** Suppose you are a policy adviser to the president. Write a letter to persuade the president to lift or impose trade barriers. Cite specific reasons for your recommendation.

Issues to Debate

Should We Allow More Offshore Drilling?

Some of the oil that belongs to the United States is found on the ocean floor. Starting in the 1970s, though, people became worried about drilling for this oil. They feared it could cause harm to the environment. In response, Congress banned drilling in about 80 percent of the country's outer continental shelf (OCS). The OCS is the seafloor near the coast. In the early 2000s, President George W. Bush supported exploring for oil in these areas. That step became a reality under President Barack Obama in early 2010.

Then, in April 2010, an oil rig in the Gulf of Mexico exploded, killing 11 workers and causing a massive oil spill. This accident and its results made many people rethink the idea of expanding offshore drilling. Should the United States continue to look for oil under the sea?

Offshore oil platforms, like this one in the Gulf of Mexico, accounted for about one-third of U.S. oil production in 2009.

Yes

The United States imports nearly 60 percent of the oil it uses. Oil imports affect the economy and the balance of trade. Supporters of offshore drilling want the nation to rely less on foreign oil.

"[O]ffshore drilling is good policy for one simple reason: America is going to use a lot of oil for many years to come, and . . . it makes sense to produce more of it at home. . . . Domestic production also creates jobs and tax revenues for state and federal coffers [government funds] that can be used for environmental purposes . . . [such as] development of clean energy technologies that might someday make oil obsolete."

—Samuel Thernstrom,
American Enterprise Institute

No

Opponents of offshore drilling think that the oil it would produce is not enough to reduce the need for foreign oil. They believe that drilling for oil also harms the environment and industries near the oil wells. They want the nation to use other fuels.

"Not only are our coastal ecosystems at stake, but so is America's ocean-based economy, which each year generates more than $230 billion. . . . If we want to boost our domestic oil supply, we should focus on enhanced oil recovery from existing fields, a process that can supply more than 10 times the amount of oil that could be produced by drilling in our oceans."

—Frances Beinecke,
Natural Resources Defense Council

Debating the Issue

1. **Identifying** How much of the oil it uses does the United States import?

2. **Identifying the Main Idea** What are the potential benefits of offshore drilling?

3. **Explaining** What are the risks of offshore drilling?

4. **Drawing Conclusions** Do you think offshore drilling should be carried out or not? Explain.

TEXT: Frances Beinecke, "What the Spill Means for Offshore Drilling" From *The New York Times*, April 29 © 2010. Reprinted with permission from the Natural Resources Defense Council.
TEXT: Samuel Thernstrom, "What the Spill Means for Offshore Drilling" From *The New York Times*, April 29 © 2010. Used by permission of Samuel Thernstrom. PHOTO: Guillen Photography/Alamy

networks
There's More Online!

☑ **GRAPHIC ORGANIZER**
Market, Command, and Mixed Economies

☑ **MAP**
GDP Per Capita, Selected Nations

☑ **SLIDE SHOW**
Post-Soviet Russia

☑ **CHART**
Comparing Economies: Russia, China, and the United States

☑ **INFOGRAPHIC**
Social Statistics Comparison, Selected Regions

☑ **VIDEO**

Lesson 2
Economic Systems and Development

ESSENTIAL QUESTION *Why and how do people make economic choices?*

IT MATTERS BECAUSE
The type of economic system determines the way in which a society organizes the production and consumption of goods and services.

Market Economies

GUIDING QUESTION *What characteristics do market economies share?*

Have you ever been to a flea market? You might see a person at one table selling used comic books. He can sell them because they are his to sell. You can choose to buy comic books from that seller, from another seller, or not at all. The seller sets the price of those comic books based on how much he thinks people will pay for them. If no one wants to buy his comic books at that price, he will probably lower the price. On the other hand, if many people are willing to pay that price, he may raise the price even more. Other tables at the flea market will have people selling other goods, which might be things they made by hand or used items they no longer want. The buying and selling in a flea market is an example of a free market economy.

A market economy is one of the several types of economies that answer the three basic questions of what to produce, how to produce, and for whom to produce. How a society answers these questions determines its economic system. In a market economy, it is individuals who answer these three questions. In answering the questions, they make economic decisions.

PHOTO: (tl) David McNew/Getty Images; (tc) AP Photo/Lu Heung Shing; (tcr) Franz-Marc Frei/Corbis; (tr) Frédéric Soltan/Corbis

---

Reading**HELP**DESK

Taking Notes: *Categorizing*

As you read, complete a graphic organizer to identify features of different types of economies.

Market	Command	Mixed

Content Vocabulary

• **privatization**
• **mixed economy**
• **developed country**
• **developing country**

How a Market Economy Works

In a market economy, individuals act in their own self-interest to answer the three basic questions. No central authority makes these decisions. Instead, the market economy seems to run itself. In a market economy, private individuals—not the government—own the factors of production. Those factors are natural resources, capital, labor, and entrepreneurship. Since they own the factors of production, individuals have the power to decide how to use them.

In a market economy, supply and demand combine to set the prices of goods and services. The way they interact is what drives a market economy.

Characteristics of a Market Economy

Market economies give people a lot of freedom. People are free to own property, control their own labor, and make their own economic decisions. Such freedom gives people who live in market economies a high level of satisfaction. Market economies work best because economies are too complex to be controlled by a single authority.

Another feature of a market economy is competition. Sellers compete with each other to attract the most buyers. Buyers compete with each other to find the best prices.

Most countries with high GDPs per capita have a market economy. As you recall, GDP per capita is the total value of goods and services produced in a country divided by the number of people in that country. GDP per capita lets us compare one nation's economic output to another's without regard to the size of the two economies. The map on GDP per capita shows the GDP per capita for selected nations.

Market economies do have some disadvantages. Although they enjoy a high degree of success, they do not grow at a steady rate. Instead, they go through periods of growth and decline. While the periods of growth are much longer than the periods of decline, people can be hurt in the down times. For example, many people lose their jobs during down times.

Lesson 2 **619**

21st Century
SKILLS

Self-Direction

A market economy gives freedom to workers and consumers. With that freedom comes responsibility. This means that people are responsible for the results of their choices. Workers can choose their careers. But they also face the risk of being laid off during market downturns, or even losing their job if the business closes. Workers may need to continuously learn new skills in order to remain competitive in the job market. So, continuing education and job training will be especially important in the twenty-first century.

One feature of a market economy is competition. These businesses, located close to one another, must compete for customers. Customers can compare prices and service and make a choice.

► **CRITICAL THINKING**
Making Connections Why is competition important to consumers?

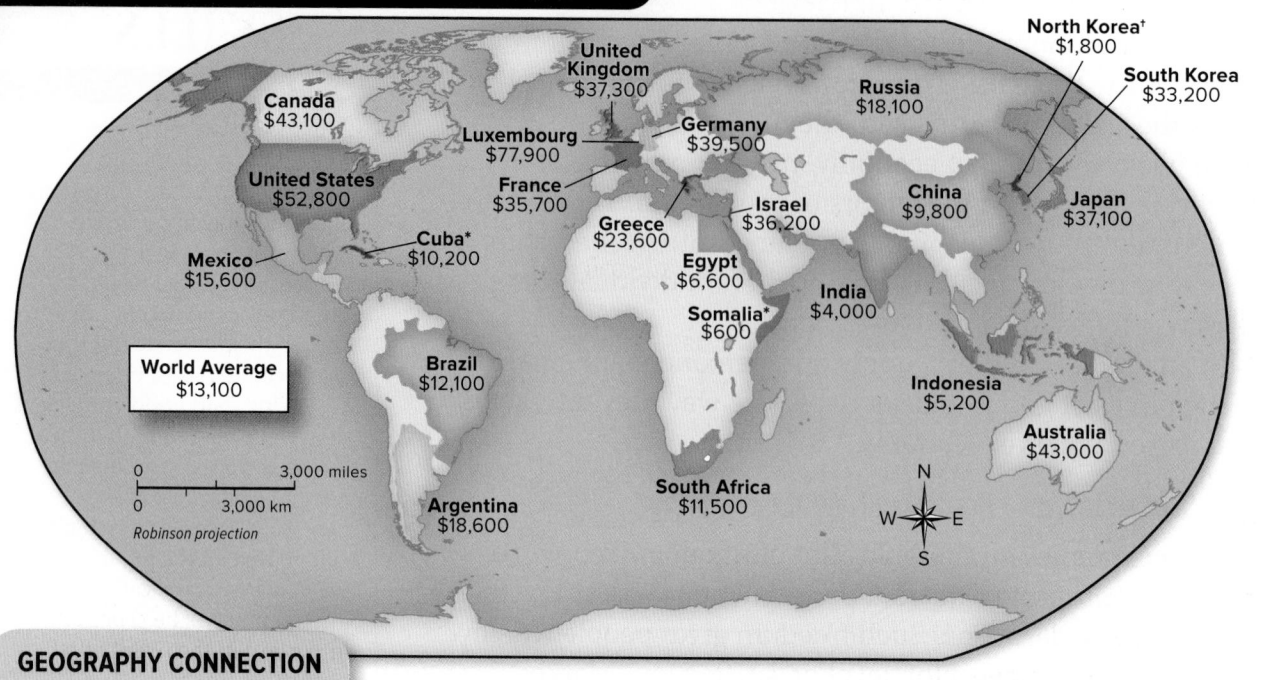

Source: CIA The World Factbook, 2014. *figures are 2010 estimates; †figure is 2011 estimate

GEOGRAPHY CONNECTION

The map shows GDP per capita for only a few of all the nations in the world.

1 **PLACE** Where does the United States rank in GDP per capita?

2 **CRITICAL THINKING**
Making Inferences Which country, North Korea or South Korea, do you think has a market economy? Why?

Another problem is that businesses, driven by profit, might not give workers good working conditions or high wages. The profit motive can also result in negative externalities. These are the harmful side effects of business activities that affect third parties. Pollution is one example.

☑ PROGRESS CHECK

Identifying the Main Idea Who owns the factors of production in a market economy?

Command Economies

GUIDING QUESTION *Who makes the basic economic decisions in a command economy?*

The opposite of a market economy is a command economy. In a command economy, the government owns the factors of production. It has powerful planning agencies that make the major economic decisions. They decide what goods will be produced, how they will be produced, and to whom they will go. Individuals have little say over how the economy operates.

Most command economies have their roots in the system known as socialism. In the early 1800s, some people came to believe that aiding oppressed workers required eliminating

Reading HELPDESK

Reading Strategy: *Summarizing*

To summarize a piece of writing, briefly restate only the most important ideas. Summarize the text under "Command Economies." Begin by noting that in command economies, governments, not individuals, make economic choices.

privatization the process of changing from state-owned businesses, factories, and farms to ones owned by private citizens

capitalism completely. They advocated socialism, the belief that the means of production should be owned and controlled by society, either directly or through the government. Socialists felt that this system would distribute wealth more equally among all citizens.

The central planning that is related to command economies can work in rare instances. In times of emergency, it can direct resources where they are needed most. For example, central planning helped the Soviet Union rapidly rebuild its economy after World War II.

Characteristics of a Command Economy

Command economies are not very efficient. As the map shows, Cuba and North Korea—which have command economies—have low GDPs per capita. In a command economy, people often face shortages of goods and services and products of poor quality. Finally, command economies tend to grow more slowly than market economies do.

Switch to a Market Economy

These problems convinced several countries with command economies to make the switch to market economies. This movement swept through Eastern Europe and Russia around 1990. The change has been difficult, especially for citizens. First, they had to go through privatization. **Privatization** is the process of changing state-owned businesses, factories, and farms into ones owned by private citizens. Second, people had to learn to make decisions in an economy based on prices. Third, businesses had to learn how to work more efficiently so that they could earn a profit. Some countries have not yet seen the positive results they had hoped for.

China has been more successful, though. Starting in the late 1970s, China began adopting some features of a market economy. The result has been a dramatic rise in GDP and GDP per capita. China now has the world's second-largest economy after the United States.

✓ PROGRESS CHECK

Identifying What is the government's role in a command economy?

PHOTO: AP Photo/Liu Heung Shing

Taking Notes

What are some of the challenges faced by societies switching from a command to a market economy? Reread the paragraph and make a list.

The Soviet Union had a command economy, and its people often faced long lines for few goods.

▶ CRITICAL THINKING

Identifying What other problems are found in a command economy?

Mixed Economies

GUIDING QUESTION *Why do most countries have a mixed economy?*

The U.S. economic system is not a pure market economy. In fact, today most nations of the world combine elements of command with market economies to form **mixed economies.** In a mixed economy, both markets and the government play a role in economic activity. The U.S. economy tends more toward a market economy so it is considered a market-**oriented** economy.

In the United States, the principles of free enterprise underlie the economy. Nevertheless, government has several important roles, too. First, the government provides some goods and services. The government builds roads and bridges and provides schooling to children. Second, the government works to make sure that markets are competitive. Third, it regulates some businesses. For example, the government has passed laws setting minimum pay for workers. Other laws try to ensure that workplaces and products are safe. Although these laws put some restrictions on business owners, the government passed them because it believed they were needed to protect citizens.

✓ PROGRESS CHECK

Explaining What are signs that the United States does not have a pure market economy?

CHART SKILLS

The United States has long enjoyed the benefits of having a market-oriented economy. Russia and China are just making the transition.

► CRITICAL THINKING

1 *Comparing* In what area does China still lag well behind the United States?

2 *Making Inferences* In what area of economic performance has China surpassed the success of the United States?

COMPARING ECONOMIES: RUSSIA, CHINA, AND THE UNITED STATES

	RUSSIA	CHINA	UNITED STATES
Population	142,478,272	1,355,692,576	318,892,103
GDP per capita	$18,100	$9,800	$52,800
Labor Force • Agriculture • Industry • Services	9.7% 27.8% 62.5%	33.6% 30.3% 36.1%	0.7% 20.3% 79.0%
Exports	$515 billion	$2,210 billion	$1,575 billion
Imports	$341 billion	$1,950 billion	$2,273 billion

Source: CIA, *The World Factbook, 2014*; Statistics based on 2009–2013 estimates.

Reading**HELP**DESK

Academic Vocabulary

orient to tend toward a certain direction

mixed economy a system combining characteristics of more than one type of economy

developed country a country with a high standard of living, a high level of industrialization, and a high per capita income

developing country a country with a low per capita income in which a large number of people have a low standard of living

Developed and Developing Countries

GUIDING QUESTION *What kinds of challenges do developing countries face?*

Most countries with modern market economies enjoy a high standard of living. Standard of living is measured by such things as having plentiful goods and good health care. The countries with these features are called **developed countries.** Only about 35 countries in the world are considered developed. Examples are the United States, Canada, Japan, and Germany.

Some countries have taken steps to join this group. They have relied on building export industries to power growth. For this reason, they are called *newly industrialized countries.* China and India are examples. They have not yet reached the level of output of the developed countries. They are growing economic powers, though. Mexico is another example.

A large number of countries, however, do not have the advanced economies of the developed countries. Nor have they seen the growth of China and India. These countries are not very productive. They have low GDPs per capita. They are called **developing countries.** Many of these countries are trying to develop market economies. They face great difficulties, though.

Obstacles to Development

One major obstacle to development is a high rate of population growth. When population grows faster than GDP, GDP per capita declines. The result is that each person has a smaller share of what the economy produces. Countries with the highest rates of population growth tend to have the lowest GDPs per capita.

Countries with high rates of population growth face another difficulty. As more people are added to the population, these countries need to create more jobs.

Many developing countries have barriers to trade. They are trying to protect domestic jobs and young industries. Trade barriers, however, usually protect industries that are not efficient. Most economists think that these barriers actually hold back the countries' ability to build their economies.

Developing nations often lack the means to extract, use, and sell their resources. Developing countries that have no access to the sea may have difficulty getting their goods to other countries.

teen citizens in action

Helping Children to Better Health

Beatrice Thaman
Toledo, Ohio

Beatrice Thaman was, for many years, the only girl in a family of four boys. Her parents' decision to adopt a baby girl from a poor region of Guatemala did more than add a sister to her family. It inspired Beatrice to act. "I realized," she explains, "how easily my little sister Rose could have been one of those children living a life of poverty."

Beatrice read about the causes and effects of hunger on young children. In Guatemala, nearly half of all children under the age of five don't get enough healthful food. Beatrice decided to help poor children in Guatemala by working to provide them with vitamin tablets. Vitamins are important elements in food that are often missing from the diets of poor people. Beatrice contacted local pharmacies and wrote to drug companies asking them to provide vitamins for free. She gave speeches at local schools and asked for donations at school football games and her church.

Her efforts have paid off. Over the past three years, Beatrice has sent more than one million vitamins to Guatemala. That total equals a year's supply of vitamins for several thousand children. Beatrice says she "felt compelled to do this. I think about how lucky we are. We have so much. I want them to have a better life."

Citizenship and Teens

Why did Beatrice decide to work to help the poor children of Guatemala?

Lesson 2 **623**

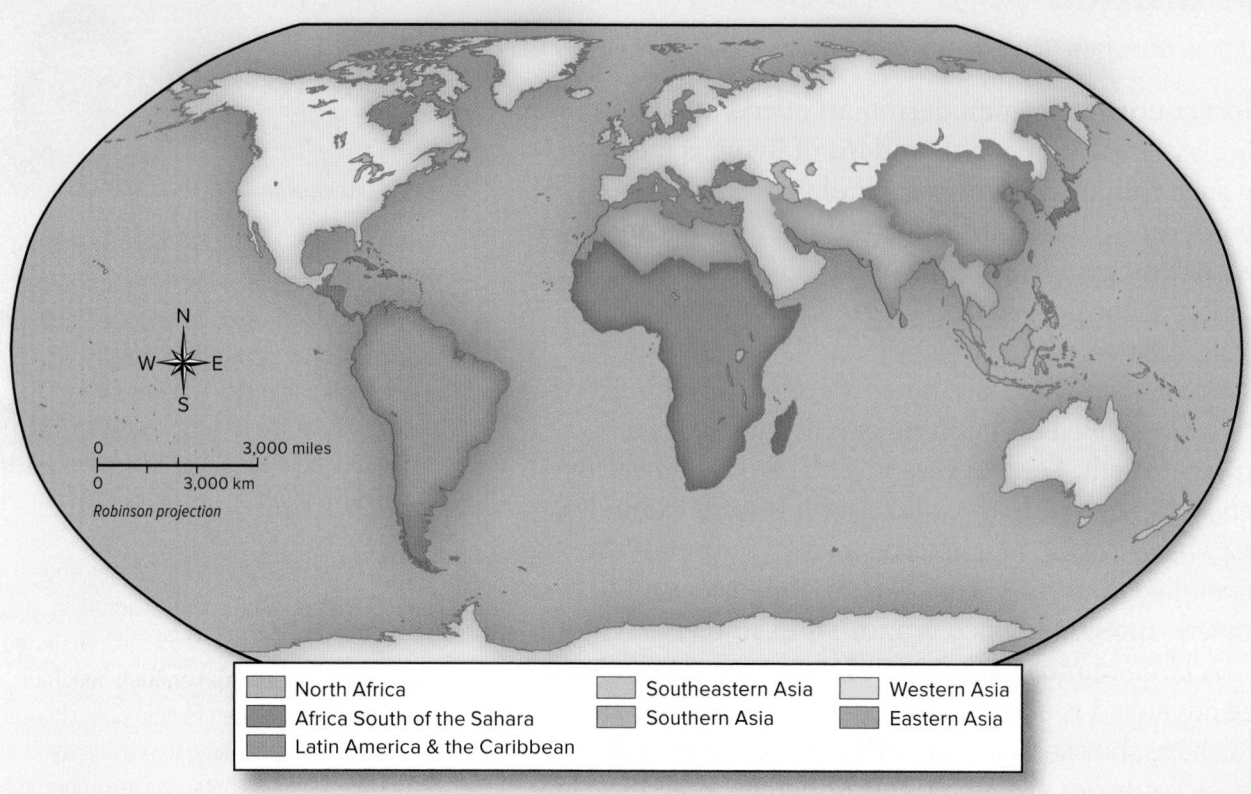

North Africa

Africa South of the Sahara

Latin America & the Caribbean

Southeastern Asia

Southern Asia

Western Asia

Eastern Asia

	Africa		Asia				Latin America & Caribbean
	Northern	South of the Sahara	Eastern	Southeastern	Southern	Western	
Health							
Proportion of undernourished population	<5%	26%	10%	14%	21%	7%	9%
Under 5 years of age mortality rate, per 1,000 live births	29	144	21	38	74	32	23
Employment							
Employment Rate	46%	65%	70%	66%	55%	44%	60%
Proportion of employed people living on less than $1.25 a day	4%	64%	13%	28%	51%	12%	8%
Education and Technology							
Enrolment in primary education	94%	76%	96%	95%	90%	88%	95%
Number of internet users per 100 population	19	6	25	14	6	24	29

Source: United Nations, The Millennium Development Goals Report, 2010.

INFOGRAPHIC

Economists use many different social statistics to determine standard of living, or how well off the people in a country are.

1 **Region** Which region has the lowest rates of enrollment in primary schools and the lowest Internet use?

2 CRITICAL THINKING

Making Inferences How might these statistics affect the economies of nations in the region?

Less-developed countries may have single-resource economies, while developed countries have diversified economies. In a single-resource economy, a nation depends on a single export product for its economic growth. A failure of a crop or a similar problem with the one resource a country exports makes it difficult for a developing country to make progress.

War is another huge obstacle in many developing countries. Fighting kills people and forces others to move away. It damages a nation's resources. Productivity slows, and people face shortages of food, health care, and education. As a result, countries have more difficulty investing in their economies.

Many developing countries also face the problem of severe debt. Many of them once borrowed large sums of money from wealthy nations to encourage economic growth. That growth was not fast enough, however, to pay off those debts. Now, they have to use too much of their income to pay off their debt.

Corruption has been a problem in some countries, too. Some leaders stole money that was meant to pay for economic development projects or other projects to help their people. Corrupt leaders base their economic decisions not on what is best for their country, but on what is best for themselves.

Any one of these problems would be difficult for any nation to solve. However, many developing nations have to deal with two or three serious problems at the same time. As a result, economic progress has been difficult for them to achieve.

PHOTO: Frédéric Soltan/Corbis

India has overcome obstacles to development by lowering trade barriers. As industry has grown, service businesses, like this architect's office, have grown as well.

▶ **CRITICAL THINKING**
Assessing How might growth in industry spur growth in services?

 **PROGRESS CHECK**

Explaining How do trade barriers hurt development?

LESSON 2 REVIEW

Review Vocabulary

1. What is *privatization* and why have some governments used it?

2. What is the difference between a *developed country* and a *developing country*?

Answer the Guiding Questions

3. ***Identifying the Main Idea*** What are some of the benefits of a market economy?

4. ***Identifying the Main Idea*** Why do command economies move toward privatization?

5. ***Explaining*** How does the government support free enterprise in a mixed economy?

6. ***Concluding*** What are some obstacles to development that face developing countries?

7. **INFORMATIVE/EXPLANATORY** Describe the economy of the United States and how its characteristics contribute to a high standard of living.

Write your answers on a separate sheet of paper.

1 Writing Activity

EXPLORING THE ESSENTIAL QUESTIONS

Why do people trade?

Why and how do people make economic choices?

Describe the role of individuals in making economic choices in a market economy. How might this role change or remain the same in a mixed economy?

2 21st Century Skills

COMPARE DATA Choose two developed countries and two developing countries. Find data on their GDP per capita, rate of population growth, type of government, type of economic system, and level of debt. Identify whether they are single-resource or diversified economies. You can find the data at the Web site for the *CIA World Factbook,* or you can consult another equally reliable source. Make a table to display your data. Finally, write two paragraphs that describe the economy of the poorest-performing country you researched and identify the obstacles to its development.

Being an Active Citizen

Where are the products you use every day made? Choose 10 items in your household that you or another family member use regularly. Choose a variety of goods, such as clothing, kitchen appliances, electronic devices, and toys. Pick goods that have labels identifying where they were made. Make a list. How many of these items were made in the United States? In what other countries were the items made? Write a paragraph explaining how you think your choices to purchase these items affect the nation's economy and whether you would make different choices in the future. Why or why not?

Understanding Visuals

Study the cartoon. What do the images of the two vessels stand for? What is the cartoonist saying about them?

REVIEW THE GUIDING QUESTIONS

Directions: Choose the best answer for each question.

1 Why do nations engage in trade?

A. to protect home industries

B. to get rid of what they do not want

C. to dump unwanted currency

D. to solve the problem of scarcity

2 What are tariffs, quotas, and subsidies all examples of?

F. free trade

G. the balance of trade

H. protectionism

I. exports

3 Why are exchange rates needed?

A. to turn all export sales into dollars

B. because each trading partner wants to use its own currency

C. to use the standard currency for trade, the euro

D. because the World Trade Organization requires it

4 What is most likely to happen to a country's economy if the value of its currency goes down?

F. Its exports go up because they become cheaper.

G. Its imports go down because they become cheaper.

H. It gains export jobs because labor becomes less costly.

I. Workers benefit because prices go down.

5 Which of these is a problem with market economies?

A. They are inefficient.

B. They cycle through periods of growth and decline.

C. They often result in shortages of consumer goods.

D. They tend to have lower GDP per capita.

6 Which nation has the second-largest economy in the world, yet a GDP per capita that is much lower than the U.S. GDP per capita?

F. China

G. France

H. Germany

I. Russia

DBQ ANALYZING DOCUMENTS

Directions: Analyze the excerpt and answer the questions that follow.

"The United States will focus our development efforts on [give aid to] countries like Tanzania that promote good governance [government] and democracy. . . . Because over the long run, democracy and economic growth go hand in hand."

—President Barack Obama, Millennium Development Goals Summit, 2010

7 **Summarizing** Which of the following best summarizes the statement by President Obama?

A. The U.S. will give aid to developing countries that are democratic.

B. Tanzania deserves aid because its government has excellent planners.

C. Tanzania is the only country to which the United States will give aid.

D. The United States refuses to give aid to any developing country.

8 **Identifying** Which statement does the excerpt support?

F. Poor countries lack resources.

G. The United States should give more money to Tanzania.

H. Population growth is bad for development.

I. Good government benefits economic growth.

SHORT RESPONSE

"The evidence points to NAFTA being mostly good for the countries involved. And if American factory workers want to see where their jobs have gone, they'd do better to look east than south. Labor may be cheaper in Mexico, but it's cheaper still in Asia. . . . In 2007, the U.S. trade deficit with China hit $256 billion. The deficit with Mexico, despite reaching an all-time high of $74 billion, was less than a third as big. . . . The U.S. trade deficit with Canada . . . was not far behind at $64 billion."

—Columnist Froma Harrop, 2008

9 According to the passage, what is the real threat to American jobs? Explain.

10 Why is the U.S. trade deficit with China more of a concern than its trade deficit with its NAFTA partners?

EXTENDED RESPONSE

11 **Informative/Explanatory** Suppose you were an economic adviser to the president. What policies would you recommend about joining trade agreements? Why?

Need Extra Help?

If You've Missed Question	**1**	**2**	**3**	**4**	**5**	**6**	**7**	**8**	**9**	**10**	**11**
Review Lesson	1	1	1	1	2	2	2	2	1	1	1, 2

TEXT: NAFTA gets a bum rap, by Froma Harrop. Published by The Providence Journal Co., February 24, 2008. By permission of Froma Harrop and Creators Syndicate, Inc.

The United States and Foreign Affairs

netw⊕rks

There's More Online about the United States and foreign affairs.

CHAPTER 24

ESSENTIAL QUESTIONS • *Why and how do nations interact with one another?*
• *Why does conflict develop?*

The Story Matters...

In the summer of 2010, monsoon rains caused the worst flooding in Pakistan's history. Thousands died. Roads, bridges, and power systems were destroyed. Over 650,000 homes washed away.

Flood victims were desperate for food, clean drinking water, shelter, and medical treatment. They also had to rebuild their country. The cost was more than Pakistan could afford.

The United Nations (UN), the largest international governmental organization in the world, asked its 192 member nations to help. Many countries, including the United States, responded. They gave money, food, water, and medical aid. They also sent construction supplies and specialists to help rebuild Pakistan.

◄ *Pakistani children wait for their food ration at a flood relief camp.*

PHOTO: Pedro Ugarte/AFP/Getty Images

629

Real-Life Civics

▶ PEACEKEEPING

Nations form governmental organizations to address international issues. The UN, for example, deals with many matters of concern to its members. One of its vital jobs is helping to maintain world peace and to rebuild war-torn nations. In 2014, the UN had peacekeeping forces in at least 16 locations around the world. One such place was Kosovo in eastern Europe. That nation had been taken over by its neighbor, Serbia, and a brutal war followed. After the war, the UN Interim Administration Mission helped Kosovo set up a new government. UN volunteers also helped citizens rebuild their lives.

Units within the UN also work to improve world health, protect children, promote education, and encourage economic development in poorer nations.

▷ These UN soldiers are on duty at the Macedonian border with Kosovo.

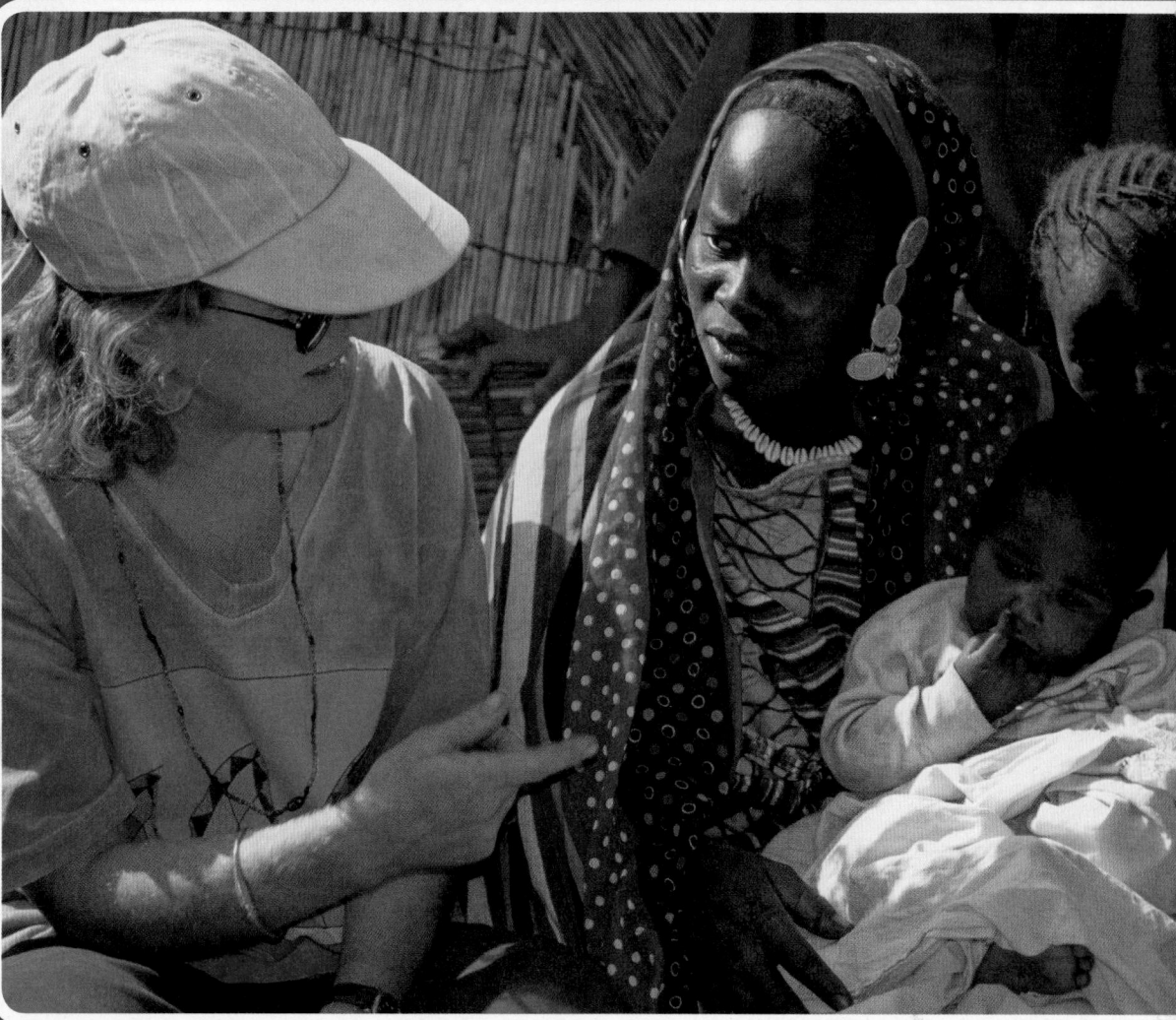

A Peace Corps volunteer gives a mother some advice about caring for her baby.

▶ **EDUCATING** Unlike the United Nations, which has many member nations, the Peace Corps is an entirely American volunteer organization run by the U.S. government. Founded in 1961, the Peace Corps now has members in 65 countries all over the world. They train and educate the people of those countries. Peace Corps volunteers perform a wide variety of tasks to meet the needs of the residents in each place. For example, they teach math to children, educate communities about health issues, train businesspeople in how to use the latest computer software, and help farmers to produce more food. They also help Americans and people in other nations to understand each other better.

CIVIC LITERACY

★ ★ ★ ★

Inferring Why might government and volunteer organizations be willing to help people in need in countries around the world?

Your Opinion Would you be willing to volunteer for an organization such as the Peace Corps? What might be some benefits and difficulties of being a Peace Corps volunteer?

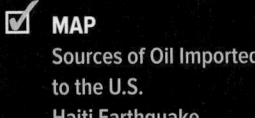

Lesson 1
Global Interdependence and Issues

ESSENTIAL QUESTION *Why and how do nations interact with one another?*

IT MATTERS BECAUSE
Growing global interdependence offers both opportunities and challenges for the people of the world.

Global Interdependence

GUIDING QUESTION *Why do nations depend upon one another?*

Would you like a banana for lunch tomorrow? If you live in the small part of the nation that is warm enough to grow bananas, you might pick one off a banana plant. More likely, though, you have to go to a store to buy a banana grown in another country. Importing bananas is one example of global interdependence. **Global interdependence** means that people and nations rely on one another for goods and services. If Americans want bananas, or other tropical fruit, they must trade with other nations to get them.

People around the world exchange what they have or make for things they do not have. This exchange involves both developed and developing nations. Developed nations usually buy raw materials and local products, such as bananas, from developing nations. Developing nations buy things like technology and medicine from developed countries.

Global Trade

Global trade occurs because nations have different needs, comparative advantages, and resources. These factors make trade among nations worthwhile—and perhaps even necessary.

PHOTO: (tl) Grant Faint/Stone/Getty Images; (tr) Brand X Pictures/Punchstock

Reading **HELP**DESK

Taking Notes: *Identifying*

As you read, complete a diagram like the one shown to list features of developing nations.

Developing Nations

Content Vocabulary
- **global interdependence**
- **trade war**
- **deforestation**
- **ethnic group**
- **terrorism**
- **refugee**

The United States is both a large exporter and a large importer. Many countries need things from the United States. The United States sells wheat, corn, computer software, aircraft, medical equipment, and machinery to nations that cannot produce these goods on their own. Poorer nations look to the United States for food, medicine, and defense weapons. People around the world are also eager to buy American entertainment products, such as movies, music, and video games.

The United States also depends on other nations for certain resources and products. For example, Americans use oil and natural gas to heat homes, to run factories, and to power cars. The United States uses almost 20 million barrels of oil per day. About 40 percent of that oil is imported. Canada, Saudi Arabia, Venezuela, and Mexico supply most of that oil.

Not all trade is based on need though. Comparative advantage also contributes to global trade. Low manufacturing costs in China, for instance, make the cost of Chinese goods attractive to other nations. As a result, China sells the electronics, textiles, plastics, furniture, and toys it makes around the world.

Finally, differing sets of natural resources play a role in global trade. The United States needs industrial diamonds to make certain goods. Since our nation does not have that resource, we must import them from South Africa, Democratic Republic of the Congo, and Botswana.

Global Economic Cooperation

Sometimes nations cooperate on trade issues. The 28 nations that belong to the European Union have few meaningful trade barriers with one another. The North American Free Trade Agreement (NAFTA) was written to end trade barriers among the United States, Canada, and Mexico. Other free trade agreements exist among nations in other parts of the world as well.

Of course, these agreements do not solve all trade-related problems. They do support global interdependence, however.

✓ PROGRESS CHECK

Summarizing What is global interdependence?

global interdependence the reliance of people and countries around the world on one another for goods and services

Bananas and other tropical fruits are exported to the United States from other nations in huge numbers.

▶ CRITICAL THINKING
Making Inferences What do you think are some of the costs involved for growers of bananas to export their crops to the United States?

PHOTO: Grant Faint/Stone/Getty Images

ARCTIC OCEAN

RUSSIA

IRAQ

CANADA

UNITED STATES

ATLANTIC OCEAN

KUWAIT

PACIFIC OCEAN

MEXICO

VENEZUELA

SAUDI ARABIA

COLOMBIA

NIGERIA

INDIAN OCEAN

ECUADOR

PACIFIC OCEAN

ANGOLA

N
W E
S

0   2000 miles
0   2000 km
Robinson projection

	70–110 million barrels per year
	110–300 million barrels per year
	More than 300 million barrels per year

Source: U.S. Energy Information Administration

GEOGRAPHY CONNECTION

The United States imports about half the oil it consumes.

1 **REGIONS** From what nations does the United States import the most oil?

2 **CRITICAL THINKING**
Inferring Based on this information, what can you infer about supplies of oil in Canada and Mexico?

Global Issues

GUIDING QUESTION *What are some consequences of global interdependence?*

Global interdependence has made people aware of issues that affect the world as a whole. Therefore, nations must cooperate, or work together, to find solutions to the challenges brought by increasing global contacts. However, a variety of political and cultural forces are also at work around the globe. Those forces do not always encourage nations to work together.

Costs of Competition and Trade

Global interdependence has increased trade and led to prosperity in many parts of the world. More and freer trade usually results in lower prices and more choices for consumers. However, trade can cause problems too. Companies may decide to move factories to other countries with lower labor costs. The cost of doing business or decreasing sales could cause some companies to close. In both cases, people lose their jobs. Many workers may not be able to find new jobs that pay as well as their former ones. They might have a difficult time learning new job skills. They might even have to sell their homes and move to other parts of the country to get jobs.

Reading**HELP**DESK

trade war economic conflict that occurs when one or more nations put up trade barriers to punish another nation for trade barriers it erected against them

Academic Vocabulary

stable not subject to major changes

Nations sometimes act to protect their industries from imports produced in countries that have cheaper labor. Countries may put up barriers to trade. These barriers have a cost, though. Tariffs may help home industries, but they hurt consumers by raising prices.

Another problem with trade barriers is that one set of barriers can lead to additional ones. In response to tariffs placed on the goods it produces, for example, a nation may put up its own trade barriers. A **trade war** could develop. In a trade war, one or more nations put up trade barriers to punish another nation for its trade barriers against them. The result is higher prices for everyone and fewer choices for consumers.

Rich and Poor Nations

A major challenge in the world today is the growing economic inequality among nations. Unequal levels of economic growth have led to a large gap between rich and poor nations. This gap is getting wider as well. Developing nations are making some economic progress, but many of them are not growing fast enough to catch up to the developed nations.

Nations that have grown wealthy because their economies are doing well are called developed nations. They generally have a high per capita GDP. They usually have political systems that are **stable,** or not subject to major changes. The United States, Germany, and Australia are examples of developed countries.

Other nations, called developing countries, have low per capita GDPs and low rates of growth. Several factors contribute to these problems. Some of these countries lack natural resources or have unskilled workers. Some struggle with political unrest. Some have poor schools. Many face serious health problems, such as a lack of clean water or high rates of infectious diseases.

One example of a developing nation is Haiti, the poorest nation in the Western Hemisphere. Haiti exports clothing, but these exports are not enough to sustain a strong, growing economy. Most of Haiti's people are poor and unskilled. Its political system has been unstable. Some elected leaders have even been illegally removed from office by military leaders. Few outside businesses want to invest in Haiti because of its history of political unrest. A devastating earthquake in 2010 caused more problems. As a result, Haiti depends on aid from other nations.

PHOTO: (tr) Courtesy of Neha Gupta; (br) Courtesy of Neha Gupta

teen citizens in action

Developing Nations by Empowering Orphans

Neha Gupta
Yardley, Pennsylvania

Neha Gupta reached across the globe to create an organization that seeks to empower children. Every year Neha and her family visit her grandparents in northern India. While there, they always volunteer at the Bal Kunj orphanage. These visits convinced Neha that the orphanage lacked the resources to provide an adequate education for the 200 orphaned or abandoned children living there.

When Neha returned home, she began raising money for the orphanage. Family and friends helped her make and sell wind chimes, as well as greeting cards created by the children at the orphanage. She sold these items door-to-door and at craft fairs.

As donations increased, Neha created Empower Orphans, a nonprofit organization that raises funds from businesses, civic groups, and charitable organizations to support the orphanage.

Every year Empower Orphans sponsors the education of 50 children at the orphanage, paying their school fees. It also holds a four-day medical clinic providing eye and dental screenings for about 350 children. In Pennsylvania, Neha has also worked with orphanages in Norristown and Warminster.

Citizenship and Teens

How is Neha helping the children at the Bal Kunj orphanage?

Develop and complete a two-column chart about conservation. Label the first column "Advantages" and the second column "Disadvantages" and list the information from your reading in the appropriate column.

Despite the harmful effects of deforestation, forests are still being cut down at an alarming rate.

▶ **CRITICAL THINKING**
Speculating Why do you think people continue to cut down forests?

Global Politics

As the global economy has spread, many political changes have taken place. East Asian countries now play a growing role in world affairs, and the nations of Europe are moving toward unity. The United States is concerned about its role in the world and the importance of working with other nations.

Nations have different forms of government and views of what is good for the world. These differences can lead to disagreements. For example, Venezuela criticizes the U.S. market economy and the influence American businesses have around the world. At the same time, the United States condemns the economic policies of Venezuela. Yet, Venezuela needs money and the United States needs Venezuela's oil. In spite of their differences, then, the two nations trade with each other. Economic interdependence can sometimes, but does not always, force nations to cooperate.

Environmental Issues

In recent years, people have become aware of dangers to the world's environment. Modern life offers many comforts, but they can come at a cost to the environment. Chemicals released by factories and cars pollute the air and water. Burning coal for energy also puts harmful chemicals into the air. These chemicals harm trees and fish when carried to the earth by rain. Most experts believe that burning coal and oil is causing dangerous changes in Earth's climate. **Deforestation,** the mass removal of trees, causes flooding, leads to mud slides, and lessens the amount of carbon dioxide that trees absorb.

Solving these problems is not easy. Protecting forests may deprive poor farmers of land they need to grow crops. Cleaner sources of energy cost more. The process of switching to those other sources can be costly, as well. Many poor nations fear that taking steps to curb pollution will slow their economic growth—growth they need in order to better the lives of their people.

Some people have turned to conservation to reduce environmental

deforestation the mass removal of trees in large areas

ethnic group a group of people who share a common national, cultural, or racial background

terrorism the use of violence or the threat of violence to compel a group of people to behave in a certain way

refugee a person who has unwillingly left his or her home to escape war, famine, or natural disaster

damage. Conservation means carefully using resources and limiting the harmful effects of human activity. For example, if people use less gasoline, then they cause less air pollution. If people recycle paper, then fewer forests need to be cleared.

Points of view about conservation differ. Some people think that conserving natural resources is less important than economic growth. They argue that limiting the ways that businesses operate drives up costs. Others claim that not conserving resources today will lead to greater future costs. They suggest that addressing the harmful effects of air, ground, and water pollution tomorrow will cost more.

Other Global Challenges

An interdependent world also faces other challenges. One serious problem is immigration. Immigrants move to a new country in search of better jobs and living conditions. Sometimes people already living in a country are unhappy about these newly arrived people who increase demands on land, services, and jobs. Differences among religious and ethnic groups can intensify these bad feelings. **Ethnic groups** are those with a common national, cultural, or racial background.

Many countries suffer from war or conflict. There is also a growing threat of international **terrorism.** Terrorism is the use of violence or the threat of violence to make people afraid and to force people—or governments—to behave in a certain way.

In addition, millions of **refugees** have been driven from their homes by famine, conflicts, or natural disasters. They now live in temporary camps. These people require a great deal of help. Many more people throughout the world suffer from lack of food, clean water, and basic health care. Meeting all of these challenges requires cooperation among nations.

 PROGRESS CHECK

Explaining Why do nations sometimes disagree?

LESSON 1 REVIEW

Review Vocabulary

1. Explain what effect trade barriers have on *global interdependence*.

2. Use the terms *terrorism, ethnic groups,* and *refugees* to explain global issues today.

Answer the Guiding Questions

3. ***Analyzing*** How do Americans benefit from a foreign policy that promotes trade?

4. ***Analyzing*** Why does the United States trade with Venezuela, even though they have disagreements?

5. **ARGUMENT** Governments, businesses, and people have different ideas on conservation. Think about the views of each of these groups. Write a letter to the editor in which you take a position on the issue. Explain what conservation efforts you think are important or are unnecessary, and why. Explain why you recommend those steps.

Lesson 2

The United States and International Organizations

ESSENTIAL QUESTION *Why and how do nations interact with one another?*

IT MATTERS BECAUSE

International organizations help nations communicate and work together to solve global problems.

The Purpose of International Organizations

GUIDING QUESTION *What is the purpose of international organizations?*

Nations often face difficult problems. Sometimes a crisis affects only one country. For example, in 2010 a severe earthquake struck Haiti. The destruction caused by the quake was too great for the country to handle by itself, so other nations sent food, water, medical supplies, and people to help.

Other concerns affect many nations. Such issues include climate change, pollution, and trade. Nations often hold talks with one another to discuss these matters. **Diplomats,** or officials who represent their country's government, meet and try to work out ways to address common concerns.

Governmental Organizations

Countries also form organizations to address international issues. These are called governmental organizations. Diplomats from member nations meet regularly, discuss problems, and try to find solutions. Sometimes they agree on a course of action. Sometimes they do not.

Reading**HELP**DESK

Taking Notes: *Classifying*

As you read, complete a chart to identify the type of organization to which different international organizations belong.

Governmental	Nongovernmental

Content Vocabulary

- **diplomat**
- **nongovernmental organization (NGO)**
- **prisoner of war**

The government of each member nation must agree to follow the rules of the organization and to support its decisions. For example, a certain number of the member nations must approve the admission of a nation that wishes to become a member of the organization. Each member must also provide part of the money that is needed to run the group.

Some governmental organizations are formed for a single purpose. The North Atlantic Treaty Organization (NATO) was first created for the defense of its member nations. The goal of the World Trade Organization (WTO) is to address issues of trade and finance among nations.

The objectives of other governmental organizations are broad. The largest governmental organization is the United Nations (UN). It has many goals, including promoting peace, fighting disease, building schools, and improving health care. The UN also provides its member countries with a place where they can present their own point of view. Members do not always agree on what actions to take, however.

Governmental organizations can create major changes in the world. For example, the European Union (EU) set up a common unit of money for most of its members. The euro is now a standard currency, which makes it easier for nations to trade. At times, group efforts are less effective. Terrorism persists, although all international organizations condemn and work to prevent it.

Nongovernmental Organizations (NGOs)

There are also international organizations that are not linked to any government. Rather, they are formed by private citizens to meet a need or to work for a cause. Such groups are called **nongovernmental organizations (NGOs).** NGOs often work with governmental organizations to provide relief in the event of a natural disaster, such as the earthquake in Haiti. These organizations usually depend on volunteers and private donations.

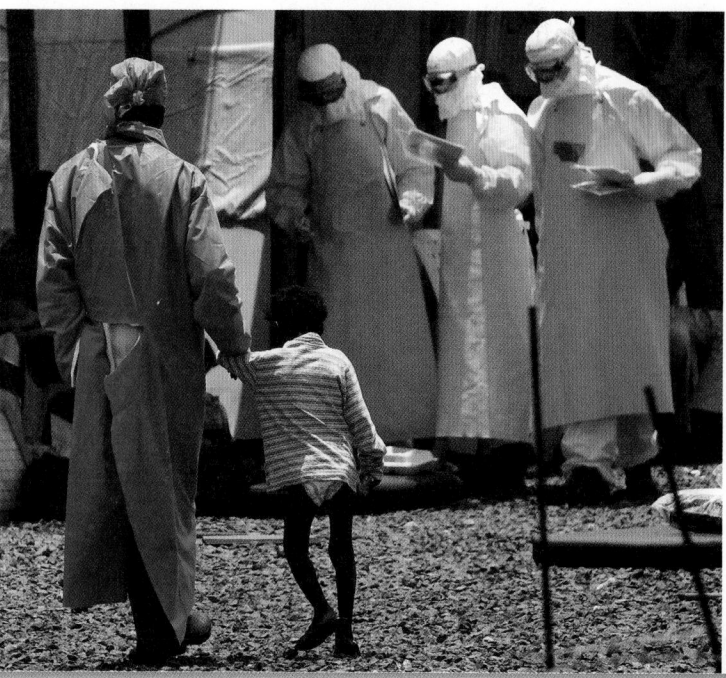

Why It MATTERS

Organizations in Your Life

The organizations that are formed among nations for the common purpose of helping others in need, or of providing protection, have a list of rules to govern their actions. What organized clubs or organizations do you belong to or are you familiar with? Find out if they have any rules that ensure that they will run smoothly.

Beginning in 2014, the nongovernmental organization Doctors Without Borders sent physicians and workers to several countries in West Africa to battle outbreaks of the deadly Ebola disease. These workers are helping patients in Liberia.

► CRITICAL THINKING
Explaining How do ordinary people help nongovernmental organizations do their work?

diplomat a representative of a country's government who takes part in talks with representatives of other nations

nongovernmental organization (NGO) an organization that operates independently of any government body, usually through individual volunteer efforts and private donations

PHOTO: Tim Sloan/AFP/Getty Images

The UN General Assembly meets at regular times during the year. Emergency meetings among smaller UN groups are also called sometimes.

▶ **CRITICAL THINKING**
Making Inferences For what reasons might an emergency meeting be called?

NGOs can do some things that governmental organizations cannot do. For example, some countries may accept aid for their people from NGOs that they would not accept from an organization connected with governments. The International Committee of the Red Cross (ICRC) is one such NGO. The Red Cross serves people in need on both sides in a war.

✓ **PROGRESS CHECK**

Explaining What is one success and one failure of governmental organizations in recent times?

International Organizations

GUIDING QUESTION *How do international organizations help people?*

Many international organizations work to improve the lives of people around the world. Some are particularly important.

The United Nations

The United Nations (UN) was founded in 1945, just after World War II. Its main goal is to keep peace among nations. The UN also seeks to support social progress, fight poverty, and protect human rights.

Reading HELPDESK

Reading Strategy: *Paraphrasing*

When you paraphrase a reading, you restate the passage in your own words. Read about the various groups within the United Nations. On a separate sheet of paper, paraphrase the makeup and purposes of these groups.

The General Assembly is the main forum for the UN's 193 member nations. Every member has a voice there. A smaller body called the Security Council deals with immediate threats to world peace. The Security Council has five permanent members. They are the United States, Russia, United Kingdom, France, and China. Ten other members are elected to two-year terms by the General Assembly. Any one of the five permanent members can veto a decision made by or block any action of the Security Council.

The UN has a number of units that handle other issues. The UN's International Court of Justice, also called the World Court, settles legal disputes between nations. The UN also tries to help developing countries make their economies more productive. The United Nations Children's Fund (UNICEF) works to improve the lives of children around the world. The United Nations Educational, Scientific and Cultural Organization (UNESCO) promotes science, education, and culture.

North Atlantic Treaty Organization

The North Atlantic Treaty Organization (NATO) is a group of 28 nations in North America and Europe. Its main goals are to keep peace and defend all members in times of war. Sometimes, NATO members send armed forces to an area where there is a crisis. For instance, NATO sent forces to Afghanistan in 2001 and to Iraq in 2003. NATO also works with nonmember nations to help prevent conflict.

World Trade Organization

The World Trade Organization (WTO) has some 160 member nations from around the world. The WTO's goal is to promote free trade. To do so, it encourages member nations to remove any trade barriers. The WTO also tries to resolve disputes between countries if they arise.

The WTO is not without critics. Some developing nations say that the WTO favors developed nations and the large businesses based in them. Some people charge that its focus on trade and profit ignores concerns about the environment.

A NATO-led peacekeeping force began patrolling war-torn Kosovo in 1999.

► CRITICAL THINKING
Identifying Central Issues Why do you think the United States would want to join with the forces of other NATO countries to respond to a conflict?

NONGOVERNMENTAL ORGANIZATIONS

► **CRITICAL THINKING**

1 *Categorizing* Many of the NGOs listed have similar areas of concern. Make a list of the categories of all of the areas of concern represented in the chart.

2 *Assessing* Based on the list you made, rank the categories in order from what you consider least important to most important, and give reasons for your decisions.

NGO	REGION	AREA OF CONCERN
Amnesty International	Worldwide	Human Rights
CARE International	Worldwide	Poverty, Education, Economic Development, Health
Cousteau Society	North America	Environment
Doctors Without Borders	Worldwide	Health, Disaster Response/Relief
Heifer International	Worldwide	Hunger, Poverty, Economic Development
Hunger Project	North America	Hunger
International Committee of the Red Cross	Worldwide	Human Rights, Public Health, Disaster Response/Relief
MacArthur Foundation	Worldwide	Human Rights, Economic Development, Peace, Education, Environment
MAP International	Worldwide	Health, Disaster Response/Relief
Nature Conservancy	Worldwide	Environment
Oxfam International	Worldwide	Poverty, Hunger, Human Rights, Economic Development
Sweatshop Watch	North America	Human Rights (specifically for workers)

World Health Organization

The World Health Organization (WHO) is part of the United Nations. It works in a variety of ways to improve health for all people. It directs the UN's efforts to fight and prevent disease in nations around the world. The WHO has formed standards for countries to meet to promote their people's health. It helps countries meet these standards. The WHO also conducts research on public health issues.

Among the WHO's successes are the ending of smallpox and teaching people about the HIV virus. The WHO has also helped achieve a 99 percent decrease in cases of polio around the world. In Africa, the WHO has helped reduce a disease called river blindness. River blindness is caused by the bite of a particular insect. Lessening the threat of this disease has allowed land that was not used because of the risk of infection to be farmed again.

Peace Corps

The Peace Corps is a volunteer group run by the U.S. government. The Peace Corps began in the 1960s when President John F.

Reading HELPDESK

prisoner of war a person captured by opposing forces during a time of war or conflict

Academic Vocabulary

neutral taking no side or part in a conflict or disagreement

Kennedy challenged students to make a difference for peace in the world. The original goal of the Peace Corps was to help Americans and the people of other nations understand each other.

Today, the Peace Corps has about 7,200 volunteers working in 65 countries. These volunteers work on several kinds of projects. Some work on public health issues, such as providing people with clean water. Some teach people ways to use modern technology and help them with local business development.

International Committee of the Red Cross

The International Committee of the Red Cross (ICRC) is an NGO. Based in Switzerland, the ICRC unites the efforts of aid societies in countries around the world. Those aid groups are called the Red Cross or the Red Crescent. The ICRC gives aid to people who are victims of war or natural disasters. During a war, the group tries to protect civilians and to make sure that prisoners of war are well treated. **Prisoners of war** are soldiers captured by enemy forces during a conflict. The ICRC tries to find missing persons. It also brings food, clothing, and medicines to people in need in war-torn areas.

The ICRC maintains a **neutral** position. That is, it does not take sides in a war. Most nations respect the efforts of the ICRC and allow it to do its work.

Other NGOs

Many NGOs are active around the world. Those that focus on public health, feeding the hungry, fighting disease, or promoting economic development typically work in developing nations. Those that focus on environmental problems may be active anywhere in the world. Some try to protect human rights. They tend to focus on nations with harsh governments.

✓ PROGRESS CHECK

Summarizing What are some main goals of international organizations?

LESSON 2 REVIEW

Review Vocabulary

1. Write a sentence about international organizations that includes the term *diplomat*.

2. Write a sentence that explains the difference between a *nongovernmental organization* and a governmental organization.

Answer the Guiding Questions

3. *Explaining* Why do nations and individuals form international organizations?

4. *Analyzing* What are some of the advantages and disadvantages of governmental organizations?

5. **INFORMATIVE/EXPLANATORY** Write an essay about the international efforts in which units of the United Nations are involved today.

netw✪rks

There's More Online!

☑ **GRAPHIC ORGANIZER**
Human Rights

☑ **POLITICAL CARTOON**
Human Rights

☑ **GRAPH**
Free and Not Free

☑ **MAP**
Global Terrorism

☑ **CHARTS**
Refugees
Types of Government

☑ **SLIDE SHOW**

Lesson 3

The United States and World Affairs

ESSENTIAL QUESTION *Why does conflict develop?*

IT MATTERS BECAUSE

Recognizing potential causes of conflict helps us to understand and address challenges facing the world.

Human Rights

GUIDING QUESTION *What are human rights?*

Governments differ around the world. **Cultures**—the ideas, customs, art, behaviors, and beliefs of a people or group of people—differ too. Yet people around the world also have many common characteristics. These shared characteristics are **universal.** That is, they apply to all people. We all want to be safe and feel secure. We all want enough food to eat and a decent place to live. We all want to raise our children in a way that seems right to us.

These shared desires form the basis for the concept of human rights. A **human right** is a basic freedom that all people should have simply because they are human. Human rights include the right to adequate food, safety, and shelter. They also include the right to be protected under the law and to exercise freedom of thought. These ideas have inspired people the world over. They have often shaped important political events, such as the American Revolution. They continue to have an impact in the world today.

PHOTO: (tl) AFP/Getty Images; (tcl) CORBIS; (tcr) Thomas Hartwell; (tr) Associated Press

Reading**HELP**DESK

Taking Notes: *Identifying*

As you read, complete a diagram identifying human rights cited by the Universal Declaration of Human Rights.

Human Rights

Content Vocabulary

- universal
- human right
- repression
- genocide
- communism
- weapon of mass destruction (WMD)

The Universal Declaration of Human Rights

Soon after the United Nations was formed, its members agreed on a list of people's basic rights. In December 1948, the UN adopted the Universal Declaration of Human Rights. The declaration was made up of 30 separate articles, or statements, that define specific human rights that all people should have.

Article 1 states, "All human beings are born free and equal in dignity and rights." They have "reason and conscience." *Conscience* means an awareness of the right or wrong nature of one's actions. Article 2 says that all people should have human rights "without distinction of any kind, such as race, colour, sex, language, religion, political or other opinion, national or social origin, property, birth or other status." These two articles form the foundation for the rest of the rights in the declaration.

The remaining articles detail other rights and protections. For instance, they say that people should be free from slavery and not be tortured. People should be free from arrest without cause and should have equal protection under the law. They should be free to marry whom they choose. They should have the right to own property, to move freely, and to take part in government as they choose.

Articles 22 through 27 focus on economic and social rights. These include equal pay for equal work and the right to a decent standard of living. Part of that standard of living includes medical care and security for children and the elderly.

Of course, there have been times when different nations have not given all their people all these rights. There have also been many times when nations have not upheld the standards in this declaration. Protecting human rights around the world is an ongoing effort.

The Kalma refugee camp in the Darfur region of Sudan provides some safety for people fleeing the civil war in that nation.

▶ **CRITICAL THINKING**
Making Inferences Why would the violation of human rights cause people to flee their homeland?

PHOTO: AFP/Getty Images

Academic Vocabulary

culture the ideas, customs, art, behaviors, and beliefs of a people or a group

universal worldwide, or applying to all

human right a protection or a freedom that all people should have

The United States and other countries sometimes refuse to trade with countries that violate human rights. Write a list of the effects that such a refusal to trade has on the government of a country charged with violating human rights and on the people living in that country.

In 2010 jailed Chinese human rights advocate Liu Xiaobo won the Nobel Peace Prize. China's communist government did not allow him to receive the prize, however.

▶ **CRITICAL THINKING**
Analyzing Visuals Does the cartoonist approve or disapprove of China's action? Why do you think so?

Violations of Human Rights

Unfortunately, some governments do not protect the rights of their own people. Some rulers use repression to stay in power. **Repression** means to prevent people from expressing themselves or from freely engaging in normal life. Some governments do not allow their people freedom of speech or the press. Many nations, such as China, Iran, and Saudi Arabia, limit their people's ability to get information. North Korea does not allow its people to leave the country or to criticize its leader.

Sometimes, tension among ethnic groups turns into violence. That violence can turn into **genocide,** the attempt to kill all members of an ethnic group, such as the Jews in WWII. During the 1990s, ethnic fighting broke out in Rwanda and Burundi, in Africa. More than a million people were killed. Since 2003, conflict has rocked the Darfur region of Sudan, in Africa. Ethnic Arabs from the northern part of the country have attacked ethnic Africans from the southern part of the country.

Protecting Human Rights

The U.S. government tries to promote human rights. It protests governments that take away people's freedoms. Sometimes it refuses to trade with such countries.

The UN Human Rights Council observes and reports on human rights. It hopes to pressure governments to respect people's rights. When governments are accused of violating the human rights of their citizens, the Security Council can refer cases to the International Criminal Court for trial.

Many nongovernmental organizations (NGOs) also work for human rights. Amnesty International and Human Rights Watch are two examples. Both publish reports identifying countries that violate rights. They, too, try to pressure countries into changing the way they act.

✅ **PROGRESS CHECK**

Defining What are human rights?

CARTOON: PARESH NATH, The Khaleej Times - UAE, and PoliticalCartoons.com

Reading**HELP**DESK

repression preventing people from expressing themselves or from freely engaging in normal life

genocide the attempt to kill all members of a particular ethnic group

communism a one-party system of government based on the idea of state ownership and government direction of property and industry

Democracy, Liberty, and Conflict

GUIDING QUESTION *Why does conflict among nations occur?*

Democratic nations, on the whole, do a better job of respecting human rights than nations that are not democratic. As more nations have become democratic, more people around the world have become free.

The Growth of Democracy

As the twentieth century began, only a few of the world's peoples lived in countries where they had the right to choose their own leaders. Today, the situation is much different. About 60 percent of the world's nations are democracies.

The spread of democracy and freedom has long been a major goal of the United States. President Woodrow Wilson hoped that World War I would "make the world safe for democracy." During World War II, President Franklin D. Roosevelt said:

PRIMARY SOURCE

"Freedom means the supremacy of human rights everywhere. Our support goes to those who struggle to gain those rights or keep them."

During that war, the United States joined with Great Britain and the Soviet Union as allies to defeat Germany, Japan, and Italy. After the war, these allies split into two camps. The two sides had very different political and economic systems. The United States and most of Western Europe had democratic governments and market-based economies. The Soviet Union and Eastern Europe practiced **communism.** There, one-party governments owned all resources and directed all economic activities. People in these countries had few freedoms, unlike the people in the United States and Western Europe.

The Cold War

The conflict between these two sides was called the Cold War. It lasted from the late 1940s to 1991. The chief nations—the United States and the Soviet Union—never fought each other. The United States and its allies tried to stop the Soviet Union from expanding its control. In doing so, the United States sometimes supported rulers who abused the rights of their people. This was the case in Chile and Iran, for instance. American actions that favored rulers in those countries were criticized by some people.

In his speech to Congress in 1917, Woodrow Wilson denounced Germany for attempting to sink any ship—military or not—that approached parts of the European coastline.

▶ **CRITICAL THINKING**
Making Inferences How were Germany's actions a violation of human rights?

Free: Political competition, civil liberties, free press

Partly Free: Restricted political rights and civil liberties

Not Free: Lacks basic political rights and civil liberties

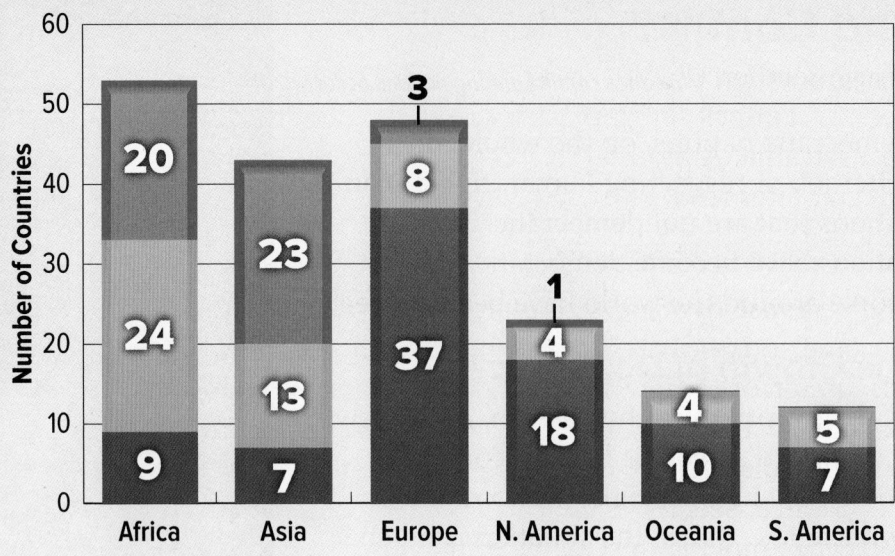

GRAPH SKILLS

The graph shows the proportion of countries in each continent with people who are free, partly free, or not free.

1 *Comparing* Which continents are the most free? The least free?

2 CRITICAL THINKING
Making Inferences Why do you think Africa has so many not free and partly free nations?

In the late 1980s, unrest spread in Eastern Europe and the Soviet Union. The people revolted against their communist governments. New leaders pushed these countries toward democracy and market economies. In 1991 the Soviet Union broke apart into 15 separate nations, one of which was Russia. The Cold War was over.

Free and Not Free

The end of the Cold War brought a rush of new democracies into the world. Since then, the move toward democratic governments has slowed. In large parts of South America and Africa, many people are only partly free. They live under governments that restrict human rights. Communist governments in North Korea, China, and Cuba continue to deny their peoples basic human rights such as freedom of speech and freedom of the press. These nations are considered not free.

At the same time, new threats to peace and freedom have emerged. Some extreme people and groups have decided to use terrorist attacks to try to influence countries. Groups such as al Qaeda and the Taliban have killed thousands of people around the world in order to impose their beliefs on others.

✓ PROGRESS CHECK

Concluding Did the policies of the United States during the Cold War advance or hold back human rights?

Reading Strategy: *Defining*

In one or two sentences, define in your own words what the Cold War was.

Recent Conflicts

GUIDING QUESTION *Why has the United States engaged in conflict in recent years?*

On September 11, 2001, members of al Qaeda carried out a terrorist attack on New York City, Washington, D.C., and Pennsylvania. Almost 3,000 people died in those attacks. The United States responded in several ways.

Homeland Security

One response by the government was to create the Department of Homeland Security in 2001. It has three main goals: to prevent terrorist attacks in the United States, to reduce the threat of such attacks, and to help in the recovery from attacks or natural disasters. The department was given many powers. For instance, security workers now check all people and inspect all luggage moving through airports. It is also taking action to increase the security of information stored on computers.

Patriot Act

Another response to the September 11 attacks was the Patriot Act of 2001. The law increased the government's power to seek information that could be related to terrorism. It allowed the government to search telephone and financial records. The act allowed federal agents to secretly search the homes of those suspected of terrorism. They did not have to obtain a search warrant from a court before making these searches.

Many people felt that this law went too far. They believed that rights people had under the U.S. Constitution were no longer protected. Congress made some changes to the law as a result. Some Americans still object to it, though.

21st Century SKILLS

Write a Blog Entry

The United States took a number of actions in response to the terror attacks of 9/11. Chose one of the responses mentioned in the text and write a blog entry describing it. Do you think the response suitable? Was it effective? Give reasons to support your opinion.

GEOGRAPHY CONNECTION

Terrorist attacks have struck many nations around the world.

1 LOCATION Where did the terrorist attack with the greatest loss of life occur?

2 CRITICAL THINKING *Making Generalizations* Why do you think terrorist attacks have been so widespread?

GLOBAL TERRORISM

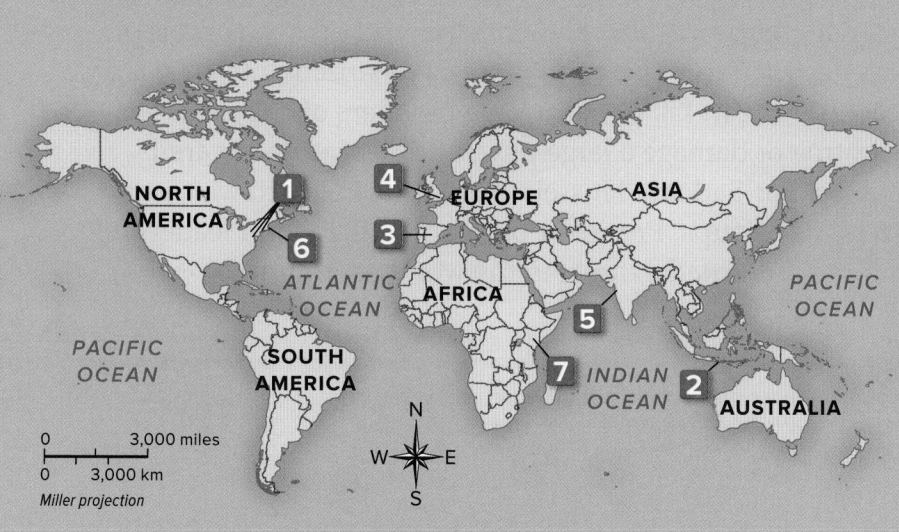

1	**2001** Four hijacked airliners flown into World Trade Center, the Pentagon, and rural Pennsylvania, more than 3,000 killed
2	**2002** Resort in Bali, Indonesia bombed, more than 200 killed
3	**2004** Train system in Madrid, Spain, bombed, 191 killed
4	**2005** London subway bombed, 52 killed
5	**2008** Attacks of Mumbai landmarks, nearly 190 killed, 300 injured
6	**2013** Boston Marathon bombings, 3 killed, 264 injured
7	**2013** Shopping mall in Nairobi, Kenya, attacked, 67 killed, 200 injured

PHOTO: Thomas Hartwell

United States government aid workers faced challenges in rebuilding Iraqi schools and other institutions following the fall of Saddam Hussein.

▶ **CRITICAL THINKING**
Making Inferences Why do you think it was so difficult to rebuild Iraq after Saddam Hussein's removal from power?

Afghanistan

The U.S. government also responded to the September 11 attacks with military force. Wars in Afghanistan and Iraq followed.

Afghanistan was ruled by the Taliban, a political group that did little to recognize the rights of the country's people. The Taliban also helped al Qaeda, the group behind the attacks on September 11. They allowed al Qaeda to train terrorists in Afghanistan. President George W. Bush demanded that the Taliban hand over the leader of al Qaeda, Osama bin Laden, so that he could be punished for the September 11 attacks. The Taliban leaders refused, however.

When that happened, the United States responded. In October 2001, U.S. planes and troops attacked Afghanistan. The Taliban were quickly ousted, but bin Laden avoided capture.

Fighting continued for many years. Attempts to form an effective new government in Afghanistan met with little success. Taliban and other fighters returned to attack again and again. More troops were sent, but clear progress was difficult. President Barack Obama sent more American forces to Afghanistan to try to end the conflict there. The government also put pressure on Afghanistan's government to solve its own problems. In May 2011, U.S. forces located bin Laden hiding out in Pakistan. They raided his compound and he was killed in the fighting.

Iraq

While fighting continued in Afghanistan, the United States also moved against Iraq. After September 11, President Bush feared terrorist groups might acquire nuclear and other weapons of mass destruction. A **weapon of mass destruction (WMD)** is a weapon that can kill or harm large numbers of people as well as destroy or damage a large physical area. Leaders feared Iraqi dictator Saddam Hussein might provide such weapons to terrorist groups. President Bush and other world leaders felt that Iraq presented a threat to the world community.

Reading**HELP**DESK

weapon of mass destruction (WMD) a weapon that can kill or harm large numbers of people as well as destroy or damage a large physical area

In early 2003, the United States and other countries attacked Iraq. Iraq's army was quickly defeated, and Saddam Hussein was overthrown. Later, he was captured, tried by Iraq's new government, and executed for crimes against his people.

Although the United States succeeded in these efforts, it still faced problems. No WMDs were found. Thus, the government was criticized for the invasion. It also proved more difficult than expected for the United States to build democracy in Iraq. In addition, rebel groups battled U.S. forces with roadside bombs and surprise attacks. Fighting among Iraq's different ethnic and religious groups made the situation worse.

In 2008 though, the addition of more U.S. troops helped reduce the level of violence. As a result, President Barack Obama later withdrew all American combat troops. Some U.S. troops remained in Iraq to train that country's new army and police.

Foreign Policy Challenges Continue

The United States continued to face a number of global challenges. While relations with Iran improved, concerns about that country's development of nuclear weapons remained. Terrorist groups based in Pakistan still posed a threat. Despite efforts to help Israel reach a peace agreement with the Palestinians, their conflict was not settled. In 2014, the United States once again carried out military operations in Iraq to battle a militant group called the Islamic State of Iraq and Syria (ISIS). That group hoped to create an Islamic state in the region and captured a number of Iraqi cities. Other nations around the world were torn by internal conflict. The U.S. government takes an active role in ending such conflicts while promoting democracy and human rights.

In 2014, attacks by the group called the Islamic State of Iraq and Syria led to further unrest in Iraq and brought about renewed U.S. involvement in the region. These ISIS fighters are using a vehicle captured from the Iraqi army.

▶ **CRITICAL THINKING**
Making Connections Why might the United States have been opposed to ISIS attacks and further unrest in Iraq?

✓ **PROGRESS CHECK**

Explaining What have been the biggest foreign policy challenges for the United States since 2000?

LESSON 3 REVIEW

Review Vocabulary

1. Write two or three sentences defining *human rights*. Include the term *universal*.

2. Write two or three sentences explaining the relationship between *communism* and *repression*.

Answer the Guiding Questions

3. ***Identifying*** What are some examples of human rights?

4. ***Identifying*** What was the Cold War?

5. ***Analyzing*** Why do some countries allow little freedom?

6. **ARGUMENT** Write a paragraph that expresses your opinion about the Patriot Act. Do you think it was right to give the government more power to prevent terrorist attacks? Be sure to explain your reasoning.

Write your answers on a separate piece of paper.

1 Writing Activity

EXPLORING THE ESSENTIAL QUESTION
Why and how do nations interact with one another?

Trade among nations is a big part of global interdependence. Consider the products and services that you use in your daily life. Identify six items that are the result of trade with other nations. Then write a paragraph explaining how you benefit from global interdependence and why international trade is important to you.

2 21st Century Skills

PREPARE A PRESENTATION Using presentation software or posters, prepare a brief presentation on the use of imported oil in the United States. Prepare at least eight slides or posters to share. Include in your presentation at least one graph, using information from Lesson 1, about sources, amounts, and percentages of foreign oil consumed in the United States. Use what you have learned to discuss ideas about energy use or to predict the consequences of current trends in the United States.

3 Being an Active Citizen

Many NGOs begin because someone sees a problem in the world and tries to solve it. Local volunteer groups often begin for the same reason. Many groups sponsor activities to raise funds or awareness for their causes. Look around your community for such events. Check newspaper, radio, television, and Internet resources for activities that rely on volunteer support. Choose one that you think is a good cause and volunteer to participate. Invite others to join you. If you cannot participate in an activity, prepare a display giving more information on the group and its efforts.

4 Understanding Visuals

The Cold War was a time of tension when many people around the world feared war. Study the cartoon. Then answer these questions. What do the flags represent in this cartoon? What does the crack in the Earth represent? How does the cartoon show the state of the world at the time?

STATE OF THE WORLD

REVIEW THE GUIDING QUESTIONS

Choose the best answer for each question.

1 Why do nations depend on one another?

　A. They want to remain friendly with all nations.

　B. They need or want things from other nations.

　C. The United Nations requires that they do so.

　D. They want to protect their own industries.

2 What is one important global issue facing nations of the world?

　F. the need for more consumer goods in developed nations

　G. the falling price of energy worldwide

　H. the overabundance of food in developing nations

　I. global damage to the environment

3 Which of the following is an example of a nongovernmental organization (NGO)?

　A. United Nations

　B. United States Army

　C. International Committee of the Red Cross

　D. European Union

4 What is one of the main purposes of the United Nations?

　F. to provide a place where nations can express their views

　G. to secure military defense for all member nations

　H. to ensure protectionism for developing nations

　I. to develop energy resources for developed nations

5 What does the Universal Declaration of Human Rights do?

　A. establishes tribunals to try cases of war crimes

　B. obligates nations to provide aid to refugees

　C. defines freedoms that all people should have

　D. protects people around the world from violence

6 Which of the following has played a major part in recent conflicts involving the United States?

　F. increased oil supply

　G. terrorism

　H. communism

　I. international trade

DBQ **ANALYZING DOCUMENTS**

Directions: Analyze the excerpt and answer the questions that follow.

"(1) Men and women of full age, without any limitation due to race, nationality or religion, have the right to marry and to found a family. They are entitled to equal rights as to marriage, during marriage and at its dissolution.
(2) Marriage shall be entered into only with the free and full consent of the intending spouses."

—Article 16, Universal Declaration of Human Rights, 1948

7 **Analyzing Primary Sources** What does Section 1 of Article 16 say about women's rights in marriage?

A. Traditional marriage roles around the world are different.

B. The article makes no statement about the role of women's rights.

C. Religion, nationality, and race must be considered in the choice to marry.

D. Women have rights equal to men as far as marriage laws should be concerned.

8 **Making Inferences** What is the intention of Section 2 of Article 16?

F. It opposes forced marriages.

G. It requires partners to sign consent forms.

H. It asserts that only people who are free can marry.

I. It bans marriages arranged by parents.

SHORT RESPONSE

"Whereas Member States have pledged themselves to achieve . . . the promotion of universal respect for and observance of human rights . . ."

—Preamble, Universal Declaration of Human Rights, 1948

9 The preamble to the Universal Declaration of Human Rights contains this section. What is the preamble's purpose?

10 Why does the preamble refer to what the Member States have pledged?

EXTENDED RESPONSE

11 **ARGUMENT** What do you think is the single biggest threat to peace and prosperity in the world today? Why do you feel that way?

Need Extra Help?

If You've Missed Question	**1**	**2**	**3**	**4**	**5**	**6**	**7**	**8**	**9**	**10**	**11**
Review Lesson	1	1	2	2	3	3	3	3	3	3	1,2,3

REFERENCE ATLAS

ATLAS KEY

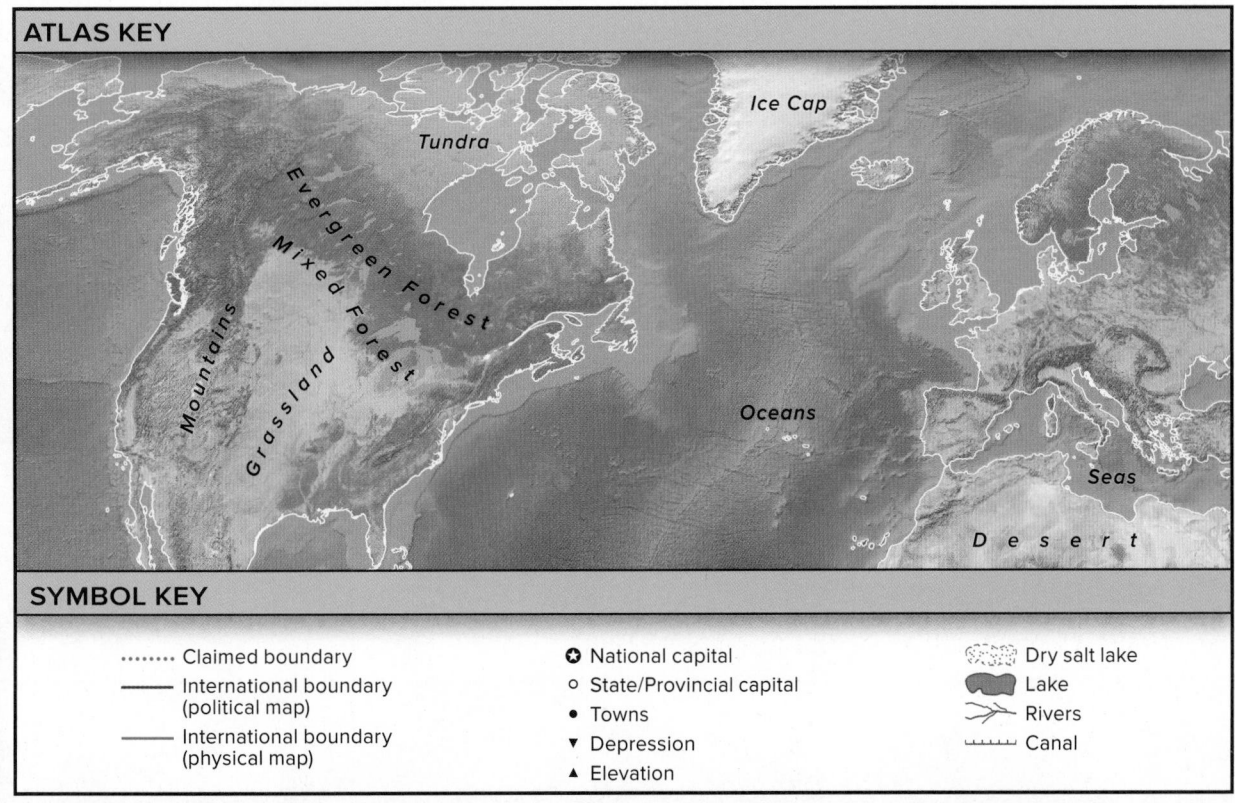

SYMBOL KEY

········· Claimed boundary	⊛ National capital	Dry salt lake
——— International boundary (political map)	○ State/Provincial capital	Lake
——— International boundary (physical map)	• Towns	Rivers
	▼ Depression	Canal
	▲ Elevation	

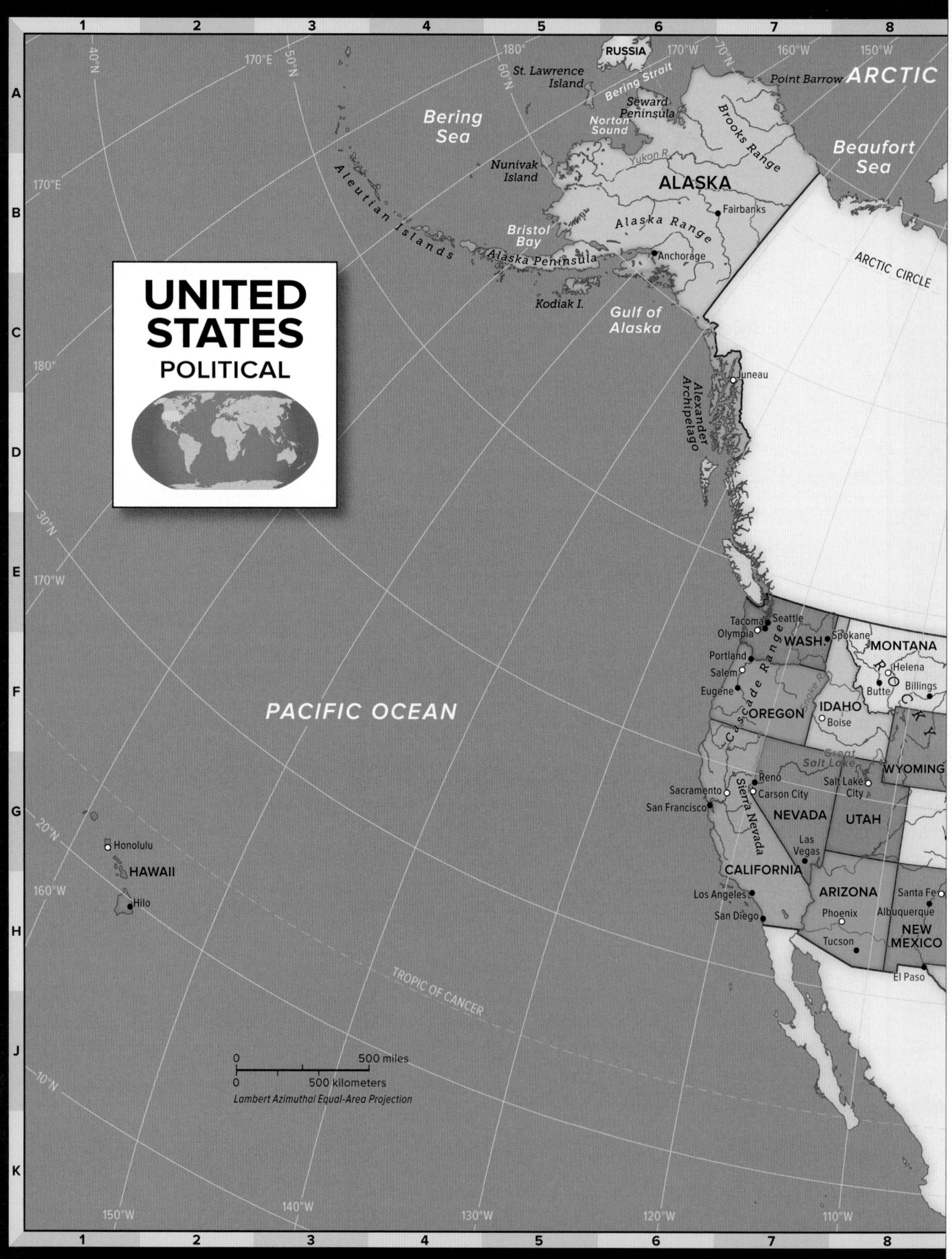

UNITED STATES POLITICAL

RUSSIA

St. Lawrence Island

Bering Sea

Bering Strait

Seward Peninsula

Norton Sound

Point Barrow   ARCTIC

Brooks Range

Beaufort Sea

ALASKA

Nunivak Island

Yukon R.

Fairbanks

Alaska Range

ARCTIC CIRCLE

Aleutian Islands

Bristol Bay

Alaska Peninsula

Anchorage

Kodiak I.

Gulf of Alaska

Alexander Archipelago

Juneau

PACIFIC OCEAN

Tacoma Seattle
Olympia WASH. Spokane
Portland MONTANA
Salem Snake R. Helena
Eugene OREGON IDAHO Butte Billings
Cascade Range Boise

Great Salt Lake WYOMING

Reno
Sacramento Sierra Nevada Carson City Salt Lake City
San Francisco NEVADA UTAH

Honolulu

HAWAII

Las Vegas

Hilo

CALIFORNIA

160°W

Los Angeles ARIZONA Santa Fe
Phoenix Albuquerque
San Diego NEW MEXICO
Tucson
El Paso

TROPIC OF CANCER

0   500 miles
0   500 kilometers
Lambert Azimuthal Equal-Area Projection

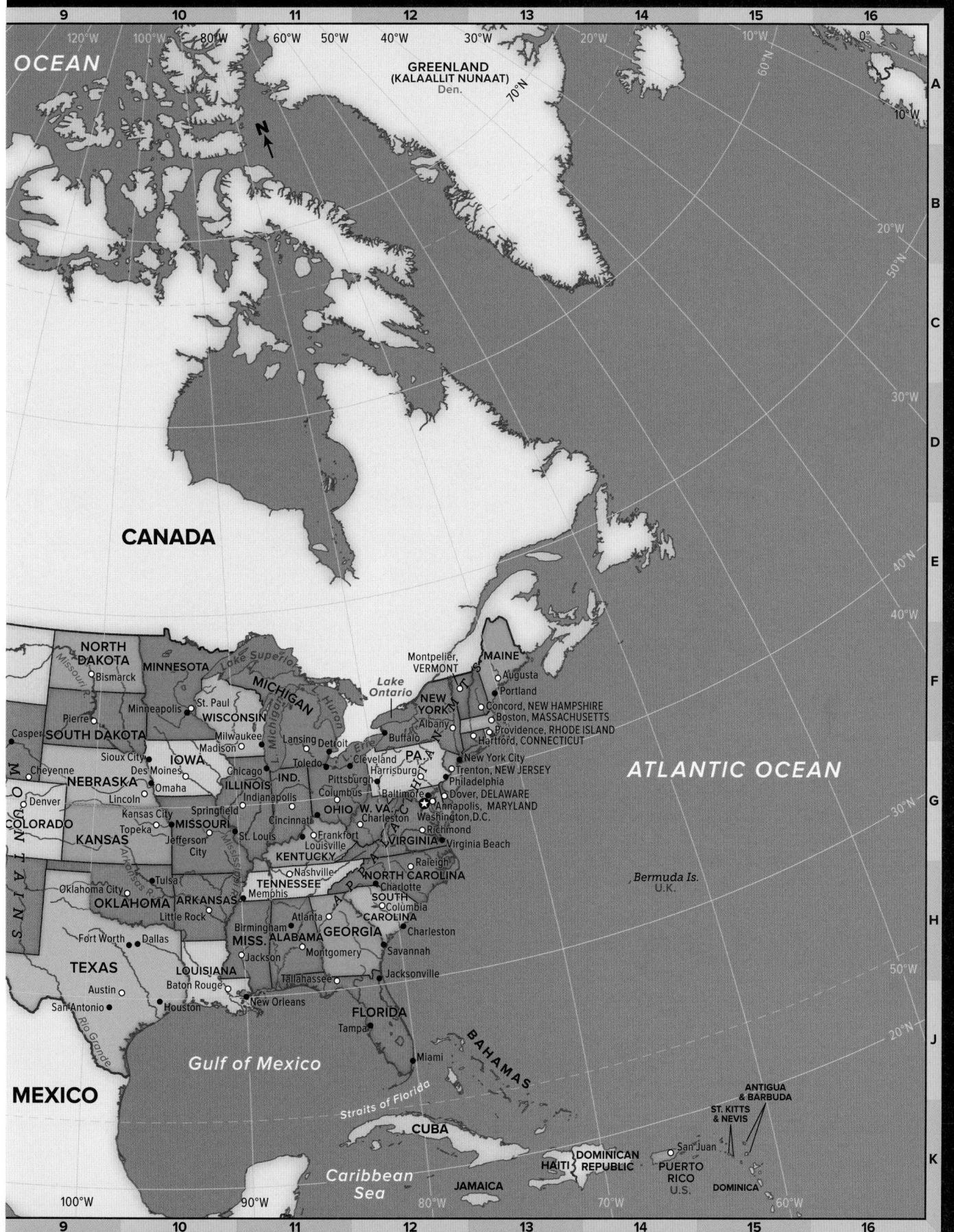

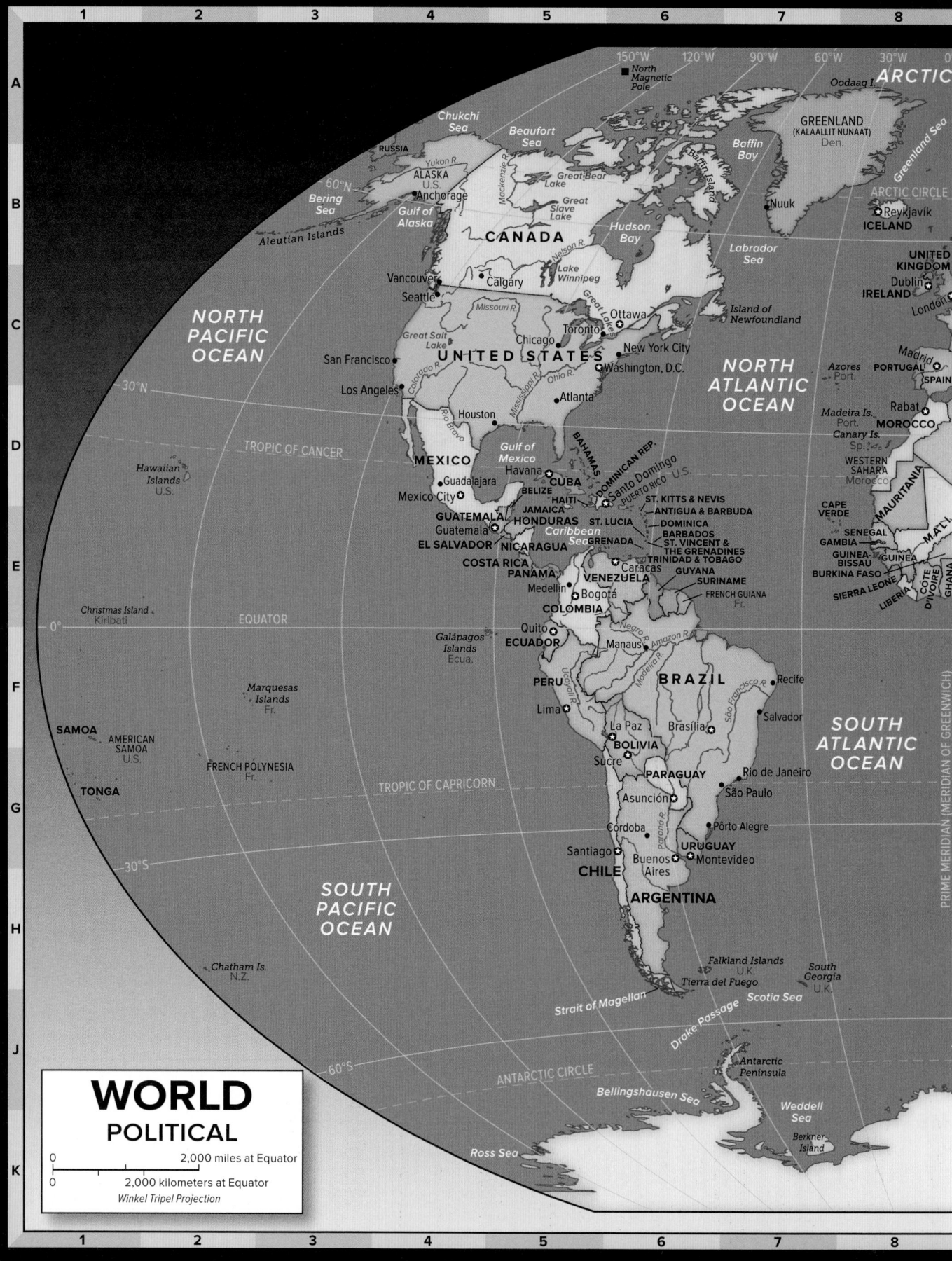

WORLD
POLITICAL

0 ————— 2,000 miles at Equator
0 ————— 2,000 kilometers at Equator
Winkel Tripel Projection

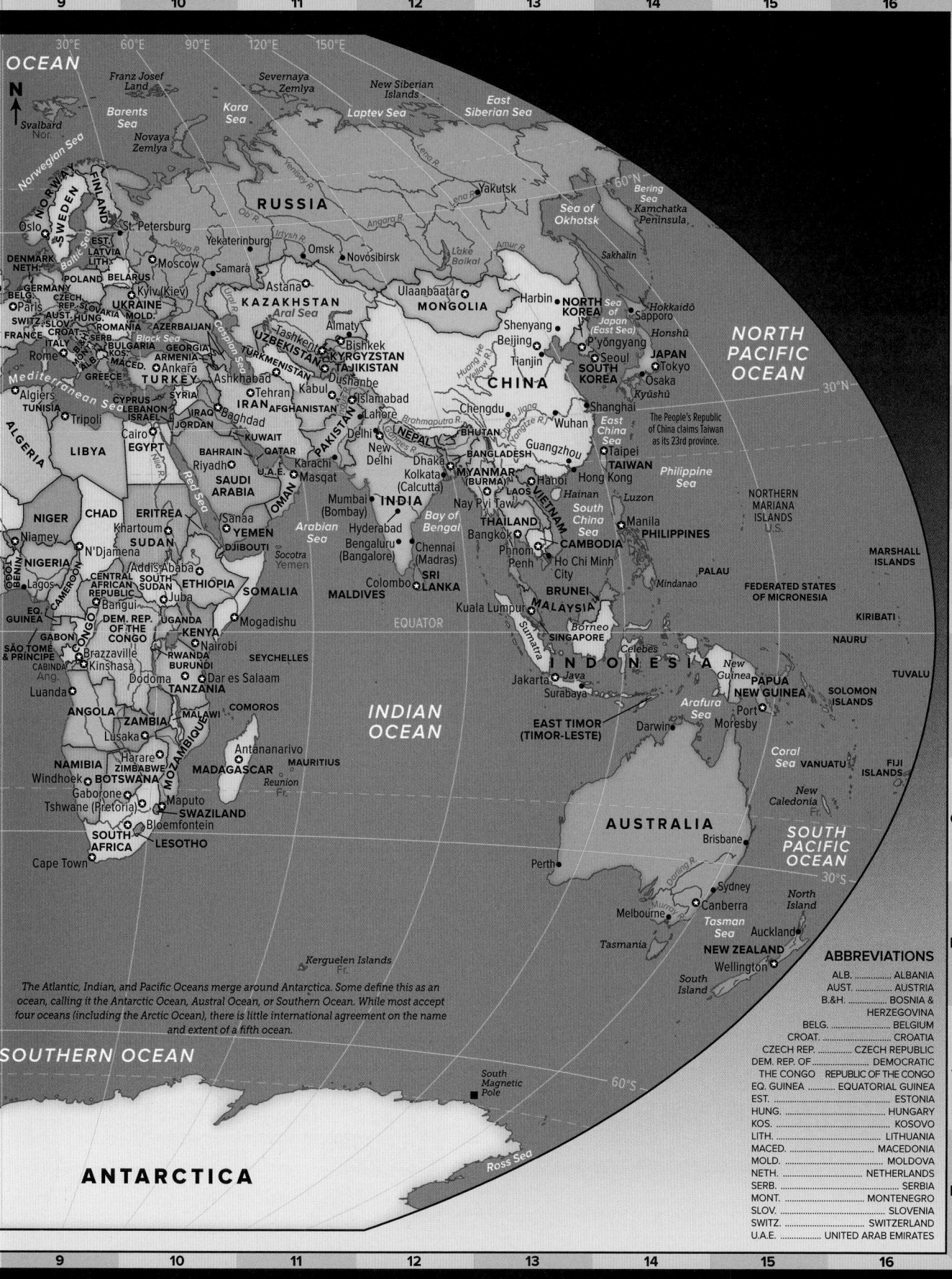

A
B
C
D
E
F
G
H
J
K

N

OCEAN
30°E 60°E 90°E 120°E 150°E

Franz Josef Land
Svalbard
Nor.
Barents Sea
Novaya Zemlya
Kara Sea
Severnaya Zemlya
New Siberian Islands
Laptev Sea
East Siberian Sea

Norwegian Sea

NORWAY
FINLAND
SWEDEN
Oslo
DENMARK
NETH.
BELG.
GERMANY
PARIS
SWITZ.
FRANCE
ITALY
Rome
Mediterranean Sea
Algiers
TUNISIA
Tripoli
LIBYA
ALGERIA
EGYPT
Cairo
Nile R.
Red Sea

St. Petersburg
Moscow
Baltic Sea
EST.
LATVIA
LITH.
POLAND
BELARUS
CZECH REP.
SLOVAKIA
AUST. HUNG.
SLOV.
CROAT.
B.&H. SERB.
MACED.
BULGARIA
ROMANIA
UKRAINE
Kyiv (Kiev)
MOLD.
Black Sea
GREECE
TURKEY
Ankara
CYPRUS
LEBANON
ISRAEL
JORDAN
SYRIA
IRAQ
Baghdad

RUSSIA
Yekaterinburg
Volga R.
Samara
Omsk
Ob R.
Novosibirsk
Irtysh R.
Ural R.
Astana
KAZAKHSTAN
Aral Sea
Caspian Sea
AZERBAIJAN
ARMENIA
GEORGIA
Tashkent
UZBEKISTAN
Bishkek
KYRGYZSTAN
Almaty
TURKMENISTAN
Ashkhabad
TAJIKISTAN
Dushanbe
IRAN
Tehran
Kabul
AFGHANISTAN
Islamabad
Lahore

Yenisey R.
Angara R.
Lena R.
Yakutsk
Lake Baikal
Amur R.
60°N
Bering Sea
Kamchatka Peninsula
Sea of Okhotsk
Sakhalin

Ulaanbaatar
MONGOLIA
Harbin
Shenyang
Beijing
Tianjin
NORTH KOREA
P'yongyang
SOUTH KOREA
Seoul
Sea of Japan (East Sea)
Hokkaidō
Sapporo
Honshū
JAPAN
Tokyo
Osaka
Kyūshū

NORTH PACIFIC OCEAN

30°N

CHINA
Huang He (Yellow R.)
Chengdu
Wuhan
Shanghai
Chang Jiang (Yangtze R.)
Guangzhou
Hong Kong
Taipei
TAIWAN
East China Sea
Hainan
Philippine Sea

The People's Republic of China claims Taiwan as its 23rd province.

NORTHERN MARIANA ISLANDS
U.S.

MARSHALL ISLANDS

KUWAIT
BAHRAIN
QATAR
U.A.E.
SAUDI ARABIA
Riyadh
OMAN
Masqat
YEMEN
Sanaa
ERITREA
DJIBOUTI
Socotra Yemen

PAKISTAN
Karachi
Delhi
New Delhi
NEPAL
BHUTAN
Brahmaputra R.
Ganges R.
Dhaka
BANGLADESH
MYANMAR (BURMA)
Kolkata (Calcutta)
INDIA
Mumbai (Bombay)
Hyderabad
Bengaluru (Bangalore)
Chennai (Madras)
Bay of Bengal
Arabian Sea
Nay Pyi Taw
LAOS
Hanoi
VIETNAM
THAILAND
Bangkok
CAMBODIA
Phnom Penh
Ho Chi Minh City
South China Sea
Manila
PHILIPPINES
Luzon

PALAU

FEDERATED STATES OF MICRONESIA

KIRIBATI

NIGER
Niamey
CHAD
SUDAN
Khartoum
N'Djamena
NIGERIA
Lagos
BENIN
TOGO
CAMEROON
CENTRAL AFRICAN REPUBLIC
SOUTH SUDAN
ETHIOPIA
Addis Ababa
Juba
SOMALIA
EQ. GUINEA
SÃO TOMÉ & PRÍNCIPE
GABON
DEM. REP. OF THE CONGO
CONGO
Brazzaville
Kinshasa
CABINDA Ang.
UGANDA
KENYA
Nairobi
RWANDA
BURUNDI
Dodoma
TANZANIA
Dar es Salaam
SEYCHELLES

Colombo
SRI LANKA
MALDIVES

BRUNEI
MALAYSIA
Kuala Lumpur
SINGAPORE
Sumatra
Borneo
Celebes
Java
Jakarta
Surabaya
INDONESIA
New Guinea
PAPUA NEW GUINEA

NAURU

TUVALU

SOLOMON ISLANDS

EQUATOR

Luanda
ANGOLA
ZAMBIA
MALAWI
Lusaka
MOZAMBIQUE
COMOROS
Antananarivo
MADAGASCAR
MAURITIUS
Reunion Fr.
NAMIBIA
ZIMBABWE
BOTSWANA
Harare
Windhoek
Gaborone
Tshwane (Pretoria)
Maputo
SWAZILAND
Bloemfontein
LESOTHO
SOUTH AFRICA
Cape Town

INDIAN OCEAN

EAST TIMOR (TIMOR-LESTE)
Arafura Sea
Darwin
Port Moresby
Coral Sea
VANUATU
FIJI ISLANDS
New Caledonia Fr.

AUSTRALIA
Perth
Murray R.
Darling R.
Sydney
Canberra
Melbourne
Tasman Sea
Brisbane

SOUTH PACIFIC OCEAN

30°S

North Island
Auckland
NEW ZEALAND
Wellington
South Island
Tasmania

Kerguelen Islands Fr.

The Atlantic, Indian, and Pacific Oceans merge around Antarctica. Some define this as an ocean, calling it the Antarctic Ocean, Austral Ocean, or Southern Ocean. While most accept four oceans (including the Arctic Ocean), there is little international agreement on the name and extent of a fifth ocean.

SOUTHERN OCEAN

South Magnetic Pole
60°S

ANTARCTICA
Ross Sea

ABBREVIATIONS

ALB.	ALBANIA
AUST.	AUSTRIA
B.&H.	BOSNIA & HERZEGOVINA
BELG.	BELGIUM
CROAT.	CROATIA
CZECH REP.	CZECH REPUBLIC
DEM. REP. OF	DEMOCRATIC
THE CONGO	REPUBLIC OF THE CONGO
EQ. GUINEA	EQUATORIAL GUINEA
EST.	ESTONIA
HUNG.	HUNGARY
KOS.	KOSOVO
LITH.	LITHUANIA
MACED.	MACEDONIA
MOLD.	MOLDOVA
NETH.	NETHERLANDS
SERB.	SERBIA
MONT.	MONTENEGRO
SLOV.	SLOVENIA
SWITZ.	SWITZERLAND
U.A.E.	UNITED ARAB EMIRATES

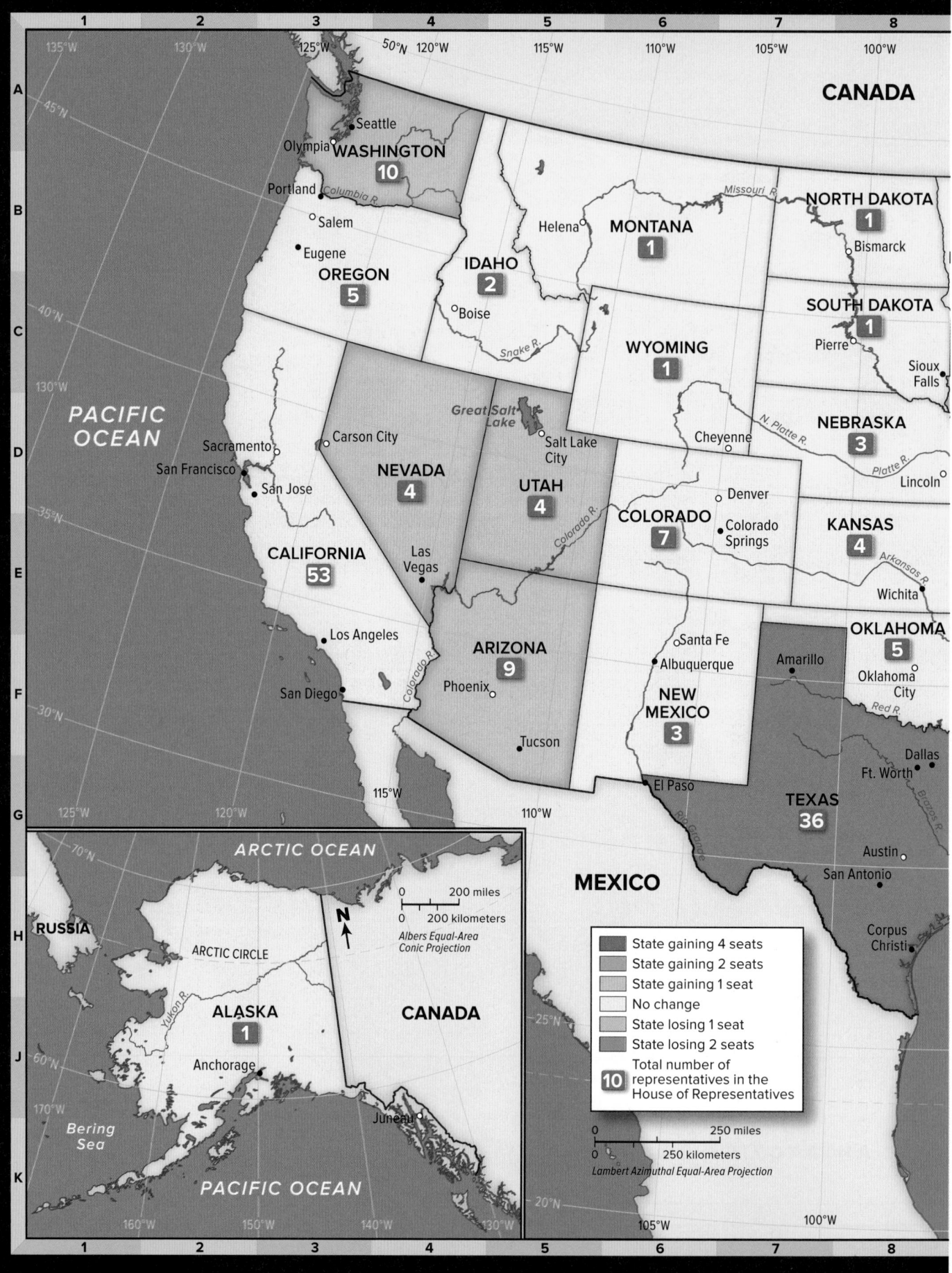

PACIFIC OCEAN

CANADA

Seattle
Olympia WASHINGTON **10**
Portland _Columbia R._
Salem
Eugene
OREGON **5**

Helena
MONTANA **1**

Missouri R.

NORTH DAKOTA **1**
Bismarck

IDAHO **2**
Boise

Snake R.

WYOMING **1**

SOUTH DAKOTA **1**
Pierre

Sioux Falls

Great Salt Lake

Sacramento
San Francisco
San Jose

Carson City

Salt Lake City

Cheyenne

N. Platte R.

NEBRASKA **3**

Platte R.

Lincoln

NEVADA **4**

UTAH **4**

Colorado R.

COLORADO **7**

Denver
Colorado Springs

KANSAS **4**

Wichita

CALIFORNIA **53**

Las Vegas

Los Angeles

ARIZONA **9**

Santa Fe
Albuquerque

Amarillo

OKLAHOMA **5**

Oklahoma City

San Diego

Colorado R.

Phoenix

NEW MEXICO **3**

Red R.

Dallas
Ft. Worth

Tucson

El Paso

Rio Grande

TEXAS **36**

Brazos R.

MEXICO

Austin
San Antonio

Corpus Christi

ARCTIC OCEAN

0 ___ 200 miles
0 ___ 200 kilometers
N
Albers Equal-Area Conic Projection

RUSSIA

ARCTIC CIRCLE

Yukon R.

ALASKA **1**

Anchorage

CANADA

Juneau

Bering Sea

PACIFIC OCEAN

	State gaining 4 seats
	State gaining 2 seats
	State gaining 1 seat
	No change
	State losing 1 seat
	State losing 2 seats
10	Total number of representatives in the House of Representatives

0 ___ 250 miles
0 ___ 250 kilometers
Lambert Azimuthal Equal-Area Projection

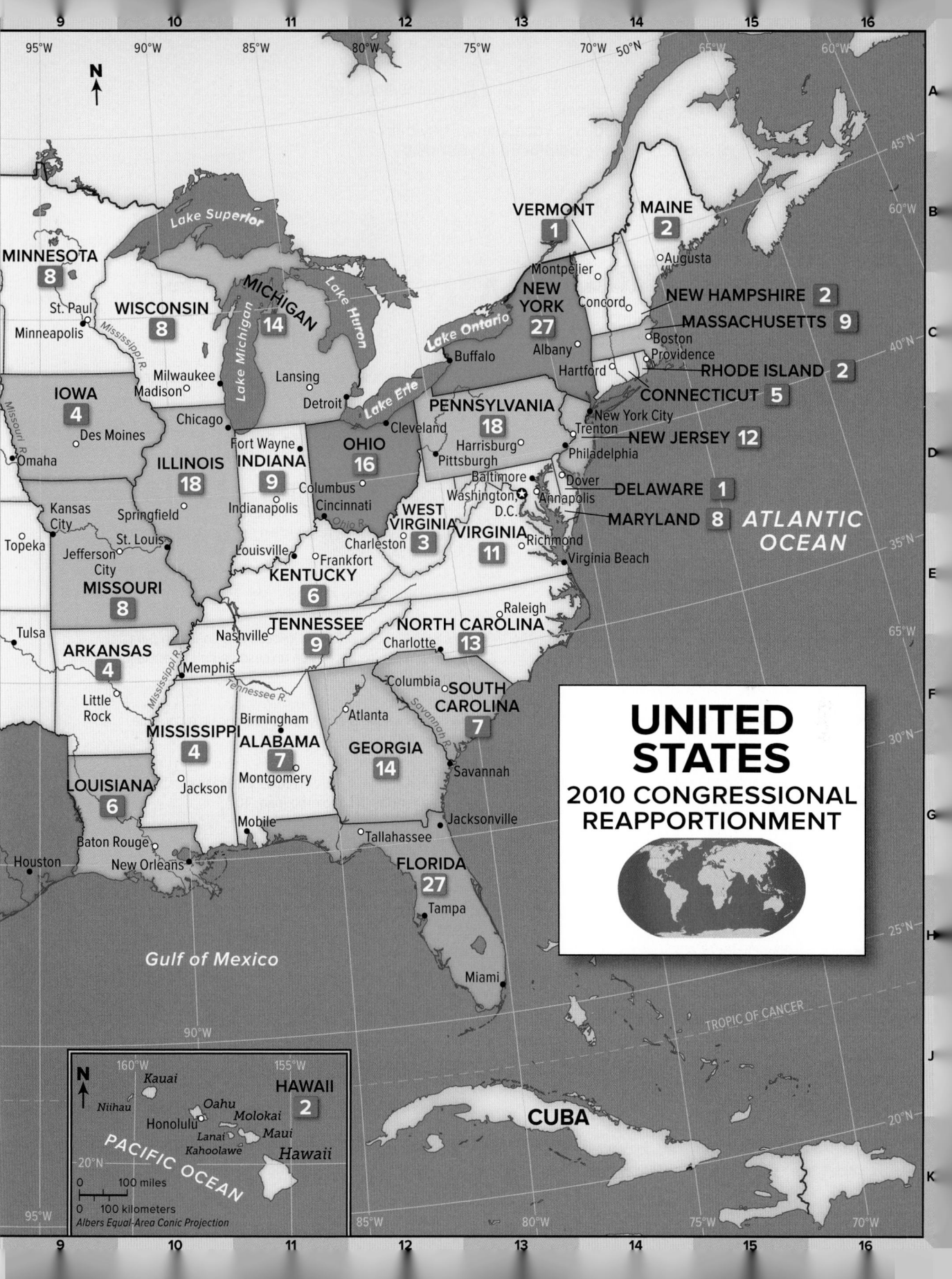

UNITED STATES
2010 CONGRESSIONAL REAPPORTIONMENT

GLOSSARY/GLOSARIO

- Content vocabulary are words that relate to civics and government content. They are **highlighted yellow** in your textbook.
- Words that have an asterisk (*) are academic vocabulary. They help you understand your school subjects and are **boldfaced** in your text.

access • annual percentage rate (APR)

ENGLISH	A	ESPAÑOL

ENGLISH	ESPAÑOL
***access** the freedom to make use of something (p. 504)	***acceso** libertad de usar algo (pág. 504)
accused a person officially charged with a crime (p. 134)	**acusado** persona a quien se le atribuye oficialmente un crimen (pág. 134)
***achieve** to accomplish or to reach (p. 601)	***lograr** alcanzar o llegar (pág. 601)
***acknowledge** to admit (p. 298)	***reconocer** admitir (pág. 298)
***adapt** to change in response to new circumstances (p. 458)	***adaptar** cambiar en respuesta a nuevas circunstancias (pág. 458)
***adjacent** located next to (p. 255)	***adyacente** situado a un lado (pág. 255)
adjudication hearing the procedure used to determine the facts in a juvenile case (p. 433)	**audiencia de resolución** procedimiento usado para determinar los hechos en un caso de delincuencia juvenil (pág. 433)
***adjust** to change or alter in order to fit or conform (p. 160)	***ajustar** cambiar o alterar para que encaje o coincida (pág. 160)
administrative law rules and regulations set by government agencies (p. 401)	**derecho administrativo** reglas y normas establecidas por las agencias del gobierno (pág. 401)
***affect** to impact; to have an effect on (p. 543)	***afectar** tener impacto; tener efecto sobre algo (pág. 543)
alien a foreign-born resident of the United States who has not been naturalized (p. 15)	**extranjero** residente de Estados Unidos nacido en otro país y que no ha sido naturalizado (pág. 15)
***alternative** another choice (p. 378)	***alternativa** otra elección (pág. 378)
ambassador an official representative of a country's government (p. 197)	**embajador** funcionario que representa el gobierno de un país (pág. 197)
amendment any change in the Constitution (p. 86)	**enmienda** cualquier cambio en la Constitución (pág. 86)
amnesty a pardon to a group of people (p. 196)	**amnistía** perdón concedido a un grupo de personas (pág. 196)
annual percentage rate (APR) annual cost of credit expressed as a percentage of the amount borrowed (p. 499)	**tasa anual equivalente (TAE)** costo anual de un crédito, expresado como porcentaje de la cantidad prestada (pág. 499)

Glossary/Glosario

Anti-Federalists those who opposed ratification of the Constitution (p. 85)

antitrust law legislation to prevent new monopolies from forming and to preserve and promote competition (p. 544)

apathy a lack of interest (p. 275)

appellate court type of court in which a party who lost a case in a lower court asks judges to review that decision and reverse it (p. 335)

appellate jurisdiction the authority of a court to hear a case appealed from a lower court (p. 224)

appropriations bill legislation that sets spending on particular programs for the coming year (p. 591)

***arbitrary** unrestrained (p. 10)

arbitration situation in which union and company officials submit the issues they cannot agree on to a neutral third party for a final decision (p. 529)

***area** a region or section (p. 74)

article one of several main parts of the Constitution (p. 86)

Articles of Confederation the first constitution of the United States (p. 73)

***assign** to dole out or give as a task (p. 94)

***assume** to take on or accept a role or responsibility (p. 90)

at-large election an election for an area as a whole, for example, statewide (p. 348)

***attain** to gain; to achieve (p. 558)

***attitude** a feeling or way of thinking (p. 383)

authoritarian regime a government in which one leader or group of people holds absolute power (p. 31)

***authority** power or influence over other people or groups; person or persons having the power of government (p. 54)

automatic stabilizer any economic feature that works to increase or preserve income without additional government action (p. 603)

anti-federalistas personas que se oponían a la ratificación de la Constitución (pág. 85)

ley antimonopolio legislación para evitar la formación de nuevos monopolios y para preservar y promover la competencia (pág. 544)

apatía falta de interés (pág. 275)

tribunal de apelaciones tipo de tribunal en el cual una parte que perdió un caso en una instancia inferior les pide a los jueces que revisen esa decisión y la revoquen (pág. 335)

jurisdicción de apelación autoridad de un tribunal para ver una causa que ha sido apelada de un tribunal inferior (pág. 224)

proyecto de ley de presupuesto legislación que fija el gasto para programas específicos durante el año siguiente (pág. 591)

***arbitrario** desmedido (pág. 10)

arbitraje situación en la cual un sindicato y los funcionarios de la compañía someten los asuntos en los que no pueden llegar a un acuerdo a un tercero neutral para que tome la decisión final (pág. 529)

***área** región o sección (pág. 74)

artículo una de las partes principales de la Constitución (pág. 86)

Artículos de la Confederación primera constitución de Estados Unidos (pág. 73)

***asignar** repartir o poner como tarea (pág. 94)

***asumir** aceptar o hacerse cargo de un rol o una responsabilidad (pág. 90)

elección general elección para un área total, por ejemplo a nivel estatal (pág. 348)

***alcanzar** obtener; lograr (pág. 558)

***actitud** sentimiento o manera de pensar (pág. 383)

régimen autoritario gobierno en el cual un líder o un grupo de personas tiene el poder absoluto (pág. 31)

***autoridad** poder o influencia sobre otras personas o grupos; persona o personas que tienen el poder del gobierno (pág. 54)

estabilizador automático factor económico que actúa para incrementar o conservar los ingresos sin que haya intervención del gobierno (pág. 603)

B

bail a sum of money used as a security deposit to ensure that an accused person returns for his or her trial (pp. 136, 408)

fianza suma de dinero usada como depósito de garantía para asegurarse de que un acusado regrese a su juicio (págs. 136, 408)

balance amount of money left over after subtracting expenses from income; money still owed on a credit card or bank loan (p. 495)

saldo dinero que queda después de sustraer los gastos de los ingresos; dinero que aún se debe en una tarjeta de crédito o un préstamo bancario (pág. 495)

balance of trade the difference between the value of a nation's exports and its imports (p. 615)

balanza comercial diferencia entre el valor de las exportaciones y las importaciones de una nación (pág. 615)

balanced budget annual budget in which expenditures equal revenues (p. 598)

presupuesto equilibrado presupuesto anual en el cual los gastos son iguales a los ingresos (pág. 598)

ballot the list of candidates for which you cast your vote (p. 274)

papeleta de votación lista de candidatos por los cuales se emite el voto (pág. 274)

barter to trade a good or service for another good or service (p. 568)

trocar cambiar un bien o servicio por otro (pág. 568)

bear market period during which stock prices decline for a substantial period (p. 556)

mercado bajista periodo durante el cual los precios de las acciones bajan por un tiempo sustancial (pág. 556)

*benefit to be useful or profitable to (p. 53)

*beneficiar ser útil o rentable (pág. 53)

benefit-cost analysis economic model that compares the marginal costs and marginal benefits of a decision (p. 451)

análisis costo-beneficio modelo económico que compara los costos marginales y los beneficios marginales de una decisión (pág. 451)

*bias good or bad feelings about a person or group that affects judgment (p. 337)

*parcialidad sentimientos buenos o malos hacia un individuo o grupo que afectan el juicio (pág. 337)

biased favoring one view (p. 306)

parcializado que favorece un punto de vista (pág. 306)

bicameral a legislature consisting of two parts, or houses (p. 73)

bicameral asamblea legislativa que consta de dos partes o cámaras (pág. 73)

bill of attainder a law that punishes a person accused of a crime without a trial or a fair hearing in court (pp. 169, 404)

ley de extinción de derechos civiles ley que castiga a una persona acusada de un crimen sin un juicio o una audiencia justa en un tribunal (págs. 169, 404)

black codes laws from after the Civil War that kept African Americans from holding certain jobs, gave them few property rights, and limited their rights in other ways (p. 142)

códigos negros leyes posteriores a la Guerra Civil que evitaban que los afroamericanos tuvieran ciertos trabajos, les daba pocos derechos de propiedad y limitaba sus derechos de otras maneras (pág. 142)

board of directors people elected by the shareholders of a corporation to act on their behalf (p. 520)

junta directiva personas elegidas por los accionistas de una compañía para actuar en nombre suyo (pág. 520)

bond interest-bearing certificate of agreement between a borrower and a lender (p. 508)

bono certificado de acuerdo entre un prestatario y un prestamista que genera intereses (pág. 508)

borrower the recipient of a loan (p. 499)

boycott the refusal to purchase certain goods or services (p. 56)

brief a written document explaining the position of one side or the other in a case (p. 238)

budget a plan for making and spending money (p. 495)

budget deficit a situation that occurs when a government spends more than it collects in revenue (p. 598)

budget surplus a situation that occurs when a government collects more revenues than it spends (p. 598)

bull market period during which stock prices steadily increase (p. 556)

business cycle alternating periods of economic growth and decline (p. 550)

prestatario beneficiario de un préstamo (pág. 499)

boicot negativa a comprar determinados bienes o servicios (pág. 56)

sumario documento escrito que explica la posición de un lado o el otro en un caso (pág. 238)

presupuesto plan para obtener y gastar dinero (pág. 495)

déficit presupuestario situación que ocurre cuando los gastos de un gobierno superan sus ingresos (pág. 598)

superávit presupuestario situación que ocurre cuando los ingresos de un gobierno superan sus gastos (pág. 598)

mercado alcista periodo durante el cual los precios de las acciones aumentan de manera constante (pág. 556)

ciclo económico periodos alternativos de crecimiento y caída de la economía (pág. 550)

C

cabinet a group of advisers to the president that includes the heads of 15 top-level executive departments (p. 207)

canvass to seek votes from voters (p. 283)

capitalism a system in which private citizens own most, if not all, of the means of production and decide how to use them within legislated limits (p. 477)

case law law established by judicial decisions instead of by legislative action (p. 401)

caseload a judge's or court's workload of cases in a period of time (p. 237)

casework the work that a lawmaker does to help constituents with a problem (p. 174)

cash crop a crop produced mainly for sale (p. 50)

gabinete grupo de asesores del presidente compuesto por los jefes de los 15 departamentos ejecutivos de alto nivel (pág. 207)

hacer campaña buscar votos de los electores (pág. 283)

capitalismo sistema en el cual ciudadanos privados poseen todos los medios de producción, o la mayoría de ellos, y deciden cómo usarlos dentro de límites establecidos por la ley (pág. 477)

jurisprudencia ley establecida por decisiones judiciales, no por acciones legislativas (pág. 401)

casos asignados carga laboral de casos asignados a un juez o a un tribunal en un periodo de tiempo (pág. 237)

asistencia social trabajo que hace un legislador para ayudar a los constituyentes con un problema (pág. 174)

cultivo comercial cultivo producido principalmente para la venta (pág. 50)

Glossary/Glosario

caucus a meeting of political party members to conduct party business (p. 254)

asamblea partidista reunión de miembros de un partido político para tratar asuntos del mismo (pág. 254)

censorship the banning of printed materials or films due to alarming or offensive ideas (p. 130)

censura prohibición de materiales impresos o películas debido a ideas alarmantes u ofensivas (pág. 130)

census a population count taken by the Census Bureau (p. 160)

censo conteo de población realizado por la Oficina del Censo (pág. 160)

central bank an institution that lends money to other banks; also, the place where the government does its banking business (p. 573)

banco central institución que presta dinero a otros bancos; también, lugar donde el gobierno realiza sus transacciones bancarias (pág. 573)

certificate of deposit (CD) a timed deposit that states the amount of the deposit, maturity, and rate of interest being paid (p. 579)

certificado de depósito (CD) depósito temporal que estipula el monto del depósito, la fecha de vencimiento y la tasa de interés pactada (pág. 579)

*__challenge__ to object to a decision or outcome (p. 233)

*__desafiar__ oponerse a una decisión o un resultado (pág. 233)

charter a government document granting permission to organize a corporation (p. 520)

escritura de constitución documento del gobierno que autoriza organizar una empresa (pág. 520)

charter school a type of school that receives state funding but is excused from meeting many public school regulations (p. 378)

escuela semiautónoma tipo de escuela que recibe fondos estatales y está exenta de cumplir muchos de los reglamentos de las escuelas públicas (pág. 378)

checking account an account from which deposited money can be withdrawn at any time by writing a check (p. 580)

cuenta corriente cuenta en la cual el dinero depositado se puede retirar en cualquier momento girando un cheque (pág. 580)

checks and balances a system in which each branch of government is able to check, or restrain, the power of the others (p. 95)

equilibrio de poderes sistema en el cual cada rama del gobierno puede controlar, o restringir, el poder de las otras (pág. 95)

circular flow model a model showing how goods, services, and money flow among sectors and markets in the American economy (p. 471)

modelo de flujo circular modelo que muestra cómo los bienes, servicios y el dinero fluyen entre los sectores y los mercados de la economía estadounidense (pág. 471)

*__circumstance__ situation (p. 527)

*__circunstancia__ situación (pág. 527)

citizen community member who owes loyalty to the government and is entitled to its protection (p. 11)

ciudadano miembro de una comunidad que le debe lealtad al gobierno y tiene derecho a recibir su protección (pág. 11)

citizenship rights and duties of citizens (p. 12)

ciudadanía derechos y deberes de los ciudadanos (pág. 12)

city charter a document granting power to a local government (p. 347)

ley orgánica de la ciudad documento que confiere poder al gobierno local (pág. 347)

civics the study of the rights and duties of citizens (p. 11)

educación cívica estudio de los derechos y deberes de los ciudadanos (pág. 11)

*__civil__ of or relating to citizens (p. 128)

*__civil__ relativo a los ciudadanos (pág. 128)

civil case court case in which one party in a dispute claims to have been harmed in some way by the other (p. 335)

caso civil caso judicial en el cual una de las partes en disputa afirma que la otra la ha perjudicado de algún modo (pág. 335)

civil liberties freedoms to think and act without government interference or fear of unfair legal treatment (p. 128)

civil rights the rights of full citizenship and equality under the law (p. 147)

civil service system the practice of hiring government workers on the basis of open, competitive examinations and merit (p. 211)

*clarify to explain; to make something more understandable (p. 518)

closed primary an election in which only the declared members of a party are allowed to vote for that party's nominees (p. 257)

cloture a procedure used in the Senate to limit debate on a bill (p. 180)

*code an organized statement of a body of law (p. 396)

coin metallic form of money, such as a penny (p. 569)

collective bargaining process by which unions and employers negotiate the conditions of employment (p. 527)

command economy an economic system in which the government makes the major economic decisions (p. 445)

commercial bank a financial institution that offers full banking services to individuals and businesses (p. 571)

common law a system of law based on precedent and customs (p. 398)

communism a one-party system of government based on the idea of state ownership and direction of property and industry (p. 647)

community policing local police force visibly keeping the peace and patrolling neighborhoods (p. 380)

commute to reduce a criminal's sentence (p. 331)

*compact an agreement, or contract, among a group of people (p. 46)

comparative advantage a country's ability to produce a good more efficiently than other countries can (p. 610)

libertad civil libertad de pensar y actuar sin intervención del gobierno ni temor a un trato injusto por parte de la ley (pág. 128)

derechos civiles derechos de ciudadanía plena e igualdad bajo la ley (pág. 147)

sistema de servicio civil práctica que consiste en contratar trabajadores del gobierno con base en exámenes abiertos y competitivos y en sus méritos (pág. 211)

*aclarar explicar; hacer que algo sea más comprensible (pág. 518)

elección primaria cerrada elección en la cual solo los miembros declarados de un partido pueden votar por los candidatos de ese partido (pág. 257)

clausura procedimiento usado en el Senado para limitar un debate sobre un proyecto de ley (pág. 180)

*código declaración organizada de un cojunto de leyes (pág. 396)

moneda forma metálica del dinero, como las monedas de un centavo (pág. 569)

negociación colectiva proceso por el cual los sindicatos y los empleadores negocian las condiciones del empleo (pág. 527)

economía planificada sistema económico en el cual el gobierno central toma las principales decisiones económicas (pág. 445)

banca comercial institución financiera que ofrece servicios bancarios completos a individuos y empresas (pág. 571)

derecho consuetudinario sistema legal basado en precedentes y costumbres (pág. 398)

comunismo sistema de gobierno de un solo partido, fundamentado en la idea de que el Estado posee y dirige la propiedad y la industria (pág. 647)

policía de proximidad fuerza policial local que mantiene la paz y patrulla los vecindarios (pág. 380)

conmutar reducir la sentencia de un criminal (pág. 331)

*pacto acuerdo, o contrato, entre un grupo de personas (pág. 46)

ventaja comparativa capacidad que tiene un país de producir un bien con mayor eficiencia que otros países (pág. 610)

Glossary/Glosario

comparison shopping the process of comparing competing products and prices in order to find the best value (p. 491)

compra comparativa proceso de comparar los productos y precios de la competencia para hallar el mejor valor (pág. 491)

compensation payment to unemployed or injured workers to make up for lost wages (p. 560)

compensación pago efectuado a los desempleados o a los obreros incapacitados para cubrir los salarios no percibidos (pág. 560)

competition efforts by different businesses to sell the same good or service (p. 454); the struggle that goes on between buyers and sellers to get the best products at the lowest prices (p. 480)

competencia esfuerzos de diferentes empresas por vender el mismo bien o servicio (pág. 454); pugna entre compradores y vendedores para obtener los mejores productos a los precios más bajos (pág. 480)

complaint a formal notice that a lawsuit has been brought (p. 419)

denuncia aviso formal de que se ha entablado una demanda legal (pág. 419)

*complex complicated or intricate; having many parts connected together (pp. 334, 361)

*complejo complicado o intrincado; que tiene muchas partes interconectadas (págs. 334, 361)

*comprise to be made up of (p. 474)

*comprender constar de o estar compuesto de (pág. 474)

concurrent jurisdiction authority for both state and federal courts to hear and decide cases (p. 222)

jurisdicción concurrente autoridad de los juzgados estatales y federales para ver causas y decidir sobre ellas (pág. 222)

concurrent powers powers shared by the state and federal governments (pp. 96, 319)

poderes concurrentes poderes que comparten los gobiernos federal y estatal (págs. 96, 319)

concurring opinion a statement written by a justice who votes with the majority, but for different reasons (p. 241)

opinión concurrente declaración escrita de un magistrado que vota igual que la mayoría, pero por razones diferentes (pág. 241)

*conduct to carry out (p. 144)

*realizar llevar a cabo (pág. 144)

confederation a group of individuals or state governments (p. 73)

confederación grupo de individuos o gobiernos estatales (pág. 73)

*consent to express willingness or to agree; approval (p. 227)

*consentir expresar voluntad o acuerdo; aprobar (pág. 227)

conservation the careful preservation and protection of natural resources (p. 384)

conservación preservación y protección cuidadosa de los recursos naturales (pág. 384)

constituent a person from a legislator's district (p. 160)

constituyente persona que forma parte del distrito de un legislador (pág. 160)

constitution a detailed, written plan for government (p. 72)

constitución plan de gobierno escrito y detallado (pág. 72)

constitutional in accordance with the Constitution (p. 232)

constitucional conforme a la Constitución (pág. 232)

Constitutional Convention meeting of state delegates in 1787 leading to adoption of a new Constitution (p. 80)

Convención Constitucional reunión de delegados estatales que tuvo lugar en 1787 y llevó a la adopción de una nueva Constitución (pág. 80)

constitutional law branch of law dealing with formation, construction, and interpretation of constitutions (p. 401)

derecho constitucional rama del derecho que se ocupa de la formación, construcción e interpretación de las Constituciones (pág. 401)

constitutional monarchy monarchy in which the power of the hereditary ruler is limited by the country's constitution and laws (p. 30)

monarquía constitucional monarquía en la cual la Constitución y las leyes del país limitan el poder del gobernante heredero (pág. 30)

*consult to seek information or advice from a person or resource (p. 516)

*consultar buscar información o consejo de una persona o fuente (pág. 516)

consumer someone who buys a good or service (p. 452)

consumidor quien compra un bien o servicio (pág. 452)

consumerism a movement to educate buyers about the purchases they make and to demand better and safer products from manufacturers (p. 488)

consumismo movimiento para educar a los consumidores sobre las compras que realizan y para exigir a los fabricantes productos de mejor calidad y más seguros (pág. 488)

contract a set of promises between agreeing parties that is enforceable by law (p. 417)

contrato conjunto de promesas entre las partes que llegan a un acuerdo, el cual la ley hace cumplir (pág. 417)

*convince to persuade or win over (p. 370)

*convencer persuadir o ganar apoyo (pág. 370)

corporation type of business organization owned by many people but treated by law as though it were a person (p. 520)

sociedad anónima tipo de organización empresarial que pertenece a muchas personas pero que la ley trata como si fuera una persona (pág. 520)

county normally the largest territorial and political subdivision of a state (p. 354)

condado normalmente, la subdivisión territorial y política más grande de un estado (pág. 354)

county seat a town where the county courthouse is located (p. 355)

capital del condado ciudad donde se localiza el palacio de justicia del condado (pág. 355)

credit permission to pay later for goods or services obtained today (p. 498)

crédito autorización para pagar posteriormente bienes o servicios adquiridos en el presente (pág. 498)

credit union nonprofit service cooperative that accepts deposits, makes loans, and provides other financial services to members (p. 571)

cooperativa de ahorro y crédito cooperativa de servicios sin ánimo de lucro que acepta depósitos, hace préstamos y presta servicios financieros a sus asociados (pág. 571)

crime an act that breaks a law and causes harm to people or society in general (p. 421)

delito acción que viola una ley y causa daño a las personas o a la sociedad en general (pág. 421)

cross-examination the questioning of a witness at a trial or hearing to check or discredit the witness's testimony (p. 426)

contrainterrogatorio interrogatorio realizado a un testigo en un juicio o una audiencia para corroborar o desvirtuar un testimonio (pág. 426)

*crucial very important, especially for its effect on something (p. 534)

*crucial muy importante, en especial por su efecto sobre algo (pág. 534)

*culture the ideas, customs, art, and beliefs of a people or group (p. 644)

*cultura ideas, costumbres, arte y creencias de un pueblo o grupo (pág. 644)

currency money, both coins and paper bills (p. 569)

moneda dinero en forma de monedas y billetes (pág. 569)

custody taking charge of someone in an official way (p. 432)

custodia encargarse de una persona de manera oficial (pág. 432)

Glossary/Glosario

D

damages money ordered by a court to be paid for injuries or losses suffered (p. 419)

daños dinero que un tribunal ordena pagar por lesiones o pérdidas sufridas (pág. 419)

*data factual information used for reasoning (p. 497)

*datos información objetiva que se usa para hacer razonamientos (pág. 497)

*debate to discuss or argue (p. 59)

*debatir comentar o argumentar (pág. 59)

debt money borrowed and not yet paid back (p. 598)

deuda dinero que se pidió prestado y aún no se ha pagado (pág. 598)

defendant the person in a civil case who is said to have caused the harm; the person who is being sued (pp. 335, 419)

acusado persona en un proceso civil que se dice que ha ocasionado un daño; persona que está siendo demandada (págs. 335, 419)

deficit a negative balance (p. 496)

déficit saldo negativo (pág. 496)

deforestation the mass removal of trees in large areas (p. 636)

deforestación eliminación masiva de árboles en grandes áreas (pág. 636)

delegate a representative to a meeting (p. 59)

delegado representante en una reunión (pág. 59)

delinquent offender a youth who has committed an offense that is punishable by criminal processes (p. 431)

delincuente juvenil joven que ha cometido un delito que se castiga por procesos criminales (pág. 431)

demand the amount of a good or service that consumers are willing and able to buy over a range of prices (p. 453)

demanda cantidad de un bien o servicio que los consumidores desean y pueden comprar dentro de una gama de precios (pág. 453)

democracy a government in which citizens hold the power to rule (p. 40)

democracia gobierno en el cual los ciudadanos tienen el poder para gobernar (pág. 40)

*deny to take away a right or privilege (p. 14)

*negar quitar un derecho o un privilegio (pág. 14)

deposit the money that customers put into a financial institution (p. 570)

depósito dinero que los clientes consignan en una institución financiera (pág. 570)

deposit insurance government-backed program that protects bank deposits up to a certain amount if a bank fails (p. 571)

seguro de depósito programa respaldado por el gobierno que protege los depósitos bancarios hasta cierta cantidad si un banco se declara en quiebra (pág. 571)

depression state of the economy with high unemployment, severely depressed real GDP, and general economic hardship (p. 551)

depresión estado de la economía que se caracteriza por alto desempleo, PIB real en situación muy crítica y dificultades económicas generales (pág. 551)

*despite regardless or in spite of (p. 79)

*a pesar de no obstante, pese a que (pág. 79)

detention hearing a juvenile court process that is much like a preliminary hearing in adult criminal law (p. 433)

audiencia de detención proceso en un tribunal juvenil que se asemeja a una audiencia preliminar en el derecho penal de adultos (pág. 433)

developed country a country with a high standard of living, a high level of industrialization, and a high per capita income (p. 623)

país desarrollado país con un alto estándar de vida, un alto nivel de industrialización y un alto ingreso per cápita (pág. 623)

developing country a country with a low per capita income in which a large number of people have a low standard of living (p. 623)

país en desarrollo país con un ingreso per cápita bajo, en el cual un gran número de personas tiene un estándar de vida bajo (pág. 623)

diplomat a representative of a country's government who takes part in talks with representatives of other nations (p. 638)

diplomático representante del gobierno de un país que toma parte en conversaciones con representantes de otras naciones (pág. 638)

direct democracy a form of democracy in which the people vote firsthand (p. 41)

democracia directa forma de democracia en la cual las personas votan directamente (pág. 41)

direct primary an election in which voters choose candidates to represent each party in a general election (p. 257)

elección primaria directa elección en la cual los votantes eligen candidatos para que representen a cada partido en una elección general (pág. 257)

discount rate the interest rate that the Fed charges on its loans to financial institutions (p. 576)

tasa de descuento tasa de interés que la Reserva Federal cobra por sus préstamos a las instituciones financieras (pág. 576)

discovery process by which attorneys have the opportunity to check facts and gather evidence before a trial (p. 419)

revelación de pruebas proceso mediante el cual los abogados tienen la oportunidad de corroborar los hechos y reunir evidencias antes de un juicio (pág. 419)

discretionary income income left after taxes on it have been paid and that you can choose to spend (p. 494)

ingresos discrecionales ingresos monetarios que quedan después de pagar impuestos, cuya destinación se puede elegir (pág. 494)

discretionary spending spending for federal programs that must receive approval each year (p. 591)

gastos discrecionales gastos para los programas federales que deben ser aprobados cada año (pág. 591)

discrimination unfair treatment based on prejudice against a certain group (p. 146)

discriminación trato injusto basado en prejuicios contra un grupo determinado (pág. 146)

*__display__ to show or list (p. 190)

*__exponer__ mostrar o enumerar (pág. 190)

disposable income income left after all taxes on it have been paid (p. 494)

ingresos disponibles ingresos monetarios que quedan después de pagar todos los impuestos (pág. 494)

*__dispose__ to get rid of; to eliminate (p. 480)

*__desechar__ deshacerse de; eliminar (pág. 480)

disposition hearing the final settlement and sentencing in a juvenile case (p. 433)

audiencia de disposición resolución y sentencia finales en un proceso juvenil (pág. 433)

dissenter one who opposes official or commonly held views (p. 49)

disidente persona que se opone a opiniones oficiales o ampliamente aceptadas (pág. 49)

dissenting opinion a statement written by a justice who disagrees with the majority opinion, presenting his or her opinion (p. 241)

opinión discrepante declaración escrita de un magistrado que no está de acuerdo con la opinión de la mayoría, en la cual presenta su opinión (pág. 241)

*__distinct__ unique, special, or different in some way; separate or noticeably different (p. 5)

*__distinto__ único, especial o diferente de alguna manera; separado o perceptiblemente diferente (pág. 5)

*__distinguish__ to see a difference in; to separate into categories (p. 493)

*__distinguir__ ver alguna diferencia; separar en categorías (pág. 493)

Glossary/Glosario

***distribute** to give out; to deliver (pp. 443, 578)

dividend a portion of company earnings paid to shareholders (p. 508)

division of labor the breaking down of a job into separate, smaller tasks to be performed individually (p. 476)

docket a court's calendar, showing the schedule of cases it is to hear (p. 237)

***document** an official paper or form that is a record of something (p. 42)

***dominate** to have great influence over (p. 348)

double jeopardy putting someone on trial for a crime for which he or she was previously found not guilty (pp. 135, 407)

***draft** to write a document in its first form (p. 241); to make an outline or a rough version (p. 173); to call for military service (p. 19)

dual court system a court system made up of both federal and state courts (p. 219)

due process following established legal procedures (pp. 136, 404)

duty an action we are required to perform (p. 18); a tax on an imported good (p. 56)

distribuir repartir; entregar (págs. 443, 578)

dividendo parte de las utilidades de una compañía que se paga a los accionistas (pág. 508)

división del trabajo separación de un trabajo en tareas independientes más pequeñas que se realizan individualmente (pág. 476)

lista de casos calendario de un tribunal, que muestra la programación de las causas que debe ver (pág. 237)

***documento** papel oficial o formato que sirve como registro de algo (pág. 42)

***dominar** tener gran influencia sobre algo (pág. 348)

doble enjuiciamiento juzgar a alguien por un crimen del cual había sido absuelto antes (págs. 135, 407)

***hacer un borrador** escribir la primera versión de un documento (pág. 241); hacer un esquema o una versión sin perfeccionar (pág. 173); el término en inglés "draft" también significa "reclutar", es decir, convocar al servicio militar (pág. 19)

sistema judicial doble sistema judicial compuesto por tribunales federales y estatales (pág. 219)

debido proceso seguimiento de los procesos legales establecidos (págs. 136, 404)

deber acción que estamos obligados a realizar (pág. 18); el término en inglés "duty" también significa "impuesto de aduana", es decir, impuesto sobre los bienes importados (pág. 56)

E

economic growth the increase in a country's total output of goods and services over time (p. 475)

economic systems a nation's way of producing things its people want and need (p. 444)

economics the study of how individuals and nations make choices about ways to use scarce resources to fulfill their needs and wants (p. 441)

economy a system for making choices about ways to use scarce resources to make and distribute goods and services to fulfill people's needs and wants (p. 50)

crecimiento económico aumento en la producción total de bienes y servicios de un país con el paso del tiempo (pág. 475)

sistema económico forma en que una nación produce lo que sus habitantes desean y necesitan (pág. 444)

ciencia económica estudio de la manera en que los individuos y las naciones toman decisiones sobre la forma de usar recursos escasos para satisfacer sus necesidades y deseos (pág. 441)

economía sistema para tomar decisiones sobre la forma de usar y distribuir los bienes y servicios para satisfacer las necesidades y los deseos de las personas (pág. 50)

elastic clause clause in Article I, Section 8 of the Constitution that gives Congress the right to make all laws "necessary and proper" to carry out its expressed powers (p. 167)

cláusula elástica cláusula del Artículo I, Sección 8 de la Constitución que le da al Congreso el derecho de crear las leyes "necesarias y apropiadas" para poner en práctica sus poderes explícitos (pág. 167)

elector person appointed to vote in presidential elections for president or vice president (p. 189)

elector persona habilitada para votar en las elecciones presidenciales por el presidente o el vicepresidente (pág. 189)

Electoral College a group of people named by each state legislature to select the president and vice president (pp. 83, 280)

colegio electoral grupo de personas nombradas por la asamblea legislativa de cada Estado para elegir al presidente y al vicepresidente (págs. 83, 280)

electronic money money in the form of a computer entry at a bank or other financial institution (p. 569)

dinero electrónico dinero en forma de registro computarizado en un banco u otra institución financiera (pág. 569)

*eliminate to take away or to end (p. 141)

*eliminar quitar o acabar (pág. 141)

embargo an agreement among a group of nations that prohibits them all from trading with a target nation (p. 204)

embargo acuerdo entre un grupo de naciones que les prohíbe negociar con una nación determinada (pág. 204)

eminent domain the right of government to take private property – usually land – for public use (p. 136)

derecho de expropiación derecho del gobierno de tomar propiedades privadas para uso público (pág. 136)

*emphasis weight or stress (p. 430)

*énfasis valor o importancia de algo (pág. 430)

*enormous very large (p. 551)

*enorme muy grande (pág. 551)

*ensure to make sure of; to guarantee (p. 93)

*asegurar cerciorarse de algo; garantizar (pág. 93)

entitlement program a government program that makes payments to people who must meet certain requirements in order to help them meet minimum health, nutrition, and income needs (p. 594)

programa de ayuda social programa del gobierno que realiza pagos a las personas que cumplen ciertos requisitos para ayudarlas a satisfacer las necesidades económicas, de salud y de alimentación mínimas (pág. 594)

entrepreneur risk-taking individual who starts a new business, introduces a new product, or improves a management technique (p. 467)

empresario individuo que se arriesga y empieza una nueva empresa, introduce un producto nuevo o mejora una técnica gerencial (pág. 467)

enumerated powers powers granted directly to the national government by the Constitution (p. 96); another name for expressed powers (p. 165)

poderes enumerados poderes que la Constitución le confiere directamente al gobierno nacional (pág. 96); otro nombre con que se conocen los poderes explícitos (pág. 165)

environmentalism movement concerned with protecting the environment (p. 382)

ambientalismo movimiento que se preocupa por la protección del medioambiente (pág. 382)

equilibrium price the price set for a good or service in the marketplace, where demand and supply are perfectly balanced (p. 455)

precio de equilibrio precio fijado para un bien o servicio en el mercado, en el cual la oferta y la demanda están en perfecto equilibrio (pág. 455)

*estimate to form a rough or general idea of the cost, size, or value of something (pp. 173, 358)

*estimar hacerse una idea aproximada o general del costo, el tamaño o el valor de algo (págs. 173, 358)

ethnic group a group of people who share a common national, cultural, or racial background (pp. 8, 637)

grupo étnico grupo de personas que comparten el mismo origen nacional, cultural o racial (págs. 8, 637)

Glossary/Glosario

*exceed to be greater than (p. 590)

exchange rate the value of a nation's currency in relation to another nation's currency (p. 616)

exclusionary rule rule that evidence gained by police in a way that violates the Fourth Amendment may not be used in a trial (p. 405)

exclusive jurisdiction authority of only federal courts to hear and decide cases (p. 222)

executive agency independent agency that deals with certain specific areas within the government (p. 210)

executive agreement an agreement between the president and the leader of another country (p. 203)

executive branch the branch of government that carries out laws (p. 87)

executive order a rule or command the president gives out that has the force of law (p. 196)

expense money spent on goods and services (p. 495)

*exploit to use unfairly for someone else's gain (p. 151)

export to sell goods to other countries (p. 610)

ex post facto law a law that would allow a person to be punished for an action that was not against the law when it was committed (pp. 169, 404)

expressed powers power that the U.S. Congress has that is specifically listed in the Constitution (p. 165)

externality an economic side effect that affects an uninvolved third party (p. 543)

*exceder ser mayor que otra cosa (pág. 590)

tasa de cambio valor de la moneda de una nación con relación a la de otra nación (pág. 616)

regla de exclusión norma que establece que las evidencias obtenidas por la policía en una forma que viole la Cuarta Enmienda no se pueden usar en un juicio (pág. 405)

jurisdicción exclusiva autoridad exclusiva de los tribunales federales para ver causas y decidir sobre ellas (pág. 222)

agencia ejecutiva agencia independiente que se ocupa de algunas áreas específicas dentro del gobierno (pág. 210)

acuerdo ejecutivo acuerdo entre el presidente y el líder de otro país (pág. 203)

poder ejecutivo rama del gobierno que hace cumplir las leyes (pág. 87)

orden ejecutiva regla o mandato impartido por el presidente que tiene fuerza de ley (pág. 196)

gastos dinero que se invierte en bienes y servicios (pág. 495)

*explotar usar indebidamente algo para el beneficio de otro (pág. 151)

exportar vender bienes a otros países (pág. 610)

ley ex post facto ley que permite que una persona sea castigada por una acción que no infringía la ley cuando se cometió (págs. 169, 404)

poderes explícitos facultad del Congreso de Estados Unidos que se enumera específicamente en la Constitución (pág. 165)

exterioridad efecto económico colateral que afecta a un tercero no comprometido (pág. 543)

F

factor market a market where productive resources are bought and sold (p. 472)

federal bureaucracy agencies and the employees of the executive branch of government (p. 209)

Federal Open Market Committee (FOMC) the most powerful committee of the Fed, which makes decisions that affect the economy as a whole by manipulating the money supply (p. 574)

mercado de factores mercado donde se compran y venden los recursos productivos (pág. 472)

burocracia federal agencias y empleados de la rama ejecutiva del gobierno (pág. 209)

Comité Federal del Mercado Abierto (en inglés, FOMC) comité más poderoso de la Reserva Federal, el cual toma decisiones que afectan la economía global controlando la oferta de dinero (pág. 574)

federal system the sharing of power between the central and state governments (p. 316)

sistema federal poder compartido entre los gobiernos central y estatal (pág. 316)

federalism a form of government in which power is divided between the federal, or national, government and the states (p. 83)

federalismo forma de gobierno en la cual el poder se divide entre el gobierno federal, o nacional, y los estados (pág. 83)

The Federalist Papers a series of essays written to defend the Constitution (p. 84)

Documentos Federalistas serie de ensayos escritos para defender la Constitución (pág. 84)

Federalists supporters of the Constitution (p. 83)

Federalistas defensores de la Constitución (pág. 83)

*fee the cost of a service (p. 499)

*honorarios costo de un servicio (pág. 499)

felony a type of crime more serious than a misdemeanor, such as murder, rape, kidnapping, or robbery (pp. 336, 422)

delito grave tipo de crimen más grave que un delito menor, como un homicidio, una violación, un secuestro o un robo (págs. 336, 422)

filibuster a tactic for defeating a bill in the Senate by talking until the bill's sponsor withdraws it (p. 180)

obstruccionismo táctica para derrotar un proyecto de ley en el Senado hablando hasta que el ponente del proyecto lo retira (pág. 180)

financial capital money used to run or expand a business (p. 517)

capital financiero dinero usado para poner en marcha o ampliar un negocio (pág. 517)

fiscal policy how the government uses taxes and spending to reach economic goals (p. 601)

política fiscal manera en que el gobierno usa los impuestos y el gasto para alcanzar las metas económicas (pág. 601)

fiscal year any 12-month period chosen for keeping accounts (p. 590)

año fiscal periodo de 12 meses escogido para llevar las cuentas (pág. 590)

fixed cost an expense that does not change no matter how much a business produces (p. 448)

costo fijo gasto que no cambia sin importar cuánto produzca una empresa (pág. 448)

fixed income an income that remains the same each month and does not have the potential to go up when prices are going up (p. 553)

ingreso fijo ingreso que permanece igual cada mes y que no tiene la posibilidad de aumentar cuando hay un alza en los precios (pág. 553)

foreign policy a nation's overall plan for dealing with other nations (p. 200)

política exterior plan general de una nación para relacionarse con otras naciones (pág. 200)

foundation an organization established by a company or an individual to provide money for a particular purpose, especially for charity or research (p. 532)

fundación organización establecida por una compañía o un individuo con el fin de proveer dinero para un propósito en particular, especialmente para caridad o investigaciones (pág. 532)

franchise a company that has permission to sell the supplier's goods or services in a particular area in exchange for a sum of money (p. 522)

franquicia compañía que tiene permiso de vender bienes o servicios en un área en particular a cambio de una suma de dinero (pág. 522)

franking privilege the right of senators and representatives to send job-related mail without paying postage (p. 171)

privilegio postal derecho de los senadores y representantes para enviar correspondencia relacionada con su trabajo sin pagar franqueo (pág. 171)

Glossary/Glosario

free enterprise economic system in which individuals and businesses are allowed to compete for profit with a minimum of government interference (p. 477)

libre empresa sistema económico en el cual los individuos y las empresas pueden competir para obtener utilidades con una mínima intervención del gobierno (pág. 477)

free speech the right to say our opinions, in public or in private, without fear of being stopped or punished by the government for those ideas (p. 129)

libertad de expresión derecho de una persona a expresar sus opiniones en público o en privado, sin temor a que el gobierno lo detenga o castigue por esas ideas (pág. 129)

free trade the lack of trade restrictions among countries (p. 612)

libre comercio ausencia de restricciones comerciales entre países (pág. 612)

*function to serve a purpose (p. 319)

*funcionar cumplir un propósito (pág. 319)

*funds money (p. 570)

*fondos dinero (pág. 570)

G

GDP per capita Gross Domestic Product on a per-person basis; GDP divided by population (p. 470)

PIB per cápita Producto Interno Bruto por persona; PIB dividido entre el número de habitantes (pág. 470)

*gender whether a person is male or female (p. 291)

*sexo condición de ser hombre o mujer (pág. 291)

*generate to produce (p. 383)

*generar producir (pág. 383)

generic good an item that does not have a brand name but is basically similar to a more expensive, well-known product (p. 491)

producto genérico artículo que no tiene una marca comercial pero básicamente se asemeja a otro producto conocido y más costoso (pág. 491)

genocide the attempt to kill all members of a particular ethnic group (p. 646)

genocidio intento de asesinar a todos los miembros de un grupo étnico en particular (pág. 646)

gerrymander an oddly shaped election district designed to increase the voting strength of a particular group (p. 160)

guerrimandaje distrito electoral formado de una manera anormal para aumentar la fuerza electoral de un grupo en particular (pág. 160)

global interdependence the reliance of people and countries around the world on one another for goods and services (p. 632)

interdependencia global dependencia mutua de las personas y los países del mundo para obtener bienes y servicios (pág. 632)

government the ruling authority for a community (p. 12)

gobierno autoridad a cargo de una comunidad (pág. 12)

government corporation a business owned and operated by the federal government (p. 210)

empresa estatal empresa de propiedad del gobierno federal, operada por el mismo (pág. 210)

*grant to allow (p. 423)

*conceder permitir (pág. 423)

grants-in-aid money awarded to the states by the federal government (p. 320)

subvención estatal dinero que el gobierno federal adjudica a los estados (pág. 320)

Great Compromise agreement providing a dual system of congressional representation (p. 81)

Gran Compromiso acuerdo que provee un sistema dual de representación en el Congreso (pág. 81)

Gross Domestic Product (GDP) total market value of all final goods and services produced in a country during a single year (p. 466)

Producto Interno Bruto (PIB) valor total de mercado de todos los bienes y servicios finales producidos en un país en un solo año (pág. 466)

*__guarantee__ to promise (p. 307)

*__garantizar__ prometer (pág. 307)

H

hate crime a violent act against a person because of his or her race, color, national origin, gender, or disability (p. 150)

crimen de odio acto violento contra una persona debido a su raza, color, origen nacional, sexo o discapacidad (pág. 150)

home rule allows cities to write their own charters, choose their own type of government, and manage their own affairs (p. 347)

autonomía gubernamental facultad que permite a las ciudades redactar sus propias leyes orgánicas, elegir su tipo de gobierno y manejar sus asuntos (pág. 347)

House of Representatives the lower house of Congress, consisting of a different number of representatives from each state, depending on population (p. 158)

Cámara de Representantes Cámara baja del Congreso, compuesta por un número diferente de representantes de cada estado de acuerdo con el número de habitantes (pág. 158)

human capital the sum of people's knowledge and skills that can be used to create products (p. 476)

capital humano suma de los conocimientos y destrezas de las personas que se pueden usar para crear productos (pág. 476)

human right a protection or a freedom that all people should have (p. 644)

derecho humano protección o libertad que todas las personas deberían tener (pág. 644)

I

ideology a body of ideas about life and society (p. 32)

ideología conjunto de ideas sobre la vida y la sociedad (pág. 32)

*__illustration__ an example that helps make something clear (p. 423)

*__ejemplificación__ ejemplo que ayuda a aclarar algo (pág. 423)

immigrant an individual who moves permanently to a new country (p. 4)

inmigrante individuo que se traslada a vivir a otro país (pág. 4)

*__impact__ to influence or affect (p. 75)

*__tener impacto__ influenciar o afectar (pág. 75)

impeach to accuse government officials of misconduct in office (p. 168)

recusar acusar a un funcionario del gobierno por mala conducta en el ejercicio de su cargo (pág. 168)

implied power power that Congress has that is not stated explicitly in the Constitution (p. 167)

poder implícito facultad del Congreso que no se haya estipulada de manera expresa en la Constitución (pág. 167)

import to buy goods from another country (p. 610)

importar comprar bienes de otro país (pág. 610)

impulse buying an unplanned, often emotional, decision to buy (p. 493)

compra impulsiva decisión de compra no planeada, por lo general emocional (pág. 493)

Glossary/Glosario

*incentive reward offered to try to persuade people to take certain economic actions (p. 480)

incorporate to receive a state charter, officially recognizing the government of a locality (p. 347)

indentured servant workers who contracted with American colonists for food and shelter in return for their labor (p. 49)

*indicate to signal (p. 550)

indictment a document issued by a body called a grand jury that formally charges someone with a crime (p. 135)

*individual a person (p. 442)

inflation a long-term increase in the general level of prices (p. 554)

infrastructure a community's system of roads, bridges, water, and sewers (p. 373)

initiative a procedure by which citizens can propose new laws or state constitutional amendments (p. 278)

injunction a court order to stop some kind of action (p. 528)

institution a key practice, relationship, or organization in a society (p. 10)

*integrate to combine multiple components into a functioning whole (p. 614)

*interaction effect of two or more things on each other (p. 459)

interest the payment people or institutions receive when they lend money or allow someone else to use their money (p. 499)

interest group a group of people who share a point of view about an issue and unite to promote their beliefs (p. 292)

intergovernmental revenue funds that one level of government receives from another level of government (p. 594)

issue a matter of debate or dispute (p. 278)

*incentivo recompensa ofrecida con el fin de tratar de persuadir a las personas para que tomen ciertas decisiones económicas (pág. 480)

incorporar recibir una carta estatal en la que se reconoce oficialmente el gobierno de un lugar (pág. 347)

sirviente por contrato trabajador que firmaba un contrato con los colonos de la América colonial para obtener alimento y refugio a cambio de su trabajo (pág. 49)

*indicar señalar (pág. 550)

formulación de cargos documento expedido por un órgano llamado gran jurado en el que se acusa formalmente a alguien de un crimen (pág. 135)

*individuo persona (pág. 442)

inflación aumento a largo plazo del nivel general de precios (pág. 554)

infraestructura sistema comunitario de carreteras, puentes, agua y alcantarillado (pág. 373)

iniciativa procedimiento por el cual los ciudadanos pueden proponer nuevas leyes o enmiendas constitucionales estatales (pág. 278)

interdicto judicial orden judicial para detener un tipo de acción (pág. 528)

institución práctica, relación u organización fundamentales en una sociedad (pág. 10)

*integrar combinar varios componentes en un todo que funcione (pág. 614)

*interacción efecto mutuo de dos o más cosas (pág. 459)

interés pago que las personas o instituciones reciben cuando prestan dinero o permiten que alguien más use su dinero (pág. 499)

grupo de interés grupo de personas que comparten un punto de vista sobre un tema y se unen para difundir sus creencias (pág. 292)

ingreso intergubernamental fondos que un nivel del gobierno recibe de otro nivel del gobierno (pág. 594)

asunto tema de debate o controversia (pág. 278)

J

"Jim Crow" laws Southern segregation laws (p. 146)

leyes de Jim Crow leyes de segregación del Sur (pág. 146)

joint resolution a resolution that is passed by both houses of Congress (p. 177)

resolución conjunta resolución aprobada por ambas cámaras del Congreso (pág. 177)

judicial branch the branch of government that interprets laws (p. 88)

poder judicial rama del gobierno que interpreta las leyes (pág. 88)

judicial review the power of the Supreme Court to say whether any federal, state, or local law or government action goes against the Constitution (p. 232)

revisión judicial facultad de la Corte Suprema de decir si una ley federal, estatal o local, o una acción del gobierno van en contra de la Constitución (pág. 232)

jurisdiction a court's authority to hear and decide cases (p. 221)

jurisdicción autoridad de una corte para ver causas y decidir sobre ellas (pág. 221)

juvenile delinquent a child or teenager who commits a serious crime or repeatedly breaks the law (p. 430)

delincuente juvenil niño o adolescente que comete un crimen grave o viola la ley en repetidas ocasiones (pág. 430)

L

labor union association of workers organized to improve wages and working conditions (p. 524)

sindicato asociación organizada de trabajadores para mejorar sus salarios y condiciones laborales (pág. 524)

laissez-faire economics a belief that government should not interfere in the marketplace (p. 481)

economía del laissez-faire creencia de que el gobierno no debe intervenir en el mercado (pág. 481)

landfill a place where garbage is dumped (p. 383)

basural lugar en donde se vierte la basura (pág. 383)

lawsuit a legal action in which a person or group sues to collect damages for some harm that is done (p. 400)

pleito acción legal en la cual una persona o un grupo entabla un proceso legal para cobrar daños por un perjuicio que se le hizo (pág. 400)

leak to release secret government information by anonymous government officials to the media (p. 298)

filtración revelación de información secreta del gobierno a los medios de comunicación por parte de funcionarios anónimos del gobierno (pág. 298)

legislative branch the lawmaking branch of government (p. 87)

poder legislativo rama del gobierno que hace las leyes (pág. 87)

legislative referendum a vote called by a legislature to seek voter approval of a law (p. 327)

referendo legislativo elección convocada por una asamblea legislativa para buscar que los votantes aprueben una ley (pág. 327)

legislature a group of people that makes laws (p. 42)

asamblea legislativa grupo de personas que hace las leyes (pág. 42)

*levy to demand and collect a tax or other payment, either by authority or by force (p. 356)

*gravar exigir y cobrar un impuesto u otro pago mediante el uso de la autoridad o la fuerza (pág. 356)

liability the legal responsibility for something, such as an action or a debt (p. 517)

responsabilidad obligación legal de responder por algo, como una acción o una deuda (pág. 517)

libel written untruths that are harmful to someone's reputation (p. 132, 301)

difamación falsedades escritas que perjudican a la reputación de alguien (págs. 132, 301)

Glossary/Glosario

liberty the quality or state of being free (p. 54)

libertad cualidad y estado de quien es libre (pág. 54)

*license a document granting the holder permission to do something (p. 138)

*licencia documento que da al tenedor permiso de hacer algo (pág. 138)

limited government the principle that a ruler or a government is not all-powerful (p. 42); a government that can do only what the people allow it to do (p. 94)

gobierno limitado principio según el cual un mandatario o un gobierno no son todopoderosos (pág. 42); gobierno que solo puede hacer lo que el pueblo le permite hacer (pág. 94)

line-item veto to veto only a specific part of a bill (p. 331)

veto de partidas específicas vetar solo una parte específica de un proyecto de ley (pág. 331)

litigant one of the parties involved in a lawsuit (p. 226)

litigante una de las partes de un pleito (pág. 226)

loan money lent at interest (p. 499)

préstamo dinero que se da a crédito con un interés (pág. 499)

lobbyist representative of an interest group who contacts lawmakers or other government officials directly to influence their policy making (pp. 172, 306)

cabildero representante de un grupo de interés que se pone en contacto con legisladores y otros funcionarios del gobierno para influir directamente en su diseño de políticas (págs. 172, 306)

lockout when management closes a workplace to prevent union members from working (p. 528)

cierre patronal cuando la administración cierra un lugar de trabajo para evitar que los miembros del sindicato trabajen (pág. 528)

long-term plan a government plan for policy that can span 10 to 50 years (p. 372)

plan a largo plazo plan gubernamental para una política que puede abarcar de 10 a 50 años (pág. 372)

M

majority a number that is more than 50 percent of the total (p. 258)

mayoría número superior al 50 por ciento del total (pág. 258)

majority party in both the House of Representatives and the Senate, the political party to which more than half the members belong (p. 161)

partido mayoritario tanto en la Cámara de Representantes como en el Senado, partido político al que pertenece más de la mitad de los miembros (pág. 161)

majority rule political principle providing that a majority of the members of a community has the power to make laws binding upon all the people (p. 31)

gobierno de la mayoría principio político que establece que una mayoría de los miembros de una comunidad tiene la facultad de legislar vinculando a todas las personas (pág. 31)

malapportionment unequal representation in state legislatures (p. 325)

desproporcionalidad representación desigual en las asambleas legislativas estatales (pág. 325)

malice evil intent (p. 301)

malicia mala intención (pág. 301)

mandatory spending federal spending required by law that continues without the need for Congressional approval each year (p. 591)

gasto obligatorio gasto federal exigido por la ley que sigue vigente sin necesidad de ser aprobado por el Congreso todos los años (pág. 591)

*manipulate to make changes to something to produce a desired effect (p. 576)

*manipular modificar algo para producir un efecto deseado (pág. 576)

marginal cost the additional or extra opportunity cost associated with each increase of one unit of sales (p. 449)

costo marginal costo de oportunidad adicional o extra asociado con el incremento por unidad vendida (pág. 449)

marginal revenue the additional income received from each increase of one unit of sales (p. 450)

market location or arrangement that allows buyers and sellers to get together and buy or sell a certain product (p. 454)

market economy an economic system in which individuals and businesses own all resources and make economic decisions on the basis of price (p. 444)

mass media a mechanism of mass communication, including television, radio, the Internet, newspapers, magazines, books, recordings, and movies (p. 292)

master plan a plan that states a set of goals and explains how the government will carry them out to meet changing needs over time (p. 374)

maturity the present time at which you may withdraw funds from a certificate of deposit (p. 506)

mediation situation in which union and company officials bring in a third party to try to help them reach an agreement (p. 529)

*medium a way to carry out an action (p. 568)

merger a combination of two or more companies to form a single business (p. 545)

merit system hiring people into government jobs on the basis of their qualifications (p. 211)

*method a procedure or process of doing something (p. 202)

metropolitan area a large city and its suburbs (p. 352)

*minimum the least quantity possible (p. 324)

*minor of comparatively less importance (p. 431)

minority party in both the House of Representatives and the Senate, the political party to which fewer than half the members belong (p. 161)

Miranda Warnings list of rights police must inform persons of before questioning, including the right against self-incrimination and the right to counsel (p. 407)

misdemeanor the least serious type of crime; minor crime for which a person can be fined a small sum of money or jailed for up to one year (pp. 335, 422)

ingreso marginal ingreso adicional proveniente del incremento por unidad vendida (pág. 450)

mercado lugar o acuerdo que permite a compradores y vendedores reunirse para comprar o vender un producto específico (pág. 454)

economía de mercado sistema económico en el cual los individuos y las empresas son dueños de los recursos y toman decisiones económicas con base en el precio (pág. 444)

medios de comunicación social mecanismo de comunicación masiva que incluye televisión, radio, Internet, prensa, revistas, libros, grabaciones y películas (pág. 292)

plan maestro plan que establece un conjunto de objetivos y explica cómo el gobierno los llevará a cabo para satisfacer las necesidades que cambian con el tiempo (pág. 374)

vencimiento fecha en la cual se pueden retirar los fondos depositados en un certificado de depósito (pág. 506)

mediación situación en la cual el sindicato y los funcionarios de una compañía acuden a un tercero para que los ayude a llegar a un acuerdo (pág. 529)

*medio forma de realizar una acción (pág. 568)

fusión combinación de dos o más compañías para formar una sola empresa (pág. 545)

sistema de méritos contratación de personas para cargos del gobierno de acuerdo con su preparación (pág. 211)

*metodo procedimiento o proceso para hacer algo (pág. 202)

área metropolitana una ciudad grande y sus alrededores (pág. 352)

*mínimo la menor cantidad posible (pág. 324)

*menor que tiene relativamente menos importancia (pág. 431)

partido minoritario tanto en la Cámara de Representantes como en el Senado, partido político al que pertenece menos de la mitad de los miembros (pág. 161)

advertencia Miranda lista de derechos que la policía debe leer a las personas antes de interrogarlas, entre ellos el derecho a no autoincriminarse y a tener un abogado (pág. 407)

delito menor tipo de delito de menor gravedad; delito menor por el cual una persona puede ser multada con una pequeña suma de dinero o encarcelada hasta por un año (págs. 335, 422)

Glossary/Glosario

mixed economy a system combining characteristics of more than one type of economy (p. 622)

mixed market economy a market economy that has elements of command and tradition (p. 445)

monetary policy manipulation of the money supply to affect the cost of credit, economic growth, and price stability (p. 576)

money market account a type of savings account that pays interest but also allows customers to write checks against the account (p. 580)

monopoly a sole provider for a good or service (p. 544)

mutual funds an investment company that sells stock in itself and uses the proceeds to buy stocks and bonds issued by other companies (p. 509)

economía mixta sistema que combina características de más de un tipo de economía (pág. 622)

economía de mercado mixta economía de mercado que tiene elementos de orden y tradición (pág. 445)

política monetaria manipulación de la oferta de dinero para afectar el costo del crédito, el crecimiento económico y la estabilidad de los precios (pág. 576)

cuenta del mercado monetario tipo de cuenta de ahorros que devenga intereses pero que también permite a los clientes girar cheques de esta (pág. 580)

monopolio cuando el mercado solo cuenta con un proveedor de un bien o servicio (pág. 544)

fondo de inversión compañía de inversión que vende acciones en ella misma y usa los ingresos para comprar acciones y bonos emitidos por otras compañías (pág. 509)

N

national committee representatives from the 50 state party organizations who run a political party (p. 254)

national security the ability to keep the country safe from attack or harm (p. 200)

natural monopoly a market situation in which the costs of production are minimized by having a single firm produce the product (p. 545)

natural rights freedoms people possess relating to life, liberty, and property (p. 45)

naturalization a legal process to obtain citizenship (p. 13)

negligence a lack of proper care and attention (p. 418)

*****neutral** taking no side or part in a conflict or disagreement (p. 643)

NIMBY an acronym that stands for "not in my backyard"; attitude of opposing landfills near one's home (p. 383)

nongovernmental organization (NGO) an organization that operates independently of any government body, usually through individual volunteer efforts and private donations (p. 639)

comité nacional representantes de las 50 organizaciones partidistas estatales que tienen un partido político (pág. 254)

seguridad nacional capacidad de mantener al país a salvo de un ataque o un perjuicio (pág. 200)

monopolio natural situación del mercado en la cual los costos de producción se minimizan teniendo una sola firma que elabore el producto (pág. 545)

derechos naturales libertades que las personas poseen con relación a la vida, la libertad y la propiedad (pág. 45)

naturalización proceso legal para obtener la ciudadanía (pág. 13)

negligencia falta de cuidado y atención apropiados (pág. 418)

*****neutral** que no toma partido en un conflicto o desacuerdo (pág. 643)

NIMBY (por sus siglas en inglés) acrónimo para "no en mi jardín"; actitud de oponerse a los basurales cercanos al propio hogar (pág. 383)

organización no gubernamental (ONG) organización que funciona independientemente de cualquier organismo del gobierno, por lo general mediante esfuerzos voluntarios individuales y donaciones privadas (pág. 639)

nonlegislative power duty Congress holds besides lawmaking (p. 168)

facultades no legislativas deberes del Congreso diferentes a la función de legislar (pág. 168)

nonpartisan free from party ties or bias (p. 304)

no afiliado que no tiene vínculos con ningún partido ni parcialidades (pág. 304)

nonprofit organization a business that does not intend to make a profit for the goods and services it provides (p. 523)

organización sin ánimo de lucro empresa que no busca obtener ganancias por los bienes y servicios que provee (pág. 523)

nonviolent resistance peaceful protest against laws believed to be unfair (p. 148)

resistencia no violenta protesta pacífica en contra de leyes que se cree son injustas (pág. 148)

Northwest Ordinance 1787 law that set up a government for the Northwest Territory and served as a model for other new territories and as a plan for admitting new states to the Union (p. 75)

Ordenanza del noroeste ley de 1787 que estableció un gobierno para los territorios del Noroeste y sirvió de modelo para otros territorios nuevos y como plan para admitir nuevos estados en la Unión (pág. 75)

nullify to cancel legally (p. 232)

anular cancelar legalmente (pág. 232)

O

*occur to happen or take place (p. 159)

*ocurrir suceder o tener lugar (pág. 159)

open market operations purchase or sale of U.S. government bonds and Treasury bills (p. 576)

transacciones de mercado abierto compra o venta de bonos del gobierno y letras del Tesoro de Estados Unidos (pág. 576)

open primary an election in which voters need not declare their party preference (p. 258)

elección primaria abierta elección en la cual no es necesario que los votantes declaren cuál es el partido de su preferencia (pág. 258)

opinion a detailed explanation of the legal thinking behind a court's decision in a case (p. 226)

dictamen explicación detallada de la justificación legal que subyace a una decisión de un tribunal en un caso (pág. 226)

opportunity cost the cost of the next-best use of time and money when choosing to do one thing or another (p. 447)

costo de oportunidad costo de la mejor alternativa de tiempo y dinero cuando se elige hacer una cosa u otra (pág. 447)

*option something that is chosen; an alternative or a choice (pp. 447, 529)

*opción algo que se escoge; alternativa o elección (págs. 447, 529)

ordinance a law, usually of a city or county (pp. 74, 348)

ordenanza ley, por lo general de una ciudad o un condado (págs. 74, 348)

Ordinance of 1785 a law that set up a plan for surveying western lands; this method is still used today. (p. 74)

Ordenanza de 1785 ley que fijó un plan para medir las tierras del Oeste; se sigue usando hoy en día (pág. 74)

*orient to tend toward a certain direction (p. 622)

*orientarse tender hacia una dirección determinada (pág. 622)

original jurisdiction the authority to hear cases for the first time (p. 223)

jurisdicción original autoridad para ver una causa por primera vez (pág. 223)

*outcome a result or consequence (p. 190)

*producto resultado o consecuencia (pág. 190)

*output amount produced (p. 466)

*producción cantidad producida (pág. 466)

Glossary/Glosario

P

pardon a declaration of forgiveness and freedom from punishment (p. 196)

perdón declaración de perdón y remisión del castigo (pág. 196)

parole to grant a prisoner an early release from prison, with certain restrictions (p. 331)

libertad condicional conceder la libertad anticipada a un prisionero con algunas restricciones (pág. 331)

partnership a business owned by two or more people (p. 517)

sociedad empresa de propiedad de dos o más personas (pág. 517)

penal code a state's written criminal laws (p. 421)

código penal leyes criminales escritas de un estado (pág. 421)

penalty fee for early withdrawal of funds (p. 506)

penalidad multa por el retiro anticipado de fondos (pág. 506)

*period a stretch of time (p. 580)

*periodo extensión de tiempo (pág. 580)

*persist to last or to continue (p. 146)

*persistir durar o continuar (pág. 146)

petition a formal request for government action (p. 131)

petición solicitud formal para una acción determinada del gobierno (pág. 131)

picketing a union tactic in which striking workers walk with signs that express their grievances (p. 528)

manifestación táctica sindical en la cual los trabajadores que están en huelga marchan con pancartas que expresan sus quejas (pág. 528)

plaintiff the person in a civil case who claims to have been harmed; person who files a lawsuit (pp. 335, 419)

demandante persona en un proceso civil que afirma haber sido perjudicada; persona que entabla una demanda (págs. 335, 419)

planning commission an advisory group to a community (p. 372)

comisión de planificación un grupo asesor para una comunidad (pág. 372)

plantation a large estate (p. 51)

plantación propiedad de gran tamaño (pág. 51)

platform a series of statements expressing the party's principles, beliefs, and positions on election issues (p. 253)

plataforma serie de enunciados que expresan los principios, creencias y posiciones de un partido con respecto a temas electorales (pág. 253)

plea bargaining the process in which a defendant agrees to plead guilty to a less serious crime in order to receive a lighter sentence (p. 425)

acuerdo de reducción de sentencia proceso en el cual un acusado acepta declararse culpable de un crimen de menor gravedad para recibir una sentencia más leve (pág. 425)

plurality the most votes among all those running for a political office (p. 258)

pluralidad mayoría de votos entre los candidatos a un cargo político (pág. 258)

pocket veto president's power to kill a bill, if Congress is not in session, by not signing it for 10 days (p. 181)

veto indirecto facultad presidencial para hundir un proyecto de ley, si el Congreso no está en sesión, absteniéndose de firmarlo en un plazo de 10 días (pág. 181)

policy a guiding course of action (p. 370)

política curso de acción que sirve como guía (pág. 370)

political action committee (PAC) political organization established by a corporation, labor union, or other special-interest group designed to support candidates by contributing money (p. 283)

comité de acción política (en inglés, PAC) organización política establecida por una corporación, un sindicato u otro grupo de interés especial con el fin de apoyar a los candidatos haciendo aportes de dinero (pág. 283)

political appointee a person appointed to a federal position by the president (p. 211)

political machine a strong party organization that can control political appointments and deliver votes (p. 256)

political party an association of voters with broad common interests who want to influence or control decision making in government by electing the party's candidates to public office (p. 248)

poll tax a sum of money required of voters before they are permitted to cast a ballot (p. 145)

polling place the location where voting is carried out (p. 273)

pollster a specialist whose job is to conduct polls regularly (p. 295)

popular referendum a question placed on a ballot by a citizen petition to decide if a law should be repealed (p. 327)

popular sovereignty government receives its power from the people (pp. 10, 93)

popular vote the votes cast by individual voters in a presidential election, as opposed to the electoral vote (p. 280)

pork-barrel project government project grant that primarily benefits the home district or state (p. 175)

*__potential__ possible; capable of being or becoming (pp. 394, 558)

Preamble the opening section of the Constitution (p. 86)

precedent a ruling that is used as the basis for a judicial decision in a later, similar case (pp. 226, 398)

precinct a geographic area that contains a specific number of voters (p. 255)

*__predict__ to forecast (p. 597)

*__preliminary__ something that introduces or comes before something else (p. 228)

*__presumed__ assumed or supposed to be true (p. 220)

*__presumption__ an attitude or belief based on likelihood (p. 404)

designado político persona escogida por el presidente para un cargo federal (pág. 211)

maquinaria política fuerte organización partidista que puede controlar los nombramientos políticos y obtener votos (pág. 256)

partido político asociación de votantes con numerosos intereses en común que desean influenciar o controlar la toma de decisiones en el gobierno eligiendo sus candidatos para cargos públicos (pág. 248)

impuesto al sufragio suma de dinero que se exige a los votantes antes de permitirles depositar su voto (pág. 145)

sitio de votación lugar donde se llevan a cabo las elecciones (pág. 273)

encuestador especialista cuyo trabajo es realizar encuestas con regularidad (pág. 295)

referendo de iniciativa popular pregunta planteada por los ciudadanos en una papeleta de votación para decidir si se deroga una ley (pág. 327)

soberanía popular idea de que el gobierno recibe su poder del pueblo (págs. 10, 93)

voto popular votos depositados por los votantes individuales en una elección presidencial, en contraste con el voto electoral (pág. 280)

proyecto clientelista auxilio del gobierno para un proyecto que beneficia principalmente al distrito o estado de origen (pág. 175)

*__potencial__ posible; susceptible de ser o llegar a ser (págs. 394, 558)

preámbulo sección inicial de la Constitución (pág. 86)

precedente fallo que se usa como base para tomar una decisión judicial en un caso futuro similar (págs. 226, 398)

distrito electoral área geográfica que contiene un número específico de votantes (pág. 255)

*__predecir__ anticipar (pág. 597)

*__preliminar__ que introduce o antecede a algo más (pág. 228)

*__presunto__ algo que se supone que es verdad (pág. 220)

*__presunción__ actitud o creencia basada en la probabilidad (pág. 404)

Glossary/Glosario

principal amount of initial deposit on which interest is earned (p. 504)

capital suma inicial de dinero depositado que produce interés (pág. 504)

*principle basic belief (p. 268)

*principio creencia básica (pág. 268)

prior restraint the act of stopping information from being known by blocking it from being published (p. 300)

censura preliminar acción de evitar que se conozca alguna información impidiendo su publicación (pág. 300)

*priority having the highest ranking on a list (p. 16)

*prioridad clasificación más alta en una lista (pág. 16)

prisoner of war a person captured by opposing forces during a time of war or conflict (p. 643)

prisionero de guerra persona capturada por las fuerzas enemigas durante una guerra o un conflicto (pág. 643)

private good an economic good that, when consumed by one person, cannot be used by another (p. 542)

bien privado bien económico que una vez consumido por un individuo no puede ser consumido por otro (pág. 542)

private property rights the freedom to own and use our property as we choose as long as we do not interfere with the rights of others (p. 480)

derecho a la propiedad privada libertad que tiene una persona de tener propiedad y usarla como lo desee siempre y cuando no interfiera con los derechos de los demás (pág. 480)

privatization the process of changing from state-owned businesses, factories, and farms to ones owned by private citizens (p. 621)

privatización proceso en el que empresas, fábricas y granjas de propiedad del Estado pasan al control de ciudadanos privados (pág. 621)

probable cause strong reasons to think that a person or property was involved in a crime (p. 134)

causa probable razones de peso para creer que una persona o propiedad están involucradas en un crimen (pág. 134)

*process an action or a series of actions directed toward a result (p. 79)

*proceso acción o serie de acciones orientadas a un resultado (pág. 79)

proclamation an official, formal public announcement (p. 55)

proclamación anuncio público oficial y formal (pág. 55)

producer a person or business that provides goods and services (p. 452)

productor persona o empresa que provee bienes y servicios (pág. 452)

product anything that is produced; goods and services (p. 466)

producto cualquier cosa que se produce; bienes y servicios (pág. 466)

product market a market where productive resources are bought and sold (p. 472)

mercado de productos mercado en el cual los productores ofrecen bienes y servicios para la venta (pág. 472)

productivity the degree to which resources are being used efficiently to produce goods and services (p. 475)

productividad grado hasta el cual los recursos se usan eficientemente para producir bienes y servicios (pág. 475)

*professional worker with much education and high-level skills (p. 372)

*profesional trabajador con educación y destrezas de alto nivel (pág. 372)

profit the money a business receives for its products or services over and above its costs (p. 479)

rentabilidad dinero que recibe una empresa por sus productos o servicios por encima del costo (pág. 479)

profit motive the driving force that encourages individuals and organizations to improve their material well-being (p. 479)

afán de lucro fuerza que motiva a individuos y organizaciones a mejorar su bienestar económico (pág. 479)

*promote to advance a cause or an idea (p. 251)

*promover impulsar una causa o idea (pág. 251)

property tax a tax on the value of land and property that people own (p. 596)

impuesto predial impuesto sobre el valor de las posesiones de tierra y propiedades de las personas (pág. 596)

*proportion the size or amount of something in relation to something else or to a whole (p. 408)

*proporción tamaño o cantidad de algo en relación con algo más o con un todo (pág. 408)

prosecution the government, which starts the legal proceedings against someone accused of committing a crime (p. 424)

fiscalía el gobierno, que da inicio a los procesos legales en contra de alguien que se acusa de cometer un delito (pág. 424)

protectionism the use of tactics that make imported goods more expensive than domestic goods (p. 612)

proteccionismo uso de tácticas que hacen que los productos nacionales sean más baratos que los importados (pág. 612)

public agenda issues considered most significant by government officials (p. 298)

agenda pública temas que los funcionarios del gobierno consideran los más importantes (pág. 298)

public good an economic good that is used collectively, such as a highway and national defense (p. 543)

bien público bien económico que se usa en forma colectiva, como una carretera o la defensa nacional (pág. 543)

public-interest group an organization that supports causes that affect the lives of Americans in general (p. 304)

grupo de interés público organización que apoya las causas que afectan la vida de los estadounidenses en general (pág. 304)

public opinion the ideas and attitudes that most people hold about elected officials, candidates, government, and political issues (p. 290)

opinión pública ideas y actitudes de la mayoría de las personas sobre los funcionarios elegidos, los candidatos, el gobierno y los asuntos políticos (pág. 290)

public opinion poll a survey in which individuals are asked to answer questions about a particular issue or person (p. 294)

encuesta de opinión pública sondeo en el cual se les pide a las personas que respondan preguntas sobre un aspecto o persona en particular (pág. 294)

public policy the decisions and actions a government takes to solve problems in the community (pp. 28, 371)

política pública decisiones y acciones que toma el gobierno para resolver problemas en la comunidad (págs. 28, 371)

*pursue to try to reach or attain (p. 283)

*perseguir tratar de alcanzar o lograr (pág. 283)

Q

quota a limit on the amount of foreign goods imported into a country (p. 612)

cuota límite de productos importados por un país (pág. 612)

R

*random by chance (p. 295)

*al azar por casualidad (pág. 295)

ratify to vote approval of (p. 74)

ratificar votar la aprobación de algo (pág. 74)

real GDP GDP after adjustments for inflation (p. 549)

PIB real PIB posterior a los ajustes por inflación (pág. 549)

Glossary/Glosario

Glossary/Glosario

Glossary/Glosario

recall a special election in which citizens can vote to remove a public official from office (p. 279); action that causes an unsafe product to be removed from store shelves (p. 547)

recession a period of declining economic activity lasting six or more months (p. 550)

recycling the process of reusing old materials to make new ones (p. 383)

redistricting the process of redrawing legislative districts (p. 325)

redress payment for a wrong or loss (p. 490)

referendum a way for citizens to vote on state or local laws (p. 278)

refugee a person who has unwillingly left his or her home to escape war, famine, or natural disaster (pp. 15, 637)

*regime a government that is in power (p. 31)

*register to record or enroll formally (pp. 19, 272)

*regulate to manage or control (p. 167)

*regulation a rule (p. 378)

*regulatory describing an agency that controls or governs (p. 301)

regulatory commission independent agency created by Congress that can make rules concerning certain activities and bring violators to court (p. 210)

rehabilitate to correct a person's behavior (p. 429)

*reluctant unwilling (p. 349)

*rely to depend on something or someone (p. 327)

repeal to cancel a law (p. 56)

representative democracy a government in which citizens choose a smaller group to govern on their behalf (pp. 30, 41)

repression preventing people from expressing themselves or from freely engaging in normal life (p. 646)

revocatoria elección especial en la cual los ciudadanos pueden votar para retirar a un funcionario público de su cargo (pág. 279); acción que hace que un producto inseguro sea retirado de los estantes de los almacenes (pág. 547)

recesión periodo de actividad económica en declive que dura más de seis meses (pág. 550)

reciclaje proceso de reutilización de materiales viejos para producir materiales nuevos (pág. 383)

redistribución proceso en el cual se vuelven a dividir los distritos legislativos (pág. 325)

reparación pago para compensar un mal o una pérdida (pág. 490)

referendo mecanismo para que los ciudadanos voten por leyes estatales o locales (pág. 278)

refugiado persona que ha dejado su hogar para escapar de la guerra, la persecución del gobierno, el hambre o un desastre natural (págs. 15, 637)

*régimen gobierno que está en el poder (pág. 31)

*registrar documentar o matricular formalmente (págs. 19, 272)

*regular manejar o controlar (pág. 167)

*reglamentación regla (pág. 378)

*regulador término que describe una agencia que controla o gobierna (pág. 301)

comisión reguladora organismo independiente creado por el Congreso que puede establecer leyes concernientes a determinadas actividades y llevar ante los tribunales a quienes las violen (pág. 210)

rehabilitar corregir la conducta de una persona (pág. 429)

*reacio que no está dispuesto a algo (pág. 349)

*confiar depender de algo o de alguien (pág. 327)

derogar cancelar una ley (pág. 56)

democracia representativa gobierno en el cual los ciudadanos eligen a un grupo más pequeño para que gobierne en su nombre (págs. 30, 41)

represión evitar que las personas se expresen o lleven una vida normal con libertad (pág. 646)

reprieve an order to delay a person's punishment until a higher court can hear the case (p. 196)

indulto orden de posponer el castigo de una persona hasta que un tribunal superior pueda ver la causa (pág. 196)

republic a representative democracy in which citizens choose their lawmakers (p. 41)

república democracia representativa en la cual los ciudadanos eligen a sus legisladores (pág. 41)

*require to have a need for or to order (p. 195)

*solicitar necesitar o exigir (pág. 195)

reserve requirement the percentage of a deposit that banks have to set aside as cash in their own vaults or as deposits in their Federal Reserve district bank (p. 577)

encaje legal determinado porcentaje de depósitos que los bancos deben separar en efectivo en sus bóvedas o en su distrito bancario de la Reserva Federal (pág. 577)

reserved powers powers that the Constitution does not give to the national government that are kept by the states (pp. 96, 319)

poderes reservados facultades que la Constitución no le confiere al gobierno nacional y que los estados ejercen (págs. 96, 319)

*resign to give up one's office or position (p. 192)

*renunciar entregar un cargo (pág. 192)

*resolve to find a solution to a disagreement (p. 26)

*resolver hallar una solución a un desacuerdo (pág. 26)

resource the money, people, and materials available to accomplish a community's goals (p. 374); all things that can be used—natural resources, labor, capital—to make goods or services (p. 441)

recurso dinero, personas y materiales disponibles para alcanzar los objetivos de una comunidad (pág. 374); todo lo que se puede usar para producir bienes o servicios, como: recursos naturales, mano de obra o capital (pág. 441)

*respond to give a spoken or written answer (p. 419)

*responder dar una respuesta verbal o escrita (pág. 419)

responsibility an obligation that we meet of our own free will (p. 18)

responsabilidad obligación que se cumple por propia voluntad (pág. 18)

*restore to bring back (p. 546)

*restaurar devolver (pág. 546)

*restriction limit placed on something (p. 132)

*restricción límite impuesto a algo (pág. 132)

*retain to keep or hold secure (p. 139)

*retener mantener o asegurar (pág. 139)

return profit earned by an investor (p. 507)

retorno ganancia que obtiene un inversionista (pág. 507)

*reveal to make something known (p. 534)

*revelar dar algo a conocer (pág. 534)

revenue the money a business receives from selling its goods or services (p. 449)

ingreso dinero que una empresa recibe por la venta de sus bienes o servicios (pág. 449)

rider a completely unrelated amendment added to a bill (p. 178)

cláusula adicional enmienda completamente independiente que se hace a un proyecto de ley (pág. 178)

right-to-work laws state laws forbidding unions from forcing workers to join (p. 527)

leyes de derecho al trabajo leyes estatales que prohíben a los sindicatos obligar a los trabajadores a asociarse a estos (pág. 527)

*role the function of a person or thing (p. 207)

*rol función de una persona o cosa (pág. 207)

roll-call vote a voting method in the Senate in which members voice their votes in turn (p. 181)

votación nominal método de votación del Senado en el cual, por turnos, los miembros anuncian en voz alta sus votos (pág. 181)

Glossary/Glosario

Glossary/Glosario

rule of law principle that the law applies to everyone, even those who govern (p. 94)

ruling an official decision by a judge or a court that settles a case and may also establish the meaning of a law (p. 225)

imperio de la ley principio según el cual la ley se aplica a todas las personas, incluso a quienes gobiernan (pág. 94)

fallo decisión oficial de un juez o un tribunal que resuelve un caso; también puede establecer el significado de una ley (pág. 225)

S

sales tax a tax paid by consumers at the time they buy goods or services (p. 594)

impuesto a las ventas impuesto que los consumidores pagan en el momento de comprar un producto o servicio (pág. 594)

savings account an account that pays interest on deposits but allows customers to withdraw money at any time (p. 579)

cuenta de ahorros cuenta que paga un interés sobre los depósitos pero les permite a los clientes retirar el dinero en cualquier momento (pág. 579)

savings and loan association (S&L) a financial institution that traditionally loaned money to people buying homes (p. 571)

asociación de ahorros y préstamos (S&L) institución financiera que tradicionalmente prestaba dinero para comprar vivienda (pág. 571)

scarcity the situation of not having enough resources to satisfy all one's wants (p. 441)

escasez no contar con suficientes recursos para satisfacer todas las necesidades (pág. 441)

search warrant a court order allowing law-enforcement officers to search a suspect's home or business and take specific items as evidence (pp. 134, 405)

orden de cateo orden judicial que permite a los oficiales encargados de hacer cumplir la ley inspeccionar el hogar o la empresa de un sospechoso y tomar artículos específicos como evidencia (págs. 134, 405)

*sector** a category or a part of a whole (p. 471)

*sector** categoría o parte de un todo (pág. 471)

segregation the social separation of the races (p. 146)

segregación separación social entre las razas (pág. 146)

self-incrimination giving evidence that could lead to one being found guilty of a crime (p. 135)

autoincriminación cuando una persona aporta evidencias que pueden llevar a que lo declaren culpable de un crimen (pág. 135)

Senate the upper house of Congress, consisting of two representatives from each state (p. 158)

Senado cámara alta del Congreso integrada por dos representantes de cada estado (pág. 158)

seniority years of service, which is used as a consideration for assigning committee members (p. 164)

antigüedad años de servicio, criterio que se tiene en cuenta para designar a los miembros de un comité (pág. 164)

sentence the punishment given to someone found guilty of committing a crime (p. 423)

sentencia castigo impuesto a una persona que es hallada culpable de cometer un crimen (pág. 423)

separation of powers the split of authority among the legislative, executive, and judicial branches (p. 94)

separación de poderes división de la autoridad en las ramas legislativa, ejecutiva y judicial (pág. 94)

session a meeting of a legislative or judicial body to conduct business (p. 326)

sesión reunión de un organismo legislativo o judicial para tratar un tema (pág. 326)

Shays's Rebellion an uprising of Massachusetts farmers who did not want to lose their farms because of debt caused by heavy state taxes after the American Revolution (p. 77)

shield law a law that protects a reporter from revealing his or her sources (p. 301)

shortage situation in which the supply of the good or service available is less than the demand for it (p. 455)

short-term plan a government policy being carried out over the next few years (p. 372)

***similar** almost the same (p. 361)

sit-in the act of occupying seats or sitting down on the floor of an establishment as a form of organized protest (p. 149)

slander spoken untruths that are harmful to someone's reputation (p. 132)

smuggling the act of importing or exporting secretly, in violation of law and especially without paying duty on goods (p. 57)

social contract an agreement among people in a society with a government (p. 44)

socialism system in which government owns some factors of production and distributes the products and wages (pp. 32, 620)

social responsibility the obligation businesses have to pursue goals that benefit society as well as themselves (p. 531)

sole proprietorship a business owned and operated by a single person (p. 516)

solid waste the technical name for garbage (p. 383)

special district a unit of government that deals with a specific function, such as education, water supply, or transportation (p. 351)

special-interest group an organization of people with some common interest who try to influence government decisions (p. 178)

special session a legislative meeting called for a specific purpose (p. 326)

specialization when people, businesses, regions, and/or nations concentrate on goods and services that they can produce better than anyone else (p. 476)

***specific** falling into a particular category; clearly specified, precise, or explicit (pp. 209, 331)

rebelión de Shays levantamiento de agricultores de Massachusetts que no querían perder sus granjas debido a las deudas generadas por los elevados impuestos estatales posteriores a la Revolución Americana (pág. 77)

ley de protección de la fuente ley que protege a los periodistas para que no revelen sus fuentes (pág. 301)

desabastecimiento situación en que la oferta de un bien o servicio disponible es menor que la demanda de estos (pág. 455)

plan a corto plazo política gubernamental que se lleva a cabo durante los siguientes años (pág. 372)

***similar** casi igual (pág. 361)

sentada acto de ocupar sillas o sentarse en el suelo de un establecimiento a manera de protesta organizada (pág. 149)

calumnia mentira en forma verbal que perjudica la reputación de una persona (pág. 132)

contrabando acción de importar o exportar en secreto, violando la ley y en especial sin pagar impuestos sobre los productos (pág. 57)

contrato social acuerdo entre los miembros de la sociedad y el gobierno (pág. 44)

socialismo sistema en el que el gobierno es propietario de algunos factores de producción y distribuye los productos y los salarios (págs. 32, 620)

responsabilidad social obligación que tiene una empresa de trazarse metas que la beneficien a ella misma y a la sociedad (pág. 531)

empresa unipersonal empresa de propiedad de una sola persona y bajo su dirección (pág. 516)

residuo sólido nombre técnico para la basura (pág. 383)

distrito especial división política que se ocupa de una función específica, como educación, abastecimiento de agua o transporte (pág. 351)

grupo de interés especial organización de personas que tienen interese comunes y tratan de influir en las decisiones del gobierno (pág. 178)

sesión especial reunión de una asamblea legislativa convocada para tratar un punto específico (pág. 326)

especialización cuando las personas, empresas, regiones o naciones se concentran en los bienes y servicios que pueden producir mejor (pág. 476)

***específico** que cabe dentro de una categoría en particular; especificado claramente, preciso o explícito (págs. 209, 331)

spoils system rewarding people with government jobs on the basis of their political support (p. 211)

***stable** not subject to major changes (p. 635)

standard of living the material well-being of an individual, a group, or a nation as measured by how well their needs and wants are satisfied (p. 470)

standing vote in Congress, when members stand to be counted for a vote on a bill (p. 181)

stare decisis the practice of using earlier judicial rulings as a basis for deciding cases (p. 240)

status offender a youth charged with being beyond the control of his or her legal guardian (p. 431)

statute a law written by a legislative branch (p. 398)

stock shares of a company held by an investor (p. 507)

***stress** to place special importance or emphasis on something (p. 250)

strike when workers deliberately stop working in order to force an employer to give in to their demands (p. 528)

***submit** to offer a bill for consideration (p. 178)

subpoena an order that requires a person to appear in court (p. 228)

subsidize to aid or support a person, business, institution, or undertaking with money or tax breaks (p. 594)

suburb a community that is near a larger city (p. 352)

suffrage the right to vote (pp. 143, 268)

summons a notice directing someone to appear in court to answer a complaint or a charge (p. 419)

supply the amount of goods and services that producers are willing and able to sell at a range of prices (p. 453)

supremacy clause the clause in Article VI of the Constitution that makes federal laws prevail over state laws when there is a conflict (pp. 97, 319)

surplus situation in which the amount of a good or service supplied by producers is greater than the amount demanded by consumers (p. 455)

sistema de botín compensar a las personas con trabajos en el gobierno por su apoyo político (pág. 211)

***estable** que no está sujeto a cambios importantes (pág. 635)

nivel de vida bienestar material de un individuo, un grupo o una nación, que se mide determinando hasta qué punto se satisfacen sus necesidades y deseos (pág. 470)

votación de pie en el Congreso, cuando los miembros se ponen de pie para votar un proyecto de ley (pág. 181)

obligatoriedad de la jurisprudencia práctica de usar fallos judiciales anteriores como base para decidir en otros casos (pág. 240)

menor infractor joven acusado de salirse del control de su tutor legal (pág. 431)

estatuto ley escrita por un cuerpo legislativo (pág. 398)

acción participaciones de una compañía que posee un inversionista (pág. 507)

***acentuar** dar especial importancia o poner énfasis en algo (pág. 250)

huelga cuando los obreros dejan de trabajar deliberadamente para obligar a un empleador a ceder a sus exigencias (pág. 528)

***someter** poner a consideración un proyecto de ley (pág. 178)

carta de emplazamiento orden judicial que le exige a una persona presentarse ante un tribunal (pág. 228)

subsidiar ayudar o sostener económicamente o con excepción de impuestos a una persona, empresa, institución o un proyecto (pág. 594)

suburbio comunidad cercana a una ciudad grande (pág. 352)

sufragio derecho al voto (págs. 143, 268)

citación aviso que le ordena a una persona comparecer en un tribunal para responder una queja o una acusación (pág. 419)

oferta cantidad de bienes y servicios que los productores desean y pueden vender a una gama de precios (pág. 453)

cláusula de supremacía cláusula del Artículo VI de la Constitución que determina que las leyes federales prevalecen sobre las estatales cuando hay un conflicto (págs. 97, 319)

excedente situación en la cual la cantidad de un bien o servicio ofertado por los productores es mayor que la cantidad demandada por los consumidores (pág. 455)

T

*target selected person or thing receiving an action (p. 204)

tariff a tax on an imported good (p. 612)

Temporary Assistance for Needy Families (TANF) welfare program paid for by the federal government and administered by the individual states (p. 560)

tenure the right to hold an office once a person is confirmed (p. 228)

terrorism the use of violence or the threat of violence to compel a group of people to behave in a certain way (p. 637)

third party a political party that challenges the two major parties (p. 251)

Three-fifths Compromise agreement providing that enslaved persons would count as three-fifths of other persons in determining representation in Congress (p. 82)

tolerance respecting and accepting others, regardless of their beliefs, practices, or differences (p. 22)

tort wrongful act, other than breaking a contract, for which an injured party has the right to sue (p. 418)

total cost the combination of all fixed and variable costs (p. 449)

totalitarian describes a system in which government control extends to almost all aspects of people's lives (p. 32)

town political unit that is larger than a village and smaller than a city (p. 359)

town meeting a gathering of local citizens to discuss and vote on important issues (p. 360)

township a subdivision of a county that has its own government (p. 359)

toxic poisonous or deadly (p. 383)

trade-off the alternative you face if you decide to do one thing rather than another (p. 446)

trade sanctions an effort to punish another nation by imposing trade barriers (p. 204)

*objetivo persona o cosa seleccionada que recibe una acción (pág. 204)

arancel impuesto a las importaciones (pág. 612)

Asistencia temporal para familias necesitadas (en inglés, TANF) programa de bienestar subvencionado por el gobierno federal y administrado por los estados individuales (pág. 560)

tenencia derecho que tiene una persona a conservar un cargo una vez que ha recibido el visto bueno (pág. 228)

terrorismo uso de la violencia o de amenazas para obligar a un grupo de personas a actuar de determinada manera (pág. 637)

partido bisagra partido político que desafía a los dos partidos principales (pág. 251)

Compromiso de las tres quintas partes acuerdo que establecía que los esclavos contarían como las tres quintas partes de otras personas para determinar su representación en el Congreso (pág. 82)

tolerancia respeto y aceptación hacia los demás sin importar sus creencias, prácticas o diferencias (pág. 22)

agravio acción ilegal, como incumplir un contrato, por la cual la parte afectada tiene derecho a demandar (pág. 418)

costo total combinación de todos los costos fijos y variables (pág. 449)

totalitarismo describe un sistema en el que el control del gobierno se extiende a casi todos los aspectos de la vida de las personas (pág. 32)

pueblo división política más grande que una aldea pero más pequeña que una ciudad (pág. 359)

cabildo municipal reunión de ciudadanos de un lugar para analizar y votar asuntos importantes (pág. 360)

municipio subdivisión de un condado que tiene su propio gobierno (pág. 359)

tóxico venenoso o mortal (pág. 383)

disyuntiva alternativa que se afronta cuando se decide hacer una cosa en lugar de otra (pág. 446)

sanción comercial intento de castigar a otra nación imponiéndole barreras comerciales (pág. 204)

Glossary/Glosario

Glossary/Glosario

trade war economic conflict that occurs when one or more nations put up trade barriers to punish another nation for trade barriers it erected against them (p. 635)

guerra comercial conflicto económico que ocurre cuando una o más naciones imponen barreras comerciales a otra nación debido a barreras comerciales que esta les impuso anteriormente (pág. 635)

***tradition** a custom; the long-followed way of doing things (p. 330)

***tradición** costumbre; manera de hacer las cosas que viene de tiempo atrás (pág. 330)

traditional economy an economic system in which the decisions of what, how, and for whom to produce are based on custom or habit (p. 444)

economía tradicional sistema económico en el cual las decisiones acerca de qué, cómo y para quién producir se basan en las costumbres o los hábitos (pág. 444)

***transfer** to move ownership of something (p. 469)

***transferir** pasar la propiedad de algo (pág. 469)

***transmit** to send a document or a message (p. 591)

***transmitir** enviar un documento o un mensaje (pág. 591)

transparency process of making business deals or conditions more visible to everyone (p. 534)

transparencia proceso que consiste en hacer que los tratos o condiciones comerciales sean más visibles para todos (pág. 534)

treaty a formal agreement between the governments of two or more countries (p. 203)

tratado acuerdo formal entre los gobiernos de dos o más países (pág. 203)

trial court type of court in which a judge or a jury listens to the evidence and reaches a verdict, or decision, in favor of one party in the case (p. 334)

tribunal juzgado en el cual un juez o un jurado escuchan las evidencias y emiten un veredicto, o decisión, a favor de una de las partes implicadas (pág. 334)

tuition voucher program providing subsidies for education payments, allowing families the option of sending students to private schools (p. 378)

bono escolar programa que suministra subsidios para los pagos de la educación, lo que brinda a las familias la opción de enviar estudiantes a escuelas privadas (pág. 378)

two-party system a system of government in which two parties compete for power (p. 248)

sistema bipartidista sistema de gobierno en el cual dos partidos compiten por llegar al poder (pág. 248)

U

unanimous opinion the Supreme Court rules on a case in which all justices agree on the ruling (p. 241)

decisión unánime fallos de la Suprema Corte en los cuales todos los magistrados coinciden (pág. 241)

unemployment rate the percentage of people in the civilian labor force who are not working but are looking for jobs (p. 553)

tasa de desempleo porcentaje de personas en la fuerza laboral civil que no están trabajando pero están buscando un empleo (pág. 553)

unicameral having a one-house legislature (p. 324)

unicameral asamblea legislativa que tiene una sola cámara (pág. 324)

universal worldwide, or applying to all (p. 644)

universal mundial, que se aplica a todos (pág. 644)

V

values the general principles or beliefs people use to make judgments and decisions (p. 9)

valores principios o creencias generales a partir de los cuales las personas emiten juicios y toman decisiones (pág. 9)

variable cost an expense that changes depending on how much a business produces (p. 448)

costo variable gasto que cambia según lo que produce una empresa (pág. 448)

*vary to change (p. 448)

*variar cambiar (pág. 448)

village smallest unit of local government (p. 362)

aldea división política local pequeña (pág. 362)

*violate to fail to keep or to break, as a law (p. 320)

*violar no obedecer o quebrantar, por ejemplo una ley (pág. 320)

voice vote a voting method in which those in favor say "Aye" and those against say "No" (p. 180)

votación oral método de votación en el cual todos los que están a favor dicen "Sí" y los que están en contra dicen "No" (pág. 180)

voluntary exchange the act of buyers and sellers freely and willingly engaging in market transactions (p. 479)

intercambio voluntario transacciones comerciales que realizan compradores y vendedores de manera libre y voluntaria (pág. 479)

volunteerism the practice of offering your time and services to others without receiving payment (p. 23)

voluntariado práctica que consiste en ofrecer a los demás tiempo y servicios sin recibir ningún pago a cambio (pág. 23)

voter turnout rate percentage of eligible voters who actually vote (p. 275)

tasa de asistencia a las urnas porcentaje de votantes habilitados que en realidad votan (pág. 275)

W

want desire individuals and nations have that can be met by getting a good or a service (p. 440)

necesidad deseo que tienen los individuos y las naciones y que se puede satisfacer con la obtención de un bien o servicio (pág. 440)

warranty the promise made by a manufacturer or a seller to repair or replace a product within a certain time period if it is faulty (p. 492)

garantía promesa hecha por un fabricante o vendedor para reparar o reemplazar un producto dentro de cierto plazo si este falla (pág. 492)

watchdog the role played by a media organization that exposes illegal practices or waste (p. 299)

organismo de control función desempeñada por una organización mediática que denuncia prácticas ilegales o gastos excecivos (pág. 299)

weapon of mass destruction a weapon that can kill or harm large numbers of people as well as destroy or damage a large physical area (p. 650)

arma de destrucción masiva arma que puede matar o herir a un gran número de personas así como destruir o dañar una amplia área física (pág. 650)

welfare the health, prosperity, and happiness of the members of a community (p. 23); aid given to the poor in the form of money or necessities (p. 560)

bienestar salud, prosperidad y felicidad de los miembros de una comunidad (pág. 23); ayuda que se brinda a los pobres en forma de dinero para cubrir sus necesidades básicas (pág. 560)

Glossary/Glosario

winner-take-all system a system in which the candidate who wins the popular vote in a state usually receives all of the state's electoral votes (p. 281)

el ganador se lleva todo sistema electoral en el cual un candidato que gana el voto popular en un estado por lo general recibe todos los votos electorales de ese estado (pág. 281)

workfare programs that require welfare recipients to exchange some of their labor in return for benefits (p. 560)

trabajo auspiciado por el gobierno programas que exigen que los beneficiarios de los subsidios de bienestar retribuyan algunas de las ayudas con su mano de obra (pág. 560)

writ of certiorari an order a higher court issues to a lower court to obtain the records of the lower court in a particular case (p. 236)

auto de avocación orden emitida por un alto tribunal a un tribunal menor para que este entregue los expedientes de un caso específico (pág. 236)

writ of habeas corpus a court order that requires police to bring a prisoner to court to explain why the person is being held (pp. 169, 403)

auto de hábeas corpus orden judicial que exige que la policía lleve a un prisionero ante un tribunal para explicar por qué ha sido detenido (págs. 169, 403)

Index

——————— **D** ———————

Index

G

Index

—————— **J** ——————

Index

Index

Index

rehabilitation: of criminals, 415, 423, *p423,* 429, 430

religion: authoritarian regimes and, 32; in colonies, 49, 50; in foundation of democracy, 40–41; freedom of, 9–10, 49, 129, *p129 (see also* First Amendment); Great Awakening movement, 54; of presidents, 188–89; of Supreme Court justices, 231; U.S. diversity of, 8, *c34. See also individual religions.*

religious institutions, 10

remand, 225

repeal, 56

representative democracy, 30, 41, 360

representative government, *c30,* 102

repression, 646

reprieve, 196

Republican Party: ballot power of, 251; campaigning activities, *p257;* history, *c249,* 250; platform of, 253; role of, 245

republics, 30, 41–42, 93, 112

reserved powers, 96, *c318,* 319

reserve requirement, 577

resident aliens, 15, *p15*

resolution, 105

Resolution of Independence, 68

resolutions, 177

resources, 441; in colonial life, 51, *m51;* in community planning, 373, 374; economic decision making, 447; economic growth and, 475; GDP and, 467; limited, 441; in market economy, 444; scarcity, 441; trade and, 632–33; war and, 625. *See also* natural resources.

responsibilities: of citizens, 18, *c21,* 21–22, *p22*

restitution, *c426*

restrictions: on civil liberty, 132

return: vs. risk, 507, 508, 509

revenues, 105, 449, 592, *g592,* 594, *g595,* 597

"reverse discrimination," 150

Reynolds, Robert, 302

Rheingold, Howard, *q309*

Rhode Island: declining Constitutional Convention, 78; governor qualifications, 329; lack of counties in, 354; state constitution in, 322

riders: on bills, 178

rights: bills of, 73 (*see also* Bill of Rights); consumer rights, 488–90; in Declaration of Independence, 65, 117; as democratic principle, *c30;* of legal aliens, 15; natural,

44–45; of other people, 22. *See also* freedom.

right-to-work laws, *m526,* 527

risk: business risk, 522; vs. return, 507, 508, 509

rivers. *See* environment, the.

robbery, 423

Roberts, John G., Jr., *q229*

Rockefeller, Nelson A., 193

Roe v. Wade, *c239*

roll-call vote, 181

Rome, ancient: republic, 41–42; Roman law, 397, 398; senate, *ptg41*

Romney, Mitt, 189, 257

Roosevelt, Franklin D., *p190;* Civilian Conservation Corps, 540; democracy declaration, *q647;* deposit protection, 582; on importance of voters, *q274;* political campaigning, 267, *p267;* on public opinion, 291; reacting to Pearl Harbor attack, 2; staff of, 205; term of office, 191; on voting, *q21;* welfare programs, 560, 601

Roosevelt, Theodore, 267

Rousseau, Jean-Jacques, *c45,* 61; *The Social Contract,* 45

rule of law, *c30,* 94

ruling, 224, 225

runoff election, 258, 278

rural, 7

Russia: Cold War and, 648; economic statistics, *c622;* privatization in, 621; treaty with, *p197;* as UN Security Council member, 641

Rwanda: genocide in, 646

S

safe deposit box: for secure storage, *p566*

safety: right to, 489

sales taxes, 327, 594

Sanford, John, 17

Saudi Arabia: human rights issues in, 646; as oil source, 633; trading partners, *m613*

savings: budgeting for, 495, 503–4, 506–7, *q512;* decision making, 486; as electronic money, 569; as a financial cushion, 487; growth of, *crt442;* profit motive, 479; purpose of, 503–4; rates of, *g504*

savings account, 504, 506, *c508,* 579

savings and loan association (S&L), 571, 583

savings bond, U.S., *c508,* 509. *See also* bonds.

Scalia, Antonin, 226, *p226*

scarcity, 441, 442–43, 610

schools: alternatives to public, 378–79; citizens' duty to attend, 20; purpose of rules in, 400; safety of, 370; as social institution, 10. *See also* education.

Schwarzenegger, Arnold, 298, *p298*

Scott, Dred, 17, *p17*

Scranton, Pennsylvania: fire department, 345

search warrant, 57, 134, 405

Second Amendment, 114, 137–38, *p138*

Second Bank of the United States, 581

Second Continental Congress, 60, 72, 73

secretaries: in president's cabinet, 207

secretary of defense, 206

secretary of state, 206, 333

secret ballot, 265, 273–74

sector, 471–74

security: government providing, 27, *c27*

segregation, 146, *c240,* 353. *See also* civil rights movement.

select committees, 163

Selective Service System, 19

selectmen, town, 361

self-incrimination, 135, 402, 405–6

Senate, U.S.: approving cabinet department heads, 208; approving Council of Economic Advisers, 207; approving federal judges, 227; approving treaties, 197, 203; committees in, *c163;* confirming ambassadors, 203; debating and voting on bills in, 180–81; electing members of, 103, 118, 144, 278; filibusters in, *crt182;* history of, 158; leadership in, 162, *p162,* 191; member requirements and benefits, 171; number of members in, 158, 159, 161; overriding president's veto, 169, 181; power of, 168; presidential succession role of, 193; Watergate investigation by, 199. *See also* Congress, U.S.

senatorial courtesy, 227

Senior Corps, 25

seniority: in congressional committees, 164

senior majority party member, 164

sentences: in criminal cases, 331, 423, *c425, c426,* 427

separation of powers, 45, 94, 347

service: redress, 492; right to, 490

Index

Index

Index